The Creeping Codification of the New Lex Mercatoria

KLUWER LAW INTERNATIONAL

The Creeping Codification of the New Lex Mercatoria

SECOND EDITION

by

Klaus Peter Berger

Published in conjunction with the Center for Transnational Law
(CENTRAL)
University of Cologne, Germany

Wolters Kluwer
Law & Business

AUSTIN BOSTON CHICAGO NEW YORK THE NETHERLANDS

Published by:
Kluwer Law International
PO Box 316
2400 AH Alphen aan den Rijn
The Netherlands
Website: www.kluwerlaw.com

Sold and distributed in North, Central and South America by:
Aspen Publishers, Inc.
7201 McKinney Circle
Frederick, MD 21704
United States of America
Email: customer.service@aspenpublishers.com

Sold and distributed in all other countries by:
Turpin Distribution Services Ltd.
Stratton Business Park
Pegasus Drive, Biggleswade
Bedfordshire SG18 8TQ
United Kingdom
Email: kluwerlaw@turpin-distribution.com

Printed on acid-free paper.

ISBN 978-90-411-3179-9

Printed in Great Britain.

Table of Contents

Preface to the Second Edition

The first edition of this book introduced the concept of the 'Creeping Codification' of the New *Lex Mercatoria*. That concept was well-received and was characterized by a renowned arbitration practitioner as an idea that is '*as close as we've come, in recent generations, to tackling the lex and wrestling it into usable shape*' (*Fortier*, Arbitration International 2001, at 121, 127).

Since the publication of the first edition in 1999, the idea of self-regulation and private governance in international business and the use of international restatements of contract law has gained increasing acceptance. Both the UNIDROIT and *Lando* Principles were published in new and expanded editions. The Draft Common Frame of Reference (DCFR), which the Joint Network on European Private Law delivered to the EU Commission in late 2007, is another example for the success of the concept of private rule-making.

Against the background of these and other new developments, the second edition of this book presents an advanced notion of the Creeping Codification which is based on the 'TransLex Principles', operated by the Center for Transnational Law (CENTRAL) of Cologne University at www.trans-lex.org. The TransLex Principles are based on the 'List of Principles, Rules and Standards of the Lex Mercatoria' which was reproduced in the Annex of the first edition of this book. This Internet-based codification method realized through the TransLex Principles corresponds to the unique character of the Creeping Codification of the New *Lex Mercatoria* which is an ongoing, spontaneous, and dynamic process which is never completed.

The Annex of this book contains a unique personal account – both in the French original and in English translation – which Professor *Philippe Kahn* wrote at the request of the author on how the 'rediscovery' of the New Lex Mercatoria by *Berthold Goldman* and the Dijon School happened in the late 1950s and early 1960s.

I am particularly indebted to my senior research fellows Bernd Scholl, Matthias Schalljo, Bettina Richter, and Oliver Froitzheim for their excellent editorial work and to my student research assistants Thomas Claeßens, Tobias Prang, Erika Theisen, Juliane Thon, Kai Mathar, Miriam Miltenberger, Julia Strerath, Nimalka Rohns, Melanie Kaspers, Nora Wisnagrotzky, and Marc Wetzig, and to my secretary Heidi Potschka for their involvement with this project. I am also indebted to Katherine Simpson who did a wonderful job in improving the readability of this book.

Any comments, critiques or suggestions are very welcome and should be sent to kp.berger@uni-koeln.de.

Klaus Peter Berger
Cologne, January 2010

Preface to the First Edition

'The life of the law has not been logic; it has been experience'.
Oliver Wendell Holmes, The Common Law, 43rd ed., at I.

This book is a revised, updated and expanded version of a study first published in German in 1996 by Walter de Gruyter Publishers, Berlin under the title '*Formalisierte oder "schleichende" Kodifizierung des transnationalen Wirtschaftsrechts*'. It addresses one of the most controversial issues of modern commercial law, the existence and viability of a doctrine of transnational commercial law, a new lex mercatoria. Unlike other studies on this subject, this book tries to provide not only an answer to the multitude of theoretical and methodical questions related to it. The study also deals with the central objection that so many have advanced against the lex mercatoria in the past; i.e., the allegation that the principles, rules and legal institutions that are said to be part of transnational commercial law are too vague and too ambiguous to be applied in every-day legal practice, that the lex mercatoria is, if any, rather a method of decision-making then a self-contained legal system.

To refute this contention and to provide international practice with a tool for the application of the lex mercatoria, this Study presents a new approach towards the 'codification' of the lex mercatoria: the 'creeping codification' through the drafting of an open-end list of principles and rules that constitute the lex mercatoria. The list is drafted and updated regularly under the auspices of a new research center for transnational commercial law, the 'Center for Transnational Law' (CENTRAL), established at Münster University, Germany. Arbitrators, counsel or other lawyers involved in international contract drafting or dispute settlement may thus have easy access to individual rules and principles, together with comprehensive comparative references, which include domestic laws, legal writings, arbitral awards and court decisions.

The practical usefulness of the list is largely depending upon its acceptance by international practitioners. Therefore, any comments as to possible improvements, additions and, most important, practical examples of how the list has been used in actual legal practice, are highly welcome.

This Study has been influenced by all those academics and practitioners who have provided me with insights into the study of international commercial law over the past years. I am particularly indebted to Norbert Horn, who first introduced me into the fascinating world of transnational commercial law. His 'transnational spirit', together with that of Pieter Sanders, Yves Derains and so many others has deeply influenced my approach to the *lex mercatoria* doctrine.

I am also indebted to Professor Michael Joachim Bonell, Rome, and Professor Ole Lando, Copenhagen, for their permission to reprint the UNIDROIT Principles of International Commercial Contracts and the Principles of European Contract Law in the Annex of this Study and for providing me with further information and materials on these projects.

A very special thank you goes to my secretaries, Sabine Holtmannspötter and Ingeborg Steinkamp, for their admirable typing efforts.

Finally, I am very grateful to Volker Nienaber, senior research fellow at the Institute for International Business Law and the Center for Transnational Law (CENTRAL), Münster University, for his excellent editorial support and to Kristie Stahnke and Alison Williams for improving the readability of this book.

Parts of this Study were written (or rewritten) while I was anxiously waiting for the birth of my daughter, Lea Katharina, to whom this book is dedicated.

Klaus Peter Berger
Münster, June 1998

List of Abbreviations

A.2nd	Atlantic Reporter, 2nd ed.
AAA	American Arbitration Association
ABAJ	American Bar Association Journal
ABGB	Allgemeines Bürgerliches Gesetzbuch – Austrian Civil Code
ABSK/RGW	Allgemeine Bedingungen für die Spezialisierung und Kooperation der Produktion zwischen den Organisationen der Mitgliedsländer des Rats für gegenseitige Wirtschaftshilfe (General Conditions for Consumer Services for Machines, Equipment and other Products, delivered between the Organizations and Member States of the COMECON)
A.C.	Appeal Cases
AcP	Archiv für die civilistische Praxis
AG	Die Aktiengesellschaft
AGBG	Gesetz zur Regelung des Rechts der allgemeinen Geschäftsbedingungen – (former) German Law on Standard Form Contracts
AJIL	American Journal of International Law
AJP	Aktuelle Juristische Praxis
Akad.St.Rwiss.DDR	Akademie für Staats- und Rechtswissenschaft der DDR – Academy for Political and Legal Science of the (former) German Democratic Republic

ALB/RGW	Allgemeine Bedingungen für die Warenlieferungen zwischen den Organisationen der Mitgliedsländer des Rats für gegenseitige Wirtschaftshilfe (General Conditions on the Delivery of Goods between the Organizations and Member States of the COMECON)
ALJR	The Australian Law Journal Report
All E.R.	All England Reports
Am.J.Comp.L.	American Journal of Comparative Law
Am.J.Int'l L.	American Journal of International Law
Am.L.Inst. Proc.	American Law Institute Proceedings
Am.Rev.Int'l Arb.	The American Review of International Arbitration
ann.	annotated
Ann.Surv.Int'l & Comp.L.	Annual Survey of International and Comparative Law
AnwBl.	Anwaltsblatt
AöR	Archiv des öffentlichen Rechts
APEC	Asia-Pacific Economic Cooperation
Arb.Int'l	Arbitration International
ArchVR	Archiv des Völkerrechts
Ariz.	Arizona
Ariz.J.Int'l & Comp.L.	Arizona Journal of International and Comparative Law
Art.	Article
Artt.	Articles
ASA	Association Suisse de l'Arbitrage – Swiss Arbitration Association
ASA Bull.	Association Suisse de l'Arbitrage Bulletin – Bulletin of the Swiss Arbitration Association
ASEAN	Association of Southeast Asian Nations
AWD	Außenwirtschaftsdienst des Betriebs-Beraters
b2b	business-to-business
b2c	business-to-consumer
BAGE	Entscheidungen des Bundesarbeitsgerichts
BB	Der Betriebs-Berater
BBl.	Bundesblatt – Swiss Law Gazette
Berkeley J.Int'l L.	Berkeley Journal of International Law
BG	Bundesgericht – Swiss Federal Court
BGB	Bürgerliches Gesetzbuch – German Civil Code
BGBl.	Bundesgesetzblatt – German Law Gazette
BGE	Entscheidungen des Bundesgerichts – Judgments of the Swiss Federal Court

BGH	Bundesgerichtshof – German Federal Supreme Court
BGHZ	Entscheidungen des Bundesgerichtshofs in Zivilsachen – Civil Judgments of the German Federal Supreme Court
BIS	Bank for International Settlements
Bl.Zuerch.Rspr.	Blätter für Zuercherische Rechtsprechung
BMJ	Bundesministerium der Justiz – German Ministry of Justice
BOT	Build Operate Transfer
Brit.Yb.Int'l L.	The British Yearbook of International Law
BT-Drucks.	Bundestags-Drucksache – Publications of the German Parliament
Build L.R.	Building Law Review
Bull.	Bulletin
Bull.Europ.Arb.	Bulletin Européen D'Arbitrage de la Cour Internationale D'Arbitrage de la CCI – European Arbitration Bulletin of the International Court of Arbitration of the ICC
Burrow's Rep.	Burrow's Reports
Bus.Lawy.	Business Lawyer
Bus LR	The Business Law Reports
BVerfG	Bundesverfassungsgericht – German Federal Constitutional Court
BVerfGE	Entscheidungen des Bundesverfassungsgerichts – Judgments of the German Federal Constitutional Court
BW	Burgerlijk Wetboek
BYIL	British Yearbook of International Law
c.	contre
Cambridge L.J.	Cambridge Law Journal
CCI	Chambre de commerce internationale – International Chamber of Commerce (ICC)
CEBS	Committee of European Banking Supervisors
CEDC	Code Européen des Contrats – European Contract Code
CENTRAL	Center for Transnational Law
cf.	confer
CFR	Common Frame of Reference
Ch.	Chapter
CHAPS	Clearing House Automated Payment System
Chi.J.Int'l L.	Chicago Journal of International Law
China FECL	China Foreign Economic Contract Law
CHIPS	Clearing House Interbank Payment System

CIDIP	Conferencia Especializada Interamericana sobre Derecho Internacional Privado – Inter-American Specialized Conference on Private International Law
Cir.	Circuit
CISG	United Nations Convention on Contracts for the International Sale of Goods
CMI	Comité Maritime International
CMR	Convention relative au contrat de transport international de marchandises par route – Convention on Contracts for the International Carriage of Goods by Road
Col.J.Europ.L.	Columbia Journal of European Law
Col.J.Transnat'l L.	Columbia Journal of Transnational Law
Col.J.W.Bus.	Columbia Journal of World Business
Col.L.Rev.	Columbia Law Review
COM	Working Documents of the European Commission
Com.	Commercial
COMECON	Council for Mutual Economic Assistance
Comp. & Int'l L.J. of Southern Africa	Comparative and International Law Journal of Southern Africa
Comp. L.Yb.Int'l Bus.	Comparative Law Yearbook of International Business
Contemp.Probl.	Contemporary Problems
Contract Code	Contract Code Drawn upon on behalf of the English Law Commission
Cowp.	Cowper's English King's Bench Reports (1774–78)
CR	Computer und Recht
CRCICA	Cairo Regional Centre for International Commercial Arbitration
CTC Rep.	Center for Transnational Corporations Reporter
CTR	Iran – United States Claims Tribunal Report
Czech LIT	The Law of International Trade of the Former Czechoslovakia
DB	Der Betrieb
D.C.	District of Columbia
DCFR	Draft Common Frame of Reference
DDR	(ehemalige) Deutsche Demokratische Republik – (former) German Democratic Republic
Dig.	Digest
DIN	Deutsches Institut für Normung

DIS	Deutsche Institution für Schiedsgerichtsbarkeit – German Institution for Arbitration
DIS Mitt.	DIS Mitteilungen
Diss.	Dissertation – dissertation, doctoral thesis
DJZ	Deutsche Juristen-Zeitung
D.L.R.	Dominion Law Reports
D.L.R. (3d)	Dominion Law Reports, Third Series (Canada)
D.P.	Dalloz périodique
DPCI	Droit et Pratique du Commerce International
DRiZ	Deutsche Richterzeitung
DZWir	Deutsche Zeitschrift für Wirtschaftsrecht
EC	European Community/Communities
ECE	United Nations Economic Commission for Europe
ECJ	Court of Justice for the European Communities
ECR	European Court Reports
ed.	edition or editor
eds.	editors
EEC Treaty	Treaty establishing the European Economic Community
e.g.	exempli gratia
EGBGB	Einführungsgesetz zum Bürgerlichen Gesetzbuch – Introductory Law to the German Civil Code
EICC	Electronic Industry Code of Conduct
EKG	Einheitliches Gesetz über den internationalen Kauf beweglicher Sachen
Eng.Rep.	English Reports
EU	European Union
EuR	Europarecht
Eur.J.L.Reform	European Journal of Law Reform
Eur.L.J.	European Law Journal
Europ.Rev.Priv.L.	European Review of Private Law
EuZW	Europäische Zeitschrift für Wirtschaftsrecht
EWCA Civ.	Court of Appeal of England and Wales, Civil Division
EWiR	Entscheidungen zum Wirtschaftsrecht
F.2d	Federal Reporter, Second Series (USA)
FECL	The Foreign Economic Contract Law of the People's Republic of China
FIDIC	Fédération Internationale des Ingénieurs Conseils – International Federation of

	Consulting Engineers
fn.	footnote
Ford.Int'l L.J.	Fordham International Law Journal
GA	United Nations General Assembly
Ga.	Georgia
Ga.App.	Georgia Appeals Reports
GAFTA	Grain and Feed Trade Association
GAOR	United Nations General Assembly Official Record
GATT	General Agreement on Tariffs and Trade
GBl. DDR	Gesetzblatt der (ehemaligen) Deutschen Demokratischen Republik – Law Gazette of the (former) German Democratic Republic
GDR	(former) German Democratic Republic
GEDEC	Groupe d'étude pour le droit européen commun
Georgetown L. & P.Int'l Bus.	Georgetown Law and Policy in International Business
German L.J.	German Law Journal
GIW DDR	Gesetz für internationale Wirtschaftsverträge der (ehemaligen) Deutschen Demokratischen Republik – Foreign Economic Contract Law of the (former) German Democratic Republic
GmbHR	GmbH-Rundschau
G.Wash.J.Int'l L. & Ec.	George Washington Journal of International Law and Economics
GYIL	German Yearbook of International Law
Harv.Int'l L.J.	Harvard International Law Journal
Harv.L.Rev.	Harvard Law Review
HGB	Handelsgesetzbuch – German Commercial Code
IAS	International Accounting Standard(s)
IASB	International Accounting Standards Board
IBA	International Bar Association
ICAO	International Civil Aviation Organization
ICC	International Chamber of Commerce
ICC Bull.	The ICC International Court of Arbitration Bulletin
ICCA	International Council for Commercial Arbitration
ICJ	International Court of Justice
ICJ Reports	International Court of Justice Reports
ICLQ	International & Comparative Law Quarterly
ICSID	International Center for the Settlement of Investment Disputes

ICSID Rev.-FILJ	ICSID Review – Foreign Investment Law Journal
id.	idem
IFLR	International Financial Law Review
IFRS	International Financial Reporting Standard(s)
IHR	Internationales Handelsrecht (International Commercial Law) – Zeitschrift für das Recht des internationalen Warenkaufs und -vertriebs
ILA	International Labour Organization
ILC	International Law Commission
ILM	International Legal Materials
ILO	International Labour Organization
ILR	International Law Report
IMF	International Monetary Fund
Inc.	Incorporated
INCOTERMS	International Commercial Terms
Ind.J.Gl.Legal Studies	Indiana Journal of Global Legal Studies
Ind.L.J.	Indiana Law Journal
Int'l Arb.	International Arbitration
Int'l Arb.Rep.	International Arbitration Report
Int'l Arb.L.Rev.	International Arbitration Law Review
Int'l Bus.Lawy.	International Business Lawyer
Int'l Com.Arb.	International Commercial Arbitration
Int'l Comp.L.Q.	The International and Comparative Law Quarterly
Int'l Constr.L.Rev.	The International Construction Law Review
Int'l Encycl.Comp.L.	International Encyclopedia of Comparative Law
Int'l Rev.L. & Econ.	International Review of Law and Economics
Int'l L.Rep.	International Law Report
Int'l Lawy.	The International Lawyer
Int'l Tax & Bus.Lawy.	International Tax & Business Lawyer
IO	International organization
IPR	Internationales Privatrecht – International Private Law / Conflict of Laws Rules
IPRax	Praxis des Internationalen Privat- und Verfahrensrechts
IPRG	Bundesgesetz über das Internationale Privatrecht – Swiss International Private Law Code
ISDA	International Swaps and Derivatives Association
ISO	International Organization for Standardization

IZPR	Internationales Zivilprozeßrecht – Law of International Civil Procedure
J.	Journal
Jahrb.NPÖ	Jahrbuch für Neue Politische Ökonomie
JBR	Journal of Banking Regulation
J.Bus.L.	Journal of Business Law
JCP	Juris Classeur Pratique
Jher.Jahrb.	Jherings Jahrbücher für die Dogmatik des bürgerlichen Rechts
JIBL	Journal of International Banking Law
J.I.B.L.R.	Journal of International Banking Law and Regulation
J.Int'l Arb.	Journal of International Arbitration
J.Int'l Bus.L.	Journal of International Business Law
J.Int'l L. & Pol.	Journal of International Law and Policy
JITE	Journal of Institutional and Theoretical Economics
J.L. & Com.	Journal of Law and Commerce
J.Legal Stud.	Journal of Legal Studies
JPS	Jahrbuch für die Praxis der Schiedsgerichtsbarkeit
JuS	Juristische Schulung
JW	Juristische Wochenschrift
JWTL	Journal of World Trade Law
JZ	Juristenzeitung
K.B.	English Law Reports, King's Bench
KWG	Kreditwesengesetz
L.	Law
LCIA	London Court of International Arbitration
L.Ed.	U.S. Supreme Court Reports, Lawyer's Edition
LFMR	Law and Financial Markets Review
LG	Landgericht
Lloyd's L.Rep.	Lloyd's Law Report
LM	Lindenmaier-Möhring – Nachschlagewerk des Bundesgerichtshofs
LMA	Loan Market Association
L. & Pol.Int'l Bus.	Law and Policy in International Business
L.Q.Rev.	Law Quarterly Review
L.R.	Law Reports
Ltd.	Limited
M&A	Mergers and acquisitions
McGill L.J.	McGill Law Journal
Md.	Maryland
MDR	Monatsschrift für Deutsches Recht

Mich.J.Int'l L	Michigan Journal of International Law
Mich.L.Rev.	Michigan Law Review
MIGA	Multilateral Investment Guarantee Agency
MNE	Multinational Enterprise
Mo.App.	Missouri Appeal Reports
MünchKomm	Münchener Kommentar
MvA	Memorie van Antwoord – 2nd Memorial Publication on the Dutch Arbitration Law of 1986
MvT	Memorie van Toelichting – 1st Memorial Publication on the Dutch Arbitration Law of 1986
n.c.p.c.	Nouveau Code de Procédure Civile – New French Code of Civil Procedure
Neth.Int'l L.Rev.	Netherlands International Law Review
NJ	Nederlandse Jurisprudentie
NJW	Neue Juristische Wochenschrift
NJW-RR	Neue Juristische Wochenschrift – Rechtsprechungsreport
NLM	New Lex Mercatoria
No.	Number
Nos.	Numbers
N.W. (2nd)	North Western Reporter (2nd series)
N.Y.U.L.Rev.	New York University Law Review
ÖBA	Österreichisches BankArchiv
OCIT	Organization for International Transport by Rail
OECD	Organisation for Economic Co-operation and Development
OHADA	Organisation pour l'harmonisation en Afrique du droit des affaires
OJ	Official Journal of the European Communities / Union
OLG	Oberlandesgericht
OR	Obligationenrecht – Swiss Law of Obligations
ORGALIME	Organisme de liaison des Industries Métalliques Européenes- Organization of the Association of the European Metal Industries
OTC	over-the-counter
Pa.	Pennsylvania
P.C.I.J.	Permanent Court of International Justice
PECL	Principles of European Contract Law
Pr.Inv.Abr.	Private Investors Abroad
P.Wms	Peere William's English Chancery Reports

PWW	Prütting/Wegen/Weinreich, BGB-Kommentar
RabelsZ	Rabels Zeitschrift für ausländisches und internationales Privatrecht
RDAI	Revue de droit des affaires internationales
Rdipp.	Rivista di diritto internazionale privato e processuale
Rec.Cours	Recueil des Cours
Rev.	Review or Revue
Rev.belge dr.int.	Revue belge du droit international
Rev.crit.dr.int.priv.	Revue critique de droit international privé
Rev.d'Arb.	Revue de l'arbitrage
Rev.dr.unif.	Revue de droit uniforme, Uniform Law Review
Rev.dr.int.dr.comp.	Revue de droit international et de droit comparé
Rev.int.dr.comp.	Revue internationale de droit comparé
RGZ	Entscheidungen des Reichsgerichts in Zivilsachen
R.I.E.J.	Revue interdisciplinaire d'études juridiques
Riv.Tr.Dir.Pr.Civ.	Rivista Trimestrale di Diritto e Procedura Civile
RIW	Recht der Internationalen Wirtschaft
RMBCA	Revised Model Business Corporation Act
RTD civ.	Revue trimestrielle de droit civil
Sb.Z.	Sbírka zákonů – Czech Law Gazette
Schw.Jahrb.Int.R.	Schweizer Jahrbuch für Internationales Recht
S.Ct.	Supreme Court Reporter
S.E.	South Eastern Reporter
Sec.	Section
SemJud.	La Semaine Judiciaire
SJZ	Schweizerische Juristen-Zeitung
S.W.2d	South Western Reporter, Second Series
SWIFT	Society for Worldwide Interbank Financial Telecommunication
Swiss ZGB	Zivilgesetzbuch – Swiss Civil Code
Syr.J.Int'l L. & Com.	Syracuse Journal of International Law & Commerce
SZW	Schweizerische Zeitschrift für Wirtschaftsrecht
TFEU	Treaty on the Functioning of the European Union
TranspR	Transportrecht
Tul.J.Int.Comp.L.	Tulane Journal of International Comparative Law

Tul.L.Rev.	Tulane Law Review
TvA	Tijdschrift voor Arbitrage
TvPr.	Tijdschrift voor Privaatrecht
UCC	Uniform Commercial Code
U.Chi. L.Rev.	University of Chicago Law Review
UCP	ICC Uniform Customs and Practice for Documentary Credits
UCJ	Union for *jus commune*
ULF	Uniform Law on the Formation of Contracts for the International Sale of Goods
ULIS	Uniform Law for the International Sale of Goods
UN	United Nations
UNCITRAL	United Nations Commission on International Trade Law
UNCTAD	United Nations Commission on International Trade and Development
UNIDO	United Nations Industrial Development Organization
UNIDROIT	Institut international pour l'unification du droit privé/International Institute for the Unification of Private Law
Unif.L.Rev.	Uniform Law Review
UNTS	United Nations Treaty Series
U.Pa.L.Rev.	University of Pennsylvania Law Review
UPICC	UNIDROIT Principles of International Commercial Contracts
URDG	ICC Uniform Rules for Demand Guarantees
U.S.	United States
v.	versus
Va.J.Int'l L.	Virginia Journal of International Law
Vand.J.Transnat'l L.	Vanderbilt Journal of Transnational Law
VersR	Versicherungsrecht
Vol.	Volume
WHO	World Health Organization
WiB	Wirtschaftsrechtliche Beratung
WIPO	World Intellectual Property Organization
WiRO	Wirtschaft und Recht in Osteuropa
Wis.	Wisconsin
W.L.R.	Weekly Law Reports
WM	Wertpapier-Mitteilungen
WPr.	Weekblad voor Privaatrecht, Notarisambt en Registratie
W.St.U.L.Rev.	Western State University Law Review
WTO	World Trade Organization

WuB	Entscheidungssammlung zum Wirtschafts- und Bankrecht
WUR	Wirtschaft und Recht
Yale L.J.	Yale Law Journal
YCA	Yearbook Commercial Arbitration
ZaöRV	Zeitschrift für ausländisches öffentliches Recht und Völkerrecht
ZBB	Zeitschrift für Bankwirtschaft und Bankrecht
ZEuP	Zeitschrift für Europäisches Privatrecht
ZfRV	Zeitschrift für Rechtsvergleichung
ZGB	see Swiss ZGB
ZGB GDR	Zivilgesetzbuch der ehemaligen Deutschen Demokratischen Republik – Civil Code of the former German Democratic Republic
ZGS	Zeitschrift für das gesamte Schuldrecht/ Zeitschrift für Vertragsgestaltung, Schuld- und Haftungsrecht
ZHR	Zeitschrift für das gesamte Handelsrecht und Wirtschaftsrecht
ZIP	Zeitschrift für Wirtschaftsrecht
ZPO	Zivilprozeßordnung – German Civil Procedure Code
ZRP	Zeitschrift für Rechtspolitik
ZRVgl.	Zeitschrift für Rechtsvergleichung
ZSR	Zeitschrift für schweizerisches Recht
ZVglRWiss.	Zeitschrift für Vergleichende Rechtswissenschaft
ZZP	Zeitschrift für Zivilprozeß

Table of Cases and Awards

A. ARBITRAL AWARDS

I. Ad Hoc Arbitration

II. Institutional Arbitration

American Arbitration Association

Arbitration Court of the Austrian Economic Chamber in Vienna

B. Decisions of Domestic Courts

Austria

England

Bundesarbeitsgericht

Lower Courts

Italy

Corte di Cassazione

Switzerland

Bundesgericht

Cantonal Courts

United States of America

Supreme Court

Other Courts

C. Decisions of Public International Law Courts

Permanent Court of International Justice

Introduction

I. THE NEW *LEX MERCATORIA* AND MODERN TRENDS TOWARDS THE CODIFICATION OF TRANSNATIONAL COMMERCIAL LAW

A. THE DOCTRINE OF A NEW *LEX MERCATORIA*

1. The Birth of the New *Lex Mercatoria* Doctrine

The New *Lex Mercatoria* doctrine would perhaps never have come into existence without the Suez Canal crisis of the mid-1950s. A newspaper article by the French comparativist *Berthold Goldman*, at that time professor of law at the University of Dijon, France[1], is said to mark the rebirth of the theory of the New *Lex Mercatoria* (NLM). The article was published in 'Le Monde' of October 4, 1956 and dealt with the nationality of the Suez Canal Company. Even though he qualified the Suez Canal Company as a juridical person of private law, *Goldman* argued in that newspaper article that the Company was not of Egyptian, English, French or mixed nationality. Due to its particular capital structure, its organization and the global effects of its business activities, *Goldman* drew parallels between the Suez Canal Company, the World Bank, and the Red Cross and characterized the Company as

1. *Berthold Goldman* was born on September 12, 1913 in Bucarest, Romania. He was Professor of Law at the University of Indochina, Faculty of Law from 1947 to 1949, at the University of Dijon, Faculty of Law from 1949 to 1960, at the University of Law, Economics and Social Sciences of Paris from 1960 to 1981, he passed away in 1993, *see Goldman*'s *curriculum vitae* in: *Fouchard/Kahn/Lyon-Caen* (eds.), Le droit des relations économiques internationales, Etudes offertes à Berthold Goldman, at V; *cf. also* the portraits by *Perrot* and *Bredin*, in: Fouchard/Vogel (eds.), L'actualité de la pensée de Berthold Goldman, at 11 *et seq.* and 15 *et seq.*

'*une société internationale, relevant directement de l'ordre juridique international*':

> '[The Suez Canal Company] is, through its capital structure and its management bodies as well as through the subject matter and the effects of its business activity, an *international company which is directly subject to the international legal order*. This is certainly a new concept – if not to say one in the process of being born – but its necessity has, to draw from an ancient reality, for many years been recognized.'[2]

Despite its 'necessarily territorial genesis and functioning'[3], the Suez Canal Company, in *Goldman*'s view, had a truly transnational character. It must be noted, however, that when writing the article, *Goldman* was not aware that his comments on the legal nature of the Suez Canal Company marked the birth of a new theory on transnational commercial law. In his account on 'Towards the Quest for the *Lex Mercatoria*: The Contribution of the Dijon School, 1957–1964', which is reprinted in Annex I of this Study, *Philippe Kahn*[4], who worked with *Goldman* as his assistant in the 1960s, reports from his memories of the work of the research team directed by *Goldman* in those days. He confirms that the team members – *Jean Stoufflet*[5], *Philippe Kahn*[6] and *Philippe Fouchard*[7] – did not purposely 'reinvent' the *lex mercatoria* and the idea of the transnationalization of commercial law in the early 1960s. Rather, the idea evolved almost 'accidentally' from their academic, very practice-oriented[8] research on documentary credits, international sales law and international commercial arbitration.

Even though the birth of the NLM doctrine was nothing but an 'accident of legal history'[9], *Goldman* and the other members of the Dijon School – unknowingly – made the first crucial step to transform the ancient notion of 'law merchant' or *lex mercatoria*, into the modern concept of the NLM. The ancient *lex mercatoria* was developed in the late thirteenth century as part of 'Colford's

---

2. *Goldman*, La Compagnie de Suez, société internationale, Le Monde, October 4, 1956, at 3, English translation reprinted in Annex II of this Study, French facsimile copy at *www.Trans-Lex.org/000009* (emphasis added).
3. *Goldman, id.*
4. *Philippe Kahn* has been the founder of the '*Centre de Recherche sur le Droit des Marchés et des Investissements Internationaux*' (CREDIMI) funded by the French research funding organization (CNRS) and attached to the *Université de Bourgogne*.
5. *Stoufflet*, Le crédit documentaire: étude juridique d'un instrument financier du commerce international.
6. *Kahn*, La vente commerciale internationale, 1964, at 365 *et seq.*; *see also Kahn*, Clunet 1975, at 467, 474; *Kahn*, Clunet 1981, at 5, 26; *Kahn*, in: Fouchard/Kahn/Lyon-Caen (eds.), Le droit des relations économiques internationales, at 97 *et seq.*; *Kahn*, in: Festschrift für Clive M. Schmitthoff, at 240, 241.
7. *Fouchard*, L'Arbitrage Commercial International, 1965, at 423 *et seq.*
8. *Philippe Kahn* emphasized the truly pragmatic approach taken by the research team in the time between 1955 and 1965 in Dijon in a personal letter to the author of July 3, 2009; *see also Kahn*, Annex I of this Study.
9. *Kahn*, *supra* note 6; *see also Kahn*, in Annex I of this Study.

Collection' in the 'Little Red Book of Bristol'[10] and was later refined by *Gerard Malynes* in his famous treatise '*Consuetudo Vel Lex Mercatoria*' published in 1622[11]. In the early 1960s, *Fragistas* and *Goldstajn* published law review articles, the first on the transnationalization of arbitral procedure[12], the second on the evolution of an autonomous law merchant across the iron curtain[13]. Beginning in 1964, *Goldman* himself articulated his view on the law merchant in various articles[14]. For him, the NLM was in fact an '*ensemble*' of general principles and legal rules growing out of a process of spontaneous institutional law-making. He argued that this process is detached from domestic legal systems and escapes the realm of domestic lawmakers which is limited to the territory of its respective jurisdiction. Instead, the law is created within the community of merchants doing cross-border trade and commerce – the *societas mercatorum*[15].

At the outset of his groundbreaking article in the 1964 *Archives de philosophie du droit*, which provides the synthesis of the research work of the Dijon School conducted between 1957 and 1964[16], *Goldman* made reference to the collection of materials of the Colloquium on 'The New Sources of the Law of International Trade with special reference to East-West trade', arranged at King's College, University of London by the International Association of Legal Science between

10. '*Incipit Lex mercatoria, Que, quando, ubi, inter quos et de quibus sit*' ('Here begins Lex Mercatoria, What, When, Where, Among Whom, and Concerning What it is'), English translation and facsimile of the first page of the Latin Original at *www.Trans-Lex.org/000008*; the Document is divided into twenty-one chapters and contains an instructional manual on how to conduct a mercantile court and a series of recommendations on how to improve the process in such courts, *see Basile/Bestor/Coquillette/Donahue* (eds.), Lex Mercatoria and Legal Pluralism: A Late Thirteenth-Century Treatise and its Afterlife, at 13 *et seq.*; another treatise published roughly at the same time is '*De legibus mercatorum apud nundinas et alibi, etc.*' ('On the Laws of Merchants at Fairs and Elsewhere, etc.'), Latin text and English translation reprinted *id.*, Appendix, at 40 *et seq.*
11. *Malynes*, Consuetudo Vel Lex Mercatoria or the Ancient Law-Merchant, at 3, who characterized the ancient *lex mercatoria* as 'customary law of merchants . . . , more ancient than any written law . . . [and] built upon the foundations of Reason and Justice', see for facsimile excerpts of the book *www.trans-lex.org/104970*; *Marquardus*, Tractatus politico-iuridicus de iure mercatorum et commerciorum singulari, Frankfurt 1662; *see* for the significance of the Lex Mercatoria in the Middle Ages *Bart*, in: Souveraineté étatique et marchés internationaux à la fin du 20ème siècle, at 9, 10 *et seq.*; *Blase*, Die Grundregeln des Europäischen Vertragrechts als Recht grenzüberschreitender Verträge, at 27 *et seq.*; *cf.* for the integration of the law merchant into the English common law *Pillans and Rose v. van Mierop and Hopkins*, [1765] 3 Burr. 1663, E.R. 97, 1035 (per *Lord Mansfield*); *Luke v. Lyde*, 2 Burr. 883, 887 ('Mercantile law is not the law of a particular country, but the law of all nations', per *Lord Mansfield*); *cf. generally Blaurock*, in: Ferrari (ed.), The Unification of International Commercial Law, at 9, 10 *et seq.*
12. *Fragistas*, Rev.crit.dr.int.pr. 1960, at 1 *et seq.*
13. *Goldstajn*, The New Law Merchant, J.Bus.L. 1961, at 12 *et seq.; Goldstaijn*, Festschrift Schmitthoff, at 171 *et seq.*
14. *See Goldman*, Frontières du droit et *lex mercatoria*, Archives de philosophie du droit 1964, at 177 *et seq.*; *Goldman*, Clunet 1979, at 475 *et seq.*; *Goldman*, Nouvelles réflexions sur la lex mercatoria, Festschrift P. Lalive, 1993, at 241 *et seq.*
15. *Goldman*, Clunet 1979, at 499.
16. *See Kahn*, Annex I to this Study.

September 24 and 27, 1962 and in particular to the 'rapport général' of *Professor Clive M. Schmitthoff*[17]. *Schmitthoff* was *Goldman's* counterpart in the common law world, the second driving force behind the revival of the ancient *lex mercatoria* in the early 1960s. The London Colloquium is generally regarded as an early milestone in the academic discussion on the NLM. In various articles *Schmitthoff* advocated the evolution of an autonomous law of international trade[18]. In his introductory speech to the London Colloquium, in which *Goldman* did not participate, *Schmitthoff* stated:

> 'The evolution of an autonomous law of international trade, founded on universally accepted standards of business conduct, would be one of the most important developments of legal science in our time. It would constitute a common platform for commercial lawyers from all countries, those of planned and free market economy, those from civil law and common law, and those of fully developed and developing economy, which would enable them to co-operate in the perfection of the legal mechanism of international trade'[19].

Schmitthoff's vision of the future of international business law was based on a pragmatic theory of self-regulation. *Schmitthoff*'s plea for the primacy of party autonomy, which he regarded as the basis of commercial custom as one element of the 'autonomous law of international trade'[20], made him sympathize with the notion of the self-regulatory contract, for which the parties adopt their own contractual regulation which is detached from any municipal law[21]. Consequently, in his 'General Conspectus' which he presented to the London Colloquium, *Schmitthoff* showed strong sympathy for the Swiss scholar *Dr. Luithlen* who, as early as 1956 – the year *Goldman* published his article on the Suez Canal Company – reversed the traditional relationship between domestic law and any form of transnational legal structures which had prevailed since then by arguing that 'autonomous commercial law no longer complements municipal law in some specialized topics but municipal and international law complement the *self-supporting legal order* where it still shows gaps or is inadequate'[22]. In the light of this almost revolutionary view, *Schmitthoff* observed that 'a strong tendency can be noted [in the reports presented at the London Colloquium] in favour of an autonomous

17. *Schmitthoff*, in: Schmitthoff (ed.), The Sources of the Law of International Trade, 1964, at 3 *et seq.*
18. *Schmitthoff*, International Business Law: A New Law Merchant, Current Law and Social Problems, 1961, at 129 *et seq.*; *Schmitthoff*, RabelsZ 28 (1964), at 47 *et seq.*; see for a later article on the NLM *Schmitthoff*, in: Horn/Schmitthoff (eds.), The Transnational Law of International Commercial Transactions, 1982, at 19 *et seq.*
19. *Schmitthoff*, in: Schmitthoff (ed.), The Sources of the Law of International Trade, 1964, at 3, 5.
20. *Schmitthoff*, *id.*, at 16.
21. *Schmitthoff*, *supra* note 19, at 33: 'No legal system that admits the principle of autonomy of choice of the proper law of contract, in the orthodox sense, can object to an attempt of the parties to make their contractual regulation self-regulatory.'
22. *Luithlen*, Einheitliches Kaufrecht und autonomes Handelsrecht, at 57 (emphasis added).

regulation [of world trade]'[23]. In spite of this very liberal approach towards the idea of an autonomous law of world trade, a fundamental difference to *Goldman's* theory of the NLM remained. For *Schmitthoff*, the autonomy of the parties existed *only by the will of the sovereign states*[24]. In his view, parties to international business contracts were free to subject themselves to sources of law other than national laws and to organize their relations as they deem fit, but only under the authority given by the state legislatures[25]. While *Goldman's* concept of the NLM was completely detached from national laws in the sense of a *de iure* autonomy, *Schmitthoff*'s view of an autonomous law of international trade related to a mere *de facto* autonomy which remains always within the boundaries of domestic legal systems[26].

In spite of their differences in principle, both *Schmitthoff* and the 'French School'[27] have inspired those who have contributed to the study of transnational commercial law since then, like *Dasser*[28], *De Ly*[29], *Horn*[30], *Lando*[31],

23. *Schmitthoff*, in: Schmitthoff (ed.), The Sources of the Law of International Trade, at 3, 36 with reference to *Schmitthoff*, Tidskrift av Juridiska Föreningen i Finland 1957, at 349, 364.
24. *Schmitthoff, supra* note 23, at 35: '... it is justified to ask whether the modern law of international trade constitutes an autonomous legal order, independent of municipal laws *but admitted in their domain by authority of the municipal sovereign*' (emphasis added). *See* for a modern view of the NLM going in the same direction *Ferrante*, in: Piergiovanni (ed.), From *lex mercatoria* to commercial law, at 121, 141; *see also Ipsen*, Private Normenordnungen als Transnationales Recht?, at 178 *et seq.*
25. *Goode*, ICLQ 2005, at 539, 548; *De Ly*, Diritto Del Commercio Internazionale 2000, at 555, 557.
26. *De Ly*, International Business Law and Lex Mercatoria, at 214; *Dasser*, Internationale Schiedsgerichte und Lex Mercatoria, at 43 *et seq.*; *Ipsen, supra* note 24, at 76 *et seq.*
27. The research conducted by *Goldman* and *Kahn* at the University of Dijon has influenced other French scholars such as *Motulsky*, *Stoufflet*, *Fouchard*, *Jacquemont*, *Oppetit*, *Loquin* and *Jehl*, *see De Ly, supra* note 26, at 220 *et seq.*; *Marrella*, La Nuova Lex Mercatoria, at 660 *et seq.*; it is not surprising that on the procedural plane, the French School advocates the radical notion of arbitration as a truly transnational, autonomous, largely self-regulating dispute resolution mechanism which exists in its own space – a non-national or transnational domain, independent of all national jurisdictions and completely detached from the law of the seat, *see Gaillard*, Recueil des Cours 2007, at 53, 101 *et seq.*; *see also* Cour de Cassation, *Société PT Putrabali Adyamulia v. Société Rena Holding et Société Mnogutia Est Epices*, Rev. d'Arb. 2007, at 507.
28. *Dasser*, Internationale Schiedsgerichte und lex mercatoria; *Dasser*, Schweizerische Zeitschrift für internationales und europäisches Recht 1991, at 299 *et seq.*; *Dasser*, in: Appelbaum/Felstiner/Gessner (eds.), Rules and Networks, The Legal Culture of Global Business Transactions, at 189 *et seq.*; *Dasser*, in: Zimmermann (ed.), Globalisierung und Entstaatlichung des Rechts, Teilband II, at 129 *et seq.*
29. *De Ly*, De lex mercatoria, Inleiding op de studie van het transnationaal handelsrecht; *De Ly*, International Business Law and Lex Mercatoria; *see also De Ly, supra* note 25, at 555 *et seq.*
30. *Horn*, Das Recht der internationalen Anleihen, at 510 *et seq.*, 522 *et seq.*; *Horn*, L.&Pol.Int'l Bus. 1977, at 753 *et seq.*, *Horn*, ZHR 1977, at 86 *et seq.*; *Horn*, in: Horn (ed.), Legal Problems of Codes of Conduct for MNEs, 1980, at 45, 59 *et seq.*; *Horn*, JWTL 1982, at 338 *et seq.*; *Horn*, RIW 1997, at 717, 723; *Horn*, The United Nations Convention on Independent Guarantees and the Lex Mercatoria; *Horn*, in: Berger (ed.), The Practice of Transnational Law, 67 *et seq.*; *Horn*, Festschrift für Karsten Schmidt, at 705 *et seq.*; *Horn*, in: Meessen (ed.), Economic Law as an Economic Good, at 139 *et seq.*
31. *See Lando*, 34 ICLQ 1985, at 34 *et seq.*; *Lando*, in: Festskrift till Stig Strömholm, at 567 *et seq.*

Langen[32], *Marrella*[33] and many others[34]. Some of them, like *François Rigaux* from Belgium, used the NLM doctrine to explain the legal impact and nature of the business activities of large, multinational companies which, due to their size and the global impact of their business activities, escape from the realm of nation states and function according to their own rules and principles[35]. The parallels to *Goldman*'s early explanation of the legal nature of the Suez Canal Company are striking.

2. Fifty Years of Debate on the New *Lex Mercatoria*

The works of *Goldman* and *Schmitthoff* published in the early and mid-1960s set the stage for what was to become a 'tumultuous'[36] debate on the NLM. No other topic of international business law has been as controversially and hotly debated as the doctrine of the NLM. Since he first published his view, *Goldman*'s idea of an autonomous third legal system has sent 'shock waves'[37] through the traditional, positivistic doctrine of legal sources[38]. This debate has divided the field of international business lawyers in two camps, the 'traditionalists' and the 'transnationalists'[39]. There is no middle ground between them.

It is therefore not surprising that almost every aspect of the NLM doctrine is highly controversial. These controversies relate to the principal justification, the legal quality, the methodical basis and the democratic legitimacy of the NLM, but

---

32. *Langen*, Transnationales Recht, 1981; *Langen*, NJW 1969, at 358 *et seq.*
33. *Marrella*, La Nuova Lex Mercatoria, 2003; *Marrella*, Vand. J. Transnat'l L. 2003, at 1137 *et seq.*; *Marrella/Yoo*, Virginia J.Int'l L. 2007, at 807 *et seq.*
34. *Schlesinger/Gündisch*, RabelsZ 28 (1964), at 4 *et seq.*; *Berman/Kaufman*, Harv.Int'l L.J. 1978, at 221 *et seq.*; *von Hoffmann*, IPRax 1984, at 106 *et seq.*; *Siehr*, in: Holl/Klinke (eds.), Internationales Privatrecht, 1985, at 103, 112 *et seq.*; *Carbonneau*, Col.J.Transnat'l.L. 1985, at 579 *et seq.*; *Jakubowski*, Festschrift Schmitthoff, at 207 *et seq.*; *Braeckmans*, TvPr. 1986, at 1 *et seq.; v. Struycken*, in: L'évolution contemporaine du Droit des Contrats, Journées René Savatier, 1986, at 209; *Goldstaijn*, in: Sarcevic/Volken (ed.), Dubrovnik Lectures, 1986, at 55 *et seq.*; *Kappus*, RIW 1990, at 788 *et seq.*; *Paulsson*, Int'l Bus.Lawy. 1990, at 4 *et seq.*; *Berman/Dasser*, in: Carbonneau (ed.), Lex mercatoria and Arbitration, at 53, 65 *et seq.*; *Weise*, Lex mercatoria, Materielles Recht vor der internationalen Handelsschiedsgerichtsbarkeit; *Ferrari*, Riv.Tr.Dir.Pr.Civ. 1994, at 893, 898; *Juenger*, Vand.J.Trans.L. 1995, at 487, 492 *et seq.*; *Berger*, Internationale Wirtschaftsschiedsgerichtsbarkeit, at 361 *et seq.*; *Berger*, International Economic Arbitration, at 525 *et seq.*; *Berger*, IPRax 1993, at 281 *et seq.*; *cf. also* the extensive studies by *Osman*, Lex mercatoria and *Stein*, Lex mercatoria.
35. *Rigaux*, Droit public et droit privé dans les relations internationales, at 344 *et seq.* and 437 *et seq.*; *cf. generally Rigaux*, Droit international privé, No. 2.35.
36. *Kahn*, in: L'actualité de la pensée de Berthold Goldman, at 25.
37. *Lagarde*, in: Le droit des relations économiques internationales, Études offertes à Berthold Goldman, 1987, at 125, 150
38. *See* the report by *Philippe Kahn*, reprinted in Annex I of this Study, emphasizing that *Philippe Fouchard*, member of the Dijon School, used the less provocative term '*community* of merchants' rather than '*society* of merchants' because of the strong opposition raised by the traditional, positivistic theory of legal sources against the NLM theory.
39. *Gaillard*, Clunet 1995, at 5, 6.

also to the terminology used[40] and the practical viability of the doctrine[41]. Some scholars are struck by the intensity of the debate and wonder whether the NLM doctrine is a 'cure-all', an 'enigma' or rather a 'chimera'[42]. Others speak of the NLM as a 'legal Loch Ness monster'[43].

The NLM doctrine is also subject to severe political criticism. It is argued that the NLM was developed by European law professors to preserve the political and economic imbalances between the North and the South because:

> 'the recognition of great principles under the name lex mercatoria . . . not only permitted Western enterprises to win time when confronted with the escalation of demands of the third world [in the petroleum conflicts of the 1960s and 1970s], but allowed its inventors [the 'European professors' as 'charismatic notables' and pioneers of international arbitration] to gain time as well, preserving their position when confronted with the new law firm offensive in this market [for international arbitration]'[44].

Even today, it is argued that all attempts to codify the NLM are merely intended to 'produce the need for greater expertise and thus more work for the few lawyers who are dedicated to its propagation'[45]. It is also argued that the NLM doctrine has facilitated the avoidance of local law of third world parties in the major petroleum arbitrations in the 1970s[46] and that its flexibility has served to overcome a strict interpretation of contracts, thereby serving in part to hold down the claims of developing countries raised against western oil and construction companies in the 1960s and 1970s[47]. These claims were, in turn, inspired by the upcoming sovereign pride and post-colonial consciousness of the ex-colonial states in the context of the New International Economic Order[48] and the emerging North-South conflict. From

---

40. *See infra* Chapter 2 I.C.
41. *See infra* Chapter 2 I.C.2.a. for details.
42. *K. Schmidt*, in: Murakami/Marutschek/Riesenhuber (eds.), Globalisierung und Recht, at 153 *et seq.*
43. *Molineaux*, J. Int'l Arb. 2000, issue 1, at 147.
44. *Dezalay/Garth*, Dealing in Virtue, at 89; *see also Nottage*, Arb. Int'l 2000, at 53, 59 *et seq.*; *Fortier*, Arb. Int'l 2001, at 121, 123 *et seq.*
45. *Wasserstein*, Chi. J. Int'l L. 2004, at 67, 82.
46. *See, e.g. The Government of the State of Kuwait v. The American Independent Oil Company (AMINOIL)*, ILM 1982, 976 *et seq.* (1982); *Texaco Overseas Petroleum Company/California Asiatic Oil Company v. The Government of the Libyan Arab Republic*, ILM 1978, 1 *et seq.* (1977); *Libyan American Oil Company (LIAMCO) v. The Government of the Libyan Arab Republic*, ILM 1981, 1 *et seq.* (1977); *Saudi Arabia v. Arabian American Oil Company (ARAMCO)*, ILR 1963, 117 *et seq.* (1958); *Sapphire International Petroleums Ltd. v. National Iranian Oil Company*, Int'l L. Rep. 1967, 136 *et seq.* (1963); *BP Exploration Co. (Libya) v. Government of the Libyan Arab Republic*, ILR 1979, 297 *et seq.*; *see* for an evaluation of these awards as 'typical examples of . . . misunderstood statelessness', *Highet*, in: Carbonneau (ed.), Lex Mercatoria and Arbitration, at 133, 137.
47. *Dezalay/Garth*, *id.*, at 109; *see also Sornarajah*, J. Int'l Arb. 1989, at 7, 17.
48. *See* Declaration on Permanent Sovereignty over Natural Resources, G.A. Res. 1803, 17 GAOR Supp. (No. 17) U.N. Doc. A/5217 (1962); Charter of Economic Rights and Duties of States, G.A. Res. 3281, 29 GAOR Supp. (No. 3) U.N. Doc., A/9030 (1974); *see generally Jiminez de*

the first generation of lawyers of the third world there was scarcely any opposition on this point to the 'grand professors', of whom quite often they had been disciples[49]. Lawyers involved in the arbitrations of those days recall that 'all believed in the *lex mercatoria* in the period 1960–1970'[50]. The biased view is known from the ancient law merchant which some regard not as a genuine blend of the mercantile usages of Europe but as 'a body of customary law of Italian origin imposed on medieval traders by the predominance in European commerce of the Italian merchants'[51].

Fifty years later, the economic conditions have changed dramatically. In an era of globalization of world trade, international business is faced with far-reaching regional and global integration of capital markets and markets for services, goods and foreign direct investment. These developments take place at high speed, fostered by the recent revolutions in information and communication technologies. The world has developed into a 'global market place' in which national boundaries do not play the role they played fifty years ago[52]. This development is of crucial importance for the NLM doctrine. The fathers of the NLM doctrine have always emphasized that economic factors – and above all the striving for enhanced productivity, rationalization of production, and for the reduction of transaction costs as well as the development from domestic and regional to world markets that results from these developments – have a significant impact on the evolution of a transnational system of law[53]. The proponents of the NLM doctrine regard themselves as 'chroniclers of the development of international commerce and its legal framework conditions, drawing their legal conclusions from the observance of real-life phenomena'[54]. The dramatic economic transformations of the world economy that have taken place and are taking place today at an enormous pace relate directly to the social and economic processes 'at the periphery' of the legal process[55] which serve as the laboratory for the creation of transnational legal structures. Therefore, the debate on the NLM has not lost much of the momentum it has gained in the early 1960s. Even though this debate was initiated by academics from France and England, the modern discourse suffers from the absence – on both sides – of a real dialogue between Francophone and Anglo-Saxon ways of discussing law in the global economy, a reciprocal deafness undoubtedly related to the hesitation of dealing with academic writings in foreign languages[56].

Arechaga, Application of the Rule of State Responsibility to the Nationalization of Foreign Owned Property, Legal Aspects of the New International Economic Order 1980, at 220 *et seq.*; *Horn*, JWTL 1982, at 338, 340.

49. *Dezalay/Garth*, *id.*, at 89.
50. *Dezalay/Garth*, *id.*, at 90, stating that there was 'an illusion of consensus' on the *lex mercatoria* at that time.
51. *Gutteridge*, Comparative Law, at 14.
52. *See Berger*, in: Berger (ed.), The Practice of Transnational Law, at 1, 14 *et seq.*
53. *Goldstajn*, J.Bus.L. 1961, at 12, 13; *Kahn*, La vente commerciale internationale, at 365.
54. *Stein*, *supra* note 34, at 13.
55. *See infra* Chapter 2 II.G.3.b.aa.
56. *Wälde*, Book Review, *www.transnational-dispute-management.com/samples/freearticles/tv1-1-bookreview_06.htm.*

B. FROM DOGMATISM TO PRAGMATISM: MODERN TRENDS TOWARDS THE CODIFICATION OF THE NEW *LEX MERCATORIA*

1. The Dogmatic Dilemma: The New *Lex Mercatoria* Trapped between Legal Positivism and the Need for Codification

From the very beginning, the academic discussion on the existence of a NLM has focused either on the justification or the denial of its theoretical foundation. The fierce 'trench fighting'[57] about the theoretical basis of the NLM doctrine has prevented any attempts to change the perspective and to search for pragmatic means of codifying the NLM. Legal doctrine was always more concerned with the provenance of legal rules than with their quality and the dogma of legal positivism left no room for non-national precepts even if they should be clearly superior to domestic law[58]. It is not surprising, therefore, that the discussion about the idea of the transnationalization of commercial law conveys the impression that the 'final issue is one of national pride'[59].

There are two aspects which are responsible for this dilemma. *Schmitthoff* described them with remarkable foresight in the Conclusion of his 'General Conspectus' delivered at the London Conference in September 1962:

> 'When we compare the modern law of international trade ... with the medieval *lex mercatoria*, we notice that the modern development has one great drawback and one great advantage: the drawback is that the modern law of international trade has to overcome the barriers created by the relatively modern concept of the national state which originated a legal order of numerous municipal systems; and the advantage is that the technique and mechanism of deliberate formulation of the law of international trade is infinitely more developed today than it was in the middle ages'[60].

Even though these seemingly contradictory aspects – the positivistic inertia of state sovereignty[61] and the need for proper codification techniques for an a-national legal system – were recognized very early in the process, it took more than forty years until they were finally reconciled[62]. Today's trend towards a 'global civil society'[63]

57. *See infra* Chapter 2 I.A.
58. *Juenger*, in: Berger (ed.), The Practice of Transnational Law, at 81, 83.
59. *Großmann-Doerth*, JW 1929, at 3447.
60. *Schmitthoff, supra* note 17, at 37.
61. *See* for a more recent view as to the 'exaggerated respect [of the US Supreme Court] for the notion of state sovereignty' as an obstacle to the recognition of a new law merchant by the American judiciary *Juenger, supra* note 58, at 89; *see also Lynch*, The Forces of Economic Globalization, at 342.
62. *See generally Bonell*, Essays in Honor of Roy Goode, at 91 *et seq.*
63. *See generally Böhm*, in: Mestmäcker (ed.), Freiheit und Ordnung in der Marktwirtschaft, 1980, at 105 *et seq.*; *Schröder*, Die neue Gesellschaft/Frankfurter Hefte 2000, at 200 *et seq.*; *see also* the vision of a 'general global legal society' of *von Savigny*, System des heutigen Römischen Rechts, Vol. VIII, 1849, at 30 *et seq.*

and the relative decline of the states' power to influence or steer national or international economic developments has lead to an erosion and irrelevance of national boundaries in markets. This global development has resulted in the decreasing significance of sovereignty in this area[64]. That phenomenon and the freedom of the parties in international contract law have caused a reconsideration of the traditional theory of legal sources which has 'moved beyond yesteryear's narrow-minded positivism'[65]. A non-positivistic notion of the law is beginning to emerge[66].

All these developments account for a marked shift from a theoretical approach regarding the nature and sources of the NLM prevailing until the mid-1990s to a more pragmatic perspective focusing on ways and means to codify the NLM[67].

2. The Pragmatic Approach: Three Projects for the Codification of the New *Lex Mercatoria*

There are three projects which reflect this shift from dogmatism to pragmatism in the context of the NLM doctrine. Two of them (*infra* a. and b.), while different in origin, are similar in nature, while the third one (*infra* c.) takes a completely different approach as an Internet-based codification platform for transnational commercial law. All three projects have a direct connection with the NLM doctrine. They reflect a change of paradigm in international commercial law, a marked shift away from formal rule-making by international formulating agencies to private codification efforts. The codification of transnational commercial law is being 'privatized'. In spite of the different attitudes of their drafters towards the existence and practical viability of the NLM, all three projects furnish proof of the fact that, in spite of the long lasting dispute about its nature and dogmatic underpinnings, legal theory and international practice have accepted today that transnational business law is open to the 'codification'[68] of its contents.

a. The UNIDROIT Principles of International Commercial Contracts

In May 1994, the International Institute for the Unification of Private Law *(Institut international pour l'unification du droit privé*, UNIDROIT)[69] seated in Rome published the official text of the 'Principles of International Commercial Contracts' (UNIDROIT Principles)[70]. The UNIDROIT Principles were first published

64. *Walker/Fox*, Global Legal Studies Journal 1996, at 375, 380.
65. *Juenger*, in: Carbonneau (ed.), Lex Mercatoria and Arbitration, at 265, 276; *see also Berman/ Dasser, supra* note 34, at 60.
66. *Canaris*, in: Basedow (ed.), Europäische Vertragsrechtsvereinheitlichung und deutsches Recht, 2000, at 5, 10 *et seq.*
67. *De Ly, supra* note 25, at 571.
68. *See* for the meaning of 'codification' in the context of the NLM doctrine *infra* Chapter 4 II.C.5.e.
69. *See infra* Chapter 4 I.A.1. for a brief survey on the history and work of UNIDROIT.
70. UNIDROIT (ed.), Principles of International Commercial Contracts, 1994.

in English and French, but are also available in various other languages[71]. In preparing the Principles, the Institute implemented the idea of drafting a 'restatement' of international contract law, an idea first presented as early as 1968 by its then General Secretary *Mario Matteucci*[72]. In 2004, UNIDROIT published a new edition of the Principles[73]. The main purpose of the new edition was to cover additional topics of interest to the international legal and business community such as authority of agents, third party rights, set-off, assignment of rights, transfer of obligations and assignment of contracts, and limitation periods[74]. The UNIDROIT Principles indicate in their Preamble that they set forth 'general rules' (*règles générales*) for international commercial contracts[75]. In presenting the Principles, UNIDROIT intended to provide academics and practitioners alike with a kind of '*ratio scripta* of a supra-national legal order'[76]. Even though the acceptance and validity of the Principles is said to depend only on their authoritative persuasiveness[77], the drafters of the UNIDROIT Principles regard them as 'a kind of modern *ius commune*... or a modern expression of what is commonly called *lex mercatoria*'[78].

b. *The Principles of European Contract Law*

In spring 1995, after more than ten years of preparation, the 'Commission on European Contract Law', under the leadership of the Danish law Professor *Ole Lando*, presented the first part of the 'Principles of European Contract Law' (PECL)[79]. A consolidated version of Part I and Part II of these Principles was published in 2000[80] and Part III was published in 2003[81]. The *Lando* Principles

71. *Cf.* the German, Italian, Spanish, Arabic, Chinese and Russian versions in *Bonell*, An International Restatement of Contract Law, at 271 *et seq.*
72. *Matteucci*, contribution to the discussion at the 4th conference of the organizations dealing with the unification of law from April 22 to 24, 1968 in Rome, in: UNIDROIT, Annuaire 1967–1968, Vol. II, at 267, 268; *see generally* for the legal nature of 'restatements' *infra* Chapter 3 I.B. and Chapter 4 I.A.4.
73. UNIDROIT (ed.), Principles of International Commercial Contracts, 2004, also available at *www.unidroit.org/english/principles/contracts/principles2004/blackletter2004.pdf.*
74. Introduction to the 2004 Edition, in: UNIDROIT (ed.), Unidroit Principles of International Commercial Contracts 2004, at VIII; *see also* the contributions in Jolivet (ed.), Unidroit Principles: New Developments and Applications, at 9 *et seq.*
75. *See* for the terminology ('commercial' or 'economic contracts') *infra* Chapter 4 I.A.6.b.
76. UNIDROIT Study L Doc. 16 (1979), at 2; *Bonell*, RDAI 1988, at 873, 874; *Kötz*, Festschrift Zweigert, at 481, 492.
77. UNIDROIT (ed.), Principles of International Commercial Contracts, at VIII *et seq.*
78. *Bonell*, RabelsZ 56 (1992), at 274, 287.
79. *Lando/Beale* (eds.), Principles of European Contract Law, Part I: Performance, Non-Performance and Remedies, 1995.
80. *Lando/Beale* (eds.), Principles of European Contract Law, Parts I and II, Combined and Revised.
81. *Lando/Clive/Prüm/Zimmermann* (eds.), Principles of European Contract Law, Part III. The *Lando* Principles are available at *http://frontpage.cbs.dk/law/commission_on_european_contract_law.*

want to contribute to the evolution of a new 'European *ius commune*'[82]. Art. 1.101(3)(a) PECL states that the PECL may be applied to a contract 'when the parties have agreed that their contract is to be governed by ... the *lex mercatoria* ...'. A similar provision is to be found in the Preamble of the UNIDROIT Principles. However, the *Lando* Principles differ from the UNIDROIT Principles in two important respects. The first difference relates to their geographical reach. While the UNIDROIT Principles aim at the global level, the *Lando* Principles are necessarily limited to the regional level, *i.e.* the Member States of the EU. The second difference relates to the nature of transactions both sets of Principles intend to cover. While the UNIDROIT Principles are limited to international b2b-transactions, the *Lando* Principles cover both b2b and b2c-contracts. This distinction is important, given that in b2c-transactions, party autonomy is not granted to the same extent as in b2b-transactions in order to allow for a high level consumer protection. In spite of the resulting limited use of the *Lando* Principles for the codification of the NLM, they claim that they are a 'modern European *lex mercatoria*'[83].

c. *The TransLex Principles*

In April 2009, the Center for Transnational Law (CENTRAL) at the University of Cologne, Germany, presented the 'TransLex Principles'[84] as part of its new online codification and research platform 'TransLex' at www.trans-lex.org. As of October 2009, the TransLex Principles contain 128 principles and rules of the NLM. Unlike the *Lando* and UNIDROIT Principles, the TransLex Principles contain the black letter text of these principles and rules and comprehensive comparative law references taken from domestic statutes, court decisions, doctrine, arbitral awards, uniform law etc., many of them in full text format. The TransLex Principles are the successor of the 'Transnational Law Database & Bibliography' (Tldb) which CENTRAL operated on the Internet from October 2001 until March 2009. The Tldb was developed by the CENTRAL Research Team out of the 'List of Principles, Rules and Standards of the *Lex Mercatoria*' which was contained in the Annex of the first edition of this book[85].

The TransLex Principles are based on the notion of the 'Creeping Codification'[86] of transnational commercial law which was likewise introduced in the first edition of this book. The concept of Creeping Codification serves two main purposes. The first is to provide international practitioners (contract negotiators, arbitrators, attorneys and other representatives of the parties in international arbitration

82. *Cf. infra* Chapter 4 I.B.1.
83. *Lando/Beale*, *supra* note 80, at XXIV; *see also Hesselink*, in: Hesselink/de Vries, Principles of European Contract Law, at 25.
84. Text reprinted in Annex III of this Study.
85. *Berger*, The Creeping Codification of the Lex Mercatoria, 1999, at 278 *et seq.*; *see* for the history of TransLex *infra* Chapter 4 II.C.5.
86. *See infra* Chapter 4 II.C.

proceedings) with an instrument to apply transnational commercial law in daily legal practice. With its depth of resources on transnational commercial law, including international arbitration and the law of expropriation, the TransLex Principles provide the hitherto missing link between the theory of transnational commercial law and international legal practice[87]. As a second and major objective, the concept of Creeping Codification, coupled with the Word Wide Web, is intended to lead the NLM doctrine out of the codification dilemma in which it has been trapped over the past fifty years. The need for extreme flexibility and openness of any process directed towards the codification of the NLM has long since been criticized as irreconcilable with the 'petrification' of the law which necessarily results from any codification process. Like the UNIDROIT and *Lando* Principles, the TransLex Principles can be applied 'if the parties have chosen transnational commercial law, general principles of law, the *lex mercatoria* or the like'[88].

II. COURSE OF THE STUDY

This Study is divided into two main parts. The first part is concerned with the theoretical and methodological foundations of the doctrine of an autonomous transnational economic law. The second part deals with the core question as to how the NLM can be codified so as to allow for its application in everyday legal practice. To this end, the Study presents a new and independent approach: the concept of 'Creeping Codification' of the NLM.

The first Chapter provides a brief survey of the principal failures of the application of domestic laws to transnational commercial transactions as well as the various proposals to overcome these failures. Particular emphasis is placed on the attempts to achieve a harmonious and interest-oriented relationship between substantive law and traditional conflict of laws doctrine. The second Chapter deals with the principal objections raised against the NLM doctrine. In discussing the various arguments advanced in favour and against the doctrine of transnational commercial law, the Study develops a comprehensive system of methodical and theoretical foundations for the NLM as an independent third legal system alongside domestic and public international law. To achieve this goal, the Study explores the various options for a spontaneous and decentralized formation and evolution of a transnational system of commercial law.

The second major part of this Study deals with the basic question of whether, how and to what extent the NLM doctrine can be used in everyday legal practice. The third Chapter surveys previous efforts to unify international contract law. The draft of a Franco-Italian Law of Obligations, the American Restatement of the Law of Contract, the efforts of the Member States of the former Council for Mutual Economic Existence (COMECON) to unify their contract law and the most recent attempts to codify European contract law all serve as examples for

87. *See Berger*, Arb. Int'l 2002, at 83, 84.
88. *See* Purpose and Concept at *www.Trans-Lex.org/000010*.

regional or bilateral projects for the unification of transnational contract law. UNIDROIT's plan for the 'progressive codification of international trade law', first presented in the 1960s, demonstrates the efforts to unify contract law on a global basis. In spite of these manifold and diverse attempts to codify transnational commercial law, this development has – for decades – only been of minor interest to international legal practice. In the eyes of many practitioners, the notion of transnational law is limited to such general and vague principles as 'good faith' and *'pacta sunt servanda'* which lack any concrete and workable content[89]. Critics of the NLM maintain that the evolution of detailed legal rules which might resolve complex legal disputes requires comprehensive and time-consuming comparative law efforts which international arbitrators cannot perform within the tight schedules of international arbitration proceedings. Also, in international contract practice, the NLM is seen with substantial scepticism. A worldwide survey among attorneys active in international commercial law revealed that most of them would strongly advise against including a provision in the contract of their client referring to the NLM as the *lex contractus*[90]. In their opinion, transnational law does not have the 'definitive' and 'provable' quality of domestic laws:

> 'By these criteria, lex mercatoria simply has not stood up. The problem is both in its "provability", and in finding a comprehensive set of principles within the lex mercatoria. For problems with determining the existence of any purported principle of lex mercatoria, just look at its sources: practices followed since time immemorial, or at least since the roman ius gentium; ancient cases in dusty tomes; writings of erudite scholars who passed away about the time the steam engine was revolutionizing industry... As a collection of commercial practices, the content of lex mercatoria has not been discoverable in any single place... Nor has lex mercatoria been "definitive" in the sense of supplying a comprehensive set of decision-making rules which can be applied to resolve a dispute'[91].

Other surveys, such as the worldwide enquiry conducted by CENTRAL between 1999 and 2000[92] revealed a substantial awareness of the NLM in the legal community[93]. At the same time, the CENTRAL enquiry showed a lack of knowledge

89. *See Berman/Dasser*, in: Carbonneau (ed.), Lex Mercatoria and Arbitration, at 53, 59, stating that it is difficult to refute these objections since most authors 'do not indicate what degree of clarity, objectivity, generality, and universality is required before a set of concepts, standards, principles, rules, procedures, and institutions can be said to constitute a system of "law"'.
90. *Selden*, Ann.Surv.Int'l &Comp.L. 1995, at 111, 113 *et seq.*
91. *Selden, id.*, at 119 *et seq.*
92. *See* for the background, methodical basis and results of this worldwide survey, which was conducted as part of a three-year research project sponsored by the Volkswagen-Foundation and entitled 'The Role of Merchants, their Lawyers and their Arbitral Tribunals in the Evolution and Development of Transnational Commercial law' *Berger/Dubberstein/Lehmann/Petzold*, in: Berger (ed.), The Practice of Transnational Law, at 91 *et seq.*; see for a copy of the questionnaire used and a graphical analysis of the result of the survey *id.*, at 135 *et seq.*
93. *See* also the empirical study by *Dasser*, in: Zimmermann (ed.), Globalisierung und Entstaatlichung des Rechts, Teilband II, at 129, 139 *et seq.*

and information on the content and background of the NLM and a resultant hesitation to apply the NLM in practice. These reservations and knowledge deficits of international practitioners must be taken seriously. These deficits have had unfortunate repercussions on the discussion of the dogmatic foundation of the NLM doctrine. Indeed, it has always been a major argument of those who oppose this doctrine that without a minimum amount of concrete workable legal rules, there is no room for a theoretical foundation of the doctrine of transnational economic law[94].

In the fourth Chapter of this Study, two concepts are presented and analysed which may serve to escape this vicious circle of dogmatic discussion and opposition from legal practice. The first concept is the drafting and implementation of restatements of international contract law through UNIDROIT on a worldwide basis and the *Lando* Commission on the level of the European Union. The second concept relates to the phenomenon of 'Creeping Codification' of the NLM through the TransLex Principles.

The Annex of this Study contains a nutshell version of the TransLex Principles. The full version is available online at www.trans-lex.org. In the online version, each principle and rule is accompanied by extensive comparative references taken from statutory law, legal doctrine, court decisions, uniform law, arbitral awards etc., many of them in full text versions. The online version is updated on a continuous basis by the CENTRAL Research Team. The Annex also contains the personal account by Professor *Philippe Kahn* on the 'discovery' of the NLM by the Dijon School in the late 1950s and early 1960s and the English translation of *Berthold Goldman*'s Le Monde article on the legal nature of the Suez Canal Company[95] which marks the beginning of the NLM doctrine.

94. *See infra* Chapter 4 II.C.2.
95. *See supra* note 2.

Part I

The Theoretical and Methodical Foundations of the New *Lex Mercatoria* Doctrine

Chapter 1

Traditional Concepts to Overcome Deficiencies in the Application of Domestic Law in Transnational Commercial Contexts

I. INADEQUACY OF DOMESTIC LAW AS A LEGAL FRAMEWORK FOR TRANSNATIONAL COMMERCIAL TRANSACTIONS

International legal practitioners and academics alike have long complained about the inadequate legal framework for international trade and commerce[1]. International contractual arrangements frequently involve a complex network of contractual provisions 'which constitute the law between the parties'[2]. Sometimes, however, judges or international arbitrators find themselves unable to resolve the conflict before them solely on the basis of the provisions and stipulations contained in the comprehensive contractual arrangement before them. Instead, they have to refer back to the applicable domestic law which is determined either on the basis of a choice of law clause contained in the contract or by reference to the applicable conflict of laws rules. This reference to domestic law, however, reveals the basic dilemma of international commercial law: the natural territorial limitation of the principles and rules contained in domestic laws necessarily leads to the nationalization of international commercial cases, a phenomenon that is irreconcilable

1. *See e.g. Dalhuisen*, Berkeley J.Int'l L. 2006, at 129, 187.
2. *See e.g.* the formula used in the contract between *MINE* and *The Republic of Guinea*, reprinted in *Schröder/Wenner*, Internationales Vertragsrecht, No. 117: 'The law between the parties is the contract itself'.

with the interests of the international commercial community[3]. The territorial limitation of domestic laws necessarily leads to a large degree of diversity of these laws which, in turn, constitutes a major obstacle to international commerce. The Joint Response prepared by the Commission on European Contract Law and the Study Group on a European Civil Code to the European Commission's Communication on European Contract Law has revealed the substantial increases in information and legal costs for market participants resulting from the diversity of contract law rules within the EU. These costs may effectively prevent certain kind of commercial activities in the EU market[4]. The problem is also discussed by economists in the context of the 'New International Economics of International Transactions'[5].

The phenomenon of the inadequacy and diversity of domestic laws is relevant to three different levels of the legal process[6]. The first relates to the determination of the applicable domestic law on the basis of the relevant conflict of laws rules. The domestic law character of these rules stands in sharp contrast to the international or transnational character and quality of the cases that are subject to these rules. This inherent conflict has been rightly characterized as the 'inveterate evil of private international law'[7]. Once the applicable domestic law has been ascertained, the second level of the dilemma relates to the determination of the relevant substantive law rules of that particular domestic law that is applicable to the case before the judge or arbitrator[8]. Problems may arise in this context when the international character of the case raises doubts as to whether the principle or rule of that particular legal system may be applied to the individual circumstances of a certain dispute. The third and final aspect of the dilemma described above relates to the question of whether the internationality of transnational commercial cases requires the modification of the methods of construction that are inherent in every legal system.

3. *See U. Hübner*, Die methodische Entwicklung des internationalen Wirtschaftsrechts, at 17 *et seq.*; *Steindorff*, Sachnormen im internationalen Privatrecht, at 11 *et seq.*
4. Communication on European Contract Law: Joint Response of the Commission on European Contract Law and the Study Group on a European Civil Code, available at *http://ec.europa.eu/consumers/cons_int/safe_shop/fair_bus_pract/cont_law/comments/5.23.pdf*; *see also Blase,* Die Grundregeln des Europäischen Vertragsrechts als Recht grenzüberschreitender Verträge, at 2 *et seq.*; *Gopalan*, J.L. & Com. 2004, at 117, 125 *et seq.*; *Meyer*, Principles of Contract Law und nationales Vertragsrecht, at 30 *et seq.*
5. This economic theory (NIIT) takes a transaction-oriented approach to international business and deals with the territorial limitations of law-making and law enforcement and the problems (coordination of economic behaviour, increase of transaction costs) arising out of this phenomenon for the property rights exchanged in international trade; *see Schmidtchen*, RabelsZ 59 (1995), at 56, 62 *et seq.*; *Schmidtchen/Schmidt-Trenz*, Jahrb.NPÖ 1990, at 3 *et seq.*; *Yarbrough/Yarbrough*, JITE 1994, at 239 *et seq.*; *see also Basedow*, Festschrift Horn, at 229, 234 *et seq.*
6. *See David*, in: UNIDROIT (ed.), New Directions in International Trade Law, at 5, 7.
7. *Kegel*, IPR, 7th ed. 1995, § 2 II.3.a., at 112 (translation by the author).
8. *See David, supra* note 6, *id.*

A. Conflict of Laws

It has always been a major concern of those who advocate the existence of a transnational commercial law to mitigate or even evade the uncertainties connected with the application of traditional domestic conflict of laws rules. The unpredictability of conflict of laws decisions has long since been criticized as a 'jump in the dark'[9]. Conflict of laws has been characterized as 'the source of problems for which it considers itself to be the solution'[10]. It is for this very reason that as early as 1964 *Kegel* brought up the issue of the 'crisis of conflicts of law'[11]. Since then, the 'murkey maze of conflict of laws'[12] has not disappeared from the agenda[13]. In fact, it lies at the root of the development towards informal and pragmatic procedures for the unification of transnational contract law:

> 'The conflict of laws of contract leaves you with the choice between two bad alternatives, between rules which the court may always invoke but which are so vague that they are more or less meaningless and clear and foreseeable rules which often lead to bad results because they disregard the outcome of the dispute. One may take this into account when one thinks about how to frame the contract law of a future integrated Europe. It may be considered best to draft substantive Principles of European Contract Law on which the lawyers in the Union may agree. Such rules may substantially reduce the conflicts of law'[14].

Traditional European conflict of laws doctrine holds that the judge or arbitrator may take account of the interests of the parties and of the general interest in an orderly application of conflict of laws (decisional harmony). These interests ('*Ordnungsinteressen*'[15]), however, do not relate to the quality of the substantive

9. *Raape/Sturm*, IPR, at 199; *see also Zweigert*, Festschrift Raape, at 35 ('atomic physics of jurisprudence'); *Schmitthoff*, JZ 1978, at 495, 497: 'Private international law, especially the search for the applicable law, is an artificial barrier to world trade created by men's hands' (translation by the author); *Rabel*, RabelsZ 50 (1986), at 303 *et seq.*: 'Indeed, there is no other branch of legal science where controversy and uncertainty hang over so many basic notions, and means and ways appear so inadequate to the scope'; *Müller-Graff*, Privatrecht und Europäisches Gemeinschaftsrecht, at 37: private international law as the 'Bermuda Triangle' of substantive law; *cf. also Stein*, Lex mercatoria, at 23.
10. *Schmidtchen*, RabelsZ 59 (1995), at 89.
11. *See* for the 'crisis of conflict of laws' *Kegel*, Rec.Cours 1964-II, at 91 *et seq.*; *cf. also Schlesinger*, Formation of Contracts, Vol. I, at 16: '...modern trend away from the play of unpredictable rules of private international law'.
12. *See* dissenting opinion in *American Motorists Ins. Co. v. ARTRA Group, Inc.*, 338 Md. 560, 659 A.2nd, at 1295, 1313.
13. *See e.g.* UNCITRAL (ed.), Legal Guide on Drawing Up International Contracts for the Construction of Industrial Works, at 301: 'The... factor producing uncertainty as to the law applicable to the contract is that even if it is known which system of private international law will determine the law applicable to the contract, the rules of that system may be too general or vague to enable the law applicable to a works contract to be determined with reasonable certainty'.
14. *Lando*, The King's College Law Journal 1996–1997, at 55, 74.
15. *See* for this aspect of private international law justice which was elaborated by the 'Cologne conflict of laws school' *Kegel*, Festschrift Lewald, at 270 *et seq.*; *Kegel/Schurig*, IPR, § 2 II.3, at

law to be applied but only to the abstract relation between the case, the applicable law, and the ideal of decisional harmony in private international law. Thus, the determination of the *lex causae*, described by *Savigny* as the search for the law 'with which the legal relationship has the closest connection due to its inherent nature'[16], does not always lead to the application of the 'best law' when compared to the practical needs and interests of international business.

To achieve more substantive law justice, a 'revolution' has taken place in the past decades in US conflict of laws doctrine. Conflict of laws scholars from all parts of the legal spectrum have advanced new conflict of laws theories which have a common goal: to abandon traditional rules in favour of more flexible approaches. Most of these theories take account of the quality of the substantive law and the interests that lie behind them, thus substituting traditional conflict of laws arguments with a vague 'policy analysis'. However, the multitude of approaches and theories, embracing traditional methods such as the 'most significant relationship test', '(governmental) interest analysis'[17], the '*lex fori* approach', 'choice influencing considerations', the 'better-law approach'[18], and other 'combined modern approaches' have caused a 'creative chaos'[19], leading to more insecurity and less foreseeability[20]:

> 'Orthodox conflicts doctrine is, in some ways, worse equipped to respond to the need for certainty in international commercial transactions than it was a century ago. Modern 'policy', 'interest' and other non-rule approaches have rewritten the subject. This is particularly true for tort matters, but the effect of the 'conflicts revolution' has been significant in contracts as well. Many commentators . . . have applauded the ability of these trends to ferret out justice in the individual case. But there is no denying that where predictability is at a premium, this helter-skelter approach advocated by American courts and some of their foreign counterparts just will not do'[21].

Decisions on conflict of laws by American courts are thus heavily criticized as so unpredictable and extraordinary 'that it is as if one encountered a practicing alchemist'[22]. Looking at the American conflict of laws scene, one is reminded of *Prosser's* famous characterization of conflict of laws as 'a dismal swamp filled with

139 *et seq.*; *Lüderitz*, Festschrift Kegel, at 31, 36 *et seq.*; *Lüderitz*, IPR, No. 101; *Lüderitz*, Festschrift der Rechtswissenschaftlichen Fakultät zur 600-Jahr-Feier der Universität zu Köln, at 271, 280; *Schurig*, Kollisionsnorm und Sachrecht, at 136, 137.

16. *von Savigny*, System des heutigen Römischen Rechts, Vol. 8, at 28.
17. *See* the critical analysis by *Juenger*, Am.J.Comp.L. 1984, at 1, 50 (interest analysis as a 'dead-end alley').
18. *See infra* II.A.1.
19. *Dasser*, in: Festschrift Anton Heini, at 103, 105 *et seq.*
20. *See* the geographical survey by *Symeonides*, Am.J.Comp.L. 1996, at 181, 193 *et seq.*; *cf. also* the general criticism by *Martinek*, Das internationale Kartellprivatrecht, at 55 *et seq.*
21. *Borchers*, in: Raisch/Shaffer (eds.), Introduction to Transnational Legal Transactions, at 139, 140 (footnotes omitted).
22. *Swan*, cited by *Symeonides, supra* note 20, at 189.

quaking quagmires and inhabited by learned but eccentric professors who theorize about mysterious matters in a strange and incomprehensible jargon'[23]. This deplorable situation has induced many attorneys to settle their cases outside of the court room, instead of relying on an unpredictable conflict of laws decision by the judge[24].

Whether traditional, mixed or progressive, the international[25] nature of transnational commercial relationships always involves special interests of merchants and businessmen active in cross-border trade and does not necessarily lend itself to a regulation through domestic laws. In view of their particular character, involving abstract considerations pertaining to the 'localization' of legal relationships, conflict of laws rules are not able to take into account the quality of the substantive law rules, the application of which they are intended to regulate. They are only subject to specific conflict of laws considerations. This monistic approach has led *Kegel* to conclude that in conflict of laws reasoning 'private international law justice prevails over the substantive law one'[26].

This one-sided approach to conflict of laws problems hinders any just and equitable resolution of international commercial disputes. Achieving an equitable decision in international commercial contexts always requires the taking into account of the nature and quality of the substantive law *ab initio*, *i.e.* in the initial phase, where traditionally conflict of laws considerations play a dominant role. The traditional approach to conflict of laws issues prevents arbitrators and judges from taking this combined view at the outset of any arbitration or judicial proceedings[27]. This leads to considerable uncertainties in the determination of the applicable law[28]. For international business and trade, these uncertainties make contractual risk management more difficult, thereby raising transaction costs[29].

A practical example demonstrates this inherent dilemma. It is generally accepted that, in the absence of a choice of law clause, the contract is subject to the law that bears the closest connection to it ('*engste Verbindung*', 'closest and most real connection' 'most significant relationship', 'centre of gravity-test', '*lien (rapport) le plus étroit*')[30]. This principle is reflected in the former Art. 28(1) of

23. *Prosser*, Mich.L.Rev. 1953, at 959, 971; *see also* the concluding statement of *Symeonides, supra* note 20, at 241: 'Thus ends another year in the life of American conflicts law in its strive for maturity'.
24. *See* the statement of Judge *Jack Weinstein (New York)*, cited by *Dasser, supra* note 19, at 105: 'I seldom get a conflicts decision anymore. As soon as I mention the fact that perhaps a brief ought to be submitted, the attorneys immediately go out and settle the case'.
25. *See* for the problems regarding the definition of 'internationality' *infra* Chapter 4 I.A.6.a.
26. *Kegel/Schurig*, IPR, § 2.I, at 131.
27. *See Meessen*, AöR 1985, at 398, 404.
28. *David*, in: UNIDROIT (ed.), New Directions in International Trade Law, at 5, 7; *de Boer*, in: Hartkamp/Hesselink/Hondius/du Perron/Vranken (eds.), Towards a European Civil Code, 1st ed., at 51, 53 *et seq.*
29. *See Lando*, in: Festskrift Birger Stuevold Larsen, at 623, 624 *et seq.*
30. *Cf. Kegel/Schurig*, IPR, § 18 I.1.d, at 658 *et seq.*; *Ferid*, IPR, No. 6-37; MünchKomm-*Martiny*, EGBGB, Art. 28, No. 6; *Delaume*, Transnational Contracts, § 3.01; *Lagarde*, Rec.Cours 1986-I, at 9 *et seq.*

the Introductory Law to the German Civil Code (EGBGB), as well as in Art. 4(1) of the Rome Convention on the Law Applicable to Contractual Obligations and Art. 4(4) of the Rome I Regulation[31]. It is considered to be a principle of the NLM[32]. However, this principle *on its own* turns out to be a non-rule. In order to be workable in individual cases it requires clarification through specific conflict of laws criteria[33]. Application of these criteria fails to provide the link to the applicable law in complex cases like swap contracts, where none of the parties performs the characteristic obligation. In international trade, these problems may arise in the context of barter or countertrade transactions[34], letters of intent[35] or complex, multilateral netting arrangements[36]. Even more intricate problems arise when arbitrators or judges have to determine the law applicable to 'Build-Operate-Transfer' (BOT)-construction projects. These transactions involve a 'network'[37] of singular contracts concluded as a part of a complex construction project. There is thus an inherent need to achieve a coordination of these contracts with regard to substantive law, since all contracts are geared towards the same economic objective. Due to their different bargaining positions and negotiating power, the parties are sometimes not able to include the same choice of law clause in all the different contracts related to the project. This may lead to considerable inconsistencies between the various contracts and sub-contracts and the rights and duties evolving out of them, *e.g.* with respect to periods of limitation or exclusion of liability. Hence, the frictions between choice of law considerations and substantive law justice become particularly apparent in these constellations. Focusing solely on the abstract 'geographical' localization of the individual contracts, traditional conflict of laws doctrine tends to ignore the economic unity of the different contracts and suggests that each contract should be subject to the law to which it has the closest connection[38]. Given the close economic interrelation of the contract, this view amounts to a '*dépeçage*'. In order to avoid these frictions, it is suggested to subject the 'secondary contracts', *i.e.* the sub-contracts, to the law that is applicable to the 'main contract', *i.e.* the construction contract which constitutes the economic centre of gravity of the whole relationship between all parties involved in the project[39]. Even though it takes account of the substantive character of the contract and of the interests of the parties involved therein, the search for an accessory connection of the secondary contracts to the main contract may be futile.

31. Regulation (EC) No. 593/2008 of the European Parliament and of the Council of June 17, 2008 on the law applicable to contractual obligations (Rome I), OJ No. L 177/6, at 11.
32. *See* TransLex Principle No. XIV.2, reprinted *infra* Annex III, available with further references at *www.Trans-Lex.org/971000.*
33. *Jayme*, in: Sarcevic (ed.), International Contracts and Conflicts of Laws, at 42.
34. *Cf.* for the problems of conflict of laws in this field *Fülbier*, Das Vertrags- und Wirtschaftsrecht des Gegenkaufs im internationalen Wirtschaftsverkehr, at 94.
35. *Cf. Lutter*, Letter of Intent, at 145 *et seq.*
36. *Cf. Berger*, Der Aufrechnungsvertrag, at 721 *et seq.*
37. *See* for the legal implications of network contracts *Rohe*, Netzverträge, at 305 *et seq.*
38. *Cf.* ICC Award No. 3043, Clunet 1979, at 1000 *et seq.* with note *Derains, id.*, at 1001 *et seq.*
39. *Cf. Jayme*, in: Nicklisch (ed.), Rechtsfragen privatfinanzierter Projekte, at 65, 66 *et seq.*

The contractual conglomerate may have its centres of gravity not only in the main construction contract, but also in the sub-contracts if they involve a substantial amount of the work to be performed on the construction site and also in the concession contract which usually forms the basis of construction projects with state parties[40]. However, applying a different law to each individual contract[41] would frustrate the economic unity of the construction project. Those parties that have not been able to agree on the applicable law would then be left with the 'closest connection test' leading to isolated conflict of laws considerations instead of taking into account the parties' interests and the suitability of the applicable law *vis-à-vis* the particular legal issues that are involved in the dispute.

The problems related to conflict of laws issues in the context of international commercial transactions reveal that even an increased emphasis on party interests[42] and/or substantive justice[43] does not provide a final and workable breakthrough in the resolution of the basic conflict between private international law rules on the one hand and substantive law and party interest on the other. This conflict is even intensified by the domestic courts'[44] homeward boundness ('*Heimwärtsstreben*') and unsystematic application of conflict of laws rules:

> 'The national courts of the world, with all that makes them the just pride of their respective countries, have dismally failed in organizing any reliable set of conflicts rules. The question of what law applies to a specific case has been left to a chaotic, if not willful, administration of justice . . . Even courts known to respect foreign law in principle often do it from case to case graciously by comity rather than by obeying a legal duty, thus impairing the certainty of the applicable law by giving way to unpredictable local policies. Freedom of the parties to determine their laws has been sacrificed to fancy theories'[45].

These theoretical problems are mirrored in everyday legal practice. The choice of law clauses contained in the usual comprehensive international contractual agreements not only serve the positive purpose of indicating the domestic law to be applied to the contract but also perform an important negative function: they are

40. *Jayme, id.*
41. *See von der Seipen*, Akzessorische Anknüpfung und engste Verbindung im Kollisionsrecht der komplexen Vertragsverhältnisse, at 319.
42. *Cf.* for this approach *Flessner*, Interessenjurisprudenz im internationalen Privatrecht, at 140 *et seq.*: 'Interest oriented jurisprudence [''*Interessenjurisprudenz*''] in private international law means that, in contrast to substantive law, the interests of the parties involved in the transaction are identified and compared with the interests that have been assumed and evaluated by the legislature' (translation by the author).
43. *Cf. Lüderitz*, Festschrift der Rechtswissenschaftlichen Fakultät zur 600-Jahr-Feier der Universität zu Köln, at 271, 281 *et seq.*
44. *Langen*, Transnationales Recht, Part I, No. 10.
45. *Cf. Rabel*, RabelsZ 50 (1986), at 324, 325; *see also Flessner*, Interessenjurisprudenz im internationalen Privatrecht, at 142: 'There is probably no other field of law with practical relevance which is denied regularly and massively its usefulness through the behaviour and attitudes of legal practice, while at the same time legal doctrine frequently and emphatically has to call for the necessary obedience to its rules and principles' (translation by the author).

intended to shield parties and arbitrators from the time-consuming and cost-intensive uncertainties of the traditional conflict of laws doctrine[46].

B. SUBSTANTIVE LAW

Inadequacies of the law-finding process in international commercial contexts are by no means limited to the field of private international law. They can also be found on the substantive law plane. In fact, it was this phenomenon which has led to the creation of the *lex mercatoria* of the Middle Ages[47]. The reason for this development is what has for a long time[48] been accused as the failure of national laws to provide just and equitable solutions to legal problems arising out of international commercial transactions. These deficiencies of domestic laws are to be found in the statutory law itself, but also in the case law of domestic courts.

1. Statutory Law

Today, domestic legislatures publish brochures to promote the advantages of their respective jurisdiction in the global 'patchwork'[49] of domestic private and commercial laws to foreign parties[50]. The goal of this 'battle of brochures' is to gain a marketing advantage in the regional and global competition of legal systems[51]. What these brochures do not state, however, is that it is often the domestic

---

46. *Horn*, in: Horn (ed.), Legal Problems of Codes of Conduct for Multinational Enterprises, at 45, 72.
47. *See Blackstone*, Commentaries on the Laws of England, Vol. I, at 273: '... whereas no municipal laws can be sufficient to order and determine the very extensive and complicated affairs of traffic and merchandise; neither can they have a proper authority for this purpose ... - For which reason the affairs of commerce are regulated by a law of their own, called the law merchant or *lex mercatoria*'; *cf. also Malynes*, Consuetudo Vel Lex Mecatoria, at 2 *et seq.*; *Blaurock*, in: Ferrari (ed.), The Unification of International Commercial Law, at 9, 11 *et seq.*
48. *See Lepaulle*, The Function of Comparative Law, Harv.L.Rev. 1921/22, at 838, 856: '... we see that law is behind the times, and has not been able to mold its methods to meet the economic changes'; *Béguin*, McGill Law Journal 1985, at 478, 482 *et seq.*; *cf. also Goldstaijn*, The New Law Merchant, J.Bus.L. 1961, at 12 *et seq.*; *Goldstaijn*, The New Law Merchant Reconsidered, in: Festschrift Clive Schmitthoff, 1973, at 171, 174 *et seq.*
49. *Horn*, in: Meessen (ed.) Economic Law as an Economic Good, at 139, 140.
50. *See* The Law Society of England and Wales (ed.), England and Wales: The jurisdiction of choice with a Foreword by Secretary of State for Justice *Jack Straw*, stating that '[t]his brochure sets out the reasons for our success and lets people know why it is in their own interest to use English law and to settle their disputes here'; *see also* the German brochure 'Law – made in Germany', edited by the major German associations for the legal profession available at *www.lawmadein-germany.de*, with a preface by Federal Minister of Justice *Brigitte Zypries*, stating that 'to a great degree, we owe [wealth and democracy] to our law. Anyone choosing continental European – German – law today makes a smart choice as "Law – made in Germany" is a guarantee for success'. *See* for the transformation of law into a 'product' which is reflected in these projects *Eidenmüller*, JZ 2009, at 641 *et seq.*
51. *See* for this competition of legal systems *Horn*, *supra* note 49, at 140.

substantive law itself which proves to be incapable of keeping pace with the development and fast evolution as well as the high degree of specialization of international commerce and the legal problems arising out of it. In the famous *IBM/Fujitsu*-arbitration, domestic copyright laws proved to be incapable of providing adequate protection for complex computer software[52]. Also, in the field of international trade finance and capital markets transactions, such as swaps and derivatives contracts, domestic laws are frequently inapt to provide workable and practicable solutions for international business[53]. In these areas, voluminous standard documentations, such as the master agreements drafted by the International Swaps & Derivatives Association (ISDA[54]) for over-the-counter (OTC) derivative contracts and by the Loan Market Association (LMA[55]) for international loan agreements, dominate the market. The ISDA master agreements have been established in response to demands for better documentation that reduces negotiating costs, addresses counterparty credit risk, and helps ensure contract enforceability. Also, they establish the rights and obligations between the parties in a comprehensive and exclusive manner. Even though they contain a choice of law clause, these contract documentations are, as much as possible, detached from the uncertainties of any applicable domestic law. It is not surprising, therefore, that it is particularly in these fields of international commercial law where the plea for the development of transnational legal rules and principles is frequently raised[56]. Also, in M & A transactions governed by German law, parties typically exclude the multitude of legal remedies for non-performance available under German law because the legal consequences of these remedies are not appropriate for such types of transactions. Instead, the parties establish their own

52. *IBM Corp. v. Fujitsu Ltd., see Bühring-Uhle*, Am.Rev.Int'l Arb. 1991, at 113, 122; *cf. generally Weidhaas/Swoboda*, CR 1988, at 104, 107 *et seq.*; *Ehricke*, CR 1989, at 665 *et seq.*; *Berger*, International Economic Arbitration, at 555.
53. *See Horn*, in: Horn/Schmitthoff (eds.), The Transnational Law of International Commercial Transactions, at 275, 288 *et seq.*; *Berger*, DZWir 1993, at 1.
54. *See www.isda.org*; *see* for the significance of the ISDA documentation *Jomadar*, *http://papers.ssrn.com/sol3/papers.cfm?abstract_id=1326520.*
55. *See www.loan-market-assoc.com*: *see also Wenzel*, Rechtsfragen internationaler Konsortialkreditverträge, at 73 *et seq.*
56. *See e.g.* for the inability of domestic legal rules to cope with the specificities and dynamic nature of international financial markets and the special nature of international financial law as a distinct legal subject matter when compared to domestic financial law, and non-financial international law *Sebastianutti*, LFMR 2009, at 64 *et seq.*; *Sebastianutti*, LFMR 2009, at 155 *et seq.*; *Sebastianutti*, LFMR 2009, at 248 *et seq.*; *see* for the transnational character of Euromarket financial instruments and the underwriting practice prevailing in the Euromarket and derived from the 'international law merchant' *Dalhuisen* on International Commercial, Financial and Trade Law, at 805; *see* also the decision of the Court of Appeal of the Canton of Zurich of 1986, in which the Court qualified the bank guarantee on first demand as an institution of 'the transnational lex mercatoria', Bl.Zuerch.Rspr. 1986, No. 23, at 44; *cf.* for a proposal to regulate the law of bank guarantees through 'supra-national law' *Coing*, ZHR 147 (1983), at 125, 127; *cf. also Nielsen*, ZHR 147 (1983), at 145, 147 (bank guarantees as 'a sort of lex mercatoria'); *cf. also Berger*, DZWir 1993, at 1; *Horn*, The United Nations Convention on Independent Guarantees and the Lex Mercatoria, at 1.

exclusive system of contractual representations, warranties and remedies ('locked box system'), thereby making use of the wide room for party autonomy granted by German contract law. Considering that most post M & A disputes are decided by arbitral tribunals and not by domestic courts, the German M & A law is shaped and developed outside the realm of the German judiciary, which contributes to an increasing gap between German contract law and M & A practice[57].

Finally, in the field of international reinsurance law, the parties to reinsurance agreements usually resort to 'the usages and customs of international reinsurance practice' in view of the absence of any adequate statutory law and the technical specificities of this highly specialized branch of the insurance industry[58]. In fact, it is the reinsurance business which, in the wake of the English *Orion*[59] and *Eagle Star*[60] cases, has paved the way for decision-making by international arbitrators that is freed from 'all judicial formalities' and from 'following the strict rules of law'. The reason for this liberalism is the very existence of an 'almost uniform [uncodified] world-reinsurance law', which makes the application of traditional conflict of laws rules superfluous[61].

2. Case Law

Arbitrators and judges must apply the case law by domestic courts as part of the law chosen by the parties or applied under the conflict of laws provisions[62]. That case law can be hostile to the basic principle of party autonomy and the idea that contracts should be upheld as much as possible in international b2b-transactions[63]. An example for this phenomenon is the long-standing case law of the German Federal Court of Justice (*Bundesgerichtshof*) on the invalidity of contract clauses in standard forms. The Court regularly declares standard form clauses, such as exclusion from liability, limitation of liability ('cap-clauses') or penalty clauses, invalid by transferring the strict protection standards it applies to b2c-contracts also to b2b-transactions[64]. As a consequence of this case law, it is almost impossible to

57. *See Duve/Keller*, SchiedsVZ 2005, at 169 *et seq.*
58. *Labes*, Schiedsgerichtsvereinbarungen in Rückversicherungsverträgen, at 93 *et seq.*; *Janott,* Festschrift Stiefel, at 370.
59. *Orion v. Belfort* [1962] 2 Lloyd's L.Rep. 257, 262 *et seq.* (per *Megaw* J.).
60. *Eagle Star v. Yuval*, [1978] 1 Lloyd's L.Rep. 357, 362 (per Lord *Denning*).
61. *Schütte*, VersR 1982, at 223, 225; *cf. also Lando*, Festskrift Till Stig Strömholm, at 567, 569 *et seq.*
62. *Cf. Loquin*, Clunet 1983, at 293, 325; *Berger*, International Economic Arbitration, at 87; *Berger*, L.&Pol.Int'l Bus. 1997, at 943, 951.
63. *See* TransLex Principle No. IV.5.3, reprinted *infra* Annex III, available with further references at *www.Trans-Lex.org/925000*; for international arbitration agreements ('*in favorem validitatis*') TransLex Principle No. XIII.1.2, reprinted *infra* Annex III, available with further references at *www.Trans-Lex.org/968902*.
64. BGH NJW 2003, 1805, 1807; BGHZ 153, 312; 150, 299; BGH NJW-RR 1993, 504; BGH NJW 2004, 1454; *cf. also Gottschalk*, NJW 2005, at 2493, 2494 *et seq.*; BGHZ 90, 273, 278; BGH NJW-RR 2005, 247, 248; BGH NJW 1996, 389.

validly include such standard form clauses in b2b-contracts governed by German law, even though these clauses are regularly used because they are of paramount importance for the parties' risk management and price calculation. In taking that approach, the Court operates *contra legem* because the German law on standard terms contained in Secs 305 *et seq.* German Civil Code expressly requires the courts to draw a distinction between b2c- and b2b-transactions and to apply different protection standards to both types of contracts. The Court also ignores the legal principle of the presumed professional competence of businessmen which is underlying German commercial law[65] and which is a principle of the NLM[66]. That principle implies that a less stringent protection standard must be applied to b2b-transactions because businessmen are supposed to be able to take care of their own affairs due to their presumed professional sophistication. In ignoring these essential legal principles, the Court has sacrificed party autonomy as well as the commercial practicability and international competitiveness of German law[67]. The 'creeping' transfer of strict consumer protection standards into the b2b-context exercised by the German Federal Court of Justice begs the question whether 'leave has been taken from party autonomy'[68] and whether the case law of the German courts in the area of standard forms law is at all suitable for domestic, let alone international business transactions for which maximum party autonomy is essential[69]. Years ago, an International Chamber of Commerce (ICC) arbitral tribunal refused to apply the case law on standard terms in b2b-contracts in a dispute concerning the effect of a cap-clause on claimant's claim for damages for non-performance that arose out of a contract for the cross-border delivery of a complex industrial machine[70]. The tribunal acknowledged that this case law runs counter to the general principle that sophisticated companies doing business in international commerce require less protection than consumers[71]. As a consequence of this restrictive case law, some companies and their legal advisors have already decided to escape the 'standard form trap' set by the German Federal Court of Justice. To achieve more certainty and predictability for their price calculation and risk management, they apply Swiss law instead of German law to their cross-border business contracts[72].

65. *Berger*, ZIP 2006, at 2149, 2151.
66. *See* TransLex Principle No. I.2.3, reprinted *infra* Annex III, available with further references *www.Trans-Lex.org/909000.*
67. *See Acker/Bopp*, Baurecht 2009, at 1040, 1041 *et seq.*; *Berger, supra* note 65, at 2149 *et seq.*; *Berger/Kleine*, BB 2007, at 2137 *et seq.*; *Lenkaitis/Löwisch,* ZIP 2009, at 441 *et seq.*; *Kessel/ Jüttner,* BB 2008, at 1350 *et seq.*
68. *Cf. Medicus*, Abschied von der Privatautonomie im Schuldrecht?, 1994, at 11 *et seq.*; *Dauner-Lieb*, NJW 2004, at 1431; *Dauner-Lieb*, AnwBl. 2006, at 430, 434; *Hillgruber*, ZRP 1995, at 6 *et seq.*
69. *Berger*, *supra* note 65, at 2153 *et seq.*
70. ICC Interim Award No. 10279 of January 29, 2001, SchiedsVZ 2005, 108 *et seq.*
71. *See Acker/Bopp*, *supra* note 67, at 1045: 'This arbitral award reflects [commercial] reality.'
72. *See Triebel*, AnwBl. 2008, at 305 *et seq.*; *Hobeck*, SchiedsVZ 2005, at 112.

II. ESCAPING THE DILEMMA OF THE INTERNATIONAL LEGAL PROCESS

The multifacetedness of the legal problems inherent in the resolution of disputes in international trade and commerce is also reflected in the variety of concepts that are offered to overcome these problems. These solutions are related either to the sphere of conflict of laws (A.) or to the field of substantive law (B.). There are also proposals which attempt to combine traditional conflict of laws and substantive law aspects in order to create innovative, 'hybrid' approaches to the resolution of transnational commercial disputes (C.). All of these solutions have one common denominator: the basic problem of modern conflict of laws doctrine[73], *i.e.* the exact determination of the relationship between substantive law and private international law.

A. Solutions on the Conflict of Laws Plane

1. The 'Better-Law Approach'

The better-law approach, developed by American conflict of laws doctrine, is intended to provide a remedy for the dilemma that is caused by the fact that traditional international private law is based on the notion of equality of all legal systems involved in a dispute. The proponents of the better-law approach suggest that the quality of the substantive law rules as 'most appropriate', 'best' or simply 'most advanced' solutions for the case should be considered as part of several 'choice-influencing-considerations'[74]. Conflict of laws considerations are thus substituted by aspects of functionality and the question as to which substantive domestic law provides the most adequate and most advanced solution for the legal problem before the judge or arbitrator.

The better-law approach may prove to be useful in the Inter-American context because the American judge is able to overlook the pros and cons of the substantive laws of the various federal states[75]. In the international context, however, the arbitrator or judge will usually not be able to conduct a functional comparison between the domestic laws that are involved in the case. This problem is aggravated by the fact that domestic legal systems do not take account of the specificities

73. *Cf. Kegel*, in: Juenger (ed.), Zum Wandel des Internationalen Privatrechts, at 35, 38.
74. *Cf. Leflar*, N.Y.U.L.Rev. 1966, at 267 *et seq.*; *Juenger*, Zum Wandel des Internationalen Privatrechts, at 21 *et seq.*; *Clark v. Clark*, 222 A 2nd. 205, 209 (1966); *Taylor v. Bullock*, 279 A.2nd 585; *Gagne v. Berry*, 290 A.2nd 624; *Woodward v. Steward*, 243 A.2nd 917, 923; *Hunker v. Royal Indemnity Co. (J. Heffermann)*, 204 NW 2nd. 897, 906 *et seq.*; *Schneider v. Nichols*, 158 N.W. 2nd 254; *cf. also Zweigert*, RabelsZ 37 (1973), at 447 *et seq.*
75. *Cf. Kropholler*, IPR, § 11 IV.3 (at 91 *et seq.*); partly, this approach is only being used to justify the 'homeward-boundness' of the court under the veil of a methodical approach, *Schödermeier*, Sonderprivatrecht für internationale Wirtschaftsverträge, at 126.

and complexities of the international context[76], thus depriving the arbitrator or judge of any guidelines that may help him in his choice between the various legal systems. In addition, criteria such as 'the most advanced solution' or 'the best solution for the case' are too open and vague and do not lend themselves to any concretization in practice, bringing the conflict of laws decision close to the equitable '*ex aequo et bono*' decisions known from the plane of substantive law[77]. It is for this very reason that the escape clauses (*'Ausweichklauseln', 'clauses d'échappement'*) contained in conflict of laws statutes of Continental European jurisdictions[78] do not have the function of guaranteeing the application of that legal system which provides the best solution for the case except in those rare cases where the regular conflict of laws considerations are already combined with substantive law issues (internal decisional harmony)[79].

Most importantly, however, the basic premise of the better-law approach stands in sharp contrast to the meaning and purpose of international private law rules. These rules are based solely on the closest connection test and do not consider the legal quality of the substantive law rules of the various legal systems. The better-law approach, however, compares the substantive law rules contained in the different legal systems and provides them with a different sphere of application depending on their usefulness in the individual case. This is hardly reconcilable with the underlying philosophy of traditional conflict of laws doctrine which is focused on an objective localization of legal relationships[80]. Therefore, the better-law approach only has a declaratory value. It serves to confirm the inherent weakness of the classical conflict of laws doctrine elaborated above[81]. At the same time, this theory confirms the view of those who oppose this traditional system: the aim of applying the law that is best suited to solve the problems of international trade and commerce cannot be achieved through the application of traditional conflict of laws doctrine.

2. The '*Comitas*' Doctrine

The proponents of the *comitas* doctrine accept that classical conflict of laws principles are inapt to improve the law-finding process in the context of international commercial transactions. Instead, they focus on the very origins of contemporary private international law, which was developed by *Story*[82] and

76. *Cf. supra* I.B.
77. *Cf. Kegel*, Festschrift Beitzke, at 551, 571 *et seq.*; *von Bar/Mankowski*, IPR, Vol. I, § 6 No. 92.
78. *See e.g.* former Art. 28(5) Introductory Law to the German Civil Code; Art. 15 of the Swiss Private International Law Statute; Art. 4(3) Rome Convention on the Law Applicable to Contractual Obligations.
79. *Heini/Keller/Siehr/Vischer/Volken-Keller-Girsberger*, IPRG, Art. 15, No. 88.
80. *Kegel*, in: Juenger (ed.), Zum Wandel des Internationalen Privatrechts, at 44.
81. *Cf. Schödermeier*, Sonderprivatrecht für internationale Wirtschaftsverträge, at 137.
82. *Story*, Commentaries on the Conflict of Laws, at 8: 'Whatever extra-territorial force [the laws] are to have, is the result, not of any original power to extend them abroad, but of that respect, which from motives of public policy other nations are disposed to yield to them, giving them

Savigny[83] out of the principles of inter-state comity: a sovereign state allows for the application of foreign private law and vice versa. Based on this notion of comity, they suggest a redefinition of the inherent objectives of private international law. They declare the 'national interest in the functioning of international commerce and trade' as the only substantive criterion that is able to avoid the formalized application of the principles and values of conflict of laws doctrine[84]. The criterion is applied to the determination of both the applicable private and public law. With this approach, the *comitas* doctrine aims to replace traditional considerations of private international law by a specific international criterion that leads to the 'friendly admission of foreign economic law'.

The *comitas* doctrine takes up the notion of mutual inter-state comity developed by Dutch scholars like *Ulricus Huber* in the seventeenth century[85]. This doctrine had a considerable influence on the development of American and European private international law-doctrine[86]. The *comitas* doctrine found its way into the American Restatement (Third) of the Foreign Relations Law of the United States. In Commentary e) to § 101 of the Restatement, the authors have adopted the definition used by the US Supreme Court in *Hilton v. Guyot*:

> 'Comity, in the legal sense, is neither a matter of absolute obligation, on the one hand, nor of mere courtesy and good will, upon the other. But it is the recognition which one nation allows within its territory to the legislative, executive or judicial acts of another nation, having due regard both to international duty and convenience and to the rights of its own citizens or of other persons who are under the protection of its laws. *Hilton v. Guyot*, 159 U.S. 113, 163–64, 16 S.Ct. 139, 143, 40 L.Ed. 95 (1895) . . .'[87]

---

effect, as the phrase is, *sub mutuae vicissitudinis obtentu*, with a wise and liberal regard to common convenience and mutual benefits and necessities'. . . . and at 35: 'There is then not only no impropriety in the use of the phrase '*comity of nations*', but it is the most appropriate phrase to express the true foundation and extent of the obligation of the laws of one nation within the territories of another' (emphasis added).

83. *See von Savigny*, System des heutigen Römischen Rechts, Vol. VIII, at 28: 'One may [describe the inherent function of private international law] as the friendly admission between sovereign states, *i.e.* the admission of originally foreign law as part of the sources from which the domestic courts derive solutions for the evaluation of legal relationships' (translation by the author).
84. *Meessen*, AöR 1985, at 398, 407 *et seq.*
85. *Cf. Scholten*, Het begrip Comitas in het internationaal privaatrecht van de Hollandse juristen-school der zeventiende eeuw, at 12 *et seq.*; *Yntema,* Festschrift Rabel, at 513, 524; *Erauw*, in Sumampouw/Barnhoorn/Freedberg-Swartzburg/Tromm/Wade (eds.), Law and Reality, at 63, 70.
86. *Cf. U. Hübner*, Die methodische Entwicklung des internationalen Wirtschaftsrechts, at 25; *cf. also* US Supreme Court in *Hilton v. Guyot*, 159 US 113 (1895); *see also von Savigny, supra* note 83, at 28, n. (f), where reference is made to *Huber*, De conflictu legum, § 2 (*'Rectores imperiorum id comiter agunt, ut jura cujusque populi . . . teneant ubique suam vim'*), to *Voet*, de statutis, § 1.12.17 (*'Dein quid ex comitate gens genti . . . liberaliter et officiose indugeat, permittat, patiatur, ultro citroque . . .'*) and to *Story*, Conflict of Laws, §§ 24–38.
87. Restatement of the Law, Third, Foreign Relations Law of the United States, Commentary e) to § 101 (1987).

In international commerce and trade specifically, the justification for the rebirth of the *comitas* doctrine is due to the fact that existing rules and sanctions of domestic laws are not enforced in order to ensure the functioning of world trade and to avoid retaliatory measures of other states, thus subordinating the legal sovereignty of states to the common economic interests of the international commercial community[88]. Therefore, claims and rights that are raised *and enforced* in the domestic context are often neutralized in the international context by overriding principles and interests[89].

The comity principle was referred to in a number of antitrust decisions of US courts, the EU Commission and the European Court of Justice which dealt with the question of jurisdiction over antitrust violations in cross-border cases[90]. Based on these considerations, the principle of 'positive comity' was embodied in Art. III of the 'Agreement Between the European Communities and the Government of the US on the Application of Positive Comity Principles in the Enforcement of Their Competition Laws' of 1998 (US-EU Agreement)[91]. The principle had already been incorporated into the 'Recommendation concerning Co-operation between Member Countries on Anticompetitive Practices Affecting International Trade' of the Organisation for Economic Co-operation and Development (OECD)[92]. In the antitrust context, the positive comity principle aims at curbing the unilateral application of domestic antitrust law by making the antitrust authority of the country which is affected by a foreign antitrust violation rely on the active collaboration with the antitrust authorities of the state which has territorial jurisdiction over the case[93].

88. *Meessen, supra* note 84, at 409.
89. *Joerges*, ZHR 138 (1974), at 549, 560.
90. *Timberlane Lumber Co. v. Bank of America, N.T.&A.*, 549 F.2nd 597 (9th Cir. 1976); *Mannington Mills Inc. v. Congoleum Corp.*, 549 F.2nd 1287 (3rd Cir. 1979); *Laker Airways Ltd. v. Sabena, Belgian World Airlines*, 731 F.2nd 909 (D.C. Cir. 1984); *Hartford Fire Insurance Co. v. California* 509 US 764, 113 S. Ct. 2891 (1993); Commission Decision of January 18, 2000 declaring a concentration to be compatible with the common market and the EEA Agreement, OJ No. L 92/1 of March 30, 2004; ECJ (November 11, 1981), Case 60/81, *IBM v. Commission*, ECR 1981, 2639.
91. OJ No. L 173/26 *et seq.* of June 18, 1998. This Agreement is intended to explain and reinforce the positive comity principle contained in a similar Agreement of 1991, OJ No. L 95/45-50 of April 27, 1995, corrected OJ No. L 131/38 of June 15, 1995.
92. *Buchmann*, Positive Comity im internationalen Kartellrecht, at 116 *et seq.*
93. *Marceau*, Anti-Dumping and Anti-Trust Issues in Free Trade Areas, at 93; *Buchmann, id.*, at 77 *et seq.*, Art. III ('Positive Comity') provides: 'The competition authorities of a Requesting Party [*i.e.* the Party adversely affected by anticompetitive activities occurring in the territory of another Party] may request the competition authorities of a Requested Party [*i.e.* the Party in the territory of which such anticompetitive activities appear to be occurring] to investigate and, if warranted, to remedy anticompetitive activities in accordance with the Requested Party's competition laws. Such a request may be made regardless of whether the activities also violate the Requesting Party's competition laws, and regardless of whether the competition authorities of the Requesting Party have commenced or contemplate taking enforcement activities under their own competition laws.'

In spite of its attractiveness, there are several reasons why the *comitas* doctrine may not serve as a means for the transnationalization of international commercial transactions. The notion of friendly admission of foreign economic law is said to apply only where there is a genuine interest on the part of the individual domestic law maker[94]. These interests are difficult to discern, let alone to formulate. The notion of comity is too broad to provide solutions in individual cases without the development of concrete and specialized criteria for individual types of conflicts[95]. Also, the US and EU decisions quoted above and the EU-US Agreement illustrate the limited effect of the *comitas* doctrine. Its effects are confined to the level of administrative cooperation between the antitrust agencies of both sides and the jurisdiction of the courts. The US-EU Agreement addresses the internationalization of antitrust procedure only. It does not concern the unification or harmonization of substantive antitrust law. This limited effect of the positive comity principle enshrined in the Agreement is underlined by the fact that the Agreement is of a bilateral, rather than of a multilateral nature[96].

All the developments described so far have one common denominator: they hint at the relativity of domestic laws in the context of international commercial relations and pave the way for the next step: the search for a way to regulate international commerce that is detached from domestic conflict of laws rules.

B. 'Hybrid' Solutions

1. Substantive Law Rules (*'Règles Matérielles'*)

The doctrine of substantive law rules in private international law suggests that in cases involving different legal systems, which offer different solutions for the same legal problem, the judge or arbitrator should adhere to classical conflict of laws considerations but should enrich them with substantive law rules[97]. In doing so he or she should either arrive at a cumulative application of all legal systems concerned, select the suitable norm among the various legal systems or create a new '*règle matérielle*' out of the solutions offered by the various domestic laws[98].

This approach is attractive in so far as it allows for the direct application of substantive law rules to individual problems of international trade, thus avoiding the uncertainties of the classical conflict of laws considerations. This, in turn,

94. *Meessen, supra* note 84, at 411.
95. *U. Hübner, supra* note 86, at 26.
96. *See Buchmann, supra* note 92, at 131 raising doubts as to whether the positive comity principle may serve as the basis for a multilateral agreement given that it requires the trust of all parties in the efficiency and reliability of the work of antitrust agencies of all other parties to such an agreement.
97. *Steindorff*, Sachnormen im IPR, at 278 *et seq.*; *cf. also Bonell*, RabelsZ 42 (1978), at 485, 498 ('transnational criteria and principles').
98. *Steindorff, id.*, at 276 *et seq.*

enables judges and arbitrators not only to save time and costs but also to arrive at economically sensible solutions for commercial disputes.

A closer examination of this approach, however, reveals that it suffers from serious methodical deficiencies. To ensure its functioning in everyday legal practice, the proponents of this theory have to grant to the judge or arbitrator the power to make policy decisions and value judgments to an extent that by far exceeds the corresponding powers in other areas of the law[99]. Decision-making by judges and arbitrators would involve 'policy decisions as to the suitability of legal rules and decisions on a case by case basis'[100]. The law-finding process would thus be shifted towards mere decisions in equity. Also, judges or arbitrators alike often find themselves in no position to decide if and how the new substantive law rule should be structured in the individual case before them. The idea of forming new substantive law rules in the context of private international law therefore does not have practical value per se. Rather, it emphasizes the necessity to develop and draft specific legal rules that take account of the specificities of commerce and trade. The NLM doctrine and the idea of materializing traditional private international law therefore have identical objectives[101].

2. General Principles of Law

As early as 1964, *Schlesinger* and *Gündisch* developed the view that international contracts that contain arbitration clauses should be made subject to general principles of law rather than to the rules and principles of any particular domestic legal system[102]. This approach is conflictual in nature in that the choice of general principles of law as an a-national legal system is dependent on the admission by the *lex fori* of the arbitral tribunal[103]. Even though this view has not gained ground in traditional private international law doctrine, it has nevertheless had considerable influence in this field of law. Thus, some authors maintain that in cases where the applicable foreign law cannot be determined by the judge, general principles of law should be applied as substitutional law instead of the *lex fori* of the court[104].

Of all concepts introduced so far in this Study, this view bears the closest resemblance to the notion of an autonomous transnational commercial law. Like the principles and rules of the NLM, general principles of law, by their very nature, have a broad scope of application. Like the NLM, general principles of law are difficult to reconcile with the traditional theory of legal sources. In their generality, they are not part of statutory law. Also, a single or a small number of court

99. *Steindorff, supra* note 97, at 278.
100. *Steindorff, supra* note 97, at 276 *et seq.*
101. *Weise*, Lex mercatoria, at 81.
102. *Schlesinger/Gündisch*, RabelsZ 28 (1964), at 9 *et seq.*; *see also Wengler*, Rev. crit. dr. int. pr. 1982, at 467 *et seq.*
103. *Schlesinger/Gündisch, id.*, at 29 *et seq.*
104. *Kötz*, RabelsZ 34 (1970), at 663 *et seq.*; *cf. also infra* Chapter 2 II.F.2.a.

decisions cannot serve as a comprehensive basis for a general principle of law whose scope is not limited to the section of the legal system to which these judgments relate but which covers and governs the legal system as a whole. Also, only some selected general principles of law assume the quality of customary law[105]. At the same time, looking at general principles of law in isolation to determine the contents of the NLM makes no sense. As will be seen later in this Study[106], general principles of law form an integral part of the autonomous transnational commercial law, but they are not the only ones. Leaving aside the problems of finding and formulating the general principles, a case that is decided solely on the basis of them is characterized by a certain 'analytical indifference' in that the traditional customs, usages and practices of international trade are being neglected. The latter, however, constitute intrinsic elements of the NLM which is geared towards the particular interests of international commercial practice[107]. The view developed by *Schlesinger* and *Gündisch* thus shows the right direction. On its own, however, it does not suffice to develop a workable autonomous legal system for international commerce and trade.

C. SOLUTIONS ON THE SUBSTANTIVE LAW PLANE

1. Special Statutes for International Trade

If neither the traditional private international law doctrine nor the development of substantive law rules provide satisfactory solutions for the legal problems of international trade and commerce, the domestic law makers themselves are called upon to supply a satisfactory statutory framework for international trade. The legislators of the countries of the former Eastern Bloc and of the People's Republic of China have filled this legislative vacuum and have enacted special statutes for international trade[108]. These laws leave maximum room for party autonomy and strive to ensure the validity of the contract as far as possible (*'favor contractus'*)[109]. Both aspects play a dominant role in contemporary international contract doctrine. The idea of drafting and implementing special statutes for international trade has therefore been advocated as an 'international business law approach' for all areas of international commercial practice[110]. In fact, it has been

105. *See generally Metzger*, Extra legem, intra ius: Allgemeine Rechtsgrundsätze im Europäischen Privatrecht, at 107.
106. *Cf. infra* Chapter 4 II.C.3.
107. *Cf. infra* Chapter 2 II.A.2.c.
108. *Cf.* for the 'International Economic Contract Law' (*Gesetz über Internationale Wirtschaftsverträge*) of the former German Democratic Republic, the 'Law on International Trade' of the former Czechoslovakia (Czech LIT) and for the 'Foreign Economic Contract Law of the People's Republic of China (China FECL) *infra* Chapter 4 I.A.3.b.aa.
109. *Cf. infra* Chapter 4.I.A.7.a.
110. *See* the approach developed by *Baxter*, ICLQ 1985, 538 *et seq.*; *Baxter*, ICLQ 1987, at 92 *et seq.*; *Baxter*, ICLQ 1990, at 288 *et seq.*; *cf. also Béguin*, McGill L.J. 1985, at 485 *et seq.*

considered whether domestic legislation should be enacted to adopt the UNIDROIT Principles which would then automatically govern international commercial contracts, unless the parties expressly choose to apply another law[111].

The suggested approach is justified in so far as the statutes of the countries of the former Eastern Bloc and the People's Republic of China prove that the comparative experience contained in international conventions and contract forms may be transformed into special statutes for international commercial transactions. This view is supported by the UNIDROIT Principles and the Principles of European Contract Law of the *Lando* Commission. One of their principal objectives is to serve as a model for domestic legislatures in their search for an adequate legislative framework for international transactions[112]. The orientation of these projects towards domestic legislatures indicates that drafting special domestic statutes on the basis of intensive comparative research will lead to a certain approximation of domestic laws and, in the end, to worldwide harmonization of domestic laws relating to international commerce[113].

In spite of this positive prognosis the international business law approach is not viable for several reasons.

First and foremost, the drafting of special statutes for international commerce does not eliminate the uncertainties that are necessarily connected with conflict of laws. In spite of their international orientation, these statutes remain part of their respective domestic legal systems. The applicability of these legal systems has to be determined according to the conflict of laws rules of the court's *lex fori*, or according to the special conflict of laws rules for international arbitrators[114]. To avoid this friction, domestic legislatures would have to accompany their special statutes for international commercial transactions with special conflict of laws rules[115]. These rules could be drafted in a way that domestic courts always have to apply the special statutes of their *lex fori*[116].

This approach, however, would run the risk of introducing a new kind of specialized law, *i.e.* special conflict of laws rules, which would lead to further complication of the law-finding process in international commercial transactions. Formulating these laws as substantive law rules ('*règles matérielles*') that contain their own conflict of laws rules ('*autolimitierte Sachnormen*') does not provide an escape from this dilemma. In this case, one would always have to decide whether the provision in question has such a special character or is subject to the general conflict of laws rules[117].

Leaving aside these intricacies of private international law, the problem still remains that domestic legislatures are traditionally reluctant to cooperate in the

111. *Selden*, Ann.Surv.Int'l Comp.L. 1995, at 111, 127 *et seq.*
112. *See infra* Chapter 4 I.A.10.f. and B.2.c.
113. *Baxter*, ICLQ 1990, at 288, 290.
114. *Kropholler*, IPR, § 1 II 2 (at 2 *et seq.*).
115. *Cf. Lüderitz*, Festschrift der Rechtswissenschaftlichen Fakultät zur 600-Jahr-Feier der Universität zu Köln, at 271, 281.
116. *Cf. Baxter*, ICLQ 1990, at 288, 289 *et seq.*
117. *Cf. Kropholler*, IPR, § 13 IV.2 (at 108).

unification of the law applicable to international commercial transactions. This reluctance is mainly due to the fact that domestic legislatures are hesitant to create different statutes concerning the same subject or similar matters[118]. In Germany, this phenomenon was on the top of the agenda during the deliberations on the 1998 German arbitration law in the 10th book of the German Code of Civil Procedure. Contrary to suggestions made by German legal doctrine[119], the Working Group on the 1998 German Arbitration Act decided to pursue a 'monistic' approach and drafted a single law to be applied both to domestic and international arbitrations[120]. In the end, the 'international usefulness' of the arbitration law that entered into force on January 1, 1998 was not affected by this decision. The German legislature decided to adopt the United Nations Commission on International Trade Law (UNCITRAL) Model Law on International Commercial Arbitration which now enjoys worldwide recognition and acceptance among arbitration practitioners[121].

Finally, an important psychological aspect should not be overlooked. The drafting of special statutes for international cases is no *panacea* to the many legal problems of international transactions. Discussion on the applicable law in international contract practice is always accompanied by certain distrust against the values, concepts and solutions found in foreign legal systems. The practical experience with the special statutes of the countries of the former Eastern Bloc has revealed that even the most liberal statutes that leave maximum room for party autonomy and contain highly practical provisions, *e.g.* on documentary credits and construction contracts, are not immune from this traditional scepticism towards domestic legislation. Special statutes on international transactions implemented by domestic legislatures would therefore always share the 'international reputation' of the whole legal system in which they are embedded. A special statute enacted in Switzerland, *e.g.* would have a much higher potential for success than special statutes issued by countries which do not enjoy a high reputation in international legal practice.

2. Internationally Useful Construction of Domestic Laws

If neither a modified approach to the traditional conflict of laws doctrine nor the drafting of special domestic statutes for international transactions provides viable solutions for the manifold problems of international commercial law, the question of whether internationally useful methods for the construction of domestic laws can be developed in order to escape the dilemma described above remains. Through these methods, domestic statutes originally drafted and

118. *Cf. Zitelmann*, DJZ 1900, at 329, 331; *but see Schödermeier*, Sonderprivatrecht für internationale Wirtschaftsverträge, at 165.
119. *Cf. e.g. Berger*, Arb.Int'l 1992, at 110 *et seq.*
120. *Cf. Schumacher,* Festschrift Glossner, at 341, 343 *et seq.*
121. *Cf.* German Ministry of Justice (ed.), Diskussionsentwurf einer Neuregelung des 10. Buches der ZPO, 1994; *see generally Berger*, Int'l Arb.Rep., January 1998, at 38; *Berger*, Int'l Arb.L.Rev. 1998, at 121 *et seq.*

promulgated solely for domestic cases could be adapted to the particularities of international commerce and trade in individual cases without involving the domestic legislatures[122]. This approach could be based on the understanding that the law-finding process is not a mere syllogism, that individual statutory provisions do not provide a predetermined result and that for this reason, the application of the law has to take account of the individual circumstances of the case[123]. It is for this very reason that the courts of many jurisdictions tend to use the blanket clauses contained in domestic laws such as 'good faith' to replace the strict application of the law with considerations of equity and fairness, thereby construing the law *praeter* or even *contra legem*[124]. The French case law on the validity of gold clauses in 'international contracts'[125] reveals that this freedom may also be used to adapt domestic laws to the particularities of international commercial transactions. Further justification for the development of a special way of construing domestic laws in international context may be derived from the fact that German legal doctrine favours a comparative method of construction and that Dutch legal doctrine has always favoured the idea of an 'anticipated method of construction'. This Study will deal with these issues in the context of the UNIDROIT Principles[126]. To clarify, under certain provisions of domestic law such as Sec. 157 of the German Civil Code (*Bürgerliches Gesetzbuch*) and Sec. 346 of the Commercial Code (*Handelsgesetzbuch*) arbitrators or judges have to take into account usages, customs and practices in construing contractual provisions or declarations of the parties. This allows the judge or arbitrator to use typical clauses of international trade as guidance for his or her task of construing the contract concluded between the parties[127].

In spite of these tendencies to de-nationalize the methods of construction, a method of construing domestic laws which would be useful in international contexts, may not provide a suitable substitute for the application of transnational commercial law. This is because judges or arbitrators who construe foreign laws are required to give an undistorted and authentic picture of that law. *W. Goldschmidt's* famous saying applies here that 'the judge is architect when applying his own law but has to behave like a photographer when he is called upon to apply or construe foreign law'. This means that in the application of foreign law,

122. *Cf. Dalhuisen, supra* note 1, at 188: '. . . English law applicable in a domestic case may turn out quite differently from English law when applied in an international case where it will meet other sources of law that prevail over it, and in any event it may not be applied in a domestic manner'; *cf. also Schödermeier*, Sonderprivatrecht für internationale Wirtschaftsverträge, at 177 *et seq.*; *Berger*, J. Int'l Arb. No. 4 1992, at 5, 10 *et seq.*
123. *Cf. Larenz*, Methodenlehre, at 211; *cf. also Lando*, in: Sarcevic (ed.), Essays on International Commercial Arbitration, at 129, 141.
124. *Cf.* for details *infra* Chapter 2 II.B.2. and G.2.c.
125. *Cf.* Cour de Cassation of May 17, 1927, *The Algier Land & Warehouse Company Ltd.*, D.P. 1928, I, at 25; October 17, 1928, *Pélissier du Besset v. Société The Algiers Land*, Clunet 1928, at 419; *Messageries Maritimes*, Civ. 1, S.Jur. 1951, at 1; *cf. generally Delaume*, Transnational Contracts, § 4.08; *cf. also infra* Chapter 4 I.A.6.a.
126. *Cf. infra* Chapter 4 I.A.10.e.bb.
127. *Schödermeier*, Sonderprivatrecht für internationale Wirtschaftsverträge, at 196.

account must always be taken of the methods of construction of that particular legal system[128].

> 'All in all, the statutory construction according to the functional considerations of international practice is embedded in the values of the respective domestic legal system – there is trust in international practice, but it is controlled and verified according to the own fundamental legal values. Domestic laws can hardly be denied this influence'[129].

Therefore, judges and arbitrators who pretend to construe the law in a way which is internationally useful, may not thrust upon the parties their ideas of a useful and equitable solution of the dispute before them. This method of construction may therefore only be implemented within the limits set by that respective domestic legal system. If the construction of the law transcends the possible meaning of the statutory wording and the limits set by the legal doctrine of that jurisdiction, the arbitrators' striving for an internationally useful solution of a particular case may not justify a modification of the law *praeter* or even *contra legem*. Instead, the limits set by the law itself or developed by the doctrine of that particular jurisdiction have to be observed[130]. The international usefulness or functionality of the law can only be brought into play by judges or arbitrators after they have been filtered through the notions and values of that particular jurisdiction. These aspects of domestic law therefore take precedence over any international business consideration and not vice versa. This strict approach to the construction of domestic law helps to prevent a distortion of statutory provisions when applied by arbitrators or judges in international cases. At the same time, however, it diminishes the value of any internationally useful construction method for international business practice.

III. THE CHANGING PARADIGM OF INTERNATIONAL COMMERCIAL LAW: PRIVATIZED LAW-MAKING

As a consequence of the intricacies of the legal process both on the plane of substantive and private international law, legal science and international practice are faced with a phenomenon that has gained increasing significance throughout the past decades: 'private governance' or 'private ordering', *i.e.* the privatization of law-making and the creation of pragmatic, sector-specific, and flexible rules that result from this process.

128. *Cf. Radbruch*, Monatsschrift für Kriminalpsychologie und Strafrechtsreform 1905/06, at 422, 425: 'We must not restrict ourselves to interpret foreign laws to our best ability, but rather find out how they are being interpreted in their home country' (translation by the author); *Ebert*, Rechtsvergleichung, § 45 V; *Aden*, RIW 1984, at 937: 'The way how in a range of possible solutions a typical judge in the relevant country arrives at his decision and how this range is limited by statutes, the law and methods of interpretation is typical for a legal order' (translation by the author).
129. *Schödermeier*, *supra* note 118, at 198 (translation by the author).
130. *Schulze*, ZfRV 1997, at 183, 191 *et seq.*; *Lüderitz*, Auslegung von Rechtsgeschäften, at 49.

A. ISO, IAS/IFRS, Basel II: From Technical Standardization to Private Law-Making

Privatized rule-making has long been used as an accepted means to unify technical and other business related standards[131]. The Geneva-based 'International Organization for Standardization' (ISO[132]), whose members are the domestic standardization institutions of 161 countries, is the institution responsible for technical standardization on the global level. The acronym 'ISO' is derived from the Greek *isos*, meaning 'equal' and is used in all member countries, irrespective of how the name of the organization is translated in the respective language. The law is not irrelevant in this context. It is telling that a soft law instrument and not a formal legal instrument links the global and the domestic level of technical standardization. The 'Code of Good Practice for the Preparation, Adoption and Application of Standards' issued by World Trade Organization (WTO) as Annex 3 to the WTO Agreement on Technical Barriers to Trade, concluded during the Uruguay Round (1986–1994)[133] is addressed to domestic standardization institutions like the Berlin-based '*Deutsches Institut für Normung*' (DIN[134]) and recommends that they adopt those technical standards which have been established on the international level.

Accounting is another area in which standardization has long since been recognized. The International Accounting Standards (IAS) and the International Financial Reporting Standards (IFRS) have been developed by the 'International Accounting Standards Board' (IASB) which is operated by a private, Delaware-based foundation[135]. These private rules have now found their way into EU law[136] and the commercial law of many jurisdictions[137]. They provide perfect examples for the fact that 'bottom up' rule-making is accepted by international and domestic legislatures in this important area of business life.

The 'Basel Committee of Banking Supervision'[138] provides another prominent example for non-legislative rule-making whose results are subsequently

131. *See Köndgen*, AcP 206 (2006) at 477, 481 who calls these rules 'expert made law' ('*Expertenrecht*'); *Röthel*, JZ 2007, at 755, 758 ('*lex technica*'); *see* for EU law the 'Council Resolution of May 7, 1985 on a new approach to technical harmonization and standards' (85/C 136/01), OJ No. C 136 of June 4, 1985.
132. *See www.iso.org*; the 'About'-section of the homepage emphasizes the 'hybrid' nature of the ISO membership: 'ISO is a non-governmental organization that forms a bridge between the public and private sectors. On the one hand, many of its member institutes are part of the governmental structure of their countries, or are mandated by their government. On the other hand, other members have their roots uniquely in the private sector, having been set up by national partnerships of industry associations.'
133. *See www.wto.org/english/docs_e/legal_e/17-tbt_e.htm#annexIII.*
134. *See www.din.de.*
135. *See www.iasb.org.*
136. Regulation (EC) No. 1606/2002 of the European Parliament and of the Council of July 19, 2002 on the application of international accounting standards, OJ No. L 243 of September 11, 2002.
137. *See e.g.* Sec. 315a German Commercial Code (*Handelsgesetzbuch*).
138. *See www.bis.org/bcbs.*

converted into domestic law[139]. The Committee is of a 'hybrid' nature. It is attached to an international institution, the Bank for International Settlements (BIS) in Basel. The BIS was established in 1930 in the context of the Young Plan which dealt with the issue of the reparation payments imposed on Germany by the Treaty of Versailles following the First World War[140]. Even though it is the most influential body on banking supervision and regulation in the world, the Basel Committee is not an official organ of the BIS. The members of the Committee are the heads of the central banks and banking supervision authorities of the G-10 states[141]. Given the traditional independence of these authorities from the political process, the Committee members' mandate is not based on political legitimacy and is not subject to the control by the political process. Instead, the Committee members are solely committed to their common goal to enhance the understanding of key supervisory issues and to improve the quality of banking supervision worldwide, thereby ensuring the stability of the world financial system. After complex consultation processes with other expert groups such as the 'Committee of European Banking Supervisors' (CEBS[142]), the Basel Committee issues important rules and regulations on the capital adequacy and supervision standards for banks and other financial institutions. Of these rules, 'Basel I' of 1988[143] and 'Basel II' of 2004[144] are the most prominent and influential ones. The Basel Accords constitute soft law[145] until they are transformed into EU-Ordinances[146] and/or domestic law[147]. In effecting this transformation, the domestic legislatures rely exclusively on the expertise of the Committee members and do not question

---

139. *Köndgen, supra* note 131, at 493 *et seq.*
140. *See* for the history of the BIS and its role in the current financial environment *www.bis.org/about/history.htm.*
141. The Basel Committee's members come from Argentina, Australia, Belgium, Brazil, Canada, China, France, Germany, Hong Kong SAR, India, Indonesia, Italy, Japan, Korea, Luxembourg, Mexico, the Netherlands, Russia, Saudi Arabia, Singapore, South Africa, Spain, Sweden, Switzerland, Turkey, the United Kingdom and the United States.
142. *See www.c-ebs.org.*
143. International convergence of capital measurement and capital standards 1988, text available at *www.bis.org/publ/bcbsc111.htm*; *see Berger* BB 1989, at 1017 *et seq.*
144. Basel II: International Convergence of Capital Measurement and Capital Standards, A revised Framework, text available at *www.bis.org/publ/bcbs107.htm*; *see M. Berger*, Hertfordshire Law Journal 2008, at 2 *et seq.*; *Angermüller/Eichhorn/Ramke*, J.I.B.L.R. 2005, at 45 *et seq.*; *Tanega*, J.I.B.L.R. 2005, at 617 *et seq.* and J.I.B.L.R. 2006, at 1 *et seq.*; *Hall*, JBR 2006, at 106 *et seq.*
145. *See* MünchKomm-*Berger*, 4th ed., Vor § 488 No. 49.
146. Directive 2006/48/EC of the European Parliament and of the Council of June 14, 2006 relating to the taking up and pursuit of the business of credit institutions (OJ No. L 177/1 of June 30, 2006); Directive 2006/49/EC of the European Parliament and of the Council of June 14, 2006 on the capital adequacy of investment firms and credit institutions (OJ No. L 177/201 of June 30, 2006).
147. *See e.g.* Secs 10 *et seq.* KWG, as modified by the German Act on the Implementation of the Revised EU Capital Adequacy Directives ('Gesetz zur Umsetzung der neu gefassten Bankenrichtlinie und der Kapitaladäquanzrichtlinie' of November 17, 2006, BGBl. I, at 2606 *et seq.*).

the legitimacy of the rule-making process within the Committee[148]. The world financial crisis of 2008/2009 has revealed weaknesses in the worldwide banking supervision systems established by the Basel Committee. However, the Committee reacted to this crisis and issued a package of consultative documents to strengthen the Basel II capital framework in early 2009. The goal of these measures is to ensure that the risks inherent in banks' portfolios related to trading activities, securitizations and exposures to off-balance sheet vehicles are better reflected in minimum capital requirements, risk management practices and accompanying disclosures to the public[149]. Thus, the world financial crisis has revealed how quickly the Basel Committee as a 'hybrid' formulating agency between private and public rule-making can react on a global level to turbulences in the world financial markets.

B. Decentralizing the Law-Making Process

It is not surprising that in light of the developments just described, the process of private governance has become a frequent phenomenon also in the area of law-making. In fact, it is the spontaneous creation of the law instead of state controlled implementation of laws and statutes which gave new momentum to the discussion on the transnationalization of commercial law already in the mid-1990s. Today, private governance furnishes an important indication for a dramatic change of paradigm in international commercial law[150]. To an ever increasing extent, legal rule-making is affected by 'formulating agencies' in the form of governmental and non-governmental institutions rather than by domestic legislatures[151]. As a consequence, harmonization and creation of the law is no longer initiated 'top down' by the legislative authority of sovereign states, *e.g.* through the transformation of international conventions or bilateral treaties. Law-making no longer appears 'in the splendid garment' of the statute[152]. Instead, it occurs 'bottom up' in a number of informal methods which create pragmatic, practice-made rules[153]. These rules are said to be economically more efficient than state legislation[154]. International organizations like UNCITRAL[155], the ICC[156], the International Institute for the

148. *Köndgen, supra* note 131, at 494.
149. *See* the announcement of the Basel Committee of January 16, 2009, at *www.bis.org/press/p090116.htm.*
150. *Kramer*, ÖBA 1991, at 621; *cf. also Boele-Woelki*, Unif.L.Rev. 1996, at 652, 659; *Béguin*, McGill Law Journal 1985, at 478, 483.
151. *Cf. Behrends*, RabelsZ 50 (1986), at 19, 23 *et seq.*
152. *Kötz*, RabelsZ 56 (1992), at 215, 217; *see also Berger*, L. & Pol.Int'l Bus. 1997, at 943, 954 *et seq.*
153. *See generally* for a collection of instruments of self-regulation in international commercial law *De Ly*, Unif.L.Rev. 1997, at 519, 530 *et seq.*
154. *Cooter*, Int'l Rev. L. & Econ. 1994, 215 *et seq.*; *Cooter*, U. Pa. L. Rev. 1996, at 1643 *et seq.*
155. *See www.uncitral.org.*
156. *See www.iccwbo.org.*

Unification of Private Law (UNIDROIT)[157], the *Organisation pour l'harmonisation en Afrique du droit des affaires* (OHADA)[158], the *Fédération Internationale des Ingénieurs-Conseils* (FIDIC)[159], the ISDA[160], the LMA[161] and the *Comité Maritime International* (CMI)[162] as the oldest formulating agency of its kind established in 1897 all function as formulating agencies. They each draft 'code-like' compilations of rules and principles for international commerce such as the 'ICC Uniform Customs and Practices for Documentary Credits' (UCP), the INCOTERMS, the UNCITRAL Arbitration Rules, and the UNCITRAL Notes on Organizing Arbitral Procedure or the UNIDROIT Principles.

'Codes of Conduct' or 'Codes of Best Practice' are other examples of the dominance of private governance in international business. This practice dates back to the 1930s. The first international code of conduct for multinationals was created by the ICC as 'Code of Standards of Advertising Practice' in 1937. Since then, this technique has become extremely popular as a means to reflect 'good practices' or policies which participants in a certain industry are expected to observe[163]. The ILO 'Tripartite Declaration of Principles Concerning Multinational Enterprises'[164], the 'Equator Principles, An Industry Approach for Financial Institutions in Determining, Assessing and Managing Environmental & Social Risk in Project Financing'[165], the 'Electronic Industry Code of Conduct' (EICC)[166] and the 'OECD Guidelines for Multinational Enterprises'[167] provide examples for the significance and diversity of these soft law instruments for international business. Private companies also issue Codes of Conduct to underline their social self-responsibility. The concept 'corporate code of conduct' refers to companies' policy statements that define ethical standards for their conduct. There is great variance in the ways these statements are drafted[168]. Even though many of these Codes of Conduct contain express provisions stating their non-binding character, the rules contained in them are frequently converted into hard law because parties incorporate them into their contracts, irrespective of their dogmatic qualification[169]. Even without such a transformation from 'soft' to 'hard' law, the bad publicity and

157. *See www.unidroit.org.*
158. *See www.ohada.org.*
159. *See www.fidic.org.*
160. *See supra* I.B.1.
161. *See supra* I.B.1.
162. *See www.comitemaritim.org.*
163. *See Horn*, in: Horn (ed.), Legal Problems of Codes of Conduct for Multinational Enterprises, at 45 *et seq.*; *Farjat*, in: Fouchard/Kahn/Lyon-Caen (eds.), Le droit des relations économiques internationales, at 47 *et seq.*; *Sanders*, *id.*, at 281 *et seq.*
164. *See http://actrav.itcilo.org/actrav-english/telearn/global/ilo/guide/main.htm#Summ.*
165. *See www.equator-principles.com.*
166. *See www.eicc.info.*
167. *See www.oecd.org/department/0,3355,en_2649_34889_1_1_1_1_1,00.html.*
168. *Cf. generally Buntenbroich*, Menschenrechte und Unternehmen, at 65 *et seq.*; *see also* ILO, Corporate Codes of Conduct, available at *http://actrav.itcilo.org/actrav-english/telearn/global/ilo/code/main.htm.*
169. *See Berger*, in: Bierbaum (ed.), So investiert die Welt, at 33, 40.

other social sanctions arising out of violations of the rules and standards contained in Codes of Conduct makes market participants adhere to these Codes.

In the area of international commercial arbitration, private governance has long presented itself through the publication of arbitration rules issued by private arbitral institutions such as the ICC, the London Court of International Arbitration (LCIA) or the German Institution of Arbitration (DIS). Today, private governance in international arbitration has assumed a new dimension. The recent publication of a large number of 'best practice standards'[170] has had a marked impact on international practice. The 'IBA Rules on the Taking of Evidence in International Commercial Arbitration' of 1999 and the 'IBA Guidelines on Conflict of Interest in International Arbitration' of 2004, both issued by the International Bar Association (IBA), provide only two examples of this important development[171]. The IBA Guidelines specifically refer to their soft law nature and the resulting relationship with domestic law:

> 'These Guidelines are not legal provisions and do not override any applicable national law or arbitral rules chosen by the parties. However, the Working Group hopes that these Guidelines will find general acceptance within the international arbitration community (as was the case with the IBA Rules on the Taking of Evidence in International Commercial Arbitration) and that they thus will help parties, practitioners, arbitrators, institutions and the courts in their decision-making process on these very important questions of impartiality, independence, disclosure, objections and challenges made in that connection. The Working Group trusts that the Guidelines will be applied with robust common sense and without pedantic and unduly formalistic interpretation.'[172]

It must be noted that the ever increasing number of these best practice standards available today in the field of international arbitration has endured considerable criticism. The question has been raised as to whether there is a risk that arbitral discretion and the inherent flexibility of the arbitral process as a major advantage of the arbitral process as compared to procedures before domestic courts, will ultimately be eliminated by an 'overdose' of private governance[173].

Finally and above all, the preserving effect of international contract practice plays an all important role in this context[174]. Businessmen active in cross-border

---

170. *See Voser*, in: Wirth (ed.), Best Practices in International Arbitration, 1, 2: ' "Best Practice" means a practice-made rule. It is, in other words, impossible to speak about Best Practice if there is an applicable authoritative rule (*i.e.* statutory provision or a binding precedent rule) on the very same issue.'
171. *See* with reference to further best practice standards *Berger*, Private Dispute Resolution in International Business, Handbook, Nos. 16-114 *et seq.*
172. Paragraph 6 of the Introduction to the IBA Guidelines on Conflicts of Interest in International Arbitration.
173. *See Morrissey/Graves*, International Sales Law and Arbitration, 311 *et seq.*; *see also Park*, in: Lew/Mistelis (eds.), Arbitration Insights, Nos. 17-91 *et seq.*; *Berger, supra* note 171, No. 16-117.
174. *Horn*, Internationale Anleihen, at 534; *cf. also Stein*, Lex mercatoria, at 37 *et seq.*

trade constantly refer to pre-drafted, standardized contracts designed to avoid disputes from the outset[175]. They create their own law through the drafting, use and refinement of general conditions of trade, standardized contracts and other clauses as well as the development of practices and usages, elevating them from regional to worldwide customs[176]. Also on this level of private contracting, the creation and unification of the law is being increasingly 'privatized'[177].

C. Legitimizing Privatized Law-Making

From the perspective of domestic legislatures, private governance as a means of de-centralized 'bottom up' rule-making appears as an expression of de-regulation of international business[178]. Due to their high degree of abstraction, domestic legal rules are inapt to provide workable regulatory frameworks for the increasingly complex business world[179]. Privatized rule-making is effected by specialists in the field. It results not in general or abstract laws, but in sector-specific rules which take account of the specificities of the business which they intend to regulate. These practice-made rules may be adjusted easily and quickly as required by those subject to them and by the business environment which today changes at an extremely high pace[180]. The high flexibility of private law-making is much better suited to 'trial-and-error' rule-making, which the fast changing world of international business often provokes, than the formalized and slow procedures of domestic legislation and international law-making through conventions[181], model laws or bilateral agreements[182]. Private governance, therefore, seems to provoke the question as to the correct delineation of the state from the market, and of the public from the private[183]. Moreover, the uniformity of substantive rules created by private governance has two advantages. On a more general level, it replaces the

175. *Cf. Kappus*, RIW 1990, at 788 *et seq.*; *Delaume*, Transnational Contracts, §§ 4.01 *et seq.*
176. *Cf.* for the contract as an independent, self-sufficient legal order *Sandrock*, ZHR 152 (1988), at 66, 83; *Verdross*, ZaöRV 1957/58, at 635 *et seq.*; *cf. also David*, in: UNIDROIT (ed.), New Directions in International Trade Law, at 5, 11.
177. *Cf. Schneider*, NJW 1991, at 1985, 1987 for the harmonization of law in the area of contracts in banking law; *Blaurock*, ZEuP 1993, at 247; *cf. also De Ly*, Europese Gemeenschap en privaatrecht, at 49; *cf. also Mertens,* Festschrift Odersky 1996, at 857 *et seq.*
178. *Köndgen, supra* note 131, at 516 *et seq.*
179. *See supra* I.B.1.
180. *Cf.* for a normative economic theory of the unification of law *Bernholz/Faber*, RabelsZ 50 (1986), at 35 *et seq.*; *Kötz*, RabelsZ 50 (1986), at 1, 3 *et seq.*; *Kötz*, RabelsZ 56 (1992), at 215, 216.
181. *See Goode*, ICLQ 2005, at 539, 558: 'The preparation of international conventions is arduous and time-consuming and calls for immense patience, mutual respect and a very great deal of hard work'.
182. *Köndgen, supra* note 131, at 512.
183. *See Zumbansen*, Transnational Law, in: Smits (ed.), Encyclopedia of Comparative Law, at 738, 742.

'failing economic productivity of private international law'[184]. On the specific level of private contracting, uniform rules of a transnational character create a 'level playing field' between the parties to international contracts[185], thereby granting equal opportunities to all participants in international commerce and trade. This aspect of ensuring equality of the parties is the major practical advantage of the unification of substantive law as compared to any conflict of laws considerations[186].

The process of private governance necessarily involves the creation of 'para-legal'[187] rules, a kind of practice-made, 'extra-state law'[188], thereby provoking the question as to the circumvention of the safeguards of the domestic legislative process. The rules resulting from private governance are developed without a formal mandate for legislation. Participants in this process do not perceive themselves as state representatives. Instead, they argue and act according to their expertise and own interests[189]. They have created their own system of internal 'checks and balances' which safeguard the integrity of the privatized rule-making process. Thus, the IASB[190] develops its accounting standards through an international consultation process, the 'Due Process', a 'thorough, open, and transparent' procedure that involves intense discussions between investors, regulators, business leaders and the global accountancy profession and collaborative efforts with the worldwide standard setting community[191]. The 'Due Process' and the six distinct stages it involves, are described in great detail in the 'Due Process Handbook' issued by the Board and available at the Board's homepage[192].

Given these privatized consultation and law-making procedures, private governance, like the notion of a transnational autonomous world trade law, has gone far beyond *anything* that the proponents of the traditional theory of legal sources ever imagined[193]. It has reached the sphere of economics. The 'Economics of Governance' theory analyses the question of why the need for private ordering arises if the state has created and enforces efficacious rules of law, as assumed by the legal traditionalists. The theory concludes that private ordering is central to the

184. *Lüderitz*, Festschrift der Rechtswissenschaftlichen Fakultät zur 600-Jahr-Feier der Universität zu Köln, at 271, 281.
185. *See Berger*, in: Bierbaum (ed.), So investiert die Welt, at 33, 36.
186. *Dölle/Wahl*, EKG, Art. 17, No. 17.
187. *Cf. Braeckmans*, Paralegale Normen en Lex Mercatoria, TvPr. 1986, at 1 *et seq.*
188. *Esser*, Grundsatz und Norm, at 344.
189. *Calliess*, Indiana Journal of Global Legal Studies 2007, at 469, 475; *see* for the conflict of the lack of democractic legitimacy and political accountability of decision-making and the increased effectiveness of rule-making within international institutions such as ISO and ICANN *Fukuyama*, America at the Crossroads, at 163 *et seq.*
190. *See supra* A.
191. *See* IASB and the IASC Foundation, Who we are and what we do, available at *www.iasb.org/NR/rdonlyres/0A5A767C-E7DE-49E5-8B12-499F62F8870C/0/WhoWeAre_Final12508.pdf.*
192. *See www.iasb.org/About+Us/How+we+develop+standards/How+we+develop+standards.htm.*
193. *Köndgen, supra* note 131, at 510; *see also Joerges*, RabelsZ 43 (1979), at 6, 40.

performance of any economy, regardless of the particular conditions of lawfulness. This is because in many instances, business actors can devise more satisfactory solutions to their problems and disputes than can professionals (lawmakers, courts) who are constrained to apply general rules on the basis of limited knowledge of the problem or the dispute[194].

In the eyes of the traditionalists, private governance, like the NLM doctrine, constitutes a veritable threat to the classical theory of legal sources[195]. In both scenarios, the problem is rooted in the discrepancy between the legal reality of international trade and commerce that exists according to its own principles and rules, and the traditional theory of the states' monopoly of law-making[196]. In the NLM context, the lack of involvement of domestic legislatures, in the eyes of legal positivists, sheds doubt on the very foundations of legal theoretical conceptions of the law as a means of social control, decreed and sanctioned by the State Supreme[197] and being an 'epitome of compulsory rules issued by a state'[198] as opposed to mere moral rules of behaviour[199]. Instead, the notion of private governance, like the creation of law in the NLM context, involves the concept of self-supervision and privatized enforcement mechanisms as the focal point of legal theoretical considerations. This self-supervision is effected by arbitral tribunals, 'black lists', withdrawal of trade associations' members' rights, forfeiture of bonds and other risks of damage to the commercial reputation of the parties. They constitute informal, social sanctions within the business community. The law is no longer created by the national sovereign and protected by sanctions; sanctions are no longer reasons for creating the law[200] but rather become an integral part of the law itself which, in turn, evidences rules of societal behaviour enforced by sanctions[201]. This view resembles the sociological school established by

194. *See Williamson*, The Economics of Governance, *www.aeaweb.org/annual_mtg_papers/2005/0107_1645_0101.pdf*, at 2 *et seq.*
195. *See* for private governance *Köndgen, supra* note 131, 508 *et seq.*; for the *lex mercatoria Béguin*, McGill Law Journal 1985, at 478, 484 *et seq.*; *Juenger*, Vand. J. Transnat'l L. 1995, at 487, 490 *et seq.*
196. *Schnitzer,* Festschrift Mann, at 289, 300.
197. *Cf.* for the function of law as *'governmental social control' Black*, The Behavior of Law, 1976, at 2.
198. *von Jhering*, Der Zweck im Recht, Vol. 1, at 249: 'Only those rules imposed by society deserve the name of law which have behind them the force of the law or . . . the force of the sovereign state, meaning that only those rules adopt the quality of legal norms that have been vested with this effect by the sovereign state or that the state is the only source of the law' (translation by the author).
199. *See Blackstone*, Commentaries on the Laws of England, Vol. I, 1809, at 46: '. . . municipal law is a rule of civil conduct prescribed by the *supreme power in a State* . . . sovereignty and legislature are indeed convertible terms; one cannot subsist without the other'; *von Jhering, id.*, at 249: *cf. also Juenger*, in: Carbonneau (ed.), Lex Mercatoria and Arbitration, at 265, 268: 'The fact that those who decide transnational commercial cases are more concerned about the quality than the sources of rules may . . . shock legal positivists, the school of thought that includes such illustrious jurists as Justice Holmes and Justice Brandeis'.
200. Distinctly *Schlosser*, Das Recht der internationalen privaten Schiedsgerichtsbarkeit, No. 197.
201. *Allen*, Law in the Making, at 60.

Eugen Ehrlich[202], which denied the classical rule that every law must necessarily originate from the state legislature and laid the basis for the theory of legal pluralism[203], or *Roscoe Pound's* 'theory of social interest'[204]. For this reason, traditional domestic doctrine regards both private governance and the NLM as 'a sociological transformation of the traditional theory of legal sources'[205] thereby exerting substantial methodological and theoretical pressure on the proponents of this view[206].

A major argument raised by those who oppose the theory of privatized law-making is always brought forth against any attempt to recognize extra-positivistic legal principles or institutional law-making. They submit that this view is nothing more than a disguised attempt to ignore the contents of the codified law and to do away with statutory values and policy decisions under the pretext of the methodical justification of the normative force of facts[207]. For them 'privatized law is non-law'[208].

However, the reality of rule-making in a modern society as expressed in the phenomenon of private governance speaks a different language. It reveals the stealth of the traditional theory of legal sources. Over the past decade, a non-positivistic notion of the law has begun to emerge[209]. The law has to take account of the complexities of society[210]. Therefore, it is not the public reason represented by the state or by inter-governmental organizations *alone* but also the power for self-regulation and coordination of the individual and of private organizations and federations which justifies normative force and contributes to a redefinition of the notion of normativity. The traditional theory of legal sources, which is centred around the notion of sovereignty of the state[211], is being replaced by a legal pluralism which accepts that society's ability to self-organize and coordinate is more than a mere factual pattern without independent legal significance[212]. Domestic laws are here to stay. Private governance takes place 'in the

202. *Cf. E. Ehrlich*, Grundlegung der Soziologie des Rechts, 1913, at 67 *et seq.*; *see also Köndgen, supra* note 131, 509 *et seq.*; for comparative law as sociological jurisprudence *see Rheinstein*, Einführung in die Rechtsvergleichung, at 28.
203. *See infra* Chapter 2 G.3.b.aa.
204. *Cf. Pound*, Col.L.Rev. 1905, at 339 *et seq.*; *Pound*, Harv.L.Rev. 1911, at 591 *et seq.*
205. *Joerges*, RabelsZ 43 (1979), at 6, 41; *cf. also Klein*, Festschrift Mann, at 617, 632.
206. *Cf. Behrends*, RabelsZ 50 (1986), at 19, 22; *Bonell*, RabelsZ 42 (1978), at 485, 491 *et seq.*
207. *Cf. Rüthers*, Die unbegrenzte Auslegung, at 453 *et seq.*
208. *Köndgen, supra* note 131, at 509 who does not share this view.
209. *Canaris*, in: Basedow (ed.), Europäische Vertragsrechtsvereinheitlichung und deutsches Recht, 2000, at 5, 10 *et seq.*
210. *See* for the 'normative force of fact' *Jellinek*, Allgemeine Staatslehre, at 338.
211. *von Jhering*, Der Zweck im Recht, Vol. 1, at 249: 'Only those rules imposed by society deserve the name of law which have behind them the force of the law or . . . the force of the sovereign state, meaning that only those rules adopt the quality of legal norms that have been vested with this effect by the sovereign state or that the state is the only source of the law' (translation by the author).
212. *See infra* Chapter 2 G.3.b.aa.

shadow of the law', *i.e.* private and public governance mechanisms work as supplements which are mutually dependent and reinforce each other[213].

IV. SUMMARY

The above considerations reveal that the law-finding process in international trade and commerce is hampered by considerable problems and uncertainties. Judges and arbitrators alike are confronted with these problems both on the plane of conflict of laws and substantive law. The solutions and approaches developed so far by legal doctrine do not provide a viable option to escape this dilemma. A major reason for this failure lies in the fact that even though international trade and commerce is particularly dependent upon the interplay of substantive and private international law, the classical conflict of laws doctrine has considerable problems in ensuring the harmonic interaction of these two branches of the law. At most, the many pitfalls of traditional conflict of laws doctrine and the tendency to resort to substantive law solutions provide further support for the necessity to develop a coherent theory of transnational commercial law[214]. Thus, the idea of a worldwide NLM reflects the 'dream of every conflict of laws lawyer, the idea of substantive decisional harmony that does away with traditional conflict of laws rules, leading to the vision of eternal peace that stands behind the idea of the law as such'[215].

There is, however, another major reason why the solutions offered so far are doomed to fail: they do not transgress the traditional boundaries of domestic doctrine and theory. In order to achieve acceptable, *i.e.* economically sensible solutions for international business people, comparative legal theory and practice have to go beyond the traditional, 'positivistic' limits of domestic doctrine in order to develop transnational solutions for transnational cases. The fight over the theoretical justification of private governance shows that every attempt to develop such transnational approaches has to meet various challenges advanced by legal theory and practice. On the one hand, it has to overcome the traditional objections which are brought forth against any attempt to modify or even overcome the classical theory of legal sources. It is this traditional theory which has always been the major stumbling block in preventing a correct appreciation of the NLM[216]. On the other hand, a practical and workable concept for the transnationalization of the legal process of international commerce has to be developed in order to make the NLM acceptable for legal practice.

---

213. *Calliess, supra* note 189, at 471.
214. *See Borchers*, in: Raisch/Shaffer (eds.), Introduction to Transnational Legal Transactions, at 139, 151: 'The lex mercatoria is simply the name most commonly given to the substantive law solution to cross-border commercial conflicts questions'.
215. *See Martinek*, Das internationale Kartellprivatrecht, at 97 (translation by the author).
216. *Blackman*, Mercantile Law and Mercantile Practice, at 3.

Private governance plays an important role in this context for two reasons: From a theoretical perspective, private governance has paved the way towards a liberalization and 'pragmatization' of the theory of legal sources and the 'de-limitation' of the law[217] as an indispensable precondition for the methodical acceptance of the NLM as a 'third' legal system between domestic and international law. From a more practical viewpoint, the plurality and diversity of practice-made rules created by private governance, such as Codes of Conducts, provide important input for the contents of the NLM[218]. From the perspective of contract law there is still another fundamental issue that has to be dealt with in any effort to justify the theory of private governance and NLM, namely whether it is possible to bring together and unify such distinct and elementary categories like 'contract' and 'legal norms'[219].

217. *Horn*, in: Brugger/Haverkate (eds.), Grenzen als Thema der Rechts- und Sozialphilosophie, at 179 *et seq.* ('*Entgrenzung des Rechts*').
218. *Horn, supra* note 163, at 61; *Sanders, supra* note 163, at 298.
219. *Cf. Martiny*, RabelsZ 50 (1986), at 730, 731; *Metzger supra* note 105, at 522; *see also Loquin*, in: Souveraineté étatique et marchés internationaux à la fin du 20ème siècle, at 23, 32 *et seq.*

Chapter 2

The Dogmatic Foundations of the New *Lex Mercatoria* Doctrine

I. THE STATUS QUO IN THE DISCUSSION ON THE CONCEPT OF A TRANSNATIONAL COMMERCIAL LAW

A. Antinomy of Viewpoints

When it comes to the discussion of the theoretical foundations and practical usefulness of the NLM, opinions are more opposed than in the case of any other question of international commercial law. The proponents of a transnational system of commercial law praise the NLM as a means to escape from the conflict of laws dilemma and as a substantive 'better-law approach'[1]. The opponents, especially those from the field of private international law, attack the NLM as 'a mere sociological phenomenon'[2], as 'a trip into legal weightlessness'[3], as 'legal utopia'[4], a 'useful illusion'[5] or 'legal dreams of the future'[6], as 'wishful thinking'

1. *Cf. e.g. Kropholler*, IPR, § 12. I. 3 (at 99): 'What *Voltaire* said about God: "If he did not exist, someone would have to invent him", also applies to this kind of transnational law' (translation by the author), *see also Hausmann*, in: Reithmann/Martiny (eds.), Internationales Vertragsrecht, No. 3525 where it is acknowledged that the parties may choose to have their contract governed by 'the lex mercatoria as a genuine source of law'; *see also supra* Introduction I.A., notes 1–9.
2. This is the view of the prevailing opinion in German legal doctrine, *see e.g. Kegel/Schurig*, IPR, § 1 IX.2.d, at 125 *et seq.*; *von Bar/Mankowski*, IPR, Vol. I, § 2 No. 76; MünchKomm-*Sonnenberger*, EGBGB, Einl. No. 268; *Schlosser*, Das Recht der internationalen privaten Schiedsgerichtsbarkeit, No. 197.
3. *Heini*, Festschrift Moser, at 67, 72, note 22.
4. *Steindorff*, in: UNIDROIT (ed.), New Directions for International Trade Laws, at 87, 100; *Schödermeier*, Sonderprivatrecht für internationale Wirtschaftsverträge, at 142.
5. *Ipsen*, Private Normenordnungen als Transnationales Recht?, at 178.
6. *Ferid*, IPR, No. 6-24; MünchKomm-*Sonnenberger*, EGBGB, Einl. No. 270.

and as a 'disguise for the marketing of own solutions'[7], as 'palm-tree justice'[8], as 'conceptionally vague and misplaced from a policy point of view'[9], as 'a laissez-faire-doctrine'[10], as a 'not always candid legal mood'[11] or simply as 'degenerated'[12] and therefore totally 'out of question'[13] and as 'the phantom of Sorbonne Professors'[14]. Banking lawyers are even said to live in a '*horror legis mercatoriae*'[15]. It is argued that the existence of the NLM, 'like the existence of God, seems to depend largely on the will to believe'[16] and that the NLM seems to be a dangerous '*lex illegitima*'[17].

It is the intrinsic evil of the NLM doctrine that the discussion about its theoretical conception and practical viability is frequently too emotional and too passionate. The way in which arguments are exchanged resembles a 'religious war'[18] and the 'military language'[19] used in the combat often prevents any clear or tension-free analysis of the real problems related to this doctrine[20]. Business practice sometimes raises the concern that the creation of supranational law is subject to subtle political and ideological influences which necessarily lead to substantial disadvantages in the application of the law[21]. At the same time, the discussion on the transnationalization of commercial law is frequently misused to promote certain philosophical conceptions about the advantages or disadvantages of extrajudicial dispute settlement through international arbitration[22]. Sometimes, both aspects are combined in that it is alleged that the NLM concept was 'invented' by arbitration specialists of the seventies in order to allow Western governments involved in the major (oil) arbitration disputes of that time to escape from the laws and regulations that were unfavourable to Western interests. At the same time, the flexibility of the NLM concept and the collective image of neutrality of its academic proponents is said to have served as a major 'marketing tool' for the arbitral process as such, preserving the inventors' position in the lucrative market for international arbitrations[23]. Finally, the multitude of approaches taken towards the justification of a transnational legal order tends to undermine the very success of this doctrine[24].

---

7. *Cf.* the remark by *Bonell*, reported by *Remien*, RabelsZ 56 (1992), at 300, 305.
8. *Mann*, Introduction, in: Carbonneau (ed.), Lex Mercatoria and Arbitration, at XX.
9. *von Bar/Mankowski*, IPR, Vol. 1, § 2 No. 75.
10. *Mustill*, Arb.Int'l 1988, at 86.
11. *Zahi*, L'Etat et l'arbitrage, at 225.
12. *Cf.* the remark by *Schanze*, reported by *Remien*, *supra* note 7, at 303.
13. *Schlosser*, Das Recht der internationalen privaten Schiedsgerichtsbarkeit, No. 197.
14. *See Marrella*, La Nuova Lex Mercatoria, at 660.
15. *Cf.* the remark by *Harries*, reported by *Remien, supra* note 7, at 310.
16. *Wasserstein Fassberg*, Chi.J.Int'l L. 2004, at 67.
17. *Teubner*, in: Teubner (ed.), Global Law Without a State, at 3, 7.
18. *Bonell*, ZRVgl. 1996, at 152.
19. *Béguin*, McGill L.J. 1985, at 478, 479.
20. *Dasser*, Internationale Schiedsgerichte und Lex Mercatoria, at 3.
21. *Schütte*, VersR 1982, at 223, 225 for international reinsurance law.
22. *Stein*, Lex mercatoria, at 6 ('postmodern dispute of ideologies par excellence').
23. *See supra* Introduction I.A.2.
24. *Goode*, ICLQ 1997, at 1, 35.

B. The Need for a Uniform Substantive Law of International Commerce and Trade

All those who oppose the doctrine of a transnational economic law must accept the fact that there have always been and still are various efforts towards the 'formalized' unification of the law on the international plane to be described below[25]. These efforts began with the drafting of the Franco-Italian Obligation Law in 1917 and found a provisional end with the publication of the UNIDROIT Principles of International Commercial Contracts in May 1994. These projects have one feature in common: they provide ample evidence for the fact that there has always been a substantial need for the transnationalization of the legal relationships of international commerce. With the progressive intensification of world trade in the past century and the foundation of UNCITRAL and UNIDROIT, a growing body of clearly identifiable general principles is being manifested and codified as 'International Trade Law'[26]. The scepticism of the mid-1960s, when practitioners and academics alike thought that there was a strong interest in perpetuating the differences in the various domestic systems and that any effort to harmonize and coordinate the unification of private law was futile[27], is no longer justified today. *Goode* has identified seven reasons why an international arbitral tribunal may resort to the NLM instead of domestic law[28].

This positive prognosis is supported by the general tendency to acknowledge the autonomous value and validity of customs and usages both in domestic and international commerce[29]. This development finds further support in the comprehensive and legally autonomous contractual agreements drafted in international contract practice that detach the parties' relationship from domestic laws. The climax of this transnationalization movement is reached when contracts with state parties[30] are made subject to general principles of law. Art. 46 of the concession contract between the Government of Iran and the 'National Iranian Oil Company' on one side and nine foreign oil companies on the other provides a typical example for this drafting technique:

> 'In view of the diverse nationalities of the parties to this Agreement it shall be governed by . . . the principles of law common to Iran and the several nations in which the other parties to this Agreement are incorporated, and, in the absence of such common principles, by . . . the principles of law recognized by civilized nations in general, including such of those principles as may have been applied by international tribunals'[31].

---

25. *Infra* Chapters 3 and 4; *see also Ferrari*, Riv.Tr.Dir.Pr.Civ. 1994, at 893, 898.
26. *Fischer*, GYIL 1976, at 143, 164.
27. *Schwarzenberger*, Rec.Cours 1966-I, at 1, 10.
28. *Goode*, ICLQ 1997, at 1, 30 *et seq.*
29. *Bärmann*, Festschrift Mann, at 547, 553.
30. *Cf. Schlesinger* (ed.), Formation of Contracts, Vol. I, at 13 *et seq.*; *Böckstiegel*, Der Staat als Vertragspartner ausländischer Privatunternehmen, at 110 *et seq.*; *see also Cistac*, DPCI 1996, at 168, 195.
31. Reported by *Wetter*, Bus.Lawy. 1966, at 967, 977; *Schwarzenberger*, Rec.Cours 1966-I, at 1, 9; *Fouchard*, L'Arbitrage Commercial International, at 425.

Subjecting international contracts to general principles of law is by no means a new idea, but rather has a long tradition. A railway contract between Turkey and the Austrian company '*Compagnie générale pour l'exploitation des chemins de fer de la Turquie Europe*' of May 18, 1872 provided that disputes be settled according to '*les principes appliqués dans les circonstances analogues dans les autres grands Etats de l'Europe, tel que l'Autriche, l'Italie, la France et l'Allemagne*'[32]. In modern contract practice this technique has enjoyed further refinement. General principles of law are declared applicable if and to the extent that the cumulative application of two different legal systems is not possible because both laws contain different provisions for the same legal problem[33]. Art. 42(1) of the International Centre for the Settlement of Investment Disputes (ICSID) Convention[34] mirrors the general drafting practice to have domestic laws applied to the contract only in so far as they conform with general principles of law[35]. The choice-of-law clause contained in the channel tunnel contract, one of the most important infrastructure projects of modern times[36], provides a perfect example of the use of general principles of law in international contract practice in those cases where the parties are unable to agree on a domestic law as the *lex causae*. Since both the English and French sides were unable to agree in the 1986 Canterbury Treaty[37] on the applicable law, the clause finally included in the construction contract provided that:

> '[t]he construction, validity and performance of the contract shall in all respects be governed by and interpreted in accordance with the principles common to both English and French law, and in the absence of such common principles by such general principles of international trade law as have been applied by national and international tribunals. Subject in all cases, with

32. *Fischer*, GYIL 1976, at 143, 154.
33. *Cf.* the case reported by *Clagett*, Pr.Inv.Abr. 1989, at 12-1, 12-22: the arbitral tribunal had to decide according to 'the laws of... and New York that are not inconsistent with each other'; in case of inconsistency the tribunal applied general principles of law.
34. Convention on the Settlement of Investment Disputes between States and Nationals of Other States of March 18, 1965, 575 UNTS 159; according to Art. 42(1) 'In the absence of... agreement [between the parties], the Tribunal shall apply the law of the Contracting State party to the dispute... and such rules of international law as may be applicable'; *cf.* for the corrective function of this formula the ICSID Ad Hoc Committee Award *Klöckner v. Cameroon*, ICSID Rev.-FILJ 1986, at 90, 112.
35. *Cf.* the arbitration *SSP (Middle East) Ltd. et al. v. Arab Republic of Egypt et al.*, ILM 1983, at 752, 771, in which the arbitrators absent a choice of law applied Egyptian laws 'in as much as they do not contravene said principles of international law'; *cf. also* the ICSID arbitration *Letco v. Liberia*, ILM 1987, at 647, 658, in which the arbitral tribunal declared: 'The rules and principles of Liberian law which it has taken into account are in conformity with generally accepted principles of public international law governing the validity of contracts and the remedies for their breach'; *cf.* for the corrective function of general principles of law *Blessing*, in: Böckstiegel (ed.), Die internationale Schiedsgerichtsbarkeit in der Schweiz (II), at 67 *et seq.*
36. *See generally* for an account of the drafting history *Morton*, Int'l Bus.Lawy. 1996, at 6 *et seq.*; *Naslin*, Int'l Bus.Lawy. 1996, at 8 *et seq.*
37. Treaty Concerning the Construction and Operation by Private Concessionaires of a Channel Fixed Link of February 12, 1986, *see Harris/Parry/Hopkins* (eds.), An Index of British Treaties, Vol. 4, at 653 *et seq.*

> respect to the works to be respectively performed in the French and in the English part of site, to the respective French or English public policy (ordre public) provisions'[38].

Even though English courts raised doubts as to the validity of this choice-of-law clause and have applied Belgian law instead[39], the clause reflects a typical scenario of modern drafting practice: the need to find a common agreement and to achieve pragmatic and workable solutions between lawyers from totally different legal cultures and backgrounds:

> 'If the two Western systems of law, common law and civil law, had no common principle, what was the meaning of the second provision [in the choice-of-law clause cited above]? How can a general principle of international trade law be applied by national and international tribunals, which would not have been accepted by both systems? Is it not rather odd to have a construction contract submitted to trade law? A truly impossible task which fortunately did not have to be resolved. But acrobatics were necessary to decide that on the matters which were dealt with, a common principle always existed... Obviously, we had to read the laws [of England and France] in the original language. We not only had to master the language but we had also to know our own law and to understand why provisions had been included in a statute, and why a decision had been rendered in such and such a manner. To know the rules was not sufficient; we had to remember or learn the basic fundamentals because it was the only way we could make the French and English rules meet. *On the face of it, the rules were different, sometimes even contradictory; yet, a common principle had to be found to exist. This daily miracle was made possible largely because all of us... decided to go beyond the mere wording of the legal provisions and find the basic principle behind them. The principles usually matched*... Obviously we Frenchmen are absolutely certain our system is the best; our English friends had exactly the same view with respect to their own system.... The motto between [the] lawyers became: "CARTESIAN PRAGMATISM"'[40].

In view of the vagueness and generality of the general principles, this drafting approach has been characterized as 'a recipe for uncertainty'[41]. Interestingly enough, in an international arbitration between the Eurotunnel company and the construction consortium, there was general agreement that on the basis of the choice-of-law clause contained in the construction contract, the UNIDROIT

---

38. *Cf. Jayme*, in: Nicklisch (ed.), Rechtsfragen privatfinanzierter Projekte, at 65, 73; *Karrer*, IPRax 1994, at 56 *et seq*.
39. *See Channel Tunnel Group v. Balfour Beatty Construction, Ltd.*, [1993] 2 W.L.R. 262: 'The proper substantive law of this contract is the law, *if such it can be called*, chosen in Clause 68' [emphasis added].
40. *Cf.* the most interesting account of the cross-cultural problems involved in the drafting process by *Nouel*, Int'l Bus.Lawy. 1996, at 22 *et seq*. [emphasis added].
41. *Goode*, ICLQ 1997, at 1, 30.

Principles, or more specifically the provision on 'hardship' in Art. 6.2.2 of the Principles, should be applied[42].

However, the choice-of-law clause contained in the channel tunnel contract is important not only because of its amalgamation of domestic laws and general principles of laws. The reference to English and French public policy provisions contained in the choice-of-law clause also hints at one of the basic problems of the NLM doctrine: the interplay of the autonomous law of international trade and mandatory provisions of other jurisdictions with *ordre public* character (*'lois d'application immédiate'*)[43].

C. Confusion of Terminology

It should be emphasized at the outset that a major reason for the existence of irreconcilable opinions on the practical and theoretical viability of transnational commercial law is caused by a basic misconception of the meaning of the term *'lex mercatoria'*[44]. It has rightly been argued that the term NLM is often used as a catch-phrase that is over-burdened with meaning[45]. The use of different languages and the fact that academics and practitioners who are involved in the discussion on the NLM come from totally different legal backgrounds have both caused a degree of terminological confusion that makes any discussion of this subject matter almost impossible[46]. The situation resembles that of trade usages and customs which are bedevilled with linguistic ambiguity[47]. The following considerations will therefore provide the reader with an understanding of the terminology on which this Study is based. The focal point for the delimitation and concretization of the terminology has to be the basic premise elaborated in the introduction of this Study that the international community of merchants creates its own law through decentralized, 'autonomous'[48] law-making processes. As is always the case in the theory of legal terminology[49], the use of the term *'lex mercatoria'* may be purely descriptive (*infra* 1.) or may have a substantive (*infra* 2.) content.

42. *Schlechtriem*, in: Festschrift v. Craushaar, at 157; *Lalive*, in: Bonell/Bonelli (eds.), Contratti Commerciali Internazionali E Principi UNIDROIT, at 73, 84.
43. *Cf. infra* II.E.
44. *See Goode*, ICLQ 1997, at 1, 2; *Goode*, ICLQ 2005, at 539, 546; *Gaillard*, in: van den Berg (ed.), Planning Efficient Arbitration Proceedings – The Law Applicable in International Arbitration, ICCA Congress Ser. No. 7, at 570, 571 *et seq.*; *Lalive*, in: Bonell/Bonelli (eds.), Contratti Commerciali Internazionali E Principi UNIDROIT, at 73, 77; *Goode/Kronke/McKendrick*, Transnational Commercial Law, No. 1.37.
45. *Brunner*, Force Majeure and Hardship under General Contract Principles, at 9.
46. *Dasser*, Internationale Schiedsgerichte und Lex Mercatoria, at 63; *cf. also Horn*, Internationale Anleihen, at 514; *Stein*, Lex mercatoria, at 183 ('brushwood of variants in the jungle of opinions').
47. *See Goode*, ICLQ 1997, at 1, 7.
48. *Cf. Ferrari*, Riv.Tr.Dir.Pr.Civ. 1994, at 893, 898.
49. *Cf. generally Wank*, Die juristische Begriffsbildung, at 38.

1. Disadvantages of Descriptive Terminology

Descriptive terminology is often used in the NLM context[50]. In the context of transnational commercial law, comprehensive terms serve a limited function in that they denote similar rules of domestic laws, international conventions or international drafting practice[51]. Since this terminology is devoid of any substantive content, it adds to the terminological confusion instead of providing a more secure terminological framework which is vital for any dogmatic discussion. However, a brief survey on this descriptive terminology is necessary to appreciate the misunderstanding and inconsistencies in the current debate on transnational commercial law. Basically, there are three different kinds of descriptive terminology to be found in this area of international commercial law.

a. De Facto Similarities of Domestic Legal Systems

Parts of international legal doctrine use the term '*lex mercatoria*' or 'transnational law' only to denote *de facto* similarities or conformities of domestic legal systems[52]. Sometimes, this term is applied only to special statutes for international commerce such as those implemented by the countries of the former Eastern Bloc[53]. Use of this terminology is dangerous in that it obscures the important methodical distinction between the determination of similarities of legal institutions or rules of different legal systems and the functional legal comparison of these rules or institutions. While the first constitutes a mere preliminary stage in the determination of an autonomous world trade, the latter serves to identify the existence or non-existence of general principles and rules of transnational commercial law[54]. The term '*lex mercatoria*' may also be used to denote the implementation of identical statutes in different countries ('*lois conformes*'). This method of coordinated implementation of identical statutes which is pursued for example in the Scandinavian countries provides a means to create a uniform law[55]. However, the legitimacy of this law is dependent upon domestic legislatures while the creation and evolution of the NLM is detached from any domestic law. Therefore, *de facto* similarities of domestic laws on one side and unified structures of an autonomous

50. *Horn*, in: Festschrift für Karsten Schmidt, at 705, 708 *et seq.*
51. *Cf. Dasser*, Internationale Schiedsgerichte und lex mercatoria, at 41.
52. *Siehr*, in: Holl/Klinke (eds.), Internationales Privatrecht, Internationales Wirtschaftsrecht, at 103, 125: 'The lex mercatoria is an independent legal order in such a way that it regulates a coherent subject. Although it is primarily national law, *it is in force with the same or a similar content in different legal orders*' (translated by the author); *see also Goode*, ICLQ 1997, at 1, 3.
53. *Enderlein*, in: UNIDROIT (ed.), New Directions in International Trade Law, at 447, 451 '... lex mercatoria is to express nothing other than a uniform and special regulation of international economic relations ...'; *cf.* for this aspect *also infra* Chapter 4 I.A.3.b.aa.
54. *Cf. Horn* in: Horn/Schmitthoff (eds.), The Transnational Law of International Commercial Transactions, at 3, 16: 'Those similarities are welcome, and are a first step towards uniformity; but by no means can we speak here of elements of an "autonomous" law of international commerce'.
55. *Cf. Kropholler*, Internationales Einheitsrecht, at 105 *et seq.*

world trade on the other side should be distinguished sharply from each other both in terms of terminology and substance.

b. Uniform Law Created by International Conventions

Sometimes, the term '*lex mercatoria*' is used to denote uniform law created by international conventions[56]. The use of this terminology also meets with considerable concern[57]. The validity of the uniform law is based on the common undertaking of the contracting states to transform the provisions contained in the convention into their own domestic law[58]. This transformation process, however, should not be confused with decentralized law-making and the creation of an autonomous legal system such as the NLM. This is not to say that the rules and principles contained in international conventions and draft conventions may not serve as an indication that a common understanding of the subject matters of these rules and principles exists in all major legal systems. This may ultimately lead to the development of general principles which become part of the autonomous world trade law[59]. Uniform law created by international conventions therefore merely serves as an indication for the possible content of the NLM, but may not be equated with it[60]. Replacing the term '*lex mercatoria*' with the terminology '*Einheitsrecht*/ Uniform Law'[61] does not provide an acceptable means to escape the terminological dilemma.

c. Unified Contractual Provisions

Finally, the term '*lex mercatoria*' is sometimes used to denote the broad array of unified contractual stipulations used in the international drafting practice. Again, use of this descriptive terminology is not useful when it comes to the substantive qualification of a NLM. In particular, it does not answer the question of how and when this drafting practice develops into autonomous substantive law[62]. As in the case of uniform law created by international conventions, the principle applies that the unification of contractual stipulations used in international commerce and trade

56. *See e.g. Popescu*, in: UNIDROIT (ed.), New Directions in International Trade Law, at 21, 44.
57. *Cf. Horn, supra* note 46, *id.*; *Goode*, ICLQ 1997, at 2.
58. *Kropholler*, Internationales Einheitsrecht, at 94; *Goode, id.*
59. *Cf. infra* II.A.2.c.
60. *Goode, supra* note 41, at 3: '. . . an international convention or a contractually adopted codification is at most evidence of the uncodified rules previously existing; and by itself it is not a very reliable evidence because the purpose of most conventions or contractual codifications is not to reproduce an existing set of universally adopted usages for in truth no such universality exists – but, rather, to build on existing usage and to provide best solutions to current problems'.
61. A proposition by *Dasser*, Internationale Schiedsgerichtsbarkeit und lex mercatoria, at 66.
62. *Cf. Horn, supra* note 46, *id.*: 'The truly crucial question comes when we find such de facto similarities and must ask whether the clauses, rules or patterns have some normative effects beyond the individual contract in which they are expressly included or referred to. Here, we return to our problem, whether international practice might have created international commercial practice or even customary law'.

may provide an important indication for the existence of a common understanding within the community of international merchants on certain principles and rules. As will be seen later in this Study, the common conviction among merchants may only be equated with the existence of an autonomous legal system of world trade law after extensive verification, *i.e.* external validation of its substantive quality[63]. As in the case of customary law, the conviction of the parties that a certain rule or principle constitutes 'the law' is only one step in a complicated process to determine the legal effect and quality of this conviction.

2. Substantive Understanding of Terminology

a. Three Possible Meanings of 'Lex Mercatoria'

If, therefore, the only viable starting point for any discussion on the existence of an autonomous world trade law is a substantive understanding of the term '*lex mercatoria*', the question remains as to the exact meaning of this term. Unfortunately, those who use the term in a substantive context are not in agreement as to the exact determination of its contents. Basically, international legal doctrine advocates three different conceptions of the term '*lex mercatoria*'.

Some authors use the term to denote a mere 'mass' of rules and principles without any internal consistency or systematic quality. It merely serves as a complement to the otherwise applicable domestic law. The mass derives its validity and enforceability from the sovereign states themselves, in that the principle of party autonomy in contract law has been accepted by almost all major jurisdictions in the world[64]. A second view regards the NLM as the totality of trade usages that are refined according to the needs of international commerce[65] and constitute a 'factual *ius commune*'[66]. Sometimes, this collection of usages and practices is denoted as an 'autonomous law of world trade'[67]. A third view regards the NLM as an

63. *See Goode/Kronke/McKendrick*, Transnational Commercial Law, No. 1.60.
64. *Cf. Fragistas*, Rev.crit.dr.int.pr. 1960, at 1, 14 *et seq.*; *Schmitthoff*, RabelsZ 28 (1964), at 47, 71; *Bonell*, RabelsZ 42 (1978), at 485, 486 *et seq.*, 495; *Braeckmans*, TvPr. 1986, at 1, 66; *Molineaux*, J.Int'l Arb., No. 1 1997, at 55, 56; *David*, in: UNIDROIT (ed.), New Directions in International Trade Law, at 5, 18: '*Le problème n'est plus . . . de savoir si les commerçants peuvent créer un droit qui leur soit propre, autonome par rapport aux droits nationaux, c'est plutôt de savoir si les législateurs nationaux l'autorisent, quelle mesure de liberté ils vont consentir aux particuliers pour que ceux-ci élaborent des règles, qui apparaissent comme intégrées aux droits nationaux, et non plus comme autonomes par rapport à ceux-ci*'; *Mertens*, Festschrift Odersky (1996), at 857, 869: party autonomy as 'umbilical cord to national law'; *see also Ferrante*, in: Piergiovanni (ed.), From *Lex Mercatoria* to Commercial Law, at 121, 141.
65. *Cf. Paulsson*, Rev.d'Arb. 1990, at 55, 60 *et seq.*; *Dasser*, Internationale Schiedsgerichtsbarkeit und Lex Mercatoria, at 63; *Martiny*, in: Reithmann/Martiny (eds.), Internationales Vertragsrecht, No. 72; *cf. also* Heymann/*Horn*, HGB, Vol. 1, Einleitung III, No. 15, 16; Vol. 4, Vor § 343 No. 114; *van Houtte*, The Law of International Trade, No. 1.35.
66. The phrase was coined by *Lüderitz*, Festschrift der Rechtswissenschaftlichen Fakultät zur 600-Jahr-Feier der Universität zu Köln, at 271, 291.
67. *Cf. Großmann-Doerth*, JW 1929, at 3447, note 4.

independent, supranational legal system which derives its justification and validity from its autonomous existence[68]. The majority of those who hold this view place the transnational legal system between domestic laws and public international law. Yet, there are also proponents of the autonomous approach who regard the NLM as part of public international law[69]. International arbitral tribunals[70] and parts of French legal doctrine[71] even want to combine all three views described above, considering the NLM as the totality of international trade usages which have the character of an independent legal system, deriving its justification from the acknowledgment by domestic laws.

However, all three views have to be sharply distinguished from one another. If one regards the autonomy of the parties which is granted by the state legislature as the basis for the development of the NLM, there is *ab initio* no contradiction to the traditional doctrine of legal sources, since the terminology means nothing more than a collection of principles and rules, the legitimacy of which is derived from the state[72]. This view is therefore based on the notion that party autonomy is always linked to a particular domestic legal system[73]. Section 346 of the German Commercial Code and similar provisions of other jurisdictions indicate that trade usages also have to be seen in the context of a particular domestic law[74]. Thus, trade usages, customary law, and transnational law have to be distinguished from each other. Trade usages do not have the quality of law[75]. Together with other

68. *See Goldman*, Archives de philosophie du droit 1964, at 177 *et seq.*; *Goldman*, Clunet 1979, at 475 *et seq.*; *Goldman*, Nouvelles réflexions sur la lex mercatoria, Festschrift P. Lalive, 1993, at 241 *et seq.*; *cf. also Larroumet*, La Semaine Juridique 1997, at 147, 149; *Berman/Dasser*, in: Carbonneau (ed.), Lex Mercatoria and Arbitration, at 53, 63.
69. *See* for this latter view *Booysen*, RabelsZ 59 (1995), at 245, 252 *et seq.*
70. *Cf.* the arbitral tribunal in ICC Award No. 5953, *Primary Coal Inc. v. Compañía Valenciana de Cementos Portland*, Rev.d'Arb. 1990, at 701, 712; *cf. also Berger*, IPRax 1993, at 281 *et seq.*
71. *Cf. Derains*, Rev.d'Arb. 1973, at 122 *et seq.*; *cf. also von Hoffmann*, Internationale Handelsschiedsgerichtsbarkeit, at 115: '. . . a-national norms, in particular international trade usages and general legal principles'; *Langen*, Transnationales Recht, Part I, No. I-24: ' The law of trade usages as so-called lex mercatoria'.
72. *Cf. von Jhering*, Der Zweck im Recht, Volksausgabe, Vol. 2, at 249: 'The right to self-legislation (autonomy) for one's own affairs . . . does not stand in contrast (to a sovereign understanding of law), because its juridical reason for existence lies in the express grant or implied toleration by the state; it is not in existence out of its own force but by derivation from the state' (translation by the author); *cf.* for the conscious or unconscious tolerance by the state legislator as precondition for the coming into being of the *lex mercatoria Böckstiegel*, Der Staat als Vertragspartner ausländischer Privatunternehmen, at 141; *cf. also Münzberg*, Die Schranken der Parteivereinbarungen in der privaten internationalen Schiedsgerichtsbarkeit, at 132; *Kropholler*, Internationales Einheitsrecht, at 122; *von Bar*, IPR, Vol. 1, § 2 No. 76.
73. *See supra* Introduction I.A.1, note 26; *Schödermeier*, Sonderprivatrecht für internationale Wirtschaftsverträge, at 113.
74. *See Goode*, ICLQ 1997, at 2 *et seq.; van Houtte*, The Law of International Trade, No. 1.35 *in fine*: 'In so far as trade usages are considered as *lex mercatoria*, the latter are recognised as standard under national law'.
75. *See Malynes*, Consuetudo Vel Lex Mercatoria, at 4: '. . . Customes cannot abridge the generall Lawes of an absolute Prince . . .'.

'factual legal sources'[76], such as general conditions of trade or customs[77], they constitute the first stage towards the development of customary law and towards the creation of a NLM[78]. 'All customary law of international trade has the quality of trade usages but not all trade usages are customary law'[79].

b. Consequences of the Different Terminological Approaches

No problem of legitimacy exists for the first two views of the NLM doctrine, which regard transnational commercial law as a mere heterogeneous collection of legal rules or principles or as mere trade usages. Here, the NLM is understood in its medieval meaning[80] as an internationally or at least regionally acknowledged commercial law that is composed of customary law, customs, and trade usages. These notions of transnational commercial law are far from assuming the quality of an autonomous legal system[81]. For the proponents of these views, the question as to the legal nature of these rules and principles loses practical significance. Instead, their legal quality is decided on a case-by-case basis according to the categories of the applicable domestic law[82]. Judges and arbitrators who follow this view therefore pursue the same approach that they would use in purely domestic cases.

This perspective of the NLM is irreconcilable with the notion of an autonomous world trade law. It must necessarily lead to a '*contrat sans loi*'[83], a result that

76. Factual legal sources are being described as those sources of knowledge that by acceptance of the addressee and the user have binding force analogous to that of legal sources, *Bühler*, Festschrift Walder, at 153 *et seq.*
77. *Cf. generally* for the historic evolution and legal quality of custom *Glenn*, Am.J.Comp.L. 1997, at 613, 615 *et seq.*
78. *Böckstiegel*, Festschrift Beitzke, 1979, at 443, 457; Heymann/*Horn*, HGB, Vol. 1, Einleitung II No. 4; *see also Blackman*, Mercantile Law and Mercantile Practice, at 3 *et seq.*; *Coquillette*, in: Petit (ed.), Del Ius Mercatorum Al Derecho Mercantil, at 143, 150; *Galgano*, Ann.Surv.Int'l & Comp.L. 1995, at 99, 108.
79. *Cf. also Dasser*, Lex Mercatoria, at 91; *see generally* for the legal quality of trade usages *Goode*, ICLQ 1997, at 1, 7 *et seq.*
80. *See Blackstone*, Commentaries on the Laws of England, Vol. I, at 75, note 8: 'The *lex mercatoria*, or the custom of merchants, like the *lex et consuetudo parliamenti*, describes only a great division of the law of England ... But the expression has frequently led merchants to suppose, that all their new fashions and devices immediately become the law of the land; a notion which, perhaps, has been too much encouraged by the courts. Merchants ought to take their law from the courts, and not the courts from the merchants; and when the law is found inconvenient for the purposes of extended commerce, application ought to be made to parliament for redress'.
81. *Cf. Bärmann*, Festschrift Mann, at 547, 557; *Steindorff*, contribution to the discussion, in: UNIDROIT (ed.), New Directions in International Trade Law, at 517 *et seq.*
82. *Bonell*, RabelsZ 42 (1978), at 485, 487; *Klein*, Festschrift Mann, at 617, 626 *et seq.*; Münch-Komm-*Sonnenberger*, EGBGB, Introduction No. 273; *Schlosser*, Das Recht der internationalen privaten Schiedsgerichtsbarkeit, No. 198; *Sandrock*, Am.Rev.Int'l Arb. 1992, at 30, 49; *id.*, in: Böckstiegel, Rechtsfortbildung durch internationale Schiedsgerichtsbarkeit, at 21, 78 ('Phenomenona that the proponents of the lex mercatoria observe, can thus be classified according to the classical doctrine of legal sources without difficulties').
83. *Popescu*, in: UNIDROIT (ed.), New Directions in International Trade Law, at 21, 35; *see generally* for the theory of '*contrat sans loi*' *Gannagé*, in: Boele-Woelki/van Erp (eds.),

is totally unacceptable both in terms of theory and practice. This use of the NLM terminology therefore turns out to be counterproductive. In this perspective, international cases are 'nationalized' in that they are subjected to domestic laws even though the main objective of the proponents of the NLM doctrine is to remedy this grievance[84].

This understanding of the NLM terminology has an important effect on the traditional private international law doctrine. The parties' reference to the NLM as the 'law' applicable to their contract, transforms the rules and principles contained therein into mere contract conditions ('*materiellrechtliche Verweisung*'[85]). In contrast to a proper choice-of-law clause, the parties are not able to override the mandatory norms of the 'otherwise' applicable law[86]. Applying this notion of the NLM therefore does not help to achieve a true transnationalization of dispute settlement in international commercial cases.

For these reasons, the term 'New *Lex Mercatoria*' will be used in this Study in line with the third view elaborated above[87]: the term NLM denotes an independent, 'third' supranational legal system between domestic law and public international law, a legal system that is created and developed by the law-making forces of the international business community. Qualifying the NLM in this manner requires the development of a profound theoretical basis. In the absence of such a basis, the idea of a transnational commercial law will be doomed to fail from the outset and will have no chance of being applied by international practitioners.

Based on this terminological clarification, the following considerations will provide answers to the main objections that are usually brought forth against this transnational and autonomous understanding of the NLM.

II. TRADITIONAL OBJECTIONS AGAINST THE NEW *LEX MERCATORIA* DOCTRINE

Not infrequently, the outright rejection of any attempts to justify the existence of the NLM as an autonomous legal system is caused by the fact that so far no one has been able to present a clear-cut conceptual theory of transnational commercial law[88]. The principal arguments against this doctrine are ventured either from a party-oriented perspective or from the viewpoint of domestic legislatures.

In the first case the arguments are centred around the theory that parties may not conclude a '*contrat sans loi*', *i.e.* may not declare themselves '*legibus soluti*'[89], leaving their contract in a legal vacuum. This view finds support in various

General Reports of the XVIIth Congress of the International Academy of Comparative Law, 275 *et seq.*

84. *Cf. supra* Chapter 1 III.A.
85. *Cf. generally Kegel/Schurig*, IPR, § 18 I.1.c, at 654.
86. *von Hoffmann/Thorn*, IPR, § 10, No. 28.
87. *See supra* a, note 68.
88. *Martiny*, RabelsZ 50 (1986), at 730, 731.
89. *See Schack*, AcP 1991, at 373, 374.

decisions of the highest courts in several European jurisdictions, which have repeatedly stated that the validity of international contracts requires their '... unqualified submission to some kind of law-making power'[90].

Those who oppose the idea of an autonomous NLM from the perspective of domestic legislatures usually argue that it is highly unlikely that these legislatures are willing to 'resign'[91] in the field of international commercial law, leaving the regulation of contractual relationships entirely to the autonomy of the parties.

The following parts of this Study will be devoted to the discussion of the classical arguments that are traditionally ventured against the idea of a transnational commercial law. The reproduction of this discussion in the Study is not intended merely to serve academic purposes. Instead, it paves the way for the analysis of possible practical applications of this theory. Examples for these practical applications will be presented in the second part of this Study.

A. The New *Lex Mercatoria* Doctrine Has No Methodical Foundation

All those who oppose the theory of transnational commercial law complain that it has an inadequate methodical foundation. In their opinion, these methodical uncertainties make it impossible to discern and apply the rules and principles that are said to form part of this legal system[92].

This concern carries much weight, as a sound methodical foundation is the *conditio sine qua non* of the legal process as a whole, regardless of whether one is dealing with a domestic or international context[93]. Leaving open the question as to the methodical starting point provides a most welcome pretext for the criticism of all those who regard the NLM doctrine as nothing more than a 'theoretical

---

90. RG JW 1936, at 2058, 2059; *cf. also* French Cour de Cassation of June 21, 1950, *Messageries Maritimes*, Rec.crit.dr.int.priv. 1950, at 609 ('... *tout contrat est nécessairement soumis à la loi d'un Etat*'); English House of Lords in *Amin Rashed Shipping Corporation v. Kuwait Insurance Co.* (1983) WLR 241, 249 ('Contracts are incapable of existing in a legal vacuum. They are mere pieces of paper devoid of all legal effects unless made by reference to some system of private law'); Permanent Court of International Justice, *Case Concerning Various Serbian Loans Issued in France* (1929) P.C.I.J., Ser. A, No. 20, at 41 ('Any contract which is not a contract between States in their capacity as subjects of international law is based on the municipal law of some country'); Vienna Court of Appeal of January 26, 1982, *NORSOLOR v. Pabalk Ticaret*, AG 1982, at 165, 166 (*lex mercatoria* as a 'world law of doubtful validity').
91. *Kropholler*, Internationales Einheitsrecht, at 123; *David*, in: UNIDROIT Annuaire 1967–1968, Vol. II., at 77.
92. *Herdegen*, Internationales Wirtschaftsrecht, § 2 No. 41; *Kropholler*, IPR, § 12 I.3 (at 100); *Spieckhoff*, RabelsZ 56 (1992), at 116, 124; *Sandrock*, Am.Rev.Int'l Arb. 1992, at 30, 50; *cf. also* the comment by *Rehbinder*, reported by *Remien*, RabelsZ 56 (1992), at 300, 304; *Martiny*, in: Reithmann/Martiny (eds.), Internationales Vertragsrecht, No. 72.
93. *K. Schmidt*, in: Behrends (ed.), Privatrecht heute und Jherings evolutionäres Rechtsdenken, at 77, 85.

abstraction'[94]. Therefore, the methodical issue provides one of the major pillars from which the NLM doctrine derives its legitimacy.

1. The Methodical Starting Point: 'Functional Legal Comparison'

a. The Basic Comparative Approach

The idea behind the NLM doctrine is closely related to the harmonization and unification of the law. In this context, the discussion on the methodology to be applied in the harmonization and unification process has always played a dominant role[95]. The methodical approach employed is the 'functional legal comparison'[96]. Being a sub-species of the general functional legal theory[97], this approach is of a topical nature[98], *i.e.* strictly problem-oriented. From its very inception at the First International Congress of Comparative Law held in Paris in 1900[99], the

94. *Joerges*, RabelsZ 43 (1979), at 6, 41 *et seq.*: 'Here the self-limitation of juridical theory leads to the use of empty phrases: the law of international economic relations remains at the level of mere etiquette; its preconditions and its functions are regarded as a kind of object of jurisprudence in itself that is beyond the reach of juridical knowledge' (translation by the author).
95. *Stone*, Tul.L.Rev. 1950/51, at 325, 330; *Wallace*, in: Horn/Schmitthoff (eds.), The Transnational Law of International Commercial Transactions, at 81 *et seq.*; *Coing*, in: Coing/Schmitthoff/Hellner/Gleichmann (eds.), Methoden der Rechtsvereinheitlichung, 1974, at 7, 16; *Lorenz*, JZ 1962, at 269, 270.
96. *See generally Michaels*, in: Reimann/Zimmermann (eds.), The Oxford Handbook of Comparative Law, at 339, 341 *et seq.*; *Rabel*, Indiana L.J. 1949, at 353, 355 *et seq.*; *Pound*, Am.J.Comp.L. 1952, at 1, 7 *et seq.*; *Esser*, Grundsatz und Norm, at 102 *et seq.*, 346 *et seq.*; *Ficker*, Rev.int.dr.comp. 10 (1958), at 701, 716 *et seq.*; *Schmitthoff*, UNIDROIT Annuaire 1967–1968, at 93, 110; *Lorenz*, JZ 1962, at 269, 271; *Bonell*, RabelsZ 42 (1978), at 485, 498 *et seq.*; *Kokkini-Latridou*, Een inleiding tot het rechtsvergelijkende onderzoek, at 11 *et seq.*; *Ancel*, Utilité et Méthodes du Droit Comparé, at 101; *Zweigert/Kötz*, Einführung in die Rechtsvergleichung, at 9 *et seq.*, 29 *et seq.*; *von Hülsen*, JZ 1967, at 629, 633; *Reinhardt*, Festschrift der Juristischen Fakultät zur 600-Jahr-Feier der Ruprecht-Karls-Universität Heidelberg, at 599, 601; *Rheinstein*, Einführung in die Rechtsvergleichung, at 27 *et seq.*; *cf. also David*, in: International Encyclopedia of Comparative Law, 1971, at 1, 35 *et seq.*; *Mänhardt/Posch*, Internationales Privatrecht, Privatrechtsvergleichung, Einheitsprivatrecht, No. 5/5 *et seq.*; critical *Kohler*, in: Congrès international de droit comparé, Procès-verbaux des séances et documents, Paris, Vol. I, at 229 *et seq.*; *Berger*, Der Aufrechnungsvertrag, at 131 *et seq.*
97. *Cf. generally Kahn*, Latente Gesetzeskollisionen, Jher.Jahrb. 30 (1891), at 107, 115; *Salomon*, Grundlegung zur Rechtsphilosophie, at 41 *et seq.*; *Hartmann*, Die philosophische Grundlage der Naturwissenschaften: Erkenntnistheorie und Methologie, at 125; *Spengler*, Der Untergang des Abendlandes, at 655; *Luhmann*, AöR 94 (1969), at 1 *et seq.*; *von Hippel*, Zur Gesetzmäßigkeit juristischer Systembildung, at 6 *et seq.*; *Engisch*, Die Einheit der Rechtsordnung, at 30 *et seq.*; *Viehweg*, Topik und Jurisprudenz, at 68 *et seq.*; *Joost*, JZ 1995, at 11, 12.
98. *Cf.* for the use of the topical concept in comparative law *Kramer*, RabelsZ 33 (1969), at 1 *et seq.*; *generally Viehweg*, Topik und Jurisprudenz, at 95 *et seq.*
99. Generally, the International Congress for Comparative Law of 1990 is regarded as the birth place of modern comparative law; *cf. Gutteridge*, Comparative Law, at 18; *Ancel*, Utilité et Méthodes du Droit Comparé, at 18; *Zajtay*, Comp. & Int'l L.J. of Southern Africa 1974, at 321.

comparative method has been employed to detect and formulate universal principles of law, an 'International Common Law'. This comparative methodology has already been applied with success in the development of general principles of public international law, particularly with respect to contracts between states and private persons. In this context, comparative law does not serve an end in and of itself[100], but rather assumes a 'supportive'[101] character in that it performs 'a highly practical'[102] function. This confirms the general experience that the value of comparative law as a legal discipline does not lend itself to abstract evaluation but may only be determined in a context-oriented manner[103]. Both in the field of the unification of private law and the transnationalization of international commercial law, the use of the functional legal comparison bears a close resemblance to the 'comparative law-making technique' employed by domestic legislatures in drafting contemporary legislation with an international connotation[104]. The analytical process of this method starts with the practical problem, collects and selects the solutions to be found in various major jurisdictions and presents a solution that is based on a synthesis of the various domestic laws. This law-making technique was not only used in the drafting process of major European codifications of 'the second generation'[105] as the Swiss Obligation Law[106], the German Civil Code and the Italian *Codice Civile*[107]. It is also employed to an increasing extent in the drafting of such 'third generation codes'[108] like the Dutch Civil Code (*Burgerlijk Wetboek*, BW)[109], the recent reform of the German Obligation Law[110]

100. *Cf. also Bekker*, Zeitung der Savigny-Stiftung für Rechtsgeschichte 6 (1885), at 90: 'Comparative law begins where the mere compilation [of legal principles of foreign legal systems] is followed by a comparative valuation process' (translation by the author).
101. *Cf. von Hülsen*, JZ 1967, at 629; *see also Loquin*, in: Souveraineté étatique et marches internationaux à la fin du 20ème siècle, at 23, 34 *et seq.*
102. *Cf.* for the change of comparative law from a pure abstract science to a functional methodology *Coing*, NJW 1981, at 2601, 2604: 'Comparative law has found a new method. We do not compare legal norms anymore, like above all in the 19th century, but we work out and weigh up legal solutions' (translation by the author); *cf. also Stone*, Tul.L.Rev. 1950/51 at 325, 329: 'Comparative Law conceived in terms of the comparison of results or solutions to specific problems is likely to prove popular with students and lawyers alike, because it has about it the appearance of practicality. It to some extent minimizes the notion that 'comparative law' is exotic or a species in dilettantism . . . '; for the connection between functional comparative methodology and the promotion of the practical application of the law *see Kötz*, RabelsZ 54 (1990), at 203, 211.
103. *Cf. Schwarzenberger*, Rec.Cours 1966-I, at 1, 9.
104. *Cf.* for the functional qualification in private international law *Sandrock*, Über Sinn und Methode zivilistischer Rechtsvergleichung, at 25 *et seq.*; *Kropholler*, IPR, § 17.
105. *Cf. Wieacker*, Festschrift Boehmer, at 46 *et seq.*
106. Especially the French Code Civil and the Austrian Civil Code, *cf. Merz*, Festschrift Zweigert, at 667, 670 *et seq.*
107. *Cf.* for the influence of the Franco-Italian Draft on Obligation Law on the Codice Civile of 1942 *infra* Chapter 3 I.A.2.
108. *Cf. Blaurock*, JZ 1994, at 270.
109. *Cf. Haanappel/Mackaay*, Nieuw Nederlands Burgerlijk Wetboek; *Blaurock*, JZ 1994, at 270; *Hartkamp*, Am.J.Comp.L. 1992, at 551, 570, note 23.
110. *Cf.* for the important role of comparative law considerations during the preparation of the German reform proposals BT-Drucks. 14/6040, at 181 *et seq.*; *Rolland*, NJW 1992, at 2377, 2380.

and the Civil Code of the Russian Federation[111]. *E. Langen* has described this method in his major treatise on 'Transnational Law'[112].

The particular practical value of the functional legal comparison for the unification and transnationalization of commercial law is based on its close relation to commercial reality[113]. The analytical process on which this method is based does not start from a certain provision or legal institution to be found in a domestic legal system or from the factual pattern of a certain case ('factual approach'[114]) but from the concrete commercial realities of a certain legal problem. The use of comparative law, thus, allows the detection of similar solutions to this problem in different legal systems. In most cases, this comparative viewpoint will lead to a common denominator that lies at the basis of all the different solutions to be found in the domestic laws:

> 'One has to bear in mind that the mere determination that a certain norm or legal institution finds no direct correspondence in a foreign legal system does not justify the assumption that the principle is not known in this jurisdiction; it is a general experience of comparative lawyers that *functionally* similar results are frequently achieved through the combined effect of several legal institutions which – from an isolated perspective and from the viewpoint of a foreign observer – seem to be beyond the ambit of the principle in question'[115].

This view has been confirmed in recent commercial practice. It has been emphasized above[116] that the French and English lawyers who negotiated and drafted the Eurotunnel construction contract had to take a 'pragmatic' approach in order to look behind the black-letter law of their respective legal systems and find common general principles of law that underlie provisions of completely different wording and dogmatic qualification.

Finally, a comparative method that operates on a global basis and strives to achieve reliable and workable results also has to take into account ethnological as well as historical and cultural aspects of foreign legal systems without amounting to 'applied anthropology'[117].

---

111. Part I entered into force on January 1, 1995; *see infra* Chapter 4 II.C.5.
112. *Langen*, Transnationales Recht, Part I, Nos. 13 *et seq.*; *cf.* the note by *Coing*, JZ 1975, at 40.
113. *See Loquin*, in: Souveraineté étatique et marchés internationaux à la fin du 20ème siècle, at 23, 39, arguing that the use of functional comparative methodology is proof of the fact that the NLM is based more on commercial reasonableness than on good faith.
114. *Cf.* for the *'factual approach' Schlesinger*, The Common Core of Legal Systems, in: XXth Century Comparative and Conflicts Law, Legal Essays in Honor of Hessel E. Yntema, 1961, at 65, 70, who says that there is no 'real contrast' between the functional method and a *factual approach*, because an overall view of the results gained by case analysis will provide respective 'functional insights'; *but see Constantinesco*, Rechtsvergleichung, Vol. II, 1972, at 347, note 63.
115. *Cf. Lorenz*, JZ 1962, at 269, 270 (italics by the author); *see also Hyland*, Va. J. Int'l L. 1993/94, at 406: 'However different things may seem, the dominant method in comparative law usually seeks to demonstrate that the differences are merely apparent. *What is to be sought is a deeper level at which the legal systems in question share a common vision*' (emphasis added).
116. *See supra* I.B.
117. *Cf. Großfeld*, Festschrift Lukes, at 655, 660: 'We can only find out about the functionality of foreign legal institutions if we can reasonably locate the foreign system of coordinates in

b. *Purpose of the Functional Legal Comparison*

The use of the functional legal comparison may have two different objectives. It may either be geared towards a mere *consolidation*, meaning the determination of a common core of the legal systems compared. It may also go further and aim at a *codification, i.e.* the development and drafting of black-letter-rules[118]. In contrast to the mere consolidation, codification will often lead to better and more progressive solutions when compared to those to be found in the domestic legal systems. Codification may lead to solutions that are better adapted to the particular needs and circumstances of the legal problem. Indeed, this is the case for such general principles as 'good faith' which, in the international context, is refined to the principle of 'good faith and fair dealing in international business'[119]. In general, therefore, the functional legal comparison may create general principles and rules that are better apt to serve the particular needs of international trade and commerce[120].

c. *Details of the Comparative Process*

In order to achieve either of the two goals mentioned above – consolidation or codification – the functional legal comparison establishes a 'step by step analysis of the comparison process'[121]. The initial and fundamental phase serves to determine the legal problem and to select the legal systems to be reviewed in the search for common or similar solutions for this problem[122]. In spite of its selective character, this first phase of the comparative process is by no means deprived of any analytical elements. The selection of the relevant legal systems and legal problems to be examined requires a substantial degree of analytical effort in order to be able to determine whether differences contained in the regulatory structure of these legal systems are of an accidental or fundamental nature. To achieve this goal, the comparatist is required to free himself from the legal and dogmatic

---

relation to our's . . . Our ideas of functionality are founded on our assumptions on rationality that are at least partly a result of our environment and our language. For this reason we must not understand the functional method in a narrow sense but we have to widen it by a regional, historical-cultural approach' (translation by the author); *Großfeld* himself concedes (*id.*, at 670) that his approach overshoots the mark of a 'socially and historically' correct picture of foreign legal institutions insofar as he argues too much in the direction of an 'anthropological' method of comparative law and for this reason sees the jurist more as a 'practicing anthropologist' in the sense of Judge *Jerome Frank* (*cf. Schlesinger*, AJIL 1957, at 734, 752).

118. *Schmitthoff*, UNIDROIT Annuaire 1967–1968, Vol. II, at 93, 110.
119. For details *see infra* Chapter 4 I.A.7.b.
120. *Cf. Bonell*, An International Restatement of Contract Law, at 45 *et seq.*
121. *Cf. Constantinesco*, Rechtsvergleichung, Vol. II, 1972, at 32; *cf. also Kropholler*, Internationales Einheitsrecht, at 160 *et seq.*
122. *Cf.* the cautious approach by *Großfeld*, Macht und Ohnmacht der Rechtsvergleichung, at 127 *et seq.*: 'We are faced with a dilemma: we have to see the foreign law in its individuality. But the more we do that, the more we pay attention to the cultural and social context, and the more questionable is the comparability' (translation by the author).

convictions of his own legal background[123], the 'substantive technicalities of domestic doctrine'[124]. Leaving aside these dogmatic technicalities of the legal institutions puts him in a position to detect common convictions and principles that are open for generalization[125]:

> 'The initial question of any comparative work has to be . . . posed in a purely functional manner, *i.e.* the problem under review has to be cleared in a hard-hearted manner from the systematic notions and values of one's own legal system and has to be formulated in a language which describes the problem in a manner that makes the inherent collision of interests understandable for every listener, whether lawyer or layman, German or not'[126].

Conversely, formulating the legal or factual problem in its socio-economic and teleological context may not only ensure the comparability of these legal or factual patterns within the different jurisdictions as a basic prerequisite for the application of comparative science[127] but may also provide the *tertium comparationis*, *i.e.* the standard to be applied in the comparative process[128].

In order to provide efficient solutions, the selection process described above has to be supplemented by a thorough evaluation of the different solutions for the legal problem to be found in the legal systems under review. This evaluation is a highly creative process. It can result in solutions that are not to be found in any of the legal systems that were the subject of the comparative review. Thus, only the combined effect of comparative work *and* the evaluation of the results brought about by this comparison may achieve the codificatory effect described above[129].

---

123. *Zweigert/Kötz*, Einführung in die Rechtsvergleichung, § 3 II, at 34 call this the 'negative side of the principle of functionality' (translation by the author).
124. *Esser*, Grundsatz und Norm, at 33; *Ripert*, Rec.Cours 1933-II, at 565, 629 ('Les différentes techniques ne doivent pas faire oublier la similitude des principes').
125. *See Esser*, Grundsatz und Norm, at 346: 'The structural strangeness in terminology and perspective must be explained genetically, so that the similarity in function, caused by the same purpose, comes to the light' (translation by the author); *cf. also Ripert*, Rec.Cours 1933-II, at 565, 579 *et seq.*
126. *Kötz*, RabelsZ 54 (1990), at 203, 209 *et seq.* (translation by the author).
127. *Cf. Rheinstein*, Einführung in die Rechtsvergleichung, at 26.
128. *Sandrock*, Über Sinn und Methode zivilistischer Rechtsvergleichung, at 46; *Drobnig*, RabelsZ 18 (1953), at 294 *et seq.*; *Esser*, *supra* note 124, at 356 *et seq.*; *Jescheck*, Entwicklungen, Methoden und Aufgaben der Strafrechtsvergleichung, at 36; *Zweigert/Kötz*, Einführung in die Rechtsvergleichung, § 3 V; probably also *Constantinesco*, Rechtsvergleichung, Vol. II, at 347, note 63 *in fine; Radbruch*, Monatsschrift für Kriminalpsychologie und Strafrechtsreform 1905/06, at 422, goes further and demands a 'transnational system of law' as a *tertium comparationis*.
129. *De Groot/Schneider*, in: Boele-Woelki/Grosheide/Hondius/Steenhoff (eds.), Comparability and Evaluation, at 53, 58 ('If research in comparative law shall not be done as a mere *l'art pour l'art*, then an evaluation at the end of the descriptive process is indispensable'); *Zweigert/Kötz*, Einführung in die Rechtsvergleichung, § 3 VII; *Schmitthoff*, Cambridge L.J. 1939, at 94 *et seq.*; *but see Rabel*, RabelsZ 16 (1951), at 357; *Kaden*, in: Schlegelberger (ed.), Rechtsvergleichendes Handwörterbuch für das Zivil- und Handelsrecht, Vol. 6, keyword 'Rechtsvergleichung', at 17, who wants to differentiate between pure comparative law and evaluation which she transfers into the field of legal criticism.

The close connection and interrelation of these two aspects is also of major importance for the determination of the standard to be applied in the comparative process (*tertium valutationis*)[130]. In the context of transnational commercial law, this standard is provided by the typical interests of international traders and businessmen.

The second and third stages of the comparative process concern the formulation and drafting of the general rules and principles which are regarded as part of the NLM. In this context, particular emphasis has to be placed on a unified and globally understandable legal terminology that avoids problems of construction from the outset. These linguistic aspects have been of particular importance for the drafting of the restatements of international contract law and the TransLex Principles which are reprinted in Annex III of this Study.

2. Benefits of the Functional Legal Comparison for the New *Lex Mercatoria* Doctrine

a. The Use of Comparative Law in the New Lex Mercatoria *Context*

The advocates of an independent transnational commercial law apply the functional legal comparative method to investigate the contents of such a legal system and to determine a possible convergence of the families of legal systems[131]. Always under the *caveat* of premature generalization[132], they attempt to go beyond the replaceable dogmatic structures and technicalities of domestic legal systems in order to determine the purpose and socio-economic conceptions of the rules and principles of those systems. Having achieved this and establishing the common factors regarding the structure and purpose of the rule, they succeed in establishing independently applicable general legal principles of a transnational legal system by referring to the 'nature of the matter'[133], *i.e.* the typical factual circumstances which are at the root of the legal problems and which are recognized by the legal community worldwide[134]. It is not surprising, therefore, that functional legal

130. *Cf. Kokkini-Latridou*, Een inleiding tot het rechtsvergelijkende onderzoek, at 180; *De Groot/ Schneider*, in: Boele-Woelki/Grosheide/Hondius/Steenhoff (eds.), Comparability and Evaluation, at 53, 60 *et seq.*
131. *See Loquin, supra* note 113, at 37 *et seq.*; *Ordtscheidt*, La réparation du dommage dans l'arbitrage commercial international, at 16.
132. *Cf. Mustill*, Arb.Int'l 1988, at 110, 113, note 95; *Berger*, Internationale Wirtschaftsschiedsgerichtsbarkeit, at 374, note 196 *in fine*.
133. *Cf. Bydlinski*, Juristische Methodenlehre und Rechtsbegriff, at 498; *Dernburg*, Pandekten I, § 38, 2; *Canaris*, Die Feststellung von Lücken im Gesetz, at 118 *et seq.*: 'Even if the "nature of the matter" as such may be regarded as the sociological reason for the coming into being of a norm, it obtains the rank of a legal reason for existence only by its reference to a legal idea. Insofar, it is also of importance for the interpretation and development of the law' (translation by the author).
134. *Cf. Esser*, Grundsatz und Norm, at 346 *et seq.*; *Berger*, Internationale Wirtschaftsschiedsgerichtsbarkeit, at 361 *et seq.*

comparison was discovered very early as an instrument for the evolution of a '*droit idéal relatif*' or a '*droit commun législatif*'[135]. The value of this comparative method for the development of general principles of law is generally recognized and has proved its effectiveness in the works of *Lauterpacht* on the creative force of 'private law analogies'[136], of *Ripert*[137], *Gutteridge*[138], *Esser*[139], *Cheng*[140] and finally *F. A. Mann* on a commercial law of nations[141]. All of these authors have based their studies on a functional comparative methodology. The results and success of these studies are particularly useful in our context because most of them have pursued the comparison of private law institutions in a public law context (Art. 38(1)(c)) of the ICJ-Statute:

> 'Les principes . . . se retrouvent semblables dans les principales législations. Il y a accord sur les principes, bien que diversité dans les règles. Les nations civilisées ont, à l'heure actuelle, un droit qui est établi sur des principes communs, bien que leur droit codifié ait un caractère technique particulier . . . Il est peu de règles du droit positif dont l'application soit strictement limitée au droit interne. Le droit contractuel, dans tous les pays, est formé de règles générales dégagées peu à peu par le progrès des idées, afin d'assurer à la volonté libre sa pleine efficacité. Dans la société des Etats, les accords ne sauraient être régis par d'autres principes que dans la société des hommes, réserver faite de la personnalité des contractants'[142].

A comparative method that has been used successfully for the development of general principles of public international law may also be used for the evolution of a transnational legal system like the NLM which is necessarily founded on a considerable number of general principles of law[143].

In choosing the comparative method, the authors mentioned above have also made an important indication as to their understanding of the legal nature of general principles of law. In this context[144] they do not have the quality of

---

135. *Cf.* the propositions by *Saleilles* and *Lambert*, printed (with critical note) by *Kaden*, in: Schlegelberger (ed.), Rechtsvergleichendes Handwörterbuch für das Zivil- und Handelsrecht, Vol. 6, keyword: Rechtsvergleichung, at 17 *et seq.*
136. *Lauterpacht*, Private Law Sources and Analogies of International Law, at 91 *et seq.*; *Schachter*, Rec.Cours 1982-V, at 79 *et seq.*
137. *Ripert*, Rec. Cours 1933-II, at 565 *et seq.*
138. *Gutteridge*, Comparative Law, at 61 *et seq.*
139. *Esser*, Grundsatz und Norm, at 37 *et seq.*
140. *Cheng*, General Principles of Law, at 29 *et seq.*
141. *F. A. Mann*, BYIL 1957, at 20 *et seq.*
142. *Ripert*, Rec.Cours 1933-II, at 565, 582, 606.
143. *Cf. von Hoffmann*, Festschrift Kegel, at 215, 220; *Gentinetta*, Die *Lex fori* internationaler Handelsschiedsgerichte, at 148; *Kropholler*, Internationales Einheitsrecht, at 159 *et seq.*; *Schmitz*, Allgemeine Rechtsgrundsätze in der Rechtsprechung des Iran-United States Claims Tribunal, at 57; *cf. also* ICC Award No. 3327, Clunet 109 (1982), at 97 *et seq.*
144. *Cf. generally* for the double meaning of 'general principles of law' in the sense of Art. 38(1)(c) of the ICJ-Statute *von Hoffmann*, Internationale Handelsschiedsgerichtsbarkeit, at 116.

objective principles imposed by natural law[145] but as common values, policy decisions, and convictions contained in the domestic laws of the world[146].

b. Functional Legal Comparison and the Legitimacy of the New Lex Mercatoria *Doctrine*

The functional legal comparison may not be denied recognition in the transnational context simply because it serves to ascertain transnational principles whose existence is highly disputed[147]. Such a view of the methodology problem in transnational commercial law suffers from a *petitio principii*: The result – 'there are no general legal principles of law because no contract can exist in a legal vacuum' – cannot be justified simply by reference to the issue of methodology. Instead, both issues have to be distinguished from each other[148]. From this perspective, the functional approach may even serve an important additional purpose for the theory of a transnational commercial law: it provides increased legitimacy to the NLM by making it necessary to refer back to the notions and values contained in domestic legal systems in the light of the particular needs of international commerce and trade. This recourse to domestic legal systems prevents premature generalizations[149] which would mean the death of every comparative legal method and also of the concept of the NLM.

c. The Dual Approach: Reception of General Principles of Law and Determination of Common Convictions of the 'Societas Mercatorum'

In addition to the above considerations, there is still another aspect which demonstrates the utility of the functional approach in the transnational commercial context. The determination of the contents of the NLM always requires a dual approach: The reception of general principles of law and the determination of common convictions of the business community.

As has been indicated above, deriving general principles of law from domestic legal systems is a well-known phenomenon and may easily be transferred to the

145. Only *Cheng, supra* note 140, at 24, understands the general principles of law as part of natural law and uses aspects of functional legal comparison merely as a methodical means to 'discover' the principles; *cf. also Wolff*, Rec.Cours 1931-II, at 483 *et seq.*
146. *Cf. Ripert*, Rec.Cours 1933-II, at 565, 573; *Constantinesco*, Rechtsvergleichung, Vol. II, at 398; *Esser*, Grundsatz und Norm, at 37.
147. *But see Sandrock*, Über Sinn und Methode zivilrechtlicher Rechtsvergleichung, at 72.
148. *Kropholler*, Internationales Einheitsrecht, at 159, note 26 *in fine*; *von Hülsen*, JZ 1967, at 629, 631.
149. *Cf. Lauterpacht*, Private Law Sources and Analogies of International Law, at 178; *Gutteridge*, Comparative Law, at 71; *cf. also Derains*, in: Sanders (ed.), ICCA Congress, Ser. No. 4, at 283, 289: 'Comparative law highlights the similarities between the systems and thus makes it possible to detect the constants. It also quite often sheds light on the divergences and thus marks the limits of the general principles'.

field of transnational commercial law[150]. The importance of the general principles doctrine for the NLM has frequently been emphasized:

> 'Among all the transnational legal approaches the theory of the general principles of law, in spite of the blurred character that is attached to it by even its most prominent proponents, leaves authors and readers alike dependent upon their own fantasy only to a relatively small extent. One is able to refer to extensive research and to tendencies of practice; one can also refute philosophical speculations in order to search for relevant legal principles instead according to methods ... which every lawyer (i.e. every comparatist who stands in the Rabelian tradition) is familiarized with and declare them to be generally applicable because they appear in the majority of the leading legal systems'[151].

General principles of law therefore serve as 'transformer of domestic contract law into international [commercial] law'[152]. Once they have been ascertained, they play an important role within the system of transnational commercial law similar to the roles they play in domestic law, where they provide the 'structural engineering'[153]. General principles of law lay down the basic maxims which are of fundamental importance for all elements of the legal process and above all for the progressive development of the law[154].

In spite of their tremendous significance, there are two major reasons why the theory of an autonomous transnational commercial law may not be based on general principles alone. First, these principles do not supply a 'ready-made' and generally applicable legal system[155]. They are therefore of little practical utility[156]. Secondly, and more importantly for the context of this Study, while it is true that general principles of law are derived directly from domestic legal systems, thereby adding additional legitimacy to them[157], their application *alone* is not able to take into account the specific commercial realities of international trade and commerce. Since general principles of law have been extracted from the commercial realities of the relevant domestic laws, they have a high degree of analytical abstraction[158]. For this reason, their application in the transnational context always requires their 'implantation' in the transnational community of merchants, *i.e.* their factual and

---

150. *Kappus*, RIW 1990, at 788, 791.
151. *Joerges*, ZHR 138 (1974), at 549, 554 (translation by the author); *see also Metzger*, Extra legem, intra ius: Allgemeine Rechtsgrundsätze im Europäischen Privatrecht, at 526 *et seq.*
152. *Horn*, Internationale Anleihen, at 516; *cf. also Fouchard*, L'Arbitrage Commercial International, at 423 *et seq.*; *Metzger*, *id.*, at 531.
153. *Rüthers*, Die unbegrenzte Auslegung, at 453.
154. *Rüthers, id.*
155. *Horn*, Internationale Anleihen, at 516.
156. *Goode*, ICLQ 1997, at 1, 18.
157. *Metzger, supra* note 151, at 531.
158. *Goode, id.*, at 16: 'It is not a great oversimplification to say that general principles of law, to the extent that they are not overriding rules of international public policy, are generalized (though not necessarily universal) expressions of former international trade usages or conventions'.

social recognition in international commerce and trade[159]. Again, the functional legal comparison provides an important supportive function in the performance of this task. This theory is also of a sociological nature since the legal institutions and provisions under review are not considered in an isolated manner, but are seen as part of the overall context of the legal and social order in which they are embedded[160]. If the comparative process is geared from the outset towards the determination of legal rules and principles relevant for international commercial cases, particular needs, usages, customs, and practices of commerce are automatically included in one way or another in this comparative approach. The reference to the 'nature of the matter' ('*Natur der Sache*') which is implied in this view and which has often been criticized as a rebellion against legal positivism[161], thus loses the 'awkward taste of an embarrassing argument'[162]. These considerations explain why, not only general principles of law, but also usages, customs, and practices of international trade must be considered as the legal sources of the NLM.

d. The Search for a 'Better' Solution

It has been emphasized above that the assessment and evaluation process may lead to the adaptation of solutions found in domestic laws to the particular needs of international business[163]. This innovative function of the comparative method is of particular importance in those cases where a variety of different solutions to a certain legal problem can be discerned from the various legal systems but no solution would be mandated by a majority of these systems. In these cases, the comparative valuation process requires a search for the most advanced or most appropriate solution under the given circumstances. In this context, the NLM becomes a 'substantive better-law approach'. As *ultima ratio* one is also allowed to develop compromise solutions, such as the mutual adaptation of solutions found in different legal systems[164]. Again, the search for a compromise does not take

159. *Basedow*, Festschrift Horn, at 229, 239; *Boele-Woelki*, IPRax 1997, at 161, 164; *Metzger*, *supra* note 151, at 531.
160. *Cf. Esser*, Grundsatz und Norm, at 341; *Mänhardt/Posch*, IPR, Privatrechtsvergleichung, Einheitsprivatrecht, No. 5/6.
161. *Cf.* from the perspective of comparative law *Strömholm*, RabelsZ 39 (1975), at 702, 711 *et seq.*
162. *Esser*, Grundsatz und Norm, at 379 *et seq.*: 'Even in case of some deviations in the concrete evaluation of interests – and don't we even encounter these within our own legal order? – the identity of a problem and the substantive claim for justice remains visible. The same necessities for order are represented in corresponding "fundamental thoughts"' (translation by the author); *cf. also Langen*, Transnationales Recht, Part II, Nos. 1 *et seq.*; for the connection between the 'economic way of evaluation' ('*wirtschaftliche Betrachtungsweise*') and the 'nature of the matter' ('*Natur der Sache*') in the rulings of the German Federal Supreme Court of Justice, BGHZ 18, 325, 332; 30, 338, 342 *et seq.*; 60, 126, 131; 60, 145, 147; *see* for a critical view *Rittner*, Die sogenannte wirtschaftliche Betrachtungsweise in der Rechtsprechung des Bundesgerichtshofes, at 31.
163. *Cf.* for the principle of 'keeping with the times' ('*Grundsatz der "Zeitgemäßheit"*') of legal norms *Langen*, Transnationales Recht, Part I, No. 36.
164. *Kropholler*, Internationales Einheitsrecht, at 160 *et seq.*; *Langen*, Transnationales Recht, Part I, No. 41; *cf. also Bonell*, RabelsZ 42 (1978), at 485, 498, although he rejects the thesis

place in a legal vacuum. Rather, the evaluation process has to come to an end where the possible result is not supported by international commercial practice. From this perspective, it becomes clear that the comparative approach resembles the development of usages and practices of international trade as a possible source of transnational commercial law. Quite often, these usages and practices are not the result of a straightforward historical evolution, but rather of a combination of common principles of domestic legal systems[165]. They may deviate from the provisions of domestic laws that deal with the same subject matter[166]. The comparative method just described therefore resembles the approach underlying the medieval *lex mercatoria*. Most of the principles and rules contained therein were not developed and structured according to the legal patterns of Roman law. Instead, they represented 'new law', which in the course of time developed into generally recognized legal institutions[167].

B. The Application of the New *Lex Mercatoria* Leads to a Decision In Equity

The practical application of the comparative method described so far resembles a 'discovery process': New rules and principles are sought, developed and modified on a case-by-case basis. In view of this particular nature of the law-finding process in transnational commercial law, the majority opinion of German legal doctrine holds that the NLM blurs the traditional distinction between decisions in law and decisions in equity[168]. The significance of this objection goes far beyond German law and constitutes one of the major reasons why the doctrine of a transnational commercial law meets with so much opposition globally[169]. This view receives further support from the increasing use of arbitration as the classical dispute settlement mechanism of international trade. In their decision-making, international arbitrators much more than state court judges tend to take into consideration the underlying interests of the parties in order to achieve equitable solutions of commercial disputes. This equitable character of arbitral decision-making is

of an autonomous world trade law and instead wants to apply to international cases 'transnational criteria and principles' as substantive law and wants to determine their contents by the application of the functional method.

165. *Fabricius*, Festschrift Schmitthoff, at 101, 141.
166. *Blaurock*, ZEuP 1993, at 247, 263 *et seq.*
167. *Cf. Zimmermann*, ZEuP 1993, at 4, 29.
168. *Cf. Ipsen*, Private Normenordnungen als Transnationales Recht?, at 103; *Sandrock*, in: Böckstiegel (ed.), Rechtsfortbildung durch Internationale Schiedsgerichtsbarkeit, at 21, 79; MünchKomm-*Sonnenberger*, Introduction IPR, No. 281; *Gottwald*, Festschrift Nagel, at 54, 65; *von Bar/Mankowski*, IPR, Vol. 1, § 2 No. 85; *von Hoffmann*, Internationale Handelsschiedsgerichtsbarkeit, at 107 *et seq.*; *Markert*, Rohstoffkonzessionen in der internationalen Schiedsgerichtsbarkeit, 1989, at 128; *Triebel/Petzold*, RIW 1988, at 249; *cf. also F. A. Mann*, BYIL 1957, at 36 (for general principles of law).
169. *Mustill*, Arb.Int'l 1988, at 86, 91; *cf. also Osman*, Lex Mercatoria, at 333 *et seq.*

enhanced by arbitrators' increasing references to behavioural standards such as 'reasonableness'[170]:

> 'This shift toward equitable standards brought an increasing wave of judicial discretion, allowing arbitration to gain new grounds over court adjudication. Resolution of disputes arising out of international commercial transactions also underwent a shift toward arbitration, revealing a strong desire to abandon the impediments of court adjudication, the most important of which was submission to rigid technical rules... This illustrates a move towards flexible standards, under which judicial discretion is both broadened and strengthened. The broader judicial discretion is, the less useful are technical rules; and the role of surrounding circumstances takes on increasing importance. Cases are decided on their facts in pursuit of '*ad hockery*' justice, where the spirit – not the technicalities of the law – is observed. Obviously, this vests the judge or arbitrator with wide discretion to define the legal effects of contracting'[171].

In the United States, this natural tendency of arbitrators has led to the assumption that 'there is inherent in the institutions of private dispute resolution an endemic disinclination to enforce legal rights rigorously'[172]. However, in spite of this increased emphasis on equitable considerations in the decision-making of international arbitrators, the traditional distinction between decisions in law and decisions in equity has by no means disappeared. Arbitrators that render a decision as *amiables compositeurs* (*ex aequo et bono*), without the consent of the parties, run the risk of having their award set aside by domestic courts at the seat of the arbitration[173]. Therefore, a decision rendered by international arbitrators and based on the NLM has to remain a decision in law in order to be accepted by the domestic courts. The general observation of an increased reference to equitable considerations in international arbitral case law therefore does not suffice as a major objection against the NLM doctrine.

It also has to be born in mind that objections of this kind are not a new phenomenon. Rather, they reflect the general scepticism against decisions based on general principles of law. It has always been assumed that reference to such principles provides nothing more than a veil for the artificial and arbitrary decision-making practice of international courts[174]. In the commercial context,

170. *Cf. infra* Chapter 4 I.A.7.b.
171. *Nassar*, Sanctity of Contracts Revisited, at 27 *et seq.*
172. *Carrington/Haagen*, The Supreme Court Review 1996, at 331, 346; *cf. also id.*, at 345: 'A Latin phrase sometimes employed to describe the spirit of much American commercial arbitration is *ex aequo et bono* – a resolution is sought that is equitable, minimizes harm to either party, and enables potential adversaries to maintain a valuable commercial relationship... It is said of the American commercial arbitrator that he "may do justice as he sees it, applying his own sense of the law and equity to the facts as he finds them to be and making an award reflecting the spirit rather than the letter of the agreement"' [footnote omitted].
173. *Cf.* BGHZ 96, 40, 45; OLG Frankfurt, RIW 1984, at 400, 401.
174. *Cf. Schlesinger* (ed.), Formation of Contracts, Vol. I, at 11: 'From the standpoint of the litigants and of the international community, judicial use of "general principles" has long been suspect because it has been regarded as a mere mask for capricious law-making by judicial fiat'.

these objections are supported by the general assumption that the reference to unclear and vague decisions in equity may serve as an instrument to circumvent the 'otherwise' applicable law and as a means to exert and enforce economic power[175]. Ultimately, this discussion leads back to the historic rules of the relationship between law and equity and the decline of the Byzantine Empire where the Emperor *Constantine* tried to put the '*aequitas*' on an equal footing with the traditional strict law, the '*ius*', and reserved the determination of what is 'equitable' to his own imperial will: '*Inter aequitatem iusque interpositam interpretationem nobis solis et oportet et licet inspicere*'[176].

From the present perspective, there are two major aspects which form the basis for these general objections to the NLM doctrine. They relate: (1) to the practical difficulties in finding and determining the contents of the NLM; and (2) to the doctrinal issue of distinguishing decisions in law and decisions in equity.

1. Practical Difficulties in the Finding of the Law

One of the aspects which form the basis for the general objections against the NLM relates to the practical difficulties in the finding of the law which is necessarily connected with the functional legal comparison described above[177]. It is alleged that these difficulties allow international arbitrators a degree of discretion that amounts to equitable decision-making without the authority of the parties[178]. This view has its roots in the broad and vague nature of such general principles as 'good faith' and '*pacta sunt servanda*', which form the basic pillars of the NLM. It was for this reason that the Vienna Court of Appeal (*Oberlandesgericht*) set aside an arbitral award in 1982 which had been rendered in a case decided solely on the basis of an 'international principle of good faith':

> 'In the case before the Court, the arbitral tribunal referred to the lex mercatoria, deduced therefrom the general validity of the principle of good faith and then based its decision *wholly* on this principle. The legal concept of good faith communicates mutual considerations between the parties, the redemption of the trust shown and claimed; by fairness one understands a weighing and settlement of interests which is fair to both contracting parties . . . No concrete decisions have yet been made based directly on such general legal views and principles. Where a decision is based *solely* on good faith, the court is only expressing that it considers the solution to be fair. This, of course, does not change the fact that the judge must decide according to the law and not only according to his convictions of what is right and fair.'[179]

175. *See Carrington/Haagen, supra* note 172, at 345 *et seq*.
176. *Codex Iustinianus* 1, 14, 1; *cf. Hedemann*, Die Flucht in die Generalklauseln, at 52.
177. *See Samuel*, Jurisdictional Problems in International Commercial Arbitration, at 244.
178. *Sandrock*, in: Böckstiegel (ed.), Rechtsfortbildung durch internationale Schiedsgerichtsbarkeit, at 21, 79.
179. Vienna Court of Appeal of January 26, 1982, *NORSOLOR v. Pabalk Ticaret*, AG 1982, at 164, 166 (emphasis added).

In this well-known case, the line between a strictly judicial decision and a decision based on fairness and equity (*ex aequo et bono*), for which an express agreement between the parties would be necessary, was completely blurred and the NLM so understood was therefore properly criticized by the Vienna Court as an 'international law of doubtful validity'.

For the evolution of the NLM doctrine, this case is of paramount importance. It reveals the difficulties that exist in the practical day-to-day application of the principles and rules of this transnational legal system. The notion of 'Creeping Codification' of the NLM through the drafting of a list of principles and rules is intended to eliminate these practical difficulties. This theory will be dealt with in the second part of this Study[180].

2. The Application of the New *Lex Mercatoria* Leads to *Ex Aequo Et Bono* Decisions Without Authorization by the Parties

More importantly, the reference to the equitable character of decisions based on the NLM touches upon one of the basic issues of international arbitral decision-making. Without any contrary indication by the parties, the competence of international arbitrators is limited to decisions in law. This means that equitable considerations may only be taken into account within the framework of the applicable law. Decisions '*ex aequo et bono*' which are detached from any domestic legal system may only be rendered by international arbitrators when the parties have expressly authorized them to do so[181]. In that case, arbitral decision-making is subject only to the will of the parties and to the international *ordre public*. Within these limits, the arbitrator may be guided in his decision-making only by his conception of what is fair and just in the case before him, *without having to ascertain and to verify the general validity of the principles applied by him*[182]. The traditional objection that a decision based on the NLM is in fact a decision in equity is nurtured by the fact that the proponents of the NLM doctrine also regard those arbitral awards as possible sources of this legal system that have been rendered by arbitrators acting as '*amiables compositeurs*'. This approach provokes the objection that a transnational *legal* system may not be created and developed by arbitrators who have been freed from their duty to apply the law[183].

180. *Cf. infra* Chapter 4 II.C.
181. *Berger*, Internationale Wirtschaftsschiedsgerichtsbarkeit, at 391 *et seq.*
182. *Jolidon*, in: Reymond/E. Bucher (eds.), Recueil de Travaux Suisses sur L'Arbitrage International, 1984, at 259, 266: 'The decision *ex aequo et bono* does not strive to become a rule. It does not provide a rule of general validity but produces only an individual decision ...' (translation by the author); *cf. also Esser*, in: Summum ius – summa iniuria, at 22, 24: 'Equity means passing over characteristic features useful for categorizing, leaving aside general situations of conflict and their just general regulation in favour of a just decision *hic et nunc*' (translation by the author).
183. *Cf. Loquin*, Clunet 1983, at 344.

a. *Differences Between Equitable Considerations Prescribed by the Law and* Ex Aequo Et Bono *Decisions*

One might argue that even the judge or arbitrator who is bound to apply the law enjoys broad discretion when this law allows him to base his decision on equitable considerations, good faith, reasonableness or similarly vague principles[184]. Also, cases like the English *Athens International Airport* decision, in which *both* sides invoked good faith to support their claims and/or defences, reveal that even high profile international business disputes related to large infrastructure projects may be dominated by the maxim of good faith and the legal principles and rules derived from it[185]. Equating the NLM with *ex aequo et bono* decisions neglects the basic difference between both types of decision-making[186]. If the domestic law, either through concrete statutory provisions or through blanket clauses, authorizes the judge or arbitrator to take into account equitable considerations, the respective arguments of the court or tribunal have to remain within the framework provided for by the policy decisions and values of this law[187]. The German Federal Supreme Court has made it clear that the thresholds for correcting the strict application of the law in order to achieve justice in individual cases through the standard of good faith are very high[188]. Maintaining these high thresholds is meant to preserve legal certainty as the overriding goal of adjudication by the courts[189]. It is for this very reason that the concept of *clausula rebus* embedded in Sec. 313 and the principle of supplementary construction under Sec. 157 of the Civil Code, which both have their origin in the principle of good faith, are applicable only in exceptional, extreme cases. Many of the decisions reached with this approach are similar to those which English courts would have reached. English law tends to achieve many of the results reached by German courts under the umbrella of good faith through the doctrine of implied duties, estoppel, unconscionability or related doctrines. The arbitrator who applies the NLM is in the same position when he seeks an

184. *Cf. infra* G.2.
185. *ABB AG v. Hochtief Airport GmbH, Athens International Airport S.A.* [2006] 2 Lloyd's Rep. 1, paras 28 *et seq.*; the case was decided by the arbitral tribunal on the basis of Greek law, the structure and content of the Greek Civil Code of 1946 is almost identical with the German Civil Code, *see Zweigert/Kötz*, Einführung in die Rechtsvergleichung, at 155; *Zepos*, J.Comp.Leg. 1946, at 56 *et seq.*
186. *See Heini/Keller/Siehr/Vischer/Volken-Heini*, IPRG, Art. 187, Nos. 7, 26.
187. *Esser*, in: Summum ius – summa iniuria, at 22, 25 *et seq.*: 'Nowadays no organ of the state judiciary can decide like a Sovereign without giving any legal reasons, *i.e.* only *ex aequo et bono*. Equity obtains its legality not as freedom from the law but by supplementing the law in a wise manner' (translation by the author); *Kriele*, Theorie der Rechtsgewinnung, at 167 *et seq.*; *David*, International Encyclopedia of Comparative Law, Vol. II, Chapter 3, at 149: 'In such case, [equity] forms part of the legal order, perfecting or supplementing it') *cf. also Derains*, note ICC Award No. 2093/3100, Clunet 1980, at 955, 959: '*Cependant, cet usage de l'equité [as provided for in domestic substantive law] reste enfermé dans un cadre limité défini par la loi elle-même, alors que l'amiable compositeur peut, et parfois doit, recourir à l'équité pour écarter certaines dispositions de la loi.*'
188. *See* BGHZ 38, 61, 65; BGH NJW 1985, at 2579, 2580.
189. PWW-*Schmidt-Kessel*, BGB Kommentar, § 242 No. 20.

equitable solution in the case before him or her: the arbitrator does not enjoy full discretion but instead considers the legal values that form the basis of each principle and rule of transnational commercial law[190]. The NLM therefore does not provide the international arbitrator with unlimited discretion to consider what is 'fair'[191] in a given case:

> 'Even though general principles of law have to be instilled with concrete meaning to be workable in individual cases, they are still legal rules which the judge has to apply. The result stands only at the very end of the legal process. Equitable considerations are in place here only in so far as they accompany the judge's decision and guide him in his efforts to find a just decision of the case. The reason why arbitral tribunals that apply general principles of law make reference to equitable considerations is simply that the general principles want to be concretized in this manner. Thus, these tribunals cannot be blamed for rendering decisions in equity'[192].

There is thus a minor but important difference between equitable decisions rendered in the context of strict law and those issued by arbitrators acting as *amiables compositeurs*. In the first case, the decision remains embedded in the doctrinal writings, case law and statutory provisions of the respective legal system. In the second case, the *amiable compositeur* may decide to be guided only by what he deems fair and equitable in order to reach a *hic et nunc* just decision. It seems that the equation of arbitration and decisions in equity is a relic from the Middle Ages when arbitrators rendered their awards according to 'equity and conscience', without being bound by the law[193].

b. Ex Aequo Et Bono *Decisions as a Source of a New* Lex Mercatoria

Even though principal differences exist between decisions in law and decisions in equity, the latter may be referred to as being among the major sources of the NLM. The reason for this observation lies in the decision-making practice of international arbitrators. It is often overlooked that international arbitral tribunals that are authorized to decide *ex aequo et bono* conduct a comparative analysis of the legal systems that are involved in the case and, on this basis, apply the law as the *ratio scripta*, instead of focusing solely on what they consider to be fair in light of the individual circumstance of the case[194]. In the eyes of international arbitrators, 'the

190. *Cf. Bucher*, in: Schwind (ed.), Aktuelle Fragen zum Europarecht aus der Sicht in- und ausländischer Gelehrter, at 11, 44; *generally* for the disclosure of these legal values, freed from dogmatic technicalities, by functional legal comparison *supra* A.2.b.
191. *Lowenfeld*, Arb.Int'l 1990, at 141; *cf. also Mustill*, Arb.Int'l 1988, at 103 *et seq.*
192. *Schmitz*, Allgemeine Rechtsgrundsätze in der Rechtsprechung des Iran-United States Claims Tribunal, at 52 *et seq.* (translation by the author).
193. *See Malynes*, Consuetudo, Vel Lex Mercatoria, Vol. I, at 305.
194. *Cf. David*, Arbitration in International Trade, at 335: 'In the vast majority of cases *amiables compositeurs* do not intend to work out a compromise, but they feel bound to decide as is

authorization to decide as *amiable compositeur* in no way excludes a competence to determine the mutual rights of the parties according to a certain legal system'[195]. This approach is in line with the *ex aequo et bono* decision according to the *usus modernus pandectarum* where the Roman law was applied as *aequitas scripta* and the rule was '*aequitas numquam contravenit legi*'[196]. In the context of international commercial law, arbitrators who follow this approach do not only equip their award with more persuasive power but also insure themselves against problems in the enforcement stage.

Thus, decisions *ex aequo et bono* are particularly appropriate to foster the evolution of a transnational commercial law as 'law in action'. The authority to act as *amiable compositeur* induces international arbitrators, much more than in proceedings under strict law[197], to combine the functional comparative analysis with a look at the legitimate commercial interests of the parties in order to arrive at a solution that is 'just' from a commercial point of view[198]. '*Ius est ars boni et aequi*'[199]. Public international law also shows a strong preference for a flexible legal process instead of considerations of equity:

> 'Treaties of public international law have a broader scope than contracts between private parties, customary public international law is much less specific than domestic law and the famous "*principes généraux*", the third source of public international law, bear the hallmark of generality. On the basis of such a law, the judge enjoys much more discretion and is not bound to the fine-tuned dogmatic rules of other legal disciplines. To me, this seems to be the major reason why international judges, on the basis of positive public international law, have the possibility to achieve just and equitable decisions in individual cases, thus escaping the dilemma "*summum ius summa iniuria*"'[200].

From the perspective of domestic law, this flexible decision-making practice is not only a characteristic of public international law tribunals or international commercial arbitration. As will be seen later in this Study[201], domestic judges,

prescribed by the law; they see in the law a kind of *ratio scripta* and do not find any good reason for departing from its application in a particular case. The *amiable compositeur* is in fact a judge, but one who enjoys greater flexibility in adopting the solution which he regards as best, even though from a strictly legal point of view it may not be absolutely correct'; *cf. also* ICC Award No. 3742, Clunet 1984, at 910; *Fouchard*, L'Arbitrage Commercial International; at 443; *Eisemann*, Festschrift Bülow, at 67 *et seq.*; *Bartels*, Contractual Adaptation and Conflict Resolution, at 113.

195. ICC Award No. 5118, Clunet 1987, at 1027, 1028.
196. *Cf. Coing*, Festschrift H. Hübner, at 35, 46.
197. *Cf. generally* for the taking into account of the legitimate interests of the parties by international arbitrators *Berger*, Internationale Wirtschaftsschiedsgerichtsbarkeit, at 354 *et seq.*
198. *Cf.* for arbitral case law *Lowenfeld*, Arb.Int'l 1990, at 140: 'I do not recall anyone arguing, in a commercial case, "The result we seek is plainly unfair, but it's just too bad, that's the law"'.
199. *Dig.*, 1, 1, 1.
200. *Schüle*, in: Summum ius – summa iniuria, at 224, 239 (translation by the author).
201. *Cf. infra* G.2.b.

to an increasing extent, tend to seek solutions which they consider just and fair under the circumstances of the case before them[202]. This means that, even in the state judiciary, the search for justice in individual cases ('*Einzelfallgerechtigkeit*') leads to the denial of a systematic unity of the institutions and principles of a legal system[203]. This phenomenon is by no means new. In the 1920s, the French judge *Magnaud* rendered equity decisions *contra legem*[204]. Even the early case law of the German Imperial Court (*Reichsgericht*) witnessed a substantial increase of equity considerations:

> 'Today, we look with astonishment at the initial, calm and stringent development [of equity decisions in the case of the Imperial Court]. A look at the number of relevant decisions reveals how much the significance of Sec. 242 [good faith] has changed in the past. Each volume of the law reports now contains a whole array of cases that make reference to the formula of good faith . . . much more important than the counting of numbers is the growth in the functional emphasis on this principle. Almost every new legal creation is garnished today . . . in one way or another with the principle of 'good faith', almost all legal problems are dealt with by reference to the principle of 'good faith' which assumes the function of a magic wand. It seems that today no one dares to render an important decision without making reference in one way or another to the principle of good faith'[205].

Since the days of the Imperial Court, there has been a boom of Sec. 242 of the German Civil Code and similar provisions of domestic law. The principle of good faith is being used to moralize the entire German legal system, thereby assuming the function of a 'super-provision'[206]. The Dutch Civil Code (BW) is even more explicit. Art. 6:248 allows the Dutch courts to ignore contractual obligations if their contents contravene the notions of equity and fairness in the individual case[207].

All this explains why it is a misunderstanding to say that international arbitrators have a much stronger tendency than domestic judges to 'split the difference'[208]. Instead, the real difference between decision-making by domestic judges and by international arbitrators is that the latter use the freedom granted by domestic law to place more emphasis on the interests of the parties and the economic values involved in the case[209]. From this perspective, there is again a clear

202. *Cf. Strömholm*, Festschrift Zweigert, at 909, 913.
203. *Smid*, Einführung in die Rechtsphilosophie, § 5 II. 1; *Jakobs*, Wissenschaft und Gesetzgebung im Bürgerlichen Recht, at 160 *et seq.*; *Mertens*, RabelsZ 56 (1992), at 219, 236.
204. *Cf. infra* Chapter 3 I.A.1.
205. *Hedemann*, Reichsgericht und Wirtschaftsrecht, at 322 *et seq.* (translation by the author); *cf. also Hedemann*, at 349: 'From a rare protective barrier, good faith has been degraded into an every-day legal institution' (translation by the author).
206. *Lando*, in: Essays in Honor of Roy Goode, at 103, 121 *et seq.*
207. *See Lando, id.*, at 122.
208. *Sandrock*, WM 1994, at 445, 446.
209. *Cf. e.g. Aden*, RIW 1984, at 934, 935: 'The agreement of the parties, to substitute the domestic judge with an arbitrator, is . . . also a decision regarding the obedience of the law which the

parallel between arbitral decision-making and the medieval *lex mercatoria*, where the courts had to decide according to the circumstances of the case before them (‘*secundum negotii veritatem*’) and the dictates of equity[210]. At all times, the notions of ‘legal certainty’ and ‘predictability of decision-making’, both being of only seemingly absolute value[211], have not been of inviolable force in international commercial law[212].

C. THE MAKING OF THE NEW *LEX MERCATORIA* DOES NOT ENJOY THE NECESSARY TRANSPARENCY

The transparency argument is another objection that is frequently raised against the validity of the NLM doctrine: ‘The law is public if it is anything’[213]. This argument has a theoretical and a pragmatical aspect. The latter relates to the view that the NLM is rather propagated than actually found and applied in international legal practice[214]. The phenomenon of ‘Creeping Codification’ through the drafting of lists of general principles and rules of the NLM provides an answer to this objection. It will be dealt with later on in this Study[215].

1. Theoretical Significance of Legal Transparency

The above reference to the idea of drafting lists of general principles and rules leads us to the theoretical significance of the publicity problem. The purpose of these lists is not only to facilitate the practical application of the NLM, but also to ensure the transparency that is necessary for every legal system. However, the drafting of these lists ensures the transparency only in so far as the contents of the rules and principles are concerned. The lists are not concerned with the methodical approach in which these principles are discerned by judges, arbitrators or academics. It is this limited understanding of legal transparency which ensures the legal certainty and continuity that is necessary for the legitimacy and survival of every superior legal system[216]. Transparency, therefore, is not only important for the practical application of the law, but also provides the basic *conditio sine qua non* of every

---

parties require from their arbitrator . . . This obedience is less strict than that which a domestic judge owes to the people, in the name of which he renders his judgments’ (translation by the author); *cf. also Berger*, J.Int’l Arb., No. 4 1992, at 5, 10 *et seq.*

210. *Cf. Zimmermann*, ZEuP 1993, at 4, 30.
211. *Wiedemann*, Festschrift Larenz, 1993, at 199 *et seq.*
212. *Berger*, J.Int’l Arb., No. 4 1992, at 5, 11; *but see Blaurock*, ZEuP 1993, at 247, 261.
213. *Kegel*, Rec.Cours 1964-II, at 87, 262; *cf. also David*, Arbitration in International Trade, at 352.
214. *Cf. Remien*, RabelsZ, 56 (1992), at 300, 304; *see also supra* I.A. for the ideological implications of the *lex mercatoria* doctrine.
215. *Cf. infra* Chapter 4 II.C.
216. *Esser*, Grundsatz und Norm, at 344.

developed legal system[217]. Consequently, the transparency of decision-making is of paramount importance for the legitimacy of the NLM concept:

> 'If the international community of merchants wants to have an autonomous legal system, this law has to be made known to all those who have an interest in it: The arbitrators should not resemble the old pontifex of ancient Rome who jealously kept the law for himself and with it the religious and political power'[218].

International commercial arbitration, as the driving force behind the evolution of a transnational commercial law[219], is, however, frequently denied this transparency[220]. It seems that at this juncture the requirements of legal theory and the practice of international commercial arbitration are irreconcilable. The confidentiality of arbitration has always been regarded as one of the major advantages of the arbitral process *vis-à-vis* adjudication by domestic courts[221]. Also, awards by international arbitral tribunals are frequently handed over from one practitioner to another in an informal way instead of being published in official collections[222]. The French courts seem to have accepted this informal procedure. They have raised no objections when arbitral tribunals did not grant the parties access to these informal sources prior to their decision-making[223].

2. Increasing Publicity of International Arbitral Awards

In recent times, the above argument has lost much of its persuasive force. Even in the context of domestic law, the past decades have revealed that the publicity of legal rules is not the only argument to justify their validity and enforceability, *i.e.* the idea of codification is not based solely on the notion of publicity and transparency[224]. In addition, modern arbitral practice is characterized by an increasing degree of transparency of decision-making. As early as 1965, *Fouchard* witnessed a systematic development of the practice of publishing international

217. *Horn*, Internationale Anleihen, at 537.
218. *Fouchard*, L'Arbitrage Commercial International, at 451 (original in French, translation by the author).
219. *See Lynch*, The Forces of Economic Globalization, at 343.
220. *Cf. Kropholler*, Internationales Einheitsrecht, at 148; *Kropholler* IPR, § 12 I.2 (at 99); *cf. also Hirte*, Wege zu einem europäischen Zivilrecht, at 16.
221. *See* the English Court of Appeal in *Emmott v. Michael Wilson & Partners Ltd.*, EWCA Civ. 2008, at 184 = Bus LR 2008, at 1361 paras 105 *et seq.*: 'The obligation [of confidentiality] is not limited to commercially confidential information in the traditional sense . . . this is in reality a *substantive rule of arbitration law* reached through the device of an implied term'; *see also Paulsson/Rawding*, Arb.Int'l 1995, at 303, 305 *et seq.*; *Fortier*, Arb.Int'l 1999, at 131 *et seq.*; *Berger*, Private Dispute Resolution in International Business, Vol. 2 (Handbook), No. 16-67.
222. *Berger*, J.Int'l Arb., No. 4 1992, at 5, 21.
223. Cour d'Appel de Paris of February 14, 1989, *Société Ofer Brothers v. The Tokyo Marine Fire Insurance Co. Ltd. et al.*, Rev.d'Arb. 1989, at 695, 697.
224. *K. Schmidt*, Die Zukunft der Kodifikationsidee, at 35 *et seq.*

arbitral awards[225]. This development has reached a new level in past decades. Since 1974, arbitral awards rendered under the auspices of the ICC have been published on a regular basis in the Journal du Droit International (Clunet), and since 1976 as well in the Yearbook Commercial Arbitration. In Clunet, the awards are published together with in-depth commentaries by noted arbitration experts, which put particular emphasis on the effect of the particular award for the evolution of the NLM doctrine. Since 1986, international arbitral awards, relevant commentaries and important information from arbitral practice have been published in the American 'Mealey's International Arbitration Report'[226]. In addition, the ICC has published collections of their awards which, through comprehensive and well structured keyword-indexes, provide easy access to the vast amount of ICC arbitral case law[227]. With these publications, the ICC has finally achieved the goal that was first promoted in the 1970s, *i.e.* the publication of a collection of arbitral awards of international arbitral tribunals concerning the legal problems of international trade under the auspices of an international organization[228]. The arbitral awards rendered by arbitral tribunals in Switzerland are being published regularly in the Bulletin of the Swiss Arbitration Association (*Association Suisse de l'Arbitrage*, ASA). Awards rendered under the auspices of the Netherlands Arbitration Institute (NAI) and other Dutch arbitration institutions are published regularly in the 'Tijdschrift voor Arbitrage'. Finally, the important awards of the Iran-United States Claims Tribunal in The Hague have been published, since 1983, in a comprehensive collection of more than thirty volumes (Iran-United States Claims Tribunal Reports). In spite of the particular political situation which has surrounded the decision-making of this Tribunal[229], these awards constitute a most valuable quarry for the development and practical application of general principles of law, the application of which is required under Art. V of the Claims-Settlement Declaration[230].

It is by no means an exaggeration to state that, in terms of size and quality, the practice of publishing international arbitral awards will soon almost equal the publication of domestic court judgments. This practice also has an important side

225. *Fouchard*, L'Arbitrage Commercial International, at 457.
226. International Arbitration Report, published by *Mealey* Publications, Wayne, PA, USA.
227. Collection of ICC Arbitral Awards, Recueil des sentences arbitrales de la CCI 1974 to 1985 and 1986 to 1990.
228. *Cf. Kos-Rabcewicz-Zubkowski*, in: UNIDROIT (ed.), New Directions in International Trade Law, at 459, 461.
229. *Cf. e.g. Carbonneau*, in: Lillich (ed.), The Iran-United States Claims Tribunal 1981–1983, at 104, 128: '. . . the awards rendered by the Tribunal have been essentially devoid of substantive legal content and, as a result, are incapable of having much precedential value'; critical also *Kahn*, The Iran-US Claims Tribunal, at 258 *et seq.*; *cf. also Dasser*, Lex Mercatoria, at 165 *et seq.*; positive on the other hand *Sandrock*, ArchVR 1991, 104, 125 *et seq.*; *Holtzmann*, Pr.Inv. Abr. 1987, at 16-5; *Straus*, J.Int'l Arb., No. 3 1986 at 57, 58.
230. *Cf. Schmitz*, Allgemeine Rechtsgrundsätze in der Rechtsprechung des Iran-United States Claims Tribunal, at 42; Art. V provides that the Tribunal has to decide, 'on the basis of respect for law, applying such choice of law rules and principles of commercial and international law as the tribunal determines to be applicable, taking into account relevant usages of trade, contract provisions and changed circumstances', *cf.* 1 CTR 9, at 11.

effect. It ensures the homogeneity and coherence of arbitral decision-making throughout different arbitral institutions[231]. In recent years, an increasing number of awards resulting from *ad hoc* arbitrations has been included in this publication practice. This shows that the publication practice reaches beyond the major arbitral institutions such as the ICC or American Arbitration Association (AAA).

This comprehensive publicity of international arbitral awards has made a major contribution to the stabilization and consolidation of the NLM doctrine[232]. In the near future, domestic courts confronted with legal problems of international commerce and trade will seek guidance for their decision-making in the published awards of international arbitral tribunals. In fact, it is suggested in German legal doctrine that courts should refer to international arbitral awards when interpreting general contract conditions issued by international formulating agencies[233].

D. The New *Lex Mercatoria* Lacks Procedural Legitimacy

The problem of the publicity of transnational commercial law discussed above necessarily implies the question as to the procedural safeguards, *i.e.* the procedural checks and balances which ensure the viability and enforceability of every developed legal system[234]. According to most authors the NLM lacks such procedural legitimacy[235]. Again, this objection is not new. It is known from public international law[236]. Customary public international law is frequently said to lack the 'democratic legitimacy' because it is 'discovered' by international judges and academics, thus lacking the necessary procedural safeguards of domestic legal systems[237].

It is beyond doubt that the development of rules and principles within an open system such as transnational commercial law requires procedural safeguards which accompany the law-making process. The consistency and continuity of a legal system is usually preserved by the legal or quasi-legal authority of judicial case law or the factual authority of judicial interpretation and doctrinal writings[238]. It is the lack of hard decisional law which casts doubt on the democratic legitimacy of

231. *Cf.* for this counter-argument *Kropholler*, Internationales Einheitsrecht, at 148 *et seq.*
232. *Cf. Lew*, in: Schultz/van den Berg (eds.), The Art of Arbitration, Liber Amicorum Pieter Sanders, at 223, 321 *et seq.*; *Berger*, J.Int'l Arb., No. 4 1992, at 22; *Molineaux*, J.Int'l Arb., No. 1 1997, at 62; *Struycken*, Journées Savatiers, at 225; *cf.* for the increased decisional harmony and continuity in international commercial arbitration *Mertens*, Festschrift Odersky, 1996, at 857 *et seq.*; *Stein*, Lex mercatoria, at 241.
233. *See infra* Chapter 4 I.A.10.e.dd.
234. *Cf.* the objection by *Drobnig*, reported by *Remien*, RabelsZ 56 (1992), at 300, 303.
235. *Cf.* the contribution by *Steindorff*, reported by *Remien*, RabelsZ 56 (1992), at 300, 304; *Schmitthoff*, RabelsZ 28 (1964), at 72; *Dasser*, Lex Mercatoria, at 123 *et seq.*; *David*, Arbitration in International Trade, at 352; *Stoecker*, J.Int'l Arb., No. 1 1990, at 101, 120.
236. *Cf. generally* for the parallels between the *lex mercatoria* concept and public international law *Goode*, ICLQ 1997, at 1; *Molineaux*, J.Int'l Arb., No. 1 1997, at 55, 66.
237. *Cf. Zamora*, GYIL 1989, at 9, 37.
238. *Esser*, Grundsatz und Norm, at 52.

public international law[239]. Similar problems arise in the NLM context. Here, domestic courts are unable to provide the necessary procedural safeguards. More than 90% of all major international commercial disputes are withdrawn from the jurisdiction of domestic courts and decided by international arbitral tribunals. Even in those instances where domestic courts retain a supervisory function over these arbitral bodies, *i.e.* in procedures relating to the setting aside and enforcement of arbitral awards, the courts' control over the arbitrators' application of substantive law is reduced to a minimum. The courts must refrain from any *de novo* examination of the merits of the case. There is no '*révision au fond*' of international arbitral awards. The courts may interfere only in those rare cases where the arbitrators have violated the notion of international public policy[240]. This severe limitation of the courts' competence in this field is intended to ensure the speed and efficiency of the international arbitral process. Speed and efficiency have always been considered a major advantage of international arbitration[241]. For this reason, the case law of domestic courts rendered in the context of setting aside or enforcement procedures does not provide procedural safeguards for the evolution of the NLM. Instead, it serves as an important indication that domestic courts tend to acknowledge the existence of this transnational legal system[242].

For these reasons the procedural legitimacy of the NLM is to be derived from different sources. These sources are: (1) the 'formulating agencies' which are involved in the drafting and formulation of international instruments for the unification of commercial law; and (2) international commercial arbitrators as the 'natural judges'[243] of international trade and commerce.

1. International 'Formulating Agencies'

International organizations such as UNIDROIT[244], UNCITRAL[245], the Hague Conference on Private International Law[246], the Inter-American Specialized

239. *Zamora*, GYIL 1989, at 9, 37: 'The lack of hard decisional law, either at the international or the national level, profoundly affects the quality of analysis of customary international law . . . '.
240. *Berger, supra* note 221, No. 28-54.
241. *Cf. Berger*, RIW 1989, at 850 *et seq.*; *cf. also* the dictum of *Leggat J.* in the English judgment *Arab African Energy Corp. Ltd. v. Olieprodukten Nederland B. V.*, 2 Lloyd's L.Rep. [1984], at 419, 423: 'True it is that formerly the Court was careful to maintain its supervisory jurisdiction over arbitration and awards. But this aspect of public policy has now given way to the need for finality. In this respect the striving for legal accuracy may be said to have been overtaken by commercial expediency'.
242. *Cf. infra* F.2.b.
243. *See Philippe Kahn* in his personal account on the 'rediscovery' of the NLM by the Dijon School in the late 1950s/early 1960s Annex I *infra.*
244. *Cf. infra* Chapter 4 I.A.1.
245. *Cf.* for the role of UNCITRAL as a 'formulating agency' *Herrmann* in: Horn/Schmitthoff (eds.), The Transnational Law of International Commercial Transactions, at 35 *et seq.*
246. The Conference convened for the first time on September 12, 1883 under the chairmanship of *T.M.C. Asser* in The Hague; *cf. Parra-Aranguren*, Festschrift P. Lalive, at 97 *et seq.*; *cf. also* the contributions relating to The Hague Conference on Private International Law 1883–1983, Neth.Int'l L.Rev. 1993, at 1 *et seq.*

Conference on Private International Law (CIDIP)[247], the ICC[248] and similar institutions[249] play an important role in the unification and evolution of international commercial law. The members of the World Bank Group, and in particular the Multilateral Investment Guarantee Agency (MIGA)[250] and the International Monetary Fund (IMF)[251] also make important contributions to the unification of law in areas which have been traditionally excluded from the global unification process due to their highly political character. It is not surprising, therefore, that *Clive Schmitthoff*, one of the fathers of the NLM doctrine, put particular emphasis on the work and influence of international formulating agencies:

> 'It is the formulating activity of these international agencies which inspires hope for the ultimate emergence of a fully autonomous law of international trade... Commercial life... is a many-splendoured thing, and out of the complementary activity of these international agencies must eventually arise the harmony of an integrated autonomous international trade law'[252].

For *Schmitthoff*, the progressive liaison and cooperation between these institutions was 'the next step in the development of an autonomous law of international trade' because, in his view, the advance of an autonomous law of international trade depended 'on the willingness of the formulating agencies to cooperate, to the benefit of all trading nations'[253]. It is not surprising, therefore, that UNCITRAL was founded upon *Schmitthoff*'s initiative in 1966[254].

a. *Objections to the Idea of 'Codification Through Formulating Agencies'*

In spite of the considerable influence that international organizations and institutions have had on the unification and evolution of international commercial law, their contribution to the unification process has been met with considerable scepticism. Critics argue that the internal procedures followed by the formulating agencies to gather the necessary information, establish working groups, and to draft international instruments are not necessarily geared towards the balancing of interests of all member countries or the cultivation of an international '*bonum*

247. *See* for a collection of materials and a list of Conventions adopted since 1975 *Rudolf*, in: Raisch/Shaffer (eds.), Introduction to Transnational Legal Transactions, at 191, 218 *et seq*.
248. *Cf. Rowe*, in: Horn/Schmitthoff (eds.), The Transnational Law of International Commercial Transactions, at 51 *et seq*.
249. *See supra* Chapter 1 III.B.
250. *Cf. Voss*, JWTL 1987, at 5 *et seq.*; *Ebenroth/Karl*, Die Multilaterale Investitions-Garantie-Agentur.
251. *Cf.* for the rule of Art. VIII(2)(b) International Monetary Fund Agreement as part of the *lex mercatoria Ebke*, Internationales Devisenrecht, at 169 and TransLex Principle No. V.2.4, reprinted *infra* Annex III, available with further references at *www.Trans-Lex.org/955000*.
252. *Schmitthoff*, in: Schmitthoff (ed.), The Sources of the Law of International Trade, 1964, at 3, 37.
253. *Schmitthoff*, *id.*, at 38.
254. Resolution 2205 (XXI), Adopted by the General Assembly at its 1497th Plenary Meeting on December 17, 1966, 'Establishment of the United Nations Commission on International Trade Law'.

commune'. The particular institutional structure, including aspects such as political influences, participation of governments, and insufficient consideration of the 'North-South' conflict, is said to be the major obstacle for a truly democratic process within these institutions[255]. As a result of these numerous external influences on the decision-making of international organizations, the consensus reached within their working groups is frequently limited to what is 'desirable and possible'[256]. The result is that the initial comprehensive plans for the unification of commercial law are reduced to the 'lowest common denominator'[257]. An additional objection is raised by international legal practitioners. They argue that the advice of academics has a decisive influence during the negotiations of international instruments, even though international commercial law is particularly dependent upon the input from international practice[258].

In addition to these general arguments, UNIDROIT is faced with a specific objection to the 'democratic legitimacy' of their Principles of International Commercial Contracts. It is argued that these Principles are the result of a 'competition of projects' and were adopted by the Governing Council of UNIDROIT in May 1994 only in an effort to be 'on the market' prior to the Principles of European Contract Law of the *Lando* Commission[259]. Due to this artificial time constraint, the members of UNIDROIT's Governing Council had no chance to formulate their concerns against the UNIDROIT Principles, let alone to introduce them in the discussion on a final version[260].

These objections to the 'democratic legitimacy' of the internal decision-making process of UNIDROIT are not new. They have also been raised against the American Law Institute, the editor of the American Restatements of the Law, which has served as a model for the UNIDROIT Principles[261]. This Institute has always been confronted with the objection that its internal structure is not designed to ensure a democratic decision-making process. Involving the best academics from major American universities only serves the empirical purpose to determine an *existing* consensus, but not the democratic task to bring this consensus about[262].

Also, the first few years following the foundation of UNCITRAL in the early 1970s were dominated by a discussion on the democratic legitimacy of its decision-making process[263].

---

255. *Dolzer*, in: Horn/Schmitthoff (eds.), The Transnational Law of International Commercial Transactions, at 61, 79 *et seq.*; see for a political perspective on the democratic deficiencies of new informal types of international cooperation which are often not legally grounded in international law, *Fukuyama*, America at the Crossroads, at 163 *et seq.*
256. *Zweigert/Kötz*, Einführung in die Rechtsvergleichung, § 2 V.1.
257. *Dolzer, supra* note 255, *id.*
258. *Goode*, Unif.L.Rev. 1991, at 54, 70 *et seq.*
259. *Cf. infra* Chapter 4 I.B.
260. *Raeschke-Kessler*, in: ICC (ed.), The UNIDROIT Principles of International Commercial Contracts, A New Lex Mercatoria?, at 172 *et seq.* with reference to the session protocols.
261. *See* for details *infra* Chapter 4 I.A.5.
262. *Rosett*, Am.J.Comp.L. 1992, at 683, 692 *et seq.*
263. *Cf. Farnsworth*, Festschrift Schmitthoff, at 144, 153 *et seq.*; *Schmitthoff*, in: Coing/Schmitthoff/Hellner/Gleichmann (eds.), Methoden der Rechtsvereinheitlichung, at 19, 20 *et seq.*

b. Increasing 'Depolitization' of the Decision-Making Process of 'Formulating Agencies'

International organizations have always regarded it as one of their main tasks to emphasize the participation of international practice in the negotiation and drafting of international instruments. Thus, both academics and practitioners were involved in the negotiations of the UCP, drafted and promulgated by the ICC in Paris. The ICC has always placed particular emphasis on the equal status of practice and theory[264]. This dual approach is reflected in the foundation of the 'ICC Institute of International Business *Law and Practice*', which is now called the 'ICC Institute of World Business Law'[265]. It is this involvement of international practice which has made the INCOTERMS[266] and the UCP an integral part of transnational commercial law[267]. It is not surprising, therefore, that *Philippe Kahn*, in his personal account on the 'rediscovery' of the NLM by the Dijon School in the late 1950s/early 1960s[268], emphasizes the significance of the UCP as 'an expression of the [New] Lex Mercatoria'[269]. The Uniform Rules for Contract Guarantees will assume the same quality[270]. UNIDROIT also presented the Draft-Principles at a series of international conferences where they were discussed by academics and practitioners alike[271]. UNIDROIT's approach in this context has been praised as a model for other intergovernmental organizations[272]. Finally, and most importantly, the adoption of the Principles did not come as a surprise to the members of UNIDROIT's Governing Council. From the outset of the drafting process, there was general agreement among the members of the Council that an *in toto* discussion of the final draft would be impracticable due to its complexity and length. Therefore, a list of controversial issues was drafted after every meeting of the

---

264. *Cf. Berger*, DZWir 1993, at 1, 11.
265. *Cf. www.iccwbo.org/business_law/id2730/index.html.*
266. Due to their trade usage-like quality, the international arbitrator may apply the INCOTERMS in order to construe the contract before him even if the parties have not expressly agreed on their application, *cf.* ICC Award No. 3130, Clunet 1981, at 931; No. 3894, Clunet 1981, at 987.
267. *Cf.* Heymann/*Horn*, HGB, Vol. 4, Anhang § 372 No. VI/25.
268. *See supra* Introduction I.A.1.
269. *See Kahn*, Annex I *infra.*
270. *Cf. Berger*, DZWir 1993, at 1 *et seq.*
271. *Cf.* the conference reported in UNIDROIT Bulletin January/April 1992, at 1 at the Miami Law School on 'Unification and Law Reform in a Changing World' and the conferences reported in UNIDROIT Bulletin January/April 1994, at 2 *et seq.* at the '*Eason-Weimann Center*' at *Tulane University School of Law*, USA and at the University Rome II (in cooperation with UNIDROIT, the 'Centre for Comparative and Foreign Law Studies', the 'Centre for Latin American Studies' of the University Rome II and the 'Association for Latin American Social Studies') and the conferences reported in UNIDROIT Bulletin July/October 1994 (in Melbourne together with 'Committee M' of the International Bar Association on the 21st International Trade Law Conference in Sydney).
272. *Goode*, Unif.L.Rev. 1991, at 54, 71: 'This is a procedure which should become standard in future work by intergovernmental organizations'.

Working Group. This list and possible solutions were then presented to and discussed by the Governing Council, together with possible solutions[273].

Apart from these general observations, it should be borne in mind that the internal procedure of international organizations is only indirectly relevant to the evolution of the NLM as a transnational legal system. Instruments drafted and adopted by these institutions do not automatically assume the quality of 'law' within the NLM context[274]. Rather, this law is created through the contract practice of the international community of merchants and the case law of international arbitration[275]. This means that rules and principles which are contained in the text of such instruments have to stand the test of international commercial practice and international arbitration in order to become acknowledged as part of the NLM[276]. Therefore, a distinction must be drawn between the democratic legitimacy of the acts and instruments of international 'formulating agencies' and the legitimacy of the NLM itself. While the resolutions of international organizations have the quality of secondary sources of international commercial law and derive their legitimacy from the procedural safeguards laid down in their charter or bylaws[277], compliance with these safeguards should not be confused with a statement as to the transnational legal quality of these principles or rules.

It seems, therefore, that any objections against the 'democratic' quality of the internal procedures of international organizations seem to be ill-founded in the NLM context. In view of its quality as 'law in action', different considerations have to be brought into play in order to determine the democratic legitimacy of transnational commercial law. These considerations are related to the inherent values and qualities of the international arbitral process.

2. International Commercial Arbitration

Legal theory and practice have long accepted that international arbitrators perform a genuine judicial function. Arbitrators are called upon by the parties to resolve a dispute within the procedural framework established by the two basic principles of equal treatment of the parties and '*audiatur et altera pars*' as the '*Magna Charta*' of the international arbitral process[278]. It is for this reason that the German legislature has repeatedly emphasized in the *travaux préparatoires* on

273. *Cf.* UNIDROIT Bulletin, July/October 1990, at 2.
274. *But see* the ambiguous statement by *Raeschke-Kessler, supra* note 260, *id.*, who maintains that in view of the inconsistencies detected by him, the adoption of the Principles could only be regarded as a 'draft', a 'draft, however, does not constitute the applicable law'.
275. For details *cf. infra* G.3.c.
276. *See* the correct view by *Raeschke-Kessler, supra* note 260, *id.* ('The Principles need to be discussed in context and in detail').
277. *Fischer*, GYIL 1976, at 143, 156.
278. *Cf. Ramm*, ZRP 1989, at 136, 138: 'The notion of adjudication covers the whole broad range of dispute settlement: not only the state judiciary and enforcement procedures, but also arbitration on all planes, *i.e.* inter-state, domestic and international' (translation by the author).

the German arbitration law of 1998 the quality of arbitration as a truly adjudicatory process[279].

Also, international arbitration has been recognized on a global basis as the dispute settlement instrument for international trade. Even those regions of the world with a traditional reluctance towards arbitration, South-America (Calvo Doctrine!) and the Arabic countries, show a strong tendency to accept arbitration clauses in their contracts today[280]. Even the international banking and finance practice, which has always refused to accept international arbitration, is now beginning to consider the advantages of the international arbitral process[281].

International arbitral tribunals, therefore, have assumed the function, which under the medieval *lex mercatoria* was performed by special courts. Due to the specialized knowledge of the judges, their informal and speedy procedure and the efficient enforcement procedures, these courts were able to meet the needs of the traders of their time[282]. The growing acceptance of international arbitration is also reflected in the liberal attitude of domestic courts *vis-à-vis* arbitration and arbitrators. In view of the fact that today almost 90% of all cross-boarder trade contracts contain arbitration clauses the German Federal Supreme Court (*Bundesgerichtshof*) has held that in certain branches of trade dispute settlement through arbitration has assumed the quality of a trade usage. This means that the courts have to refer the parties to arbitration even though they have not concluded an arbitration agreement[283]. This decision has been heavily criticized as being irreconcilable with the consensual basis of arbitration[284] and is irreconcilable with the written form requirement of the 1998 German Arbitration Law[285]. In fact the German Federal Supreme Court has recognized the new quality of the international arbitral process. Parties who are doing business in a particular branch of international trade where arbitration has become the natural dispute settlement system know, or

---

279. *See* Kommission zur Neuordnung des Schiedsverfahrensrechts (ed.), Bericht mit einem Diskussionsentwurf zur Neufassung des Zehnten Buches der ZPO, at 91; Bundestags-Drucksache No. 13/5274 of July 12, 1996, at 34: 'If one regards *arbitration as a means of adjudication that has, in principal, equal weight to adjudication before domestic courts*, then it is only natural to exclude arbitration only insofar as the state has reserved for himself a monopoly of adjudication in view of the weight and significance of the interests involved' (translation by the author, emphasis added).
280. *Cf. Berger*, Internationale Wirtschaftsschiedsgerichtsbarkeit, at 5.
281. *Cf. Berger*, LFMR 2009, 54 *et seq.; see also Sandrock*, WM 1994, at 405 *et seq.*; 445 *et seq.*; the American banking industry has long since turned towards arbitration as a standard dispute settlement technique; the American Arbitration Association has set up a '*Commercial Financial Disputes Arbitration Panel*' and has issued a special set of arbitration rules for this purpose, *cf. American Arbitration Association* (ed.), Resolving Commercial Financial Disputes, A Guide to Alternative Dispute Resolutions, at 4 *et seq.*; *Moller/Rolph/Ebener* (eds.), Private Dispute Resolution in the Banking Industry, at 16 *et seq.*
282. *Zimmermann*, ZEuP 1993, at 4, 29 *et seq.*
283. BGH NJW 1993, at 1798 = LM H. 7/1993, § 1027 ZPO, No. 18 with note *Kappus*; *cf. also Schütze*, WuB VII A. § 1027 ZPO 1.93; *Berger*, DZWir 1993, at 466 *et seq.*
284. *See Carbonneau*, Am.Rev.Int'l Arb. 1993, at 217 *et seq.*
285. *Raeschke-Kessler/Berger*, Recht und Praxis des Schiedsverfahrens, No. 229.

should have known, that this trade usage exists. As in other areas of international trade, the parties in this case may not deny the application of that trade usage[286].

In spite of this growing acceptance of international arbitration as a dispute settlement mechanism in international trade, two major reasons are advanced why arbitration is not able to legitimize the NLM doctrine. One of these arguments relates to the lack of an organizational structure that is typical for the domestic court system:

> 'Il n'existe aucun système organisé de juridictions arbitrales; les organismes permanents d'arbitrage sont nombreux, mal coordonnés entre eux, mal répartis du point de vue géographique, exagérément soumis parfois à la tutelle étatique, et beaucoup d'arbitrages, par surcroît, sont organisés en dehors eux. En raison de ces circonstances il est difficile d'attendre d'eux la formation d'une jurisprudence cohérente . . . '[287].

Secondly, there is a general suspicion that the alleged potential for misuse inherent in the arbitral process constitutes a threat to domestic legal systems and to the interests of the parties involved: '*arbitration is power*'[288]. It is this fear which has exerted considerable pressure on the US Supreme Court's extremely liberal case law on arbitration which can be boiled down to the formula: 'whenever there is agreement there is arbitration'[289].

a. Lack of Forensic Quality of the International Arbitral Process

There is a substantial quality problem involved in the increasing competition between domestic legal systems for international arbitrations, the growing quality of the international arbitral process as a 'forensic industry', and the increase of delaying tactics and confrontational atmospheres between the parties. In the eyes of those who oppose the NLM doctrine, all these phenomena have raised doubts as to the forensic quality of the international arbitral process as such[290]. This view maintains that international arbitration no longer provides the degree of legal culture and sophistication that is necessary to serve as a guarantor for the procedural legitimacy of the NLM[291]. However, these concerns are devoid of any basis, since we are dealing here with phenomena which are also typical for adjudication by courts. Thus, no one would deny the common law courts' ability to develop and shape the law simply because of the Anglo-American procedural tradition to create an adversarial atmosphere between the parties ('winning the battle')[292]. It is fair to say that it is this parallel development between arbitration

286. *Cf. Berger*, DZWir 1993, at 466 *et seq.*; *cf. also Kappus*, WiB 1994, at 189, 190.
287. *David*, in: UNIDROIT (ed.), New Directions in International Trade Law, at 5, 16.
288. *See Kronstein's* article in N.Y.U.L.Rev. 1963, at 661 *et seq.*
289. *See Carrington/Haagen*, The Supreme Court Review 1996, at 334 *et seq.*
290. *Cf.* for this scenario *Berger*, Internationale Wirtschaftsschiedsgerichtsbarkeit, at 8 *et seq.*
291. *Cf. Kropholler*, IPR, § 12 I.2 (at 100).
292. *Cf.* for the 'litigation battle' the treatises by *King, Denbin* and *Arkin*, in: Campbell/Summerfield (eds.), Effective Dispute Resolution for the International Commercial Lawyer, at 55 *et seq.*

and adjudication by domestic courts which provides another indication for the growing adjudicatory quality of the international arbitral process. Additionally, in the past decades international arbitration practitioners have reached a basic consensus about the basic professional and ethical principles to be observed in international arbitration. The 'IBA Rules on the Taking of Evidence' of 1999 and the 'IBA Guidelines on Conflicts of Interest in International Arbitration' of 2004[293] as well as the (partly overruled) 'Rules of Ethics for International Arbitrators'[294] issued by the IBA in 1987 are not per se binding upon the parties. Instead, they serve the important function of a 'source of positive inspiration' for a worldwide uniform understanding of the arbitrators' procedural rights and duties[295].

b. No Stages of Appeal

Apart from special arbitration procedures in international commodity trade, international arbitration lacks the stages of appeal that are a main characteristic of domestic court systems. The reason for this phenomenon is a basic structural difference between adjudication by international arbitrators and by domestic judges. International arbitrators are not subject to the regular supervision by appeal tribunals and become *functus officio* after they have performed their decision-making function. It is for this very reason that international arbitrators are much more able to take account of the commercial realities of the case and the interests of the parties than state court judges who have a multitude of cases on their dockets[296]. This basic difference between adjudication by domestic courts on the one side and by international arbitral tribunals on the other relates to the treatment of individual cases, but it also has an important impact on the development of the law in general. Only the scrutiny of court decisions on appeal creates the factual (in civil law systems), or legal (in common law systems which apply the *stare decisis* doctrine), precedential value of court decisions. A major function of appeal courts is to ensure the uniform application of the law. The binding force of their decisions endows these appeal courts with the power to act as 'quasi legislatures'[297]. Also, 'the public', *i.e.* the parties to the dispute, their attorneys and advisors expect the lower courts to follow the law as it is shaped and developed by the higher courts in order to ensure predictability, certainty and economy of decision-making, as well as uniformity of case law.

293. *See supra* Chapter 1 III.B..
294. IBA, *Rules of Ethics for International Arbitrators*, YCA 1987, at 199 *et seq.*
295. *See Berger*, *supra* note 221, Nos. 16-114 *et seq.*; *cf. also Hunter/Paulsson*, Int'l Bus.Lawy. 1985, at 153 *et seq.*; *Craig/Park/Paulsson*, ICC Arbitration, at 225; *cf. also Stein*, Lex mercatoria, at 171.
296. *Cf. Redfern*, Priv.Inv.Abr. 1989, at 11-1, 11-12 *et seq.*
297. *Cf. Kriele*, Theorie der Rechtsgewinnung, at 195; *Meyer-Cording*, Die Rechtsnormen, at 69; *Kruse*, Das Richterrecht als Rechtsquelle, at 12; *Larenz*, in: Festschrift für Hans Schima, at 247, 249; *Roellecke*, in: Roellecke (ed.), Zur Problematik höchstrichterlicher Entscheidung, at 1, 18.

The international arbitral process lacks the checks and balances created by the existence of a permanent appeal system. In their decision-making, international arbitrators do not have to take into account the question of whether their decision will be upheld by a higher court. It has often been argued that the lack of such control mechanisms is a major deficiency of the NLM doctrine[298]. Even those who have always supported the idea of a transnational commercial law have called for the creation of a hierarchy of international arbitral tribunals and of an appeal tribunal for international arbitral awards[299].

The development of the international arbitral process in recent years reveals that these arguments no longer have the force they had ten years ago. Today, the case law of international arbitral tribunals may no longer be characterized as a more or less unsystematic 'reservoir of examples'. The notion of a vertical control mechanism through appeal tribunals, which is a typical characteristic of a court system created, financed and controlled by the state, cannot be transferred to the field of international commercial arbitration, which is based solely on the will of the parties. By agreeing to dispute settlement through international arbitration, the parties ('the public') strive for a speedy and efficient resolution of their disputes. At the same time, their agreement to arbitrate is intended to avoid the long-lasting, multi-instance appeal procedures of domestic court systems[300]. It is this presumed intention of the parties which has led domestic courts to refrain from trying to control the substantive decision-making of international arbitrators, except for those rare cases where they have violated the international *ordre public*[301].

In spite of this far-reaching retreat of domestic courts from the substantive control of arbitral awards, parties to international commercial arbitrations do not renounce their right for the arbitrator's correct application of the law. To this end, internal, horizontal control mechanisms have been developed within the international arbitral system that have assumed the function of vertical controls through courts of appeal. Today, increased value is attached to international arbitral awards as precedents for future disputes[302]. They provide arbitrators with the means for the mutual control of their decision-making. With the increasing publication of international arbitral awards[303], international arbitrators have shown a

298. *Cf. Redfern/Hunter*, Law and Practice of International Commercial Arbitration, 1st ed. 1986, at 92: '. . . there is generally no hierarchy of appeal tribunals to ensure consistency of decisions as between one arbitral tribunal and another. Therefore any international trade law built up from arbitral decisions is not likely to be generally applied until it acquires reasonable consistency and reasonable content, and it will then only succeed in becoming established to the extent that it accords with common sense and the realities of international commercial trade'; *cf. also Lorenz*, ZHR 126 (1964), at 151; *Schmitthoff*, RabelsZ 28 (1964), at 72; *Kropholler*, Internationales Einheitsrecht, at 148.
299. *Cf. Schmitthoff*, RabelsZ 28 (1964), at 72.
300. *Cf. Berger*, RIW 1989, at 850, 852.
301. *Cf. Domke*, Festschrift A. Bülow, at 49 *et seq.*
302. *See Berger*, J.Int'l Arb., No. 4 1992, at 5 *et seq.*
303. *Cf.* for the interrelation between the publication of arbitral awards and the self-control of arbitrators *Moehle v. Hoffmannswaldau*, TranspR 1990, at 15.

growing inclination to refer to the decisions of other arbitral bodies as precedents. Even though this precedential value of arbitral awards does not (yet) have the quality of court precedents[304], the substantial factual precedential value which arbitral awards enjoy today justifies the assumption that a 'crypto-system of precedents'[305] is developing within the international arbitral system. But also, in a more general context, the psychological factors which lend persuasive authority to court precedents operate in the case of arbitral awards[306]. As the arbitral case law becomes more extensive, the ideas and concepts contained therein are regarded as valuable knowledge by other international arbitrators. Arbitrators, therefore, tend to regard awards rendered by other arbitrators in related cases as veritable precedents, which are consequently put on an equal footing with the decisions of state courts. An international arbitral tribunal composed of highly renowned comparative lawyers and academics has described this development in the following words:

> 'The decisions of these tribunals progressively create case law which should be taken into account, because it draws conclusions from economic reality and conforms to the needs of international commerce, to which rules specific to international arbitration, themselves successively elaborated should respond'[307].

This practice has reached a new dimension in recent years. There is an increasing tendency of international arbitrators to refer to published arbitral awards *rather* than to relevant court decisions to justify their holding or to reject the allegations and legal views of the parties[308].

The habits, convictions, and constraints on which this particular decision-making practice of international arbitrators is based have led to a hierarchy of arbitral awards. Since arbitral awards are often published together with the names of the arbitrators who have rendered them, their authority and reputation serves to create a certain ranking of arbitral awards within the extensive arbitral case law[309]. In addition, many awards are known not only for the names of the arbitrators who have rendered them, but also for the basic considerations on important issues of

---

304. *Schütze*, Festschrift Glossner, at 333, 339 speaks of a 'prejudicial effect in a wider sense'; *cf. also Kaufmann-Kohler*, Arb.Int'l 2005, at 631 *et seq.*
305. *Cf.* for this observation in relation to state courts *Hedemann*, Reichsgericht und Wirtschaftsrecht, at 287 *et seq.*
306. *Cf. Lando*, in: Festschrift Zweigert, at 157, 159; *Cremades*, in: Horn (ed.), Legal Problems of Codes of Conduct for Multinational Enterprises, at 87; *Paulsson*, Rev.d'Arb. 1990, at 56, 76 *et seq.*; *Siehr*, in: Holl/Klinke (eds.), Internationales Privatrecht, Internationales Wirtschaftsrecht, at 123 *et seq.*; *Rubino-Sammartano*, International Arbitration, at 78 *et seq.*; *Lalive*, Rev.d'Arb. 1986, at 333; *Norton*, AJIL 1991, at 474, 505; *Berger*, International Economic Arbitration, at 522 *et seq.*
307. ICC Award No. 4131 (*Dow Chemical France et al. v. ISOVER Saint Gobain*), YCA 1984, at 131, 136.
308. *Cf. e.g.* for the interpretation of Art. 67 FIDIC *Berger*, J.Int'l Arb., No. 4 1992, at 5, 20 and the ICC Award No. 5277, YCA 1988, at 80, 85.
309. *Berger, see supra* note 283, *id.*

international commercial law on which they are based, thus attaching additional precedential value to them[310].

These developments within the international arbitral system have had a considerable impact on the evolution of the NLM. A legal system that is based on a functional methodology and on a case-by-case analysis of its principles and rules is dependent upon the belief that its 'court' decisions will serve as precedents for future disputes, similar to the *stare decisis* doctrine of common law court systems[311]. The increasing mutual reference of international arbitral tribunals, the critical analysis and acceptance, modification or rejection of legal ideas, institutions or values within the context of international commercial arbitration, is gradually leading to the coordination of those legal principles, rules and notions which form the basis of the NLM. This development has been intensified by the increasing scientific discussion of individual arbitral awards[312].

All of these developments serve to justify *Langen's* thesis that 'theory should finally take account of arbitration which has become rampant in the past'[313]. Today, this view derives its justification both from arbitral practice and legal theory. From the practical perspective, the flexibility and autonomy of the arbitral system which, in the eyes of its critics, lie at the root of all the problems and developments described above, are firmly based upon the will of the parties as the creators of the international arbitral system. From the perspective of legal theory, the above developments are a natural consequence of the general observation that substantive and procedural law are always intertwined and interconnected in any adjudicatory process, be it before domestic courts or before international arbitral tribunals[314]. This cross-fertilization of procedural (arbitration) law and substantive (transnational) law is the major reason why international arbitration is of paramount importance for the creation and evolution of the NLM. The flexibility and '*souplesse*' of the international arbitral process not only allows the arbitrators to take account of the interests and economic realities of the case, but also leaves enough room and leeway for the arbitrators to 'detect' principles and rules of transnational law within this flexible procedural framework[315]. At the same time, these arbitrators, being aware of their enormous responsibility *vis-à-vis* the parties in particular and the transnational commercial community in general,

310. *Cf. Schütze/Tscherning/Wais*, Handbuch des Schiedsverfahrens, Nos. 14 *et seq.*; *Schütze*, Festschrift Glossner, at 333 *et seq.* who refers to the *Aramco* and *Sojusneftexport* Awards; *Berger, supra* note 283, *id.*

311. *Steindorff*, in: UNIDROIT (ed.), New Directions in International Trade Law, at 87, 101.

312. *Cf. e.g. Rabe*, TranspR 1989, at 356; *Rabe*, TranspR 1990, at 15 *et seq.*; *Moehle v. Hoffmanswaldau*, TranspR 1990, at 15.

313. *Langen*, Transnationales Recht, Part I, No. 10 (translation by the author).

314. *Cf. Zöllner*, AcP 1990, at 471, 482 *et seq.*

315. *Cf. Schmitthoff*, International Trade Usages, 1987, No. 71: 'Substantive law is often born in the womb of procedure. In keeping with their international character, the law which these international arbitral bodies create is transnational. It is the new lex mercatoria'; *Fouchard*, L'Arbitrage Commercial International, at 401 *et seq.*; *Berman/Dasser*, in: Carbonneau (ed.), Lex Mercatoria and Arbitration, at 53, 65 *et seq.*; *Langen*, NJW 1969, at 358, 359; *Stein*, Lex mercatoria, at 254; *Goode*, ICLQ 1997, at 1, 6.

create their own control standards which supply the transnational legal system, the NLM, with the necessary legitimacy.

E. THE NEW *LEX MERCATORIA* RESULTS IN THE CIRCUMVENTION OF PROVISIONS WITH ORDRE PUBLIC QUALITY

Those who deny the existence of an autonomous transnational commercial law claim that the NLM allows the parties to circumvent the mandatory *ordre public* provisions of the 'otherwise applicable law'. In their eyes, this problem is aggravated by the fact that the NLM does not itself contain provisions of *ordre public* quality[316]. This view is based on the concern that arbitral decisions based solely on an autonomous transnational commercial law may evade the socio-economic values and policy decisions which stand behind mandatory provisions of domestic law that has an *ordre public* quality.

These concerns have to be viewed from two different perspectives. First, those who raise these concerns in order to uphold the notion of consumer protection (NLM as a 'means to dominate the weak party'[317]) misunderstand the true quality of transnational commercial law. Transnational commercial law, like the UNIDROIT Principles[318], does not apply to consumer contracts. Secondly, those who intend to safeguard the general notion of *ordre public* inherent in any domestic legal system likewise misunderstand the true quality of the NLM. One has to bear in mind that parties to an international contract may choose a law that has no connection with the transaction[319], thereby derogating from the mandatory rules of the 'otherwise applicable domestic law'[320]. The requirement set up by English[321] and Swiss[322] courts in the past that the law chosen by the parties needs to have some 'sensible connection' with the case, has long since been abandoned. In addition, given the uncertainties of conflict of laws methodology described above[323], it is difficult to speak of an 'otherwise applicable law'.

This does not mean, however, that mandatory provisions of third legal systems are irrelevant in the context of private international law. Based on *Savigny's* ideas[324], contemporary doctrine has developed special rules to deal with those

316. *Cf. Sandrock*, in: Böckstiegel (ed.), Rechtsfortbildung durch internationale Schiedsgerichte, at 56; *Sandrock*, Am.Rev.Int'l Arb. 1992, at 30, 34 *et seq.*; *van Hecke*, Internationaal Privaatrecht, No. 860.
317. *Cf. Bonell*, in: UNIDROIT (ed.), New Directions in International Trade Law, at 109, 129; *cf. also* the note by *von Hippel*, reported by *Remien*, RabelsZ 56 (1992), at 300, 303.
318. *Cf. infra* Chapter 4 I.A.6.b.
319. *Cf.* Soergel-*Kegel*, EGBGB, vor Art. 7, No. 331.
320. *Cf.* already *Langen*, Transnationales Recht, Part I, No. 8.
321. *See Vita Food Products, Inc. v. Unus Shipping Co. Ltd.*, [1939] A.C. 277.
322. *See* the decision rendered by the Swiss Federal Tribunal BGE 91 II 44, 51, requiring a 'reasonable interest' of the parties in the application of the law chosen by them.
323. *Cf. supra* Chapter 1 I.A.
324. *von Savigny*, System des heutigen Römischen Rechts, Vol. 8, at 33 *et seq.*

mandatory provisions of third legal systems which, due to their inherent economic values, apply to a contract irrespective of the *lex causae* (*'lois d'application immédiate'*; *'lois de police'*[325]). It is of primary importance that the NLM doctrine takes account of these important developments, since principles of international public policy even override trade usages[326]. A major weakness of transnational commercial law is that it is developed by international commercial practice even though this practice does not necessarily meet the ethical and socio-economic standards of modern society[327]. '[I]n the absence of any "*ius cogens*" international trade would be ruled by jungle law'[328].

This objection may be addressed through two different perspectives. From a progressive point of view, it may be questioned as to whether the existence of such rules requires the assumption of a mere 'relative' autonomy of transnational commercial law which remains dependent upon the application of such *'lois d'application immédiate'*. In spite of their quality as 'soft law', the various Codes of Conduct drafted by international organizations[329] provide evidence for the existence of a uniform ethical understanding in international commercial affairs[330]. This mass of ethical and moral rules and principles may be used to provide the NLM with the necessary ethical underpinnings[331]. In doing so, the doctrine of a transnational commercial law is supplemented by the creation of an a-national, *i.e.* transnational *ordre public* (*'ordre public réellement international'*)[332].

325. *Cf. Berger*, Acts of State and Arbitration: Exchange Control Regulations, in: Böckstiegel (ed.), Acts of State and Arbitration, at 99, 110 *et seq.*; *Horn*, SchiedsVZ 2008, at 209 *et seq.*; *Schiffer*, Normen ausländischen 'öffentlichen' Rechts in internationalen Handelsschiedsverfahren, at 44 *et seq.*; *Drobnig*, Festschrift Kegel, at 95 *et seq.*; *Juenger*, Festschrift Rittner, at 233 *et seq.*
326. *Goode*, ICLQ 1997, at 1, 18.
327. *Horn*, in: Horn (ed.), Legal Problems of Codes of Conduct for Multinational Enterprises, at 45, 61; *Goldman*, contribution to the discussion, in: UNIDROIT (ed.), New Directions in International Trade Law, at 498, 499.
328. *Tallon*, cited by *Kropholler*, IPR, § 52 II.3.e) (at 464).
329. *Cf.* OECD Declaration On International Investment and Multinational Enterprises of June 21, 1967 and its various revisions, reprinted in: Horn (ed.), Codes of Conduct, at 45 *et seq.*; ILO, Tripartite Declaration of Principles Concerning Multinational Enterprises and Social Policy of 1977, UN Doc. E/C.10/AC.2/3 (Annex II); Code of Conduct on Transnational Corporations, last draft of June 2, 1983, UN ESCOR Doc. E/C.10/1983/S/5.
330. *Langen*, Studien zum Internationalen Wirtschaftsrecht, Nos. 24 *et seq.*
331. *Horn, see supra* note 327, *id.*; *Horn*, AöR 1985, at 398, 409: 'basically, the international ordre public formulated in the universally accepted soft law constitutes the modern version of a common Christian ethical standard' (translation by the author); *Goldman*, Festschrift Lalive, at 241, 252; *A. Bucher*, in: Schwind (ed.), Aktuelle Fragen zum Europarecht, at 11, 55 *et seq.*; *Kassis*, Théorie Générale des Usages de Commerce International, at 473 *et seq.*; *Lalive*, Rev.d'Arb. 1986, at 329 *et seq.*; *Dasser*, Internationale Schiedsgerichte und Lex Mercatoria, at 11 *et seq.*, 100; *Struycken*, in: Journées René Savatier, at 207, 223; *cf. also Schlesinger*, Am.J.Int'l L. 1957, at 734, 745 *et seq.*; *see generally* for the development of 'soft law' into *ius cogens* of public international law *Shihata*, Legal Treatment of Foreign Investment: 'The World Bank Guidelines', at 42.
332. *Goldman*, contribution to the discussion, in: UNIDROIT (ed.), New Directions in International Trade Law, at 498, 499; *cf. also Stein*, Lex mercatoria, at 241, 250.

Admittedly, the existence of such an a-national notion of public policy is still vividly disputed. But even on the basis of the traditional approach, the NLM doctrine does not serve to circumvent the public interests and policy decisions underlying provisions of domestic law with public policy quality. Arbitrators who apply the NLM, as if they applied any domestic law, have to take account of those provisions of domestic law which need to be applied to a given case irrespective of the *lex causae*. Arbitrators who evade this task run the risk of threatening the legitimacy of the NLM:

> 'If the arbitrator evades the task of implementing the notions of fairness and justice reflected in these [mandatory] norms, this task will necessarily be taken over by the domestic courts. They will try to counterbalance this development through non-recognition of arbitral awards. In other words, if arbitral tribunals do not adhere to the demands of international fairness and justice, they put into question the validity of their own decisions . . . This task also serves to provide legitimacy to the arbitral process as such and strengthens the confidence in the fairness of this institution. One should not assume that ethical aspects and the notion of responsibility towards international commerce do not play a role in the arbitrators' decision-making'[333].

Regardless of whether the arbitrator applies domestic or transnational law, international comparative studies and arbitral practice have developed criteria under which mandatory norms of third legal systems must be applied irrespective of the *lex contractus*:

(1) The provision in question must be qualified as a mandatory norm.
(2) The prerequisites of this norm have to be met.
(3) The legislature wants the provision to be applied irrespective of which law is applicable to the contract.
(4) There must be a 'close' connection between the contract and the jurisdiction that has promulgated the provision.
(5) The contents of the provision, *i.e.* the socio-political values and policy considerations inherent in it, must be in accordance with the general opinion of the international community of states ('shared values'–test)[334].

From this traditional conflict of laws perspective, the NLM is put on an equal footing with any domestic law[335], thereby underlining its quality as an independent, autonomous legal system.

333. *See Juenger*, in: Festschrift Rittner 1991, at 233, 249 (translation by the author); *see also* ICC Award No. 2216, Clunet 1974, at 917.
334. *Cf.* for details *Berger*, International Economic Arbitration, at 690 *et seq.*; *Berger*, in: Herrmann/Berger/Wackerbarth (eds.), Deutsches und Internationales Bank- und Wirtschaftsrecht im Wandel, at 322, 330; *Berger*, ZVglRWiss 96 (1997), at 316 *et seq.*
335. *Cf. Grundmann*, Jahrbuch Junger Zivilrechtswissenschaftler 1991, at 43, 49.

F. Domestic Legislatures and Courts Do Not Acknowledge the New *Lex Mercatoria*

Those who oppose the doctrine of transnational commercial law argue that domestic legislatures and courts show a traditional hostility towards any attempt to transnationalize the application of the law in an international commercial context[336].

1. The Classical Conflict of Laws Doctrine Does Not Accept the Idea of the Transnationalization of Commercial Law

Those who follow this view can refer to a considerable number of decisions of the highest European courts cited above[337] and to general principles of private international law. Among these principles is the *Magna Charta* of conflict of laws which states that domestic courts may not apply a-national law. In applying the conflict of laws provisions of their *lex fori*, the domestic courts have to ensure that the case before them is governed by substantive domestic law instead of vague notions of an a-national NLM[338]. Also, the parties themselves may not exclude the application of any domestic law through a 'negative choice of law'[339]. From this perspective, the relevance of the NLM doctrine within the traditional conflict of laws system is limited to the effect that the decision on the applicable law may be left open if the application of all legal systems which bear a connection to the case before the judge would lead to the same result[340].

2. Approximation of Traditional Conflict of Laws Doctrine and Transnational Law

a. Approximation in the Field of International Commercial Arbitration

Various developments of the recent past have shown that the NLM doctrine and classical conflict of laws principles are no longer regarded as being as

336. *Triebel/Petzold*, RIW 1988, at 246; *Schödermeier*, Sonderprivatrecht für internationale Wirtschaftsverträge, at 142; *Schlosser*, RIW 1982, at 857, 867: 'So far no court in the world has recognized something like the lex mercatoria as the basis of its decision' (translation by the author).
337. *Cf. supra* note 90.
338. *Bonell*, RabelsZ 42 (1978), at 485, 495; *von Hoffmann/Thorn*, IPR, § 10, No. 28; *Kropholler*, IPR, § 12 I.3 *in fine* (at 100); *A. Bucher*, in: Schwind (ed.), Aktuelle Fragen zum Europarecht aus der Sicht in- und ausländischer Gelehrter, at 11, 55; *Martiny*, in: Reithmann/Martiny (eds.), Internationales Vertragsrecht, No. 73; *von Bar/Mankowski*, IPR, Vol. 1, § 2 No. 86; MünchKomm-*Sonnenberger*, EGBGB, Introduction No. 268; *van Hecke*, Internationaal Privaatrecht, No. 696.
339. *Bonell*, Uniform Law and Party Autonomy: What is Wrong with the Current Approach?, in: UNIDROIT (ed.), International Uniform Law in Practice, 1988, at 433; *Heini*, IPRG-Kommentar, Art. 187, No. 9.
340. MünchKomm-*Sonnenberger*, EGBGB, Introduction No. 271.

irreconcilable, as they were twenty years ago[341]. The major reason for the approximation of traditional private international law and NLM lies in the increasing sophistication of international arbitral practice and legislation. For more than a decade, international arbitrators have been freed from the constraints of domestic substantive law[342]. Those legislatures who have modernized their arbitration laws in recent years and the drafters of the UNCITRAL Model Law on International Commercial Arbitration[343] have included special conflict of laws rules in their laws which allow the arbitrator to apply the 'rules of law' (*'règles du droit'*; *'Rechtsvorschriften'*; *'regelen des rechts'*) instead of 'the law'[344]. It is generally recognized in international legal doctrine and arbitral practice that this terminology indicates that arbitrators may apply transnational legal principles such as the NLM[345]. The Dutch legislature has even indicated the parties' option to have the NLM applied to their contract in the official *travaux préparatoires* of the 1986 Netherlands' Arbitration Act. To support this view a reference was made to a similar provision of the French Decree on International Arbitration of 1981[346]. In view of its value as a standard point of reference for every comparative research in the field of international commercial arbitration[347], Art. 28(1) of the UNCITRAL Model Law which was incorporated into German law on January 1, 1998[348], provides sufficient indication of a general global tendency of domestic legislatures to accept the application of transnational law in the context of international commercial arbitration, provided that the parties to the contract have

341. *See generally Lando*, in: Festskrift till Stig Strömholm, at 567, 570 *et seq.*
342. *Kropholler*, Internationales Einheitsrecht, at 158.
343. The Model Law was recommended to its Member States for transformation by the General Assembly of the United Nations on December 11, 1985. GA Res. 40/72, O.U.N. GAOR Supp. (No. 53), at 308, UN Doc. A/4053 (1985); the Model Law has by now been adopted by a multitude of states throughout the world; *see* for the draft of the German arbitration law adopting the Model Law *supra* Chapter 4 I.A.6.a.; *cf. generally* for details of the Model Law *Calavros*, Das UNCITRAL-Modellgesetz über die internationale Handelsschiedsgerichtsbarkeit; *Hußlein-Stich*, Das UNCITRAL-Modellgesetz über die internationale Handelsschiedsgerichtsbarkeit; *Granzow*, Das UNCITRAL-Modellgesetz über die internationale Handelsschiedsgerichtsbarkeit von 1985.
344. Article 1496 of the French n.c.p.c.; Art. 1054 Secs. 1 and 2 of the new Netherlands Arbitration Act of 1986; Art. 187 Sec. 1 of the new Swiss Law on Private International Law (official French version); *cf. Heini/Keller/Siehr/Vischer/Volken-Heini*, IPRG-Kommentar, Art. 1987, No. 7); Art. 12 Djibouti Code on International Arbitration; Art. 28 Sec. 1 of the UNCITRAL Model Law for International Commercial Arbitration (in case of choice of law by the parties); *cf. Berger*, Internationale Wirtschaftsschiedsgerichtsbarkeit, at 385 *et seq.*
345. *Redfern/Hunter* on International Arbitration, Nos. 3.194 *et seq.*; *Delaume*, Transnational Contracts, 1988, at 32 *et seq.*; *Schmitthoff*, International Trade Usages, No. 73 *in fine*; *Loquin*, Clunet 1983, at 293, 305; *Gaillard*, in: van den Berg (ed.), Planning Efficient Arbitration Proceedings – The Law Applicable in International Arbitration, ICCA Congress Ser. No. 7, at 570, 581; *Lando*, in: Šarčević (ed.), International Commercial Arbitration, 1989, at 129, 154; *Dasser*, Lex Mercatoria, at 347; *Goode*, ICLQ 1997, at 1, 32.
346. *Cf.* Memorie van Toelichting, TvA 1987, at 40.
347. *Cf. Gaillard*, in: Sanders (ed.), ICCA Congress Ser. No. 4, at 283, 284 ('standard point of reference').
348. *See Berger*, Int'l Arb.Rev. 1998, at 121 *et seq.*

chosen a-national legal principles as the *lex causae*. It is for this reason that the UNIDROIT Working Group stated in the Preamble of the Principles of International Commercial Contracts that they may be applied 'when the parties have agreed that their contract be governed by general principles of law, the *lex mercatoria* or the like'. The official UNIDROIT commentary states that this terminology gives the parties the freedom to chose the Principles as the 'rules of law' according to which the arbitrators would decide the dispute, thereby excluding any national law[349].

Unfortunately, the same liberal view does not apply in those cases where the parties have not made a choice of (transnational) law. In these cases, there seem to be good arguments for the mandatory application of domestic law only[350]. Thus, absent a choice of law by the parties, Art. 28(2) of the UNCITRAL Model Law demands that the arbitrators determine the applicable 'law' and not the 'rules of law'. On the other hand, conflict of laws provisions in domestic arbitration laws allow the arbitrators to apply 'rules of law' even in those cases where the parties have not made a decision as to the applicable law. The official *travaux préparatoires* of the Dutch Arbitration Act follow the same view[351].

In spite of their ostensibly different approaches to the transnationalization of the law-finding process in international commercial arbitration, these two views are not irreconcilable. Allowing the arbitrators to determine 'the law' was not meant to prevent any transnational considerations within the arbitrators' 'law-finding process'. Similarly to the deliberations of the UNCITRAL Arbitration Rules[352] the drafters of the Model Law took this cautious approach to protect the parties from any arbitrary choice-of-law decisions of the tribunal[353]. The UNCITRAL Secretariat agreed that the parties can widen the scope of the arbitral tribunals' determination of the applicable law and that the term 'law' should be interpreted in a broad sense, taking account of recent developments in international economic arbitration[354]. This general concern of the UNCITRAL Working Group is in line with the efforts of international doctrine to determine the limits of the application of transnational law in order to prevent any misuse to the detriment of one of the parties of the arbitration[355]. Admittedly, there is a need in international arbitral practice for such a cautious approach to the application of transnational law where the parties have not chosen their own law. International arbitral tribunals

349. *Cf. UNIDROIT* (ed.), Principles of International Commercial Contracts, at 3.
350. *Samuel*, Jurisdictional Problems in International Commercial Arbitration, at 241 *et seq.*; *von Hoffmann*, IPRax 1984, at 107; *Tschanz*, RDAI 1988, at 448.
351. *Cf.* Memorie van Toelichting, *see supra* note 346, *id.*, where reference is made to Art. 1496 of the French n.c.p.c., stating that: 'According to French practice, the arbitrators may apply the lex mercatoria which, in principal, does not have the quality of domestic law'; reference is made to *Delvolvé*, Arbitration in France, at 30, note 46; in this footnote, Delvolvé states that the parties 'may free themselves from any reference to domestic law (*lex mercatoria*)'.
352. *Cf. Klein*, Festschrift Mann, at 617, 638 ('*souci de sécurité*').
353. *Cf.* UN Doc. A/CN.9/264, para. 5.
354. UN Doc. A/CN.9/SR.326, para. 33; *Berger*, International Economic Arbitration, at 559.
355. *Kropholler*, IPR, § 12 I.3 (at 100).

sometimes prematurely resort to the application of transnational law in situations where no law has been chosen by the parties simply because of the international character of the contract[356] and the high competence of transnational law for the resolution of international disputes[357].

These practical problems, however, may not serve as a general objection to the theory of a transnational commercial law. Many of the awards in which arbitrators have had resort to transnational law were rendered in the context of 'state contracts', where the sovereignty of one of the parties involved and the stabilization clause and other clauses contained in the contract justified the 'internationalization' of the contractual relationship[358]. In other areas of international commercial law the premature application of the NLM is evidence that arbitrators, like the judges of domestic courts, may go astray in the application of conflict of laws principles. Sometimes, these mistakes are induced not so much by the negligence of the arbitrators themselves, but by the domestic legislatures that have gone too far in the liberalization of conflict of laws for international arbitrators. It is particularly telling in this respect that the arbitral tribunal in the *Compañía Valenciana* case misinterpreted the parties' intention to have transnational principles of law applied to their contract. The tribunal was acting under the liberal conflict of laws provisions[359] of the French international arbitration law, which allows the arbitrator to determine the applicable law absent a choice of law by the parties by way of the '*voie directe*', *i.e.* without applying any conflict of laws considerations. The tribunal's decision may also have been influenced by the view of *Berthold Goldman*, the *spiritus rector* of the NLM doctrine, who maintains that the international

356. *Cf. e.g.* ICC Award No. 3572 *Deutsche Schachtbau- und Tiefbohrgesellschaft mbH et al. v. The Government of the State of R' as Al Khaimah and The R' as Al Khaimah Oil Company (Rakoil)*, YCA 1989, at 111 *et seq.*, where the arbitral tribunal decided that the application of the law of one of the parties on the *Operating Agreement* 'would be inappropriate for various reasons' and the dispute should therefore be decided on the basis of '*internationally accepted principles of law governing contractual relations*'; *see* for a comment on this decision *Lando*, in: Festskrift till Stig Strömholm, at 567, 577; *cf. also Sapphire International Petroleums Ltd. v. National Iranian Oil Company*, International Law Reports 1967, at 136, 172 ('If no positive implication can be made from the arbitral clause, it is possible to find there a negative intention, namely to reject the exclusive application of Iranian law'); *TEXACO Overseas Petroleum Company (TOPCO)/California Asiatic Oil Company (CALASIATIC) v. The Government of the Libyan Arab Republic*, ILM 1978, at 1, 16: 'It is therefore unquestionable that the reference to international arbitration is sufficient to internationalize a contract, in other words, to situate it within a specific legal order – the order of international law of contracts'; the arbitrator based his decision also on the stabilization clause contained in the contract, which, in his view, indicated clearly and unambiguously the parties' intention '*to remove all or part of the agreement from the internal law*'), *id.*, at 17; ICC Award No. 5953 (Partial Award), *Primary Coal Inc. (USA) v. Compañía Valenciana de Cementos Portland*, Rev.d'Arb. 1990, at 701, 711.
357. *Goldman*, Festschrift Lalive, at 241, 250 *et seq.*
358. *Cf.* only *Sandrock/Steinschulte*, Handbuch der Internationalen Vertragsgestaltung, Vol. 1, at 10 *et seq.*; *cf. generally Kischel*, State Contracts.
359. Article 1496 n.c.p.c.: 'The arbitrator decides the dispute according to the rules of law chosen by the parties; absent such choice, the arbitrator decides according to the rules of law which he considers appropriate'.

character of the contract in itself justifies the application of transnational legal principles[360]. This liberal approach is also reflected in the 'Resolution on Transnational Legal Principles' adopted by the International Law Association (ILA) at its 65th Conference on April 26, 1992, in Cairo. It states that the validity or enforceability of an arbitral award based on transnational legal rules should not be questioned if 'the parties have remained silent concerning the applicable law'[361]. Art. 1.101(3)(b) of the *Lando* 'Principles of European Contract Law' provides that these Principles may be applied 'when the parties have not chosen any system or rules of law to govern their contract'. The official commentary justifies this approach by arguing that the Principles are much more able to provide solutions for international commercial conflicts than any domestic law and that this particular quality of the Principles is sufficient to justify their application in a given case even without a choice by the parties[362]. This view is drawn to its extreme by *Langen* who maintains that the mere participation of legal advisors with international experience during the negotiations of a contract justifies the application of transnational legal principles and rules:

> '. . . It is undisputed between the parties that no consensus has been reached on the applicable law even though this question has been the subject of negotiations. In addition, this is clear from the fact that attorneys from both sides have been involved in the conclusion of the contract. The arbitral tribunal cannot assume that one of the attorneys or even both have failed to inform the parties of the need to discuss this question'[363].

There is a substantial danger inherent in this approach. Equating the parties' failure to include a choice-of-law clause in their contract with the positive choice of transnational legal principles tends to endanger the legitimacy of the NLM doctrine in that it neglects the complex network of interests involved in international contract negotiations. The lack of a choice-of-law clause may be due to a number of reasons, none of which necessarily indicating the parties' intention to 'transnationalize' their contract. For example, the equal bargaining position of the parties or

---

360. *Goldman*, Clunet 1990, at 433, 440: '*S'il est vrai, en effet, que la désignation de la lex mercatoria implique nécessairement une qualification de la matière litigieuse, elle découle immédiatement de cette qualification, lorsque celle-ci fait apparaître que le contract (ou le délit) s'inscrit dans les relations économiques internationales. La méthode est théoriquement conflictuelle, mais elle échappe aux incertitudes et aux complexités du fonctionnement de la règle de conflit, lorsque celle-ci est utilisée dans son domaine traditionnel, pour désigner une loi nationale*'.
361. *Cf.* the 'Resolution on Transnational Rules Adopted at the 65th International Law Association Conference in Cairo on April 26, 1992', reprinted in: Gaillard (ed.), Transnational Rules in International Commercial Arbitration, at 247; *see also Lando*, in: Festskrift till Stig Strömholm, at 567, 578.
362. *Cf. Lando/Beale* (eds.), The Principles of European Contract Law, at 42.
363. *See* the reasoning in a (fictitious) award reported by *Langen*, Studien zum Internationalen Wirtschaftsrecht, No. 15c (translation by the author).

their conviction that the issue of the applicable law does not require a stipulation in the contract, may have caused the parties to omit a choice-of-law clause:

> 'Although they did, indeed, deliberately keep silent on the applicable law, it was because they thought that, when the time came, the arbitrator would make a choice between the possible municipal laws, which seldom exceed two.
>
> In other words, the parties deliberately took the risk that the arbitrator would choose the law of their contracting partner or at worse that of a third country linked through law with the contract. The parties did not generally take the risk that the arbitrator would make a break with all municipal law. It is often through a misunderstanding of negotiation that some arbitrators take it for granted that, where the contract is silent, they should refrain from selecting a municipal law since they would, in such a case, be doing exactly what the parties had decided not to do. In any event, it would be the proper policy, before reaching a decision, for the arbitrator to get the parties to explain what they expect'[364].

There may also be more psychological reasons for omitting a choice-of-law clause. Not mentioning the law applicable to the contract may be a way to preserve the prestige of a party whose domestic law would be excluded from application through a choice-of-law clause[365]. Finally, state parties have always been reluctant to agree to the application of foreign law which is regarded as a violation of their sovereign rights[366].

The 'plurilocalization'[367] of international contracts *alone*, combined with an arbitration clause, may not be equated with an automatic application of transnational legal rules and principles to a contract[368]. Instead, the judge or arbitrator faced with the absence of an express or implied choice of law by the parties should look for positive, objective criteria which justify the application of transnational law. To achieve this, the arbitrator or judge has to ascertain whether 'the parties, fully aware of the necessity to find an agreement as to the applicable law have created a sphere totally detached from any domestic law'[369]. These subjective criteria have to be accompanied by objective circumstantial proof indicating the need to apply transnational law. For example, the special character of the legal problems involved which would be difficult to solve under domestic law[370] or the

364. *Robine*, J.Int'l Arb., No. 2 1992, at 31, 36.
365. *Kropholler*, IPR, at § 52 II 1 (at 460).
366. *Delaume*, Law and Practice of Transnational Contracts, 1988, § 1.02.
367. *I.e.* the necessary connection with more than one jurisdiction, *see Kassis*, Théorie Générale des Usages du Commerce, at 394.
368. *See Böckstiegel*, in: Gaillard (ed.), Transnational Rules in International Commercial Arbitration, at 49; *Berger*, IPRax 1993, at 281, 287 *et seq.*; *Raeschke-Kessler*, in: Institute of International Business Law and Practice (ed.), The UNIDROIT Principles of International Commercial Contracts – A New Lex Mercatoria?, at 167, 170; *cf. also* ICC Award No. 5118, in: Jarvin/Derains/Arnaldez (eds.), Collection of ICC Arbitral Awards 1986–1990, at 318 with approving note *Jarvin, id.*, at 319, 320; No. 6500, Clunet 1992, at 1015 *et seq.*
369. *Langen*, Studien zum Internationalen Wirtschaftsrecht, No. 15c; *Berger, id.*
370. *Cf. e.g.* for the inadequacy of domestic copyright law to resolve complex problems of international computer software disputes the *IBM Corp. v. Fujitsu* arbitration, which was of

conduct of the parties during the long-lasting contract negotiations may provide sufficient and clear evidence of the parties' rejection of any domestic law[371]. Thus, in the ICC Award No. 8365, the parties' agreement to have their (guarantee) contract governed by 'international law' was considered by the arbitral tribunal to express the clear will of the parties not to have any national law applied to their contract. At the same time, the tribunal considered this terminology an implied choice of 'the usages of international commerce and the general principles of law (lex mercatoria)'[372]. Also, the NLM may not be applied where the contract shows a clear connection to a particular domestic legal system[373].

The phenomenon of a 'negative choice of law' and the related problem of a premature application of the NLM therefore do not necessarily justify an outright rejection of the theory of transnational commercial law. Instead, they make it necessary to reiterate the practical importance of the transnational approach for international contract drafting. In those cases where the parties are unable to reach an agreement on the applicable law, they should have resort to general principles of law, the NLM or the like, and indicate this choice in their contract. This would avoid any uncertainty when it comes to a conflict about the contractual rights and duties[374]. Even in those cases where the parties – unaware of these problems – have not made any precautions during the drafting process, international arbitrators should be allowed to apply transnational law absent a choice of law by the parties. For this reason, various legislatures that have adopted the UNCITRAL Model Law on International Commercial Arbitration have allowed arbitrators to apply the 'rules of law' in these cases, thereby opening the way for the application of the NLM[375].

b. *Approximation in the Field of Classical Conflict of Laws Doctrine*

The trend towards the universal recognition of the NLM is confirmed by a long line of court decisions that have accepted arbitral awards based on general principles of

---

particular relevance for the international software market due to the market power of the parties; *cf. Weidhaas/Swoboda*, CR 1988, at 104, 107 and the statement by the Lead- Counsel for *Fujitsu, Robert R. Raven*: 'Existing copyright doctrine is not particularly well-suited . . . to resolutions of computer software development issues'; *cf. also Bühring-Uhle*, Am.Rev.Int'l Arb. 1991, at 113 *et seq.*

371. *Berger*, IPRax 1993, at 281, 287; *cf. also Derains*, note to ICC Award No. 2438, Clunet 1976, at 971; *see also Mertens*, Festschrift Odersky, at 857 *et seq.*
372. ICC Award No. 8365, Clunet 1997, at 1078, 1079.
373. ICC Award No. 6500, Clunet 1992, at 1015 *et seq.*
374. *Langefeld-Wirth*, Joint Ventures, at 130; *Zweigert/von Hoffmann*, Festschrift M. Luther, at 203, 210 for joint venture agreements; *Allison/Coe*, Protecting Against The Expropriation Risk, § 2.03; *Bartels*, Contractual Adaptation, at 110 for investment contracts; *see* for service, licensing and credit contracts *Wälde*, J.Int'l L. & Pol. 1977/78, at 33, 66.
375. *Nöcker*, Das Recht der Schiedsgerichtsbarkeit in Kanada, at 14 *et seq.* for the arbitration law of the Canadian common law provinces.

transnational commercial law[376]. Based on these decisions, international legal doctrine has developed the view that an arbitral award, in which the arbitrators have followed the parties' agreement to apply the NLM, may not be set aside by domestic courts[377]. The situation is different, however, if the arbitrators have applied transnational law without the authorization of the parties. It is alleged that in such cases, domestic courts may set aside the ensuing award[378]. The awards rendered in these arbitrations are said to have assumed the quality of *ex aequo et bono* decisions without authority of the parties[379]. It is generally accepted that domestic courts may set aside arbitral awards when the arbitrators have rendered a decision in equity even though the parties have not authorized them to do so. In these cases, the arbitrators have violated the principle of party autonomy in that they have not followed the directions given to them by the parties[380].

As has been explained above[381], a decision based on the NLM may not be equated with a decision based on equity. Therefore, domestic courts may set aside these arbitral awards only in those rare cases where they are able to ascertain that the arbitrators have applied the 'wrong' law. In this context, the domestic courts

376. French Cour de Cassation, *Société Fougerolle v. Banque de Proche Orient*, Rev.d'Arb. 1982, at 183; Austrian Supreme Court, *NORSOLOR S. A. v. Pabalk Ticaret Ltd.* of November 18, 1982, YCA 1984, at 159; English *Court of Appeal, Deutsche Schachtbau- und Tiefbohrgesellschaft m.b.H. v. R' as al Khaimah National Oil Company* ('*Rakoil*') [1987] 2 Lloyd's L.Rep. at 246, 252; (*cf. Lalive*, ASA Bull. 1987, at 164 *et seq.*); Italian *Corte di Cassazione, Fratelli Damiano s.n.c. v. August Töpfer GmbH*, Rdipp. 1982, at 529; Cour d'Appel Paris of July 13, 1989, *Compañía Valenciana de Cementos Portland v. Primary Coal*, Rev.d'Arb. 1990, at 663 with note *Lagarde, id.*, at 666 *et seq.* (= Clunet 1990, at 430 *et seq.* with note *Goldman, id.*, at 433 *et seq.*); Cour de Cassation of October 22, 1991, *Société Compañía Valenciana de Cementos Portland v. Société Primary Coal Inc.*, Rev.d'Arb. 1992, at 457 with note *Lagarde; id.*, at 458 *et seq.*; *cf. generally Mertens*, Festschrift Odersky, at 857 *et seq.*
377. *Martiny*, in: Reithmann/Martiny (eds.), Internationales Vertragsrecht, No. 73 *in fine*; *Samuel*, Jurisdictional Problems in International Commercial Arbitration, at 255; *Lagarde*, in: Etudes offertes à Berthold Goldman, at 148; *Lando*, in: Šarčević (ed.), Essays in International Commercial Arbitration, at 154; *Dasser*, Lex Mercatoria, at 297 (for the UNCITRAL Model Law), at 303 (for German law), at 320 (for Dutch law), at 340 (for Swiss law).
378. This is the prevailing opinion in German legal doctrine, *cf. Schlosser*, Das Recht der internationalen privaten Schiedsgerichtsbarkeit, No. 863; *von Bar/Mankowski*, IPR, Vol. 1, § 2 No. 85; *von Hoffmann*, IPRax 1984, at 108; *Gottwald*, Festschrift Nagel, at 65; *Schlosser*, RIW 1982, at 867; *Raeschke-Kessler*, NJW 1988, at 3048; *Triebel/Petzold*, RIW 1988, at 249; *cf.* for Swiss law *A. Bucher*, Die neue internationale Schiedsgerichtsbarkeit in der Schweiz, No. 292 *in fine*; *Tschanz*, RDAI 1988, at 448; *cf. also van Hecke*, Internationaal Privaatrecht, note 860; *Klein*, Festschrift Mann, at 617, 622 *et seq.*
379. *Cf. von Bar/Mankowski*, IPR, Vol. 1, § 2 No. 85, who, following the prevailing view in German legal doctrine, transforms the parties' agreement to decide according to the *lex mercatoria* into an agreement for an *amiable composition*, thus shielding the award from any court review; *cf. also Kappus*, RIW 1990, at 793.
380. *Cf.* the German Federal Supreme Court in BGHZ 96, 40, 45; OLG Frankfurt, RIW 1984, at 400, 401; Swiss Federal Tribunal BGE 110 Ia 57; *Schwab/Walter*, Schiedsgerichtsbarkeit, Ch. 24 No. 22.
381. *Cf. supra* B.2.a.

must respect the prerogative of the arbitrators in the determination of the applicable law. This limits court control to the truly evident, blatant cases[382].

The above considerations reveal that domestic legislatures and courts have shown a growing tendency to accept the application of the NLM in the context of international economic arbitration. This is highlighted in a decision of the Italian *Corte di Cassazione* of 1982 in which the Court stated:

> 'A law within which arbitration works independently of the laws of various states should be considered a transnational law. This is the case of the 'mercantile' law that exists through the adhesion of the business community to the values of its environment, through its conforming to those values induced by the opinio necessitatis that it has with regard to these values, i.e. the prevailing conviction that they are binding. Since the business community . . . agrees upon some basic values regarding its business and agrees upon the aforementioned opinio necessitatis (even for simply practical reasons) *we should admit that the lex mercatoria exists*'[383].

The question, however, whether these domestic courts themselves may apply transnational commercial law remains. A comparison of the terminology used in the conflict of laws rules for international arbitrators ('rules of law') with the terminology of classical conflict of laws provision of domestic laws ('law') seems to imply that this question has to be answered in the negative. A purely terminological approach, however, neglects the existing interactions between arbitral and court adjudication. In view of these interactions, it is hard to imagine that the important developments that have taken place in the past years in the field of international economic arbitration have not had any repercussions on the treatment of conflict of laws issues by domestic courts. It is possible, therefore, that in view of the far-reaching recognition of party autonomy in international contract law, domestic courts, in applying the domestic conflict of laws rules of their *lex fori*, allow parties to have transnational legal principles applied to their contract[384]. It is for this very reason that the local court of Grenoble has applied the UNIDROIT Principles to decide a contractual dispute[385].

This prognosis is supported by the various attempts that have been made in the past to achieve a transnationalization of the legal process within the traditional system of conflict of laws. *Rabel's* theory of an autonomous qualification in private international law provides a perfect example for these efforts. His idea was to qualify legal relationships for the purpose of conflict of laws not according to the

382. *Cf. Berger*, Internationale Wirtschaftsschiedsgerichtsbarkeit, at 484.

383. Italian Corte di Cassazione of February 8, 1982, Cass., 1982 Foro It. I, 2285, translated by *Galgano*, Ann.Surv. Int'l & Comp.L. 1995, at 99, 108, note 18 (emphasis added); *see also* the decision of the Commercial Court of Nantes of July 11, 1991, applying 'the general principles of law, usages of international trade, and the lex mercatoria', Clunet 1991, at 330; *see also Lando*, in: Festskrift till Stig Strömholm, at 567, 574.

384. *Martiny*, in: Reithmann/Martiny (eds.), Internationales Vertragsrecht, No. 73.

385. *See Bonell*, Unif.L.Rev. 1997, at 30, 37.

lex fori, but according to autonomous notions and principles that have been developed on the basis of comparative research[386]. *Rabel's* transnational approach had a substantial indirect influence on the work towards the UNIDROIT Principles. The terminology employed in these Principles is regarded as being in line with the '*Rabelian* tradition of private international law'[387]. It has to be emphasized, however, that *Rabel's* approach was not truly transnational. He understood conflict of laws to be of 'domestic origin and [only] of international orientation'[388].

In spite of this limited significance of *Rabel's* approach to qualification for the approximation of traditional conflict of laws methodology and the transnationalization of commercial law, there is a general trend towards transnationalization in this field that goes beyond mere problems of terminology. Generally speaking, there is a natural tendency in international conflict of laws doctrine to denationalize legal relationships through functional comparative analysis in order to overcome the 'inveterate evil'[389] of conflict of laws, *i.e.* its quality as part of domestic law. From this perspective, *Rabel's* approach paved the way for a far-reaching transnationalization of the legal process in private international law. Some have used this approach to arrive at the application of a 'universally reasonable law' ('*universell sachvernünftiges Recht*')[390]. Based on these considerations, *Kötz* has made the step from a mere internationalization of conflict of laws to a true transnationalization of the legal process on the basis of traditional private international law doctrine. He maintains that the domestic judge, unable to determine the law applicable to the case before him or her, should apply general principles of law developed on the basis of comparative research as 'substitute law' (*Ersatzrecht*)'[391]. Taking a more careful approach to transnationalism, *De Ly* wants to attach a 'corrective function' to transnational legal principles, thereby supplementing the conflict of laws rules of the *lex fori*[392]. Modern private international law doctrine rejects these solutions, not because they are irreconcilable with traditional conflict of laws doctrine, but because of the uncertainty and vagueness which they tend to introduce into conflict of laws doctrine[393]. These uncertainties, however, may be alleviated or even eliminated through the drafting of lists of general principles of law. The courts could then resort to them in their search for a quick and reliable transnationalization of the *lex causae*[394]. The domestic courts

386. *Rabel*, RabelsZ 5 (1931), at 241, 249 *et seq.*; *but see Sandrock*, Über Sinn und Methode zivilistischer Rechtsvergleichung, at 25 *et seq.*
387. *Hyland*, Am.J.Comp.L. 1992, at 541, 550.
388. *Kropholler*, IPR. § 2 III.3., note 15.
389. *Kegel*, IPR, 7th ed. 1995, § 2 II.3.a., at 112 (translation by the author).
390. *Cf. Joerges*, ZHR 138 (1974) at 549, 552.
391. *Kötz*, RabelsZ 34 (1970), at 663, 671 *et seq.* with reference to the works of *F.A. Mann*, *Schlesinger*, and *Lorenz*; *cf. also supra* Chapter 1 II.B.2.
392. *De Ly*, De Lex Mercatoria, at 375.
393. *Kropholler*, IPR, § 31 III.2.c) (at 218 *et seq.*).
394. *Cf.* for the 'Creeping Codification' through the drafting of lists of general principles and rules of the lex mercatoria' *infra* Chapter 4 II.C.

are also familiar with this approach and the application of general principles, because they have long since employed the functional legal methodology[395].

Finally, domestic legislatures themselves directly acknowledge the existence of transnational legal principles by concluding project contracts or special arbitration agreements which refer to 'general principles of international law' or even 'general principles of international trade law'[396]. Even though these clauses were not drafted with the intention of acknowledging the existence of a transnational legal *system*, their significance in the context of the NLM doctrine should not be underestimated. The same applies to Art. 9(1) of the Mexico City Convention on Private International Law (CIDIP) which allows the judge to take account of 'general principles of international commercial law recognized by international organizations' in determining the closest connection of a legal relationship. Thus, for the first time in legal history, drafters of an international convention on private international law have brought together the classical 'seat-of-the-relationship' test developed by *Savigny* in the last century and modern ideas of transnational commercial law[397]. The rule results from the general intention of the drafters to give parties before domestic courts the same liberty and freedom in the determination of the law applicable to their contract as they would enjoy before international arbitral tribunals[398]. Interestingly enough, this rather progressive provision is still a compromise solution since the American delegation initially intended to have the UNIDROIT Principles applied in the absence of a (valid) choice of law by the parties[399]. Still, the rule as it stands embraces the UNIDROIT Principles[400]. In any event, the approach chosen in the Mexico Convention can be rightly characterized as the climax in the approximation of classical conflict of laws doctrine and transnational commercial law. In Europe, the time seems to be ripe for similar developments.

In the mid-1990s, it was suggested that the Rome Convention on the Law Applicable to Contractual Obligations should be revised so as to allow for the parties' choice of a-national legal rules and more specifically the UNIDROIT and *Lando* Principles[401]. As a response to these proposals, Art. 3(2) of one of the EU

395. *Cf. Großfeld*, Macht und Ohnmacht der Rechtsvergleichung, at 69 *et seq.*; *Bonell*, RabelsZ 42 (1978), at 485, 499 *et seq.*

396. *Cf.* the choice-of-law clause in the Channel Tunnel construction contract, *supra* I.B.

397. *See Juenger*, Am.J.Comp.L. 1997, at 195, 206; *cf. also Boele-Woelki*, Unif.L.Rev. 1996, at 652, 674.

398. *Juenger, id.*, at 205: 'Why should individuals or enterprises who choose to *arbitrate* their differences be allowed to enjoy the benefit of selecting a body of rules, drafted by a distinguished group of experts, which are specifically designed to meet the needs of international transactions, whereas parties who choose to *litigate* are relegated to national laws? It is certainly difficult to understand what interests (other than those of a doctrinal nature) would be served by impeding the parties from denationalizing their agreement in this fashion'; *but see* the more sceptical view of *Lando*, The King's College Law Journal 1996/97, at 55, 63.

399. *Juenger, id.*

400. *Juenger, id.*, at 207, stating that 'the parties certainly have no reason to complain if their failure to agree on the law they wish to govern invokes a law of superior quality', *id.*, at 206.

401. *Boele-Woelki*, Principles en IPR, at 15 *et seq.*; *see also Lando*, The King's College Law Journal 1996/97, at 55, 61; *Blase*, Die Grundregeln des Europäischen Vertragrechts als Recht grenzüberschreitender Verträge, at 234.

Commission's first drafts of the new Rome I Regulation which has converted the Rome Convention into primary EU law contained a provision allowing the parties to 'choose as the applicable law the principles and rules of the substantive law of contract recognised internationally or in the Community'[402]. The EU Commission justified that proposal with reference to the basic principle of party autonomy as one of the corner stones of conflict of laws in the area of contractual obligations:

> 'To further boost the impact of the parties' will, a key principle of the [Rome] Convention, paragraph 2 authorises the parties to choose as the applicable law a non-State body of law. The form of words used would authorise the choice of the UNIDROIT Principles, the *Principles of European Contract Law* or a possible future optional Community instrument, while excluding the *lex mercatoria*, which is not precise enough, or private codifications not adequately recognised by the international community'[403].

That statement of the EU Commission does not reject the NLM concept *in principle*, but merely for lack of specificity and precision[404], a long standing argument raised against the NLM that will be dealt with in Chapter 4 of this Study. In spite (or maybe 'because') of this rather progressive approach to the idea of the transnationalization of the parties' choice of law, the reference to non-state rules was deleted in the final version of Art. 3(2) of the Rome-I Regulation[405]. This step was made in response to concerns that allowing parties to choose the UNIDROIT Principles would allow them to opt for rules which were not subject to any legislative scrutiny[406]. The Preamble of the Rome I Regulation states that the Regulation 'does not preclude parties from incorporating by reference into their contract a non-State body of law or an international convention'[407]. That comment reveals that the parties' option to agree on a-national principles of law was downgraded in the final version of the Regulation from a genuine choice of law to a mere '*materiellrechtliche Verweisung*' in which the principles assume the quality of contract conditions which remain governed by a domestic legal system. Obviously, the EU Commission was hesitant to make the 'last step' by allowing parties to agree on transnational law *via* a genuine choice of law.

402. Commission of the European Communities, document COM (2005) 650 final of December 15, 2005, at 14.
403. *Id.*, at 5.
404. *See* for a critical view of this approach of the EU Commission *Metzger*, Extra legem, intra ius: Allgemeine Rechtsgrundsätze im Europäischen Privatrecht, at 543.
405. Regulation (EC) No. 593/2008 of June 17, 2008 on the law applicable to contractual obligations (Rome I), OJ No. L 177/6, 10.
406. *See Goode* ICLQ 2005, at 539, 545: '... to permit selection of the Principles of International Commercial Contracts as the applicable law raises an issue of legitimacy, for its effect would be to enable the parties to displace the domestic mandatory rules of the forum State by a set of rules in the preparation of which neither business interests nor governments were involved and which were not subject to any legislative scrutiny'; *see also Goode/Kronke/McKendrick*, Transnational Commercial Law, No. 1.40.
407. Preamble, para. 13, *supra* note 405.

In light of the above considerations, one can state with confidence that the *status quo* in the relationship between domestic legislatures and transnational commercial law is not proof that the two cannot be reconciled. Rather, the *status quo* recognizes the similarities between the two. In the end, the application of the NLM by domestic courts and its recognition as an autonomous legal system by domestic legislatures will be achieved if and to the extent that the traditional source of law doctrine overcomes the classical dogma of state sovereignty as the only legitimate source of law.

G. THE NEW *LEX MERCATORIA* DOES NOT HAVE THE QUALITY OF AN 'AUTONOMOUS LEGAL SYSTEM'

All the arguments discussed so far may be traced back to one basic objection which is always brought forth against the viability of the NLM doctrine: transnational law does not constitute a genuine 'legal system'. It is argued that mercantile practice, *i.e.* the mere reference to the principle '*ubi commercium, ibi ius*', based on the pragmatic conception of Roman law that the primary purpose of the legal system is to provide society with a means for conflict resolution ('*ubi societas, ibi ius*'[408]), does not suffice to serve as a theoretical foundation for a transnational legal system. In addition, the efforts to provide these theoretical underpinnings are said to be 'rather sparse'[409]. From the perspective of the traditional theory of legal sources, a severe problem of legitimization emerges from what is claimed to be the existence of a *tertium genus*, *i.e.* a third legal system between domestic law and public international law. According to the classical doctrine of legal sources, only two legal systems exist, the various domestic legal systems and public international law[410]. Traditional conflict lawyers argue that '[t]he final word always rests with state law; whatever it fails to authorize has no prospect of recognition – especially within a democratic state'[411]. From their perspective, transnational law threatens the very existence of the conflict of laws because once supranational rules emerge, choice-of-law rules and principles become superfluous. This is another reason why conflict lawyers must put so much emphasis on the state-centred view of the law:

> 'Those who question the parties' freedom to choose the law governing their contract are likely to feel even more uncomfortable about the emergence of

408. *Cf. Cicero, De legibus*, 1, §§ 2 *et seq.* and 4 *et seq.*; *De officis* 1 §§ 20–22 and 3 §§ 21–38, cited by *Liebs*, Lateinische Rechtsregeln und Rechtssprichwörter, at 237; *cf. also* the (oral) doctrine of *Samuel Pufendorf*: '*socialitatem esse principium juris sufficiens, adaequatum, et tamen invalidum, ut vim legis demum acceperit a Deo*'; *cf. also A. Kaufmann*, Tendenzen im Rechtsdenken der Gegenwart, at 8.
409. *Bonell*, RabelsZ 42 (1978), at 485, 491, note 17.
410. *See Booysen*, RabelsZ 59 (1995), at 245, 249: 'Today, the world knows only two types of legal systems, the various domestic ones and public international law'; *see also Köndgen*, AcP 206 (2006), 477, 501.
411. *von Bar/Mankowski*, IPR, Vol. I, § 2 No. 76 (translation by the author).

> rules that owe their existence to the realities of an international marketplace, rather than a sovereign's fiat. Such a law is inexplicable in their terms of reference, its "brooding omnipresence" must be anathema to those who believe that the raison d'état must control international as well as purely domestic transactions'[412].

It has to be born in mind[413] that this criticism is not meant as an outright rejection of the existence of general principles of law derived through 'private law analogies' from the legal systems of the world. Rather, a different legal quality is attached to them. General principles of law are regarded not as components of an autonomous legal system, but rather as a mass of coherent legal convictions and notions, derived from similar legal provisions of domestic laws as shaped and refined by the case law of international arbitral tribunals[414]. This traditional reluctance to overcome the law-making monopoly of the state sovereign has reduced *Langen's* 'transnational law'[415] to a mere 'lex mercatoria *en route*'[416]. The same applies to the UNIDROIT Principles of International Commercial Contracts and the *Lando* Principles of European Contract Law. The rules and principles contained in them also echo the notion of transnationalism without untying the Gordian Knot of transnationalism.

The objections which are traditionally raised against the NLM as an autonomous legal system are based either on structural or theoretical assumptions. Both kinds of arguments will be dealt with in the next part of this Study.

1. The New *Lex Mercatoria* as a Legal 'System'

Over and over again, the proponents of the NLM are confronted with the allegation that the common legal convictions and notions which undoubtedly exist on the transnational plane do not present themselves in a systematic order, which is the typical characteristic of any legal system[417]. If the general principles of law to be found in domestic legal systems do not have any systematic quality, but rather are essential elements for the jurisdiction in which they are embedded, the same must be true for transnational principles and rules. The inherent quality of any legal system is that it is not just the agglomeration of principles and rules. Instead, they are lifted on a higher and more sophisticated plane in that statutes, case law and

412. *Juenger*, Vand. J. Transnat'l L. 1995, at 487, 498.
413. *Cf. already supra* A.2.c.
414. MünchKomm-*Sonnenberger*, EGBGB, Introduction, No. 269 *in fine*; *Samuel*, Jurisdictional Problems in International Commercial Arbitration, at 247.
415. *Cf. Langen*, Transnationales Recht, Part 1, No. 1: 'This transnational law is first a case law, not a system or legal order' (translation by the author).
416. *Coing* in his review of the English version of *Langen's* book, JZ 1975, at 40.
417. *Cf. von Hoffmann*, Internationale Handelsschiedsgerichtsbarkeit, at 11 *et seq.*; *Samuel*, Jurisdictional Problems in International Commercial Arbitration, at 24 *et seq.*; *Lagarde*, in: Etudes offertes à Berthold Goldman, at 133; *Kassis*, Théorie Générale des Usages du Commerce, at 375 *et seq.*; *Klein*, Festschrift Mann, at 617, 633.

legal doctrine provide them with a systematic order: a doctrinal and theoretical framework within which the courts are able to deduct coherent and consistent solutions for individual cases[418].

a. *Ambiguity of the Notion of 'System'*

Very often, objections against the systematic quality of the NLM have to be rejected from the outset since they fail to indicate the precise meaning of this term. Conventional wisdom has it that the term 'system' is characterized by its intrinsic ambiguity. This also holds true for legal science, where three different categories of 'systems' can be distinguished: deductive, categorical and teleological[419]. The first two are based on unrealistic premises[420] and are therefore not discussed here. Thus, the Study's focus can be limited to the teleological quality of a legal system. This teleological aspect has two primary functions. First, it serves as an order for the application of the law. Second, it provides a means to implement unified structures that link together the multitude of decisions of individual cases by domestic courts and arbitral tribunals[421].

Within a legal system, the individual rule or principle has its place within a teleological framework that is formed by logical and grammatical rules leading to the grouping and coordination of legal institutions that form the basis of this system[422]. Systematizing the law in this way enables the lawyer or judge to select the suitable rule for the case before him from the multitude of possible options available. This is the basic distinction between an unmethodical legal mass and a highly sophisticated legal system[423]. At the same time, this system provides the necessary framework not only for the application of the law to individual cases, but also for the evolution and refinement of this legal system as a 'law in action'[424].

The question as to the quality and nature of this systematic framework remains. It is a common misunderstanding, based on a positivistic notion of the law, that provisions promulgated by domestic legislatures play a dominant role in the creation of a legal system[425]. This view would oversimplify the legal process as such. The search for legal rules and principles may not be reduced to a mere logical deduction from a predetermined normative system[426]. Otherwise, every system

418. *von Hoffmann*, Internationale Handelsschiedsgerichtsbarkeit, at 117.
419. *Cf. Sandrock*, Über Sinn und Methode zivilistischer Rechtsvergleichung, at 42 *et seq.*
420. *Cf. Horn*, RIW 1967, at 601, 602 *et seq.*
421. *Canaris*, Systemdenken und Systembegriff in der Jurisprudenz, at 155.
422. *Strömholm*, Festschrift Zweigert, at 909, 910.
423. *Smid*, Einführung in die Philosophie des Rechts, § 4 I.2.
424. *K. Schmidt*, in: Behrends (ed.), Privatrecht heute und Jherings evolutionäres Rechtsdenken, at 77, 87 *et seq.*
425. *Cf. e.g. Pawlowski*, Methodenlehre, Nos. 160 *et seq.*
426. *Horn*, NJW 1967, at 602 *et seq.*; *Bydlinski*, Juristische Methodenlehre und Rechtsbegriff, at 142.

would run the risk of leading law into 'mechanical jurisprudence'[427]. As *Holmes* has stated in his 'Path of the Law':

> 'The danger of which I speak is not the admission that the principles governing other phenomena also govern the law, but the notion that a given system, ours, for instance, can be worked out like mathematics from some general axioms of conduct. This is the natural error of the schools, but it is not confined to them... [T]he logical method and form flatter that longing for certainty and for repose which is in every human mind. But certainty generally is illusion, and repose is not the destiny of man. Behind the logical form lies a judgment as to the relative worth and importance of competing legislative grounds, often an inarticulate and unconscious judgment, it is true, and yet the very root and nerve of the whole proceeding... We do not know how large a part of our law is open to reconsideration upon a slight change in the habit of the public mind'[428].

Thus, what really makes a legal system is its *unwritten* framework of values and convictions that enrich it with the necessary logical consistency and internal unity[429]. Most importantly, the reference to unwritten general principles of law has, to a large extent, replaced positivistic approaches to decision-making, thereby introducing a new pluralism into the classical and largely positivistic theory of legal sources[430].

b. Increasing Systematization of the New Lex Mercatoria

An important conclusion can be derived from the above considerations. The importance of the notion of 'system' is only relative. In view of the multitude of legal problems of modern society, it merely serves as a standard point of reference in the search for the applicable principles and rules which then lead to a just decision in a given case[431]. This means that the existence of a 'ready-made' and 'complete' system is not a *conditio sine qua non* for the qualification and application of legal principles and rules[432]. In everyday legal practice, this phenomenon becomes particularly apparent in those cases where the courts of civil law jurisdictions – which are traditionally more inclined to follow a systemic approach – assume law-making functions[433].

---

427. *See Roscoe Pound*, Yale L.J. 1909, at 454, 462 *et seq.*: 'The effect of all system is apt to be petrification of the subject systematized. Legal science is not exempt from this tendency... when... legal theories have come to maturity, jurisprudence tends to decay. Conceptions are fixed. The premises are no longer to be examined. Everything is reduced to simple deduction from them. Principles cease to have importance. The law becomes a body of rules.'
428. *Holmes*, in: Holmes (ed.), Collected Legal Papers, at 167, 180 *et seq.*
429. *Canaris, see supra* note 421, at 1 *et seq.*; *Larenz*, Methodenlehre, at 165 *et seq.*; *cf. also von Savigny*, System des heutigen römischen Rechts, Vol. 1, at 214.
430. *Watt*, Clunet 1997, at 403, 405 with express reference to the parallel development in the field of the *lex mercatoria*, *id.*, note 19.
431. *Larenz, supra* note 429, at 165 *et seq.*; *Horn*, NJW 1967, at 601, 605.
432. *Cf. Horn*, NJW 1967, at 601, 602 *et seq.*
433. *Larenz, supra* note 429, *id.*

When applying these considerations to the transnational plane, one has to start by taking into account the particular characteristic of this law which makes it different from any domestic legal system. The NLM is not a 'complete' and self-contained sophisticated legal system. Instead, the NLM provides the example *par excellence* for a 'law in the making'. Consequently, the systematic requirements to be found in domestic legal systems cannot be automatically transferred to the transnational plane[434]. Instead, the actors of international trade and commerce have to create their own systematic underpinnings which are capable of coping with the complex and multifaceted problems of international commercial relationships. This is done by the decision-making practice of international arbitrators. Their search for interest-oriented and commercially sound solutions of individual disputes, the increasing publication of their case law and the discussion of individual awards by international practitioners and academics[435] create the necessary framework of value judgments and systematic structures necessary to ensure the viability of a transnational legal system. This approach takes the particular nature of transnational commercial law into account in that it combines comparative, topical, and sociological aspects, thereby enabling lawyers and arbitrators to deduce principles and rules of transnational commercial law from the case law of international arbitrators. Here, transnational methodology meets with traditional domestic doctrine which assumes that the creation of general principles of law is based on a 'value judgment directed towards the discovery of general principles of law in individual cases' as a first step towards the systematic consolidation of a legal system[436]. Therefore, international trade has created its own systematic framework within which the international community of merchants and their dispute settlement system create and develop an autonomous system of transnational law, the NLM[437].

2. The New *Lex Mercatoria* Does Not Constitute a 'Self-contained' System

Those who oppose the existence of a transnational legal system have frequently argued that the NLM is too incomplete and too rudimentary[438]. In their eyes, the

434. *Langen*, Transnationales Recht, Part I, No. 18.
435. *Cf. supra* C.2. and D.2.
436. *Canaris*, Systemdenken und Systembegriff in der Jurisprudenz, at 157, 160; *cf. also Horn*, NJW 1967, at 601, 607.
437. *Cf. Joerges*, ZHR 138 (1974), at 549, 561 and *infra* 3.b.
438. *Klein*, Festschrift Mann, at 617, 633; *Schlosser*, Das Recht der internationalen privaten Schiedsgerichtsbarkeit, No. 200; *Sandrock*, in: Böckstiegel (ed.), Rechtsfortbildung durch Internationale Schiedsgerichtsbarkeit, at 21, 77; *Bärmann*, Festschrift Mann, at 547, 569; *von Hoffmann*, IPRax 1984, at 106, 107; *Triebel/Petzold*, RIW 1988, at 245, 250; *Paulsson*, Rev.d'Arb. 1990, at 55; *Schwander*, Lois d'application immédiate, at 397; *van den Berg/van Delden/Snijders*, Arbitragerecht, at 100; *Redfern/Hunter*, Law and Practice of International Commercial Arbitration, No. 3.172; *Merkt*, Investitionsschutz durch Stabilisierungsklauseln: zur intertemporalen Rechtswahl in State Contracts, at 127; *Schödermeier*, Sonderprivatrecht

NLM does not constitute a self-contained legal system but a mere 'legal mass'[439]. Again, this objection is derived from a comparison of the NLM with modern codifications and legal systems which are said to have a self-contained character, allowing the judge to deduce from its rules and principles solutions for every conceivable legal problem. Practical experience of continental lawyers in the past century, however, has revealed that the idea of an axiomatic self-contained character of modern legal systems is a positivistic myth and 'has never been more than purely theoretical book learning'[440].

a. Incomplete Character of Domestic Legal Systems

Even though their drafters intended them to be 'complete and exhaustive'[441] ('*ius semper loquitur*'), the major codifications of private laws such as the German '*Bürgerliches Gesetzbuch*' or the French '*Code Civil*' by no means qualify as self-contained legal systems in terms of logical and conceptual consistency. No legal system should be completely open and no system can be completely closed[442]. In view of the multitude of legal problems that present themselves in practice, every codification – no matter how complete it was intended to be by its drafters – is nothing more than a preliminary collection of possible rules and principles[443]. Even with the help of the traditional instruments of deductive reasoning, these codes may not cover the 'thousand unexpected questions'[444] presented by real life. As *Portalis* suggested, only general principles, not details can be aptly codified[445]. Therefore, these codes necessarily remain open and incomplete, leaving room for the development and refinement of the law by courts and legal doctrine[446]. It is precisely this built-in flexibility which has allowed these

---

für internationale Wirtschaftsverträge, at 140 *et seq.*; *Martiny*, in: Reithmann/Martiny (eds.), Internationales Vertragsrecht, No. 72; *van Houtte*, The Law of International Trade, No. 1.35.

439. *Cf. Böckstiegel*, Der Staat als Vertragspartner ausländischer Unternehmen, at 144; *Coing*, NJW 1981, at 2602; *Esser*, Grundsatz und Norm, at 378; *von Hülsen*, JZ 1967, at 629, 632.
440. *Ehrlich*, Grundlegung der Soziologie des Rechts, at 362; *K. Schmidt*, Die Zukunft der Kodifikationsidee, at 19: 'This dogma [of the self-contained character of legal systems] does not reflect the force of the codification, but a lack of sense for reality' (translation by the author).
441. *Thibaut*, Über die Notwendigkeit eines allgemeinen bürgerlichen Rechts für Deutschland, at 1 *et seq.*; *see K. Schmidt, id.*, at 18.
442. *Miller*, 12 W. St. U. L. Rev. 1984, at 93, 115.
443. *See Zimmermann*, Columbia Journal of European Law 1994/1995, at 61, 89: '[The drafters of these codes] were no longer obsessed with the idea that they had to provide an exhaustive regulation – from first principles down to the finest details – for every imaginable set of facts. They did not aim at comprehensiveness, nor did they contemplate the abolition of legal science.'
444. *See* the famous words of *Portalis*, one of the fathers of the French Code Civil.
445. *Miller*, *supra* note 442, at 115.
446. *Coing*, Grundzüge der Rechtsphilosophie, at 353; *Esser*, Grundsatz und Norm, at 7; *Engisch*, Studium Generale 10 (1957), at 173 *et seq.*; *Larenz*, Methodenlehre, at 173; *Bydlinski*, Methodenlehre, at 483; *Lando*, in: Šarčević (ed.), Essays on International Commercial Arbitration, at 149; *Böckstiegel*, Der Staat als Vertragspartner ausländischer Privatunternehmen, at 112; *cf. also Kötz*, Modern Law Review 1987, at 1, 11.

codes to survive for nearly one-hundred years and to adapt to the ever-changing realities of life. Indeed, the doctrine of '*clausula rebus*' is among the most prominent examples of non-regulated legal principles[447]. In the field of contract law, modern innominate contracts provide a perfect example for this phenomenon. Modern computer-, leasing-, management- or production sharing-agreements are widely used in domestic and international business but do not fit in the traditional pattern of codified contract law[448]. Instead, general contract conditions have long since assumed the function of 'substitute law' created by the parties[449]. Based on these practical experiences, the character of the classical private law codifications has changed in the past years. They are no longer based on the ideal of completeness but are geared towards completion and evolution by the courts and legal doctrine[450]. The same approach has been taken by the drafters of the third generation codes such as the new Dutch Civil Code[451]. As a consequence of this development, some domestic legislatures have followed the strategy of 'conscious incompleteness'[452] in drafting their codes. Others are currently discussing the issue of 'de-codification'[453] and are looking for new ways to create 'lean law'.

b. *Approximation of the Courts' Function in Civil and Common Law Jurisdictions*

In view of the incompleteness of every codification even in civil law jurisdictions there are substantial areas of the law in which 'the statutory origin has been overlaid by mass of case law'[454]. Thus, the civil law practitioner, just as his counterpart in common law jurisdictions, has to refer to court precedents and to the notions of '*ratio decidendi*' and '*obiter dictum*'[455] in order to be able to predict a court's decision and reasoning in a given case[456]. This means that the rules and principles developed by the courts in civil law jurisdictions may be equated with 'genuine statutory law'[457]. The teleological values and assessments in everyday legal practice therefore lead to the development of new law out of the concrete factual

---

447. *Zimmermann, supra* note 443, at 91.
448. *Cf. Martinek*, Moderne Vertragstypen, Vol. III, § 22.1.
449. *Schaub*, Gewährleistung für Standardsoftware, at 232.
450. *Stern*, Das Staatsrecht der Bundesrepublik Deutschland, Vol. I, at 106; Dölle-*Wahl*, EKG, Art. 17, Nos. 1 *et seq.*
451. *Cf. Hartkamp*, Am.J.Comp.L. 1992, at 551, 553 *et seq.*
452. *Cf.* for Switzerland *Noll*, Gesetzgebungslehre, at 274; *Zweigert/Kötz*, Einführung in die Rechtsvergleichung, § 13 II.
453. *Cf. K. Schmidt*, Die Zukunft der Kodifikationsidee, at 13 *et seq.*
454. *Lord Goff of Chieveley*, The Wilberforce Lecture 1997, ICLQ 1997, at 745, 749.
455. *See* for the functioning of these notions in English law *Cross and Harris*, Precedent in English Law, at 39 *et seq.*
456. *Cf. Kötz*, Modern Law Review 1987, at 1, 6 *et seq.*
457. *Hedemann*, Reichsgericht und Wirtschaftsrecht, at 286; *Llewellyn*, Präjudizienrecht und Rechtsprechung in Amerika, at 112 ('...the Imperial Court is de facto a law-making institution...'); *cf. also Rüthers*, Die unbegrenzte Auslegung, at 467; *see* for arbitration as 'quasi-lawmaker in international commerce and trade' *Stein*, Lex mercatoria, at 242.

circumstances of a given legal relationship[458], thereby creating the openness and dynamic character as the major characteristics of a modern legal system. In actual legal practice, this distinctive change in the function of the civil law courts is hardly visible. The creation of new legal institutions and rules is effected under the disguise of 'statutory construction' (*praeter* or even *contra legem*) or the application of blanket clauses such as 'good faith' ('*boni mores*')[459]. In German law, the broad notion of good faith under Sec. 242 of the Civil Code, intended to mitigate the rigors of the Civil Code by way of a 'moralization' of contractual and non-contractual legal relationships, gives a tremendous degree of law-making power to the domestic judge[460]. German courts and German legal doctrine have developed a wide array of principles and rules based on groups of cases in which the principle has previously been applied. These groups of cases serve to establish a system of specific good faith rules. It is this system which makes the general principle of good faith workable in everyday legal practice[461]. It is by virtue of this function as the source of individual rules and principles that Sec. 242 of the Civil Code has assumed the function of a 'super-provision'[462]. Providing even a rough overview of these rules and principles would be a hopeless undertaking. Suffice it that the principle of good faith and the legal rules derived from it can have a dual effect on the exercise of the parties' rights. On the one hand, the principle may serve to supplement the contractual rights and duties of the parties, *e.g.* by enabling the judge or arbitrator to develop additional, 'implied' legal duties, such as an ancillary duty to take care of the assets of the other side, a duty to inform the other side about events that might be of significance for that side or a duty to provide correct information if the other side has asked for that information. On the other hand, the principle of good faith serves as a means to restrict the exercise of legal rights if

458. *Cf. Ehrlich*, Grundlegung der Soziologie des Rechts, at 363: 'In applying a code, the lawyers, as they have done at all times, derive new law for new circumstances from the concrete structure of legal relationships, *i.e.* above all from the declarations of the parties, from documents and from typical behavioural standards, enriched by generalizations and norm-like formulations, which are then weighed against the contents of the codes ... The codes make the task easier for jurisprudence ... in a very efficient manner through the extreme flexibility of the provisions contained therein ... In addition, the codes always include a number of notions which allow the courts to develop new legal rules for new institutions' (translation by the author).
459. *Canaris*, Systemdenken und Systembegriff in der Jurisprudenz, at 6 *et seq.*; *Esser, supra* note 446, at 63 *et seq.*; *Larenz, see supra* note 446, at 173; *cf.* also for the case law of the German superior courts BVerfGE 34, 269, 286 *et seq.*; 49, 304, 318 *et seq.*; 65, 182, 190 *et seq.*; BGHZ 3, 308, 315 *et seq.*; 4, 153, 157 *et seq.*; 26, 349; BAGE 1, 279, 280 *et seq.*
460. *See Schlechtriem*, Good Faith in German Law and in International Uniform Laws, at 7: '... one cannot avoid the impression that those scholars who advocate an abandonment of most concrete legal provisions in favor of Sec. 242 BGB have already succeeded, for one can find a court decision or a scholarly theory applying the provision to almost every situation governed by the Civil Code and in addition very often overriding the text and the meaning of special provisions.'
461. *See Hesselink*, in: Hesselink/de Vries (eds.), Principles of European Contract Law , at 474 *et seq.*
462. *Lando*, 'Eight Principles of European Contract Law', in Essays in Honour of Roy Goode (1997), at 103, 121 *et seq.*

such exercise appears as unfair or unjustified under the given circumstances of a case. Examples of the 'limiting function' of the principle of good faith include the prohibition to contradict oneself in one's own legal conduct ('*venire contra factum proprium*'), the principle of forfeiture of rights after expiry of a certain amount of time during which the right has not been invoked by the party possessing the right ('*Verwirkung*') and the prohibition to exercise rights which have been acquired in an unlawful way ('*nemo auditur propriam turpitudinem allegans*')[463].

Section 242 also has an important corrective function to allow the court to take account of aspects of individual justice. The blanket clause obligates parties to do all that is possible to further their contractual relationship – even if doing so is contrary to their immediate short-term interests[464]. Objective values such as reliability, loyalty, fairness, reasonableness and good conduct are essential elements of the behavioural standard required from contract parties by the principle of good faith[465]. There is an inherent correlation between these blanket clauses and the 'discretion' of the judge in applying the law. In allowing the judge to escape from the application of abstract black-letter law and to take account of the particularities of individual cases[466], these clauses manifest the legislatures' will not only to allow for the adaptation of the law to changed needs and social convictions[467] but also and above all to leave enough leeway for the development and evolution of statutory law[468]. *Arndt* has summarized this function of the courts as follows:

> 'It is a one-sided and incorrect conception of the judiciary that it sees its main function in the preservation and conservation of the law, even though it considers this law to be questionable and subject to correction according to the laws of reason. In my view, it is the primary purpose of the repetitive and innovative work of the courts to detect the open character of all statutory law through a problem oriented approach to decision-making and to create a core of new law, taking into account legal reality and the solidarity of the legal community of the people. For this reason it is the basic task of the judiciary to cooperate on a case by case basis in the development of the law. This is exactly what happens in Anglo-Saxon legal systems. *Esser's* comprehensive comparative research has proven it is a misunderstanding to regard the precedents rendered by Anglo-Saxon courts as basic principal decisions. This view would also ignore how close the finding of the law and its application are intertwined'[469].

463. *See* for a discussion of these principles Palandt-*Grüneberg*, BGB, § 242 Nos. 38 *et seq.*
464. *Nassar*, *supra* note 171, at 168.
465. PWW-*Schmidt-Kessel*, BGB Kommentar, § 242 Nos. 9 and 12: good faith as an 'instrument for transporting external (social) values' (translation by the author).
466. *Cf. Weber*, AcP 192 (1992), at 516, 559; *Beater*, AcP 194 (1994), at 82 *et seq.*
467. *Cf. Oertmann*, DJZ 1931, column 265.
468. *Hedemann*, Die Flucht in die Generalklauseln, at 35, 55 *et seq.*; *Beater*, AcP 194 (1994), at 89.
469. *Arndt*, in: Böckenförde/Lewald (eds.), Adolf Arndt, Gesammelte juristische Schriften, at 59, 84 (translation by the author).

This statement demonstrates that the traditional functional distinction between common law and civil law judges is steadily disappearing[470]. Irrespective of the particular nature of the legal system, this development will be the same all over the world[471]. More and more, the view has gained ground that a major emphasis in the work of civil law judges lies in the development and evolution of the law[472]: 'Case law is our destiny'[473]. The courts no longer understand their task as being limited to the construction and application of the written common statutory law alone. Increasing emphasis is placed on the evolution and supplementation of statutory value judgments through the creation of judge-made norms[474]. The former case law of the German Federal Supreme Court (*Bundesgerichtshof*) concerning groups of companies ('*qualifiziert faktischer Konzern*') is a typical example of this development. It has been criticized as an impermissible development of the law *praeter legem*[475] and has been cited as proof for the general tendency of German commercial law to 'neglect legal principles in favour of individual circumstances of the case'[476]. This critique of the German courts merely confirms the general phenomenon that, on all levels of the judicial process, the courts are no longer responsible for the 'accurate' solution of a legal problem, but rather for the just decision of a given case[477]. The case law on groups of companies, thus, furnishes a typical example for the result-oriented approach of the German Federal Supreme Court[478]. The same phenomenon can be observed in the practice of the German Federal Constitutional Court, where new rules and principles are developed 'through the traditional methods of construction and

470. *Cf. Zajtay*, AcP 165 (1965), at 97 *et seq.*; *Rheinstein*, Einführung in die Rechtsvergleichung, at 103; *Lord Goff of Chieveley*, The Wilberforce Lecture 1997, ICLQ 1997, at 745, 749; *cf. already Llewellyn*, Präjudizienrecht und Rechtsprechung in Amerika, at 45: 'It may be of great theoretical significance that the prejudicial value of the decisions of the highest German courts is not binding from a dogmatic point of view, while such a binding force is part of the legal system in America . . . One only needs to open one's eyes to realize that the situation is strikingly similar and is getting even more similar for counsel in drafting practice and before the courts' (translation by the author).

471. *Lord Goff of Chieveley*, *id.*, at 752: 'In codified systems, as in common law systems, the substantive law has to develop in some degree from case to case; and as the world diminishes in size, and as our cultures coalesce, in all countries of the world, despite differences in legal background, the judicial reaction is likely to be similar'.

472. *Rüthers*, Die unbegrenzte Auslegung, at 457.

473. *Gamillscheg*, AcP 164 (1964), at 385, 445; *see also Radbruch*, Der Geist des Englischen Rechts, at 15.

474. *Rüthers, supra* note 472, at 469.

475. *Cf. Flume*'s note to the 'Video'-judgment of the German Federal Supreme Court in DB 1992, at 25 *et seq.*; *see* for an attempt to justify the development of the law *praeter legem* by the courts in this field of German company law *Basten*, Zur Frage einer Konzernbildungskontrolle für Aktiengesellschaften als faktische Konzerntöchter, at 465 *et seq.*

476. *Knütel*, ZEuP 1994, at 244, 248 *et seq.*

477. *Cf. Smid*, DZWir 1993, at 485, 488; *Berger*, ZIP 1994, at 173, 181.

478. *Cf. von Becker*, Methodologische Probleme des qualifiziert-faktischen GmbH-Konzerns, at 141 *et seq.*

gap-filling'[479]. Also, before *culpa in contrahendo* was codified in Sec. 311 of the German Civil Code, the various types of *culpa in contrahendo* liability developed by the German courts gave the impression that 'the German private law is not codified but assumes the quality of case law similar to the English and American jurisdictions'[480]. It has already been emphasized that modern legislatures have made this open approach part of their legislative philosophy. Thus, the Dutch Civil Code (BW) grants domestic courts a considerable degree of discretion in the development of the new law and in its adaptation to the particularities of individual cases[481].

This observation, however, does not mean that the function of a statutory legal system has been reduced to a mere '*façade*'[482]. The problem is that the overt and/or covert development of statutory law is no longer guided by the *ratio legis* alone, but by notions and value judgments that go beyond the wording of the statute and the intention of the drafters[483]. At the same time, this procedure serves to confirm the thesis of the incomplete character of domestic statutory law[484]. Thus, blanket clauses which leave room for the application of general principles of law serve as loop holes for legislatures[485] in the fulfilment of their task to avoid gaps in the law by guaranteeing sufficient abstraction and flexibility in the statutes themselves[486]. We are faced here with the phenomenon of 'substitute law-making by the courts'[487]: the development and creation of the law is frequently effected by 'arguing from case to case'[488]. Even in civil law countries, court precedents assume a higher ranking within the hierarchy of domestic legal systems than is attached to them by traditional doctrine[489]. While civil law jurisdictions lack the *stare decisis* doctrine of common law countries, legal practice in these jurisdictions is frequently based on a presumptive law-like validity of court precedents In addition, the courts' duty to substantiate their reasoning ('*Begründungslast*'[490]) requires the

---

479. BVerfGE 94, at 197, 203: 'The technical problems that arise out of the lack of a direct contractual relationship between the owner of the premise and the lessor do not justify a reduction of the standard of protection for the lessor' (translation by the author).
480. *Horn*, JuS 1995, at 377, 387.
481. *Hartkamp*, Am.J.Comp.L. 1992, at 551, 568.
482. *Strömholm*, Festschrift Zweigert, at 909, 913.
483. *Schmitz*, Allgemeine Rechtsgrundsätze in der Rechtsprechung des Iran-United States Claims Tribunal, at 54.
484. *Horn*, NJW 1967, at 601, 607.
485. *Cf. Hedemann*, Die Flucht in die Generalklauseln.
486. *Cf. K. Schmidt*, Die Zukunft der Kodifikationsidee, at 21.
487. *Cf. K. Schmidt*, in: Behrends (ed.), Privatrecht heute und Jherings evolutionäres Rechtsdenken, at 83.
488. *Zimmermann*, ZEuP 1993, at 4, 7.
489. *Cf. already Hedemann*, Reichsgericht und Wirtschaftsrecht, at 287 *et seq.*: '[The significance of precedents] today surmounts large part of legal doctrine not only in terms of practical value but also with respect to their historic significance to such an extent that a learned judge once said: "Thus, we have no precedential system *de iure*, but such a system is finding its way with such a force that one is right to speak of a crypto-precedential system" (Heinrich Gerland)' (translation by the author).
490. *Cf. Krebs*, AcP 195 (1995), at 171 *et seq.*

judge to provide the parties with adequate and comprehensive reasons for his decisions. It is through this procedure that domestic courts manage to attach an effect to their decisions that is, even if not legally, at least factually similar to that of common law courts[491].

As in common law jurisdictions, the quality of the finding of the law in civil law countries depends not so much on the quality of the codified law, but on the wisdom of the judges[492]. This development has a striking parallel in the arbitral process, where the quality of the arbitrators is the decisive factor for the quality of the arbitration and the finding of the law: '*l'arbitrage vaut l'arbitre*'.

c. 'Opening Clauses' in Domestic Legal Systems

The Dutch Civil Code mirrors this shift in emphasis from the strict application of statutory law to a more flexible adjudicatory approach. Art. 6:248(2) of the Dutch Civil Code (BW)[493] allows the judge to disregard stipulations contained in the contract if this is required by the principles of fairness and equity ('*redelijkheid en billijkheid*'). Interestingly enough, Dutch courts used these principles even before the entering into force of the new code to develop the law *contra* or *praeter legem*[494]. The Civil Code of Québec[495] is another example for that fact that modern codifications depend upon the 'opening' effect of blanket clauses. The special provision on good faith[496], drafted along Art. 1134(3) of the French Code Civil, was introduced in the law of obligations of the new Québec Civil Code and is regarded as a major innovation of this legislative project. Establishing the principle in the law of obligations instead of the general introductory part of the new law is intended to ensure increased consideration of the principle of good faith in the context of the conclusion, the implementation, the construction and the termination of contracts[497]. The Québec legislature's approach to the problem of good faith is of particular significance since the Code is heavily influenced by common law doctrine, which has always maintained that there is no such general principle as good faith and instead looks for implied terms in the contract[498]. Nevertheless,

---

491. *Krebs, id.*, at 210.
492. *Cf. Hartkamp*, Am.J.Comp.L. 1992, 571 (citing *Sauveplanne*).
493. Article 6:248(2) BW provides that contractual rules agreed upon by the parties are to be disregarded if their application appears to contravene equity and justice in light of the circumstances of the case; *see* for a comment on these provisions *Lando*, in: Weyers (ed.), Europäisches Vertragsrecht, at 81, 84: 'These are sensational provisions . . . The Dutch legislator says . . . to the courts: "We know that we cannot embrace everything. We cannot guarantee that the written law will always do justice. We trust the courts. They may derogate from the Code and from the contract when in order to do justice they find it absolutely necessary"'.
494. *van den Berg/van Delden/Snijders*, Arbitragerecht, at 9 *et seq.*; *Hartkamp*, Am.J.Comp.L. 1992, at 551, 556.
495. *Cf. infra* Chapter 4 I.A.3.b.bb.
496. Article 1375 Code Civil du Québec: '*La bonne foi doit gouverner la conduite des parties, tant au moment de la naissance de l'obligation qu'à celui de son exécution ou de son extinction*'.
497. *Cf.* the official commentary of the Ministry of Justice of Québec, reprinted in Code Civil du Québec, Commentaires du Ministre de la Justice, Publications DAFCO, 1993, at 459.
498. *See infra* Chapter 4 I.A.7.b.

contrary to this traditional common law view, the Québec legislature chose to follow the civil law approach and made it clear in the code itself that the judge may follow the general principles of good faith when deciding on the validity or construction of contractual stipulations. With this provision, the Québec legislature acknowledged the pivotal role of the notions of equity and good faith as 'roaming elements in the shaping of the law'[499].

Apart from these blanket clauses there are also explicit references to general principles of law contained in domestic legal systems which serve to confirm the thesis of the necessary open quality and character of any sophisticated legal order. Interestingly enough, one of the first provisions of this kind was Sec. 49 of the Introduction of the Prussian General Law Of The Land ('*Allgemeines Landrecht*', ALR), a code which, through its multitude of detailed provisions, constitutes the ideal example of a self-contained, logical and systematic codification. In addition, Sec. 1 of the first draft of the German Civil Code provided that where a conclusion by analogy was not possible the judge 'should apply the principles that result from the spirit of the legal system'[500]. Among the contemporary codes, Art. 1(2) of the Swiss Civil Code (*Zivilgesetzbuch*, ZGB) allows the judge to apply the principles 'which he would establish if he were the legislature'. Other examples of this kind are provided by Sec. 7 of the Austrian Civil Code, Art. 12(2), 2nd Sentence of the Italian '*Disposizioni sulla legge generale*' of the Codice Civile, Art. 6(2) of the Spanish Codigo Civil, and Art. 1 Sec. 2 of the Egyptian Civil Code[501]. According to Art. 4 of the French Code Civil, the judge who denies to decide a case because the law does not contain a solution is guilty of a denial of justice ('*deni de justice*')[502]. Finally, Art. 10 of the Inter-American Convention on the Law Applicable to International Contracts, adopted by the Inter-American Specialized Conference on Private International Law (CIDIP) at its Mexico City Session on March 17 and 18, 1994[503], provides that the judge shall apply 'the guidelines, customs and principles of international commercial law as well as commercial usages and practices generally accepted *in order to discharge the requirements of justice and equity in the particular case*'[504]. This reference is meant to encompass the rules and principles of the NLM[505]. A similar reference to 'international practice' can be found in Art. 5 of the 1985 Foreign Economic Contract Law of the People's Republic of China[506]. Again, this reference may be qualified as a legislative acknowledgment of the NLM[507].

---

499. *Esser*, in: Summum Ius – Summa Iniuria, at 22, 23.
500. *Cf. K. Schmidt*, Die Zukunft der Kodifikationsidee, at 46.
501. *Cf. also* the (partly outdated) collection of *Cheng*, General Principles, at 400 *et seq.*; *Schlesinger*, AJIL 1957, at 734, 742 *et seq.*
502. *Cf.* Dölle-*Wahl*, EKG, Art. 17, No. 2.
503. Reprinted at ILM 1994, at 733 *et seq.*
504. *Goode*, ICLQ 1997, at 1, 29 (emphasis added).
505. *Boele-Woelki*, Unif.L.Rev. 1996, at 652, 674 with reference to the *travaux préparatoires*; *see also Lando*, in: Festskrift till Stig Strömholm, at 567, 573.
506. *See Horn/Schütze* (eds.), Wirtschaftsrecht und Außenwirtschaftsverkehr der Volksrepublik China, at 438, 439.
507. *Ferrari*, Rev.int.dr.comp. 1996, at 813, 817.

d. Consequences for the New Lex Mercatoria *Doctrine*

Self-contained, strictly systematic codes are not workable in everyday legal practice. Instead, every modern legal system is based on a substantial degree of openness and flexibility. This conclusion is important for a deeper understanding of the quality of the NLM as an autonomous legal system. The overall structure of the Franco-Italian Draft on Obligation Law[508] and of the UNIDROIT Principles shows that the unification of contract law must be accompanied by blanket clauses such as good faith and other provisions which allow for the necessary flexibility and '*souplesse*' in the application of the law. It is this drafting approach which brings about the important interplay between general principles of law and individual rules to be discussed below[509]. Flexibility and openness are, therefore, of utmost importance for the viability of the NLM. In view of the multitude of legal problems of international trade and commerce, the dynamic evolution of contract practice, and the varying character of the usages and customs of the different branches of trade, it would be an illusion to expect that every possible factual pattern could be predicted from the outset and solutions for these problems could be supplied in advance on a transnational plane[510]. Rather, the resolution of concrete disputes always requires the concretization of general legal principles on a case-by-case basis[511].

This approach to transnational decision-making does away with the general criticism[512] that the principles contained in the NLM are too platitudinous to permit a detailed evaluation of conflicting interests[513]. Instead, one may state with confidence that the NLM, as it stands today, has a comprehensive potential for the solution of legal conflicts similar to that of any domestic legal system[514]. It is a basic misunderstanding to assume that the autonomous character of the NLM necessarily requires the completeness of its rules and principles[515].

Finally, there is another important aspect which explains why transnational commercial law, in spite of its openness and incomplete character, is a viable legal system. Influenced by Anglo-American drafting techniques, international contracts usually constitute comprehensive, multi-page arrangements which allow for the resolution of legal conflicts solely on the basis of the contractual stipulations

508. *Cf. infra* Chapter 3 I.A.
509. *Cf. infra* Chapter 3 II.A.2.c. and Chapter 4 I.A.7.b.
510. *Bonell*, RabelsZ 42 (1978), at 485, 502; *see also Goode*, ICLQ 1997, at 1, 33.
511. *Dasser*, Lex Mercatoria, at 117.
512. *F.A. Mann*, BYIL 1957, at 36: 'They may, on occasion, be useful to fill a gap but in essence they are too elementary, too obvious and even to platitudinous to permit detached evaluation of conflicting interests, the specially legal appreciation of the implications of a given situation. In short, they are frequently apt to let discretion prevail over justice'.
513. *Berman/Dasser*, in: Carbonneau (ed.), Lex Mercatoria and Arbitration, at 53, 59.
514. *Cf. Bucher*, in: Schwind (ed.), Aktuelle Fragen zum Europarecht aus der Sicht in– und ausländischer Gelehrter, at 11, 44; *cf. also Mertens*, Festschrift Odersky, at 857 *et seq.* who attaches a 'virtually complete dispute settlement potential' to the *lex mercatoria* in view of its inherent 'norm-creation potential'; *see* for a similar view *Stein*, Lex mercatoria, at 241 *et seq.*
515. *But see Béguin*, McGill Law Journal 1985, at 478, 487.

contained therein[516]. In drafting their contracts, the parties act like legislatures[517]. The famous formula employed in Art. 1134 of the French Code Civil (‘*Les conventions légalement formées tiennent lieu de loi à ceux qui les ont faites*’) expresses the law-making force of the contractual consensus[518]. It is this particular nature of international contracts which makes vast parts of domestic law inapplicable or useless in the international context. This problem will be discussed again when we analyse the significance of the contract for the development of transnational commercial law[519]. However, the construction and application of contractual stipulations do not take place in a legal vacuum. Instead, they have to be supplemented by general principles of law that take account of the international spirit of the contract. These principles relate to the construction and interpretation of contractual stipulations[520] and to the general problem of determining the complicated equilibrium between the principle of ‘*pacta sunt servanda*’ and the necessity to modify or even discharge an obligation in case of unforeseen circumstances (*hardship, force majeure*)[521].

3. The New *Lex Mercatoria* as a ‘Transnational’ Legal System

All of the objections raised against the NLM doctrine are based on one general assumption: the international community of merchants is not able to ‘create’ its own legal system because this law cannot guarantee justice in the same way as a domestic legal system[522]. The proponents of the NLM doctrine vividly oppose this view[523], arguing on the basis of an institutional and functional understanding of the

516. *Cf. Schlosser*, RIW 1982, at 867.
517. *Cf. Popescu*, in: UNIDROIT (ed.), New Directions in International Trade Law, at 21, 34 (‘*comme de véritables législateurs particuliers*’).
518. Article 1134(1) of the French Code Civil; the sole purpose of this provision is to indicate that the French judge may not, immaterial of how reasonable and fair this would be under the circumstances of a given case, interfere with the contractual stipulations of the parties; *cf.* also Art. 1372 Italian Codice Civile, Art. 1091 Spanish Código Civil; *see generally Hyland*, Va. J. Int’l L. 1993/94, at 406, 427.
519. *See infra* 3.c.
520. *Cf.* TransLex Principles No. IV.5.1–IV.5.6, reprinted *infra* Annex III, available with further references at *www.Trans-Lex.org*.
521. *Cf.* for these principles as part of the *lex mercatoria infra* Chapter 4 II.C.4.b.
522. *Cf. von Hoffmann/Thorn*, IPR, § 2, No. 56.
523. *Cf. Goldstajn*, in: Šarčević (ed.), International Contracts and Conflicts of Laws, 1990, at 14, 22: ‘. . . studies on the sociology of law emphasize the difference between the traditional notion of law in books, *i.e.* embodied in statutes and case law, and living law. Whereas traditional law is concerned with all the legal rules in force, living law focuses only on those legal norms which can be enforced in practice. In many aspects living law is the product of the creative ability and the inventiveness of traders to adapt to changing conditions’; *cf. also David*, UNIDROIT Annuaire 1967–1967, Vol. II, at 259; *Horn*, in: Horn (ed.), Legal Problems of Codes of Conduct for Multinational Enterprises, at 45, 60; *Juenger*, Festschrift Rittner, at 233, 237; *Berman/Dasser*, in: Carbonneau (ed.), Lex Mercatoria and Arbitration, at 53, 58 *et seq.*; *Coing*, in: Klein/Vischer (eds.), Colloque de Bâle sur la Loi Régissant les Obligations Contractuelles, 1983, at 29, 50; *Kahn*, La Vente Commerciale Internationale, at 265 *et seq.*;

law. In their view, the identification of 'state' and 'law' is not necessary. Instead, the social interaction between international merchants as an autonomous group has direct law-making power:

> 'Le théoricien du droit doit dépasser l'illusion archaïque de l'identification de L'Etat et du droit. Partout où s'exerce un pouvoir social, celui-ci prend une forme juridique, à moins qu'il ne se laisse défaire par l'anarchie ou ne projette un rêve spontanéiste. Dans les deux cas, il n'a plus de droit mais pas davantage de pouvoir. Dès lors, il faut reconnaître le pouvoir social – et par conséquent la forme particulière d'ordre juridique – que nous voyons à l'œuvre dans la domaine du sport, celui des relations économiques, dans l'activité des entreprises transnationales, sur le marché des euro-devises et des euro-obligations . . . '[524]

The problem is not new. It is present in public international law[525]. To answer this question, one has to look at the notion of the law itself. If the notion of the law necessarily implies the order of human conduct decreed by a sovereign, then the law necessarily requires the existence of the state as a meta-legal being which creates and administers the principles and rules that constitute the domestic legal system[526]. Unlimited party autonomy and the legal sovereignty of domestic legislatures would be irreconcilable[527]. The evolution of a world trade law would thus require the creation of a 'world state'[528].

This view, however, is based on a predetermined and positivistic[529] notion of the law. It does not take account of the true functions of legal institutions and rules[530]. The law is automatically equated with 'the statute' promulgated by the state legislature[531]. Regarding the state as the *conditio sine qua non* of the law renders this theory of the law contradictory in itself. The state is not only the creator

---

Braeckmans, TvPr. 1986, at 1, 69; *de Vries*, in: ICC (ed.), Hommage à Eisemann, at 115, 122; *Schneider*, NJW 1991, at 1985, 1986; *cf. also Kelsen*, Reine Rechtslehre, at 9.

524. *Cf. Rigaux*, cited by *Braeckmans*, TvPr. 1986, at 1, 67; *cf. Schnitzer*, Festschrift Mann, 1972, at 289, 300; *Berman/Dasser, id.*
525. *See Goode*, ICLQ 1997, at 1, 4: 'Transnational commercial law shares with public international law the characteristic that it raises fundamental jurisprudential questions such as 'What is law?' and 'What are the sources of law?'.
526. *Kelsen*, Reine Rechtslehre, at 288; *von Jhering*, Der Zweck im Recht, Vol. 1, at 125; *Fabricius*, in: Festschrift Schmitthoff, at 101, 108; *see also Jansen/Michaels*, RabelsZ 71 (2007), at 345, 347 dealing with the European perception of law and law-making prevailing in the 19th and 20th century in Europe: 'Was it not obvious that *all* law's validity depended on the state?'.
527. *Bärmann*, Festschrift Mann, at 547, 567.
528. *Fabricius*, Festschrift Schmitthoff, at 101, 105 *et seq.*, who does not follow this view.
529. *Cf. Jakobs*, Wissenschaft und Gesetzgebung im bürgerlichen Recht, at 12 *et seq.*
530. *Cf. Hart*, The Concept of Law, at 1 *et seq.*; *Kant*, Metaphysik der Sitten, Vol. 8, at 338; *Stammler*, Wirtschaft und Recht, at 495; *Rühl*, Rechtsschöpfung durch die Wirtschaft, at 7; *Mertens*, RabelsZ (56) 1992, at 219, 230; *Smid*, Einführung in die Philosophie des Rechts, § 3.I: ' . . . what the law really is can only be said at the end of the philosophy of law, when all of its phenomena have been explained' (translation by the author).
531. *Cf.* the critical statement by *Hoeren*, The Legal History Rev. 1993, at 493, 494.

of the law but is also subject to it. Without the law, the existence of the state as a well-ordered community would be unthinkable[532]. Therefore, there was a time in the history of all people when there was not yet a 'state', but norms were obeyed that could be qualified as law[533]. The enforcement of these norms was not effected by the state judiciary or state power but through private 'judges'. The penance compensations of the Nordic Sagas serve as a typical example for these early mechanisms of 'law'-enforcement[534]. The ancient law merchant also evolved out of mercantile practice. It was 'understood to come out of the market' and 'always followed there'[535]. As a natural consequence of this fact, the ancient *lex mercatoria* was characterized by its far reaching jurisdictional and normative autonomy. As *Baldus de Urbaldis* has stated: '*inter mercatores non convenit de iuris apicibus disputare, sed de mera veritate et consuetudine mercatorum*'[536].

a. *The Functional Notion of Law*

A different perspective is required when seeking an answer to the question as to what is the true nature of 'law'. Functional criteria have to be applied to distinguish binding legal norms from non-binding moral commands[537]. Legal norms fulfil a dual role. They represent the general conviction of what is right or wrong and, as such, form part of the consciousness of those who apply them. At the same time, legal rules and principles form a 'peacekeeping order'. It was *Pufendorf* who understood that legal norms exclude the use of force, the '*bellum omnium contra omnes*' as a means of conflict resolution. Instead, they ensure a fair and just decision of individual disputes. The application of these norms results in a decision that meets the requirements of equal treatment of all those who are subject to the law and that is free from arbitrary considerations[538]. The particularities of state law are thereby reduced to special techniques of the implementation of legislative policies through an organized enforcement procedure[539].

---

532. *Rehfeldt*, Die Wurzeln des Rechts, at 9; *Stammler*, Wirtschaft und Recht, at 496.
533. *Rehfeldt, id.*, at 8; *cf. also Berman/Dasser*, in: Carbonneau (ed.), Lex Mercatoria and Arbitration, at 53, 54 *et seq.*; *Juenger*, Vand. J. Transnat'l L. 1995, at 487, 490 *et seq.*; *cf. also Malynes*, Consuetudo Vel Lex Mercatoria, at 2: '. . . the Lex Mercatoria may well be as ancient as any humane Law . . .'.
534. *Cf. Prausnitz*, Die Geschichte der Forderungsverrechnung, at 17; *Ehrlich*, Grundlegung der Soziologie des Rechts, at 126.
535. *Coquillette*, in: Petit (ed.), Del Ius Mercatorum Al Derecho Mercantil, at 143, 167 (citing from The Little Red Book of Bristol); *see also Mitchell*, Essays on the Early History of the Law Merchant, at 161 stating that the ancient merchant has created the *lex mercatoria* 'out of his own needs and his own views'.
536. *Santarelli*, in: Petit (ed.), Del Ius Mercatorum Al Derecho Mercantil, at 237, 255.
537. *See* for a functionalist view of the law as a means to achieve particular social, political or economic ends, *Zumbansen*, Am.J.Comp.L. 2008, at 769, 783.
538. *See Hyland*, Va. J. Int'l L. 1993/94, at 406, 423; *Strömholm*, Festschrift Zweigert, at 909, 910; *Meyer-Cording*, Die Rechtsnormen, at 7; *Welzel*, Die Frage nach der Rechtsgeltung, at 232; *Smid*, Einführung in die Philosophie des Rechts, at 33.
539. *Zippelius*, Juristische Methodenlehre, § 2.

The state's role in the qualification of the true nature of the law is thus determined by its quality as an association of individuals. This does not mean, however, that the state is the only social organization that is capable of creating and preserving positive law[540]. From a practical perspective, the alleged monopoly of the state in the creation of the law becomes doubtful in view of the ever-growing need for legal decisions in modern societies[541]. From a more theoretical point of view, it has to be emphasized that enforcement mechanisms which guarantee the effectiveness of every legal system can also be implemented by means other than those of the state judiciary[542]. There may also be other compliance guarantees which ensure that the law is adhered to[543]. This preservative function may be performed by a permanent and homogenous structure that provides a framework for the compliance with and the enforcement of the law. A typical example for such a framework would be an organized group or association which unites a certain number of people for the implementation of a certain 'idea'[544].

b. *The Pluralistic Theory of Legal Sources: The New* Lex Mercatoria *as 'Reflexive Law'*

aa. Rule-making at the 'Periphery' of the Legal Process

The founding fathers of the NLM, *Goldman* and *Kahn*, developed the idea of the NLM out of a new[545] pluralistic theory of legal sources[546]. That theory acknowledges that legal rules and principles can be equally produced by political, legal or social processes, *i.e.* spontaneously by specialized, invisible, neatly defined global networks of a cultural, economic, scientific or technical nature. In more recent times, the idea that specific societal groups or associations can create law and that the state is not a necessary component of law-making was developed by

540. *Coing*, Grundzüge der Rechtsphilosophie, at 283.
541. *Mertens*, RabelsZ 56 (1992), at 219, 236.
542. *Cf. Stammler*, Wirtschaft und Recht, at 506.
543. *Coing*, Grundzüge der Rechtsphilosophie, at 285; *cf. also Fabricius*, Festschrift Schmitthoff, at 101, 110 *et seq.*
544. *Cf. Hauriou*, Die Theorie der Institution, at 20 *et seq.*; *Meyer-Cording*, Die Rechtsnormen, at 5.
545. *See* for the plural system of legal sources in Roman law *Jansen/Michaels*, RabelsZ 71 (2007), at 345, 359 *et seq.* '... the [Roman] law's validity was neither related to a "state" as such nor – at least until *Justinian* put the law into a new, comprehensive *corpus iuris* – to the general will of a "sovereign". It was the product of different and independent actors' (footnotes omitted).
546. *See Goldman*, Archives de la philosophie du droit, at 177, 179 *et seq.*; *Kahn*, in: Fouchard/Kahn/Lyon-Caen (eds.), Le droit des relations économiques internationales, at 97, 99, quoting from *Francescakis'* preface to the French translation of *Romano's* treatise on the legal order; *see also Lagarde, id.*, at 125, 134 *et seq.*; *see generally Romano*, L'ordinamento giuridico, 23 *et seq.*

Gunther Teubner in his studies on a 'global law without a state'[547]. His theory was later developed and refined by his academic pupils *Calliess* and *Zumbansen*[548].

Teubner pointed at the basic and fundamental reasons why the NLM doctrine meets with such strong opposition from the proponents of the traditional, positivistic theory of legal sources. The notion of an autonomous transnational commercial law breaks with two classical taboos:

(1) private agreements cannot produce law without authorization or control by the states; and
(2) law cannot exist beyond the realm of domestic states and international relations without a 'global rule of recognition'[549].

In *Teubner's* view, both arguments must be rejected. According to this pluralistic theory of the law, there is no 'naturally given' relation between private law and the state[550]. The NLM is produced as para-legal law at the 'periphery' of the legal process, at the 'contact zones' to international business as a distinct area of society, not in the centre of the traditional sovereign or international law-making institutions. The NLM is created by way of a 'self-reproducing legal discourse of global dimension' in close interaction with globally operating legal entities and transactions which are negotiated at the global level[551]. According to *Teubner*, the 'global villages' formed by autonomous, self-referential subsystems of our society such as international business create the 'new Bukowina'[552] of world society in which

547. *Teubner*, Rechtshistorisches Journal 1996, at 255 *et seq.*; *Teubner*, Law as Autopoietic System, 1993, at 25 *et seq.*; *Teubner*, in: Teubner (ed.), Global Law without a State; *Teubner* in: Ladeur (ed.), Public Governance in the Age of Globalization, at 71, 72 *et seq.*; *cf. also Wiethölter*, in: Teubner (ed.), Dilemmas of Law in the Welfare State, at 221 *et seq.*; *Macaulay*, Private Government in: Lipson/Wheeler (eds.), Law and the Social Sciences, at 445 *et seq.*; *Merry*, 22 Law & Society Rev. 1988, at 869 *et seq.*

548. *Calliess*, German L.J. No. 17 2001, *Calliess*, Zeitschrift für Rechtssoziologie 2002, at 185 *et seq.*; *Calliess*, Grenzüberschreitende Verbraucherverträge, at 220 *et seq.*; *Calliess*, Ind.J.Gl.Legal Studies 2007, at 469, 472; *Zumbansen*, RabelsZ 67 (2000), at 637 *et seq.*; *Zumbansen*, Eur.L.J. 2002, at 400 *et seq.*; *Zumbansen*, Ind.J.Gl.Legal Studies 2007, at 191 *et seq.*; *Zumbansen*, Am.J.Comp.L. 2008, at 769, 789 *et seq.*

549. *Teubner*, Rechtshistorisches Journal 1996, at 255, 267; *see* for the necessity of a 'rule of recognition' as the foundation of a legal system *Hart*, The Concept of Law, at 97 *et seq.*

550. *Jansen/Michaels*, *supra* note 526, at 397.

551. *Teubner*, *supra* note 549, at 268 *et seq.*; *see also Goode*, ICLQ 2005, at 539, 549: 'Lex mercatoria as practice is thus almost as potent as a true law, and this is why it has been described by some leading scholars as operating at the periphery of the legal process and as soft law but not weak law'.

552. Bukowina is a historic landscape in the eastern part of Central Europe. Today, the northern part belongs to the Ukraine, the southern part to Rumania. *Eugen Ehrlich* was born in 1862 in *Czernowitz*, Bukowina, which at that time belonged to Austria-Hungary and is now in the Ukranian part of the Bukowina. *Ehrlich* observed the first traces of his notion of 'living law', which is created by groups of society and not by the domestic legislature, in the life of the different ethnic groups in the Bukowina, which lived their everyday life according to their own self-made rules and not according to Austrian law, *see Ehrlich*, Das lebende Recht der Völker der Bukowina, in: Ehrlich (ed.), Recht und Leben, at 43.

Eugen Ehrlich's 'living law'[553] is transposed to our modern times[554]. The boundaries of that global law are formed not by maintaining a core 'territory' and expanding on a 'federal' basis as *Kant* perceived the nation-state. Instead, this global law is formed by invisible colleges, markets and branches, professional communities, and social networks that transcend territorial boundaries but nevertheless press for the emergence of genuinely legal forms. It is not the state, but the force of the contractual agreement and the function of international arbitral tribunals which stand in the centre of this law-making process. The contract 'makes the impossible possible' and becomes a genuine source of law[555]. International arbitral tribunals are the most important factors for this autonomous legal system. They provide an external control mechanism for the validation of the principles and rules which are contained in these contracts and which are part of the NLM. At the same time, however, these tribunals are an 'internal product' of the contract itself due to the consensual nature of arbitration which is typically based on an agreement of the parties. Together with private governance[556] by international formulating agencies like the ICC or UNIDROIT which the parties to international contracts tend to regard as 'private law makers'[557], these tribunals establish the necessary 'reflexive mechanism' as the basis for any autonomous legal system[558]. In *Teubner's* view, recognition of this 'silent revolution of the NLM' by domestic legislatures is only a secondary question. Recognition of the NLM by domestic legislatures is not a constitutive element of a legal system[559].

The NLM thus provides a perfect example of '*reflexive law*': while domestic legislatures impose on society as a whole and in a 'top down' fashion how life should be, the NLM is generated by a sector-specific, 'bottom up' law-creation process that reacts to and mirrors the facts and developments of real life, *i.e.* the habits and contract practices of international business[560].

553. *See Ehrlich*, Grundlegung der Soziologie des Rechts, at 415: 'The living law is the law which dominates life itself even though it has not been posited in legal propositions. The source of our knowledge of this law is, first the modern legal document; secondly, direct observation of life, of commerce, of customs and usages, and of all associations, not only of those that the law has recognized but also of those that it has overlooked and passed by, indeed even of those that it has dissapproved.'
554. *Teubner, supra* note 549, at 261.
555. *Teubner, id.*, at 274 *et seq.*; *see also Lieckweg*, Das Recht der Weltgesellschaft, at 6 (the contract as a 'conditional program of global validity').
556. *See supra* Chapter 1 III; *see also* for the significance of private governance in the NLM context *Calliess*, Ind.J.Gl.Legal Studies 2007, at 469, 481.
557. *See supra* I 4. for *Clive Schmitthoff's* emphasis on formulating agencies and *infra* I 7. for the changing paradigm of international trade and commerce.
558. *Teubner, supra* note 549, at 276; *see also Stein, supra* note 46, at 164 *et seq.*
559. *Teubner, id.*, at 278 *et seq.*
560. *But see Wasserstein Fassberg*, Chi.J.Int'l L. 2004, at 67, 81, arguing that all attempts to formulate the NLM are intended to 'prescribe, on the basis of what is common to some indefinite number of legal systems, what businessmen (and other contracting parties) should do, rather than describing what merchants do in fact. In this sense, far from being a "spontaneous outgrowth", it is a product, artificially manufactured by outsiders who are occupied not with recording behaviour but rather with selecting rules that should govern behaviour'.

bb. Globalization and the Law

There is a close link between the development of transnational legal structures in business and trade and the globalization of the world economy[561]. It would certainly be far too easy to explain the theory of the plurality of legal sources and the present state of the doctrine of transnational commercial law through the notion of globalization. This abstract term has become a *cliché* rather than a term with substantive content[562]. When we look behind the diffuse and abstract notion of 'globalization', we find a concrete phenomenon which has four common denominators:

(1) the trend towards a 'global civil society'[563];
(2) the erosion and irrelevance of national boundaries in markets which can truly be described as global and the decreasing significance of sovereignty in this area[564];
(3) the relative decline of state power to influence or steer national or international economic developments[565]; and
(4) the strong trend towards informal approaches to international rule- and decision-making, especially the practice of 'private governance'[566].

This process of the de-nationalization of the legal process both in the sphere of public international[567] and international commercial law[568] has an important impact on legal theory. This redefinition of the relationship between global rule-making and legal theory, in turn, is of great importance for the doctrine of transnational law since 'this is one of those rare instances where practical legal decisions are directly dependant upon theoretical preconceptions'[569]. The states' loss of their formerly dominant position in international policy and rule-making inherent in this process, the decreased significance of sovereignty, and the freedom of the parties in international contract law have caused a reconsideration of the traditional theory of legal sources which has 'moved beyond yesteryear's narrow-minded positivism'[570]. The traditional theory of legal sources which was centred

---

561. *See Lynch*, The Forces of Economic Globalization, at 309 *et seq.*
562. *See generally Delbrück*, Ind.J.Gl.Legal Studies 1993, 9 *et seq.*; *Walker/Fox*, Ind.J.Gl.Legal Studies 1996, at 375, 379 *et seq.*; *Luhmann*, Das Recht der Gesellschaft, at 571 *et seq.*
563. *See generally Böhm*, in: Mestmäcker (ed.), Freiheit und Ordnung in der Marktwirtschaft, at 105 *et seq.*; *Schröder*, Die neue Gesellschaft/Frankfurter Hefte 2000, at 200 *et seq.*; *see also* the vision of a 'general global legal society' of *von Savigny*, System des heutigen Römischen Rechts, Vol. 8, at 30 *et seq.*
564. *Walker/Fox*, *supra* note 562, at 380.
565. *See e.g. von Bredow*, in: Globalisierung und nationale Souveränität – Festschrift für Röhrich, at 159, 161 *et seq.*
566. *See supra* Chapter 1 III.
567. *See Hobe*, Global Legal Studies Journal 1997, 191, 207 who points at the development of a 'global society as opposed to the world of states'.
568. *See supra* I.7.
569. *Teubner*, *supra* note 549, at 264.
570. *Juenger*, in: Carbonneau (ed.), Lex Mercatoria and Arbitration, at 265, 276; *see also Berman/Dasser*, *supra* note 68, at 60.

around the notion of sovereignty[571] is being replaced by a legal pluralism which accepts that society's ability for self-organization and coordination is more than a mere factual pattern without independent legal significance. Today, it assumes a normative quality of its own.

cc. Early Examples of Transnationalism

It must be emphasized that this fundamental change of legal theory is by no means new[572]. What we are facing today is a return to the views of the relationship between state sovereignty and the theory of legal sources of the early twentieth century, albeit in a totally different geo-political and economic setting. Three examples serve to exemplify the notion of transnationalism which flourished during these days.

(a) *Raiser*

The German academic *Ludwig Raiser*, though being a proponent of a traditional positivistic view of the theory of legal sources, summarized these views in his famous treatise on general contract conditions published in 1935 as follows:

> 'Since it turns out to be impossible to qualify general contract conditions as parts of contracts or as parts of the traditional catalogue of the sources of objective law, the option remains to put into question the distinction between a legal norm and a legal transaction. Is the thinking correct that parties, in concluding a transaction, are merely setting a factual pattern, to which the law attributes or denies legal effect at its will? Aren't the parties themselves able to regulate their living conditions without the intermediation of the legal order of the state, *thus creating law among themselves*?...
>
> From this perspective, the *principle of party autonomy*... means: reluctance of the state and the legal system to intervene in the regulation of the legal relationships of private parties and instead, far reaching recognition of all specialized legal regimes, *i.e. dezentralization of lawmaking*... It is not the decentralization of the creation of the law which displays a weakness of the state which is dangerous for legal life...
>
> The state may neither reach nor claim the position as the sole guarantor of the law. It need not be concerned with the thousand written and unwritten conventions within the various social groups of society, which are secured by them through moral force, as long as these groups do not develop into a political power factor... In empirical reality, the degree of dependence of the transaction from the recognition of the state depends upon political and

571. *von Jhering*, Der Zweck im Recht, at 249: 'Only those rules imposed by society deserve the name of law which have behind them the force of the law or... the force of the sovereign state, meaning that only those rules adopt the quality of legal norms that have been vested with this effect by the sovereign state or that the state is the only source of the law' (translation by the author).

572. *See Michaels/Jansen*, Am.J.Comp.L. 2006, at 843, 874.

economic factors and consequently, may vary from case to case, from decade to decade'[573].

(b) *Zitelmann* and *Lambert*

In the late nineteenth and early twentieth centuries, the enthusiasm for nationalism and the industrial revolution led the German academic *Ernst Zitelmann* to develop the idea of a world private law ('*Weltprivatrecht*')[574]. Based on comprehensive comparative research among the legal systems of all civilized nations, the 'world private law' was supposed to be superior to any domestic legal system both in its formal structure and substantive content. In the view of its proponents, this law should be implemented through a treaty of public law. The idea was fostered by the birth of comparative law as an independent legal science at the First International Congress of Comparative Law which took place in Paris in 1900, the venue of the World Exposition[575]. In fact, it was at this Congress that *Saleilles*, proponent of the French 'Natural Law School' which was influenced by the writings of *Stammler*, and *Lambert*, introduced the idea of a 'universalist view of law' by ascertaining 'general principles which are common to all civilized legal systems' ('*droit idéal relatif*', *Saleilles*) and of creating an 'International Common Law' (*Lambert*) consisting of rules which are applicable to the needs of such communities as have attained the same standard of civilization[576]. In fact, *Édouard Lambert* described in 1935 his idea of a new international commercial law in a way which is said to be 'the strongest proclamation ever written of what we call today the *lex mercatoria*'[577]:

> 'Né comme la loi marchande médiévale de la seule force des faites économiques, et sans aucune consécration d'autorités étatiques territoriales, ce nouveau droit commercial fait par les commerçants a, comme la loi marchande médiévale, l'aptitude à se répandre librement par dessus les frontières des Etats et des nationalités. Il prend dès sa naissance un caractère accusé de cosmopolitisme, parce que les activités commerciales ou industrielles, dont il est appelé à régler le jeu, sont elles-mêmes des activités internationales. Dès aujourd'hui les commerces les plus avancés dans la voie de la rationalisation sont arrivés, non pas en général à une unification systématique et complète des usages juridiques de leurs branches commerciales, mais du moins à une uniformisation suffisante pour les besoins essentiels du commerce international'[578].

573. *Raiser*, Das Recht der Allgemeinen Geschäftsbedingungen, 1935, at 63, 74.
574. *Zitelmann*, Allgemeine Österreichische Gerichts-Zeitung 39 (1888), at 193, 201 *et seq.*; *Klein*, in: Festschrift für Ernst Zitelmann, 1913, at 3 *et seq.*
575. *See Gutteridge*, Comparative Law, at 5.
576. *Gutteridge*, *id.*
577. *Lagarde*, in: Fouchard/Kahn/Lyon-Caen (eds.), Le droit des relations économiques internationales, at 125, 136, note 43.
578. *Lambert*, Sources du droit comparé ou supranational. Législation uniforme et jurisprudence comparative, at 478, 498.

Zitelmann's progressive idea was, of course, a legal utopia. It was doomed to fail from the outset due to its broad scope, covering all areas of private law, the geopolitical framework of the early twentieth century and the strengthening notion of sovereignty and nationalism.

(c) *Duguit*

Similarly, *Duguit* adopted the notion of decentralized law-making and of the decreasing significance of the sovereign state in the theory of legal sources in the early twentieth century. He emphasized that the proposition that law, being a command, was always a unilateral act and that law and agreement were two mutually exclusive terms and that therefore, there could be no such thing as laws existing by mere agreement, cannot be considered true in the modern state[579]. Today, the effects of private ordering for the creation of norms by decentralized societal self-organization are verified by application of game theory and computer modelling techniques[580].

c. *The International Community of Merchants as a Source for the Creation of Transnational Law*

It is a standard argument against the NLM doctrine that a homogenous group, a 'global village' in the language of *Teubner's* reflexive law theory[581], does not exist as such. Rather, the international community of merchants has a heterogeneous character, composed of trade associations, individual traders and businessmen, and unorganized groups of merchants, thus lacking a coherent social pattern and the structural unity necessary for the institutional creation of the law[582]. This reminds us of the medieval *lex mercatoria* which evolved out of the particular usages of the major trading centres of that age and never constituted a uniform, self-contained system of commercial law[583]. The problem with this view is that it attaches a dual function to the usages developed in a particular branch of international trade. While they serve to provide unified contract practices for all those merchants who do business in that particular field of international trade, they are also said to stand in the way of the development of a worldwide uniform commercial law. It has to be born in mind, however, that vertical usages and contract practices of a particular branch of international trade may achieve general recognition within the international community of merchants, thereby developing into horizontal usages which apply on a global basis and are not limited to businessmen that are active

579. *Duguit*, Les Transformations du Droit Public, at 85 *et seq.*; *but see* for a different view *Allen*, Law in the Making, at 485.
580. *See* for a fascinating '*in silico*' approach to norm making *Picker*, U.Chi.L.Rev. 1997, at 1225 *et seq.*
581. *See supra* text at note 552.
582. *Kassis*, Théorie Générale des Usages du Commerce, at 398 *et seq.*; *Bärmann*, Festschrift Mann, at 547, 564; *Lynch*, The Forces of Economic Globalization, at 321 *et seq.*; *see also Lagarde supra* note 577, at 137 *et seq.*
583. *Cf. Bärmann, id.*, at 547, 555 *et seq.*; *Stoecker*, J.Int'l Arb., No. 1 1990, at 101, 102 *et seq.*

only in one particular industry[584]. Thus, many practices which are reflected in the INCOTERMS have their origin in certain branches of international trade and have gradually developed into generally recognized commercial practices.

This horizontal approach meets with the objectives of the proponents of a transnational commercial law. Their intention is not to advocate the existence of a multitude of '*leges mercatoriae*'. Instead, their doctrine is based on the assumption that a single uniform system of commercial law exists on the transnational plane and is in a constant state of flux and evolution[585].

d. *The Contractual Consensus as the Core of Decentralized Law-Making*

The mere fact that the '*societas mercatorum*' has an interest in achieving commercial profits through cross-border trade, does not suffice to justify the law-making power of the international community of merchants. The assumption of a transnational legal system requires more than a simple pragmatic policy of reasonable self-interest[586]. It would be wrong to assume that there are transactions which have the transaction itself as their sole end, rather than, *e.g.* the accomplishment of a useful step in a chain from producer to consumer[587]. Also, transnational law has to be distinguished from a mere social structure organized through conventional rules[588]. In order to be recognized as the basis for a true legal system, the collective expectations of the members of that community with respect to compliance with certain rules of behaviour have to be intensified in a way that these rules and principles are regarded as binding and mandatory upon each member[589]. This requires a basic consensus of common values and convictions and the readiness of every member of that community to comply with the relevant rules and principles *even at the risk of losing or doing damage to individual interests*[590]. From an individual perspective, the 'validity' of a legal system means nothing more than 'being motivated through the existence of legal principles and rules'[591]. With this mandatory element, the law carries an 'unfriendly moment'[592] in the regulation of social life.

584. *Eisemann/Melis*, INCOTERMS, at 18; *Kropholler*, Internationales Einheitsrecht, at 124.
585. *See Lagarde*, in: Fouchard/Kahn/Lyon-Caen (eds.) Le Droit des Relations Économiques Internationales, at 125, 135.
586. *Wieacker*, Festschrift Zweigert, at 575, 592; *cf. also Molineaux*, J.Int'l Arb., No. 1 1997, at 55, 58.
587. *Molineaux, id.*
588. *Stammler*, Wirtschaft und Recht, at 529.
589. *Meyer-Cording*, Die Rechtsnormen, at 6 *et seq.*; *cf. also Mertens*, RabelsZ 56 (1992), at 219, 231; *cf. generally* for an agent-based computer model for the study of social patterns of norms *Picker*, U.Chi.L.Rev. 1997, at 1225, 1234 *et seq.*
590. *Wieacker*, Festschrift Zweigert, at 575, 592.
591. *Rühl*, Rechtsschöpfung durch die Wirtschaft, at 9.
592. *Stammler*, Wirtschaft und Recht, at 532.

This is also true in international trade where the business persons' consciousness of the validity of trade usages, customs, contract practices, and similar rules is guaranteed through 'black lists', withdrawal of membership rights, forfeiture of bonds, and similar dangers to the commercial reputation[593]. Above all, it is the inherent danger of losing commercial good will and standing within the community of merchants – and with it the 'membership' of this closely knit community – which provides the necessary incentive to adhere to the self-made law of international business[594]. The necessary coordination of the wills of the individual market participants is brought about in the context of 'conflict avoidance' during the drafting of the contracts themselves[595]. In participating in the contractual consensus ('*consensus ad idem*'), each party expresses the confidence that its counterpart will comply with the terms and conditions of the contract[596]. Thus, the contract becomes the most important means to implement the will of the parties in practice because, in the absence of any need to ensure consumer protection, international trade and commerce constitutes an ideal climate for the free development of contractual structures[597]. The notion of 'private governance'[598] is thus extended to the contract itself. Contractual governance or 'governance by contract' occurs at the level of society[599], in our context within the society of merchants who take part in the global exchange of goods, services and money. The contract becomes the means of 'auto-regulation' within the de-territorialized and, by virtue of modern IT-technology, de-materialized global marketplace[600].

The realization of this eminent force of the contractual consensus goes back to *Grotius* and *Pufendorf*, who realized that the keeping of one's word is in harmony with the social nature of humans and the principle of good faith[601]. Through these authors, this realization then penetrated into classical contract law doctrine[602]. The ancient *lex mercatoria* of the middle ages was thus built on the faith in a given word, thereby allowing the actionability of *pacta nuda 'in curia*

593. *Rühl*, Rechtsschöpfung durch die Wirtschaft, at 16.
594. *See generally Cooter*, U.Pa.L.Rev. 1996, at 1643, 1694 *et seq.*; *Bernstein*, U.Pa.L.Rev. 1996, at 1765 *et seq.*; *Scott*, J.Legal Stud. 1990, at 597, 613 *et seq.*; *Charny*, Harv.L.Rev. 1990, at 373 *et seq.*; *Posner*, U.Chi.L.Rev. 1996, at 133, 159 *et seq.*
595. *Fabricius*, Festschrift Schmitthoff, at 101, 115; *cf. also Ripert*, Rec.Cours 1933-II, at 565, 588: '*C'est . . . une règle fondamentale du droit reconnue par tous les peuples que le consentement réciproque de deux sujets de droit suffit à créer, à transformer ou à éteindre un rapport juridique. Cet échange de volontés, c'est le contrat. Toute liberté est, en principe reconnue aux hommes pour contracter, et leur volonté est dite autonome en ce qu'elle crée la règle*'; *cf. also Ferrari*, Riv.Tr.Dir.Pr.Civ. 1994, at 893, 898 *et seq.*
596. *Cf. Ripert*, Rec.Cours 1933-II, at 565, 589.
597. *See Kahn*, in: Bonell/Bonelli (eds.), Contratti Commerciali Internazionali E Principi UNIDROIT, at 41, 42.
598. *See supra* Chapter 1 III.
599. *Zumbansen*, Ind.J.Gl.Legal Studies 2007, at 191, 211.
600. *See Loquin*, in: Souveraineté étatique et marchés internationaux à la fin du 20ème siècle, at 23, 31; *see also Berger*, in: Berger (ed.), The Practice of Transnational Law, at 1, 14 *et seq.*
601. *Hyland, supra* note 538, at 425 *et seq.* citing from *Pufendorf, De jure naturae et gentium libri octo* and *Grotius, De jure belli ac pacis libri tres.*
602. *See Atiyah's* Introduction to the Law of Contract, at 9 *et seq.*

mercatorum'[603]. At the fairs, seaports, and market towns of the Middle Ages, 'purchase and sale of merchandise was continually made' and 'the law merchant or law of the market was always followed there continuously'[604].

Today, this ancient contract practice forms the basis of the 'promise principle' as the underlying idea of modern contract law[605]. The trust of one side in the promise of the other ('my word is my bond') provides the essential basis for modern international trade transactions[606]: 'The morality of business turns the promise into a categorical imperative'[607]. The legal obligation that requires performance from every party to a contract is nothing other than the moral duty to respect one's word[608]. This notion of the contractual consensus, like the classical contract doctrine[609], is characterized by a lack of concern with distributive questions. However, the NLM only applies outside the consumer context. Also, international merchants bear an increased responsibility for the conduct of their business affairs, resulting in a transnational principle which presumes their professional competence[610]. It is thus in the field of transnational business activities, where the force of the contractual consensus can flourish and develop its law-making quality, unhampered by consumer protection laws and notions of distributive justice that go beyond the general principle of 'good faith and fair dealing in international trade'.

A typical example of this process, albeit in a closely knit commercial community, is the diamond trade in Antwerp, Belgium and other places of the world[611]. Each day, diamonds worth thousands or even millions of US dollars are traded there. The contracts between the diamond traders, frequently concluded through professional intermediaries, are based solely on the consensus of the parties, the mutual trust in the other party's performance, a handshake, and a special trading formula. Breach of these informal, unwritten contracts, however, will result in worldwide suspension from trading which will be publicly announced. This provides a strong incentive for the parties to meet their contractual obligations. Similar examples of informal, trust-based contract practices can be found in the commodity trade. When written contracts are required in international, arm's length transactions, the mutual trust of the parties is made possible and enhanced by the

603. *Zimmermann*, ZEuP 1993, at 4, 30; *cf. also* for the principle '*ex pacto nudo datur actio*' *Hyland, supra* note 538, at 417.
604. *Coquillette*, in: Petit (ed.), Del Ius Mercatorum Al Derecho Mercantil, at 143, 168 (citing from the Little Red Book of Bristol).
605. *See Kötz*, Europäisches Vertragsrecht, Vol. I, at 11.
606. *Braeckmans*, TvPr. 1986, at 1, 16; *Storme*, in: Hartkamp/Hesselink/Hondius/du Perron/Vranken (eds.), Towards a European Civil Code, 1st ed., at 159, 184.
607. *Hyland*, Am.J.Comp.L. 1992, at 541, 545.
608. *Hyland, id*., at 427 *et seq*. (citing *Flour* and *Aubert*).
609. *See Atiyah, supra* note 602, at 9 *et seq*.; *cf*. for the classical 'trust theory' ('*Vertrauenstheorie*') as the means to bind a party to its promise *Schermaier*, ZEuP 1998, at 60, 73 *et seq*. (with reference to *Grotius* and *Domingo de Soto*).
610. *See* TransLex Principle No. I.2.3, reprinted *infra* Annex III, available with further references at *www.Trans-Lex.org/909000*.
611. *See generally Bernstein*, J.Legal Stud. 1992, at 115 *et seq*.

multitude of standard form contracts and uniform contractual models that are circulated in the worldwide business community.

This understanding of the transnational legal process requires the redefining of the traditional theory of legal sources. In modern business relationships, it is the contract which assumes the genuine function of a source of law:

> 'It is the contract which now constitutes a legal change. Tradititional legal concepts do not include the contract among the sources of law. But if we continue to conceive of the contract as a mere application of the law, and not as a source of law, we will preclude the possibility of understanding how the law of our times is changing. The contract is taking the place of the law, even in the organization of society. Some decades ago Millibad wrote that, more than ever, people considered the state as source of all provisions and even as a source of their happiness. Today we must say that this notion is dissappearing. Society now looks after itself and tends towards self-organization...
>
> The inadequacy of the law to make changes derives from two characteristics of contemporary economy. The first is the meta-national nature of the economy which is antithetical to the national character of the legal systems. The second is that the economy is in continuous change which demands flexible instruments of adaptation from the law to change, in antithesis to the rigidity of the laws'[612].

This process implies that the contractual consensus which assumes a law-making force of its own, is shaped, influenced and validated by external criteria other than the parties' self-interests in making a profitable deal[613]. This process of external validation may be effected by the parties' adhesion to certain general or sector-specific market standards, by the reconciliation of the contract with unwritten cultural and/or ethical standards existing in the parties' home jurisdictions, in third countries (*e.g.* the place of performance) or on the regional and global level, or by the transformation of written standards contained in soft law instruments such as Codes of Conduct[614] of the relevant industry in which the parties are operating into 'binary' contractual obligations. This 'objectivation' of the parties' subjective contractual consent receives additional force if they base their contract not (only) on terms which they negotiate on an *ad hoc* basis, but on standard forms prepared by industry organizations or formulating agencies operating at the regional or global level, such as the 'United Nations Economic Commission for Europe (ECE)-General Conditions for the Supply of Plant And Machinery For Export

612. *Galgano*, Ann.Surv.Int'l & Comp.L. 1995, at 99, 102 *et seq.*; *see also Gandolfi*, RTD civ. 1992, at 707, 710 stating that this law-making through contract practice is tending towards an '*éloignement progressif d'une vision étatiste du droit*'.

613. *Loquin*, in: Souveraineté étatique et marchés internationaux à la fin du 20ème siècle, at 23, 33 *et seq.*; *see also* for the view that a contract which is considered as a source of transnational law 'must be open to challenge as not inherently rational and, indeed, as oppressive or injurious to the wider public interest' *Goode/Kronke/McKendrick*, Transnational Commercial Law, No. 1.43.

614. *See supra* Chapter I III.B.

(LW 188)' or the International Federation of Consulting Engineers (FIDIC) Conditions or the model contracts for distributorship, agency and international sales issued by the ICC[615].

If the confidence of one side in the compliance with the contractual terms by the other is disappointed, the arbitrators, whose jurisdiction is based on the consensus of the parties, assume the function of a control instance. The parties' confidence is no longer focused on the counter-party's will to comply with the contractual terms but on the competence of the arbitral tribunal as a privately constituted and 'genuine'[616] court for international trade. The transfer of the case from the plane of the individual bargain to the arbitral tribunal also leads to a change of perspective. The neutrality of the arbitrators requires them to take an objective view of the case, applying objective commercial standards such as 'fair dealing', 'reasonableness' and 'trade usages', thereby enriching the abstract contractual consensus ('*pacta sunt servanda*') with commercial life[617]. The private character of the arbitral process may therefore not be used as an argument to deny the control competence of international arbitrators[618]. Rather, the contractual character of their competence guarantees the homogenous character of the transnational legal process in that not only the participation in it but also the compliance control is based on the same legal notion, *i.e. the contractual agreement as such.* It is not surprising, therefore, that both general contract law and arbitration are characterized by the same principle: '*in favorem validitatis*'[619].

Again, the consensus-based dispute settlement system has important repercussions on the development of transnational law. The drafting practice of international trade, geared towards the ideal of conflict avoidance, reacts to the case law of international arbitral tribunals[620] and thereby consolidates and stabilizes the general structure of the NLM which, in turn, is shaped and influenced by international drafting practice.

615. *Loquin, supra* note 613, 34; *Mustill*, Arb.Int'l 1988, at 86. 89; *Goode/Kronke/McKendrick, id.*, No. 1.50: '.... standard-term contracts drawn up by trade or professional bodies which are designed to balance the competing interests may give a guide to the legitimate expectations of the market and can form the basis of a legal norm.'
616. *Cf.* for the genuine adjudicatory function of arbitral tribunals *supra* D.2.a.
617. *Cf. Bonell*, ICLQ 1978, at 413, 428: '... in interpreting commercial transactions, particularly when concluded at an international level, it is not sufficient to base oneself on the confidence which the parties might have established between themselves; due consideration must also be given to the expectation which the generality of the operators has of fair dealing in the respective trade sector'; *cf. also infra* Chapter 4 I.A.7.b.bb.; *Kahn*, in: Gaillard (ed.), Transnational Rules in International Commercial Arbitration, at 237, 242: 'On constatera que l'introduction de la notion de professionalisme donne une coloration spécifique à la règle générale que le contract tienne lieu de loi aux parties'; *cf. also David*, Le Droit Du Commerce International, at 127 *et seq*.
618. *But see Kassis*, Théorie Générale des Usages du Commerce, at 406.
619. *Cf. infra* Chapter 4.I.A.7.a.
620. *Goldstaijn*, Festschrift Schmitthoff, at 171, 179: '... it is a fact that Standard Contracts and the General Conditions have often been corrected through competition and therefore constitute rational solutions'.

This phenomenon of 'consensual regulation of international commerce'[621] is well known from the field of investment contracts:

> 'It belongs to the regrettable weaknesses of public international law that its norms – frequently still in the *status nascendi* – are difficult to put in a concrete form. Every arbitral award, every other solution of such a conflict – and every drafting technique adopted to solve such problems – contribute to the finding of the law. One should not be impatient. The 'actors' ... generally know about the consequences of their conduct. Irrational conduct from one or the other side will always have catastrophic consequences for the party ... there is a major chance for the consolidation of public international law of expropriation because the parties usually behave in a rational manner'[622].

It is at this juncture that the circle of consensual law-making is closed. Dispute settlement through arbitration or other dispute resolution techniques forms the vital link between spontaneous and reactive drafting techniques and the formation and evolution of the NLM. Transnational law may therefore be traced back to the consensus of the participants of international trade[623]. This consensus has a legal force of its own without the need of a prior acknowledgment by domestic legislatures.

e. *Necessity of a 'Multi-Party Agreement'?*

International legal doctrine maintains that the legal force of 'para-legal norms' requires a 'multi-party consensus'[624]. The multilateral character of the consensus, found in statutes of a commercial association[625], by-laws of a commercial corporation or other rules and regulations that have been implemented by that community, is said to provide the necessary consensual density that justifies the legal force of rules and norms issued on the basis of these agreements. In international commerce, such multilateral contractual arrangements take the form of joint venture contracts, syndicate transactions, international financial contracts and contracts

621. The term was coined by *Schanze*, Investionsverträge im Internationalen Wirtschaftsrecht, at 151.
622. *Sandrock*, ZHR 152 (1988), at 66, 86 (translation by the author); *cf. also Gramlich*, Rechtsgestalt, Regelungstypen und Rechtsschutz bei grenzüberschreitenden Investitionen, at 527: 'Without a minimum degree of convergence with respect to the systematic categorization of the multitude of cross-border transactions and operations, which have their common denominator in the typical activities of international investment ... – the criteria of which have to be deduced not only from domestic law but also from rules developed on the international plane, and not necessarily only those derived from public international law – the law, especially in the sphere of transnational economy, runs the risk of not being able to follow the realities of meta-legal facts, of being reduced to a mere mechanical image of these facts without being able to assume the function of reflecting these facts, let alone to serve as a device to influence and structure transnational economy' (translation by the author).
623. *Cf. generally Stammler*, Wirtschaft und Recht, at 508.
624. *Braeckmans*, TvPr. 1986, at 1, 38 *et seq.*
625. *Cf. Rühl*, Rechtsschöpfung durch die Wirtschaft, at 20.

concluded in the context of major construction projects[626]. These contracts, however, only bind a fraction of those who participate in international trade and commerce. By themselves, they do not establish the necessary multi-party consensus. This lack of direct consensual density is made good by the repetitive use of contractual clauses and stipulations in international commercial drafting practice[627]. Commercial practice consistently adopted is a guide to what reasonable members of the commercial community regard as a proper response to a particular fact situation and may therefore be indicative of a legal norm[628]. Also, each contract has to be seen as one link in a chain of similar transactions concluded by other businesspersons for the purpose of bringing about that particular transaction[629] or of delivering a product from producer to consumer[630]. Similar to a direct multi-party consensus, the multiplying effect of the drafting practice of international trade and commerce echoes the basic consensus with respect to legal values and phenomena[631], thereby providing the necessary prerequisite for the institutional creation of transnational commercial law. There is an obvious correlation between this phenomenon and the increased professional responsibility of international businesspersons[632].

This interaction of drafting practice and law-making is by no means new. *von Jhering* has already characterized the inclusion of standardized contractual arrangements into positive law as an incentive to develop the law from the outside social world[633]. In the context of the NLM, however, a superior legal quality is attached to this phenomenon. The combined effect of the recurring bilateral or multilateral contractual consensus and the decision-making of international arbitral tribunals which is also based on the consensus of the parties, is re-enforced through the 'codifying' efforts of international formulating agencies[634]. This process should not be confused with the evolution of customary law. We are not

626. *Cf.* for a 'multiparty-connection' in large industrial projects *Dorner*, in: Nicklisch (ed.), Rechtsfragen privatfinanzierter Projekte, at 75 *et seq.*; *Berger*, Internationale Wirtschaftsschiedsgerichtsbarkeit, at 206; *Osman*, Lex Mercatoria, at 228 *et seq.*
627. *Loquin, supra* note 613, at 30. '*On ne peut être que frappé par la répétition de processus de formation de normes et d'autorégulations, qui ont été constatés dans toutes les branches émergentes du commerce international, à savoir la production d'une innovation juridique modélisée proposée aux opérateurs du marché, lesquels répondent à l'offre en l'utilisant massivement. Ainsi se forme dans le vide des législations étatiques une pratique contractuelle homogène globale qui s'impose indépendamment de la localisation géographique des opérateurs et de leur appartenance à un système juridique donné*'.
628. *Goode/Kronke/McKendrick*, Transnational Commercial Law, No. 1.48.
629. *Radbruch*, Einführung in die Rechtswissenschaft, at 110; *Ferrari*, Riv.Tr.Dir.Pr.Civ. 1994, at 893, 899; *cf.* for the notion of contract as a 'social institution', whose effects go well beyond the parties, and for the idea of 'contractual networks' *Kessler*, Festschrift M. Wolff, at 67 *et seq.*
630. *Molineaux*, J.Int'l Arb., No. 1 1997, at 58.
631. *Cf. Braeckmans, see supra* note 624, at 51.
632. *Cf. Radbruch*, Einführung in die Rechtswissenschaft, at 110.
633. *Cf. K. Schmidt*, in: Behrends (ed.), Privatrecht heute und Jherings evolutionäres Rechtsdenken, at 77, 95.
634. *Cf. supra* D.1.

dealing here with the practice of legal norms but merely with the general conviction of the international community of merchants that the previous practice shall have the quality of legal norms in the future[635]. There is a parallel to the development of trade usages. They do not require the awareness of businesspersons as to their legal force (*necessitas iuris*) either[636]. This explains the statement made above[637] that not all trade usages are part of the NLM.

The presence and strong force of principles and rules of transnational commercial law also explain why approximately 90% of international arbitral awards are voluntarily complied with by the losing parties[638]. This high degree of acceptance of the arbitral process by international businesspersons is underlined by the fact that today almost 90% of major international contracts contain an arbitration clause[639]. These clauses insulate the overwhelming majority of commercial disputes from the jurisdiction of domestic courts. Commercial law, in terms of drafting practice, implementation of contracts and dispute settlement, has therefore assumed a life of its own, *i.e.* the quality of an autonomous system intended to provide a comprehensive legal framework for the development of transnational commercial law[640]. This development is stimulated by domestic legislatures who have granted international arbitrators the authority to decide on their own competence (*Kompetenz-Kompetenz*)[641]. It has reduced[642] or even excluded[643] the domestic courts' control standards with respect to the international arbitrators' decision-making. Finally, domestic courts have even acknowledged the legitimacy of the application of transnational legal principles of commercial law by international arbitrators[644]. The domestic courts' control of the international arbitral process is therefore reduced to the question of whether certain basic procedural due process standards have been complied with by the arbitrators. With this severe restriction of the courts' competence, the argument of the supremacy of domestic legal systems over transnational law loses much of its

635. *Ehrlich*, Grundlegung der Soziologie des Rechts, at 83.
636. *Cf. von Caemmerer/Schlechtriem-Junge*, CISG, Art. 9, No. 3; *cf. also Berman/Dasser*, in: Carbonneau (ed.), Lex Mercatoria and Arbitration, at 53, 65: '. . . what may be called normative customs is assimilated to what may be called behavioral custom, and the presumed expectations of the participants in the usage are sufficient to give rise to the obligation to observe it. The result is to broaden significantly the scope and the enforceability of mercantile understandings in international commerce'; *see also supra* I.C.2.a.
637. *See supra* I.C.2.a.
638. *Cf. Berger*, Internationale Wirtschaftsschiedsgerichtsbarkeit, at 17.
639. *Cf. van den Berg/van Delden/Snijders*, Arbitragerecht, at 134.
640. *See* (even though he rejects the notion of an autonomous world trade law) *Bärmann*, Festschrift Mann, at 547, 573: 'This is certainly the real nucleus of international commercial law, *i.e.* the ousting of domestic courts through resorting to arbitration'.
641. *Cf.* BGHZ 68, 356; *see* the critical statement by *Berger*, Internationale Wirtschaftsschiedsgerichtsbarkeit, at 252 *et seq.*
642. *Cf.* BGHZ 98, 70, 74; BGH NJW 1988, at 3090, 3092; WM 1990, at 12; Swiss Bundesgericht BGE 101 Ia 526; *generally Domke*, Festschrift Bülow, at 49 *et seq.*; *Baur*, Neuere Probleme der privaten Schiedsgerichtsbarkeit, at 15; *cf. also supra* II.D.2.b.
643. *Cf.* for this problem *Berger*, Internationale Wirtschaftsschiedsgerichtsbarkeit, at 503 *et seq.*
644. *Cf. supra* F.2.b.

persuasive force[645]. Consequently, international arbitration does not have to develop into an a-national[646], 'floating' process detached from the procedural constraints of domestic law and based solely on the consensus of the parties ('*pactum facit arbitrum*') in order to be able to contribute to the evolution of a transnational commercial law[647]. Substantive 'mercatorism' does not necessarily pre-suppose procedural 'transnationalism'.

III. SUMMARY

In the field of international commercial law a new, transnational, autonomous legal system is coming into being by way of decentralized, 'spontaneous' law-making. This legal system is the NLM. It receives impetus from public international law, uniform commercial law, and domestic law without sharing the legal qualities of any of these systems[648].

It is important to note that this transnational approach to international commercial law is not based on a purely sociologic or some kind of Darwinist understanding of the law. Nor are we dealing here with a commercial view of the law in the sense of a diffuse 'judicial subjectivism'[649]. Rather, the theory of the NLM developed so far in this Study results from a pragmatic view[650] of the relationship between economy and the law. They are not regarded as antipodes but as complementary elements which in their combined effect and through the law-making force of the parties' contractual consensus create commercial law[651]. This notion of commercial transnationalism is based on a dialectical understanding of the interaction between commercial practice and the law as it has been described by *Radbruch* in his 'Introduction Into Legal Science':

> 'More than in any other field of law, the rules of commercial law, a living law, not paper law, can be found not in the statutes themselves, but must be derived

---

645. *Cf. Coing*, Grundzüge der Rechtsphilosophie, at 283.
646. Like the *lex mercatoria* doctrine, the idea of an a-national arbitral procedure, detached from the constraints of domestic law, was developed in the 1960s in France, *cf. Fouchard*, L'Arbitrage Commercial International, at 22 *et seq.*; *Holleaux*, Rev.crit.dr.int.priv. 1956, at 179; the complete freedom from the arbitration law at the seat of the arbitration was not intended to support the *lex mercatoria* doctrine, but served as a means to escape from the rigid rules of French arbitration law that were in force at that time; it was only later on that this idea was elevated to a universal principle, especially with respect to arbitrations with state parties, where aspects of sovereignty play a special role, *cf. Dasser*, Lex Mercatoria, at 272, note 6; Arbitral Award *Société Européenne d'Études et d'Entreprises v. République de Yougoslavie*, Clunet 1959, at 107 *et seq.*; *cf. von Mehren/Kouridis*, Am.J.Int'l L. 1981, at 476 *et seq.*
647. This seems to be the opinion of *Mustill*, Arb.Int'l 1988, at 86, 89 *et seq.*
648. *Schnitzer*, Festschrift Mann, at 289, 301; *Blaurock*, ZEuP 1993, at 247, 267; *Goldstaijn*, in: Šarčević (ed.), International Contracts and Conflicts of Law, at 14, 18.
649. *Rittner*, Die sogenannte wirtschaftliche Betrachtungsweise in der Rechtsprechung des Bundesgerichtshofes, at 56.
650. *See* for the 'new Cartesian pragmatism', *supra* I.B.
651. *Cf. Seelmann*, Rechtsphilosophie, § 3, Nos. 51 *et seq.*

> from the legal process as such. More than in any other field of law, commercial law provides an example for the struggle of the law with the interest and the influence of the interest on the law, a limited control of the norms over the facts and the ultimate normative force of the facts – in short, commercial law reveals what economic history has always taught us about the relationship of commerce and law. It also teaches us to understand that in an individualistic era, commercial law assumes a pioneer role for the whole field of private law'[652].

Thus, the phenomenon of law-making through commercial practice has begun in the context of domestic laws. It is known, *e.g.* in the field of technical norms and standards where it has lead legal theory to rethink the notion of 'codification'[653]. In the transnational commercial context, this phenomenon is lifted onto a higher plane. A transnational understanding of modern commercial law has an important effect on the doctrine of private international law. Neither the parties' agreement to have the NLM applied to their contract nor the application of this transnational law by international arbitrators in the absence of a choice of law by the parties lead to a '*contrat sans loi*'. International arbitrators who apply the NLM do not act in a legal vacuum, nor do they render a decision in equity. Instead, they apply the rules and principles of a transnational legal system, and their award will be respected by domestic courts[654].

---

652. *Radbruch*, Einführung in die Rechtswissenschaft, at 113 *et seq.* (translation by the author).
653. *See* Chapter I III.A.
654. *Coing*, in: Colloque de Bâle, at 53; *Goldman*, Festschrift Lalive, at 241, 253; *Drobnig*, in: Volken/Šarčević (eds.), Drubovnik Lectures, at 305, 309; *Kappus*, RIW 1990, at 791; *see also Heymann/Horn*, HGB, Vol. 1, Einleitung III, No. 15; *Loquin*, Clunet 1983, at 336; *Gentinetta*, AWD 1970, at 113, 117; *A. Bucher*, in: Schwind (ed.), Aktuelle Fragen zum Europarecht aus der Sicht in- und ausländischer Gelehrter, at 14; *but see Böckstiegel*, Der Staat als Vertragspartner ausländischer Privatunternehmen, at 144, for state contracts; *see also Goode/Kronke/McKendrick*, Transnational Commercial Law, No. 1.47.

Part II

The New *Lex Mercatoria* in Practice: New Approaches towards the Codification of Transnational Commercial Law

Chapter 3

Previous Projects for the Codification of Transnational Contract Law

In the course of the last century, comparative scientists or private institutions have made various efforts towards the unification of transnational contract law. These projects play a pivotal role in the discussion on the codification of transnational commercial law. They provide the vital link between the theoretical basis of the NLM discussed in the first part of this Study and modern trends towards the 'codification' of the NLM to be discussed in Chapter 4.

From the outset, all those approaches that are geared towards the development of a '*droit commun*', '*fonds commun,*' or '*tranc commun*' of the legal systems are excluded from this Study. This is because they are mere methods of decision-making in international commercial cases[1] but do not constitute methods of codifying transnational commercial law. Instead, we are dealing here with two basic types of approaches towards the codification of the NLM. Towards the end of this Study[2] a method of 'Creeping Codification' of transnational commercial law will be presented which derives its legitimacy from the methodical underpinnings developed in the first part of this Study. Secondly, this Study will discuss projects which, based on the functional comparative methodology[3], have established a somewhat formalized procedure for the codification of transnational commercial law on a regional or even global basis. The UNIDROIT Principles of International Commercial Contracts provide an example of this kind of codificatory approach. This second group of efforts towards the codification of transnational commercial law has one common feature. The establishment of working groups, the

1. *See infra* Chapter 4 II.B.2. for a discussion of whether the *lex mercatoria* is a mere *ad hoc* method of decision-making or a codifiable body of law.
2. *Cf. infra* Chapter 4 II.C.
3. *See supra* Chapter 2 II.A.1.

designation of *rapporteurs* for certain areas of law, and similar efforts are designed to provide additional 'legitimacy through procedure' to these approaches.

In discussing these efforts, one has to distinguish between (I.) bilateral or regional and (II.) global projects. While the first group provides functional prototypes for every effort towards the codification of transnational commercial law, the latter group is much more ambitious, thereby indicating the chances for the realization of such projects.

I. BILATERAL AND REGIONAL PROJECTS

A. The Draft of a Franco-Italian Obligation Law

1. History and Contents

During the First World War, the Italian Professor *Vittorio Scialoja*[4], the later initiator and first director of UNIDROIT[5], launched the idea of a bilateral, Franco-Italian code of contract law (*Projet de code des obligations et des contrats*)[6]. In 1917, two private commissions in Italy (chaired by *Scialoja*) and France (chaired by *Larnaude*) began work on the project. The first unofficial draft together with a commentary was presented in 1928 by a Franco-Italian Commission for the Legislative Unification of the Law[7]. The draft consisted of 739 articles which dealt with general contract law and special types of contracts (sale, rent, agency, loan, bailment, transport, guarantee, etc.). Apart from these detailed provisions, the draft also contained general principles of law such as articles on '*lésion*', impermissible exercise of rights, unjust enrichment and general provisions on liability[8]. These blanket clauses were intended to provide the judge with the necessary legal framework for the weighing of interests in individual cases. This drafting approach also intended to eliminate the outright reference to equity (*équité*) which was extensively practiced by the French courts of that time[9]. For example, the French judge *Magnaud* had rendered a long line of judgments in the 1920s which were *contra legem*, but which he regarded as justified under the principles of equity and fairness[10]. In fact, the practice of the contemporary courts to refer to blanket clauses in

4. *Scialoja*, Per un'alleanza legislativa fra gli Stati dell'Intesa, Nuova Antologia 1916, at 450.
5. *Cf. infra* Chapter 4 I.A.1.
6. *Cf. Rotondi*, Am.J.Comp.L. 1954, at 345 *et seq.*
7. Commissione reale per la Riforma dei Codici – Commission Française d'Etudes de L'Union Législative entre les Nations Alliées et Amies (ed.), Projet de Code des Obligations et des Contrats, Rome 1928.
8. *Rotondi*, Am.J.Comp.L. 1957, at 345, 351 *et seq.*; the provisions were later found in Arts 833, 1448, 1467, 2041 and 2047, 2059 of the Italian *Codice Civile* of 1942.
9. *Rotondi*, Am.J.Comp.L. 1957, at 345, 351 *et seq.; cf.* for this tradition of the French courts, especially in the field of contract law *Esser*, in: Summum ius – summa iniuria, at 22, 28.
10. *Cf. Ripert*, Rec. Cours 1933-II, at 569, 575, footnote 1.

order to find a just and equitable solution for individual cases has its origin in this early practice of French courts[11].

2. Reasons for the Failure of the Project

In view of the changed political climate between the two World Wars, work on the project was ultimately abandoned by the French and Italian government[12]. In spite of its failure, the draft code nevertheless had an influence on the Italian *Codice Civile* and on other codifications of that time such as the Polish Civil Code of 1937, the Albanian Civil Code of 1927, the Romanian Civil Code of 1934, and the Greek Civil Code of 1940[13]. This influence is still felt today because modern approaches towards the unification and codification of European contract law are based on the Italian *Codice Civile*[14].

Regardless of the political changes of that time[15], *Scialoja's* project was doomed to fail from the outset because it was both too narrow and too broad. Limiting the project to two legal systems that were rooted in the Roman legal tradition made the drafting work easier but reduced the chances of the project of having a unifying effect that went beyond the French and Italian legal systems. There were simply not enough systems involved to provide the project with the necessary comparative legitimacy[16]. At the same time, however, the project was too ambitious both in terms of size and drafting approach. The unification of private law necessarily infringes upon the sovereignty of the states involved. It is therefore best achieved in small steps and in clearly defined areas of the law[17]. The answer to the question as to the unification of general contract law and particular types of contract may only be 'either . . . or' but not 'both . . . and'. It is therefore not surprising that the UNIDROIT Working Group has taken account of this important principle and has limited its project to general principles of contract law, while the unification of the law for particular types of contracts has been left for future projects.

11. *See supra* Chapter 2 II.B.2.a. and G.2.b.
12. *Bonell*, ICLQ 1978, at 413.
13. *Cf. Rotondi*, Am.J.Comp.L. 1954, at 345, 346; *Kötz*, Festschrift Zweigert, at 481, 492.
14. *See infra* D.
15. Even though political reasons dominate any dogmatic objections, *cf.* the statement of that time cited by *Rotondi*, Am.J.Comp.L. 1957, at 345, 357: 'Assuredly, it is not in this period of exacerbated nationalism that such an endeavor to unify law among the nations can succeed, but this period will have only space of time; the peoples will undoubtedly return, under the compulsion of necessity, to more reasonable economic ideas, and on that day they will comprehend how immense a progress it would be to unify certain parts of their legal systems'.
16. *See supra* Chapter 2 A.II.1.
17. *Cf. Gutteridge*, Comparative Law, at 157: 'It would seem that much of the blame for the failure to achieve more definite and permanent results [in the unification of law] must be attributed to an excess of zeal fostered by an exaggerated belief in the need for unification and overconfidence for its feasibility'.

B. The American 'Restatement of the Law of Contracts'

The UNIDROIT Principles, to be discussed in Chapter 4 of this Study, have often been compared with the 'Restatement of the Law of Contracts' issued by the American Law Institute that was founded in 1923[18]. In fact, there are not only striking parallels between the two projects, but the American[19] Restatement of the Law of Contracts has also served as a systematic model for the UNIDROIT Working Group[20].

1. Drafting History, Contents and Legal Effect

The initiative[21] for the drafting of the American Restatement of the Law of Contracts, which was issued for the first time in 1932[22], came from lawyers active in inter-American commerce and trade. They wanted to overcome the legal uncertainty and complexity of the law that was caused by the strictly federal character of the American legal system. Like the UNIDROIT Principles, the Restatement was drafted by a private organization which appointed *rapporteurs* for the various fields of contract law and adopted the final draft in 1932[23]. The legal rules and principles contained in the Restatement are drafted like black-letter law. They are supplemented by the series 'Restatement in the courts', which indicate the number of times and ways in which the Restatement is cited by American courts, and 'State Annotations' which indicate if and to what extent the principles laid down in the Restatement have been applied in the various American states.

It was a basic policy decision of the Institute not to follow the practice of the National Conference of Commissioners on Uniform State Laws which issues model laws, *e.g.* in the field of company law (Revised Model Business Corporation Act, RMBCA; Uniform Partnership Act, Uniform Limited Partnership Act) or general private and commercial law (Uniform Commercial Code, UCC)[24]. The reason for this special drafting technique was to maintain the necessary flexibility in the application of general contract law[25]. Similar to the UNIDROIT Principles, the Restatement is drafted in the form of black-letter law and

18. *Bonell*, RDAI 1988, at 873; *Bonell*, An International Restatement of Contract Law, at 11 *et seq.; Goode*, Unif.L.Rev. 1991, at 54, 59; *Remien*, RabelsZ 56 (1992), at 300, 312.
19. Apart from the American Restatements, there is also an African Restatement, the function of which is merely to reproduce African customary law, *cf. Allot* (ed.), Restatement of African Law, 1968; *Rheinstein*, Einführung in die Rechtsvergleichung, at 108.
20. *Cf. infra* Chapter 4 I.A.4.
21. The initiative to establish the American Law Institute goes back to Professor *William Draper Lewis* from the University of Pennsylvania, *cf. Honnold* (ed.), The Life of the Law, at 144; *Schindler*, ZEuP 1998, at 277, 278 *et seq.*
22. The Restatement of the Law of Contracts was adopted at the Annual Session of the American Law Institute on May 6, 1932; later, Restatements on eight other fields of law were passed and published (Conflict of Laws, Torts, Agency, Property, Trusts, Restitution, Security, Judgments).
23. *Cf.* for details *Lewis*, in: Honnold (ed.), The Life of the Law, at 150, 153.
24. *See Gray*, RabelsZ 50 (1986), at 111, 117 *et seq.*
25. *Clark*, Yale L.J. 1933, at 643, 649.

accompanied by commentaries and examples. Similar to a statute, there is no reference to the historic origins of each individual principle or rule. The name '*Restatement*' was chosen to indicate from the outset that the drafters' intention was merely to ascertain 'the law as it is': as it had been determined by the courts[26]. Thus, the principles and rules were not 'discovered' in the Restatement but merely reproduced in order to enhance its application in everyday legal practice[27]. Like the UNIDROIT Principles[28], the Restatement reflects the law 'as it is' and not 'as it should be'[29]. With this limited function, the Restatement resembles the '*Grandes Ordonnances*' of King Louis XIV[30] or the '*communis opinio doctorum*' of the European *ius commune*[31] from which the courts never deviated[32].

In spite of this reproductive function, the principles and rules contained in the Restatement are formulated like black-letter law in order to ensure a maximum degree of 'clarity, brevity, consistency, uniformity and accessibility'[33]. This, however, is only a question of wording and does not change the character of the Restatement as a mere reproduction of the common law of contracts, the practical validity of which depends entirely on the authority of the American Law Institute[34]. In view of the *stare decisis* doctrine, any reproduction of the common law that has evolved out of the case law of American courts also contains a prediction about future decisions of the courts in the field of contract law[35]. The differences between both functions of the Restatement are only marginal since, in the words of *Oliver Wendell Holmes*, '[t]he prophecies of what the courts will do in fact, and nothing more pretentious, are what [is] mean[t] by the law'[36]. The practical influence and the 'law-like' quality of the Restatement therefore depends upon

26. In Anglo-American law, the court decision serves as a source of law, *i.e.* as a means to detect the law as it is; the court judgment therefore has the force of law 'because it is a correct statement of the law'; *cf. Allen*, Law in the Making, at 273; in civil law-countries, however, court judgments merely provide a possible interpretation of the statute; court decisions therefore do not serve as a genuine source of law but as a means for the recognition of the law as it is'; *cf. Montesquieu*, De l'esprit des lois, Vol. XI, Chapter 6, who calls the judge the '*bouche qui prononce les paroles de la loi*', (also available at *http://classiques.uqac.ca/classiques/montesquieu/de_esprit_des_lois/partie_2/esprit_des_lois_Livre_2.pdf*); *Larenz*, Methodenlehre, at 430.
27. *Patterson*, Columbia Law Review 1933, at 397, 399.
28. *Cf. infra* Chapter 4 I.A.4.
29. *Patterson, supra* note 27, at 403.
30. *Grimm*, RabelsZ 50 (1986), at 61, 62.
31. *Coing*, in: Coing/Schmitthoff/Hellner/Gleichmann (eds.), Methoden der Rechtsvereinheitlichung, at 14; generally *Coing*, 1 Ius commune (1967), at 1.4.
32. *Cf. Knütel*, ZEuP 1994, at 244, 245.
33. *Cf.* the statement of the 'Reporter on Contracts', Professor *Samuel Williston* of Harvard Law School, in ABAJ 1932, at 775, 777.
34. *Cf.* the characterization of the Restatement of the Law of Contracts, 1st ed. 1933, Vol. 1, at XI-XII: 'The accuracy of the statement of law made rests on the authority of the Institute. They may be regarded both as the product of expert legal opinion and as the law by the legal profession'; *cf. also David/Brierley*, Major Legal Systems in the World Today, 1985, at 438.
35. *Patterson, supra* note 27, at 403.
36. *Holmes*, The Path of the Law, 1897: 'The prophecies of what the courts will do in fact, and nothing more pretentious, are what I mean by the law', cited by *Großfeld*, Festschrift Lukes, at 655, 659, footnote 15.

the courts' willingness to follow the rules and principles reproduced therein[37]. According to reports of the American Law Institute, American courts deviate from the Restatement in only 2% of all cases in which the Restatement is cited[38].

2. Creative Function of the Restatements

Both from a theoretical and practical perspective, the function of the Restatements is not limited to a mere reproduction of the law. In exceptional cases, the drafters do not content themselves with restating the common law as it is. Here, the Restatements no longer reflect the common law *de lege lata*, but *de lege ferenda*[39], a drafting approach that is hardly reconcilable with the initial idea of a 'Restatement'[40]. Going beyond their function as a mere collection of statutes and decisions, the drafters had the idea that the Restatements should accompany the development of the common law in an 'analytical, critical and constructive' way[41]. Even though this initial broad approach was taken back during the drafting process[42], there are still three ways in which the Restatements perform a more creative function within the common law system. First, the drafters, in finding a solution for a certain legal problem, followed an isolated court decision of American case law which appears to them to be more 'just' than the prevailing opinion. Secondly, they extracted the *ratio* of a certain legal problem out of a row of seemingly incongruent and contradictory court decisions and put the resulting legal principle in the wording of black-letter law. Finally, the drafters took legal principles developed by case law to create a new rule by analogy for legal problems that have not yet been decided[43]. Ultimately, this mixed approach follows the American legal tradition that, due to

---

37. *Coing*, in: Coing/Schmitthoff/Hellner/Gleichmann (eds.), Methoden der Rechtsvereinheitlichung, at 7, 15; *cf. also Patterson, supra* note 27, at 405: 'A rule deduced, for an actual or possible litigated situation, from the Restatement rules, is at best a tentative conclusion. It must be tested by the trained intuition of the jurist and by a pragmatic evaluation of the facts. The Restatement purports to offer no more than a *prima facie* conclusion, and it is to be hoped that this qualification will be carefully observed by those who use it'; critical also *Clark, supra* note 25, at 654: 'There is no sovereign power behind them to compel the courts to breathe meaning into them. If they do not seem to have meaning the courts should turn to something else and are doing so'.
38. *Blumenwitz*, Einführung in das anglo-amerikanische Recht, at 82.
39. *Cf.* the definition of 'restatement of law' in Black's Law Dictionary, 8th ed. 2004, at 1339: 'One of several influential treatises published by the American Law Institute describing the law in a given area and guiding its development'.
40. *Gray*, RabelsZ 50 (1986), at 111, 119, footnote 40 therefore speaks of a 'methodological embarassment'.
41. *Cf.* the 'Report of the Committee on the Establishment of a Permanent Organization for the Improvement of Law', reprinted in: Honnold (ed.), The Life of the Law, at 145, 149.
42. *Cf.* the working hypothesis of the reporters in *Goodrich*, in: Honnold (ed.), The Life of the Law, at 170 *et seq.*: 'We are not restating the law as we would like to make it, but as it is'.
43. *Clark*, Yale Law Journal 1933, at 415; *Gray*, RabelsZ 50 (1986), at 111, 119; Report of the Committee on the Establishment of a Permanent Organization for the Improvement of the Law Proposing the Establishment of an American Law Institute, Am.L.Inst.Proc. 1923, Vol. I, at 1, 14 *et seq.; cf. also Farnsworth*, Columbia Law Review 1981, at 5 *et seq.*

its case law nature, tends to blur the traditional distinction between the law that is in force and the law that is still in the process of development[44].

Opinions are divided as to the value of this *de lege ferenda* orientation of the American Restatements. Some maintain that they assume the greatest degree of effectiveness with this creative function[45]. Others contend that the Restatement of the Law of Contracts in particular has met with a considerable degree of mistrust because it contained innovations that were too far-reaching[46]. This latter view is probably too severe because the limited success of the first Restatement of the Law of Contracts was due to its rudimentary character. It only contained rules and principles formulated as black-letter law, accompanied by short commentaries and examples. It was only in the following editions of the Restatement that '*Explanatory Notes*', '*Special Notes*', '*Statutory Notes*' and '*Rational Comments*' were included in order to enhance the practical usefulness of the Restatement and its authority[47]. Particular emphasis was placed on these notes and comments during the drafting of the Restatement (2nd)[48].

Even though the above considerations reveal that the function of the American Restatements is sometimes geared not towards the mere reproduction but towards the 'gentle pushing'[49] of the common law, the authority of the Restatements, initially intended by their drafters to form the basis of a future codification of American law[50], 'is just above that of a leading textbook'[51].

C. The Project of the Former Council for Mutual Economic Assistance for a General Law on International Commercial Contracts

In the mid-1980s, the COMECON developed the plan to draft a general law on international commercial contracts[52]. This general law was intended to supplement

44. *Cf.* generally *Rheinstein*, Einführung in die Rechtsvergleichung, at 65.
45. *Gray*, RabelsZ 50 (1986), at 111, 120 for the principles of 'consideration' embedded in Sec. 90 as a basic requirement for the enforceability of a contractual promise.
46. *Cf. Berg*, Report on the discussion, RabelsZ 50 (1986), at 233, 244.
47. *Cf. Leach*, in: Honnold (ed.), The Life of the Law, at 162, 163 *et seq.*
48. *Cf. American Law Institute* (ed.), Restatement of the Law Second, Contracts, Tentative Draft No. 1, April 13, 1964, at XI.
49. *Schlesinger*, in: XXth Century Comparative and Conflicts Law, Legal Essays in Honor of Hessel E. Yntema, at 65, 78; *Lorenz*, JZ 1962, at 269, 274.
50. *Cf. Williston*, ABAJ 1931, at 39, 41: 'It has been the history of law in every other civilized country that after customary or common law has developed to a certain degree, or for a long period of years, and become unwieldy, a code has followed... Whether it be in fifty or one hundred or two hundred years, my own belief is that we shall repeat that history of other countries... This Restatement... will serve as a better foundation for a code, if one should be needed, than any country has had before.'
51. *Zweigert/Kötz*, Einführung in die Rechtsvergleichung, Chapter 17 III; *David/Brierley*, Major Legal Systems in the World Today, at 439: 'The *Restatement* is no more than a kind of systematic digest in which one only finds the judicial decisions on point'.
52. *Cf.* Akademie für Staats- und Rechtswissenschaften der DDR, Institut für ausländisches Recht und Rechtsvergleichung (ed.), Grundzüge einer wissenschaftlichen Konzeption des generellen

the general economic conditions which were in force between the Member States[53]. The drafting process stood in the tradition of the 'Socialist Economic Integration' which was expressed, *inter alia*, in the complex program for the further consolidation and improvement of the cooperation and development of socialist economic integration between the COMECON Member Countries[54].

Apart from general provisions on the substantive, territorial and personal ambit, the draft contained specific rules on the conclusion, contents and performance of contracts, on the payment of damages, on the adaptation of contracts, on the change of parties to the contract, and on limitation. The draft also contained provisions on set-off, on the calculation of deadlines and on unjust enrichment[55]. The draft law was intended to fulfil two purposes. First, it was intended to provide guidelines and substitute law for those cases where the General Economic Conditions did not provide a solution for a legal problem. Thus, the primary purpose of the law was to avoid recourse in those cases to domestic legal systems and to provide a model for the drafting of new General Economic Conditions for the trade within the COMECON[56] to which a norm-like quality was attached in legal practice of that time[57]. Secondly, this draft for a general part of international contract law was geared towards bringing together the various efforts for the unification of international contract law, such as the project of the *Lando* Commission and of UNIDROIT, 'within one single system'[58]. Consequently, the draft was based on these projects and on the United Nations Convention on Contracts for the International Sale of Goods (CISG)[59]. In view of the political and economic turmoil in Eastern Europe in the 1990s, the project was not brought to an end.

D. THE PROJECT OF A EUROPEAN CIVIL CODE OF THE PAVIA GROUP

In October 1990, a Working Group called the '*Groupe d'étude pour le droit européen commun*' (GEDEC) of the European Academy of Private Lawyers in Pavia, Italy, decided to engage upon the drafting of a European Civil Code[60]. The Group was chaired by the Italian law professor *Gandolfi*[61]. The initiative was

Teils der rechtlichen Regelung internationaler Wirtschaftsverträge zwischen den Organisationen der Mitgliedsländer des RGW, 1986; *Bonell*, RDAI 1988, at 873, 887 *et seq.*

53. *Cf. infra* Chapter 4 I.A.3.b.bb.
54. *See Seiffert et al.*, Sozialistische Ökonomische Integration, at 5 *et seq.*; *Enderlein*, in: UNIDROIT (ed.), New Directions in International Trade Law, at 447, 449.
55. *Maskow/Stargardt*, in: Akademie für Staats- und Rechtswissenschaften der DDR, *supra* note 52, at 7, 13 *et seq.*
56. *Cf. Maskow/Stargardt, id.*, at 10 *et seq.*
57. *Cf. infra* Chapter 4 I.A.3.b.bb.
58. *Maskow/Stargardt, supra* note 55, at 11.
59. *Cf.* the draft of 'general rules of contract law' of *Maskow*, in: Akademie für Staats- und Rechtswissenschaften der DDR, *supra* note 55, at 38 *et seq.*
60. *See Sturm's* report on the conference held in Pavia on October 20–21, 1990, where the question of drafting a unified contract law was discussed intensively, JZ 1991, at 555.
61. *See Gandolfi*, RTD civ. 1992, at 707, 720 *et seq.*

triggered by the 1989 Resolution of the European Parliament on the drafting of a European Civil Code[62]. The Group decided not to embark upon the drafting of an informal, restatement-like collection of legal rules and principles[63]. Instead, the objective of the project was to set up a 'basic scheme' which may serve as a basis for a European Civil Code. Towards this end, the Working Group decided to have recourse to two existing legislative 'models', the first title of the Fourth book of the Italian *Codice Civile* and the 'Contract Code' drafted by *McGregor* for the English Law Commission[64]. The Italian Code was chosen on *Gandolfi*'s initiative for two reasons. First, it was chosen because of its 'intermediary' position between the classical civil codes of continental Europe and the common law system. Secondly, it was chosen for its intrinsic modernity which, unlike other European codes, has not suffered from any set-backs in terms of antiquated legislative reform approaches[65].

The drafting of the First Part of the Code was based on the following seven principal assumptions:

(1) The Code was drafted with a view to domestic and international transactions in order to avoid the inconvenience of double-regulation.
(2) The drafters refrained from drafting a 'General Part', modelled on the 'Allgemeiner Teil' of the German Civil Code.
(3) The drafters decided to uphold the uniform approach to civil and commercial law of the Italian *Codice Civile.*
(4) The Code was to be drafted in the French language in order to emphasize the 'Euro-communitarian' character of the Code. The English language was seen to have a more 'inter-continental' character.
(5) The Code was not drafted by sub-committees, set up for the drafting of certain specialized parts of the draft. Instead, the Working Group as a whole discussed every article of the project.
(6) In order to avoid the painstaking drafting processes of the CISG, it was seen necessary to draft a completely 'new' Code, thereby reducing the dangers of compromise solutions.
(7) The drafting process was based on a series of three 'questionnaires' which were sent to the members of the Working Group for their comments[66].

It is important to note that for the drafting of the Second Part of the Code, the Working Group used the Italian *Codice Civile* and the English Contract Code merely as a starting point for a more comprehensive comparative research that

62. *See infra* Chapter 4 I.B.2.
63. *Gandolfi*, Introduction, in: Académie des privatistes européens (Academy of European Private Lawyers) (ed.), Code Européen des Contrats, Avant-Projet, Vol. I, at LV *et seq.*; *Canaris*, Vorbemerkung, *id.*, at XXVII, XXIX.
64. *See McGregor*, Contract Code Drawn up on behalf of the English Law Commission, at 1 *et seq.*; *cf. also Gandolfi, supra* note 61, at 718; *Gandolfi, supra* note 63, at LIX.
65. *Gandolfi, supra* note 61, at 731 *et seq.*; *Sturm, supra* note 60; *Stein*, Preface, in: Académie des privatistes européens (ed.), Code Européen des Contrats, Avant-Projet, Vol. I, at XLVII.
66. *Cf. Stein*, *id.*, at XLVII *et seq.*

also took into account the Swiss, French, Spanish, Austrian, German, and Dutch Civil Codes, as well as certain provisions of other domestic laws and EU law[67].

Based on these directives, the Draft Code contains almost one hundred articles, divided into nine chapters ('titles') and dealing with preliminary provisions, formation of contracts, contents of contracts, formal validity of contracts, interpretation of contracts, effects of contracts, performance and non-performance of contracts.

E. The Study Group on a European Civil Code

In 1998, a Study Group on a European Civil Code was set up by a Steering Committee, composed of the Danish law professor *Ole Lando* together with the Dutch professor *Hartkamp* and the German law professors *Drobnig* and *Basedow* and others, to draft a European Civil Code. The project was based on the 1989 and 1994 Resolutions of the European Parliament[68]. It received further impetus from the Conference 'Towards a European Civil Code', organized by the Dutch Ministry of Justice, during the Dutch EU Presidency, in February 1997. Subsequently published research on the possibility and necessity of creating a European Civil Code was funded by the EU Parliament's Directorate General for Research in 1999. In the same year, the Directorate General for Research of the European Parliament published a Report entitled 'The Private Law Systems in the EU: Discrimination on Grounds of Nationality and the Need for a European Civil Code'[69]. Following that Report, a hearing took place before the Parliament's Committee on Legal Affairs and the Internal Market in November 2000. The Study Group on a European Civil Code was organized as a network of academics, from across the EU, conducting comparative law research in private law in the various legal jurisdictions of the Member States[70]. The work of the Study Group was conducted by two principal sets of bodies. The 'Working Teams' operated on a permanent basis with responsibility for research and proposals within the particular fields of private law assigned to them. The Working Teams were supported by the assistance of a panel of Advisors. These were national experts in the field of private law under review who met at regular intervals with the Working Teams to advise on the preparation of the Working Teams' Position Papers. A 'Coordinating Group', a body of almost fifty professors from virtually all the EU Member States which meets biannually,

67. *Cf. generally Canaris, supra* note 63, at XXX; *Carbonnier*, Réflexions marginales, *id.*, at XX.
68. *See infra* Chapter 4 I.B.2.
69. The Private Law Systems in the EU: Discrimination on Grounds of Nationality and the Need for a European Civil Code, Comparative study of the systems of private law of the EU Member States with regard to discrimination on grounds of nationality and on the scope and need for the creation of a European Civil Code, *www.europarl.europa.eu/workingpapers/juri/pdf/103_en.pdf.*
70. *See www.sgecc.net/pages/en/introduction/index.introduction.htm.*

was charged with reviewing the content of submissions made by the Working Teams[71]. Organizational questions were addressed by the Steering Committee[72].

It was always envisaged that the *Lando* Principles would be incorporated into the model rules to be prepared by the Study Group[73]. However, it was also agreed from the outset of the Study Group's work that the envisaged Code was to contain not only principles of contract law, but also provisions on tort law, secured transactions and real property[74] law. In this way, the rules were to be going well beyond the scope of the *Lando* Principles. Due to this broad approach, the Study Group is composed of present and future Working Teams on Sales, Services and Long-term Contracts, on Financial Services, on Credit Securities, on Extra-Contractual Obligations, on Rental of Moveable Property and on Trust Law[75]. In order to arrive at its goal to develop clear and consistent concepts and legal terminology, the Study Group deviated in some areas from the language and terminology used in the *Lando* Principles. One reason for many of the drafting changes is the clearer distinction now drawn by the Study Group between a contract (seen as a type of agreement or judicial act) and the relationship usually consisting of reciprocal rights and obligations to which it gives rise[76].

The major goal in the research efforts of the Study Group was accomplished in December 2007, when the Joint Network on European Private Law delivered to the EU Commission the Academic Draft Common Frame of Reference (DCFR) prepared by the Study Group on a European Civil Code and the Research Group on EC Private Law (Acquis Group). At the same time, a set of additional drafts prepared by other participants of the Network, namely the Principles of European Insurance Contract Law by the Project Group Restatement of European Insurance Contract Law (Insurance Group) and works on Terminology, Guiding Principles and a Revision of the *Lando* Principles by the *Association Henri Capitant des Amis de la Culture Juridique Française* and the *Société de Législation Comparée* were submitted to the EU Commission[77]. The primary purpose of the DCFR is to serve as a draft for the drawing up of a 'political' Common Frame of Reference which was first called for by the EU Commission's 'Action Plan on a More Coherent European Contract Law' of February 2007[78]. According to the EU Commission, the CFR is intended to be a 'toolbox' or handbook for the EU legislator, to be used

71. *See www.sgecc.net/pages/en/organisation/index.overview.htm.*
72. The Steering Committee is composed of *Christian von Bar, Guido Alpa, Hugh Beale, Ulrich Drobnig, Jacques Ghestin, Sir Roy Goode, Arthur Hartkamp, Johnny Herre*, and *Ole Lando.*
73. *See* for this vision *Lando*, The Harmonization of European Contract Law through a Restatement of Principles, at 19 *et seq.*; *Lando*, in: Weyers (ed.), Europäisches Vertragsrecht, at 81, 101.
74. The different notions of 'property' in the legal systems of the EU Member Countries may constitute the major stumbling block for the realization of the project, *see* the remark by *Gambaro*, reported by *Schulze*, NJW 1997, at 2742, 2743; for a more optimistic view *see Hondius*, in: Weyers (ed.), Europäisches Vertragsrecht, at 45, 57.
75. *See www.sgecc.net/pages/en/organisation/91.working_teams.htm.*
76. *von Bar, et al.* (eds.), Draft Common Frame of Reference (DCFR), Outline Edition, at 30.
77. *See Schulze*, in: *Schulze/von Bar/Schulte-Nölke* (eds.), Der akademische Entwurf für einen gemeinsamen Referenzrahmen, at 1 *et seq.*
78. COM(2003) 68 final, OJ 2003, C 63/01; *see* also *von Bar, et al.* (eds.), *id.*, at 4.

when revising existing and preparing new EU legislation (Regulations, Directives) in the area of contract law[79]. An Interim Outline Edition of the DCFR was published in early 2008[80]. The revised and final Outline Edition of the DCFR was published in early 2009[81]. Similar to the *Lando* Principles, the full edition of the DCFR, which was submitted to the EU Commission at the end of December 2008, is accompanied by 'Comments' explaining the underlying rationale of each rule and providing examples for its application and 'Notes' which reflect the legal position with respect to that particular rules in the national legal systems of the EU Member States and, where relevant, the current Community law[82]. The comparative materials contained in the Notes are intended to provide the EU legislator with detailed information about the different laws in the various EU Member States as an indispensable prerequisite for the further harmonization and unification of European private law[83]. It must be, however, noted that the DCFR does not claim to be the draft of a European Civil Code[84].

II. PROJECTS FOR THE GLOBAL UNIFICATION OF CONTRACT LAW

A. THE 'COMMON CORE OF LEGAL SYSTEMS' OF CORNELL LAW SCHOOL

1. History and Substance of the Project

In 1968, a team from Cornell Law School presented the results of a ten-year research project devoted to the discovery of a 'common core' of the major legal systems of the world ('General Principles of Law Project')[85]. The project was inspired by the convictions and ideas of its mentor, Professor *Schlesinger*. For him, the existence of a common core of all legal systems 'could hardly be disputed today'[86].

79. *See* EU-Parliament Resolution of December 12, 2007 on European contract law, OJ No. C 323 E/364.
80. *von Bar/Clive/Schulte-Nölke* (eds.), Draft Common Frame of Reference (DCFR) Interim Outline Edition, at 71 *et seq.*
81. *von Bar/Clive/Schulte-Nölke* (eds.), Draft Common Frame of Reference (DCFR) Outline Edition, at 131 *et seq.*
82. *von Bar/Clive* (eds.), Principles, Definitions and Model Rules of European Private Law. Draft Common Frame of Reference (DCFR) Full Edition, 6 Vols.
83. *von Bar/Clive/Schulte-Nölke* (eds.), *supra* note 81, at 43.
84. *Schulte-Nölke*, NJW 2009, at 2161, 2166.
85. *Schlesinger* (ed.), Formation of Contracts: A Study of the Common Core of Legal Systems, 2 Vols.; *cf. Kahn-Freund*, Am.J.Comp.L. 1970, at 429 *et seq.*; *Tallon*, Rev.int.dr.comp. 1968, at 729 *et seq.*, also available at *www.persee.fr/web/revues/home/prescript/article/ridc_0035-3337_1968_num_20_4_17233?_Prescripts_Search_isPortletOuvrage=false.*
86. *Cf. Schlesinger*, AJIL 1957, at 734 *et seq.*; *Schlesinger*, The Common Core of Legal Systems, in: XXth Century Comparative and Conflicts Law: Legal Essays in Honor of Hessel E. Yntema, 1961, at 65 *et seq.*

The term 'common core' was intended to denote the general principles of law indicated in Art. 38 of the Statute of the International Court of Justice (ICJ) as one possible source of public international law. In *Schlesinger*'s view, the significance of this provision was not limited to the field of public international law. Apart from those general principles that take account of the specificities of public international law, Art. 38 also refers to those general principles of law that are to be found in the private law of almost all developed legal systems. Due to this private law origin, these principles can easily be applied to the relationship between private legal subjects[87]. It is for this very reason that they form a vital element of the NLM[88].

In spite of its global research approach, the project was never intended to provide a full picture of the general principles of international contract law. Instead, its purpose was to ascertain those general principles of contract law that relate to '*offer and acceptance*'. The reason for this strict limitation of the research project was not only the practical significance of the conclusion of contracts. It was also induced by the fact that legislatures worldwide have devoted a self-contained and clearly defined area of their legal system to problems relating to offer and acceptance. Indeed, from the outset of the project, this made the comparative research much easier[89]. In the initial phase of the project, the research team took great efforts to avoid any misunderstandings that might have been caused by different terminology used by the lawyers in the different legal systems who were involved in the project. Towards this end, working papers were produced that were based on concrete 'fact situations' which were derived from the official law reports of American, German and Italian courts. These papers did not only contain specific questions as to particular legal problems ('issues') but also referenced case law and provisional answers to these questions[90]. Upon their completion, these 'working papers' were sent to legal experts from the various legal systems involved in the project[91], who were requested to base their country reports on these papers. The country reports were then analysed in seminar hearings at Cornell Law School, using a 'comparative cross-examination-technique'[92].

Based on the direct dialogue among the scientists that were involved in the project, these seminar hearings were intended to provide a 'pool of information and experience'[93]. After further intensive discussions between the *rapporteurs* that were responsible for the respective legal problems and the whole team, the results of the research were summarized in 'general reports'[94]. The sequence of these

87. *Schlesinger*, The Common Core of Legal Systems, *id.*, at 65, 70; *Schlesinger* defines the 'common core' as 'a norm common to all of the legal systems considered'; *cf. also Schlesinger*, AJIL 1957, at 734, 739 *et seq.*; *Schlesinger* called the project 'Research on General Principles of Law', *id.*, at 751.
88. *See supra* Chapter 2 II.A.2.c.
89. *Schlesinger* (ed.), Formation of Contracts, Vol. I, at 18.
90. *Cf. Schlesinger*, AJIL 1957, at 734, 752.
91. Ten law professors from ten different legal systems worked on the project.
92. *Lorenz*, JZ 1962, at 269, 273.
93. *Schlesinger*, AJIL 1957, at 734, 751.
94. *Cf. Schlesinger, id.*, at 751 *et seq.*

discussions is reflected in the final study published by the research team. It consists of a General Part which contains the 'General Reports' and a special part which reproduces the 'Country Reports'. The Cornell research team did not attempt any 'codification' or progressive development of that particular field of international contract law. *Schlesinger*'s research approach was merely to reproduce the common legal principles of all legal systems in the field of offer and acceptance as they were at that time. It was only in this context that possible trends and development options were indicated[95].

2. Limited Use of the Project

The study published by the research team of Cornell Law School has been rightly characterized as a 'milestone of comparative research'[96] and proof for a functioning 'comparative law in action'[97]. The study therefore provides a rich quarry for the drafting of Restatements of international contract law and for the 'Creeping Codification' of transnational commercial law[98]. Also, the materials on which the study is based may be used as reference points for general comparative research in the field of private law and for the qualification and solution of legal problems that are related to the conclusion of 'state contracts'[99]. However, a comparison with the UNIDROIT Principles reveals various formal and methodical deficiencies of the project. From a formal point of view the Cornell project takes a different approach to the problem of international contract law in that it does not contain rules and principles formulated as black-letter law[100]. In order to provide workable solutions, these rules and principles would have to be distilled out of the reports contained in the study, provided that these reports have a sound and reliable methodical basis. There are, however, three reasons which shed doubt on the methodical reliability of the study as a whole.

a. Important Legal Systems Were Not Covered by the Study

From the perspective of comparative law, a first methodical deficiency of the project is caused by the fact that important Islamic legal systems and legal systems from Africa, Latin America and Asia were not covered by the research team[101]. This approach was apparently influenced by *Schlesinger*'s attitude that the modern contract law contained in Islamic and other legal systems was influenced and shaped through legal ideas and notions of the Western hemisphere. Also, according to *Schlesinger*, ascertaining 'general principles recognized by civilized nations' as

95. *Schlesinger* (ed.), Formation of Contracts, Vol. I, at 4.
96. *Rheinstein*, Einführung in die Rechtsvergleichung, at 116.
97. *See* the title of the book review by *Kahn-Freund*, Am.J.Comp.L. 1970, at 429 *et seq.*
98. *See infra* Chapter 4 II.C.
99. *Cf.* for the legal problems related to 'state contracts' *Delaume*, ICSID Rev.-FILJ 1988, at 79 *et seq.*; *Böckstiegel*, Der Staat als Vertragspartner ausländischer Privatunternehmen, at 35 *et seq.*
100. *Lorenz*, JZ 1962, at 274.
101. Also critical *Constantinesco*, Rechtsvergleichung, Vol. II, at 348.

provided for in Art. 38 of the ICJ Statute did not necessarily require the application of a quantitative standard and the recognition only of those general principles that are contained or reflected in *all* legal systems of the world[102].

Although it is obvious that comparative research may never be based on all relevant legal systems[103], outright exclusion of certain areas of the world or types of legal systems may certainly have an arbitrary influence on the result of the research. A comparison between the 'Western' legal system and Islamic law (*shi'ah*) in the field of conclusion of contracts reveals these problems. While the classical Western doctrine is based on a factual determination of the party's respective contractual expressions in a chronologically sequential order, Islamic legal systems determine *in advance* for every type of contract which party has to declare the offer (*ijáb*) and which has to declare the acceptance (*qabúl*), so that no further generalizations can be derived from this strictly formalized procedure of conclusion of contracts[104].

b. The Project Does Not Take Account of Social Reality

The scope of the Cornell Research Project was limited to the determination of the legal and mechanical problems relating to the conclusion of contracts. The 'common core' was therefore not understood as a collection or even systematic order of principles and standards but merely as a collection of legal *techniques.* In order to ascertain these techniques and technical legal problems, a research field was required that was freed as much as possible from any teleological considerations and influences:

> '...to carry out the experiment it was necessary to choose a set of legal doctrines or institutions not fundamentally affected by their social environment. The "common core"... does not consist of legal policies, but of legal techniques, of tools of legal thinking, not of purposes pursued in the formulation and application of the law. Each problem confronting a lawyer, whether he be a judge or an administrator, an adviser or an advocate, is two-faced: It looks towards the past, towards the rules and principles, the "authorities" and the traditions, the concepts and the techniques which must be brought to bear on the solution of the problem. But the problem also looks to the future, to the social, political, economic, cultural effects its solution can be expected to have, to the "desirability" of that solution in the light of what the person called upon to solve it considers as expedient, wise and just. It would be possible, though futile, to group legal problems or "branches" of the law on an ascending scale in accordance with the significance which the "teleological" element has in their solution as compared with the "deductive"

---

102. *Schlesinger*, The Common Core of Legal Systems, in: XXth Century Comparative and Conflicts Law, Legal Essays in Honor of Hessel E. Yntema, 1961, at 65, 70.
103. *See supra* Chapter 2 II.A.1.c.
104. *Cf. Owsia*, Formation of Contract, A Comparative Study under English, French, Islamic and Iranian Law, at 385 *et seq.*

> element. Clearly, Professor Schlesinger and his team were compelled to concentrate their work on problems as low as possible on that scale'[105].

This means that possible interdependencies between law and social reality were excluded from the outset from the research approach chosen by the Cornell team[106].

This technical approach to comparative science does not provide a sound methodical basis for the development of general principles of transnational commercial law. Law as a cultural phenomenon may not be analysed and developed without taking account of its social sources and effects. On the international plane, any comparative research effort requires a look at the economic interests that form the basis of many rules and principles of contract law[107]. Comparative research on the transnational plane therefore has to deal with the social realities (trade usages, customs) as they have developed within the international community of merchants (*societas mercatorum*):

> 'The comparative lawyer's investigations cannot stop at what in his own or in any other legal order happen to be frontiers of the law. To compare law and non-law . . . may be one of his principal tasks. If he fails to do so, he may see the law in a distorting mirror'[108].

To get this overall picture, comparative research has to take account of non-legislative materials[109], and has to discuss the results not only in academic circles but also among practitioners[110]. The drafters of the UNIDROIT Principles took account of this need to include social reality in comparative research in that they included general conditions of trade, standard form contracts and other examples of self-made law of international commerce in their research[111].

c. *The Project Neglects the Interaction Between General Principles of Law and Concrete Norms as the 'True Basis of a Realistic Approach to Comparative Law'*

There is another, even more serious objection to the methodical approach chosen by the Cornell Research Team[112]. Again, this objection is based on the restriction of the study to the technicalities of the formation of contracts, excluding other important legal problems of general contract law such as the influence of mistakes,

105. *Kahn-Freund*, Am.J.Comp.L. 1970, at 429, 430.
106. *Cf. Rheinstein*, Einführung in die Rechtsvergleichung, at 123.
107. *Rabel*, in: Gesammelte Aufsätze, Vol. III, Arbeiten zur Rechtsvergleichung und zur Rechtsvereinheitlichung 1919–1954, at 1, 10.
108. *Kahn-Freund*, L.Q.Rev. 1966, at 40, 51.
109. *Cf. infra* Chapter 4 I.A.3.b.bb.
110. *Cf.* for the possibility to develop the *lex mercatoria* through a 'law finding community' *infra* Conclusion.
111. *Cf. Kötz*, Festschrift Zweigert, at 481, 495.
112. *Cf. Constantinesco*, Rechtsvergleichung, Vol. II, at 347 *et seq.*; *cf. also generally Zweigert/Puttfarken*, in: Zweigert/Puttfarken (eds.), Rechtsvergleichung, at 395, 420.

issues of representation, and liability for damages. Limiting the research project to a small and purely technical field of general contract law was not only intended to ensure the feasibility of the project but was also due to a problematic understanding of the relationship of legal norms and general principles of law. For *Schlesinger*, a common core of legal principles contained in all major legal systems could only be developed 'from the bottom up'. By that he meant an inductive approach: the development of solutions for concrete legal problems which could then serve as the basis for a general comprehensive system of rules, principles and standards[113]. A deductive approach, *i.e.* the deriving of specific solutions for legal problems from general principles of law, was refuted by *Schlesinger* as an impermissible speculation:

> 'When we deal with a multitude of legal systems... the first of these two methods [*i.e.* the deductive method] is unworkable. A priori speculation will not help us to ascertain what standards and principles are in fact recognized by the civilized nations of the world; and intuitive insights, however valuable in expounding one's national law, necessarily elude us when we enter an arena which by virtue of its global nature is beyond the experience and intuition of any single man.
>
> It is submitted, therefore, that the structure of the common core cannot be built from the top down. The only feasible method is to lay a firm foundation of specific solutions found in more than one legal system, and then, brick by brick, to build on this foundation until ultimately there will rise the lofty spire of common principles and standards'[114].

This one-sided, rigorous, and seemingly mathematical view of the interaction of general principles of law ('*Allgemeine Rechtsgrundsätze*'; '*principes généraux*') and norms ('*rules*'; '*règles*'; '*Regeln*') bears a striking resemblance to the proposals of *Malintoppi* who suggested that the inclusion of identical general principles of law in various legal systems would, as a mechanical consequence, lead to the creation of similar rules for identical legal problems[115]. This view is apparently influenced by *Schlesinger*'s idea to start his research from a 'factual approach', involving individual legal or factual problem situations instead of superior social or economic principles. The latter approach is chosen by the functional comparative methodology[116]. Ultimately, *Schlesinger*'s approach to comparative law provides the comparative mirror image to the 'reasoning by example' as the principal law-finding method of common law[117].

The differences between both approaches may only be of a marginal nature[118]. However, they provide an example of the decisive weakness of a comparative law

113. *Schlesinger*, in: XXth Century Comparative and Conflicts Law, Legal Essays in Honor of Hessel E. Yntema, at 65, 79; *cf. also Schlesinger* (ed.), Formation of Contracts, Vol. I, at 9.
114. *Schlesinger, id.*
115. *Malintoppi*, UNIDROIT Annuaire 1967–1968, Vol. II, at 43, 54.
116. *See supra* Chapter 2 II.A.1 for details.
117. *See Rheinstein*, Einführung in die Rechtsvergleichung, at 167.
118. *See Schlesinger, supra* note 102, at 72.

methodology that is based solely on individual cases. It fails to take into account the important interaction between legal axioms and individual norms, between legal principles and the law. Certainly, the general principles of law alone do not provide a norm-like legal program that can be applied to individual cases. They may even stand in contradiction to each other. To be workable in practice, they require the creation of sub-principles and difficult legal evaluations[119]. Once they have been 'discovered'[120] in an individual case, general principles of law constitute a decisive reference point for the application of the law as a teleological system[121]. Such general principles may also be ascertained for individual parts of a legal system. Thus, German contract law is built on the principles of party autonomy, of liability for damages, of freedom of form and other fundamental legal notions[122].

The interaction between general principles of law and legal rules and norms is revealed in everyday legal practice. Here, the thought process of the person applying the law does not go only in one direction but in opposite directions: First, from general principles to the specific individual case and secondly, from there over the typically known cases and specific legal views back to the general principles[123]. In this way, a circle is completed in all legal cultures dealing with discovering the problem, forming the principles, and strengthening the system[124]. The general principles of law therefore constitute the *substratum* for the interaction between the application of the law in individual cases and the overriding formation of the system which can, in turn, result in the derivation of precise, specific legal rules[125]. The drafters of the UNIDROIT Principles were aware of this important relationship at an early stage of the drafting process and directed their research project towards the creation of a system of rules and general principles of law[126]. The UNIDROIT Working Group was aware of the fact that a comparative methodology that is limited to the analysis of isolated legal problems is not able to reflect a close interconnection and resemblance of different legal institutions and rules[127], thereby reducing the value of the method as a means to provide legitimacy to transnational law[128]. Legal rules and principles, no matter how technical or mechanical their nature may be, can only be understood, analysed, and applied in practice when they are seen in the context of the general principles of law on

119. *Cf. Canaris*, Systemdenken und Systembegriff in der Jurisprudenz, at 52 *et seq.*; *Esser*, Grundsatz und Norm, at 5 *et seq.*, 267 *et seq.*; *Larenz*, Methodenlehre, at 137 *et seq.*, 168 *et seq.*; *Engisch*, Studium Generale 10 (1957), at 173 *et seq.*; *cf. also Dworkin*, Law's Empire, 1986, at 210 *et seq.*
120. *Esser*, Grundsatz und Norm, at 267; *cf. also Berger*, International Economic Arbitration, at 571.
121. *Engisch*, Studium Generale 10 (1957), at 173, 177 *et seq.*
122. *Sandrock*, Über Sinn und Methode zivilistischer Rechtsvergleichung, at 44.
123. *Larenz*, Methodenlehre, at 292.
124. *Esser*, Grundsatz und Norm, at 7.
125. *Cf. Kropholler*, Internationales Einheitsrecht, at 159.
126. *Cf. infra* Chapter 4 I.A.7.b.
127. *Coing*, Grundzüge der Rechtsphilosophie, at 353.
128. *See supra* Chapter 2 II.A.

which they are based. Conversely, the 'functioning' of a legal system that is based on functional comparative methodology requires that technical legal rules are accompanied by general principles of law. Through their flexible legal content ('*notions à contenu variable en droit*'[129]), these principles provide the necessary flexibility for every legal system as 'law in action'. Thus, the significance and functioning of *force majeure* and hardship clauses in international contracts can only be understood in the context of the general principle '*pacta sunt servanda*'. This principle as well as the notion of 'good faith and fair dealing'[130] or the standard of 'reasonableness' constitute important maxims for the further development and interpretation of transnational commercial law.

The Cornell Project did not and in fact was never intended to take account of this particular character of the NLM. Its scope was limited to the technical rules of offer and acceptance without consideration of the broader context of international contract law. The project has therefore not paved the way towards the evolution of a system of transnational commercial law.

B. THE PLAN OF THE UNIDROIT SECRETARIAT FOR THE 'PROGRESSIVE CODIFICATION' OF INTERNATIONAL TRADE LAW

1. The Report of the UNIDROIT Secretariat on the 'Progressive Codification of the Law of International Trade'

In 1971, the Secretariat of UNIDROIT presented its idea for the drafting of general principles of international contract law in its report to UNCITRAL on '*Progressive codification of the law of international trade*'[131]. The report was prepared in four conferences of all institutions that were concerned with the unification of the law[132], *i.e.* UNIDROIT, UNCITRAL, the United Nations Commission on International Trade and Development (UNCTAD) and the sub-committee on fundamental legal concepts as an organ of the European Committee on Legal Cooperation. The report called for a combined effort of all institutions and emphasized the urgent necessity to develop principles and rules of international contract

129. *Cf. Perelman* (ed.), Les notions à contenu variable en droit, 1984.

130. *Cf. Dasser*, Lex Mercatoria, at 109: 'The principle of good faith gives the necessary completion and fine-tuning to an existing legal system. It becomes dangerous if a dispute is resolved solely on the basis of good faith . . . In this case, the discretion of the arbitral tribunal is almost as wide as in the case of a decision in equity, which requires, and not by coincidence, an express agreement of the parties' (translation by the author); *cf. also* the Vienna Court of Appeals in *Pabalk v. NORSOLOR*, AG 1982, at 165, 166; *cf. also supra* Chapter 2 II.B.1.

131. *Cf.* the Report of the UNIDROIT Secretariat on the '*Progressive codification of the law of international trade*', in: United Nations Commission on International Trade Law, Yearbook I (1968–1970), at 285 *et seq.*, also available at *http://www.uncitral.org/pdf/english/yearbooks/yb-1968-70-e/yb_1968-1970_e.pdf.*

132. *See* the survey by *Kropholler*, Internationales Einheitsrecht, at 43 *et seq.*

law which could serve as a reference point for the construction of private contracts and international conventions without recourse to domestic laws[133]. The report of the UNIDROIT Secretariat emphasizes the supportive function of the project as a guide for the construction of international legal instruments and domestic law. In fact, in presenting the idea UNIDROIT's initial intention went much further than that. The report emphasized that its inherent objective was to lay down the basis for a 'code of international world trade law'[134], *i.e.* for a genuine transnational legal system:

> '... international trade needs its own ordinary law with its own particular role and full range of functions... The very fact that the legal relationships of international trade are international in character puts them outside the jurisdiction of municipal law and makes them governable by a law removed from any national contingencies, that is, *an ordinary law of international trade*, which alone can provide the legal framework which international trade needs in order to develop... Consequently, international trade now, as much as ever, needs a real *ius commune mercatorum*, a material law that can govern international relations... It would be unthinkable... either to allow international trade to continue to be governed by a host of national laws, since that places it in an impossible position, or to leave all legal problems arising in international trade to be solved simply by practice... So the first task will be to prepare a draft for the general section containing the basic principles which will form the foundations and the framework of the unification'[135].

This comprehensive approach was intended to transform the various efforts to unify the law within certain branches of international trade into a global project for the creation of uniform law[136] for contracts of international commerce and trade. Influenced by proposals from *David*[137], *Schmitthoff*[138], and *Blagojevic*[139] made on the IVth Conference of the Organizations Concerned with the Unification of Law that was held in Rome from April 22 to 24, 1968[140], the project was geared towards the drafting of a 'Model Basic Code' ('*code modèle de base*')[141] made up

133. UNIDROIT Report, *supra* note 131, *id.*
134. *See* the proposal by *Schmitthoff*, JZ 1978, at 495, 498.
135. Report of the UNIDROIT Secretariat, *supra* note 131, at 286 *et seq.*
136. *Cf.* for this definition *Kropholler*, Internationales Einheitsrecht, 1975, at 4.
137. *David*, UNIDROIT Annuaire 1967–1968, Vol. II, at 77, 87: '... le nouveau droit commun doit se présenter comme un droit législatif; il ne saurait être de nos jours un droit de la doctrine'; *cf. also David, id.*, at 254, 256 *et seq.*
138. *Schmitthoff*, UNIDROIT Annuaire 1967–1968, Vol. II, at 93, 115: 'The gradual establishment of a codified world trade law, essentially identical in all national jurisdictions, can only be achieved by a series of international conventions'.
139. *Blagojevic*, UNIDROIT Annuaire 1967–1968, Vol. II, at 119, 139 *et seq.*
140. *Cf.* the summary of the results of the conference in: UNIDROIT (ed.), Annuaire 1967–1968, Vol. II, at 317 *et seq.*, stating that the unification efforts through international agreements 'still constitute the most appropriate method for the achievement of a certain degree of uniformity in the various domestic laws'.
141. *David, supra* note 137, at 257.

of international conventions and model laws and accompanied by special domestic statutes for international commercial contracts (*'lois uniformes'*[142]).

2. The Plan to Draft a 'Restatement' Anchored in Public International Law

a. René David's *Proposal for a* 'Code Modèle de Base'

The French law Professor and initiator of the work towards the UNIDROIT Principles, *René David*, always favoured a progressive approach towards the development of an international *ius commune*[143]. In the 1960s, based on this general conception, *David* presented far-reaching ideas for the unification of international commercial law. He believed that a transnational '*droit commun*' should enter into force *automatically, i.e.* without the need to transform it into domestic law, because he regarded this field of law to be outside the competence of domestic legislatures. To achieve this goal, he argued that international conventions should be drafted with the goal of transferring the 'natural competence of law-making on the international plane' to international organizations for particular regions of the world or special fields of law[144]. Instead of having to fight with a multitude of problems related to the *active* participation of states in the unification of international commercial law, this construction was intended to make it 'as difficult as possible for domestic legislatures *not* to participate in the unification of private law'[145]. In spite of the substantial delegation of sovereign rights implied in this idea, *David* maintained that his plan did not infringe upon the sovereignty of those states that would participate in his plan. First, by ratifying the international convention these states would have to transfer their 'law-making power' for international matters to the respective international organization. Secondly, the domestic legislatures should retain the right to declare restrictions, modifications or even the rejection of certain principles *vis-à-vis* the international organization which would be responsible for the drafting and monitoring of that respective uniform law[146]. This part of *David*'s idea was based on the 'opting out-provisions' contained in the charters of the World Health Organization (WHO), the International Civil Aviation Organization (ICAO) and the 'Central Office for International Transport by Rail' (OCIT).

The inherent objective of this proposal was to foster the unification process by necessitating activities of domestic legislatures not for the unification process as

142. *Cf.* for this source of international uniform law *Kropholler, supra* note 136, at 105 *et seq.*
143. *Cf. Schmitthoff*, JZ 1978, at 495, 497 *et seq.*; *cf.* above all *David*, Le droit du commerce international, at 49 *et seq.*
144. *David*, UNIDROIT Annuaire 1967–1968, Vol. II, at 254, 257; *David*, Le droit du commerce international, at 66 *et seq.*; *cf. also Farnsworth*, Festschrift Schmitthoff, at 145, 148; *Jakubowski*, Festschrift Schmitthoff, at 207, 208, footnote 4; *Kos/Rabcewicz/Zubkowski*, in: UNIDROIT (ed.), New Directions in International Trade Law, at 459, 465.
145. *David*, UNIDROIT Annuaire 1967–1968, Vol. II, at 256.
146. *David, id.*, at 88 *et seq.* and at 257.

such but only for those cases where a state wanted to reject or modify certain parts of the uniform law[147]. According to *David*, the collection of general uniform principles of commercial law, together with modifications notified to the international organization by domestic legislatures, should be published in a '*code modèle de base*' that was to be structured like the American Restatements. There was, however, one important difference between both projects. Contrary to the American Restatement, *David*'s Model Codes were not intended to be of a mere doctrinal nature but rather of a legislative nature. The public law nature of the underlying international convention was supposed to provide this project with a direct binding effect upon all legislatures that would participate in it[148].

b. France's Proposal for the Drafting of a Framework Convention for the Ius Commune *of International Trade Law*

Under the leadership of the French delegation to UNCITRAL, *David*'s plan was refined to a proposal for the drafting of a framework convention for the *ius commune* of international trade law[149]. The basic purpose of the framework convention was to establish a 'Union for *jus commune*' (UJC)[150]. The General Assembly of this Union should adopt the texts which were supposed to form part of this *ius commune* of international trade law[151]. A three-quarter majority should suffice for the adoption of each text[152]. The decisions of the General Assembly should enter into force after three years. With the expiration of this deadline, the texts adopted in the General Assembly should assume the status of statutes in the Member States[153]. Each state should retain the right to make a declaration before the General Secretary of the Union that certain provisions that have been declared part of the international *ius commune* by the General Assembly should not be applicable in its territory. At the same time, this state should be obliged to declare which provisions of its internal law should be applied instead[154]. The French delegation to UNCITRAL indicated that in view of the 'spirit of international cooperation' between the Member States of the Union, such declarations should only be made

147. *David*, UNIDROIT Annuaire 1967–1968, Vol. II, at 256 *et seq.*; *David*, Le Droit Du Commerce International, at 51 *et seq.*; *Kos/Rabcewicz/Zubkowski*, in: UNIDROIT (ed.), New Directions in International Trade Law, at 459, 465.
148. *David*, UNIDROIT Annuaire 1967–1968, Vol. II, at 257.
149. *Cf.* Draft basic convention establishing a common body of international trade law: proposal by the French delegation, UNCITRAL Yearbook 1968–1970, at 288 *et seq.*; the text of the *Draft Convention* together with a the official commentary is reprinted in UNCITRAL Yearbook 1971, at 139, 140; *cf. also Schmitthoff*, in: Coing/Schmitthoff/Hellner/Gleichmann (eds.), Methoden der Rechtsvereinheitlichung, at 19, 24 *et seq.*; *David*, Le Droit Du Commerce International, at 66 *et seq.*
150. Article I Draft Convention, UNCITRAL Yearbook 1971, at 139, 140.
151. Article VI (4) Draft Convention, *id.*
152. Article VII Draft Convention, *supra* note 150.
153. Articles VIII and IX Draft Convention, *supra* note 150.
154. Article X Draft Convention, *supra* note 150.

in exceptional cases where serious reasons prohibited the application of certain provisions of the international *ius commune* in a certain country[155]. In any event, replacing the *ius commune* by the domestic law of a particular state was seen as running counter to the underlying purpose of the framework convention, because it would introduce a considerable degree of uncertainty in the application of the law even though it was the basic purpose of the Union to avoid these uncertainties[156]. The General Secretary of the Union was supposed to issue a collection of those texts that had been adopted by the General Assembly on an annual basis. This report should also list those states that had excluded the application of certain provisions and indicate as far as possible the provisions of domestic law which this particular state wanted to have applied instead[157].

c. Clive Schmitthoff's Proposal for an 'Approval Committee' of UNCITRAL

Professor *Clive Schmitthoff* welcomed the progressive proposals of *René David* as a new methodical approach to redefine 'the difficult course between the Scylla of the consensual principle and the Charybdis of the principle of sovereignty'[158]. However, he rejected the idea of establishing a Union for the *ius commune* of International Trade Law. Instead, he suggested transferring *David*'s ideas to the existing structures of UNCITRAL. UNCITRAL should set up an 'Approval Committee' in which the five regions of the world of which UNCITRAL is composed should receive a proportionate share[159]. This Approval Committee should attach the status of *ius commune* to the relevant texts. This approval should be effected either on the basis of a unanimous vote or, following the proposals of the French delegation, based on a three-quarter majority[160]. The Approval Committee should receive the necessary legitimacy through a resolution of the UN General Assembly. This resolution should state that the members of the United Nations would be bound automatically by the text approved by the committee and that each Member State should retain the right to exclude the application of the text *in toto* or of individual provisions in its territory within a certain period of time[161].

---

155. Draft Convention, *supra* note 150, at 290.
156. Draft basic convention establishing a common body of international trade law: proposal by the French delegation, UNCITRAL Yearbook 1968–1970, at 291: 'The countries which did not comply with it would be the losers, for they would thus expose themselves to the danger that their own legislation would not be applied or would be applied incorrectly'.
157. Article XI Draft Convention, *supra* note 150.
158. *Schmitthoff*, in: Coing/Schmitthoff/Hellner/Gleichmann (eds.), Methoden der Rechtsvereinheitlichung, at 19, 25 *et seq.*
159. *Schmitthoff, id.*, at 26.
160. *Schmitthoff, supra* note 158, *id.*
161. *Schmitthoff, supra* note 158, *id.*

3. First Steps towards the Drafting of an American-Style Restatement of International Contract Law

Already in the initial phase of the deliberations, UNIDROIT's far-reaching plans for the 'progressive codification of the law of international trade' were diluted to the drafting of general principles for international contract law without direct binding effect[162]. This modification of the drafting approach was in line with the general weakening of the unification euphoria of that time[163] and the doubts that were being raised as to the suitability of that decade for the codification of general principles of international contract law[164]. It was for this reason that the progressive proposals ventured by *David* and *Schmitthoff* were doomed to fail from the outset. The substantial delegation of legislative powers that was necessarily implied in these 'utopic'[165] proposals was regarded as an unacceptable intrusion into state sovereignty[166]. It was and still is regarded as the fundamental sovereign right of every state to make a sovereign and independent decision on the acceptance or rejection of international conventions and the uniform law that is contained in them[167]. The 'opting out' procedures implemented in the ICAO and WHO charters contain important safeguards for the sovereignty of the Member States. Thus, the recommendations made by ICAO ('standards and recommended practices') have the quality of soft-law. They are not accompanied by any enforcement mechanisms, thereby enabling the individual Member States to deviate from these practices. Also, the 'opting out'-procedures in the ICAO and WHO charters have a limited scope. They have been designed for the implementation of technical standards in the Member States and do not lend themselves to the regulation of contract law[168]. For these reasons, any proposal to make use of these procedures in the context of the unification of international commercial contract law by UNCITRAL could not succeed[169]. In the end, *David* had to accept with resignation that the sovereignty of the states was the major reason for the substantial delay of the

162. *Bonell*, RDAI 1988, at 873, 878.
163. *Cf. Constantinesco*, Rechtsvergleichung, Vol. II, 1972, at 426.
164. *Bärmann*, Festschrift Mann, at 547, 565.
165. *Loewe*, UNIDROIT Annuaire 1967–1968, Vol. II, at 261, 262.
166. *Cf. Loewe, id.*
167. *Dolzer*, in: Horn/Schmitthoff (eds.), The Transnational Law of International Commercial Transactions, at 61, 77: 'It is indicative of the present state of international law that at present there is no international organization which has the power to establish rules binding for all member states on the basis of majority voting in the organization's organ in which the individual states are represented. Apparently, notions of sovereignty have become more important in the past decades: majority voting with binding effect was sometimes accepted by the member states of organizations founded during the second half of the nineteenth century'.
168. *Dolzer, id.*, at 80: 'Private economic law has in fact never been placed on the same level as technical issues with which, for instance, the organizations in the field of aviation law or health law deal; the legislative powers of organizations in the field of economic law have been strictly tied to the formal approval of all states concerned'.
169. *Dolzer, supra* note 167, *id.*

general process for the unification of international commercial law and for the rejection of his progressive ideas:

> '. . . l'indépendance nationale a été et demeure invoquée en dehors de tout bon sens pour refuser la coopération internationale qui s'impose en notre temps . . . Au moment, où, dans une époque de dirigisme, on attend du droit, dans chaque Etat, un renouvellement des structures annonciateur de vie heureuse, c'est un échec du droit que l'on enregistre dans la vie internationale. Le droit étant mis dans chaque pays au service de politiques nationales, on éprouve une certaine suspicion ici et là à l'encontre de tout ce qui risque d'apparaître comme une restriction de la souveraineté nationale; et pour plus de sûreté, on récuse l'idée même d'un droit international, qui ne serait pas exclusivement l'œuvre et la chose du législateur national'[170].

In spite of this failure, the effects of *David*'s proposals are still felt today. It was on the basis of his ideas that *Matteucci* made his suggestions for a drafting of a Restatement of international contract law[171] which formed the basis for the drafting of the UNIDROIT Principles. In fact, it was in the 1960s that the adoption of the Restatement technique was propagated for the international unification of law[172]. *David* himself had already recognized the usefulness of the Restatements for the unification of European law[173]. These ideas, together with the proposals of *van Hecke*[174] laid the methodical and instrumental foundation stone for the drafting of the 'Principles of European Contract Law' by the *Lando* Commission[175]. It is not surprising, therefore, that the IVth Conference of the Institutions Concerned with the Unification of Law held in Rome in April 1968 emphasized the enormous significance of the Restatements for the development and evolution of general principles for a global '*ius gentium*'[176].

With this renunciation of the idea of transforming international uniform law into domestic legal systems, an important opportunity for the fostering of the unification of international commercial law was missed. Also, the question as to how the unification of genuine legal principles ('*règles juridiques proprement dites*')[177] should be effected on the international plane, was left to be decided by a future generation of international and comparative lawyers.

---

170. *David*, in: UNIDROIT (ed.), New Directions in International Trade Law, at 5, 10; *cf. also David*, Le Droit Du Commerce International, at 67 ('Je n'ai jamais cru, en présentant cette proposition, qu'elle serait acceptée d'enthousiasme par les divers Etats: elle heurte trop la routine').
171. *Cf. supra* Introduction B.2.a.
172. *Cf. van Hecke*, in: De Conflictu Legum, at 198, 207 *et seq.* for the European Union.
173. *David*, UNIDROIT Annuaire 1967–1968, Vol. II, at 276; *David*, International Encyclopedia of Comparative Law, Vol. II, Chapter 5, at 180.
174. *van Hecke, supra* note 172, *id.*
175. *Cf. infra* Chapter 4 I.B.
176. *Cf. Summary of the Debates*, UNIDROIT Annuaire 1967–1968, Vol. II, at 316, 318 *et seq.*
177. *Cf. Malintoppi*, in: UNIDROIT Annuaire 1967–1968, Vol. II, at 43, 48.

III. SUMMARY

This survey on previous projects for the 'codification' of international or regional contract law, lasting over much of this century, provides a clear picture of the many problems that are connected with such efforts. It is ironic that this particular field of law lends itself so well to unification[178] and yet all the efforts so far have had only such limited success.

Important consequences may also be drawn from this survey for the 'codification' of the NLM. Even though there are voices today that call for the drafting of a 'Convention on the *lex mercatoria*' under the auspices of UNCITRAL[179], it remains highly doubtful whether this is the proper codification technique for this field of law. In view of the many problems and pitfalls connected with these techniques, international conventions or model laws may not be the best way for the codification of the NLM. However, the consolidation and evolution of contract law through the drafting of Restatements has been practiced with success in the past decades in the US and could show the way for the codification of transnational law.

Having determined on a preliminary basis the right approach towards the unification of transnational law, the question remains as to the possible success of such projects. This depends entirely on the political and economic conditions of the time. The end of the East-West conflict that was caused by the political and economic turmoil in Eastern Europe in the early 1990s and the weakening of the North-South conflict that came along with it[180] are both indications for the breaking down of barriers. They show that the opportunity for a codification of the NLM has never been as promising as it is today.

---

178. *Cf. infra* Chapter 4 I.A.3.a.
179. *See* the proposal by *Raeschke-Kessler*, in: Institute for International Business Law and Practice (ed.), UNIDROIT Principles for International Commercial Contracts, at 167, 175.
180. *Cf.* the rather sceptical prognosis by *Fischer*, GYIL 1976, at 143, 176.

Chapter 4

Informal Approaches towards the Codification of the New *Lex Mercatoria*

From the perspective of international legal practice – which plays a decisive role in the evolution of the NLM – many of the objections discussed in the first part of this Study are based on the same principal argument: the considerable problems that attorneys, in-house counsel[1], arbitrators or judges[2] have in determining the contents of this legal system through application of the functional comparative methodology:

> 'The arbitrator would . . . face a formidable task of comparative research. Instead of having to consult, after application of the appropriate rule of conflict of laws, the rules of one single – no more – national system of law, he would have to assume the rule of a full-fledged comparatist in charge of a research into perhaps a multitude of different national jurisdictions whose

1. *Mustill*, Arb.Int'l 1988, at 86, 114 *et seq.*: 'Our hypothetical adviser is not an academic lawyer, established at an institution of learning in one of those European cities where the *lex* is most at home'; *cf. also Schlesinger* (ed.), Formation of Contracts, Vol. I, at 10 *et seq.*: 'In the absence of available comparative studies, it is exceedingly difficult for counsel to assemble the necessary data for the ad hoc purpose of a particular case pending before an international tribunal'.
2. *See Samuel*, Jurisdictional Problems, at 249: ' . . . one can not interview a significant sample of the business community during the course of every arbitration'; *Mustill*, Arb.Int'l 1988, at 86, 92: 'How could any tribunal, however cosmopolitan and polyglot, hope to understand the nuances of the multifarious legal systems?'; *cf. also* the statement of a Canadian judge cited by *Dasser*, Internationale Schiedsgerichte und lex mercatoria, at 14, on the comparative references provided by counsel who appear before him: 'C'est intéressant. Mais pour ma part, je laisse à des chercheurs aisés la captivante étude du droit comparé'; *Siehr*, in: Holl/Klinke (eds.), Internationales Privatrecht, Internationales Wirtschaftsrecht, at 103, 124; *Stein*, Lex mercatoria, at 174, footnote 385.

> rules might be phrased in a language of which he is not in command. There might be fields of law, it is true, where such comparative research would have already been done, where a specific rule would therefore be easily detectable or where arbitral awards would have already flattened some paths in the jungle of the different national laws to be consulted. But an unforeseeable number of legal questions for which such research has never been carried out, would still have to be answered by arbitrators who, despite their often unusually extensive experience with foreign and international laws, would mostly be ill equipped to perform this kind of a more academic function'[3].

This situation is similar to that encountered when determining the contents of customary public international law[4]. International arbitrators in particular, when faced with the necessity to enter into time-consuming comparative research, find themselves in the dilemma 'speed versus thoroughness'[5]. Not infrequently, comparative research conducted under extreme time and money constraints turns out to be 'an excellent knowledge of an individual legal system, combined with a good dose of fantasy and wishful thinking'[6]. Under these circumstances, international arbitrators, mindful of the fact that they will not be able to meet the quantitative requirements of the functional comparative methodology, content themselves with the determination of the general principles of those legal systems that have a connection with the case before them, most often the laws of the parties and of the seat of the arbitration[7].

From the perspective of the parties who are under a contractual duty to pay for the services of the arbitrators, considerable problems in the determination of the contents of the transnational law usually lead to a domestic legal system being applied to their contract[8]. In fact, both the arbitrators and the parties and their counsel would find it very hard to determine, general principles or rules of transnational law within the time-limits set by the arbitral tribunal. These principles and rules would have to be determined on the basis of a time-consuming, global research, taking into account not only the legal implications but also the realities

3. *Sandrock*, Am.Rev.Int'l Arb. 1992, at 30, 50 *et seq.*; *cf. also* the statement by *Tilman*, reported by *Remien*, RabelsZ 56 (1992), at 300, 304; *cf. also De Ly*, Lex Mercatoria, at 365; *Triebel/Petzold*, RIW 1988, at 247; *van den Berg*, TvA 1984, at 200; *Markert*, Rohstoffkonzessionen, at 127; *Toope*, Mixed Arbitration, at 95; *von Hoffmann/Thorn*, IPR, § 2, No. 56; *Schneider*, NJW 1991, at 1986, 1987; *Spickhoff*, RabelsZ (56) 1992, at 124; *Martiny*, in: Reithmann/Martiny (eds.), Internationales Vertragsrecht, No. 72; *cf. also Schmitz*, Allgemeine Rechtsgrundsätze in der Rechtsprechung des Iran-United States Claims Tribunal, at 93: 'The case load necessarily sets limits to the possibilities of extensive comparative research'.
4. *Zamora*, GYIL 1989, at 9, 37: '...as a practical matter, U.S. judges cannot be expected to conclude accurately, on the basis of haphazard assessment of imperfect evidence, that a rule of customary international law exists'.
5. *Cf. Spickhoff*, RabelsZ 56 (1992), at 116, 124.
6. *Schlesinger* (ed.), Formation of Contracts, Vol. I, at 11.
7. *Cf. Fouchard*, L'Arbitrage Commercial International, at 424.
8. *Kropholler*, IPR, § 12.I.3 (at 100).

of international commerce and trade[9]. Instead of making the decision-making easier for arbitrators and counsel, every methodical instruction for the determination of general principles and rules of transnational law on an *ad hoc* basis would lead to an 'agglomeration of difficulties' for international practice[10].

These concerns raised by legal practice are of paramount importance for the viability and legitimacy of the NLM doctrine. Even the EU Commission referred to the lack of precision and specificity of the NLM when it refused to allow a choice of the NLM by the parties in one of the first drafts of the Rome I Regulation on the Law Applicable to Contractual Obligations[11]. The extreme difficulties in determining the contents of the NLM have always stood in the way of a serious discussion about the practical usefulness of transnational law. Also, the frequent statement of international practitioners that the NLM is not useful in practice has had serious negative repercussions on the methodical discussion on the existence of transnational commercial law. The discussion between those who vehemently oppose the NLM for lack of workable content and those who have tried to develop the doctrinal underpinnings for the NLM without dealing with its content has resulted not in synthesis but in stalemate[12].

The 'need for a realistic approach' and the 'issue of practicability' have always been important factors in discussions on any legal theories[13]. The task of legal science, therefore, does not end with providing the theoretical and methodical underpinnings for a theory of transnational commercial law. Instead, legal theory has to develop working tools for the international legal practitioners, enabling them to apply the NLM within the time and money constraints of everyday legal practice. Approaching the NLM from both theoretical and pragmatic viewpoints also helps to ease the problems that arise out of the case law character of transnational commercial law. In order to justify the application of a certain legal principle or rule of transnational law, international arbitrators may refer to a collection of the NLM developed by 'neutral' scientists and practitioners instead of having to base their decision on a single arbitral award which may suffer from an ideological or economic bias:

> '. . . the process [of Creeping Codification] may lead to better and more transparent application of transnational commercial law. No longer must arbitrators who apply lex mercatoria draw from a grab bag of unwritten rules; they may now identify the source of the applicable transnational law. In resolving international commercial disputes involving parties from disparate legal and cultural traditions, the use of concrete, neutral, pragmatic principles can only lead to greater certainty, predictability, and fairness'[14].

9. *Cf.* for the methodological problem *supra* Chapter 2 II.A.1.
10. *Martiny*, RabelsZ 50 (1986), at 730, 733.
11. *See supra* Chapter 2 II.F.2.b.
12. *Fortier*, Arb.Int'l 2001, at 121, 122.
13. *Joerges*, ZHR 138 (1974), at 549, 556.
14. *See Brower/Sharpe*, Va. J. Int'l L. 2004, at 199, 220; *cf. generally* for this aspect *Schlesinger* (ed.), Formation of Contracts, Vol. I, at 11.

The remaining part of this Study is devoted to the analysis of the function, contents and prospects of success of the two different options that can be followed to provide international practice with these working tools. The work of UNIDROIT and of the *Lando* Commission follow the example of the American Law Institute and have drafted Restatements for international contract law on a global or European basis. The idea of drafting a list of general principles and rules of transnational law presented in the last section of this Study presents a new and independent approach to the codification of the NLM.

I. RESTATEMENTS OF INTERNATIONAL CONTRACT LAW

A. THE UNIDROIT PRINCIPLES OF INTERNATIONAL COMMERCIAL CONTRACTS

1. UNIDROIT's Organizational Framework

The International Institute for the Unification of Private Law (UNIDROIT) was founded in 1926 on the joint initiative of *Ernst Rabel*, who in the same year founded the Max Planck Institute for Comparative and Private International Law[15], and the Italian comparative lawyer *Vittorio Scialoja*. The two founded UNIDROIT based on a resolution of the League of Nations and the Italian government. UNIDROIT commenced its work on May 30, 1928, under the leadership of *Scialoja* and *Rabel*, who was the first German member of the Administrative Council. The initial statutes dating from 1927 established a close interdependence between UNIDROIT and the League of Nations. They were replaced by a new version in 1940 after Italy's withdrawal from the League of Nations and are in effect today in a revised version dating from November 19, 1984[16]. Since then, UNIDROIT has been organized as an independent, intergovernmental institution which is funded by the Italian state and its more than fifty Member States. UNIDROIT's main task is 'to examine methods for the harmonization and coordination of the private law of states and groups of states and to prepare for the progressive application of uniform private law'. In performing this task, UNIDROIT has drafted numerous international conventions in the past[17] such as the 'Convention on Stolen or

15. *Cf. Rabel*, JW 1932, at 2225 *et seq.*
16. *Cf. Siehr*, in: Forstmoser/Tercier/Zäch (eds.), Innominatverträge, at 25, 28; *Nelle*, JuS 1990, at 775 *et seq.*; *cf. generally UNIDROIT* (ed.), Forty Years of Service in the Cause of the Unification of Law 1926–1966, at 7 *et seq.*; *Matteucci*, Rev.dr.unif. 1976 I, at 14 *et seq.*
17. *Cf.* the survey on the 'first fifty years' in *Monaco*, in: UNIDROIT (ed.), New Directions in International Trade Law, at XXVII *et seq.*; *cf. also* the UNIDROIT Convention on International Financial Leasing of May 28, 1988, the UNIDROIT Convention on International Factoring of May 28, 1988 and the UNIDROIT Convention on Agency in the International Sale of Goods of February 17, 1983; *cf. generally Siehr*, in: Forstmoser/Tercier/Zäch (eds.), Innominatverträge,

Illegally Exported Cultural Objects' and the 'Cape Town Convention' (Convention on International Interests in Mobile Equipment)[18], or the 'Model Law on Secured Transactions' and the 'Legal Guide to International Franchising'[19].

2. Steering Committee and UNIDROIT Working Group

a. The Steering Committee

The idea to draft general principles for international commercial law was taken up by UNIDROIT in 1973 through the establishment of a 'Steering Committee'[20]. Prior to this step, Professor *Tudor Pospescu*, a member of UNIDROIT's Administrative Council, had prepared several studies on the international unification of general contract law[21]. He had presented a first provisional draft which was based on the Uniform Law for the Conclusion of International Sales Contracts About Movables of July 1, 1964[22]. The Committee was composed of Professor *Tudor Pospescu*[23] as a member of the formerly communist legal systems, Professor *René David*[24] for the civil law systems and Professor *Clive M. Schmitthoff*[25] for the common law systems. From the outset, the Committee limited its task to the drafting of a general part of international contract law[26]. Special types of contracts, such as sales and transport contracts, were excluded from the Committee's work because they had been the subject of unification efforts by other institutions[27]. The Committee also

---

at 25, 28 *et seq.*; *Martinek*, Moderne Vertragstypen, Vol. III, at 359 *et seq.*; *Nelle*, JuS 1990, at 776.

18. Available at *www.unidroit.org/english/conventions/mobile-equipment/main.htm.*
19. *Cf.* UNIDROIT News Bulletin, July/October 1994, at 3 *et seq.*
20. *Monaco*, in: UNIDROIT (ed.), New Directions in International Trade Law, at XX–VII, XL *et seq.*; *Bonell*, An International Restatement of Contract Law, at 37 *et seq.*
21. *Cf. Bonell*, ICLQ 1978, at 413, 414.
22. *Monaco, see supra* note 20, at XLI.
23. *Cf. Popescu*, Les Contrats économiques en Roumanie comme instruments d'exécution du plan, Annales de la Faculté de droit de Liège, 1971; *Popescu*, in: UNIDROIT (ed.), New Directions in International Trade Law, at 21 *et seq.*
24. Professor *René David* (1900–1990) was one of the most renowned comparative lawyers of his time, who has always emphasized the necessity of world-wide legal unification, *cf. David*, Int.Encycl.Comp.L., Vol. II, Chapter 5: The International Unification of Private Law, 1971; his major opus 'Les Grands Systèmes de Droit Contemporains', which has been translated into all major languages of the world, has introduced the notion of 'legal families' ('familles de systèmes juridiques'), by which he understood all legal systems that make use of the same legal principles and techniques; *cf. generally Grasmann*, RabelsZ 55 (1991), at 1 *et seq.*
25. Professor *Clive M. Schmitthoff* (1903–1990) was not only the protagonist of a practical commercial law (his standard treatise '*Schmitthoff's* Export Trade' appeared in its 11th ed. in 2007), but also one of the major proponents of a transnational commercial law in the form of a modern '*law merchant*', a new '*lex mercatoria*', *cf. supra* Introduction I.A.1; the foundation of UNCITRAL is based on his initiative, *cf. Broches*, in: Broches (ed.), Selected Essays, at 359 *et seq.*; *cf. generally* for a valuation of *Schmitthoff's* life and work *Horn*, NJW 1991, at 1399; *Fabricius*, Festschrift Schmitthoff, at 11 *et seq.*
26. *Monaco*, in: UNIDROIT (ed.), New Directions in International Trade Law, at XLI.
27. *Bonell*, ICLQ 1978, at 413, 414 *et seq.*; *Monaco, id.*

decided that the rules and principles of general contract law should be preceded by an introductory section which would clarify the general objective of a codification and would define basic notions and principles that would be used throughout the draft[28]. Finally, the Committee discussed and fixed the methodical basis and general organizational framework for the drafting process. Towards this end, the three Committee members could refer to the work of the four conferences of all institutions concerned with the unification of law (1956 in Barcelona and 1959, 1963 and 1968 in Rome[29]). The fourth conference held in Rome in April 1968 was of particular importance in this respect because its primary purpose was to discuss and evaluate the criteria for the choice between the various methods for the unification of the law[30].

b. The Working Group

In spite of these intensive methodical and organizational preparations it was not until 1980 that UNIDROIT established a first Working Group[31]. The Group had seventeen permanent members from all major legal systems of the world[32]. *Rapporteurs* for the individual chapters of the Principles were chosen from within the group. They presented a first draft with explanations which was then discussed by the Working Group and redrafted, taking into account the amendments that were adopted by the group[33]. The Working Group finalized the draft at its 18th session in Tulane from January 31 to February 3, 1994. The final text of the UNIDROIT Principles was then adopted at the 73rd session of UNIDROIT's

28. *Monaco, supra* note 26, *id.*
29. *Cf. Matteucci*, UNIDROIT Annuaire 1965, at 53, 55; *Matteucci*, in: UNIDROIT (ed.), New Directions in International Trade Law, Vol. I, at XVII, XXI *et seq.*
30. *Cf.* the presentations on the general topic 'The criteria governing the choice between the various methods' by *Malintoppi* ('Les Relations entre L'Unification et L'Harmonisation du Droit et la Technique de L'Unification ou de L'Harmonisation par la voie d'Accords Internationaux'), *David* ('L'Unification ou L'Harmonisation Législative sans Engagement International'), *Schmitthoff* ('The Unification or Harmonisation of Law By Means of Standard Contracts and General Conditions'), *Blagojevic* ('Les Procèdes D'Unification ou D'Harmonisation les plus Appropriés dans les Relations entre Pays ayant des Régimes Economiques et Juridiques Différentes'), UNIDROIT Annuaire 1967–1968, Vol. II, at 43 *et seq.*; the principal significance of these methodical preparatory works is emphasized in the report of the UNIDROIT Secretariat on the 'Progressive codification of the law of international trade', UNCITRAL Yearbook I (1968–1970), at 285, 287.
31. *Cf. Bonell*, An International Restatement of Contract Law, at 38 *et seq.*; *Zimmermann*, JZ 1995, at 477, 480.
32. *P. Brazil* (Canberra), *P.-A. Crépeau* (Montréal), *S.K. Date-Bah* (Accra, London), *A. Di Majo* (Rome), *U. Drobnig* (Hamburg), *E.A. Farnsworth* (New York), *M. Fontaine* (Louvain-La-Neuve), *M.P. Furmston* (Bristol), *A. Garro* (New York), *A.S. Hartkamp* (The Hague), *H. Hirose* (Tokio), *A.S. Komarov* (Moscow), *O. Lando* (Copenhagen), *D. Maskow* (Berlin), *D. Tallon* (Paris), *Huang D.* (Beijing) and *Michael Joachim Bonell* (Rome) as Coordinator of the Working Group; in addition, the following members have in the past belonged to the Working Group: *C.M. Bianca* (Rome), *J. Rajski* (Warsaw), *T. Wade* (The Hague) and *Wang Zhenpu* (Beijing).
33. *Cf. Bonell*, RabelsZ 56 (1992), at 274, 278.

Administrative Council. At the same time its widest possible dissemination was strongly recommended[34].

3. The Method Adopted by the Working Group

a. The Functional Comparative Methodology

From the outset, the UNIDROIT Working Group decided[35] to base its work on the functional comparative methodology[36]. It has been demonstrated above that the law of international contracts is particularly suitable for such comparative efforts[37]. This hope is nourished by the nineteenth century common law judges' extensive application of the doctrine of contracts as developed in the late Spanish Scholasticism of the sixteenth and seventeenth centuries and popularized by *Grotius* and *Pufendorf*[38]. In spite of all the differences in detail, this early contract practice has produced a mass of common basic terms and, above all, fundamental notions and principles. In addition, international trade customs have influenced modern European codifications as well as the Anglo-American common law so that 'there are well-founded hopes as to the existence of far-reaching common grounds'[39]. Lord *Mansfield's* famous words in *Luke v. Lyde*, rendered in 1759, still hold true today that 'Mercantile Law is not the law of a particular country but the law of all nations'[40]. The likelihood of a '*praesumptio similitudinis*' as a basic requirement for the comparison process is the greatest here.

34. *Cf.* UNIDROIT News Bulletin, July/October 1994, at 2.
35. *Bonell*, ICLQ 1978, at 413, 440; *Furmston*, in: Institute of International Business Law and Practice (ed.), UNIDROIT Principles of International Commercial Contracts: A New Lex Mercatoria?, at 199, 203: 'The debate [within the UNIDROIT Working Group] was lively and vigorous but totally free of any acrimony. It was striking indeed what a high degree of group coherence was achieved. The enterprise can perhaps best be described as an exercise in applied comparative law'.
36. *Cf. generally supra* Chapter 2 II.A.1.
37. *Gutteridge*, Comparative Law, at 32 *et seq.*: 'The law of obligations . . . appears to provide one of the most promising fields for comparative study and research . . . [i]t deals with . . . the "mobile" elements in human relationships; in other words, it is the law of everyday life . . . The conclusions arrived at are, in general, more or less identical, although the method of arriving at them may differ considerably . . . The law of contract furnishes the necessary groundwork for a comparison of the commercial laws of the world; it is also the essential prelude to any proposal for the unification of these laws'.
38. *Cf. Zimmermann*, The Law of Obligations – Roman Foundations of the Civilian Tradition, at 143 *et seq.*; *Zimmermann*, ZEuP 1993, at 4, 49 *et seq.* (especially with respect to the origins of the 'doctrine of offer and acceptance' in the research of *Grotius* and *Pufendorf*); *generally Gordley*, The Philosophical Origins of Modern Contract Doctrine, 1991.
39. *Lorenz*, JZ 1962, at 269, 272; *cf. also Gutteridge*, Comparative Law, at 32 *et seq.*
40. Lord *Mansfield* in *Luke v. Lyde*, 2 Burrow's Rep. [1759] 883, 887; *cf. also* Judge *Story* in *Swift v. Tyson*, 41 US (16 Pet.) [1842] 1, 19: '[Commercial law] may be truly declared in the language of Cicero . . . to be in great measure not the law of a single country only, but of the commercial world'.

It is important to note that the UNIDROIT Working Group was not only concerned with the consolidation of common rules and principles contained in domestic legal systems, but also with the 'codification', *i.e.* the shaping and modification of solutions to be found in domestic laws in order to create new rules and principles which are more suited to meet the needs of international trade[41]. In fact, any attempt to 'codify' transnational law necessarily leads to the creation of 'new' rules:

> 'The notion that "codifiers" sit down faithfully to reproduce rules of customary law is pure mythology, particular at the international level, where there are likely to be significant differences between the rules of one legal system and those of another... What those involved in the project seek to achieve is best solutions to typical problems, being solutions which are not so far removed from existing practice as to make them unacceptable. Accordingly, change is inherent in any redaction of rules, whether written or unwritten. The resulting text will thus be a combination of rules that existed before, modifications of existing rules and entirely new rules'[42].

Thus, the methodical approach chosen by the Working Group even led to the modification of certain provisions of the CISG, which has so deeply influenced the drafting of the Principles[43]. As far as the substance of this comparative research is concerned, two points should be emphasized. First, the research included the legal systems of communist or formerly communist countries. Secondly, the Working Group decided to include in its comparative research so-called 'hybrid' legal systems in order to use the natural comparative potential inherent in these systems. These two important aspects will be addressed in the following section of this Study.

b. *Methodical Particularities*

aa. Foreign Trade Laws of (Formerly) Communist Legal Systems

The law of international trade depends upon the free will and the autonomy of the parties. Therefore, it may seem contradictory to include in the comparative research, legal systems from communist countries which have excluded the autonomy of the party altogether or diluted it to a mere empty shell such as Sec. 8(2) of the Civil Code of the former German Democratic Republic (GDR)[44]. In spite of these fundamental differences between the goal of the Principles and the nature

41. *Bonell*, An International Restatement of Contract Law, at 21 *et seq.*; *cf.* for this dual function of the functional comparative methodology Chapter 2 II.A.1.b.
42. *Goode*, ICLQ 1997, at 1, 19 *et seq.*
43. *See Bonell*, Unif.L.Rev. 1996, at 26, 30 *et seq.*; *Perales Viscasillas*, Ariz.J.Int'l & Comp.L. 1996, at 383, 404 *et seq.*
44. The 'freedom of contract' granted to the people of the GDR merely served as a means to determine the ways by which they could have access to the limited public resources and excluded any further party autonomy in the sense of Western legal systems, *cf.* for details *Horn*, Das Zivil- und Wirtschaftsrecht im neuen Bundesgebiet, § 7, No. 2.

of these legal systems, their inclusion in the comparative process by the UNIDROIT Working Group was perfectly legitimate. To justify this approach one does not need to debate the principal question of whether legal systems from totally different economic cultures should be included in the functional comparative process[45]. Those states that were considered by the Working Group had promulgated special laws for international trade in order to remain competitive in international business. These laws contained surprisingly detailed and advanced provisions on almost all legal problems of international trade and could therefore serve as a model for the drafting of a 'codification' of transnational commercial law. Including these laws in the research is also justified for another reason, namely that the legislators of these statutes kept them free from socialist legal ideology[46] in order to ensure 'legal competitiveness' in the international markets[47].

(a) The International Commercial Contracts Act of the Former GDR

The 1976 International Commercial Contracts Act of the former GDR Act[48] contained provisions guaranteeing unlimited party autonomy (Sec. 4), requiring consideration of trade usages in general (Sec. 5) and in the construction of contracts in particular (Sec. 6(2)), and prohibiting the misuse of rights and legal positions (Sec. 7)[49]. In addition, Sec. 3 of the Act provided for the autonomous interpretation of the law in that it required the analogous application of individual provisions of the Act in those situations which were not directly regulated by the Act. It also called upon the judge or arbitrator to determine the principles and rules to be applied to international commercial contracts 'out of the principles on which the Act is based'. This latter principle is embodied in Art. 7(2) CISG. It also plays an important role in the interpretation of the UNIDROIT Principles and is of paramount importance for the evolution of the NLM as an 'open' legal system[50]. The GDR Act also contained a multitude of provisions for sixteen different innominate contracts of international trade (assembly contract, construction contract, guarantee contract, letter of credit, etc.). Most of these provisions had no equivalent in Western legal systems.

---

45. *Cf. generally Loeber*, RabelsZ 26 (1961), at 201 *et seq.*
46. *Cf.* for the Law of International Economic Contracts of the former GDR *Horn*, Das Zivil- und Wirtschaftsrecht im neuen Bundesgebiet, § 7, No. 7; for the Czech Law on International Trade *Luby*, in: Luby (ed.), Le droit civil czécoslovaque, at 179, 181.
47. According to its Art. 1, the main objective of the Chinese Law is 'the promotion of China's foreign trade relations'; *cf. also* in a similar sense Sec. 1 of the Czech Law on International Trade.
48. Law on International Economic Contracts – GIW – of February 5, 1976, GBl. I No. 5, at 61 (= *Horn* (ed.), Das Zivil- und Wirtschaftsrecht der DDR, No. 2.5); the Law remained in force in the transitional period up to the German Reunification as the 'Law on Economic Contracts' (GW) and was applied to all contracts concluded since July 1, 1990 up to October 10, 1990; *cf. Horn*, Das Zivil- und Wirtschaftsrecht im neuen Bundesgebiet, § 7, No. 15.
49. *Cf. generally Stargardt*, ZIP 1990, at 471, 474.
50. *Cf. infra* 7. (for the UNIDROIT Principles), B.2.b. (for the Principles of European Contract Law) and *supra* Chapter 2 II.A.2. (for the *lex mercatoria*).

The drafting history of the GDR Act is another important aspect to be taken into account in evaluating the Act's significance for comparative research. The GDR Act was drafted after substantial comparative preparation which included the legal systems of many Western industrialized countries. It was this modern approach which led the GDR legislature to include in the law, ideas and provisions which were in line with the CISG and its predecessor, the Uniform Law on International Sales[51]. Due to its innovative and liberal approach to the legal problems of international trade the GDR Act was considered a model for possible legislation on international trade law in Western countries[52]. In fact, the Act was used as the applicable contract law to German-German transactions in the context of German Reunification.

(b) The Law of International Trade of the Former Czechoslovakia

The same considerations apply to the Czechoslovakian Law of International Trade of 1963 (Czech Law)[53]. The drafters of the Czech Law realized that the need for a sensible regulation of international trade had 'undoubtedly' led to an increasing unification of the law and to initial indications for the development of a uniform world trade law. At the same time, it was acknowledged that the major domestic codifications of trade law such as the German Commercial Code, the French Code de Commerce and the 'Bourgeois' civil codes such as the Swiss Code of Obligations or the Italian *Codice Civile* could not do justice to the 'objective tendency towards the internationalization' of commercial relationships[54]. Consequently, the Czech Law contained more than 700 sections on a multitude of legal problems in international trade relating to almost all types of contracts. The principle of freedom of contract (Sec. 5.722(1))[55] and the principle of inherent interpretation and supplementation of the law (Sec. 723) formed the foundation stones of the statute, thereby demonstrating completeness of this particular statute, compared to other domestic laws of the former Czechoslovakia. Furthermore, the statute was based on comprehensive functional legal comparative studies which were influenced not only by communist legal systems but also took 'capitalist legal thinking' into account through consideration of the preliminary work relating to The Hague Uniform Sale of Goods Law, the Swiss Obligation Law, the Italian and Greek Civil Codes and even the American UCC[56]. The legal notions and ideas contained in these laws were not automatically adopted by the Czech legislature. Instead, they were adapted and, where necessary, modified or developed to the extent that

51. *Enderlein*, in: UNIDROIT (ed.), New Directions in International Trade Law, at 447, 450.
52. *Cf. Horn*, Das Zivil- und Wirtschaftsrecht im neuen Bundesgebiet, at 110.
53. Law on the Legal Relationships in International Trade (The Law of International Trade) of December 4, 1963, Sb.Z. 101/1963.
54. *Cf. Kalensky*, Bulletin de Droit Tchécoslovaque 1964, at 299, 300 *et seq*. where reference is made to the research of *Schmitthoff* and *Goldstajn*.
55. *Cf. Luby*, in: Luby (ed.), Le droit civil czécoslovaque, at 179, 181; *Kalensky*, Bulletin de Droit Tchécoslovaque 1964, at 299, 310 *et seq*.
56. *Cf. Luby, id.*

they could contribute to the establishment of a coherent legal system that would be apt to overcome the problems of international trade[57]. On account of this quality of the Czech Act, the statute also served as a model in the preparation of the International Commercial Contract Act of the former GDR[58].

(c) The Foreign Economic Contract Law of the People's Republic of China

The 1985 Foreign Economic Contract Law of the People's Republic of China[59] was also included in the comparative research of the UNIDROIT Working Group[60]. Like the other laws mentioned above, it was also based on the principle of functional comparative methodology and is characterized by a far-reaching reception of Western legal thinking[61].

bb. 'Hybrid' Laws and 'Extralegal Phenomena'

The UNIDROIT Working Group's primary objective in preparing the draft principles was to achieve a realistic picture of the worldwide practice of transnational contract law. To achieve this goal, it could not limit its research to international conventions such as the CISG[62] or the major civil law codifications with substantial comparative potential such as the Dutch Civil Code[63] or the American UCC[64]. To provide the research with more comparative persuasiveness, the Working Group decided to include in its research so-called 'hybrid'[65] domestic laws. In these laws, the legal and cultural influences of different systems are merged into a single statute, thereby providing a particularly useful and valuable *substratum* for comparative research[66]. The comparative value of these laws was not created 'artificially', through a comparative drafting technique initiated by domestic legislatures who wanted to bring their laws in line with international standards. Instead, comparative law influences left their mark in the drafting process almost automatically due to the particular ethnologic and cultural conditions in these jurisdictions.

Examples of these 'hybrid' laws include: the Algerian and Egyptian Civil Codes both of which were influenced by the laws of Continental Europe, the South-African Civil Code with its strong Roman-Dutch and Common Law

57. *Kalensky, supra* note 54, at 311.
58. *Cf. Maskow/Wagner et al.*, Kommentar zum GIW, at 29.
59. Foreign Economic Contract Law of the People's Republic of China (China FECL), adopted at the Tenth Session of the Standing Committee of the National People's Congress on March 21, 1985; the Law entered into force on July 1, 1985.
60. *Bonell*, RabelsZ 56 (1992), at 280.
61. *Horn*, RIW 1985, at 688, 689.
62. *Cf.* for the Influence of the CISG on the drafting of the UNIDROIT Principles *Hartkamp*, in: Boele-Woelki/Grosheide/Hondius/Steenhoff (eds.), Comparability and Evaluation, at 85 *et seq.*
63. *Cf. supra* Chapter 2 II.A.1.a.
64. *Cf. Gray*, RabelsZ 50 (1986), at 111, 137 *et seq.*
65. *Cf. Lawson*, Judicial Review 1949, at 16, 24.
66. *Cf. Bonell*, An International Restatement of Contract Law, at 47.

influences[67], the Civil Code of Sri Lanka with its Islamic, Buddhist, Hinduist, Roman-Dutch and Common Law traditions[68], the Civil Law of the American Federal State of Louisiana, which has French, Spanish and Common Law influences[69], and the Civil Code of Quebec, which is based on French and Common Law influences and which came into force on January 1, 1994[70].

However, in preparing the methodical basis for the drafting of the UNIDROIT Principles, the Working Group could not stop here. To complete the full picture of the worldwide practice of international trade law, it had to resort to 'extralegal phenomena'[71] which are considered as a source of transnational commercial law[72]. They include[73], but are not limited to, general conditions of trade, standard contracts, the Incoterms[74], the UCP issued by the ICC[75], the ECE-General Delivery and Assembly Conditions for the Import and Export of Machines and Plans[76], the FIDIC-Conditions of Contract for Works of Civil Engineering Construction (the so-called 'red book')[77], and bilateral and multilateral conditions for foreign trade contracts negotiated and implemented with the force of law between the member countries of the former COMECON[78]. Finally, the UNIDROIT Working Group referred to the work of the *Lando* Commission on European Contract Law[79].

---

67. *Cf. Zimmermann*, Das römisch-holländische Recht in Südafrika, at 73; *Sanders*, Comp. & Int'l L.J. of Southern Africa 1981, at 328 *et seq.*
68. *Cf. Cooray*, Comp. & Int'l L.J. of Southern Africa 1974, at 295 *et seq.*
69. *Cf. Zekoll*, ZVglRWiss. 1994, at 323 *et seq.*
70. Code Civil du Québec; the text of the law, together with the official commentary, is reprinted in: DAFCO (ed.), Code Civil du Québec, Commentaires du Ministre de la Justice, 1993.
71. *Zweigert/Kötz*, Einführung in die Rechtsvergleichung, § 26 III.
72. *Cf.* for the necessity to include these sources of the *lex mercatoria* in the preparation of the restatements of European and international contract law *Kötz*, RabelsZ 50 (1986), at 1, 17.
73. *Cf.* the comprehensive list by *Bonell*, An International Restatement of Contract Law, at 48 *et seq.*
74. The Incoterms are standard trade definitions most commonly used in international sales contracts and published by the ICC; *see* Incoterms 2000, ICC Publ. No. 560; *cf. also Ramberg*, ICC Guide to Incoterms 2000 and *Bredow/Seiffert*, Incoterms 2000.
75. ICC Uniform Customs and Practices for Documentary Credits (UCP 600), in effect as of July 1, 2007, ICC Publ. No. 600; *cf. ICC* (ed.), Commentary on UCP 600, ICC Publ. No. 680.
76. *Cf. Dünnweber*, Vertrag zur Erstellung einer schlüsselfertigen Industrieanlage im internationalen Wirtschaftsverkehr, at 5.
77. *Cf. Corbett*, FIDIC 4th – A Practical Legal Guide; in 1999 FIDIC released four 'New Major Books' intended to replace the previous editions of FIDIC's construction standard forms, *cf. Bunni*, The FIDIC Forms of Contract, 2005 and *Mallmann*, Bau- und Anlagenbauverträge nach den FIDIC-Standardbedingungen.
78. *Cf. e.g.* the 'General Conditions on the Delivery of Goods between the Organizations and Member States of the COMECON 1968/88' (ALB/RGW 1968/1988) – Announcement of March 3, 1989, GBl. DDR II No. 4, at 41; 'General Conditions for Customer Services for Machines, Equipment and other Products, delivered between the Organizations and Member States of the COMECON' (AMB/RGW 1973), Announcement of December 15, 1973, GBl. DDR II, No. 18, at 277; 'General Conditions for the Specialization and Cooperation of the Production of the Member States of the COMECON' (ABSK/RGW), Announcement of May 3, 1979, GBl. DDR II, No. 3, at 49; *cf. generally Enderlein et al.*, Der Außenhandelskaufvertrag, at 103.
79. *See Bonell*, Unif.L.Rev. 1996, at 229, 233: 'Naturally the Commission on European Contract Law was from the outset aware of the work being conducted by the UNIDROIT Group and vice-versa. Moreover, as the two groups were dealing with the individual chapters at different times,

4. The Basic Decision: 'Restatement' Versus International Convention or Model Law

From the outset of the drafting process, the UNIDROIT Working Group refrained from following the traditional approach to the unification of international commercial law[80] through international conventions or model laws. This strategy was a natural consequence of the discussion on the unification of international commercial law initiated by the report of the UNIDROIT Secretariat on the 'progressive unification of the law of international trade'[81]. Adopting the restatement technique for the unification of transnational contract law resulted in both an advantage and a disadvantage for the efficiency of the whole process in general, and the acceptance of the UNIDROIT Principles in particular. By refusing to draft an international convention, the Working Group avoided the often complicated and time-consuming negotiations at international conferences[82]. The sovereign rights of the potential Member States of that convention[83] were left untouched. This helped to prevent long lasting ratification procedures from the outset. Finally, the restatement technique helped to escape the 'hardly comprehensible mess'[84] of reservation clauses which Member States usually use to restrict the scope of international conventions, thereby diluting the concept of the international unification of law[85].

The Working Group also chose not to draft the Principles in the form of a model law. A model law[86] is a 'statutory text negotiated on the international plane

---

it was inevitable that each group was influenced by the work of the other. While the UNIDROIT Group started its work with the chapter on formation, followed by those on interpretation, validity, performance and non-performance, the Commission took these topics in the inverse order. Consequently each group, as it proceeded from one topic to another, profited by having at its disposal the results of the other's work, at least in the form of a preliminary draft'; *cf.* for the *Lando*, Principles of European Contract Law, *infra* B.

80. *Cf.* for this classical approach *Kropholler*, Internationales Einheitsrecht, at 93 *et seq.*; *Borum*, Convention or Model Law, Festschrift Fragistas, at 1 *et seq.*; *Riese*, ZSR 1967, at 1, 17 *et seq.*; *Nadelmann*, UNIDROIT Annuaire 1967–1968, Vol. II, at 173 *et seq.*
81. *Cf. Bonell*, RDAI 1988, at 873, 886.
82. *Cf. Goode*, Unif.L.Rev. 1997, at 231, 233; *Zamora*, GYIL 1989, at 9, 10: 'Unfortunately, it has become increasingly difficult in multilateral conferences to negotiate specific, binding rules that would govern economic relations between States. This is due to structural changes . . . : in a world economy of heightened interdependency, the stakes at such multilateral conferences are considerably higher than those of earlier decades; because economic power is dispersed among powerful competitors, it has become harder to achieve agreement on new multilateral treaties, amendments to existing treaties, or new economic codes'; *see also Goode*, ICLQ 2005, at 539, 558: 'The preparation of international conventions is arduous and time-consuming and calls for immense patience, mutual respect and a very great deal of hard work. Even where these qualities are present . . . tensions can arise which are not related to the quality of the work'.
83. *Cf. David*, in: UNIDROIT Annuaire 1967–1968, at 77, 78 *et seq.*
84. *Müller*, Die Vorbehalte in Übereinkommen zur Privatrechtsvereinheitlichung, at 3.
85. This phenomenon is aggravated by the fact that domestic courts often interpret identical rules of uniform law in a different manner, *cf. supra* Chapter 1 II.C.2 and *infra* 10.d.
86. The procedure of model law legislation has its origins in the (internal) unification of the law in Germany in the nineteenth century ('General Laws', 'Allgemeine Gesetze'), *e.g.* in the field of

and intended to be adopted *in toto* or in part and to supplement domestic law in all those states whom it may concern'[87]. The adoption of the model law is therefore depending solely on the persuasive authority of those who have drafted it. There is thus an inherent risk in the model law technique: the unification efforts may be frustrated by the states' refusal to adopt the law or by substantial modifications made by the legislatures who adopt it[88].

Abandoning the traditional ways to the unification of law helped to ensure speed and efficiency of the 'codification process', but also had its price. By drafting a restatement-like collection of general principles and rules of international contract law, UNIDROIT stopped midway between the creation of directly applicable substantive rules of international contract law and the creation of decisional harmony through the unification of the rules of private international law[89]. The initial approach of 'unification by codification'[90] would have led to the creation of international uniform law through the drafting of an international convention or model law which, by their transformation into domestic law, would have led to special statutes for international commercial law[91]. This approach would have confirmed the view frequently ventured in international legal doctrine, that the transnationalization of commercial law may be best effected, not by striving towards the evolution of an autonomous legal system, but by the implementation of special domestic statutes for international commercial cases. Indeed, this approach would have followed the example of the International Commercial Contracts Act of the former GDR[92] and of other states of the former Eastern Bloc[93]. In contrast, UNIDROIT's idea for the comprehensive unification of the law of international trade[94] would have had the advantage of creating one single set of rules for international commercial cases, thereby doing away with the 'jump into the dark'[95] of private international law. Yet, diluting this concept to the drafting of

---

bills of exchange (Draft of a Model Law of 1847 through the German Customs Union), *cf. Hudson/Feller*, Harv.L.Rev. 1931, at 333, 335 *et seq.*, and the classical Scandinavian and Anglo-American unification procedures, *Coing*, Einführung, in: Coing/Schmitthoff/Hellner/Gleichmann (eds.), Methoden der Rechtsvereinheitlichung, at 7, 10 *et seq.*; *Kropholler*, Internationales Einheitsrecht, at 105 *et seq.*; *Ekeberg*, The Scandinavian Co-operation in the Field of Legislation, in: UNIDROIT (ed.), Unification of Law, 1948, at 321, 329.

87. *Philipps*, Erscheinungsformen und Methoden der Privatrechtsvereinheitlichung, at 52 *et seq.*
88. *Cf. Holtzmann*, in: Festschrift P. Lalive (ed.), 1993, at 257; *cf. also David*, UNIDROIT Annuaire 1967–1968, Vol. II, at 77, 83 *et seq.*
89. *Cf. generally Coing, supra* note 86, at 7, 12; *Malintoppi*, in: UNIDROIT Annuaire 1967–1968, Vol. II, at 43, 44.
90. *Cf.* the report of the UNIDROIT Secretariat on the 'Progressive codification of the law of international trade', in: UNCITRAL Yearbook I (1968–1970), at 285, 287; *cf. supra* Chapter 3 II.B.1.
91. *Cf. generally* for the 'embedding' of unified substantive law in the respective domestic legal system *Constantinesco*, Rechtsvergleichung, Vol. II, 1972, at 430; *David*, L'unification internationale du droit privé, at 277.
92. *Cf. supra* 3.b.aa.(a).
93. *Cf. supra* 3.b.aa.(b) and (c).
94. *Cf. supra* Chapter 3 II.B.
95. *See supra* Chapter 1 I.A.

a collection of non-binding rules and principles of international contract law does not answer the question as to the existence of a transnational commercial legal system. The answer to this question depends to a large extent on the determination of the legal character of the UNIDROIT Principles. They can be qualified as metalegal rules and principles existing on the transnational plane which are *merely reflected and put into 'statutory' form* in the UNIDROIT Principles, which thereby assume a normative quality. One may also go a step further and attach to the UNIDROIT Principles a normative quality of their own which is then extended to the individual norms and principles contained therein[96].

In any event, the informal approach taken by the UNIDROIT Working Group has had a decisive influence on the success of the Principles:

> '... [P]aradoxically the impact of the two sets of principles [UNIDROIT and *Lando*] may prove to be greater than that of an international convention, for a convention has no force at the time it is concluded and represents at most a provisional indication of support by participating States which may or may not crystallize, whereas the Principles represent the unconditional commitment and consensus of scholars of international repute from all over the world'[97].

Therefore, suggestions that the Principles should at some point in time be transformed into an international convention[98] should be seen with utmost scepticism. Informal, not formalized codification of transnational commercial law, is the order of the day.

5. Common Features and Differences Between the UNIDROIT Principles and the American Restatements

It has been emphasized above[99] that the American Restatements are used not only to 're-state' the law as it is but also to 'gently push' the common law into a direction that is favoured by the American Law Institute. In preparing the UNIDROIT Principles, the Working Group pursued a similar approach. It adopted solutions that were not necessarily common to all legal systems that were included in the research. Instead it adopted those solutions that were found in the research and which were best suited to the needs of international trade and commerce[100]. In the context of transnational commercial law, there are two justifications for this progressive drafting approach. First, it is in line with the particular nature of international commercial law which is in a process of constant evolution and development. Every attempt to codify this law, therefore, must take account of possible future developments, thereby assuming a creative rather than a descriptive

96. *See infra* 10.b.
97. *Goode*, Unif.L.Rev. 1997, at 231, 234.
98. *See* the proposal by *Béraudo*, La Semaine Juridique 1995, I (3842), at 194.
99. *See supra* Chapter 3 I.B.2.
100. *Cf.* for this 'codification dilemma' of transnational commercial law and the possible ways to overcome it *infra* II.

quality. This flexible character of transnational law also has serious consequences for any attempt to 'codify' the NLM. Depending on how many progressive elements the drafters included in the codification, this collection of legal principles and rules of the NLM will sooner or later necessarily lag behind the true *status quo* of the NLM. Secondly, the approach taken by the UNIDROIT Working Group confirms the general experience that *every* effort to codify the law necessarily implies a creative quality, *i.e.* the overt or covert evolution and development of the law that is to be codified[101]. The World Bank has made this experience when drafting the 'Guidelines on the Treatment of Foreign Direct Investment':

> 'Progressive developments evolve into codified law and codification exercises cannot ignore proposals *de lege ferenda* totally. As a practical matter, the process of codification often combines both the restatement of existing principles and some formulation of new principles . . . The approach adopted by the Working Group . . . was in line with this general process. It meant to use the general trend distilled from existing legal instruments as their initial building blocks, and to add to them certain elements of best practice, thereby emerging with a set of guidelines which represent in part law in the process of development (*de lege ferenda*) and in part established and accepted law (*lex lata*)'[102].

This 'gentle pushing' of transnational commercial contract law by the UNIDROIT Working Group did not happen in a legal vacuum without any methodical underpinnings. The functional comparative methodology is not simply a mere interpolation of the legal systems under review or a mere ascertainment of compromises[103]. Rather, it is generally acknowledged that research based on a functional approach to the comparative method leads to a definition of rules and principles which are not to be found in the legal systems that are the subject of the research[104]. Although misinterpreting the true character of the American Restatements, *Mario Matteucci*, the initiator of UNIDROIT's work towards the restatement of international contract law[105], had already hinted at such far-reaching progressive effects of the restatement technique on the 'codification' of international contract law:

> 'Enfin, je demande si on ne pourrait, tout en s'inspirant du procédé des Etats-Units, essayer de donner au travail de restatement un caractère plus constructif

101. *See Selden*, Ann.Surv.Int'l & Comp.L. 1995, at 111, 122: '[The UNIDROIT Principles] are not only a "restatement", but also an effort toward harmonization, which implies that they may lean in the perceived direction of "progress", and may not always reflect the actual trading practices now in use'.
102. *Cf. Shihata*, Legal Treatment of Foreign Investment: 'The World Bank Guidelines', at 62 *et seq.*
103. *See Lando*, Am.J.Comp.L. 1983, at 653, 657 for the work of the 'Commission on European Contract Law'.
104. *Rabel*, RabelsZ 16 (1951), at 357; *Lorenz*, JZ 1962, at 269, 271; *Zweigert/Kötz*, Einführung in die Rechtsvergleichung, § 3 VII.
105. *See supra* Introduction I.B.2.a.

que le restatement américain. Alors qu'en Amérique on se borne plus ou moins à constater quel est l'état objectif de la jurisprudence, ici il faudrait essayer de tirer de cette constatation quelque chose de plus avancé, des règles plus parfaites, en tenant compte du dernier cri de la jurisprudence des différents pays'[106].

Regardless of these similarities between the American Restatements and the UNIDROIT Principles, there are also two basic differences between both projects. The first difference relates to the jurisdictions, the law of which is restated in these 'codifications'. The scope of the American Restatements is limited to the jurisdiction of the US. Thus, the Restatements cover an area with a more or less homogeneous socio-economic structure. The UNIDROIT Principles on the other hand, are geared towards the global unification of international contract law, thereby covering totally different legal cultures with heterogeneous dogmatic and methodical structures. This broad scope of the UNIDROIT Principles has made the Working Group's research much more demanding[107]. This applies also to the practical usefulness of the Principles. Any 'codification' of transnational commercial law will be accepted by international legal practice only if and to the extent that it contains a delicate balance between general principles and concrete norms and rules[108]. This necessity exists in spite of the fact that in the field of international contract law, the far-reaching acknowledgement of the principle of party autonomy has to a certain extent reduced the difference between principles and rules.

The second principal difference between the UNIDROIT Principles and the American Restatement of the Law of Contracts relates to the fact that the American common law of contracts is based on a long-standing and generally acknowledged methodical framework created by the '*stare decisis* doctrine' and the 'weight of authority test' while in the context of the UNIDROIT Principles, the very existence of the rules and principles reproduced therein is vividly disputed[109]. In this respect it must be conceded that the American Restatements assume a higher degree of authoritative force than the UNIDROIT Principles.

6. Scope of the Principles

In preparing the drafting of the Principles, the Steering Committee made two principal decisions with respect to their scope. These decisions have been upheld throughout the deliberations of the Working Group. They relate to two classical questions of international commercial and uniform law, the definition of 'international contracts' (*infra* a.) and the determination of the 'commercial' character of a contract (*infra* b.).

---

106. *Matteucci*, UNIDROIT Annuaire 1967–1968, Vol. II, at 267, 268.
107. *Cf. Kötz*, Festschrift Zweigert, at 481, 496 for the Principles of European Contract Law.
108. *Cf.* for the implementation of these objectives *infra* 7.b.
109. *Cf. Hartkamp*, in: Hartkamp, *et al.* (eds.), Towards a European Civil Code, at 125, 127.

a. No Definition of 'International' Contracts

Contrary to earlier proposals made by *David* in the 1960s[110], the Steering Committee decided from the outset to refrain from any definition of the 'international' character of those contracts that would fall within the scope of the Principles. This decision was taken in view of the general experience that the definition of those criteria that determine the 'international' character of a contract would lead to a substantial delay of the unification process or would even bring this process to a halt[111]. This pragmatic approach proved to be the only way to avoid the controversial discussions that have accompanied the definition of internationality in Art. 1 of The Hague Sales Law[112], Art. 1 CISG[113], Art. 1(3) of the UNCITRAL Model Law on International Commercial Arbitration of 1986[114] and the general efforts to find an acceptable and all-inclusive definition of the 'international contract'[115].

Various reasons account for the controversies surrounding the definition of internationality in international commercial law. As far as international contract law is concerned, the international character of the subject matter has two important consequences. On the one hand, it determines the parties' freedom to choose the applicable law and to evade the application of the mandatory norms of the 'otherwise' applicable legal system. In the general context of the unification of international commercial law, the criteria that are applied to define the international character of a certain subject of international commercial law set the framework within which the states involved in the unification process are willing to accept the loss of sovereignty that is necessarily connected with the creation of uniform commercial law[116]. On the other hand, the criterion of 'internationality' serves as a measuring stick for the quality of international uniform law. This relates to the simplicity and clarity, the maximization of the scope, and the transparency for the parties of the relevant instruments of international uniform law[117]. In view of the fast development of international contract practice, it is particularly difficult to find a common and generally applicable denominator for the last three of these criteria. Not infrequently, their evolution has to be left to the case law of domestic courts or international arbitral tribunals[118].

Due to the particular legal nature of the Principles, the criteria just described apply to them only to a limited extent. As far as their scope is concerned, it was generally acknowledged by the Working Group that, in spite of the omission of a

110. *David*, UNIDROIT Annuaire 1967–1968, Vol. II, at 254, 257 still assumed that it would be necessary to define the 'internationality'.
111. *Cf. Kötz*, Festschrift Zweigert, at 481, 493.
112. *Cf. Dölle-Herber*, EKG, Art. 1, Nos. 4 *et seq.*
113. *von Caemmerer/Schlechtriem-Herber*, CISG, Art. 1, Nos. 7 *et seq.*
114. *Cf. Berger*, Internationale Wirtschaftsschiedsgerichtsbarkeit, at 51 *et seq.*, especially for the possibility to have the parties agree on the internationality of the arbitration proceedings, thereby opening the door for a 'fictitious internationality' of the proceedings.
115. *Cf. de Nova*, Festschrift Ferid, at 313 *et seq.*; *cf. also Delaume*, ICLQ 1979, at 258 *et seq.*
116. *Cf. Honnold*, ULIS, at 58; *Matteucci*, UNIDROIT Annuaire 1965, at 53, 54.
117. *Cf. Goode*, Unif.L.Rev. 1991, at 54, 65.
118. *Cf. de Nova*, Festschrift Ferid, at 307, 320; *Delaume*, ICLQ 1979, at 258, 279.

definition of internationality in the Principles, the concept of 'international' contracts should be given the broadest possible interpretation, so as ultimately to exclude only those situations where no international element at all is involved, *i.e.* where all the relevant elements of the contract in question (nationality of the parties, applicable substantive law, place of performance, etc.) are connected with one country only[119]. Yet, even in a purely domestic contract, parties are not prevented from agreeing, if they so desire, to apply the UNIDROIT Principles to their contract. Such an agreement would of course be subject to the mandatory rules of the *lex causae*[120].

b. *No Definition of 'Commercial' Contracts*

The Steering Committee also refrained from the outset to delimit in the Principles 'commercial' from purely 'civil' contracts[121]. To ensure the widest possible application of the Principles, only those contracts which relate to so-called 'consumer transactions', *i.e.* transactions involving a party which is not acting in the course of its trade or profession, were excluded from their scope[122]. The protection of consumers was not an objective that the Working Group had in mind[123].

This broad ambit has ensured that the UNIDROIT Principles apply not only to the classical exchange contracts of cross-border trade but also to more complex contracts such as investment, concession and service contracts[124]. The manifold variations of this latter type of contract, such as 'contractual joint venture', 'licencing', 'technical assistance', 'management', 'franchising', 'turnkey', 'product-in-hand', 'production sharing', 'risk-service', 'leasing' and other highly specialized innominate contracts[125] have gradually blurred the traditional distinction between commercial 'trade' transactions and equity investments[126]. This is also reflected in the broad definition of 'investment' in the OECD Multilateral Agreement on Investment (MAI)[127]. Here, on the international

---

119. *Cf. UNIDROIT* (ed.), Principles of International Commercial Contracts, at 2.
120. *Bonell*, An International Restatement of Contract Law, at 76; *cf. infra* 10.a.
121. *Bonell*, RDAI 1988, at 873, 876.
122. *Bonell*, An International Restatement of Contract Law, at 70 *et seq.*
123. *Furmston*, in: Institute of International Business Law and Practice (ed.), UNIDROIT Principles of International Commercial Contracts: A New Lex Mercatoria?, at 199, 201.
124. *UNIDROIT* (ed.), Principles of International Commercial Contracts, at 2.
125. *Cf.* for some of these modern contract forms *Martinek*, Moderne Vertragstypen, Vols. II, III; *see* for the modern innominate contracts of international commercial practice in the context of the *lex mercatoria* doctrine *Goldstajn*, in: Šarčević (ed.), International Contracts and Conflicts of Laws, at 14, 15 *et seq.*
126. *Cf.* for this phenomenon *Horn*, in: Horn (ed.), Legal Problems of Codes of Conduct for Multinational Enterprises, at 69; *Oman*, CTC Rep. 1986, No. 22, at 47 *et seq.*; *Oman*, in: Moran (ed.), Investing in Development: New Roles for Private Capital, at 131 *et seq.*; *Berger*, Syr.J.Int'l L. & Com. 1988, at 13, 16 *et seq.*; *Rubin:* in: Rubin/Nelson (eds.), International Investment Disputes, at 1, 5 *et seq.*; *Friedmann*, Col.J.W.Bus. 1972, at 57, 58 *et seq.*; *Shihata*, Legal Treatment of Foreign Investment: 'The World Bank Guidelines', at 70.
127. *See Karl*, RIW 1998, at 432, 433.

plane, the problem of the traditional narrow concept of 'commercial' transactions is even more accentuated than in the domestic arena, where countries which have a separate 'commercial' law have long considered revising the criteria used to delimit 'ordinary private' from 'commercial' law[128].

From this perspective, it might have been sensible to adopt the terminology 'international *economic* contracts'[129] in the Principles. This would have been in line with the view that general principles of contract law constitute an inherent element of the codification of international economic law[130]. Presumably, this terminology was not chosen in order to avoid from the outset any confusion with economic law of a public international law nature such as General Agreement on Tariffs and Trade (GATT) or WTO. This may seem understandable from the perspective of German law which maintains the traditional distinction between private and public law and uses the terminology 'economic law' to denote those provisions which the legislature employs to maintain the internal economic order, thereby assuming a public law nature[131]. German law thus still reflects *Montesquieu*'s[132] idea of the strict separation of private and public law. Nevertheless, if the parties receive the freedom to regulate those legal relationships that form part of general economic order, then private and commercial law instruments will become part of general economic law[133]. From that perspective, it would seem perfectly legitimate to use the term 'international economic contract law'.

Use of this terminology would also take into account the *status quo* of the discussion on what really constitutes 'international' economic law. The traditional view which regards this field of law as part of public international law[134] is gradually being abandoned and substituted by a comprehensive perspective which transcends the traditional boundaries between commercial law, public international law and private international law, combining them to an all-embracing legal framework for the regulation of cross-border commercial relationships[135]. This progressive view of international economic law is based on a pragmatic approach that takes into

128. *Cf. K. Schmidt*, Die Zukunft der Kodifikationsidee, 1985, at 63 *et seq.*; *Bydlinski*, Handels- oder Unternehmensrecht als Sonderprivatrecht, at 9 *et seq.*; *Preis*, ZHR 1994, at 567 *et seq.*
129. *See* for international 'economic' arbitration *Böckstiegel*, RIW 1984, at 671 *et seq.*; *Nöcker*, RIW 1990, at 28, 30; *Berger*, Internationale Wirtschaftsschiedsgerichtsbarkeit, at 50; *Berger*, International Economic Arbitration, at 68.
130. *Tilmann*, Wirtschaftsrecht, at 25 *et seq.*
131. *Cf. Rittner/Dreher*, Wirtschaftsrecht, § 1, Nos. 66 *et seq.*; *Quack*, Wirtschaftsrecht, at 224; *Fikentscher*, Wirtschaftsrecht, Vol. I, § 1 I. 1; *cf. also* from a comparative perspective *Rinck* (ed.), Begriff und Prinzipien des Wirtschaftsrechts, 1971.
132. *Montesquieu*, De l'Esprit des lois, Vol. XXVI, at 15: 'Il ne faut point régler par les principes du droit politique les choses qui dépendent des principes du droit civil'.
133. *Rittner/Dreher, see supra* note 131, § 1, No. 67.
134. *Cf.* for this narrow understanding of the terminology *Carreau/Juillard*, Droit International Economique, Nos. 8 *et seq.*; *Schwarzenberger*, Rec.Cours 1966-I, at 1, 7 *et seq.*
135. *Erler*, Grundprobleme des internationalen Wirtschaftsrechts, at 13 *et seq.*; *P. Fischer*, GYIL 1976, at 143, 158 *et seq.*; *Langen*, Studien zum Internationalen Wirtschaftsrecht, No. 42; *Horn*, Internationale Anleihen, at 514; *Böckstiegel*, Der Staat als Vertragspartner ausländischer Privatunternehmen, at 136; *Meessen*, AöR 1985, at 398, 403; *Zamora*, GYIL 1989, at 9, 13

account the increasing participation of states and state corporations in international commerce and the substantial economic power of multinational corporations which justifies, at least to a limited extent, regarding them as subjects of public international law[136]:

> 'It would be illogical if, despite increasingly direct involvement of government in private business enterprises (from energy production to transportation and tourism), the rules governing private transactions (the modern *lex mercatoria*) would be excluded from the definition of international economic law. In modern international economic transactions, issues of "public law" are often mixed with issues of "private law" and it would be unproductive to consider them separately. While a broad definition of international economic law may not be doctrinally neat, the realities of international economic relations in the late twentieth century dictate an inclusive definition'[137].

This view draws the necessary legal consequences from the fact that international legal relationships, regardless of whether states or private parties are involved, have long since gone beyond the traditional scope of public international law, thereby rendering 'international economic law' a denominator for the law of cross-border legal relationships[138]. This comprehensive conception of this field of law comes close to *Philip Jessup's* idea of a 'Transnational Law'[139].

Finally, use of the terminology 'international economic contracts' would have made it much easier from the outset to exclude consumer transactions. In fact, the discussion on a modern international economic law is centred around the exclusion of 'consumer transactions', which is exemplified in Art. 2(a) CISG[140], § 9-109 (1) of the American UCC[141], Art. 120(1) of the Swiss Federal Law on

---

et seq.; *Jakubowski*, Festschrift Schmitthoff, at 209; *U. Hübner*, Die methodische Entwicklung des internationalen Wirtschaftsrechts, at 26 *et seq.*; *Joerges*, RabelsZ 43 (1979), at 6, 17 *et seq.*: *Herdegen*, Internationales Wirtschaftsrecht, § 1, No. 10 *et seq.*

136. *Cf. Friedmann*, The Changing Structure of International Law, at 70; *Seidl-Hohenveldern*, Rev.belge dr. int. 1975, at 567, 570; *TOPCO-Award*, ILM 1978, at 3, 17 ('. . . for the purpose of the interpretation and performance of the [Concession] Contract, the private parties have the quality of subjects of public international law').
137. *Zamora*, GYIL 1989, at 9, 15.
138. *Siehr*, in: Holl/Klinke (eds.) Internationales Privatrecht, Internationales Wirtschaftsrecht, at 103, 109.
139. *Jessup*, Transnational Law, at 2: 'All law which regulates actions or events that transcend national frontiers. Both public and private law are included, as are other rules which do not wholly fit into such standard categories'.
140. 'This Convention does not apply to sales: a) of goods bought for personal, family or household use, unless the seller, at any time before or at the conclusion of the contract, neither knew nor ought to have known that the goods were bought for any such use'; *cf. von Caemmerer/Schlechtriem-Herber*, CISG, 1990, Art. 2, Nos. 5 *et seq.*
141. § 9–109 UCC: 'Goods are (1) "consumer goods" if they are used or bought for use primarily for personal, family or household purposes'; *cf.* for the difference between the UCC-definition and the definition used in the CISG, which does not refer to a factual use for private purposes *Honnold*, ULIS, at 86.

Private International Law[142] and the former Art. 29 of the German Introductory Law to the German Civil Code[143], which was drafted upon Art. 5 of the Rome Convention on the Law Applicable to Contractual Obligations[144], and Art. 6(1) of the Rome I Regulation. The experiences with consumer protection law on the EU-level[145] prove that the sensitive socio-political implications that are necessarily inherent in this field of law are hardly reconcilable with the creation of international uniform law[146]. In accordance with the aim of creating a coherent system of international economic law[147], the UNIDROIT Principles are applicable to all contracts which are concluded with a view towards the direct or indirect making of profits and which are related to the cross-border movement of goods, currencies, services, technologies or other financial or economic assets, provided that no 'typical element of consumer transactions' can be ascertained.

7. Contents of the Principles

a. *Structure*

The 1994 edition of the UNIDROIT Principles consisted of 120 articles which were divided into seven chapters. The 2004 edition of the Principles has not changed this basic structure but has lead to the addition of three new chapters and new subsections in Chapters 2 and 5[148]. The 2004 edition consists of 185 articles. The first chapter ('general provisions') of the UNIDROIT Principles contains basic legal notions and principles that deal with such fundamental notions as freedom of contract, freedom of form and proof, *pacta sunt servanda*, good faith

---

142. 'Contracts pertaining to goods or services of ordinary consumption intended for a consumer's personal or family use, provided that such use is not connected with the consumer's professional or business activity, are governed by the law of the state of the consumer's habitual residence'; *cf. Heini/Keller/Siehr/Vischer/Volken-Keller/Kren Kostkiewicz*, IPRG-Kommentar, Art. 120, Nos. 10 *et seq.* emphasizing that in view of the general problems to define the 'consumer contract', the term 'contracts with consumers' was included in the margins of the new law, which covers a variety of contracts.
143. Art. 29 applied to a contract the object of which is the supply of goods or services to a person ('the consumer') for a purpose which can be regarded as being outside his trade or profession, or a contract for the provision of credit for that object.
144. Rome Convention on the Law Applicable to Contractual Relationships of June 19, 1980, BGBl. II 1986, at 180.
145. *Cf. infra* B.I.
146. *Cf. Constantinesco*, Rechtsvergleichung, Vol. II, 1972, at 427; *Goode*, Unif.L.Rev. 1991, at 54, 66.
147. *Cf. Mertens/Kirchner/Schanze*, Wirtschaftsrecht, at 83 *et seq.*; *Petersmann*, Constitutional Functions and Constitutional Problems of International Economic Law, at 1 *et seq.*; *Zamora*, GYIL 1989, at 9, 15; *cf. also Herdegen*, Internationales Wirtschaftsrecht, § 1, No. 11; generally for the 'heterogeneity' of commercial law as a functional notion for the legal order of commercial relationships *Hedemann*, Reichsgericht und Wirtschaftsrecht, 1929, at 1 *et seq.*; *Klausing*, Wirtschaftsrecht, 1931, at 4 *et seq.*; *Tilmann*, Wirtschaftsrecht, at 3 *et seq.*; *L. Raiser*, ZHR 1979, at 338 *et seq.*
148. *See infra* 11.

and fair dealing and the primacy of usages and practices in international trade. The other chapters contain provisions relating to the conclusion of contracts, the effect of contracts, the construction of contractual stipulations[149], the contents of contracts, performance and the legal consequences of non-performance. The structure of the Principles follows the American Restatement of the Law of Contracts[150] in that a basic rule or a general legal principle formulated as black-letter law is followed by a short commentary-like explanation and explanatory illustrations. However, in contrast to the Restatement (2nd) of the Law of Contracts, there are no 'notes' specifying the comparative references (statutory provisions of domestic laws, court judgments, arbitral awards, conventions, doctrinal writings, etc.) on which the wording of the relevant rule or principle is based. The drafters intentionally left out such references to national legal systems in order to emphasize the international character of the UNIDROIT Principles, which are detached from any domestic legal system[151]. Also, the omission of comparative references was intended to avoid highlighting the fact that in the preparation of the Principles, some legal systems played a more significant role than others[152]. The first version of the American Restatement also did not contain any references to the practice of the common law in the various American states[153]. However, in order to enhance its acceptance, such notes were included in the second edition of the Restatement. It was for this very reason that the 'Principles of European Contract Law' drafted by the *Lando* Commission contain comprehensive comparative references[154]. A collection of comprehensive comparative references may attach increased legitimacy and authority to a list of general principles and rules of international commercial law and may serve as a starting point for their differentiation and diversification[155]. This issue will be looked at in more detail when the 'Creeping Codification' through the drafting of lists of general principles and rules of the NLM is discussed[156].

A particular characteristic of many of the provisions contained in the Principles is the attempt to uphold the contract as much as possible[157]. The assertion of the Principle '*in favorem validitatis*' reflects a general concern of economic

149. These provisions are of extreme relevance for international arbitration where the issue of contract interpretation plays a role far more important than that of determining the applicable law, *see Lalive*, in: Bonell/Bonelli (eds.), Contratti Commerciali Internazionali E Principi Unidroit, at 73, 81.
150. *Cf. supra* Chapter 3 I.B.1.
151. *Bonell*, An International Restatement of Contract Law, at 68.
152. *Bonell*, An International Restatement of Contract Law, at 57 *et seq.*; *Bonell*, Unif.L.Rev. 1996, at 29, 234.
153. *Cf. supra* Chapter 3 I.B.l.
154. *Cf.* for details *infra* B.2.b.
155. *See Huet*, in: Institute of International Business Law and Practice (ed.), UNIDROIT Principles of International Commercial Contracts: A New Lex Mercatoria?, at 275, 280: '... the danger is that by avoiding any national references, the Principles, which seek to satisfy everyone, may actually end up being chosen by no one at all'.
156. *Cf. infra* II.C.5.c.
157. *Bonell*, RabelsZ 56 (1992), at 274, 281 *et seq.*; *Bonell*, An International Restatement of Contract Law, at 102 *et seq.*

practice perceived in the general international law of contracts ('*favor contractus*')[158] and also in the area of international commercial arbitration[159]. Whether formulated as a comprehensive regulatory framework of the parties or drafted by reference to general conditions of trade, the contract detaches the legal relationship between the parties from the 'otherwise' applicable domestic law. Due to its self-sufficient character the contract becomes the 'substitute law' for the parties[160]. Influenced by Anglo-American drafting techniques, the comprehensive contractual arrangements 'autonomize' the parties' legal relationship from the direct application of substantive law[161]. In both long term business relationships and arms' length bargains, the parties have a vital interest in upholding their contract. The validity of the contract becomes all the more important since aspects of consumer protection do not play any role in this context[162]. From the perspective of legal theory, the principle of '*favor contractus*' correlates with the general significance of the contractual consensus of the parties as the driving force behind the creation and evolution of transnational commercial law[163].

A survey of those provisions which reflect the principle '*favor contractus*' may give an indication of the significance which it has played in the drafting of the Principles. These provisions include acceptance of a contractual offer by performing an act without notice to the offeror (Art. 2.6)[164], the modification of contractual terms by writings in confirmation (Art. 2.12), contracts with terms deliberately left open (Art. 2.14), the battle of forms (Art. 2.22), the validity of a mere contractual agreement without consideration (Art. 3.2), the validity of a contractual relationship in spite of initial impossibility (Art. 3.3), the rule of interpretation '*favor negotii*' (Art. 4.5), the rule to supply an omitted contractual term (Art. 4.8) and finally the right of the non-performing party to cure (Art. 7.1.4). Also, the principles on re-negotiation in case of hardship (Arts 6.2.1 *et seq.*[165]) and of excuse of non-performance in case of *force majeure* (Art. 7.1.7)[166] are inspired by the principle of '*favor contractus*'[167]. The last two principles are characterized by their inherent vagueness and lack of clarity. They are workable in practice, only

158. *Cf. Bianca/Bonell-Bonell*, Commentary on the International Sales Law, Art. 7, No. 2.3.2.2.
159. *Cf. Berger*, Internationale Wirtschaftsschiedsgerichtsbarkeit, at 115 (in the context of the applicable law) and at 502 (in the context of the continuing validity of the arbitration agreement after the setting aside of the arbitral award); *cf. also Bühler/Waiz von Eschen*, IPRax 1990, at 62, 64.
160. *Cf.* for details *supra* Chapter 2 II.G.3.d.
161. *Schanze*, Investitionsverträge im internationalen Wirtschaftsrecht, at 135 ('consensual regulation of commerce').
162. *Cf. supra* 6.b.
163. *Cf.* for details *supra* Chapter 2 II.G.3.d.
164. *Cf.* for the evolution of a general principle of law in this area *Lorenz*, JZ 1962, at 269, 274.
165. *Cf.* for the 'hardship' principle as part of transnational law TransLex Principles Nos. VIII.1 and VIII.2, reprinted *infra* Annex III, available with further references at *www.Trans-Lex.org/951000* and *www.Trans-Lex.org/951500.*
166. *Cf.* for the '*force majeure*' principle as part of transnational law TransLex Principle No. VI.3, reprinted *infra* Annex III, available with further references at *www.Trans-Lex.org/944000.*
167. *Cf. generally Bonell*, An International Restatement of Contract Law, at 117 *et seq.*

when they are embedded in a comprehensive legal system which is based on such fundamental legal notions as '*pacta sunt servanda*'[168].

b. Constituent Elements of a Legal System: The Interaction Between 'General Principles' and 'Rules'

aa. The Differentiation Between 'General Principles' and 'Rules'

The differentiation between 'general principles' ('*principes généraux*'; '*allgemeine Rechtsgrundsätze*') and 'rules' ('*règles*', '*Regeln*')[169] or between 'general principles', 'rules' and 'standards'[170] is an integral part of legal theory. According to the doctrine of legal sources, all these terms may be grouped under the heading of 'norm'[171]. This does not mean, however, that the UNIDROIT Principles obtain the quality of a legal norm in the proper sense. Like the American Restatements[172] they are merely *drafted like norms* so that the principles relevant to the drafting of norms of domestic law may always be applied here by analogy.

Whereas with respect to a rule, there are definite guidelines directing what conditions must be met before the rule can be applied, and there is a determined central area of application surrounded by a fringe of vagueness, *i.e.* a more or less wide, less distinct peripheral scope of possible applications[173], general principles are much less precise even at their core, the guidelines for their application are unclear and formulated in a general and vague manner[174]. General principles do not necessarily have pre-set conditions for application. Instead, they merely constitute 'rules of optimal application' which means that they may be complied with in varying degrees. The required degree of compliance depends not only on the actual but also on the legal options open to the target group. Application of general principles therefore requires a substantial process of weighing up contradictory principles and rules[175]. General principles are therefore always subject to a continual discussion about their effectiveness and scope[176].

168. *Cf. generally* for the interaction of the principle of '*pacta sunt servanda*' with other rules of general contract law *Lando*, in: Cranston (ed.), Essays in Honor of Roy Goode, at 103, 106 *et seq.*
169. *Dworkin*, Taking Rights Seriously, at 12 *et seq.*; *Dworkin*, Law's Empire, at 210 *et seq.*; *Benditt*, Law as Rule and Principle, at 61 *et seq.; Dillard*, Rec.Cours 1957, at 449, 477 *et seq.*; *Esser*, Grundsatz und Norm, at 3.
170. *Pound*, Tul.L.Rev. 1933, at 475; *cf. also Perelman* (ed.), Les notions à contenu variable en droit.
171. *Schneider*, Gesetzgebung, § 2, No. 16; *Atienza/Manero*, in: Festschrift Valdés, at 109, 114.
172. *Cf. supra* Chapter 3 I.B.
173. *Cf. Dillard*, Rec.Cours 1957, at 449, 478.
174. *Atienza/Manero*, in: Festschrift Valdés, at 109, 112; *cf. also Rheinstein*, U.Chi. L.Rev. 1957, at 597, 600: '1. Rules. They are precepts attaching a definite, detailed legal consequence to a definite, detailed state of facts . . . 2. Principles. These are authoritative starting points for legal reasoning, employed continually and legitimately where cases are not covered or are not fully or obviously covered by rules in the narrower sense . . . '.
175. *Alexy*, Theorie der Grundrechte, at 116; *Atienza/Manero, id.*, at 116; *Dillard*, Rec.Cours 1957, at 449, 479.
176. *Dworkin*, Law's Empire, at 210 *et seq.*

General principles of law express a general truth which serves as a basic guideline for the application of the law, whereas rules are the practical formulation of the principle and, for reasons of expediency, may vary and depart from the principles from which they spring. This teleological aspect reduces the level of foreseeability with respect to cases in which general principles are applied, as well as their practical workability. However, general principles of law also have the important task of explaining the function of individual legal institutions in the context of a legal system. They assist the legal institutions in that they appear not only as a (simple) group of standards and rules, but as a group with meaning and therefore as a 'system'[177]. Reference to general principles of law, therefore, allows for a certain degree of self-control of the decision-maker in that the solution found for an individual legal problem has to be integrated into the network of coherent general principles enunciated so far[178]. It is for this reason that in the judgments of domestic courts, general principles of law today take the place of standard references to vague blanket clauses of substantive law, thereby investing the courts with a kind of 'quasi law-making power', enabling them to find more modern, more contemporary solutions for the legal problems of today[179].

bb. Consequences of this Differentiation for the UNIDROIT Principles

The UNIDROIT Principles make use of this dialectic between a rule and a general principle of law. They keep to very definite rules with a clearly defined scope of application. In addition to the provisions relating to the conclusion of contracts (Arts 2.1 *et seq.*), the following articles should be mentioned in this context: Articles relating to the mode of payment (Arts 6.1.7 *et seq.*), to the currency of payment (Art. 6.1.9.9), to the costs of performance (Art. 6.1.11), to the right to withhold performance (Art. 7.1.3), to a party's right to require payment (Art. 7.2.1), to a party's right to claim damages for non-performance (Art. 7.4.1), to the calculation of damages (Art. 7.4.6), and to the rules governing the calculation of interest claims (Art. 7.4.9). The latter provision is of utmost economic relevance, given the enormous amounts that are frequently in dispute in international commercial cases[180]. However, the UNIDROIT Principles are not restricted to the reproduction of the technicalities of conclusion of contracts by offer and acceptance[181] and the performance of contracts and possible secondary claims. Instead, a number of general principles in the form of general clauses take precedence in the first chapter

177. *Atienza/Manero*, in: Festschrift Valdés, at 109, 121; *Esser*, Grundsatz und Norm, at 7; *Watt*, Clunet 1997, at 403, 408.
178. *Watt, id.*, at 409.
179. *Watt, id.*, at 403, No. 3, for French private international law.
180. *Cf. Berger*, RabelsZ 61 (1997), at 313 *et seq.*; *see also* for interest as an item of damages TransLex Principle No. VII.6, reprinted *infra* Annex III, available with further references at *www.Trans-Lex.org/956000.*
181. *Cf.* the project of Cornell Law School, which excluded any teleological valuation processes *supra* Chapter 3 II.A.2.

over the specific provisions in Chapters 2–7 and are then worked through by the UNIDROIT Principles as a central theme, making assessments and comparisons between rules and general principles possible. This is in accordance with the general experience that in the field of law of contracts, the application of the law always oscillates between the strict principle '*pacta sunt servanda*' and general fairness considerations and is therefore largely dependent on the consideration of a number of flexible principles[182].

In addition, general principles perform an important gap-filling function[183]. Art. 1.6(2) of the Principles takes up this idea and states that issues within the scope of the Principles but not expressly settled by them 'are as far as possible to be settled in accordance with their underlying general principles'. These general principles are either expressly contained in the individual articles of the Principles ('good faith', 'reasonableness' etc.) or must be derived from specific provisions by way of autonomous interpretation, detached from any domestic laws[184]. This concept of an autonomous uniform interpretation without reverting to any domestic law, constitutes an important leading principle in international uniform law. It formed the basis of Art. 17 of the Uniform Sales Law and Art. 7(2) CISG[185] both of which were drafted on the basis of corresponding provisions of domestic legal systems[186]. UNIDROIT's official commentary to the Principles accordingly makes it clear that in order to promote uniformity in the application of the principles, gaps should be filled 'whenever possible, within the system of the principles itself before resorting to domestic laws'[187]. Through this statement, the Working Group directly recognized the 'openness' of the 'system'[188] and the important function of the general principles contained therein.

The need to weigh legal principles against legal rules becomes obvious when such provisions in the UNIDROIT Principles are applied which, though having the characteristics of rules, allow wide scope for teleological considerations by using broad legal language which requires extensive interpretation and elaboration. The following are examples of such provisions: Duty to pay damages in case of breaking off of negotiations in bad faith (Art. 2.15(2)), supplying an omitted contract term (Art. 4.8), possible sources of implied contractual obligations (Art. 5.2), the duty to cooperate with the other party in the performance of that party's obligation (Art. 5.3), which, if it can reasonably be expected under the circumstances, may even amount to a duty of active cooperation notwithstanding contractual

182. *Hyland*, Am.J.Comp.L. 1992, at 541, 545 *et seq.*
183. *Cf. already supra* Chapter 2 II.A.2.c. and Chapter 3 II.A.2.c.
184. *Bonell*, An International Restatement of Contract Law, at 83 *et seq.*
185. *Cf. Dölle-Wahl*, EKG, Art. 17, Nos. 13 *et seq.* (with reference to the '*ius gentium*' of classical Roman law); Bianca/Bonell-*Bonell*, Commentary on the International Sales Law, Art. 7, Nos. 2.3 *et seq.*
186. Bianca/Bonell-*Bonell*, Commentary on the International Sales Law, Art. 7, No. 2.3.2.
187. *UNIDROIT* (ed.), Principles of International Commercial Contracts, at 15.
188. *Cf.* for the importance of such provisions which ensure the 'openness' of domestic codifications *supra* Chapter 2 II.G.2.c.

provisions to the contrary[189], and the duty to re-negotiate in the event of hardship (Art. 6.2.3)[190].

The general principles which serve as important reference points for the assessment process described above are: the principle of party autonomy as the *Magna Charta* of international contract law (Art. 1.1), the principle of '*pacta sunt servanda*' (Art. 1.3), the notion of 'good faith and fair dealing in international trade' which the parties have to observe during the negotiations of the contract and for the whole duration of the contract and which may not be excluded or limited by them according to Art. 1.7 of the UNIDROIT Principles[191].

The notion of good faith in particular belongs to the common core of the legal systems of the civil law countries[192] and is also acknowledged by the American UCC and the Restatement (2nd) of Contracts[193] and other common law jurisdictions such as Australia[194]. The German Federal Supreme Court has stated 'that the notion of good faith is a supranational legal principle that is inherent in all legal systems'[195].

English courts, however, have always rejected the idea of a general principle of good faith ever since *Lord Mansfield* described the notion of good faith as 'the governing principle... applicable to all contracts and dealings' in 1766[196]. In the English courts' view, such a general principle of law would run counter to the parties' respective positions during contract negotiations and over the duration of the contract and would also be impracticable[197]. Thus, the English *House of Lords*

189. *Cf.* The Official Commentary, reprinted in: UNIDROIT (ed.), Principles of International Commercial Contracts, at 102 *et seq.*
190. *Cf.* for the application of the principle of good faith on re-negotiation *UNIDROIT* (ed.), Principles of International Commercial Contracts, at 153; generally *Horn*, AcP 1981, at 255 *et seq.*
191. *UNIDROIT* (ed.), Principles of International Commercial Contracts, at 19.
192. *Cf.* Sec. 242 of the German Civil Code (German BGB) ('The debtor is bound to perform according to the requirements of good faith, ordinary usage being taken into consideration'), *see Ebke/Steinhauer*, in: Beatson/Friedmann (eds.). Good Faith and Fault in Contract Law, at 171 *et seq.*; *see also* Art. 1366 of the Italian *Codice Civile* and Art. 1134(3) of the French *Code Civil.*
193. *Cf.* § 1-201 (19) UCC: 'Good faith means honesty in fact in the conduct or transaction concerned'; § 1-304: 'Every contract or duty within [the Uniform Commercial Code] imposes an obligation of good faith in its performance and enforcement'; *see also* Sec. 205 of the Restatement (2nd of the Law of Contracts; *cf. also Diamond v. Oreamuno*, 287 NYS 2nd. 300, affd. 24 NY 2nd 494; *cf. also Farnsworth*, Contracts, § 3.26 (especially at 190) ('duty to bargain in good faith'); the notion of good faith was introduced into the UCC by Professor *Karl Llewellyn*, Chief Reporter for the UCC, who was inspired by the good faith ('Treu und Glauben') provision of Sec. 242 of the German Civil Code, *see Farnsworth*, in: Beatson/Friedmann (eds.), Good Faith and Fault in Contract Law, at 153, 155.
194. *Farnsworth, id.*, at 156 *et seq.*
195. BGH, NJW 1993, at 259, 263.
196. *Carter v. Boehm* 3 Burrow's Rep. [1766] 1905, 1910; *see also Farnsworth*, in: Beatson/Friedmann (eds.), Good Faith and Fault in Contract Law, at 153, 154.
197. *Cf. Smith v. Hughes* LR 6 Q.B. [1871] 597; *see also* the *House of Lords* (per Lord *Ackner*) in *Walford v. Miles* 2 A.C. [1992] 128, 138 ('A duty to negotiate in good faith is unworkable in practice as it is inherently inconsistent with the position of a negotiating party'); *Banque Keyser Ullmann SA v. Skandia (U.K.) Insurance Co. Ltd.*, 1 Q.B. [1990] 665, 772; *Interfoto*

has ruled that an express agreement that parties must negotiate in good faith is unenforceable[198]. From the perspective of a functional comparative analysis[199], however, the assumption of a general principle of good faith and its inclusion in the UNIDROIT Principles is justified[200] and has also found its way into Art. 7 CISG. The reason for this is that English courts have applied the principle of good faith as an 'implied term of the contract' *in individual cases*[201], thereby indirectly acknowledging the existence of a principle of 'good faith in the performance of the contract'[202]. Also, the principle of good faith lies at the roots of such important legal institutions of the common law systems as '*promissory estoppel*' or '*estoppel in pais*'[203]. Finally, it seems that under the influence of European law, especially with respect to the EU Directive on Unfair Terms in Consumer Contracts, implemented in the Unfair Terms in Consumer Contracts Regulations 1994, and continental legal traditions, the long-standing hostility against the principle of good faith will soon be overcome by English lawyers and courts[204].

Thus, it may be said that the principle of good faith is a perfect example for the basic drafting approach of the UNIDROIT Working Group, which has always been rather pragmatic than purely dogmatic[205].

Library Ltd. v. Stiletto Ltd., 1 Q.B. [1989] 433, 439; *Chitty on Contracts*, Vol. 1, No. 1-022 ('. . . at least some English judges have not been attracted by the idea of a general ground for relief for unfairness . . . '); *generally O'Connor*, Good Faith in English Law, at 15 *et seq.*; *Goode*, Unif.L.Rev. 1997, at 231, 239.

198. *Walford v. Miles*, 2 A.C. [1992] 128 (per Lord *Ackner*).
199. *Cf.* for the 'functional comparative method' *supra* Chapter 2 II.A.1.
200. *Cf.* Art. 5.2 UNIDROIT Principles; *see Lalive*, in: Bonell/Bonelli (eds.), Contratti Commerciali Internazionali E Principi Unidroit, at 73, 81.
201. *Chitty* on Contracts, Vol. 1, No. 1-032.
202. *O'Connor*, Good Faith in English Law, at 15 *et seq.*; *Scally v. Southern Health and Social Services Board*, 1 A.C. [1992] 294; *Algussein Establishment v. Eton College*, 1 W.L.R. [1988] 587; *Interfoto Library Ltd. v. Stiletto Ltd.*, 1 Q.B. [1989] 433, 439: 'English law has, characteristically, committed itself to no such overriding principle [as good faith] but has developed piecemeal solutions in response to demonstrated problems of unfairness'; *but cf.* Judge *Steyn:* 'In my respectful view the body of rules, which are described as the uberrima fides principle, are rules of law developed by the judges . . . In my judgment it is incorrect to categorize them as implied terms . . . '; *see also Lando*, in: Cranston (ed.), Essays in Honor of Roy Goode, at 103, 124.
203. *Chitty* on Contracts, Vol. 1, No. 1-034.
204. *See Steyn*, L.Q.Rev. 1997, at 433, 440: 'Given the needs of the international market place, and the primacy of European Union law, English lawyers cannot avoid grappling with the concept of good faith . . . where in specific contexts duties of good faith are imposed on parties our legal system can readily accommodate such a well tried notion. After all, there is not a world of difference between the objective requirement of good faith and the reasonable expectations of parties'; *cf. also Goode, supra* note 197, at 240: 'The fact that two separate groups of scholars working largely independently of each other, and including lawyers from the United Kingdom, the United States and Ireland, produced restatements embodying in almost identical terms a general requirement of good faith should give powerful spur to reconsideration of the traditional perspective of English law, at least in international transactions'; *Beatson/Friedmann*, in: Beatson/Friedmann (eds.), Good Faith and Fault in Contract Law, at 3, 15.
205. *See Storme*, Rev.dr.int.dr.comp. 1995, at 309, 322; *see also Lalive*, in: Bonell/Bonelli (eds.), Contratti Commerciali Internazionali E Principi Unidroit, at 73, 81.

In any event, the influence of the Principles in this respect has already been felt. In an unpublished award of 1996, an arbitral tribunal made reference to the Principles in order to demonstrate to the parties that the enforceability of the parties' agreement to negotiate in good faith under the applicable New York law was in line with international contract practice[206].

Within the UNIDROIT Principles, the notion of good faith is qualified in that it is mentioned in Art. 1.7(1) simultaneously with the idea of 'fair dealing in international trade'[207]. This was done in order to make it clear from the outset that the conduct of the parties is not to be measured according to the subjective standards of their bilateral (or multilateral[208]) contractual relationship, or according to the standards of their respective domestic legal systems, but rather according to a far-reaching, objective standard to be found among businesspersons in international trade, amounting to a 'fairness in the market place'[209]. This objective understanding of the notion of good faith in international business is not only in line with the approach taken in § 1-201 (b) (20) UCC and § 2–103 (1) (j) UCC[210], but is also reflected in English legal practice where the principle of good faith is always seen in the context of the standards of honesty, fairness and reasonableness that prevail in the relevant legal community[211]. In any event, the standard reflected in Art. 1.7 of the UNIDROIT Principles has to be understood in a transnational sense. It is detached from the particularities of domestic legal systems and has to be seen in the socio-economic environment in which multinational enterprises usually operate[212]. This confirms the general observation that it is impossible to compile a common stock of concrete rules, principles, and applications that are related to the

---

206. *See Bonell*, Unif.L.Rev. 1997, at 34, 40 *et seq.*

207. *Cf. generally Kramer*, in: Bonell/Bonelli (eds.), Contratti Commerciali Internazionali E Principi Unidroit, at 163, 164 *et seq.*

208. *Cf. supra* Chapter 2 II.G.3.e.

209. *Cf. Hyland*, Am.J.Comp.L. 1992, at 541, 549 (with reference to *Llewellyn's* ideal of sales law as 'practical issues between practical [businesspeople]'); *Bonell*, ICLQ 1978, at 413, 428; *Bonell*, An International Restatement of Contract Law, at 131 *et seq.*; *Schlechtriem*, Good Faith in German Law and in International Uniform Laws, at 20.

210. Both provisions define good faith as 'honesty in fact and the observance of reasonable commercial standards of fair dealing in the trade'.

211. *Cf.* for the definition of 'good faith' *O'Connor*, Good Faith in English Law, at 120: 'The principle of good faith in English law is a fundamental principle derived from the rule *pacta sunt servanda*, and other legal rules, distinctively and directly related to honesty, fairness and reasonableness, the application of which is determined in a particular time by the standards of honesty, fairness and reasonableness prevailing in the community which are considered appropriate for formulation in new or revised legal rules'; *cf. also Chitty* on Contracts, Vol. 1, Nos. 1-026 *et seq.; Steyn, supra* note 204, at 438: '... good faith additionally sets an objective standard, *viz.*, the observance of reasonable commercial standards of fair dealing in the conclusion and performance of the transaction concerned'.

212. *Cf. UNIDROIT* (ed.), Principles of International Commercial Contracts, at 18; *Bonell*, An International Restatement of Contract Law, at 353); *see* for the CISG *von Caemmerer/Schlechtriem-Herber*, CISG, Art. 7, No. 18.

principle of good faith. Instead, this broad and vague notion always has to be interpreted and applied in a context-oriented manner[213].

In spite of its general and vague character, Art. 1.7 of the UNIDROIT Principles may rightly be characterized as the *Magna Charta* of international commercial law. The principle of good faith and fair dealing performs a central function in the interpretation of the Principles and in transnational commercial law in general[214]. By stating in general terms that each party must act in accordance with this standard, the article makes it clear that even in the absence of special provisions in the Principles, the parties' behaviour throughout the life of the contract, including the negotiation process, must meet certain requirements which are generally accepted within the international business community[215].

The *Magna Charta* of international trade law does not stand alone within the system of the UNIDROIT Principles. It is supplemented by the parties' commitment to trade usages to which they have agreed[216] or which are widely known to and regularly observed in international trade by parties and to practices which they have established between themselves (Art. 1.8)[217]. The general terminology used in this article was adopted from Art. 9 CISG[218] and Art. 9(2) of the Uniform Sales Law[219]. The basic difference between the approach chosen in the Principles and in the Uniform Sales Law is that the standard of reasonableness which leads to the exclusion of the application of trade usages, has been changed. The heavily criticized[220] subjective test of the Sales Law ('... usages, which reasonable persons in the same situation as the parties' usually consider to be applicable to their contract ... ') is replaced by an objective test of reasonableness ('... except where the application of such a usage would be unreasonable').

This principle of 'reasonableness' plays a dominant and recurrent role in almost all of the provisions of the UNIDROIT Principles even though, contrary

213. *Schlechtriem*, Good Faith in German Law and in International Uniform Law, at 6 *et seq.*
214. *Cf. supra* Chapter 2 II.B.1.; *see also Kramer*, in: Bonell/Bonelli (eds.), Contratti Commerciali Internazionali E Principi Unidroit, at 163, 164 *et seq.*
215. *Bonell*, An International Restatement of Contract Law, at 127 *et seq.*; *Bonell*, ICLQ 1978, at 413, 428; *see also UNIDROIT* (ed.), Principles of International Commercial Contracts, at 17.
216. Article 1.8 UNIDROIT Principles refrains from adhering to the 'subjective' theory of Anglo-American law employed in Art. 9(2) CISG ('The parties are considered ... to have impliedly made applicable to their contract a usage ... '); if, however, trade usages are applicable if both parties or one of them 'ought to have known them', there is no room left for subjective criteria and the trade usages apply *ipso iure*, thereby rendering the 'implied' agreement-requirement into a mere fiction, *cf.* Bianca/Bonell-*Bonell*, Commentary on the International Sales Law, Art. 9, No. 2.2.1; *cf. also Bonell*, An International Restatement of Contract Law, at 142 *et seq.*; *Bonell*, ICLQ 1978, at 413, 432.
217. *Cf. also van Houtte*, in: Institute of International Business Law and Practice (ed.), The UNIDROIT Principles of International Commercial Contracts, A New Lex Mercatoria?, at 181, 186.
218. *Cf.* Bianca/Bonell-*Bonell, supra* note 216, Art. 9, Nos. 1.3 *et seq.*
219. Uniform Law on the International Sale of Goods of July 17, 1973 (BGB1. I at 856); *see generally Dölle*, EKG, Art. 9, Nos. 2 *et seq.*
220. *Cf.* Bianca/Bonell-*Bonell, supra* note 216, No. 1.4.1.

to the 'Principles of European Contract Law' of the *Lando* Commission[221], the UNIDROIT Principles do not contain a blanket clause which defines the notion of reasonableness. Under the Uniform Sales Law[222] and the CISG, the 'reasonableness test' ('reasonable person'; 'reasonable time'; the juxtaposition of 'reasonable' and 'unreasonable') has been used as a general criterion for the evaluation of the parties' conduct in those cases where there is no specific provision to be applied to their legal relationship[223]. The Dutch Civil Code also contains specific provisions on the standard of reasonableness which it links to the principle of good faith ('*redelijkheid en billigheid*', Arts 6:1, 6:248, 6:285 BW)[224]. The notion of 'reasonableness' thus provides the classical standard which attaches an objective quality to the principle of good faith[225]. The standard thereby performs an important prohibitive function which, under German law, is effected by the prohibition of the improper exercise of legal rights under the blanket clause of good faith contained in Sec. 242 of the German Civil Code[226].

Inclusion of this standard in the general section of the UNIDROIT Principles reflects the particular character of international commercial law. It is composed not only of clearly defined legal duties but also and to a large extent of general standards and duties of conduct ('*obligations de comportement*')[227]. They allow for the adaptation of the law to the changing circumstances of international trade and commerce. Under the standard of 'reasonableness', it is irrelevant whether or not a party has acted upon what it honestly believed to be reasonable. Instead, it is decisive whether one has put forth his best efforts, exercised due diligence in performing one's contractual obligations, upheld the common contractual goals, avoided abuse of rights required under the contract, and facilitated the other party's performance[228]. The flexibility and '*souplesse*' of the standard of reasonableness also reflects its major virtue: It allows arbitrators and judges to focus on the search for a fair and 'equitable' solution to international commercial disputes[229]. At the same time, the standard provides a further[230] indication for the 'openness' of a legal system in general and of the NLM in particular, proving the quality of

221. *Cf. infra* B.2.b.
222. *Cf. Dölle-Wahl*, EKG, Art. 17, Nos. 59 *et seq.*
223. *Bianca/Bonell-Bonell, supra* note 216, Art. 7, No. 2.3.2.2; *Ferrari*, Rev.int.dr.comp. 1996, at 813, 849.
224. *Cf. Hartkamp*, Am.J.Comp.L. 1992, at 551, 554; *Hartkamp*, in: CJHB/Brunner-Bundel, at 127, 129.
225. *Nassar*, Sanctity of Contracts Revisited, at 145 *et seq.*; *cf. also Storme*, in: Hartkamp, *et al.* (eds.), Towards a European Civil Code, 1st ed., at 159, 183.
226. *Joachim*, Comp.L.Yb.Int'l Bus. 1992, at 341, 353: 'The notion of reasonableness implies a reasonable use of rights. The reasonable man would not carry a legal interest to an extreme. The reasonable man test is, therefore, employed by judges as a means against abuse of rights. This thought relates to the "doctrine of reasonable use" in the United States'.
227. *Cf. Carreau/Flory/Juillard*, Droit International Economique, 1st ed., at 20.
228. *Nassar, see supra* note 225, *id.*
229. *Joachim*, Comp.L.Yb.Int'l Bus. 1992, at 341, 359; *cf. also* from the common law perspective *Jones*, International Sales Quarterly, March 1995, at 8 *et seq.*
230. *Cf. supra* Chapter 2 II.G.2.

transnational commercial law as a 'law in action'. The standard of reasonableness has its origin in a sociological understanding of the contract[231] which is also the basis for the idea of an institutional development of the law through the international community of merchants[232]. This view is confirmed by the fact that reasonable behaviour usually means nothing more than keeping one's word in all circumstances or at least in the manner (commonly) intended by the parties[233]. The idea of reasonable conduct is therefore inextricably linked to the principle of '*pacta sunt servanda*' and to the notion of a general transnational liability for breach of confidence as a basic pillar of the NLM[234].

In the context of the UNIDROIT Principles, the reasonableness test is of particular relevance for all those provisions which require a flexible interpretation and application in individual cases. They include those relating to the application of usages and practices (Art. 1.8(2)), the time of acceptance in case no time has been fixed by the offeror (Art. 2.7), the interpretation of the contract in cases where no common intention of the parties can be determined (Art. 4.1(2)), the determination of the quality of performance which is neither fixed by, nor determinable from, the contract (Art. 5.6), the determination of the contract price where the contract does not fix or make provisions for determining the price (Art. 5.7[235]), the determination of the time of performance absent an agreement by the parties (Art. 6.1.1(c)). The reasonableness test is also relevant for those articles dealing with 'hardship' (Art. 6.2.2) and '*force majeure*' (Art. 7.17). In the context of these provisions, the standard of reasonableness frequently takes the place of party agreements, thereby reflecting the drafters attitude of the existence of a general standard of conduct in international trade. However, the abstract and general provisions contained in the UNIDROIT Principles do not themselves provide this standard. Therefore, the construction of international contracts and the determination of the conduct of the parties depends upon a close interaction between the criterion of good faith (Art. 1.7) and the objective test of fair dealing in international trade and reasonableness on the one hand, and the usages and practices of international trade (Art. 1.8) on the other. A contract as well as a unilateral statement or conduct of a party shall be interpreted under the UNIDROIT Principles according to the intention of the party or parties and, where no such intention can be established, according to the meaning that a reasonable person of the same kind as the parties or party would give to it under the circumstances (Arts 4.1 and 4.2). Art. 4.3 of the Principles states that in applying the standard, all the circumstances, including preliminary negotiations between the parties, practices which

231. *Nassar, see supra* note 225, at 146; *Joachim*, Comp.L.Yb.Int'l Bus. 1992, at 341, 359 *et seq.*
232. *Cf. supra* Chapter 2 II.G.3.d.
233. *Storme*, in: Hartkamp, *et al.* (eds.), Towards a European Civil Code, 1st ed., at 159, 184: 'Certainly the prevailing view has been that reasonable behavior consists of nothing more than keeping to one's word in all circumstances, or least to keep to one's word in the manner (commonly) intended by the parties'; *cf. also supra* Chapter 2 II.G.3.d.
234. *Cf. supra* Chapter 2 II.G.3.d and *infra* II.C.3.b.
235. *Cf.* Art. 55 CISG; *cf.* for a commentary on this provision *von Caemmerer/Schlechtriem-Hager*, CISG, Art. 55, Nos. 8 *et seq.*

the parties have established between themselves, the conduct of the parties subsequent to the conclusion of the contract, the nature and purpose of the contract and, most importantly, 'the meaning commonly given to terms and expressions in the trade concerned' shall be considered. With this latter provision the UNIDROIT Principles refer to Art. 9(3) of the Uniform Sales Law[236]. The UNIDROIT Principles refer the judge or arbitrator who has to interpret the contractual stipulations to the meaning of typical trade clauses as reflected in the INCOTERMS issued by the ICC[237]. The Principles are therefore even more detailed than the CISG which contains a reasonableness test in Art. 8(2) but has not adopted a provision such as Art. 9(3) of the Uniform Sales Law which refers the judge or arbitrator to the meaning of contractual stipulations commonly given to terms and expressions in the trade concerned[238].

Further examples from commercial reality may serve to illustrate the functioning of this principle.

Schlechtriem provides the example of Internet communication not envisaged by the drafters of the Principles. In this case, the question may arise as to the time within which the recipient of an Internet sales confirmation has to object. Does it run only from the time the Internet message is reproduced in tangible form or from the moment of receipt in the addressee's computer? In this case, good faith and fair dealing require that the 'undue delay requirement' of Art. 2.19 has to be interpreted so as to give the recipient a reasonable opportunity to take notice of the recorded message regardless of whether and when it is printed[239].

It is also said that, from the perspective of international business practice, Art. 3.10 of the Principles, dealing with a party's right to avoid the contract or individual terms of it in case of excessive advantages for one party, would allow a seller who offered products at a low price because it had temporary cash-flow problems to ask the court at a later date to increase the contractually agreed price on the grounds that when the contract was made, this party was under 'economic distress' and had an 'urgent need' for cash (Art. 3.10(1)(a))[240]. This view would indeed go against free market principles and the fundamental rule of *pacta sunt servanda* in that it overrules the natural distribution of bargaining powers within each contractual equilibrium[241]. However, Art. 3.10 is not intended to provide the parties with a means to escape their contractual commitments. Even a considerable disparity in the value of the price of performance and counter-performance is not sufficient to permit avoidance of the contract[242]. The application of this provision

236. Article 9(3): 'Where expressions, provisions or forms of contract commonly used in commercial practice are employed, they shall be interpreted according to the meaning usually given to them in the trade concerned'; *cf. Dölle*, EKG, Anhang.
237. *Cf. Dölle id.*, No. 18.
238. *Cf.* for a criticism of this omission Bianca/Bonell-*Bonell*, Commentary on the International Sales Law Art. 9, No. 3.5.
239. *Schlechtriem*, Good Faith in German Law and in International Uniform Laws, at 12.
240. *Hill*, J.Int'l Arb., No. 2 1996, at 163, 165.
241. *Hill, id.*, at 166.
242. *See UNIDROIT* (ed.), Principles, at 78 (Commentary).

requires much more than this. Under the circumstances of the case and in the light of reasonable business practice, the disequilibrium 'has to be so great as to shock the conscience of a reasonable (business) person'[243]. This, of course, does not apply to mere cash-flow problems of one of the parties to the contract.

The same is true for the hardship provision of Art. 6.2.2. It is alleged that this provision allows the adaptation of the contract in case of currency fluctuations or because of an unexpectedly high failure rate under warranty[244]. Again, this would contravene usual business practice and again, the answer to these objections must be that the hardship provision has to be read and construed in a context-oriented manner. Thus, Art. 6.2.1 expressly states that 'where the performance of a contract becomes more onerous for one of the parties, that party is nevertheless bound to perform its obligations subject to the following provisions on hardship'. In other words, in cases of doubt, the principle of *pacta sunt servanda* prevails and performance must be rendered as long as it is possible and regardless of the economic burden it may pose on the performing party[245]. This principle is a constituent element of international commercial contract practice[246] and is also reflected in the 'ICC Guide on Force Majeure and Hardship'[247]. Currency fluctuations are a common element of commercial reality. They are usually regarded as typical business risks which cannot be shifted to the other party in case the contract does not contain a special provision and the pricing structure does not imply a certain 'currency risk premium'[248].

Finally, it has been argued that the provisions on public permissions (Arts 6.1.14 *et seq.*) are impracticable and not in line with international business practice. Art. 6.1.17(1), which states that the refusal of a permission affecting the validity of a contract renders the contract void, is alleged to be unacceptable since it would enable a state-controlled entity to evade its contractual duties simply by arranging for the refusal of the public permission. Also, it is claimed that in such cases there should be some claim for non-performance for the aggrieved party[249]. This objection is unjustified for two reasons. First, the public entity's conduct in this case would violate the general principle of good faith (*venire contra factum proprium*) which has to be observed in the interpretation of the Principles according to Art. 1.7. Also, Art. 6.1.7(2) calls for the application of the rules on non-performance in

243. *Id.*
244. *Hill, supra* note 240, at 167.
245. *UNIDROIT* (ed.), Principles, at 145 (Commentary).
246. *See e.g.* ICC Award No. 5485, YCA 1989, at 156, 168; ICC Award No. 5953, Clunet 1990, at 1056; *Fouchard*, L'Arbitrage Commercial International, at 442; *Paulsson*, Rev.d'Arb. 1990, at 55, 82 *et seq.*
247. ICC Publication No. 421, at 22.
248. *See* Ad Hoc Award of September 10, 1975, YCA 1977, at 156, 158; ICC Award No. 8486 (unpublished); *Nassar*, Sanctity of Contracts Revisited, at 205.
249. *See Raeschke-Kessler*, in: Institute of International Business Law and Practice (ed.), UNIDROIT Principles of International Commercial Contracts: A New Lex Mercatoria?, at 167, 176.

cases of refused public permissions that render the contract void, thus opening the way for a claim for damages under Art. 7.4.1.

These examples reveal that the black-letter law of the Principles cannot be applied in a mechanical way without having regard to the general framework and thrust of the Principles as clarified in the official commentary[250]. Instead, the provisions always have to be construed in the light of their underlying guiding notions, of which '*pacta sunt servanda*' and 'reasonableness' are the most important.

The generality of the principles and rules contained in the UNIDROIT Principles, the complex assessment process and the weighing of interests that is necessary for their proper application are by no means proof of a lack of practicability. Rather, they are indications for the quality of international commercial law as a 'law in action' which is in a state of constant evolution through international practice. In the context of international commerce and trade, this important function is performed by international arbitrators striving to reach equitable and reasonable solutions for commercial disputes[251]. It is through their decision-making that the UNIDROIT Principles 'are filled with life'[252]. This reflects the general experience that general principles of law and standards of conduct do not have legal effects *in abstracto*, but have to be integrated into a law-finding and norm-creation process[253]. In the context of transnational commercial law, this is the functional comparative methodology and the institutional creation of the law[254].

8. Dispositive Character of the UNIDROIT Principles

The UNIDROIT Principles have been designed as a non-mandatory legal order. Art. 1.5 allows the parties to exclude the application of the Principles or to derogate from or vary the effect of most of their provisions[255]. Derogation may be express or implied. An example for the latter would be the adoption of contract terms that are in conflict with certain non-mandatory provisions of the Principles[256]. A typical case where the parties will expressly modify certain provisions contained in the Principles are long-term contractual commitments, such as construction contracts, where the complex contractual arrangements are tailored to the specific needs of the parties and their project. The parties' right to modify the provisions of the Principles is a natural consequence of the basic principle of party autonomy as the *Magna Charta* of international contract law which the drafters of the Principles have enunciated in Art. 1.1. The mandatory character of the principle of good faith

250. *See Bonell*, An International Restatement of Contract Law, at 36; *Perales Viscasillas*, Ariz. J.Int'l & Comp.L. 1996, at 383, 389; *cf. also Boele-Woelki*, Unif.L.Rev. 1996, at 652, 655.
251. *Cf. supra* Chapter 2 II.C.2 and D.2.
252. *Cf. van Houtte, supra* note 217, *id.*
253. *Esser*, Grundsatz und Norm, at 69 *et seq.*
254. *Cf.* for details *supra* Chapter 2 II.A. and G.
255. *Cf.* Art. 6 CISG.
256. *Perales Viscasillas*, Ariz.J.Int'l & Comp.L. 1996, at 383, 427.

laid down in Art. 1.7(2) as well as in other provisions based on this notion does not contravene the liberal character of the Principles. These provisions relate to such important legal principles as a party's right to avoid a contract in case of fraud (Art. 3.8 and Art. 3.19), in case of threat (Art. 3.9 and Art. 3.19) or where contract terms give an unfair advantage to the other party (Art. 3.10 and Art. 3.19) as well as to provisions dealing with manifestly unreasonable price determination by one party (Art. 5.7(2)), with grossly excessive agreed payment for non-performance (Art. 7.4.13(2)) and with exemption clauses (Art. 7.1.6)[257]. In the latter case, the mandatory character of the provision is only implicit and follows from the content and purpose of this provision itself.

All the articles cited above carry with them the notion of good faith or are at least based on equitable considerations. They all deal with the distortion of the contractual equilibrium that goes beyond the mere difference in bargaining positions, thereby destroying the very basis of the principle of party autonomy and the equality of the parties in negotiating and performing their contract. This idea of protecting the parties' free will as the basic ingredient of party autonomy is itself part of the transnational *ordre public* which applies irrespective of a contrary agreement of the parties[258].

9. Influence of Mandatory Provisions of Other Domestic Legal Systems

The notions and values that form part of the transnational *ordre public* as well as the mandatory rules of domestic or international origin (*lois d'application immédiate*[259]), always take precedence over the UNIDROIT Principles (Art. 1.4). The broad wording of this provision ('. . . mandatory rules, whether of national, international or supranational origin . . .') was intended to ensure that the socio-economic value judgments of domestic legislatures or transnational 'shared values'[260] shall in all circumstances prevail over the provisions contained in the UNIDROIT Principles immaterial of their precise legal character[261].

10. Functional Scope of the Principles: The Options Contained in the Preamble

The substantive scope of application of the UNIDROIT Principles with respect to 'international commercial contracts' has already been analysed above. Since the

257. *Cf. UNIDROIT* (ed.), Principles of International Commercial Contracts, at 13.
258. *Cf. Lalive*, Rev.d'Arb. 1986, at 329 *et seq.*
259. *See supra* Chapter 2 II.E.
260. *Cf. supra* Chapter 2 II.E.
261. *UNIDROIT* (ed.), Principles of International Commercial Contracts, at 11; *see also Goode*, Unif.L.Rev. 1997, at 231, 244 *et seq.*; *cf. also Lando*, in: Bonell/Bonelli (eds.), Contratti Commerciali Internazionali E Principi Unidroit, at 109, 114 *et seq.*

Principles do not have the quality of statutory law, we also have to look at their functional scope. The report of the UNIDROIT Secretariat of 1971 on the 'progressive codification of the law of international trade' emphasized the necessity to include specific provisions in the codification which would provide precise indications as to the intended purpose and function of the codification[262]. For the UNIDROIT Principles, this function is performed by the Preamble. Like on a descending scale, it lists five possible ways in which the Principles may affect international commercial contracts. They will be discussed immediately below. Interestingly enough, within three years of their promulgation by UNIDROIT, international arbitrators have used the Principles in their decision-making practice with respect to the most important of these options[263].

However, the list contained in the Preamble is not meant to be exhaustive. Other options not listed in the Preamble are also conceivable. Thus, the Principles may be used as a 'checklist' for the drafting of international contracts even though this option is not directly referred to in the Principles[264]. Such checklists are also known from other fields of international commercial law. Thus, the *Fédération de l'Industrie Européenne de la Construction* (FIEC) has prepared a 'reference memorandum' to be used in the preparation of construction contracts[265]. These checklists and their effect as 'voluntary codes of conduct' in international contract drafting provide further ample evidence for the general phenomenon of self-regulation and harmonization of international commercial law[266].

An inquiry undertaken by the Secretariat of UNIDROIT has revealed that two thirds of the practitioners that had been in contact with the Principles since their promulgation in 1994 have used them as a guideline in contract negotiations[267]. Finally, the purpose of the Principles to provide guidelines for the construction of domestic law, which will be discussed below, is not directly mentioned in the Preamble.

---

262. Report of the UNIDROIT Secretariat on the '*Progressive codification of the law of international trade*', UNCITRAL Yearbook I (1968–1970), at 285, 287; *cf. supra* Chapter 3 II.B.1.
263. *See Bonell*, An International Restatement of Contract Law, at 277 *et seq.*; *Bonell*, Unif.L.Rev. 1997, at 30 *et seq.*; *Berger*, Am.J.Comp.L. 1998, at 129 *et seq.*
264. *Cf. Hartkamp*, in: Hartkamp, *et al.* (eds.), Towards a European Civil Code, at 125, 129; *cf. also* the contributions by *Farnsworth/Fontaine/Gaymer/Razumov* in: ICC (ed.), The New UNIDROIT Principles of International Commercial Contracts; *Bonell*, An International Restatement of Contract Law, at 248 *et seq.*; *Perales Viscasillas*, Ariz.J.Int'l & Comp.L.1996, at 383, 420.
265. *Helps*, Int'l Constr.L.Rev. 1997, at 524, 535.
266. *See supra* Chapter 1 III..
267. *UNIDROIT* (ed.), The Use of the UNIDROIT Principles in Practice, at 2; *see Bonell*, An International Restatement of Contract Law, at 271 *et seq.* One-Third used the Principles to overcome language barriers, another third as a checklist of issues to be addressed during the negotiations and a final third as a model for specific contract provisions.

a. *Application of the Principles in Cases Where 'the Parties Have Agreed That Their Contract Be Governed by Them'*

The first two options mentioned in the Preamble refer to the application of the Principles based on the will of the parties, either through a direct or indirect reference in the contract. Their common denominator is that the Principles do not apply because they have the force of law but because the parties want them to be applied, in one way or another, to their contractual relationship[268]. The difference between them lies in the way in which the parties call for the application of the Principles in the contract and consequently also in the force with which the Preamble directs the judge or arbitrator to apply them. The first option requires that in those cases where the parties have expressly agreed on their application, the Principles *shall* be applied by the judge or arbitrator. The consequences of this formula for the determination of the legal nature of the Principles will be addressed *infra* b.

b. *Application of the Principles in Cases Where 'the Parties Have Agreed That Their Contract Be Governed by General Principles of Law, the* Lex Mercatoria *or the like'*

In view of their transnational quality, the UNIDROIT Principles may not only be applied where the parties have made an express agreement. Arbitrators may also consider applying the Principles in those cases where the parties have clearly indicated in their contract that they do not want their contract to be subject to domestic law. The second option contained in the Preamble therefore provides that if the parties have referred in their contract to the application of 'general principles of law', the '*lex mercatoria*' or the like[269], the Principles *may* be applied to their contract. Application of the Principles is justified in these cases because they claim to be the *ratio scripta* of international commercial contract law. The arbitrators in the Channel Tunnel arbitration have pursued this approach[270]. In German legal doctrine, such references by the parties to transnational legal principles are either considered to be without effect due to their inherent vagueness or are qualified as an agreement of the parties to have a decision in equity (*ex aequo et bono*)[271]. The detailed rules and provisions contained in the UNIDROIT Principles may finally serve to dry out this traditional view which has always met with strong opposition from those who have advocated the existence of a transnational legal system.

---

268. *Larroumet*, La Semaine Juridique 1997, at 147, 148.
269. This includes reference to the 'usages and customs of international trade', *cf. UNIDROIT* (ed.), Principles of International Commercial Contracts, at 4.
270. *See supra* Chapter 2 I.B.; *see also Furmston*, in: Institute of International Business Law and Practice (ed.), UNIDROIT Principles of International Commercial Contracts: A New Lex Mercatoria?, at 201, 205 ('It is reasonable to hope that the Principles will be of major assistance to arbitrators in such cases [like the Channel Tunnel arbitration]').
271. *Cf.* for details *supra* Chapter 2 II.B.

This option has already been applied by international arbitral tribunals[272]. Thus, in two ICC arbitrations, the choice of law clauses contained in the contracts provided for the application of 'Anglo-Saxon principles of law' and 'principles of natural justice', respectively[273]. In both cases, the arbitrators did not hesitate to refer to the UNIDROIT Principles, supplemented by the contractual provisions and the relevant trade usages, as the law applicable to the contract[274]. In one of these cases, the arbitrators expressly referred to the fact that in contrast to the vague notion of 'general principles of law', that has hitherto been used to escape from the realm of domestic laws[275], the Principles have a concrete and workable content and constitute the 'central component . . . regarding international contractual rules and principles and enjoying wide international consensus'[276]. Also, in an award rendered under the auspices of the National and International Court of Arbitration of Milan, Italy, the parties, at the outset of the proceedings, agreed to have their dispute settled 'in conformity with the UNIDROIT Principles tempered by recourse to equity'[277]. Consequently, the arbitrator in his decision on the merits made numerous references to the Principles. The arbitral tribunal in the Channel Tunnel arbitration decided to have the UNIDROIT Principles applied to the contract which called for the application of the principles common to French and English law and in the absence of such conformity, for the application of general principles of international trade law as have been applied by national and international tribunals[278]. In the famous *Arthur Anderson* arbitration, in which the parties had agreed, due to the truly global character of their agreement, that the arbitral tribunal shall 'not be bound to apply the substantive law of any jurisdiction, but shall be guided by the policies and considerations set forth in the Preamble' of that agreement, taking into account general principles of law', the sole arbitrator decided to apply the UNIDROIT Principles to interpret the parties' contractual agreement, stating that:

> 'The UNIDROIT Principles of International Commercial Contracts are a reliable source of international commercial law in international arbitration for they contain in essence a restatement of those "*principes directeurs*" that

272. *See Berger*, Am.J.Comp.L. 1998, at 129 *et seq.*; *Bonell*, An International Restatement of Contract Law, at 283 *et seq.*
273. *See Bonell*, ZRVgl. 1996, at 157; *Bonell*, Unif.L.Rev. 1997, at 34, 42 *et seq.*; *Boele-Woelki*, Principles en IPR, at 12; *Lalive*, in: Bonell/Bonelli (eds.), Contratti Commerciali Internazionali E Principi Unidroit, at 73, 85 *et seq.*
274. *Bonell, id.*; *Boele-Woelki, id.*
275. *See supra* Chapter 2 I.B.
276. *Boele-Woelki, supra* note 273, *id.; Brazil*, Int'l Arb. Rep., April 1996, at 31, 36 *et seq.*; *cf. also* the extract of one of the awards reported by *Bonell*, ZRVgl. 1996, at 152, 157: '. . . general legal rules and principles enjoying wide international consensus . . . are primarily reflected by the UNIDROIT Principles . . . In consequence, without prejudice to taking into account the provisions of the Contract and relevant trade usages, this Tribunal finds that the [Contract is] governed by, and shall be interpreted in accordance to, the UNIDROIT Principles with respect to all matters falling within the scope of such principles . . .'; *see also Lalive*, in: Bonell/Bonelli (eds.), Contratti Commerciali Internazionali E Principi Unidroit, at 73, 87.
277. *Bonell*, Unif.L.Rev. 1997, at 34, 43.
278. *See supra* Chapter 2 I.B.

have enjoyed universal acceptance and, moreover, are at the heart of those most fundamental notions which have consistently been applied in arbitral practice'[279].

It has to be emphasized that neither option a. discussed above nor option b. implies an answer to the question as to the legal nature of the UNIDROIT Principles. From the perspective of private international law, the parties' direct or indirect reference to transnational legal principles may be regarded as being either a genuine choice of law supervening the mandatory provisions of the 'otherwise' applicable domestic law and giving effect, by way of a genuine choice of law, to what is commonly called the '*kollisionsrechtliche Verweisung*'[280]. The reference may also lead to the mere inclusion of the Principles in the contract as general contract conditions, thus giving effect to the '*materiellrechtliche Parteiautonomie*'[281]. In the latter case, the parties' reference to transnational law may not supervene the mandatory provisions of domestic law otherwise applicable to the dispute[282]. The reference contained in the Preamble may, thus, have two different meanings *vis-à-vis* the doctrine of transnational law. It could mean that the NLM has a strictly contractual nature and does not possess the quality of an independent legal system since the Principles may only be applied if the parties have agreed to have the NLM applied to their contract[283]. It could also mean that the NLM is an autonomous legal system but that the Principles do not (yet?) share this quality and are therefore applicable only if and to the extent that the parties have agreed on them, subject always to the law which would otherwise be applicable[284].

In answering this question, a distinction is usually drawn between adjudication before domestic courts and dispute settlement before international arbitrators. In the first case, the terminology of Arts 3(1) and 4(1) of the Rome Convention on the Law Applicable to Contractual Obligations ('*law*' instead of '*rules of law*'[285]) was seen to prevent the application of transnational legal principles[286]. One may also argue that under the Convention, parties could have chosen a-national legal principles as

279. ICC Award No. 9797, excerpt reproduced in *Marrella*, La Nuova Lex Mercatoria, 424; *see also Bonell*, Arb.Int'l 2001, at 249, 252.
280. *See* Reithmann/Martiny (eds.), Internationales Vertragsrecht, Nos. 71 (*Martiny*), 3526 (*Hausmann*) stating that the UNIDROIT Principles acknowledge the possibility of a genuine choice of law ('*kollisionsrechtliche Verweisung*') of the *lex mercatoria* by the parties; *see* for a similar view *Wichard*, RabelsZ 60 (1996), at 269, 290.
281. *See Ferrari*, Rev.int.dr.comp. 1995, at 985, 988; *Boele-Woelki*, Unif.L.Rev. 1996, at 652, 663; *Berger*, ZVglRWiss. 1995, at 224; *Drobnig*, in: Institute of International Business Law and Practice (ed.), Principles of International Commercial Contracts: A New Lex Mercatoria?, at 223, 225; *Giardina, id.*, at 145, 146.
282. *Cf. supra* Chapter 2 I.C.2.b.
283. *Larroumet, supra* note 268, at 149; *see also Goode*, ICLQ 1997, at 1, 26; *Perales Viscasillas*, Ariz.J.Int'l & Comp.L. 1996, at 383, 397; *Ferrari*, Rev.int.dr.comp. 1995, at 985, 988.
284. *Larroumet, id.; Goode*, Unif.L.Rev. 1997, at 231, 245.
285. *See* for the significance of this terminology *supra* Chapter 2 II.F.2.a.
286. *von Hoffmann/Thorn*, IPR, § 10, No. 28; *Lagarde*, Rev.crit.dr.int.priv. 1991, at 288, 300; *Blase*, Die Grundregeln des Europäischen Vertragsrechts als Recht grenzüberschreitender Verträge, 221 *et seq.*

the 'law' to be applied under Art. 3, while absent a choice of law, the judge may not apply such transnational rules, since Art. 4(1) requires the application of the 'law of a country', thereby preventing recourse to the NLM[287]. Under the final version of the Rome I Regulation, choice of a-national legal principles is excluded for the reasons explained above[288]. International arbitrators, on the other hand, are regarded as being authorized to apply the Principles as *lex causae* due to the particular nature of the arbitral process.

From the perspective of the present Study, a line has to be drawn between the NLM on one side and the Principles on the other. The Principles are an *indication* of the existence of a transnational legal rule, they are therefore *a possible source of the lex mercatoria*, but should not be confused with the NLM[289]:

> 'If one adopts a narrow definition whereby transnational law basically consists of generally recognized principles of law and trade usages, it may be difficult to consider the UNIDROIT Principles as a whole as falling in one category or the other. On the contrary, on the basis of a broader definition whereby transnational law includes virtually all principles and rules other than those established by a particular domestic law, the UNIDROIT Principles, like other "private" instruments such as the INCOTERMS or the UCP, are definitely part of it'[290].

It is true that the Principles were not adopted by UNIDROIT's Governing Council with the intention to have the publication applied 'as *the codified lex mercatoria* by arbitrators'[291]. The careful language of the second option ('may' instead of 'have to be' applied) is therefore justified. The parties' reference to the '*lex mercatoria*' refers to a transnational legal system which may or may not be reflected in the Principles[292]. If, however, it has been verified that a rule reflected in the Principles is part of the NLM[293], then the international arbitrator should be allowed to apply it as the *lex causae* and not simply as part of the contract. An international arbitral tribunal has described this important, but limited function of the UNIDROIT Principles for the NLM doctrine in a 'landmark case' involving a dispute between the Iranian government and the US *Westinghouse* corporation in the following terms:

> 'The Tribunal will apply those general principles and rules of law applicable to international contractual obligations which qualify as rules of law and which have earned a wide acceptance and international consensus in the international

287. *See Wichard, supra* note 280, at 282 and 294.
288. *See supra* Chapter 2 II.F.2.b.
289. *See Kahn*, in: Bonell/Bonelli (eds.), Contratti Commerciali Internazionali E Principi Unidroit, at 41, 45; *Meyer*, Principles of Contract Law und nationales Vertragsrecht, at 118 *et seq.*; *cf. also infra* II.A.1; *Ortscheidt*, La réparation du dommage dans l'arbitrage commercial international, at 10 *et seq.*; *Baron*, Arb.Int'l 1999, at 115 *et seq.*
290. *Bonell*, in: Berger (ed.) The Practice of Transnational Law, at 23, 24.
291. *Raeschke-Kessler*, in: Institute of International Business Law and Practice (ed.), UNIDROIT Principles of International Commercial Contracts: A New Lex Mercatoria?, at 167, 173 (emphasis added).
292. *See Kahn, supra* note 289, *id.*
293. *See* for this process *infra* II.C.5.

> business community, including notions which are said to form part of the *lex mercatoria*, also taking into account any relevant trade usages as well as the UNIDROIT Principles, *as far as they can be considered to reflect generally accepted principles and rules*'[294].

That award is an example of an increasing number of cases in which arbitral tribunals apply the UNIDROIT Principles as the rules governing the substance of the dispute even in the absence of any choice of law clause in the contract or in cases where the choice of law clause was manifestly invalid because the parties had made a reference to non-existing legal sources of law governing their contract[295]. In one of these awards, the arbitral tribunal explained in great detail why it saw itself entitled to refer to the UNIDROIT Principles as the rules governing the contractual relationship before it:

> 'The reasons why this Tribunal considers the UNIDROIT Principles to be the central component of the general rules and principles regulating international contractual obligations and enjoying wide international consensus, which constitute the proper law of the contract, are manifold: (1) the UNIDROIT Principles are a restatement of international legal principles applicable to international commercial contracts made by a distinguished group of international experts coming from all prevailing legal systems of the world, without the intervention of States or governments, both circumstances redounding to the high quality and neutrality of the product and its ability to reflect the present state of consensus on international legal rules and principles governing international contractual obligations in the world, primarily on the basis of their fairness and appropriateness for international commercial transactions falling within their purview; (2) at the same time, the UNIDROIT Principles are largely inspired by an international uniform law text already enjoying wide international recognition and generally considered as reflecting international trade usages and practice in the field of the international sale of goods, which has already been ratified by almost 40 countries, namely CISG; (3) the UNIDROIT Principles are especially adapted to the contracts being the subject of this arbitration, since they cover both the international sale of goods and supply of services; (4) the UNIDROIT Principles have been specifically conceived to apply to international contracts in instances in which as it is the case in these proceedings, it has been found that the parties have agreed that their transactions shall be governed by general legal rules and principles; (5) rather than vague principles or general guidelines, the UNIDROIT Principles are mostly constituted by clearly enunciated and specific rules coherently organized in a systematic way ...'[296]

---

294. ICC Award No. 7375, excerpt reproduced in Mealey's Int'l Arb.Rep, Dec. 1996, A-1 *et seq.* (emphasis added); *Marrella*, La Nuova Lex Mercatoria, 417; *Bonell*, An International Restatement of Contract Law, at 286, footnote 78 (emphasis added).
295. *Bonell, id.*, at 286 *et seq.*
296. ICC Award No. 7110, excerpt reprinted in *Gopalan*, J.L. & Com. 2004, at 117, 161.

c. *The Principles May Provide a Solution to an Issue Raised When It Proves Impossible to Establish the Relevant Rule of the Applicable Law*

The third option was contained in the Preamble of the 1994 edition of the Principles, but was deleted from the Preamble in the 2002 edition. However, the third option is still listed as 'another possible use of the Principles' in the official commentary to the 2004 edition[297]. It states that the Principles may provide a solution to an issue raised when it proves impossible to establish the relevant rule of the applicable law. This option refers to the situation where the judge or arbitrator may be faced with a 'documentation gap'[298] with respect to the applicable law. This means that, in spite of the application of traditional conflict of laws principles, if it proves extremely difficult to establish the relevant rule of a particular domestic law with respect to a specific issue, domestic courts usually refer back to the substantive law of the *lex fori*[299]. The Swiss legislature has put this principle into legislative form in Art. 16(2) of the Swiss Statute on Private International Law[300]. This doctrine results from the heavily criticized 'homeward boundness' ('*Heimwärtsstreben*') of domestic courts and necessarily leads to arbitrary decision-making, in that the law of the *lex fori* need not necessarily have a close connection to the case. In view of the uncertainty and injustice connected with this traditional doctrine *Kötz* has developed the view that the judge or arbitrator who is not able to determine the relevant rule or provision of the applicable law should resort to general principles of law as 'substitute law'[301]. In many cases, deciding a legal dispute on the basis of general principles common to the jurisdictions that have a connection to the case, may be more in line with the interests of the parties than the automatic reference to the substantive law of the *lex fori*. Even under Swiss law, recourse to general principles of law is allowed in spite of the statutory *lex fori*-rule if it can be assumed with sufficient probability that these principles are part of the law which would have to be applied according to general principles of private international law, or if the mandatory character of these principles makes them part of the '*ordre public international*'[302].

In legal practice, however, judges or arbitrators will find it very difficult to implement this approach in court or arbitration proceedings. Domestic court proceedings or international commercial arbitrations do not allow for the time-consuming research efforts necessary to determine the contents of general

297. *UNIDROIT*, UNIDROIT Principles of International Commercial Contracts 2004, at 7.
298. Problems in procuring *materials on the foreign law* have to be distinguished from *gaps* in the foreign law; in the latter case, the principles have to be applied which this legal system has developed for gap-filling.
299. *Cf.* BGHZ 69, 387; *Kropholler*, IPR, § 31 III.1 (at 216).
300. Article 16: 'Swiss law applies if the contents of the foreign law cannot be applied'; *cf.* Heini/Keller/Siehr/Vischer/Volken-*Keller/Girsberger*, IPRG-Kommentar, Art. 16, Nos. 69 *et seq.*
301. *Kötz*, RabelsZ 34 (1970), at 663, 674.
302. Heini/Keller/Siehr/Vischer/Volken-*Keller/Girsberger, supra* note 300, Art. 16, No. 74.

principles of law[303]. The UNIDROIT Principles may help to overcome this deficiency in that they provide the necessary basis for the verification of general principles of law as 'substitute law'.

d. The UNIDROIT Principles as a Means to Interpret or Supplement International Uniform Law Instruments

The fourth option provides that the Principles may be used to interpret or supplement international uniform law instruments. International uniform law, based on international conventions or model laws always runs the risk of being diluted and 'nationalized' once it is transformed into a domestic legal system and made subject to the traditional methods of construction of that particular jurisdiction[304]. This has always been considered as the major weakness of the creation of international uniform law through international conventions or model laws[305]. Also, it is a natural consequence of the legal process that different courts will interpret identical rules differently[306]. It is therefore of utmost importance to construe and apply provisions of uniform law from a comparative perspective even after their transformation into domestic law[307]. It is for this very reason that Art. 7(1) CISG provides that in the interpretation of the Convention, 'regard is to be had to its international character and to the need to promote uniformity in its application . . .'[308]. Art. 7(2) CISG provides that '[q]uestions concerning matters governed by this Convention which are not expressly settled in it are to be settled in conformity with the general principles on which it is based . . .'. In this context, the UNIDROIT Principles perform the important function of providing a collection of 'broad principles of general acceptation'[309] which may serve as guidelines for an autonomous and comparative method of construction and of gap-filling of all

303. *Kropholler*, IPR, § 31 III.2.c (at 218 *et seq.*).
304. *Cf.* the statement of Lord *Diplock* in *Fothergill v. Monarch Airlines Ltd.*, A.C. [1981] 251: 'The language of an international convention is addressed to a much wider and more varied judicial audience than is an Act of Parliament dealing with purely domestic law. It should be interpreted as Lord *Wilberforce* put it in *Buchanan's* case, unconstrained by technical rules of English law, or by English legal precedent, but on broad principles of general acceptation'; *cf. also de Boer*, in: Hartkamp, *et al.* (eds.), Towards a European Civil Code, 1st ed., at 51, 59: 'It must be feared . . . that uniform law is doomed to be "nationalized" if its application is not supervised by an international court, or if national courts are unwilling or unable to take judicial notice of foreign decisions and international scholarly sources'; *cf. also Schmitthoff*, Trade Usages, at 31 *et seq.*; *Bonell*, An International Restatement of Contract Law, at 11 *et seq.*
305. *Cf. Schwarzenberger*, Rec.Cours 1966-I, at 1, 9 *et seq.*: 'As is proved by the practices of multilateral conventions which depend for their application on national organs, in particular courts, the attempts made at the unification of diverging national laws have proved less promising than expected. The strength of centrifugal trends in the application of conventions such as those on carriage by sea and air bears on this skepticism'.
306. *See Ferrari*, Rev.int.dr.comp. 1996, at 813, 831.
307. *Kropholler*, Internationales Einheitsrecht, at 287 *et seq.*; *Diedrich*, Autonome Auslegung von Internationalem Einheitsrecht, at 73 *et seq.*; *Roth/Happ*, Unif.L.Rev. 1997, at 700, 702 *et seq.*
308. *Cf. von Caemmerer/Schlechtriem-Herber*, CISG, Art. 7, No. 14.
309. *Schmitthoff*, Trade Usages, at 33.

instruments of uniform law relating to international contract law in general[310] and the CISG in particular[311], thereby fulfilling *Esser's* vision of a 'coordinated case law on supranational laws'[312]. A typical example for this function would be the apodictic and highly controversial interest provision of Art. 78 CISG. It states that a creditor is entitled to interest but leaves open the important question as to the interest rate and the time from which interest runs. To fill this gap, arbitrators may[313] refer to Art. 7.4.9 of the Principles. Thus, in the ICC Award No. 8128[314], rendered in 1995, the arbitrator, in applying Art. 78 CISG, referred to Art. 7.4.9(2) of the Principles for guidance in his efforts to determine the rate of interest. However, instead of applying it literally, the tribunal only drew inspiration from this article, deducing from it the underlying premise of interest law according to which it is the damage of the creditor and not the enrichment of the debtor which determines the rate of interest[315]. This principle also underlies the rule articulated in Art. 7(2) CISG[316]. To determine the rate, the tribunal referred to the London Interbank Offered Rate (LIBOR), but added 2% since it was not dealing with interbank credits but with regular commercial borrowers with a lower credit standing and increased credit costs. A similar approach has been followed in two arbitral awards rendered by the same arbitrator under the auspices of the Arbitration Court of the Austrian Economic Chamber in Vienna[317].

Even prior to the promulgation of the Principles, an arbitral tribunal acting under the auspices of the Berlin Court of Arbitration cited the hardship provision of the Draft UNIDROIT Principles as an expression of international commercial practice, serving as an additional argument to justify hardship and its consequences under the General Conditions of Delivery of Goods between Member Countries

310. *Cf. Bonell*, An International Restatement of Contract Law, at 174 *et seq.*
311. *See Burkart*, Interpretatives Zusammenwirken von CISG und UNIDROIT Principles, at 211 *et seq.*
312. *Cf.* the concluding comment in *Josef Esser's magnum opus*, Grundsatz und Norm in der richterlichen Fortbildung des Privatrechts, at 381.
313. *See supra* b.
314. ICC Award No. 8128, Clunet 1996, at 1024 with note by *Hascher, id.*, at 1028 *et seq.*; *cf. also Bonell*, Unif.L.Rev. 1997, at 2, 10; *Bonell*, An International Restatement of Contract Law, at 247.
315. *Cf. Bonell*, Unif.L.Rev. 1996, at 26, 37: 'Art. 7.4.9 ... clearly intends to make sure that the interest to be paid covers to the greatest possible extent the loss actually suffered by the aggrieved party as a consequence of the non-payment of the sum of money due'; *see generally Berger*, RabelsZ 61 (1997), at 313, 332; *Berger*, International Economic Arbitration, at 624 *et seq.*; *Lew*, in: Cranston (ed.), Essays in Honor of Roy Goode, at 543, 554.
316. *See Honnold*, ULIS, Art. 78, No. 421: 'The principle underlying [Art. 78] is like that of Article 74 which provides for the recovery of damages ... equal to the loss ... suffered as a consequence of the breach'.
317. Awards of June 15, 1994, reprinted in RIW 1995, at 590 *et seq.* with note by *Schlechtriem, id.*, at 592; in the awards, the arbitrator emphasized the 'full-compensation principle' embodied in Arts 74 and 78 CISG; *see also Boele-Woelki*, Principles en IPR, at 23; *Perales Viscasillas*, Ariz.J.Int'l & Comp.L. 1996, at 383, 402; *Bonell*, Unif.L.Rev. 1997, at 2, 9; *Bonell*, An International Restatement of Contract Law, at 247.

of the Council for Mutual Economic Assistance which did not contain such provisions[318].

This transnational approach to gap-filling allows arbitrators to avoid imposing a purely national rule upon parties to an international contract[319] or to provide the parties with no justification at all for their decision-making, as in some cases of interest adjudication[320].

This function of the Principles envisaged by the Working Group finds a parallel in recent developments of public international law relating to the commercial activities of states and private parties. There, the collection of rules and principles drafted as non-binding 'soft law' forms the counterpart to the restatement technique of private law. The 'Guidelines on the Treatment of Foreign Investment', drafted by the World Bank as non-binding 'soft law', constitute the '*ratio scripta*' of international investment protection law. In spite of their non-binding character, the Guidelines are supposed to assume a gap-filling function if the applicable investment protection treaty does not contain relevant provisions regarding a certain legal problem of international investment protection law[321]. Thus, in both public international law and international contract law, non-binding instruments assume important functions for the gap-filling and interpretation of 'hard' uniform law. It is not surprising, therefore, that suggestions have been made to include express stipulations in international commercial contracts which allow for the application of international uniform law and, in case this law does not cover a certain issue, of the UNIDROIT Principles[322].

e. *The UNIDROIT Principles as a Means for the Internationally Useful Interpretation or Supplementation of Domestic Laws*

It was argued in the first edition of this book that the list of options contained in the Preamble of the 1994 edition of the Principles is not exhaustive and that, therefore, it should be considered whether the Principles' purpose is in fact limited to providing guidelines for the interpretation and construction of international uniform law instruments. It was suggested that the international spirit and comparative wealth contained in the Principles may also be used to develop a method for the internationally useful construction of domestic laws[323]. That option

318. *See Maskow*, Am.J.Comp.L. 1992, at 657, 665 *et seq.*
319. *Goode*, Unif.L.Rev. 1997, at 231, 245.
320. *See* for an example of 'splitting the difference' Ad Hoc Award of July 23, 1981, YCA 1983, at 89, 94: 'The agent is claiming 10%, the shipowner is offering 8%. Arbitrators fix the rate [of interest] at 9% per annum'.
321. *Cf. Shihata*, Legal Treatment of Foreign Investment: 'The World Bank Guidelines', at 71; the text of the 'Guidelines' is reprinted *id.*, at 155 *et seq.*
322. *See Bonell*, Unif.L.Rev. 1996, at 26, 38 for the CISG, suggesting the following stipulation: 'This contract shall be governed by CISG, and with respect to matters not covered by this Convention, by the UNIDROIT Principles of International Commercial Contracts'.
323. *Berger*, The Creeping Codification of the Lex Mercatoria, 1st ed., at 183 *et seq.; see also Storme*, Rev.dr.int.comp. 1995, at 309, 316 *et seq.* stating that in this respect the UNIDROIT

had not been considered by the drafters of the 1994 edition[324]. A survey of the actual practice under the 1994 edition of the Principles revealed that in almost half of the reported cases in which the Principles had been referred to by judges or arbitrators, they had been used to interpret or supplement the otherwise applicable domestic law[325]. The father of the UNIDROIT Principles himself acknowledged that this role of the Principles, not expressly stated in the Preamble of the 1994 edition, was widely acknowledged in legal writings[326]. Therefore, it was included as a fifth option in the Preamble of the 2004 edition of the Principles.

We have already seen above[327] that one of the major reasons for the development of the doctrine of transnational commercial law is the inability of domestic legal systems to provide adequate solutions for the settlement of international commercial disputes. Since most domestic legislatures have always been hesitant to develop special statutes for foreign trade contracts[328], and since the classical doctrine of legal sources is said to stand in the way of the evolution of a transnational commercial law, the development of a special method of interpretation provides the only useful means to reconcile domestic laws with the requirements of international trade and commerce. This approach is also of tremendous importance for the NLM doctrine. In those cases where the NLM does not (yet) provide a transnational legal principle or rule, recourse must be had to the applicable domestic law. The internationally useful method of construction inspired by the UNIDROIT Principles could help to avoid frictions between transnational and domestic law, thereby bridging the gap between domestic legal systems and the NLM.

Every attempt to develop a new method of construction that is designed to be incorporated in the classical canon of construction has to start from a sound methodical basis. In our context, these methodical underpinnings may be provided by two existing methods: (aa) the comparative and (bb) the 'anticipatory' method of interpretation.

aa. Comparative Method of Construction

A comparative approach to the interpretation of domestic law has long been advocated as a 'fifth' or 'universal' method of interpretation[329]. This view is a reaction

Principles are less explicit than the *Lando* Principles; *see also Wichard*, RabelsZ 60 (1996), at 269, 299 *et seq.*

324. *Bonell*, ICC Bull. 2002, at 29.
325. *Bonell*, An International Restatement of Contract Law, at 294 *et seq.* pointing out that the domestic laws governing the individual contracts in the cases in question were far from being only those of less developed countries but included, *inter alia*, the laws of Australia, England, Finland, France, Greece, Italy, the Netherlands, New Zealand, Switzerland and the state of New York; *see also Horn*, in: Berger (ed.), The Practice of Transnational Law, at 67, 76 referring to a 'surprisingly great number of cases'.
326. *Bonell*, in: Berger (ed.), The Practice of Transnational Law, at 23, 37.
327. *Cf. supra* Chapter 1 I.B.
328. *Cf. supra* Chapter 1 II.C.1.
329. *Cf. Zweigert*, RabelsZ 3 (1949/50) at 5, 17 *et seq.*; *Coing*, Die juristischen Auslegungsmethoden und die Lehren der allgemeinen Hermeneutik, at 22; *Aubin*, RabelsZ 34 (1970), at 458,

to the changed law-making techniques of domestic legislatures and draws methodical consequences from this phenomenon for the construction of these domestic laws. The 'comparative law-making method'[330], deliberately applied by domestic legislatures, calls for a corresponding approach from those who apply these laws in everyday legal practice[331]. As has been shown above, dogmatic structures rooted in domestic particularities stand in the way of an interest-oriented, primarily commercially sensible solution of international disputes[332]. A comparative approach to the construction of domestic laws may help to remedy the situation in that it detaches a certain legal institution or legal notion from the constraints and understandings shaped by that particular domestic doctrine[333]. It goes without saying that such a comparative approach is permissible only where it is required by the circumstances of the individual case and where uniform and acceptable interpretation of a legal principle or notion can be found in the relevant legal systems.

This approach should not be confused with discarding generally recognized dogmatic constructions and ideas of domestic laws[334]. Rather, the use of comparative law in the construction of domestic laws is intended to provide a more international orientation to domestic legal doctrine[335].

Irrespective of the ranking that this comparative method of interpretation assumes within the classical canon of construction[336], the comparative knowledge contained in the UNIDROIT Principles provides the necessary reference order which, similar to the determination of transnational commercial law[337], helps to mitigate the efforts necessary to establish a comparative method of construing domestic laws[338]. Through this procedure, a 'step by step process' can be established to 'familiarize judges and practitioners with this new method of construction'[339]. This aspect leads us to the second technique which may serve as a

---

459; *Horn*, Das Recht der internationalen Anleihen, at 500 *et seq.*; *Bydlinski*, Juristische Methodenlehre und Rechtsbegriff, at 461 *et seq.*; *Kriele*, Theorie der Rechtsgewinnung, at 86; *Zweigert/Kötz*, Einführung in die Rechtsvergleichung, Vol. 1, § 2.II; *Häberle*, JZ 1989, at 913, 916 *et seq.*; *Schulze*, ZfRV 1997, at 183, 192 *et seq.* (with reference to German legal doctrine of the nineteenth century, when the Prussian General Law of the Land (*'Allgemeines Landrecht'*) was frequently analysed in the light of the French *Code Civil*); *Meyer*, Principles of Contract Law und nationales Vertragsrecht, at 193 *et seq.*

330. *See Meyer, id.*, at 148 *et seq.*
331. *Cf.* for this interaction *Berger*, Internationale Wirtschaftsschiedsgerichtsbarkeit, at 19.
332. *Goode*, Unif.L.Rev. 1991, at 54, 59; *Malintoppi*, UNIDROIT Annuaire 1967–1968, Vol. II, at 43, 56 *et seq.*; *cf. also Berger*, J.Int'l Arb., No. 4 1992, at 5, 10 *et seq.*
333. *Cf.* for the problem of preconceptions of legal terms, shaped by domestic legal doctrine, *Esser*, Vorverständnis und Methodenwahl in der Rechtswissenschaft, at 121 *et seq.*
334. *Cf.* the warning of *Großfeld*, Festschrift Lukes, at 655, 656: 'The smell of the great wide world should not mislead us to see things too simple and to regard the world as a supermarket of legal cultures'.
335. *Cf. Großfeld*, Macht und Ohnmacht der Rechtsvergleichung, at 31 *et seq.*
336. *Cf. Berger*, Internationale Wirtschaftsschiedsgerichtsbarkeit, at 19 *et seq.*
337. *Cf. infra* II.C.
338. *Cf.* for the similar problem of ascertaining legal rules and principles of transnational law through the comparative method *infra* II.C.3.
339. *Matteucci*, UNIDROIT Annuaire 1967–1968, Vol. II, at 267, 268.

methodical basis for the development of the idea of an internationally useful construction of domestic laws.

bb. 'Anticipatory' Method of Construction

(a) **Methodical Basis**

The idea of an 'anticipatory' construction of domestic laws provides an additional underpinning for the establishment of an internationally useful method of construing domestic laws on the basis of the UNIDROIT Principles. This approach is effected by reversing the classical historic method of construing domestic laws. Instead of looking *back* at the *travaux préparatoires* and the motives of the drafters of the laws, the lawyer or judge looks *forward* to the contents of draft laws which are supposed to take the place of the statute that is being construed. Anticipatory construction involves the anticipation of legal principles and ideas contained in draft laws or international draft conventions for the purpose of construing domestic law.

This approach is recognized in two different fields of law.

First, it is used by international arbitrators in their decision-making. International arbitral tribunals frequently refer to international conventions that have not (yet) been ratified in their search for indications of the existence of general principles of law[340]. This anticipatory reference to international (draft) conventions has become a well-known and frequently used means to determine general principles of conflict of laws[341]. It is also familiar to domestic courts in the field of private international law ('*Vorwirkung*')[342].

Secondly, this approach is to be found in Dutch law. Since the early 1960s, the Dutch Supreme Court (*Hoge Raad*) has construed and developed the Dutch Civil Code on the basis of the new draft civil code for the Netherlands[343]. By way of this '*anticiperende interpretatie*', the Dutch courts have gradually managed to adapt the old law to the new provisions, although it took more than thirty years for the new law to be enacted[344]. With this innovative approach, the Dutch courts were close to the borderline between mere statutory interpretation and development of the law *praeter* or even *contra legem*. The concept of anticipatory construction goes well beyond the classical canon of interpretation. It does not merely determine the legislature's intention as laid down in the law. Instead, it refers the judge or arbitrator to the abstract solutions found in the new law which are then transposed into the statute that is still in force[345]. The Dutch courts used this method of anticipatory interpretation not only for the construction of the Dutch statutes in the literal sense but also to fill gaps in the old law[346].

340. *Cf.* ICC Award No. 5713, YCA 1990, at 70, 71; *cf.* also ICC Award No. 2438, Clunet 1976, at 969; No. 6281, YCA 1990, at 96, 97.
341. *Cf. Basedow*, Jahrbuch für die Praxis der Schiedsgerichtsbarkeit 1987, at 3, 18; *Walter/Bausch/Brönnimann*, Internationale Schiedsgerichtsbarkeit in der Schweiz, at 193.
342. *See Schröder*, Internationales Vertragsrecht, 1st ed., at 4.
343. *Cf.* the basic considerations of *Scholten*, WPr. 1969, at 111 *et seq.*
344. *Cf. e.g. Hoge Raad* of March 7, 1980, NJ 1980, No. 353.
345. *Scholten, supra* note 343, *id.*
346. *Scholten, supra* note 343, at 123.

In spite of these far-reaching effects and consequences of the anticipatory approach to statutory interpretation, this approach may still be classified as 'interpretation'. It has already been emphasized above[347] that it is almost impossible to draw a clear-cut borderline between those cases where the law is being construed and those cases where the law is being developed. Also, the Dutch courts have only applied this doctrine under very limited circumstances. Thus, an anticipatory interpretation of the old Dutch Civil Code was impermissible if this would have led to new solutions, *i.e.* to a development of the old law *praeter* or even *contra legem*[348]. The method of anticipatory interpretation could thus not be used to introduce clear deviations from the old civil code or to circumvent mandatory rules merely by reference to a different intention expressed in the new draft law[349]. As a positive side effect, this 'reform before the reform' made the transition from the old to the new civil code much easier[350]. In any event, it was possible that two different solutions could be found for the same legal problem over a longer period of time, one under the literal meaning of the old law and the other under the old law as construed against the background of the new draft civil code[351].

(b) Limited Use of the Anticipatory Approach for the UNIDROIT Principles

The theory of anticipatory interpretation of domestic laws is based on the premise that a new law will be promulgated in the near future. The closer the judge or arbitrator is to the moment of implementation of this law or convention, the stronger his justification for applying the idea of anticipatory interpretation. The time element is therefore of decisive importance for this approach to the construction of domestic law. This idea cannot be readily transferred to the UNIDROIT Principles which do not constitute a codification in the proper sense. Also, a technical codification of international contract law on a worldwide basis is not foreseeable in the near future[352]. Therefore, the UNIDROIT Principles do not assume the character of a draft law of a worldwide code of contract law which would justify the application of the anticipatory method of interpretation. The situation may be different in the European Union where the European Parliament has issued resolutions calling for the drafting of a European Civil Code. The Principles of European Contract Law drafted by the *Lando* Commission as well as the Draft European Civil Code drafted by the *Gandolfi* Working Group[353] and the Academic DCFR[354] may be regarded as

347. *Cf. supra* Chapter 2 II.G.2.b.
348. *Cf. van Buchem-Spapens/Nieuwenhuis*, Inleiding Privaatrecht, at 11; *Scholten, supra* note 343, at 111.
349. *Scholten, supra* note 343, *id.*
350. *Cf. Scholten, supra* note 343, at 111 *et seq.*; *Hartkamp*, Voorwoord, in: Burgerlijk Wetboek, at V.
351. *Hartkamp, id.*
352. *Cf. supra* Chapter 3 II.B.3.
353. *See supra* Chapter 3 I.D.
354. *See supra* Chapter 3 I.B.3.

first drafts of this code which would justify application of the anticipatory method of interpretation.

cc. Consequences

There is a basic methodical *substratum* for the development of an international methodology of interpretation based on the UNIDROIT Principles[355]. This view finds support in the general experience that the choice of the 'correct' method of interpretation in an individual case is always based on a teleological evaluation of the possible results with a view to ensuring the acceptability of the solution within a given social order[356]. The usefulness of the method of construction within the context of the individual legal problem and the socio-economic context of the case always plays an important role in any methodical question that is related to the issue of statutory interpretation. The idea of developing an autonomous, internationally useful method of interpretation derives additional justification from the principles that govern the application of foreign law by domestic judges or international arbitrators. The domestic judge who applies foreign law does not do this in a mechanical sense without regard to the international character of the case before him. Rather, the blanket clauses[357] contained in this law as well as the general competence to assess the interests of the parties involved granted by this law allow the judge or arbitrator to take account of these international particularities of the case before him:

> 'The rule to be applied in the individual case does not present itself "ready-made" in the foreign law any more than in the system of the *lex fori*. It is unlikely that the court of the forum will find a foreign precedent which covers the case before it completely. Moreover the court of the forum can in no circumstances adopt the solution given by the foreign court without first interpreting, with the help of the usual process, the general rule which the foreign court has applied in the case before it. On the other hand, it is necessary to stress, in particular, that the foreign law applied by the court constitutes only one element of its judicial reasoning. The court, in applying foreign law, remains the same court as when it applies the *lex fori* and retains the conviction that the judgments is its own product. It is wrong to believe that application of the foreign law entails a kind of dual character to the court, and that the court is the responsible authority when the *lex fori*, but becomes an impersonal onlooker when it comes to applying foreign law. The application of the *lex fori* or of the foreign law is a means, not an end; the end is the solution of the dispute in accordance with certain principles of law. If, in applying foreign law, the court seeks a just and equitable result, it will pursue this purpose if it applies foreign law'[358].

355. *See Wichard*, RabelsZ 60 (1996), at 269, 299 *et seq.*
356. *Cf. Esser*, Vorverständnis und Methodenwahl in der Rechtsfindung, at 123.
357. *Cf. supra* Chapter 2 II.G.2.b.
358. *Zajtay*, The Application of Foreign Law, in: Lipstein (ed.), Int'l Encycl.Comp.L., Vol. III (Private International Law), ch. 14, at 27.

The domestic judge or international arbitrator that applies a foreign domestic law may, therefore, use this discretion to strive towards an internationally useful interpretation of that law[359]. In transborder trade and commerce such would be a solution which is sensible under the economic circumstances of the case. If the parties have included a choice of law clause in their contract, it can be assumed that they will accept a certain margin of possible decisions based on this law:

> 'In choosing a certain domestic legal system a party does not mean certain foreseeable solutions for legal problems that may arise out of the contract; rather, he accepts the characteristic margin of possible and correct decisions which is typical for the solution of these legal problems under that particular legal system'[360].

Within this natural 'margin', the judge or arbitrator may decide to apply an internationally useful method of construction to find a solution for the case before him or her which takes account of the particularities of international trade and the economic interests of the parties[361]. Ultimately, the German Federal Supreme Court has sanctioned such a reasonable method of interpretation 'in a common sense manner' as a generally recognized method of construction[362].

In spite of its attractiveness, however, this methodology may not provide an equivalent for the development of a transnational commercial law. Every method of construction remains subject to the constraints of the relevant domestic law[363]. Thus, developing a theory for the internationally useful interpretation of domestic law may foster and accompany the evolution of a transnational commercial legal system but does not provide an adequate substitute for it.

dd. Application of the Concept in Arbitral Practice

Even though it has been seen above that a careful approach is required to develop the concept of an internationally useful interpretation or supplementation of domestic laws, it has already been used in numerous international arbitral awards[364].

In an unpublished ICC Award No. 8240 of 1995[365], the sole arbitrator, in a dispute between Swiss and Singaporean claimants and Belgian respondents, had to

359. *See Wichard, supra* note 355, at 300 suggesting that under German law, the Principles might influence the 'internationally useful interpretation' of Secs 254 (duty to mitigate damages) and 275 (impossibility) of the Civil Code.
360. *Aden*, RIW 1984, at 934, 937.
361. *Berger*, J.Int'l Arb., No. 4 1992, at 5, 14.
362. *Cf.* BGH, NJW 1986, at 1436, 1437; *cf. also* the lower instance OLG Frankfurt, RIW 1984, at 400; *cf.* for a comparative method of construction BGHZ 101, 337, 342 *et seq.*; *cf. also Canaris*, System und Systemdenken in der Jurisprudenz, at 154.
363. *Cf. supra* Chapter 1 II.C.2; *Schödermeier*, Sonderprivatrecht für internationale Wirtschaftsverträge, at 198.
364. *See* the most recent survey on arbitral case law under the UNIDROIT Principles by *Bonell*, An International Restatement of Contract Law, at 294 *et seq.; Marrella*, La Nuova Lex Mercatoria, at 435 *et seq.*; *Meyer*, Principles of Contract Law und nationales Vertragsrecht, 228 *et seq.; see also* the arbitral awards in the UNILEX Database at *www.unilex.info*.
365. *See Berger*, Am.J.Comp.L. 1998, at 129, 140 and L. & Pol.Int'l Bus. 1997, at 943, 982 *et seq.*

decide on the exchange rate to be applied to the agreed purchase price to be paid by the respondents, for the re-purchase of inventory from the claimants, in a foreign currency after termination of a distribution agreement, which was subject to Swiss law. The arbitrator reasoned that each party had to pay its debt at the nominal value previously agreed upon and that currency fluctuations could not lead to a modification of the principle of nominalism. To justify this view, the arbitrator referred not only to Swiss court decisions and legal doctrine, but also to Art. 6.1.9(3) of the Principles. This provision allows a debtor who has to pay a money debt expressed in a currency of the place for payment to make payment at the 'rate of exchange prevailing there when payment is due'.

In another ICC Award No. 8486 of 1996[366], the sole arbitrator[367], having before him a dispute between a Dutch and a Turkish party, was confronted with the Turkish respondent's allegation that exchange rate fluctuations in his country had discharged him from his payment obligation *vis-à-vis* the claimant under the hardship provision of Art. 6:258 of the applicable Dutch Civil Code. The arbitrator was thus faced with a task which is typical in international transactions: the reconciliation of the principle of 'sanctity of contracts' with the doctrine of excuse from performance, as reflected in the notions of *force majeure* and hardship.

To justify their decision that these doctrines, even under Dutch law, only apply in very rare and extraordinary circumstances, the sole arbitrator referred not only to Dutch legal writings but also to Art. 6.2.1 of the Principles. Thus, with reference to them, the arbitrator arrived at a restrictive and internationally useful interpretation of Dutch domestic law. Interestingly enough, he found support for this approach in Dutch legal doctrine. A Dutch scholar maintains that in interpreting Dutch legal rules in international contexts and the provisions on hardship and *force majeure* contained in the new Civil Code in particular, Dutch judges should draw inspiration from the UNIDROIT Principles[368]. This approach is the completion of the circle. The Principles have not only inspired the Dutch legislature when drafting the new Code[369], but they are also resorted to when interpreting the new law. Thus, in this case, the UNIDROIT Principles stand at the very beginning and at the very end of the legal process, confirming their central position as a standard reference point for judges, arbitrators and counsel.

For the sole arbitrator in the ICC Case No. 8486, the view advanced in Dutch legal doctrine is of the utmost importance. It provided him with the necessary justification for the international construction of domestic law. Had he not received such support from the relevant domestic law, he would have risked being accused

---

366. ICC Award No. 8486, Clunet 1998, 1047 (English translation in YCA 1999, at 162); *see Berger*, Am.J.Comp.L. 1998, at 129, 140 *et seq.* and L. & Pol.Int'l Bus. 1997, at 943, 983; *Meyer*, Principles of Contract Law und nationales Vertragsrecht, at 229 *et seq.; Brower/ Sharpe*, Va. J. Int'l L. 2004, at 199, 215; *Marrella, supra* note 364, at 447 *et seq.*
367. The sole arbitrator was the author of this book.
368. *Cf. Kuijer*, Ars Aequi, April 1996, at 16, 19.
369. *See infra* f.

of distorting the applicable law, acting no longer as 'photographer', but as 'architect': an approach which arbitrators, like domestic judges, are not allowed to take when applying and construing foreign law[370].

A similar approach may be taken to arrive at an internationally useful construction of German contract law. German legal scholars have long suggested that in international cases, the Principles should be used to achieve a more adequate interpretation of the contract law of the German Civil Code[371]. This approach has also been extended to the German law on standard contract conditions in Secs 305 *et seq.* of the German Civil Code. Sec. 307(2) No. 1 of the Civil Code provides that general contract conditions may be void 'if they contravene basic principles of the statutory law, from which the conditions are deviating'. Since contract law is of a dispositive nature, this non-mandatory quality of the law belongs to the 'basic principles' of German contract law. Therefore, the yardstick for the control of general contract conditions under the German Act in international cases is not domestic German contract law, but rather 'the stock of legal principles that is common to the average majority of states'[372]. It is suggested that the Principles reflect this stock of legal principles in the field of contract law and they should, therefore, be used not only as a guideline for the control of general contract conditions in international contexts[373], but also for the interpretation of the contract law of 2002 which was based on international models like the CISG and the UNIDROIT Principles[374].

This approach is consistent with the view maintained in German legal doctrine that in international business transactions, general contract conditions should be construed according to the prevailing international understanding and meaning of the clause[375]. Thus, a clause that has different meanings under the INCOTERMS and under domestic trade-term definitions should be construed according to the INCOTERMS, if it is contained in an international contract[376]. It is also suggested that, if general contract conditions, drafted by an international 'formulating agency'[377], are combined with an arbitration clause, the interpretation of these clauses should also take into account the case law of international arbitral tribunals. The reason for this suggestion is that the interpretation of the contract conditions through international arbitrators not only reflects in an ideal way the *opinio juris* of those who use the clause (*i.e.*, the *societas mercatorum*), but also leads to the expectation that the acceptance of this interpretation will ultimately create or enhance the understanding of this clause within the business community[378]. It is

370. *See supra* Chapter 1 II.C.2.
371. *Wichard,* RabelsZ 60 (1996), at 269, 299 *et seq.*
372. *Wichard, id.*, at 300.
373. *Wichard, id.*, at 301; *Meyer,* Principles of Contract Law und nationales Vertragsrecht, at 241 *et seq.*
374. *Meyer, id.*, at 175.
375. *Hau,* in: Wolf/Lindacher/Pfeiffer, AGB-Recht, IntGV, No. 64.
376. *Hau, id.*
377. *See supra* Chapter 2 II.D.1.
378. *Hau, supra* note 375, No. 65, *see also von Hoffmann,* AWD 1970, at 247, 251; *Wolf,* ZHR 1989, at 300, 305 *et seq.*; *cf. also* BGH, AWD 1968, at 228; *but see Schmidt,* in: Ulmer/

for this reason that an ICC arbitral tribunal, composed of three German arbitrators, refused to apply the extremely restrictive case law of the German Federal Supreme Court on the invalidity of standard terms on standard forms in b2b-contracts in an international sales dispute, acknowledging that this case law is contrary to the general principle that international businessmen require less protection as compared to consumers[379]. With this approach, German legal doctrine has abandoned its traditional hostility towards transnational legal thinking[380] and has put arbitral awards and international commercial instruments on the same footing with German court decisions and doctrinal writing. Thus, a leading German scholar has referred to the award of the ICC tribunal as if it were a German court decision to support his arguments concerning the 'practical necessity for a more flexible handling of the statutory text' of the German law on standard forms in b2b-disputes[381]. The idea of the internationally useful interpretation of domestic law therefore also performs the important function of bridging the gap between domestic positivism and the NLM.

f. The UNIDROIT Principles as a Model for National and International Legislatures

The last option listed in the Preamble of the Principles relates to their function as a model for national and international legislatures. This option, of course, has only an indirect influence on individual international commercial contracts. Legislatures of developing countries or the changing economies of Eastern Europe may refer to the Principles in their efforts to draft new modern laws on international trade through a 'comparative law-making method'[382]. Thus, the new Civil Code of the Czech Republic has been influenced by the Principles. The Dutch legislature has also sought guidance in the Principles for the drafting of the new Dutch Civil Code. Similarly, the Principles have influenced the drafting of the new Civil Code of the Russian Federation[383], and similar projects are in China, Estonia, Indonesia, Israel, New Zealand, Iran, Pakistan, Turkey, and Mongolia[384]. The drafts of § 2 of the American UCC also make reference to the Principles[385], and the same holds true for the Report of the Commission for the 2002 Reform of German Obligation Law[386].

Brandner/Hensen, AGB-Recht, Anh. § 305, No. 32, stating that there is no general principle of an internationally uniform interpretation of general contract conditions.

379. *See infra* B.III *in fine*.
380. *See supra* Chapter 2 II.B.2.
381. *Schlosser*, in: Staudinger, Kommentar zum BGB, 2006, § 305 No. 36a.
382. *Cf. supra* Chapter 2 II.A.1.a.
383. *See* for the various influences on the new Civil Code of the Russian Federation *Solotych*, Das Zivilgesetzbuch der Russischen Förderation, at 73.
384. *Bonell*, An International Restatement of Contract Law, at 268 *et seq.*
385. *Cf. Gordley*, An American Perspective on the UNIDROIT Principles, at 1 *et seq.*; *see also Rosett*, Improving the Uniform Commercial Code, at 3 *et seq.*
386. *See Meyer*, Principles of Contract Law und nationales Vertragsrecht, 155 *et seq.*

In addition, international institutions concerned with the unification of international commercial law may refer to the Principles for the 'mental preparation of the unification process' (*'préparation spirituelle à l'unification'*)[387]. This function is in no way a particularity of the UNIDROIT Principles, but is an inherent quality of all legal instruments negotiated on the international plane[388]. Thus, the World Bank 'Guidelines on the Treatment of Foreign Investment' are said to have a prototype-function for the drafting of domestic investment protection laws[389]. The Australian government has already acknowledged the potential function of the UNIDROIT Principles as a model for legislation in the ASEAN and APEC countries[390]. The Principles also served as a model for the *'Acte uniforme sur le droit des contrats'* of the OHADA and have influenced the ICC Force Majeure Clause 2003 and the ICC hardship Clause 2003[391].

11. The 2004 Edition of the UNIDROIT Principles

At its 76th Session in 1997, the UNIDROIT Governing Council decided 'that work should be resumed with priority with a view to publication of an enlarged second edition of the Principles'[392]. The Working Group for the preparation of the second edition held its first session at the UNIDROIT headquarters from March 16 to 20, 1998. Two special *rapporteurs* were appointed to prepare a draft model clause for the choice by the parties of the UNIDROIT Principles as the law governing their contract and to examine possible adaptations of the Principles in the light of electronic commerce[393]. The second edition was published in April 2004 – ten years after the publication of the first edition[394]. In the 2004 edition, certain existing provisions were revised in order to adapt them to the ever increasing important practice of electronic contracting. The Preamble contains a reference to the text of a model clause for those parties that wish to provide that their contract be governed by the Principles. Also, the text in the official comments to the individual provisions of the principles was amended. Most importantly, the new edition includes new chapters with sixty-five new articles on authority of agents (new Section 2 of Chapter 2), third party rights (new Section 2 of Chapter 5), set-off (new Chapter 8), assignment of contractual rights, obligations and of contracts as a whole (new Chapter 9) and on limitation of actions (new Chapter 10)[395].

387. *Matteucci*, UNIDROIT Annuaire 1967–1968, Vol. II, at 267, 268.
388. *Cf. generally* for the model function of international texts *Holtzmann*, Festschrift P. Lalive, at 257, 260.
389. *Shihata*, Legal Treatment of Foreign Investment: 'The World Bank Guidelines', at 71.
390. *Bonell*, An International Restatement of Contract Law, at 171 *et seq.*
391. *Bonell, id.*, at 270 *et seq.*
392. *Bonell, id.*, at 256.
393. *See Bonell, id.*, at 39 *et seq.*; *see also* the contributions by *Kronke, Reynolds, Berger, Wiegand, Bernardini, C. Ramberg, Bortolotti* and *Jolivet* in: Jolivet (ed.), UNIDROIT Principles: New Developments and Applications.
394. *UNIDROIT* (ed.), Principles of International Commercial Contracts, 2004, also available at *www.unidroit.org/english/principles/contracts/principles2004/blackletter2004.pdf.*
395. *Bonell, id.*, at 256 *et seq.*

12. Towards the 2010 Edition of the Principles

The Governing Council of UNIDROIT, when approving the 2004 edition of the Principles, recommended that the Principles become an ongoing project on UNIDROIT's work programme and instructed the Secretariat to solicit comments and suggestions with respect to additional topics to be dealt with in a future edition of the Principles. In 2005, the Governing Council decided to set up a new Working Group for the preparation of a future third edition of the Principles while at the same time limiting the scope of the work to no more than four or five topics[396]. The UNIDROIT Working Group has discussed new draft chapters on unwinding of failed contracts, illegality, plurality of obligors and/or obligees, and conditional obligations in four sessions. It was recommended that a draft chapter on termination of long-term contracts for just cause be included in a possible fourth edition of the Principles which will focus on long-term contracts in general[397]. The Working Group will hold its 5th plenary session in Rome from May 24 to 28, 2010.

B. The Principles of European Contract Law of the *Lando* Commission

1. Heterogeneous Character of 'European Private Law'

The EU Commission does not regard, Arts 114 and 115 TFEU (former Art. 3(1) h and Arts 94 and 95 of the EC Treaty) as a sufficient basis for the creation and implementation of a comprehensive European contract law[398]. The various measures taken by the Commission to unify civil and commercial law are based on superior considerations of general community policy such as consumer protection, protection of employees or socially weak parties, implementation of the four fundamental freedoms of the EC Treaty or, *e.g.* in the field of banking or insurance supervision law, the creation of a 'level playing field', *i.e.* the creation of identical conditions for all participants in the EU-market[399]. As a necessary side effect,

396. *Bonell, id.*, at 363 *et seq.* with a list of possible topics; *see also* 'Unidroit Principles of International Commercial Contracts – Study L', *www.unidroit.org/english/workprogramme/study050/main.htm.*

397. *See* Working Group for the Preparation of Principles of International Commercial Contracts (3rd ed.), Fourth Session, May 25–28, 2009, *www.unidroit.org/english/workprogramme/study050/wg03/wg-2009.htm.*

398. *Cf.* for the missing legislative competence of the EU for the private law regulation of commerce and trade *Rittner*, JZ 1990, at 838, 842; *R. Schmidt*, WUR 1990, at 1, 5; *Immenga*, EuZW 1993, at 169; and the contribution of *Taschner*, reported by *Berg*, Diskussionsbericht, RabelsZ 50 (1986), at 233, 244.

399. *Cf.* the 'White Paper from the Commission to the European Council ('Completing the Internal Market') of June 14, 1985, Doc. COM (85) 310; *De Ly*, Europese Gemeenschap En Privaatrecht, at 26; *Berger*, BB 1989, at 1017, 1020.

measures such as the Council Directive on Self-Employed Commercial Agents[400], the Directive on Unfair Terms in Consumer Contracts[401] and other directives in the field of consumer protection (on contracts negotiated away from business premises, on consumer credits, on package holidays and package tours, etc.)[402], and the numerous measures in the field of corporate law[403] lead to the unification of the law in the individual Member States[404]. Even the various measures to unify banking supervision law[405] have led, at least to a limited extent, to a unification of those areas of contract law that are relevant to the bank-customer relationship[406]. It must be borne in mind, however, that this unifying effect is a mere reflex of the socio-political policy decisions which stand behind each measure taken by the Commission. Also, this effect is limited to a certain region of the world. Therefore, this experience cannot be generalized and taken as a model for the unification of the laws of countries that do not have the same political and economic background[407]. The harmonization policy is based on the Commission's White Book on the Completion of the Single European Market[408] which has prescribed certain minimum standards and has implemented the principle of the neutral recognition of private law provisions as 'a minimum form of harmonization'[409].

In view of the persisting differences in legal culture and tradition in the various member countries of the EU, the process of harmonization just described cannot serve as a model for a genuine unification of international commercial contract law. In certain sensitive areas such as consumer protection law, the progressive harmonization policy of the Commission has led to the elimination of the principle

400. Council Directive on the Coordination of the Laws of the Member States Relating to Self-Employed Commercial Agents of December 18, 1986, OJ EC of December 31, 1986, No. L 382/17; German implementing law of October 23, 1989, BGBl. I, at 1910 *et seq.*; *cf. Hopt*, Handelsvertreterrecht, § 84 No. 3 and at p. 211 *et seq.; Kindler*, RIW 1990, at 358 *et seq.*
401. Council Directive on Unfair Terms in Consumer Contracts of April 5, 1993, OJ EC of April 21, 1993, No. L 95, at 29 *et seq.* (= NJW 1993, at 1838 *et seq.*); *cf. Michalski*, DB 1994, at 665 *et seq.*; *Nassall*, WM 1994, at 1645 *et seq.*; *Frey*, ZIP 1993, at 572 *et seq.*; *Heinrichs*, NJW 1993, at 1817 *et seq.*; *Eckert*, WM 1993, at 1070 *et seq.*
402. *Cf. generally Reich*, Europäisches Verbraucherschutzrecht, at 250 *et seq.*
403. *Cf.* the compilation of these measures by *Lutter*, Europäisches Gesellschaftsrecht; *cf.* for the limited effect of these measures with respect to the unification of the law *Vagts*, in: Rubin/Hufbauer (eds.), Emerging Standards of International Trade and Investment, at 17 *et seq.*; *Großfeld*, WM 1992, at 212 *et seq.*; *Behrens*, GmbHR 1993, at 129 *et seq.*; *Hauschka*, ZRP 1990, at 179 *et seq.*
404. *See Müller-Graff*, in: Hartkamp, *et al.* (eds.), Towards a European Civil Code, at 77 *et seq.*
405. *Cf.* for details *Horn*, ZBB 1989, at 107 *et seq.*; *Horn*, ZBB 1994, at 130 *et seq.*; *Berger*, BB 1989, at 1017 *et seq.*; *Grundmann*, Das Europäische Bankaufsichtsrecht wächst zum System.
406. *Schneider*, NJW 1991, at 1985 *et seq.*; *Wolf*, WM 1990, at 1941 *et seq.*; *cf. also* (from a global point of view) *Hirsch*, in: Buxbaum/Herting/Hirsch/Hopt (eds.), European Business Law, at 347 *et seq.*
407. *Gleichmann*, in: Coing/Schmitthoff/Hellner/Gleichmann (eds.), Methoden der Rechtsvereinheitlichung, at 35, 42; *Vagts, supra* note 403; *cf. also Buxbaum/Hopt*, Legal Harmonization and the Business Enterprise, at 193 *et seq.*
408. *Cf. supra* note 399.
409. *Blaurock*, JZ 1994, at 270, 273.

of party autonomy, in favour of special provisions designed to protect the equality and parity of the parties within the contractual relationship[410]. Also, the regulation technique employed by the Commission in certain areas of the law, such as banking supervision or corporate law, which gives leeway to the EU Member States and imposes only minimum requirements, does not lend itself well to the unification of private law, which always requires a certain degree of precision, workability and systematic coherence[411]. The Commission's directives, however, usually focus only on the approximation of certain technical rules while related areas of law are left untouched[412]. The case law of the European Court of Justice and the Court's limited competence to develop general principles of law under Art. 340(2) TFEU[413] cannot serve as a starting point for the development of unified European contract law. The European Court uses comparative law merely as an empirical technique which is employed sporadically and in an incomplete manner[414], leading to piece-meal harmonization instead of an EU wide unification of private law. While a relatively firm body of general principles of public law has been developed, *e.g.* in the field of effective judicial protection of individual rights[415], the Court has not dealt extensively with private law, let alone general contract law. Even the implementation of primary EU legislation may not serve as a means for the comprehensive and all embracing unification of private law. The creation of unified law in certain specialized areas of international trade such as transport law[416], which has traditionally been subject to various unification efforts[417], is only of sectoral significance, and the numerous gaps that still exist in the unified law always make it necessary to have recourse to the applicable domestic law[418]. It seems at least highly doubtful whether an extensive judicial interpretation of EU law may ultimately serve to create common notions and conceptions that lead to a European '*ius commune*'[419]. In any event, in spite of the persisting similarities

---

410. *Müller-Graff*, NJW 1993, at 13, 23; *Brandner/Ulmer*, BB 1991, at 701, 702.
411. *Müller-Graff, id.*, at 23.
412. *See Schulze*, DRiZ 1997, at 369, 373.
413. *Cf. Lecheler*, Der Europäische Gerichtshof und die allgemeinen Grundsätze, 1971; *Rüber*, Der Gerichtshof der Europäischen Gemeinschaften und die Konkretisierung allgemeiner Rechtsgrundsätze.
414. *Constantinesco*, Rechtsvergleichung, Vol. II, at 404; *cf. also Kötz*, RabelsZ 50 (1986), at 1, 8; *Everling*, RabelsZ 50 (1986), at 192, 214 *et seq.*; *Lorenz*, Am.J.Comp.L. 1964, at 1 *et seq.*
415. *van Gerven*, Ford.Int'l L.J. 1997, at 680, 681 *et seq.*
416. *Cf.* the 'Convention relative au contrat de transport international de marchandises par route', CMR; BGBl. II 1961, at 1119 with revising protocol of July 5, 1978, BGBl. II 1980, at 793; last revision through law of April 11, 1980, BGBl. II 1980, at 586; *cf. generally Thume*, Kommentar zum CMR.
417. *Cf. K. Schmidt*, in: Behrends (ed.), Privatrecht heute und Jherings evolutionäres Rechtsdenken, at 77, 95 *et seq.*
418. *Cf.* the German case law, BGH VersR 1975, at 610, 611; VersR 1979, at 276; TranspR 1992, at 100, 102; *Koller*, Transportrecht, CMR vor § 1 Nos. 5 *et seq.*; *see* for the determination of the applicable law in case of choice of law by the parties BGHZ 83, 96, 101; BGH TranspR 1990, at 418, 420; OLG Düsseldorf TranspR 1989, at 10, 11; OLG München TranspR 1989, at 280, 287.
419. *But see* the rather optimistic view of *Storme*, Rev.dr.int.dr.comp. 1995, at 309, 319 *et seq.*

between the European legal systems[420], there is a strange contrast between the ancient Roman-Canon *ius commune* which up to the so-called *usus modernus pandectarum* had a truly European character[421] and the present status of private law within the EU[422]. Today, a coherent body of European contract law does not exist, despite *Kötz's* publication of a text book on the subject[423].

Another way to achieve decisional harmony and to avoid friction in the application of the different substantive laws within the EU would be the creation of a uniform European conflict of laws system. The first step in this direction has already been taken with the 1980 Rome Convention on the Law Applicable to Contractual Obligations[424] which was transformed into the Rome I Regulation in June 2008[425]. This approach to harmonization is in line with the general philosophy of the Commission which is to acknowledge the equality of all legal systems within the EU and to foster their mutual recognition[426]. In view of the substantial uncertainties connected with traditional conflict of laws methodology[427], which even the Rome Convention has not been able to do away with[428], unification of the rules of private international law does not provide an escape out of the harmonization dilemma within the EU. The Commission's policy to favour the harmonization of the law through the adoption of directives may even foster the fragmentation of domestic contract laws since they leave it to the individual Member States to decide how they will transform the provisions of the directives into their domestic law[429]. This view was confirmed by Joint Response of the Commission on European Contract Law and the Study Group on European Civil Code on the EU Commissions inquiry as to the current status of European private law[430].

420. *See Hirte*, Wege zu einem Europäischen Zivilrecht, at 11 *et seq.*
421. *See Zimmermann*, Col.J.Europ.L. 1994/95, at 63, 82 *et seq.*
422. *See Dolfen*, in: Laum/Klein/Strauch (eds.), 175 Jahre Oberlandesgericht Köln, at 257, 267 *et seq.*
423. *See Kötz*, Europäisches Vertragsrecht, Vol. I, at VI.
424. Rome Convention on the Law Applicable to Contractual Obligations of June 19, 1980, OJ EC of October 9, 1980, No. L 266 (= BGBl. II 1980, at 810); *cf. generally Firsching*, IPRax 1981, at 37 *et seq.*
425. *See supra* Chapter 1 I.A. note 31.
426. *See Taupitz*, Europäische Privatrechtsvereinheitlichung heute und morgen, § 5; *Taupitz*, JZ 1993, at 533, 538 *et seq.*; *Remien*, JZ 1992, at 277, 281; *cf. also Müller-Graff*, Privatrecht und Europäisches Gemeinschaftsrecht, at 37 *et seq.*
427. *Cf. supra* Chapter 1 I.A.
428. *Cf.* for the highly controversial direct application of third country provisions of public law (*'lois d'application immédiate'*) according to Art. 7 of the Rome Convention, which has not been transformed into German law 'for reasons of legal certainty', *von Bar*, IPR, Vol. II, No. 263.
429. *Remien*, JZ 1992, at 277, 282; *cf.* from the perspective of German law *Lieb*, AcP 183 (1983), at 344; *Rolland*, NJW 1992, at 2377, 2379.
430. *See* Communication on European Contract Law: Joint Response of the Commission on European Contract Law and the Study Group on European Civil Code, available at *http://ec.europa.eu/consumers/cons_int/safe_shop/fair_bus_pract/cont_law/comments/5.23.pdf;*

In view of this highly selective and amorphous policy, the harmonization of contract law on the EU level 'has created tiny islands of unified law within a vast ocean of domestic laws'[431]. The major problem with the Commission's approach to the harmonization of contract law has always been that it is not governed by an overriding general concept which is always necessary to ensure the effectiveness of any effort to harmonize or unify the law[432]. Also, the Commission's policy suffers from a major deficiency in that it 'covers highlands of contract law which are lit by the sun of topicality while the depressions of its general notions and concepts are left untouched'[433]. It is due to this lack of conceptual clarity that domestic legislatures within the EU do not (yet) see a reason to 'refrain from modifications of domestic law which they consider necessary'[434].

To escape the harmonization dilemma described above, the European Parliament adopted a Resolution on May 26, 1989, which emphasized the economic relevance of a 'common private law for all Member States' and called for the preparation of a 'Common European Code of Private Law'[435]. This Resolution was reiterated on May 6, 1994[436]. In this second Resolution, the work of the *Lando* Commission on European Contract Law was expressly endorsed.

2. The Principles of European Contract Law as the Foundation Stone for a 'European *Ius Commune*'

a. Drafting History

The Principles of European Contract Law take up the idea raised in the Resolution of the European Parliament in 1989 and 1994. They provide the first step towards the evolution of a workable network of principles of a common European private law[437].

In pursuing this objective, the Principles serve four primary functions. First, they are intended to provide the basis for the codification of European contract law that is relevant for transborder commercial activities. Over the past two decades

---

see also Blase, Die Grundregeln des Europäischen Vertragsrechts als Recht grenzüberschreitender Verträge, at 2 *et seq.*; *Gopalan*, J.L. & Com. 2004, at 117, 125 *et seq.*

431. *Kötz*, RabelsZ 50 (1986), at 1, 12 (translation by the author); *cf. also Lando*, Am.J.Comp.L. 1983, at 653.
432. *See Müller-Graff*, Privatrecht und Europäisches Gemeinschaftsrecht, at 29; *cf. also Blaurock*, JZ 1994, at 270; *Blaurock*, in: Starck (ed.), Rechtsvereinheitlichung durch Gesetze, at 90, 103 *et seq.*; *cf. also Taupitz*, JZ 1993, at 533 *et seq.; Schulze*, DRiZ 1997, at 369, 373.
433. *Kötz*, Festschrift Zweigert, at 481, 485.
434. *Rolland*, NJW 1992, at 2377, 2383.
435. Resolution on action to bring into line the private law of the Member States, OJ EC of May 26, 1989, No. C 158/400 (= RabelsZ 56 (1992), at 320 *et seq.*); *cf. also Kramer*, in: Schluep, *et al.* (eds.), Recht, Staat und Politik am Ende des zweiten Jahrtausends, at 729, 730 *et seq.*
436. *Cf. Tilmann*, ZEuP 1995, at 534 *et seq.*
437. *Lando*, RabelsZ 56 (1992), at 261, 265; *cf. also Zimmermann*, JZ 1995, at 477 *et seq.*; *Blase, supra* note 430, at 65 *et seq.*

many have called for such a codification[438], but it has always been regarded as a myth rather than as a realistic possibility[439]. Even though work is now underway to draft a European Code of Obligations[440], the Principles are intended to constitute an informal alternative[441]. Secondly, the Principles will provide a praetorian '*corpus* of law' that will serve as a basic reference point in order to avoid the contingencies of isolated and piece-meal measures of the EU Commission concerning the harmonization of contract law[442]. Thirdly, the Principles may provide guidelines for the interpretation of harmonized law within the EU. The question as to the correct modus of interpretation of harmonized EU law triggered an intensive discussion on the 'correct' approach to this sensitive problem of EU law[443]. Similar to the *ius commune* of the middle ages with its uniform fundus of notions, principles, traditions and rules, the *Lando* Principles will provide a valuable *substratum* for a more advanced, EU wide uniform approach to the interpretation of harmonized EU law[444]. This requires that the practice of the European Court of Justice and the various approaches to the interpretation of EU law developed in the EU Member States be reconciled with the general thrust and informal character of the Principles. Fourthly, the *Lando* Principles, like their counterpart, the UNIDROIT Principles, aim to make a major contribution to the formation of a European *ius commune*[445], *i.e.* a NLM, the scope of which is limited to the Member States of the European Union[446].

For all the objectives mentioned above, drafting a restatement of European contract law is of utmost importance in view of its flexibility and the possibility to include legal sources from outside the EU[447]. The first proposal to draft a restatement of European Contract Law was made by *van Hecke* in the early 1960s:

> 'Les Restatements sont en définitive une codification officieuse et non-obligatoire du droit américain. Pourquoi ne pourrait-on en Europe également songer, à condition évidemment que la documentation et l'enseignement aient

---

438. *See Tilmann*, Wirtschaftsrecht, at 308 *et seq.*; *Tilmann*, Festschrift Oppenhoff, at 495, 507; *Kötz*, Festschrift Zweigert, at 481 *et seq.*
439. *Cf.* for the *status quo Blaurock*, JZ 1994, at 270, 271: 'Our time is not yet ripe for any attempt to achieve legal unification through a comprehensive codification of civil law'.
440. *See supra* Chapter 3 I.D (the *Gandolfi* project) and E (the *Lando* Commission).
441. *Storme*, Rev.dr.int.dr.comp. 1995, at 309, 318 *et seq.*
442. *Müller-Graff*, NJW 1993, at 13, 23; *Lando*, Am.J.Comp.L. 1983, at 653, 654 ('backbone of common principles'); *Kötz*, Festschrift Zweigert, at 481, 486 *et seq.*
443. *Cf.* only *Lutter*, JZ 1992, at 593, 596 *et seq.*; *Hommelhoff*, AcP 192 (1992), at 71, 95 *et seq.*; *Kötz*, Festschrift Zweigert, at 481, 489.
444. *Cf. Hartkamp*, in: Hartkamp, *et al.* (eds.), Towards a European Civil Code, at 125, 130.
445. *Cf. Kötz*, Festschrift Zweigert, at 481 *et seq.*
446. *Lando, see supra* note 437, at 266.
447. *Cf.* already *David*, contribution to the discussion on the IV. Conference of those Institutions Concerned with the Unification of the Law, held in Rome from April 22 to 24, 1968, UNIDROIT Annuaire 1967–1968, Vol. II, at 274, 276; *Lando*, in: Cappelletti (ed.), New Perspectives for a Common Law of Europe, at 267, 286 *et seq.*; *Müller-Graff; supra* note 442, *id.*; *Blaurock*, JZ 1994, at 270, 276; *cf. also Ulmer*, JZ 1992, at 1, 7; *Kötz*, RabelsZ 50 (1986), at 16 *et seq.*; *Kötz*, Festschrift Zweigert, at 481, 495 *et seq.*

frayé la voie pendant de nombreuses années, à rédiger des Restatements similaires pour certaines matières, telles que la représentation, les règles générales des contrats, le droit des sociétés, les régimes matrimoniaux?'

Some years later, Professor *René David* submitted a similar proposal to the French Ministry of Justice, albeit without success[448]. Ten years later, in the mid-1970s, the Danish law Professor *Ole Lando*[449] brought up the idea of drafting a European Restatement of Contract Law as an alternative drafting approach to a European UCC, which proved to be too ambitious at that time[450]. The 'Commission on European Contract Law'[451], established in 1980 and chaired by Professor *Lando*, stands in the tradition of these proposals. The Commission worked as a non-governmental Working Group[452] and is therefore dependent upon financial support from the EU Commission and individual European scientific foundations. The Commission was composed of professors and practitioners active in comparative law[453]. Similar to the UNIDROIT Working Group, the *Lando* Commission realized that the field of general contract law is the most promising area in which to initiate its unification efforts. Many of the legal institutions and principles contained in the individual domestic contract laws of the EU Member States have always had a European character which is due to a common origin in the common law of the middle ages and in the doctrine of natural law[454]. The creation of general principles of law is therefore not limited to European administrative[455] and constitutional law:

> 'What is problematic . . . is not the *existence* of a series of general principles of European private law. To the contrary: If the existence of a large number of general legal principles is acknowledged in the field of constitutional and

448. *David, id.*; *cf. also van Hecke*, in: Bundel opstellen Kollewijn and Offerhaus, at 198, 201; *Kötz*, Festschrift Zweigert, at 481, 495 *et seq.*; *Drobnig*, Festschrift *Steindorff*, at 1141, 1150.
449. *See* for the vita of *Ole Lando, von Bar*, in: Newsletter European Private Law, No. 2, 1997, at 1 *et seq.*
450. *Lando*, in: Cappelletti (ed.), New Perspectives for a Common Law of Europe, at 267, 284 *et seq.*; *cf. also Lando's* account of a dinner with a prominent member of the European Commission in 1974, when the idea was raised 'we need a European Code of Obligations. Somebody should start drafting such a code', in: Cranston (ed.), Essays in Honor of Roy Goode, at 103.
451. The members were: *Hugh Beale* (since 1987), *Alberto Bercovitz* (since 1986), *Brigitte Berlioz-Houin* (until 1986), *Massimo Bianca, M.J. Bonell, I. de Magelhaes Collaco* (since 1986), *Ulrich Drobnig, André Elvinger, Dimitri Evrigenis* (until 1986), *Roy M. Goode, Guy Horsmans, Roger Houin* (until 1986), *K. Kerameus* (since 1986), *Ole Lando, Bryan McMahon, Georges Rouhette* (since 1987), *Denis Tallon, J.A. Wade, Frans J.A. van der Velden* and *William Wilson, cf. Lando/Beale* (eds.), The Principles of European Contract Law, at XIII.
452. The proposal to establish a 'European Law Commission' was never implemented, *cf.* for this project *Chloros*, Int'l Comp.L.Q. 1968, at 849, 876.
453. *Lando*, Am.J.Comp.L. 1983, at 653, 655.
454. *Zimmermann*, The Law of Obligations. Roman Foundations of the Civilian Tradition.
455. *Cf. Kadelbach*, in: von Danwitz, *et al.* (eds.), Auf dem Weg zu einer europäischen Staatlichkeit, at 131, 143 *et seq.*; *Schoch*, JZ 1995, at 109, 111 *et seq.*

> administrative law, this must also be true for private law with its rich common tradition, the multitude of recent international connections and the functional equivalent to be found in the various domestic legal systems'[456].

This necessarily leads to the methodical basis for the comparative research found by the *Lando* Commission: the functional comparative methodology[457]. In applying this methodology, the Commission not only resorted to European civil codes. It also looked at materials from outside Europe such as the American UCC, the American Restatement of the Law of Contracts and The Hague and CISG[458]. This comprehensive approach taken by the *Lando* Commission is also proof for the increasing interconnection of comparative efforts on the international plane. As a consequence of this approach, the *Lando* Commission, just like the UNIDROIT Working Group, found solutions for individual legal problems that are not to be found in the domestic European legal systems[459]. In taking this approach, the Commission benefited from the flexible, 'bottom up' rule-making of the restatement technique, as opposed to more formalized and inflexible 'top down' legislative efforts, two contrasting approaches which the founder of the Commission once analogized with the famous dispute between the two German scholars *Thibaut* and *Savigny* on the codification of German private law in the German Civil Code[460].

The first visible result of the *Lando* Commission's research efforts was published in 1995 under the title 'Principles of European Contract Law, Part I: Performance, Non-Performance and Remedies'[461]. This, however, was only the preliminary result of the Commission's work. In 1992, a Second Commission on European Contract Law began work on the formation, validity, interpretation, and content of contracts and on the authority of agents. The last meeting of this Second Commission was held in May 1996[462]. After some editorial fine-tuning and renumbering, Parts I and II of the *Lando* Principles, a synthesis of the work of the two Commissions, was finally published in early 1999[463]. Even before the promulgation of Parts I and II of the *Lando* Principles in early 1999, the *Lando* Commission had begun to prepare research for a third part of the Principles. That research focused on set-off, assignment of claims, transfer of contract, assumption of debts, plurality of parties, periods of limitation, capitalization of interest,

---

456. *Schulze*, in: Müller-Graff (ed.), Gemeinsames Privatrecht in der EG, at 127, 145 (translation by the author); *see also Metzger*, Extra legem, intra ius: Allgemeine Rechtsgrundsätze im Europäischen Privatrecht, at 157 *et seq.*
457. *Cf. Drobnig*, Festschrift Steindorff, at 1141, 1150 *et seq.*; *cf. generally supra* Chapter 2 II.A.1.
458. *Lando, supra* note 453, at 657.
459. *Drobnig*, Festschrift Steindorff, at 1141, 1151.
460. *Lando*, European Rev. Priv. L. 1997, at 525.
461. *Lando/Beale* (eds.), The Principles of European Contract Law. The *Lando* Principles are available at *http://frontpage.cbs.dk/law/commission_on_european_contract_law*.
462. *See Lando*, in: Cranston (ed.), Essays in Honor of Roy Goode, at 103, 105.
463. *Lando/Beale* (eds.), Principles of European Contract Law, Parts I and II, Prepared by The Commission on European Contract Law.

invalidity of contracts due to illegality and immorality, and the effects of infringement of mandatory rules[464]. The Third Part of the *Lando* Principles was published in 2003[465].

b. *Structure and Contents*

The first part of the Principles published in 1995 was only half of the length of the UNIDROIT Principles. It consisted of only fifty-nine articles which were divided into four chapters. The reason for this was that the first part of the *Lando* Principles was limited to general provisions and chapters on performance, non-performance, and remedies in case of non-performance. Apparently, the Commission wanted to have at least a major part of the Principles 'on the market' as soon as possible after the publication of the UNIDROIT Principles in May 1994. It was announced at that stage of the drafting process that the missing areas were to be covered at a later stage of the Commission's work[466].

Parts I and II of the Principles, prepared by the Second Commission and published in early 1999, are structured like the UNIDROIT Principles. They consist of 131 articles and contain chapters on General Provisions, on Formation, Validity, Interpretation, Contents and Effects and Performance of Contracts, on Non-Performance and Remedies in General and on particular Remedies for Non-Performance. In addition to these rules, which are also contained in the UNIDROIT project, Chapter 3 of the *Lando* Principles deals with the important issue of Authority of Agents. Part III of the Principles of 2003 consists of sixty-nine articles divided into eight chapters, dealing with Plurality of Debtors, Assignment of Claims, Substitution of New Debtor, Set-off, Prescription, Illegality, Conditions and Capitalization of Interest.

Like the UNIDROIT Principles[467], the *Lando* Principles want to be seen as more than a mere collection of general legal principles and rules. Instead, their purpose is to present a 'system' of European contract law[468]. In those areas where the UNIDROIT Working Group and the *Lando* Commission have worked on the same subject matters they have also achieved basically the same results[469]. This becomes obvious, *e.g.* in the field of hardship and *force majeure*, where both the *Lando* (Arts 6.111, 8.108) and the UNIDROIT Principles (Arts 6.2.1 *et seq.*, Art. 7.1.7)

464. The present version of the *Lando* Principles does not deal with the invalidity of the contract due to illegality, immorality or lack of capacity (Art. 4.101).
465. *Lando/Clive/Prüm/Zimmermann* (eds.), Principles of European Contract Law, Part III, Prepared by The Commission on European Contract Law.
466. *Cf. Lando/Beale* (eds.), The Principles of European Contract Law, at XXI; *cf. also Zimmermann*, JZ 1995, at 477, 480.
467. *Cf. supra* A.7.b.
468. *Lando/Beale* (eds.), *supra* note 466, at XX.
469. *Cf.* for a more detailed account of the technical and substantive divergences between the UNIDROIT and *Lando* Principles *Bonell*, in: Cranston (ed.), Essays in Honor of Roy Goode, at 91, 95 *et seq.*

arrive at similar solutions in substance, sometimes even in legal terminology. The same similarities can be found in the field of contract formation (Arts 2.101 *et seq. Lando* Principles and Arts 2.1.1 *et seq.* UNIDROIT Principles), of breach of confidentiality (Art. 2.302 *Lando* Principles and Art. 2.1.16 UNIDROIT Principles) and of the infamous battle of forms where both projects adhere to the 'knock-out' doctrine and abandon the classical 'last shot' doctrine (Art. 2.209 *Lando* Principles and Art. 2.1.22 UNIDROIT Principles). Sometimes, the rules included in the *Lando* Principles are less detailed than their UNIDROIT counterpart. This is the case for example with the provision on interest (Art. 9.508 *Lando* Principles and Art. 7.4.9 UNIDROIT Principles)[470] or proof of harm by current price (Art. 9.507 *Lando* Principles and Art. 7.4.6 UNIDROIT Principles). Sometimes, the Principles drafted by the *Lando* Commission are more explicit than the UNIDROIT Principles. For example, Art. 1.302 contains the definition of what has to be understood as 'reasonable' under the Principles. The UNIDROIT Principles do not contain such a provision. The contents and direction of this definition, especially with respect to the reference to 'the usages and practices of the trades or professions involved', however, does not exceed the (objective) standard of reasonableness that lies at the basis of many provisions of the UNIDROIT Principles[471].

Sometimes, however, the similarity between both sets of rules is not clear from the black letter text itself but has to be derived from the commentaries. Like the UNIDROIT Working Group[472], the *Lando* Commission included a provision on the relationship of the Principles to mandatory rules of domestic law. Art. 1.103(2) of the *Lando* Principles makes it clear that the Principles may not override mandatory rules of domestic, supranational or international law. However, Art. 1:103(1) also provides that where the otherwise applicable law so allows, the parties may choose to have their contract governed by the *Lando* Principles, 'with the effect that national mandatory rules are not applicable'. This provision therefore allows for the application of the Principles *via* a genuine choice of law of the parties, thus giving way to the '*kollisionsrechtliche Parteiautonomie*'[473]. This supports the view that the application of the Principles is governed by the general rules of conflicts of laws[474].

There are very few instances where one set of rules contains provisions which are not contained in the other. This applies, *e.g.* to the articles on public permissions contained in Arts 6.1.14 *et seq.* of the UNIDROIT Principles, which are not included in the *Lando* Principles since they do not deal with the invalidity of a contract arising from illegality (Art. 4.101).

---

470. *See* generally for the significance of interest claims in international arbitration *Berger*, 61 RabelsZ (1997), at 314 *et seq.*
471. *Cf. supra* A.7.b.
472. *Cf.* Art. 1.4; *cf. supra* A.9.
473. *See supra* A.10.b.
474. *Lando/Beale* (eds.), The Principles of European Contract Law, at 41.

The structure of the *Lando* Principles consists of rules and principles formulated as black-letter law and accompanied by explanations and examples. This is in line with the American Restatement of the Law of Contracts and the UNIDROIT Principles. However, there is an important structural deviation from the latter in so far as the *Lando* Principles also contain comparative 'Notes'[475]. These Notes summarize a wealth of comparative reference material pertaining to the relevant rule or principle[476]. The Notes perform two important functions. First, they attach an increased degree of authority and persuasiveness to the principle or rule to which they refer. We have dealt with this phenomenon in the context of the American Restatement of the Law of Contracts[477]. The Notes prove to be useful in those cases where the drafters of the Principles have adopted solutions that are not to be found in the European legal systems[478]. Secondly, the Notes provide an important reference point for the autonomous development and evolution of the Principles. Like the UNIDROIT Principles[479], the *Lando* Principles contain a provision providing that issues in the scope of the principles but not expressly settled by them 'are so far as possible to be settled in accordance with the ideas[480] underlying the Principles' (Art. 1.106(2)). The drafters attached a decisive role to this provision with respect to the 'creative function' of the *Lando* Principles[481]. It is through the wealth of comparative material contained in the Notes that this comparative potential of the Principles and their quality as a 'functioning system'[482] can be used in practice. Also, Art. 1.106(1) of the *Lando* Principles provides that in interpreting the Principles, the need to promote good faith and fair dealing, certainty in contractual relations and uniformity of application must always be considered. The UNIDROIT Principles refer only to the 'international character' of the Principles. However, the official commentary makes it clear that Art. 1.7, although addressed to the parties, may also be seen as an expression of the underlying purpose of the Principles, *i.e.* 'to promote the observance of good faith and fair dealing in international business'[483]. Art. 1.106(1) of the *Lando* Principles is perhaps more explicit in that it provides that not only the interpretation but also the 'development' of the Principles should be guided by their underlying purpose, thereby placing additional emphasis on the creative potential inherent in this set of rules[484].

---

475. *See Storme*, Rev.dr.int.dr.comp. 1995, at 309, 311; *Blase, supra* note 430, at 93 *et seq.*
476. *Cf. Drobnig*, Festschrift Steindorff, at 1141, 1151.
477. *Cf. supra* Chapter 3 I.B.
478. *Cf. Lando/Beale* (eds.), The Principles of European Contract Law, at XX.
479. Article 1.6; *cf. supra* A.7.b.bb.
480. The difference in terminology ('general principles of law' in the UNIDROIT Principles, 'ideas' in the *Lando* Principles) does not seem to have any substantive implications.
481. *Lando/Beale* (eds.), *supra* note 478, at XXI.
482. *Lando/Beale* (eds.), *id.*
483. *UNIDROIT* (ed.), Principles of International Commercial Contracts, at 15.
484. *See Lando*, in: Weyers (ed.), Europäisches Vertragsrecht, at 478, 93, emphasizing that 'interpretation' under the Principles has a static *and* a dynamic aspect.

c. Options for the Application of the Principles

Like the Preamble of the UNIDROIT Principles[485], Art. 1.101 of the *Lando* Principles contains a non-exhaustive list of options relating to possible fields of application. The list is based on the basic idea that the Principles are non-binding. Like the UNIDROIT Principles, the *Lando* Principles constitute a collection of rules which are considered by the drafters to form parts of the contract laws of the EU Member States[486]. The Principles may be applied to an individual contract only in those cases where the parties have concluded an expressed or implied agreement to that extent. It is important to note that Art. 1.101(2) differentiates between a genuine choice of law and the incorporation by reference. In case of an expressed choice, the parties are free, as in the case of the UNIDROIT Principles[487], to modify certain provisions or to deviate from them except in those cases where the provisions are of a mandatory *ordre public* character (Art. 1.102(2)). The Principles may also be applied when the parties have agreed that their contract be governed by 'general principles of law', the '*lex mercatoria*' or the like. Reference to the NLM in the Principles does not imply a judgment as to the legal nature of this phenomenon but merely aims to avoid the substantial problems in the finding of the law which are usually related to such clauses[488].

In drafting the list of possible options for application, the *Lando* Commission went beyond the approach chosen by the UNIDROIT Working Group. It allowed for the application of the Principles in those cases where 'the parties have not chosen any system or rules of law to govern their contract' (Art. 1.101(3)(b)). According to this formula, the Principles can be applied in case of a 'negative' choice of the parties. It has already been shown above that the assumption of such a negative choice of law involves considerable dangers especially with respect to the disregard of the parties' intention[489]. Finally, the *Lando* Principles are also of considerable significance in the development of an anticipatory method of interpretation[490]. First, Art. 1.101(4) is more explicit in that it allows for the search for new solutions when the applicable law does not do so, thus embracing the possibility of developing a comparative method of construction of domestic law[491]. Secondly, in view of their more regional character, their potential to serve as a

485. The Principles are not intended to be in competition with the UNIDROIT Principles. Art. 101 (1) makes it clear that their scope is restricted to the European sphere, while in transnational context involving at least one non-European party, the UNIDROIT Principles will apply, *see Bonell*, Unif.L.Rev. 1996, at 229, 243; *Bonell*, in: Cranston (ed.), Essays in Honor of Roy Goode, at 91, 99 *et seq.*
486. *Drobnig*, Festschrift Steindorff, at 1141, 1151.
487. Article 1.5.
488. *Cf. Lando/Beale* (eds.), The Principles of European Contract Law, at 41.
489. *Cf. supra* Chapter 2 II.F.2.a.
490. *Cf. Hartkamp*, in: Hartkamp, *et al.* (eds.), Towards a European Civil Code, at 125, 131; *cf. also supra* A.10.e.bb.
491. *Storme*, Rev.dr.int.dr.comp. 1995, at 309, 316: 'Cette idée pourrait être considerée comme une élaboration de la méthode comparative comme méthode d'interpretation du droit national . . . '.

point of comparative orientation for construing domestic European laws is much higher than that of the UNIDROIT Principles.

Finally, Art. 107 provides that the Principles apply with appropriate modifications to agreements to modify or terminate a contract, unilateral promises and other statements, and conduct indicating intention. The UNIDROIT Principles do not contain such a general provision. Instead, they contain specific provisions such as Art. 4.2, which concerns the interpretation of statements and other conduct. This provision is almost identical with Art. 8 of the CISG.

The scope of the *Lando* Principles is not limited to commercial transactions. While consumer protection was never an object of the UNIDROIT Working Group[492], consumer contracts are not automatically excluded from the scope of the *Lando* Principles[493]. Art. 1.101(1) states unequivocally that 'the Principles are intended to be applied as general rules of contract law in the European Communities'. This difference in scope explains a number of substantive divergences between both Principles[494]. It is for this reason that the good faith provision of Art. 1.201(1) requires the parties to comply with 'good faith and fair dealing', omitting the reference to 'international trade' contained in the corresponding Art. 1.7(1) of the UNIDROIT Principles[495]. Conversely, Art. 2.210, dealing with writings in confirmation and having its counterpart in Art. 2.1.12 UNIDROIT Principles, provides that it applies only to a 'professional's' written confirmation. Art. 1.105(2), dealing with the binding force of usages, does not make use of the formula employed in Art. 9(2) CISG and Art. 1.8(2) of the UNIDROIT Principles. Instead, it merely refers to usages 'which would be considered generally applicable by persons in the same situation as the parties, except where the application of such usage would be unreasonable'. Since the last part of this sentence takes up the formula used in the Sales Convention and the UNIDROIT Principles, the *Lando* Commission has simply 'de-commercialized' the trade usage provisions of the CISG and the UNIDROIT Principles.

The importance of the notion of good faith led the drafters to include the duty to cooperate in the first chapter on general provisions while the UNIDROIT Working Group decided to be more specific and to include the corresponding provision of Art. 5.3 in the chapter on the contents of the contract. This systematic difference may also have been influenced by the fact that the UNIDROIT Group was more influenced by English legal doctrine which regards good faith as an implied term of the contract while the *Lando* Commission followed the traditional European approach which qualifies good faith as a general principle of law that applies irrespective of whether a term can be implied into the contract concluded between the parties[496]. Finally, the significance of the notion of good faith is reflected in the provision on liability for breaking off negotiations in bad faith

492. *See supra* A.6.b.
493. *Lando*, Am.J.Comp.L. 1983, at 653, 656; *Blase, supra* note 430, at 110 *et seq.*
494. *See Bonell*, in: Cranston (ed.), Essays in Honor of Roy Goode, at 91, 96 *et seq.*
495. *See* for the meaning of this standard of conduct *supra* A.7.b.
496. *See supra* A.7.b.

which the drafters included in a special section on 'liability for negotiations' in the second chapter on formation of contracts (Art. 2.301). The UNIDROIT Working Group included an identical rule, but placed it in the general provisions on contract formation (Art. 2.1.15). Also, the *Lando* Principles do not contain a provision implementing the principle of freedom of form, reflected in Art. 1.2 of the UNIDROIT Principles.

The *Lando* project is not necessarily limited to international legal relationships[497]. The drafters shared the general aversion to special domestic statutes for international cases[498]. This may be a feasible approach for the unification of contract law on the EU-level, where the notion of consumer protection has always played a pivotal role[499]. However, this approach would mean the certain death for a worldwide restatement of international contract law.

d. The Lando Principles as a First Step towards a European Civil Code

It was always envisaged that in the long run, the non-binding, restatement-like principles and rules contained in the *Lando* Principles would form the basis of a European Civil Code[500]. As indicated above[501], the 'Study Group on a European Civil Code' which was established in 1998 as the successor of the *Lando* Commission, has submitted in December 2007 the Academic DCFR into which the *Lando* Principles have been incorporated in a partly revised form[502]. The approach taken by the Study Group shows that informal codification techniques, the '*Savigny*-like approach'[503], have played an important role within the work on the evolution of a European Civil Code[504]. The Study Group itself has emphasized that the DCFR is 'an academic, not a politically authorized text':

> 'It must be stressed that what we refer to today as the DCFR originates in an initiative of European legal scholars. It amounts to the *compression into rule form* of decades of independent research and co-operation by academics with expertise in private law, comparative law and European community law. The independence of the two Groups and of all the contributors has been maintained and respected unreservedly at every stage of our labours... [The DCFR] does not contain a single rule or definition or principle which has been approved or mandated by a politically legitimate body at European or national level...'[505]

497. *Lando, supra* note 493, *id.*
498. *Cf. supra* Chapter 1 II C.1.
499. *Cf. supra* 1.
500. *See supra* Chapter 3 I.E.
501. *See supra* Chapter 3 I.E.
502. *See supra* Chapter 3 I.E.
503. *See supra* note 460.
504. *See Meyer*, Principles of Contract Law und nationales Vertragsrecht, at 62.
505. *von Bar/Clive/Schulte-Nölke* (eds.), Principles, Definitions and Model Rules of European Private Law, Draft Common Frame of Reference (DCFR), Outline Edition, at 6 (emphasis added).

From the technical perspective of legal rule-making, the DCFR stands in the tradition of the UNIDROIT and *Lando* Principles in that it constitutes 'a set of rules in the form of a codification, which could be enacted by a legislature with relevant political authority'[506]. The clear preference for 'soft law' has also been acknowledged by the EU Parliament in its resolution on European contract law of December 12, 2007[507]. The Study Group on a European Civil Code also stressed the force of written legal rules[508] and expressed a preference for a 'soft law' approach to the unification of European private law by stating that the Common Frame of Reference to be developed out of the DCFR might be used as 'the basis for an additional set of legal rules which parties might choose to govern their mutual rights and obligations'[509]. In fact, in its 'Stockholm Programme' of 2009[510], the EU Commission has revived the idea of an optional purely European contract law which would not supersede the domestic contract law of the EU Member States, but to which the contracting parties may agree in lieu of the otherwise applicable contract law ('Optional Instrument').

The *Lando* Principles, their successor, the DCFR, and the underlying goal of their drafters to contribute to an 'informal Europeanisation of private law'[511] all demonstrate that the new pragmatism, which drives the creation and unification of the law on the global level[512], now also plays a major role in the development towards a European Civil Code. The idea of the persuasive force of a compilation of legal principles, definitions, and rules, derived from comparative research, has been accepted and adopted by the Study Group on a European Civil Code and the Research Group on Existing EC Private Law ('Acquis Group') as the basis of their work on the DCFR[513].

506. *Eidenmüller/Faust/Grigoleit/Wagner/Zimmermann*, JZ 2008, at 529, 533 (translation by the author).
507. *See* EU-Parliament Resolution of December 12, 2007 on European contract law, OJ of December 18, 2008, No. C 323 E/364, stating that 'the Common Frame of Reference (CFR), which the Commission intends to be a "toolbox" or handbook for the EU legislator, to be used when revising existing and preparing new legislation in the area of contract law, is not intended at present to have any binding legal effect and thus remains in the nature of soft law'.
508. *See von Bar*, in: Schulze/von Bar/Schulte-Nölke (eds.), Der akademische Entwurf für einen gemeinsamen Referenzrahmen, at 35: 'The time of a heated debate about how to deal with national legal cultures (!) has been over *due to the formulation of common rules of private law*... Today, we are finally dealing with *something concrete*, and that is a major step forward' (translation by the author, emphasis added).
509. *von Bar/Clive/Schulte-Nölke* (eds.), *supra* note 505, at 46.
510. COM(2009) 262 final; *cf. also Schulte-Nölke*, ZGS 2009, 337.
511. *See* Introduction, in: *von Bar/Clive/Schulte-Nölke* (eds.), Principles, Definitions and Model Rules of European Private Law, Draft Common Frame of Reference (DCFR), Interim Outline Edition, 2008, at 8.
512. *See supra* Chapter 2 I.B. note 40.
513. In the introduction to the 'Draft Common Frame of Reference' (DCFR), which was published in early 2008, the drafters state: 'The drafters of the DCFR nurture the hope that it will be seen... as a text from which inspiration can be gained for suitable solutions for private law questions... If the content of the DFCR convinces, it may contribute to a harmonious and

The *Lando* Principles have to be seen in a wider context. Even though initially drafted as non-binding instruments, they have provided the framework for the statutory consolidation of European private law. This development is in line with the initial impetus of *Lando's* initative towards a Restatement of European Contract Law which was seen as an alternative to, rather than a precursor of the ambitious project of drafting of a European Code of Obligations raised in 1974[514]. The restatement technique avoided the intricate technicalities of unified law-making on the EU plane, thus serving as a catalyst for the implementation of the ambitious plans to create unified European private law on a statutory basis. Now that the project for a European Civil Code has reached an advanced stage, the non-binding *ratio scripta* embodied in the *Lando* Principles is on its way to become binding statutory law as part of the envisaged EU legislation based on the DCFR, the ultimate victory of informal codification techniques over any attempt to adhere to traditional ways and means of formalized law-making.

However, one essential difference between informal rule-making on the EU level and with respect to the NLM will always remain. Within the EU, any attempt to formulate general principles of European contract law *must* take account of the legitimate expectations of the main addressees of these rules: the consumers in the EU-Single Market[515]. For that reason, the notion of freedom of contract is necessarily overshadowed by the idea that the weaker party (the consumer) must enjoy special protection *vis-à-vis* his commercial contract partner. Consumer protection requires that the non-consumer party is obliged to be more considerate of the other side's interests, and that the very concept of contract is reformulated and turned into a legal relationship with obligations for the commercial party to inform, to cooperate, and to show an enhanced degree of solidarity with the concerns and needs of the consumer-party[516]. It is for that reason that the DCFR has been heavily criticized by German scholars as paving the way for a 'massive reduction of party autonomy' and the 'transformation of dispositive contract law into mandatory and regulatory *ius cogens*'[517]. That situation is completely different in transnational business. The NLM is the transnational law of b2b-transactions. It has nothing to do with consumer protection. It is based on the idea of the presumed professional competence of merchants[518] who are capable of taking account of their own affairs. This is one of the reasons why the *Lando* Principles and any other instrument

informal Europeanisation of private law', *see von Bar, et al.* (eds.), Principles, Definitions and Model Rules of European Private Law, Draft Common Frame of Reference (DCFR), Interim Outline Edition, 2008, at 7 *et seq.; see also Schulze*, in: Schulze (ed.), The Common Frame of Reference and Existing EC Contract Law, 2008, at 3 *et seq.*

514. *See supra* 2.a. note 437.
515. *Staudenmayer*, Die Richtlinien des Verbraucherprivatrechts, in: Schulte-Nölke/Schulze (eds.), Europäische Rechtsangleichung und nationale Privatrechte, at 63 *et seq.*
516. *See e.g. Kötz*, European Contract Law, Vol. I, at 12; *von Bar/Clive/Schulte-Nölke* (eds.), at 14 *et seq.* for the DCFR.
517. *Eidenmüller/Faust/Grigoleit/Jansen/Wagner/Zimmermann, supra* note 506, at 549.
518. *See* TransLex Principle No. I.2.3, reprinted *infra* Annex III, available with further references at *www.Trans-Lex.org/909000.*

intended to reflect the European *acquis communautaire* alone do not and cannot reflect the contents of the NLM[519].

II. ESCAPING THE CODIFICATION DILEMMA: THE 'CREEPING CODIFICATION OF THE NEW *LEX MERCATORIA*'

For the NLM doctrine, the informal codification techniques discussed above cannot be the final word. In the past decades, transnational commercial law has been trapped in a codification dilemma. The experiences that have been made since the drafting of the Franco-Italian Obligation Law in 1917 revealed that a joint effort of all domestic legislatures in the codification of transnational commercial contract law is nothing but a myth. At the same time, every attempt to codify transnational commercial law would introduce a static element into this legal system which would contravene the character of the NLM as a 'law in action'. The drafting of restatements of international or European contract law is regarded as a *panacea* of this dilemma. It transforms transnational contract law into black-letter-rules while at the same time maintaining a certain degree of openness and flexibility, thereby taking account of the special character of transnational contract law. Thus, the restatements provide international legal practice with a workable set of rules and principles that can easily be applied to the solution of individual legal problems of transnational commercial law.

A. Deficiencies of the Restatement Technique

Undoubtedly, both the UNIDROIT and *Lando* Principles play a pivotal role in the movement towards the codification of the NLM. They have made practitioners aware of the necessity to codify this transnational legal system in order to achieve more predictability and legal certainty that is necessary for decision-making and dispute resolution within the international business community[520]. The restatements also provide the ideal starting point for further comparative research which is necessary to ascertain the existence of rules and principles of transnational commercial law[521] and vital for the credibility of the NLM doctrine as such[522].

In spite of the attractiveness of the restatement technique, however, there are two major reasons why this approach is not the last word in the discussion on the codification of the NLM.

---

519. *Blase, supra* note 430, at 263 *et seq.*
520. *See e.g. Raeschke-Kessler*, in: Institute of International Business Law and Practice (ed.), UNIDROIT Principles of International Commercial Contracts: A New Lex Mercatoria?, at 167, 175.
521. *Raeschke-Kessler, id.*; *see also infra* C.5.e.
522. *See supra* Chapter 2 II.A.1.

1. No Positive Statement by the Drafters as to the Existence of the New *Lex Mercatoria*

In view of the serious discussion on the viability of the NLM concept[523], the drafters of the UNIDROIT and *Lando* Principles refrained from taking an unequivocal position as to the existence of an autonomous world trade law. Taking a position in favour or against the NLM in the Principles themselves would have endangered the success of both projects.

The price paid by the drafters is high. There is considerable uncertainty among practitioners as to the legal quality of the restatements. Some even doubt that there can be 'different leges mercatoriae claiming to be the law'[524], thus misinterpreting the true legal nature of the Principles. The restatements cannot serve *in and of themselves* as a sufficient indication for the existence and the contents of transnational commercial law[525]. In order to be considered part of the NLM, every rule and principle contained in them needs to be verified against international commercial and arbitral practice, one of the major sources of transnational law[526]. This time- and cost-intensive procedure, however, would lead to considerable law-finding problems which the restatements were intended to avoid.

2. Restatements as a 'Comparative Snapshot'

The second problem with the restatement technique relates to the fact that both the UNIDROIT and *Lando* Principles are nothing more than a 'comparative snapshot' of that part of transnational contract law which was discernible during the drafting process. Every attempt 'to capture [the lex mercatoria] in the tight meshes of a codification'[527] as well as every effort to force the NLM into a rigid system of legal concepts and notions[528] would not do justice to the flexible character of the NLM:

> '... the new transnational lex mercatoria is likely to be of a dynamic nature, often expressed in practices that may change overnight if business logic or market forces so require. The search is therefore on for a forward-moving set of internationalized, uniform principles and rules that may be largely

523. *See supra* Chapter 2 I.A.
524. *See Raeschke-Kessler*, in: Institute of International Business Law and Practice (ed.), UNIDROIT Principles of International Commercial Contracts: A New Lex Mercatoria?, at 167, 174.
525. *See supra* I.A.10.b.
526. *Cf. Kahn*, in: Bonell/Bonelli (eds.), Contratti Commerciali Internazionali E Principi Unidroit, at 41, 45; *Giardina*, in: Institute of International Business Law and Practice (ed.), UNIDROIT Principles of International Commercial Contracts: A New Lex Mercatoria?, at 145, 151; *see generally supra* Chapter 2 II.G.3.c.
527. *Bärmann*, Festschrift Mann, at 547, 549.
528. *Cf. Horn*, NJW 1967, at 601, 608.

> articulated by participants themselves and draws widely from their practical needs, established ways of dealing, best practices, trade organization rules, and from the innate rationality of their international dealings'[529].

The requirements of the NLM doctrine for extreme flexibility and openness of any process directed towards the codification of its principle and rules has long since been criticized as irreconcilable with the 'petrification' of the law which necessarily goes along with any codification process. From the outset, drafting a collection of rules and principles of the NLM in the form a self-contained 'codification' would exclude, at least for a certain period of time, a magnitude of legal issues and solutions which a topical, *i.e.* case law oriented and open-ended method of codification would be better able to cover[530]. In other words, more than in any other field of law, codification of the NLM is dependent upon the creation of an irreconcilable balance: the untying of the Gordian Knot created by the need for legal certainty on one hand and the quest for maximum flexibility on the other.

It follows from this that in order to provide international legal practice with the necessary working tools to handle the NLM, a redefinition of the traditional 'codification' techniques is required. 'Codification' of the NLM should not be understood in the technical, literal sense. Instead, we have to look for new, progressive codification techniques which can be reconciled with the flexible and elastic nature of the NLM.

B. 'Codification' Versus 'Progressive Development': Irreconcilable Contradiction or Redefinition of Traditional Codification Techniques?

Those who acknowledge that the law and traditional codification techniques cannot keep pace with the dynamism inherent in modern commerce ask whether one should not accept that: (1) domestic law provides a stable framework within which businessmen can act; (2) codification of the NLM is useless and, in any event; (3) the NLM's role is limited to supplementing and filling of gaps in domestic law[531]. That view clearly reveals that the discussion on possible ways to codify the NLM has serious repercussions on the question whether the NLM exists. While the initial ideas and initiatives related to the codification of the NLM have caused a marked shift away from dogmatic trench fighting to pragmatic rule-making[532], this view reintroduces the purely theoretic debate based on the allegation that the NLM is not apt for codification.

529. *Dalhuisen*, Berkeley J. Int'l L. 2006, at 129, 133.
530. *Cf. Osman*, Lex Mercatoria, at 459; *cf.* for the evolution of a European *ius commune Knütel*, ZEuP 1994, at 244, 268.
531. *Ipsen*, Private Normenordnungen als Transnationales Recht?, at 171.
532. *See supra* Introduction B.2.

We now have before us the basic dilemma of every attempt to codify transnational commercial law. Practical necessities require the codification of the NLM, *i.e.* the transformation of common legal convictions and notions into black-letter law. Such a collection of rules and principles of the NLM would not only lead to clarity and transparency. It would also ensure a certain degree of substantive control of this legal system. That would allow for protection of that system against the danger of the unilateral preservation of interests in purely contractual arrangements. However, the flexible and versatile nature of the NLM is resistant to the application of traditional codification techniques.

Acknowledging that intrinsic dilemma of the NLM doctrine does not mean that nothing can be done to overcome it. Before accepting the dominant role of domestic laws in international commerce, one should look for innovative methods to codify the NLM. The same problem is known from public international law (*infra* 1.). Based on the observations made in this Study, a new and progressive codification technique will be developed which does justice to the nature and character of the NLM (*infra* 2.).

1. The Codification of Public International Law Through the International Law Commission

The parallels between the NLM concept and public international law have been frequently emphasized[533]. Even though the streams of literature on the two systems have developed in almost total isolation from each other, public international law provides a rich field of inspiration for the transnational commercial lawyer[534]. Some even contend that the NLM is part of public international law, since the classical dual approach to legal sources – domestic legal systems on the one hand, public international law on the other – does not allow for the existence of a 'third' legal system[535]. In view of these parallels between the NLM and public international law, important cross-fertilizations can be achieved in the area of 'codification'. In the field of public international law, it is the task of the International Law Commission (ILC)[536] to work towards the 'codification' and 'progressive development' of public international law through negotiating and drafting international treaties[537]. For example, since 2000 the ILC has been

533. *Goode*, ICLQ 1997, at 1; *Molineaux*, J.Int'l Arb. 1997, issue 1, at 55, 66.
534. *Goode, id.*
535. *Booysen*, RabelsZ 59 (1995), at 245, 252 *et seq.*; this view is based on the assumption that identical legal sources cannot lead to two different legal systems, *id.*, at 253. However, even though there is no exact borderline between transnational 'private' law and 'public' international law, the sources of the *lex mercatoria* and public international law are by no means identical, in particular with respect to the case law of international commercial arbitration.
536. *Cf.* UN Doc. A/Res. 174 (II) of November 21, 1947 Establishment of an International Law Commission, GAOR 2d Sess. Res. 105.
537. *Cf. generally Thirlway*, International customary law and codification, at 61 *et seq.*

attempting to codify, in a series of draft articles, the law on the responsibility of international organizations (IOs). These draft articles address the nature of internationally wrongful acts committed by IOs[538].

Parts of legal doctrine consider this task as a *contradictio in se*. In their eyes, it is impossible to combine the functions of codifying and developing the law in one institution. They argue that such an approach must lead to confusion, since it remains unclear whether a convention drafted by the ILC has a mere declaratory character reflecting existing public international law or whether the draft would be intended to create new rules or at least to consolidate rules and principles of public international law[539].

It goes without saying that there are obvious parallels between the work of the ILC and the codification of transnational commercial law, because also in the NLM context, the use of the functional comparative methodology does not only lead to the consolidation but also to the creation of new or 'better' rules of commercial law that are not to be found in domestic legal systems[540].

2. The Search for a New Codification Method

It would be premature to deduce from the above considerations that transnational commercial law cannot be codified, that it is 'by its very nature un-codified'[541] and that international legal practice has to cope with the considerable problems relating to the determination of the rules and principles that form part of the NLM.

Instead, one has to look for possible ways to adjust the traditional means of codification to the particular needs of the transnational legal system. These adaptations must comply with two basic prerequisites. First, the openness of the legal system requires an open method of codification. Besides meeting the needs of an open legal system, the new method of codification also has to ensure the practicability of the NLM doctrine in everyday legal practice. Secondly, the method of codification has to ensure that legal principles and rules do in fact belong to the NLM and do not just constitute preliminary stages such as customs or trade usages. Since the idea of the institutional creation of the NLM involves its acceptance by international legal practice, the new method of codification has to include recourse to the extensive case law of international arbitral tribunals and to international drafting practice. Since this case law and drafting practice are much more diversified and voluminous than in public international law, the chances of developing a successful and workable method for the codification of transnational commercial law should not be underestimated.

538. *See http://untreaty.un.org/ilc/guide/9_11.htm.*
539. *Zamora*, GYIL 32 (1989), at 9, 22.
540. *Cf. supra* Chapter 2 II.A.1.b.
541. *Goode, supra* note 137, at 2; *cf. also Perales Viscasillas*, Ariz.J.Int'l & Comp.L. 1996, at 383, 397, stating that judges may find it difficult to apply the UNIDROIT Principles as *lex mercatoria*, since the latter 'is generally identified as a source of unwritten law'.

C. THE NEW CONCEPT: THE 'CREEPING CODIFICATION' OF THE NEW *LEX MERCATORIA*

Since the publication of the first edition of this book, academics and practitioners alike have acknowledged that the idea of the 'Creeping Codification'[542] through the drafting of lists of rules and principles of the NLM may provide an escape out of the codification dilemma of transnational commercial law, a dilemma which has trapped the NLM doctrine for decades[543]. It has been argued by renowned international arbitrators that the process of privatized law-making 'has aptly been described as the "Creeping Codification of the lex mercatoria" '[544] and that:

> '[The Creeping Codification of the NLM through a] list . . . is a tremendous achievement . . . It perfectly represents the trend associated with the development of what has been identified as the new, new *lex mercatoria.* For its scholarship, detail and thoroughness, the list puts the lie to the claim that it is not possible to point to, and thus not possible to consider basing commercial relationships on, a discrete body of transnational commercial norms. Berger's "creepy code" is undeniably a major contribution to the field of transnational law. . . . the most significant contribution is not the list *per se*, but the *technique* that gave rise to it and is meant to ensure its open-endedness and continuing evolution: the technique of Creeping Codification.
>
> *. . . it is evident that the idea of "the list" . . . is as close as we've come, in recent generations, to tackling the lex and wrestling it into usable shape'*[545].

---

542. *See* for the introduction of this terminology *Berger*, International Economic Arbitration, at 543; *Berger*, Am.Rev.Int'l Arb. 1993, at 1, 29; *see also Lando*, The Harmonization of European Contract Law through a Restatement of Principles, at 20.
543. *See e.g. Redfern/Hunter* on International Arbitration, No. 3.174; *Ipsen*, Private Normenordnungen als Transnationales Recht?, at 45 *et seq.*, at 86 ('There seems to be agreement that these lists portray the core of the *lex mercatoria*') and 96 *et seq.*; *Lando*, Am.J.Comp.L. 2005, at 379, 384: '[The] list is well documented and a remarkable achievement; its usefulness cannot be underestimated'; *Frischkorn*, Eur. J. L. Reform 2005, at 331, 338 *et seq.; Lando*, Europ.Rev.Priv.L. 1997, at 525: 'The *Savignys* want a creeping harmonization of [European] private law, to use an expression borrowed from the German writer Klaus Peter Berger'; *Molineaux*, J. Int'l Arb. 2000, issue 1, at 147, 150: ' . . . the list looks forward and provides an incentive for the future evolution of transnational commercial law as an open legal system . . . There can be no doubt that this is a list which will become a *sine qua non* reference and . . . a launch point for research for international arbitration practitioners and arbitrators'; *Pryles*, Mealey's Int'l Arb. Rep., February 2003, at 1, 21, 25 *et seq.*; *Blase*, Die Grundregeln des Europäischen Vertragsrechts als Recht grenzüberschreitender Verträge, at 275, footnote 307; *Brunner*, Force Majeure and Hardship under General Contract Principles, at 12; *see* from the perspective of the Iran-US Claims Tribunal *Brunetti*, Arb. Int'l 2002, at 355 *et seq.* surveying the Tribunal's jurisprudence relating to selected rules of the author's list; *see also Gopalan*, J.L. & Com. 2004, at 117, 145; *Metzger*, Extra legem, intra ius: Allgemeine Rechtsgrundsätze im Europäischen Privatrecht, at 530, 543; *Winiger*, ASA Bull. 1992, at 565; *Addor*, AJP 1993, at 357, 358; *Bungert*, VersR 1993, at 36, 37; *Hausmann*, in: Reithmann/Martiny (eds.), Internationales Vertragsrecht, No. 3522; *see generally* for the drafting of 'systematic surveys on the autonomous law practiced by arbitrators' *Stein*, Lex mercatoria, at 167.
544. *Brower/Sharpe*, Va. J. Int'l L. 2004, at 199, 201.
545. *Fortier*, Arb. Int'l 2001, at 121, 127 (= ICSID Rev.-FILJ 2001, at 10, 18).

The Creeping Codification has been the subject of comparative academic research[546]. The list reproduces all those rules and principles of the NLM as black-letter law which have been accepted in international arbitral and contract practice together with comprehensive comparative references. The list unifies the various sources that have fostered the evolution of a transnational commercial legal system into one single, open-ended set of rules and principles: reception of general principles of law, codification of international trade law by 'formulating agencies'[547], case law of international arbitral tribunals, the law-making forces of international model contract forms and general conditions of trade, and the analysis of comparative legal science. Scientific research in this area of highly practical law is of particular relevance because many authors of case notes, articles, and books on transnational commercial law are themselves active in the field of international commercial arbitration[548]. It is, therefore, not necessary to advocate the acceptance and promotion of the efforts of international practice through legal doctrine[549]. The often heard prejudice that the NLM doctrine is purely theoretical[550] is unjustified as long as the list reflects comparative research *and* the comprehensive case load of international arbitral tribunals which play a pivotal role in the evolution of transnational commercial law. It is this comprehensive coverage of all possible sources of the NLM which provides the necessary legitimacy and authority to the rules and principles contained in the list.

With this approach, the idea of the list stands in the tradition of the Digests of common law published in the first half of the twentieth century. What was stated by *Edward Jenks* in the Preface of his 'A Digest of English Civil Law' of 1921 applies with equal justification to the idea of the Creeping Codification through a comprehensive list of principles and rules of the NLM:

> 'A Digest differs from a Code, mainly in that it professes merely to state the rules which are covered by existing authority. It claims – at least, when it is the work of purely private authors – no other respect than that which is derived from a belief that it represents an honest, intelligent, and industrious attempt to reduce the chaos of existing materials to simplicity and order.
>
> [...]

546. *See e.g. Ipsen, supra* note 543, at 96 *et seq.*; *see also* the Master Thesis by *Emmanuel Lamaud*, 'Comparison between the CENTRAL List and the Vienna Convention for the International Sale of Goods – Specific Topics', available at *www.trans-lex.org/850000*.
547. *Cf. supra* Chapter 2 II.D.1.
548. Thus, *Paulsson* and *Mustill* (*see infra* notes 577, 578), who have both drafted lists of general principles and rules of transnational commercial law, are both active in the practice of international commercial arbitration.
549. *Cf. Langen*, Studien zum Internationalen Wirtschaftsrecht, No. 11.
550. *Cf. also* from the perspective of public international law *Baade*, in: Horn (ed.), Legal Problems of Codes of Conduct for MNEs, at 407, 413: '... whenever the volume of learned comment outstrips the supply of "hard" decisional law, and especially wherever scholarly discussion starts to feed on itself, it loses touch with reality'; *cf. also supra* Chapter 2 II.D.1.

> The chief intellectual effort demanded of the authors of the work has been to extract, by appropriate treatment, from this formless heap of statutes and judicial decisions, the rules which such authorities enunciate and expound, and to arrange those rules in the most convenient and accessible form'[551].

The emphasis on arbitral case law distinguishes the list from the UNIDROIT Principles. For the work of the UNIDROIT Working Group, awards of international arbitral tribunals played only a subordinate role. Even though they provide a clear, detailed, and analytical picture of the present state of international commercial contract law, the UNIDROIT Principles are characterized by a certain degree of 'analytical indifference' resulting from the fact that the international business community and its dispute settlement techniques were not a major focus of its research. It has already been emphasized above that international commercial arbitration provides a particularly fertile ground for the development and evolution of principles and rules of transnational commercial law because it is an inherent characteristic of the arbitral process itself that counsel and arbitrators alike present arguments based on comparative research[552]. In this manner, arbitration showcases views, arguments and background information which are necessary for a topical method of the finding of the law[553]. Arbitral procedures therefore perform a dual function in the context of the Creeping Codification of the NLM. First, parties and arbitrators are the primary addressees of the rules and principles contained in the list. Secondly, international arbitral procedures provide the procedural *substratum* for the 'discovery' of new rules and principles of the NLM which will then be included in the list.

This open-end character requires the constant updating and extension of the list and thus meets the needs of the NLM as dynamic 'law in action'. Conversely, it could also restrict the effectiveness and usefulness of the list. Practical problems will arise in those cases where an arbitrator or international practitioner is faced with a legal problem and finds no relevant rule or principle in the list. Similar to the UNIDROIT Principles[554] however, the 'new' rule or 'new' legal principle that is necessary to solve the issue may be derived out of the material that is already contained in the list. The principal purpose of the list is not only to look back and provide a picture of the *status quo* of the NLM, but also to look forward and provide an incentive for the future evolution of transnational commercial law as an open legal system[555].

---

551. *Jenks* (ed.), A Digest of English Civil Law (1921), at iii *et seq.; see also Broom*, A Selection of Legal Maxims (1939), at v: 'If, then, it be true that a knowledge of first principles is at least as essential in Law as in other sciences, certainly in none is a knowledge of those principles, unaccompanied by a sufficient investigation of their bearing and practical application, more likely to lead into grievous error.'
552. *Cf. Berger*, Internationale Wirtschaftsschiedsgerichtsbarkeit, at 371.
553. For '*per omnes locos tractare*' *cf. Zippelius*, Juristische Methodenlehre, at 88; *cf. also Stein*, Lex Mercatoria, at 168.
554. *Cf. supra* I.A.7.b.bb.
555. *Cf.* for details *supra* Chapter 2 II.G.2.

A danger may also arise if parties to an international arbitration base their transnational legal arguments on different lists, thereby initiating a 'battle of lists'[556]. In view of the special character of the NLM, however, the scenario should rather be considered as a chance for the further evolution and development of transnational commercial law. If the lists do not just reflect rules and principles of the NLM '*in abstracto*' but contain comprehensive comparative references, arbitrators and counsel are given the opportunity to analyse these references and to come to the conclusion that in spite of textual discrepancies the rules and principles contained in both lists are equal in substance. Admittedly, even the Creeping Codification through a list of principles and rules of the NLM may not remove all the uncertainties connected with the application of transnational commercial law. These uncertainties are a natural consequence of the openness of the NLM as 'law in action'. The constant evolution and changing picture of international trade and commerce require a corresponding flexibility of the applicable transnational law.

Another basic difference between the UNIDROIT and *Lando* Principles on the one hand and the Creeping Codification through a list of principles and rules on the other relates to the fact that the list is not limited to the field of international commercial *contract* law. Rather, the list follows the decision-making practice of international arbitration and therefore contains legal principles that are related to those fields of law which play a predominant role in international arbitral case law, such as international company law, conflict of laws, rules of evidence, the international law of expropriation and general arbitration law. The list thereby provides an additional indication for a wider understanding of the notion of 'international economic law'[557]. At the same time, the idea of an open-ended list shows that the progressive Creeping Codification of the NLM is not adequately reflected in the restatement technique in view of its limited coverage. The Creeping Codification of the NLM through the drafting of lists of rules and principles of transnational commercial law may not be substituted by the publication of restatements of international contract law. Each project has different objectives. The restatements only provide valuable incentives and starting points for the extension and evolution of the list.

1. Previous Efforts to Draft Lists of General Principles and Rules of the New *Lex Mercatoria*

Even in the ancient law merchant, collections of rules and principles of the *lex mercatoria* were published for use by the community of merchants. The most famous among them are the fifteenth century Catalonian compilation edited by the Consulate of Barcelona and known as '*The Consulate of the Sea*'[558] and the

556. *See Brunner*, Force Majeure and Hardship under General Contract Principles, at 21.
557. *Cf. supra* I.A.6.b.
558. *See Iglesia Ferreirós*, in: Petit (ed.), Del Ius Mercatorum Al Derecho Mercantil, at 109, 112 *et seq.*; *cf. also Goode*, ICLQ 1997, at 1, 17.

'*Little Red Book of Bristol*' published in the thirteenth century and containing the famous text '*Incipit lex mercatoria, que, quando, ubi, inter quos et de quibus sit.*'[559]. The '*Rôles d'Oléron*', a compilation of maritime principles and decisions dating back to the eleventh century consolidated principles and rules defining the rights and obligations of the parties to an outward sea voyage carrying a cargo of wine from La Rochelle or Bordeaux to Brittany, Normandy, England, Scotland or Flanders[560].

Drafting lists of general principles and rules of transnational law also has a certain tradition in the context of the NLM. However, the far-reaching consequences of this procedure for the 'Creeping Codification' of transnational law have never been realized. In almost all of these cases, the lists merely served as a means to prove that the NLM is not devoid of contents[561]. In many cases these lists were not included in a special annex, but rather formed part of the text of the study. Consequently, a codifying effect of these lists was never discussed and no attempts were ever made to develop these list procedures into an independent and autonomous codifying technique for transnational commercial law. In fact, international legal practice has criticized the fact that the existing lists were not found in the normal places to which judges, arbitrators and lawyers could turn: '[t]he occasional law review article is no substitute for a code or, in common law jurisdictions, line of judicial opinions'[562].

Lists of this kind were drafted both in the field of public international law (on the basis of Art. 38(1)(c) of the ICJ Statute) and in the area of transnational commercial law. The first substantial effort in this direction was made by *Georges Ripert*. In 1933 he presented a comprehensive collection of general principles of private law which, in his view, could also be utilized in the field of public international law[563]. He referred to 'modern trends towards the unification of domestic private laws' and referred in this context to the work of the newly founded UNIDROIT and the drafting of the Franco-Italian Obligation Law[564]. *Ripert* regarded these developments as a strong indication for the existence of common principles and rules ('*fonds commun*') in the legal systems of the world[565].

---

559. *See Coquillette*, in: Petit (ed.), Del ius Mercatorum Al Derecho Mercantil, at 143 *et seq.*; facsimile of the first page reproduced at *www.Trans-Lex.org/000008*.
560. *See Shephard*, in: Piergiovanni (ed.), From *Lex Mercatoria* to Commercial Law, at 207, 212 (with a compilation of the texts of the various versions *id.*, at 213 *et seq.*); *cf. also http://chapiteaux.free.fr/les%20roles.htm; see* for the Flemish version *www.tzwin.be/waterrecht.htm*.
561. *Cf. Bonell*, RabelsZ 42 (1978), at 485, 498, note 41; *Bucher*, in: Schwind (ed.), Aktuelle Fragen zum Europarecht aus der Sicht in- und ausländischer Gelehrter, at 11, 15 *et seq.*
562. *Selden*, Ann.Surv.Int'l & Compl.L. 1995, at 111, 119.
563. *Ripert*, Les Règles du Droit Civil Applicables Aux Rapports Internationaux, Rec.Cours 1933-II, at 569, 588 *et seq.*
564. *Ripert, id.*, at 585; as to UNIDROIT *see supra* I.A.; *see* for the draft of a Franco-Italian Law of Obligations *supra* Chapter 3 I.A.
565. *Ripert, supra* note 563, at 586.

In 1956, *Josef Esser*, who was strongly influenced by the works of *Ripert*[566], was amazed to see 'what a long list of such universal institutions could be found in the field of private law alone'[567] and used this research for his own collection of general principles of private law[568]. In 1953 *Bin Cheng* devoted a *maius opus* to the collection of general principles of public international law[569]. This collection included principles that were derived not only from private law but also from general procedural law and genuine public international law. All of these studies were limited to the collection of general principles of law which are mentioned in Art. 38(1)(c) of the ICJ Statute. They do not take account of the economic aspects of transnational law such as customs, usages and the case law of international arbitral tribunals which play such a pivotal role in the evolution and development of the NLM[570]. These lists therefore only reflect one aspect of the NLM doctrine: the reception of general principles of law[571]. Nevertheless, for this limited purpose, these studies present valuable guidelines for the development of a modern theory of 'Creeping Codification' of transnational commercial law.

In the field of international commercial arbitration, various attempts have been made in the past to draft lists of general principles and rules of an autonomous world trade law. In 1993, the 'Institute of International Business Law and Practice' of the ICC and the Committee for International Commercial Arbitration of the International Law Association presented a study on 'transnational rules in international commercial arbitration' which contained a detailed analysis of various principles of the NLM[572]. The fathers of the NLM doctrine, *Goldman*[573], *Fouchard*[574], and *Schmitthoff*[575], always included in their theoretical considerations a list of rules and principles of transnational commercial law. These lists have been completed and refined[576] through the studies of *Mustill*[577], *Paulsson*[578],

566. *Cf. Esser*, Grundsatz und Norm, at 14, note 40, at 37, note 119 and at 379, notes 191–194.
567. *Esser, id.*, at 37.
568. *Esser, supra* note 566, at 346 *et seq.*
569. *Bin Cheng*, General Principles of Law as applied by International Courts and Tribunals, published first in 1953, reprinted in 1987.
570. *Cf. Esser, supra* note 566, at 342: 'The evolution of principles that are freed from the constraints of domestic legal history and law, is directly connected with international arbitral practice'; *cf. also Stein*, Lex Mercatoria, at 169 *et seq.*
571. *Cf. supra* Chapter 2 II.A.2.c.
572. *Cf.* the contributions of *van Houtte* (changed circumstances and *pacta sunt servanda*), *Bowden* (L'interdiction de se contredire au détriment d'autrui), *Bernardini* (Duty to cooperate), *O'Neill/Salam* (Exceptio non adimpleti contractus), *Rivkin* (*Force majeure*), *Hanotiau* (Principles on calculation of damages) and *Karrer* (Interest) in: Gaillard (ed.), Transnational Rules in International Commercial Arbitration, at 105 *et seq.*
573. *Goldman*, in: Lew (ed.), Contemporary Problems in International Arbitration, at 113, 125 *et seq.*
574. *Fouchard*, L'Arbitrage Commercial International, at 423 *et seq.*
575. *Schmitthoff*, International Trade Usages, at 47.
576. *Cf. Kahn*, in: Gaillard (ed.), Transnational Rules in International Commercial Arbitration, at 237, 241.
577. *Mustill*, Arb.Int'l 1988, at 86 *et seq.* (reprint from: *Liber Amicorum for Lord Wilberforce*, 1987).
578. *Paulsson*, Rev.d'Arb. 1990, at 82 *et seq.* (limited to the case law of ICC arbitral tribunals).

Blessing[579], and other authors from the field of international commercial arbitration[580]. *Molineaux* has presented a list of principles that is said to be part of a '*lex constructionis*' as a distinct legal area from or within the NLM[581]. *Magnus* and *Ferrari* and others have derived general principles from the CISG[582]. Academics from the *Garrigues* Chair of Global Law at the University of *Navarra* in Spain have published a voluminous list of 1,000 principles, rules and aphorisms of 'Global Law'[583]. It is this process of refinement and consolidation which makes the idea of an open-ended list of the NLM so valuable for international legal practice.

In its January 1997 Newsletter, the Cairo Regional Centre for International Commercial Arbitration (CRCICA) presented a list of twenty-six legal principles that were up to then adopted by the arbitral tribunals in cases arbitrated under the auspices of the Centre[584]. Interestingly enough, the structure of CRCICA's list is very similar to the TransLex Principles reprinted in Annex III of this Study. Starting with such basic notions as '*pacta sunt servanda*' and 'good faith', the list also comprises more concrete rules relating to such basic and fundamental issues as 'penal clauses', '*force majeure*', 'navigation agents of shipping lines', 'interest for delay', 'the causality relation', 'responsibility of the consulting engineer' and 'contractual liability'. It is important to note that this is the first time that a renowned international arbitral institution has made use of the list-idea to publish a compilation of principles without recourse to any domestic legal system. A more recent list has not been published by the Centre. However, since 1985, the awards rendered under the auspices of the CRCICA have been published in two collections[585], thereby creating more transparency with respect to the way in which the arbitral tribunals acting under the rules of the Centre have reached their conclusions.

Finally, in an ICC Award rendered in 1996, the arbitral tribunal applied the NLM and listed eight principles and rules which, in its view, form part of

579. *Blessing*, in: Böckstiegel (ed.), Die internationale Schiedsgerichtsbarkeit in der Schweiz (II), at 13, 68 *et seq.*
580. *Braeckmans*, TvPr. 1986, at 55 *et seq.*; *Lowenfeld*, Arb.Int'l 1990, at 148; *Crook*, Am.J.Int'l L. 1989, at 292 *et seq.*; *Langen*, Transnationales Recht, Part I, No. 19 *et seq.*; *Craig/Park/Paulsson*, International Chamber of Commerce Arbitration, at 621 *et seq.*; *Note*, Harv. L. Rev. 1988, at 1816 *et seq.*; *Seidl-Hohenfeldern*, AJIL 1959, at 853, 854 *et seq.*; *Berger*, Internationale Wirtschaftsschiedsgerichtsbarkeit, at 374 *et seq.*; *Berger*, International Economic Arbitration, at 544 *et seq.*
581. *Molineaux*, J.Int'l Arb. 1997, issue 1, at 55, 64 *et seq.*; *see* also for the application of 'international rules of construction contracts' in arbitral practice ICC Award No. 4650, YCA 1987, at 113.
582. *Magnus*, RabelsZ 59 (1995), at 469, 475 *et seq.*; *Ferrari*, JZ 1998, at 9, 11 *et seq.*
583. *Domingo/Ortega/Rodriguez-Antolin/Zambrana*, Principios de Derecho Global, 1000 reglas, principios y aforismos jurídicos comentados, at 31 *et seq.*
584. The Cairo Regional Centre for International Commercial Arbitration (ed.), A Newsletter of CRCICA, January 1997, at 2 *et seq.*, also available at *www.trans-lex.org/400300.*
585. *Alam-Eldin*, Arbitral Awards of the Cairo Regional Centre for International Commercial Arbitration, two volumes.

the NLM[586]. This is the first international arbitral award, in which the arbitral tribunal did not content itself with a mere definition of the NLM and the restatement of one single rule which it needed for the resolution of the particular legal issue before it. Instead, it listed a whole number of these principles and rules in order to make its award more palatable and persuasive for the parties and the courts which will be called upon to enforce the award[587].

The inherent potential of this codification technique is not only reflected by its adoption by international arbitral institutions but also in the substantial growth which these lists have witnessed in the past years. While the initial lists contained only five, seven or nine principles[588], *Mustill* was able to present a list in 1987 that included twenty principles and rules of transnational commercial law[589]. *Goldman's* view[590] that the principles and rules contained in these lists would provide sufficient material to solve the overwhelming majority of legal issues that occur in international commercial disputes appears overly optimistic. *Mustill* himself acknowledges that his list merely reflects the contents of the NLM as it is *alleged* by the proponents of transnational commercial law. *Mustill* himself had considerable reservations about some of the principles[591].

2. Contribution of the Lists to the Discussion of the New *Lex Mercatoria* Doctrine

The lists do not only perform an important function as a bridge over the 'abyss between doctrinal formula and practical thinking'[592]. They also have an independent scientific value for the further evolution of transnational commercial law. Through abstraction from the various sources of transnational commercial law[593], they provide a realistic picture of the contents of the NLM, thereby filling the theoretical discussion with practical life and verifying the thesis of the

586. ICC Award No. 8365, Clunet 1997, at 1078, 1079 *et seq.*; the principles listed in the award are: (1.) pacta sunt servanda; (2.) good faith; (3.) duty to negotiate in good faith; (4.) resolution of contract in case of substantial breach by one of the parties; (5.) prohibition to prevent the performance of one's own obligation through a wilful act; (6.) venire contra factum proprium; (7.) interpretation of contracts according to the principle of 'ut res magis valeat quam pereat'; and (8.) principle of implied consent by conduct.
587. *See Arnaldez*, Comment to ICC Award No. 8365, Clunet 1997, at 1080, 1081.
588. *Cf. Schmitthoff*, International Trade Usages, at 47 (five); *Note*, Harv. L. Rev. 1988, at 1816, 1826 *et seq.* (seven); *Molineaux, supra* note 581, *id.* (nine).
589. *Mustill*, Arb. Int'l 1988, at 110 *et seq.*; *Molineaux*, J. Int'l Arb. 1997, issue 1, at 55, 56 *et seq.*; *cf. also Magnus*, RabelsZ 59 (1995), at 469, 480 (for UN Sales Law).
590. *Goldman*, Festschrift Lalive, at 241, 243.
591. *Mustill*, Arb. Int'l 1988, at 86, 110, footnote 82; *cf. also Weise*, Lex Mercatoria, at 124.
592. *Esser*, Grundsatz und Norm, at 335.
593. General principles of law, international conventions, standard-form contracts, domestic laws, general conditions of trade, trade usages, customs, international arbitral case law and scientific sources, *see* for the sources of the *lex mercatoria Goldman*, Festschrift Lalive, at 241, 242; *Mustill*, Arb.Int'l 1988, at 86, 109; *Goldstajn*, in: Volken/Sarcevic (eds.), International Sale of Goods, Dubrovnik Lectures, at 55, 99.

existence of an autonomous transnational commercial legal system[594]. This theoretical aspect has important repercussions on transnational legal practice. The list provides a clearly defined, flexible legal framework for the controlled application of the NLM[595]. It has been characterized as the '*coup de grâce*' for the NLM doctrine that the tremendous amount of academic attention devoted to it has only given rise to a very limited number of principles[596]. The consolidation and autonomization of transnational commercial law that goes along with the drafting of these lists can therefore be viewed as a basic prerequisite in regarding the parties' reference to the NLM as a genuine choice of law[597]. The resulting inclusion of the NLM doctrine in traditional conflicts of law concepts ensures that arbitral awards based on autonomous world trade law will not be set aside by domestic courts. The same applies to a refusal of recognition and enforcement of international arbitral awards abroad unless the award suffers from a general grave mistake in the application of the law that has been described above[598]. This is in line with the 'Resolution on Transnational Legal Principles', adopted by the International Law Association on its 65th conference on April 26, 1992, in Cairo[599]. This Resolution established a direct link between the validity of international arbitral awards based on the NLM and the consolidation and stabilization of transnational commercial law.

Finally and most importantly, the idea of drafting an open-ended list of principles and rules of the NLM does away with one of the major objections raised against the NLM doctrine: the criticism[600] that this allegedly unstructured and heterogeneous legal mass poses considerable problems for everyday legal practice because its contents are so difficult to determine. These lists therefore prove that the NLM doctrine is still alive and in a process of constant evolution.

3. The Role of General Principles of Law

Transnational commercial law which is focused solely on general principles of law or on technically detailed legal rules is not viable. This is reflected in the experience with the project of the American Cornell Law School, which focused solely on the technical issue of the formation of international contracts[601], and the

---

594. *See Schwab*, ZZP 107 (1994), at 118; *cf.* for a more careful view *Magnus*, RabelsZ 59 (1995), at 469, 491: '. . . they seem to reflect generalized notions of the basic structure of mutual contractual relationships as a whole' (translation by the author).
595. *Cf. generally Horn*, NJW 1967, at 601, 608.
596. *Gaillard*, in: van den Berg (ed.), Efficient Arbitration Proceedings – The Law Applicable in International Arbitration, at 570, 571.
597. *Böckstiegel*, Der Staat, at 144; *cf. also Kappus*, RIW 1990, at 788, 791.
598. *Cf. supra* Chapter 2 II.F.2.a.
599. 'Resolution on Transnational Rules Adopted at the 65th International Law Association Conference in Cairo on April 26, 1992', reprinted in: Gaillard (ed.), Transnational Rules in International Commercial Arbitration, at 247.
600. *See e.g. Spickhoff*, RabelsZ 56 (1992), at 116, 126 *et seq.*; *cf. also supra* before I.
601. *Cf. supra* Chapter 3 II.A.

judgment of the Vienna Supreme Court, which set aside an arbitral award that was based solely on the principle of good faith[602]. General principles such as 'good faith' and '*pacta sunt servanda*', although prominent in every list, do not constitute vague *formulae* that are intended to invite decisions in equity that are totally detached from any legal considerations[603]. While vagueness and flexibility do not necessarily constitute attractive elements of transnational commercial law[604], it is impossible to regard transnational commercial law as a set of clearly defined, detailed legal rules. Rather, every attempt to codify the NLM involves a sound mixture of detailed legal rules and general principles as well as standards of conduct ('*obligations de comportement*')[605]. In spite of their necessary vagueness and generality these general principles provide a vital function within the system of transnational commercial law:

> 'Le droit international économique connaîtra rarement la précision méticuleuse du droit des traités. Il est « impressionniste » et non « pointilliste ». Cette malléabilité n'empêche pas les normes du droit international économique d'exister, d'être strictement appliquées, de faire preuve d'effectivité et enfin d'être sanctionnées – sans doute grâce à des techniques inusitées et inconnues du droit international classique'[606].

These general principles of law play an important, dual role in the drafting of lists of the NLM.

a. Genetic Function of General Principles of Law

The origin of many of the rules and principles contained in the various lists may be traced back to the basic notion of good faith. For example, the right to set-off mutual claims is based on the idea that it would be against good faith if a creditor were to require performance of an obligation from his debtor if the creditor would have to immediately return what he has received from the debtor ('*dolo agit, qui petit, quod statim redditurus est*')[607]. A particularly important aspect of good faith is the prohibition of contradictory conduct ('*venire contra factum proprium nemini licet*'). Even though the latter principle is 'still far away from a sufficient normative solidification'[608], it lies at the roots of many of the more detailed rules and

602. *Cf. supra* Chapter 2 II.B.1; *cf. also Riese*, RabelsZ 29 (1965), at 66; *but see* ICC Award No. 5065, Clunet 1987, at 1039; Ad Hoc Award of November 3, 1977, YCA 1082, at 77.
603. *Cf. supra* Chapter 2 II.G.2.
604. *Zamora*, GYIL 32 (1989), at 9, 39: 'Vagueness and flexibility may be desirable characteristics for political and cultural relations; they are not particularly attractive in the competitive world of economic relations, however'.
605. *Cf. supra* Chapter 2 II.A.2.c.
606. *Carreau/Flory/Juillard*, Droit International Economique, 1st ed., at 20.
607. *Cf. already* Dig. 50, 17, 173 = 44, 4, 8 pr. (*Paulus*); RGZ 42, 138, 141; *Dernburg*, Geschichte und Theorie der Kompensation, at 361; MünchKomm-*Schlüter*, BGB, § 387, No. 1; *see* for the *lex mercatoria* (even though reluctantly) *Mayer*, Festschrift P. Lalive, at 543, 554.
608. *Canaris*, Die Vertrauenshaftung im deutschen Privatrecht, at 287.

principles contained in the list. The principle thereby serves as a perfect example for the inductive development of special rules within the system of transnational commercial law. Thus, the principle of '*volenti non fit iniuria*' as well as the general prohibition of a state or state-controlled entity to deny its contractual obligations with the reference to its internal law, is based on the idea of '*venire contra factum proprium*'. That principle forms part of public international law and is reflected in Art. 46 of the Vienna Convention on the Law of Treaties. As one of the first principles of the NLM, it has been codified in domestic law in Art. 177(2) of the Swiss Statute on Private International Law[609]. The idea of liability for breaking off negotiations in bad faith can be traced back to the prohibition of '*venire contra factum proprium*' and its Anglo-American counterpart, the idea of '*promissory estoppel*'[610]. The general principle, as well as the detailed rules derived from it, all hint at a subordinate idea pertaining to the codification of transnational law. They provide strong indications for the development of a general principle of transnational liability for disappointing the confidence of the other party in the performance of one's own obligations[611]. From the perspective of German law, this development finds further support in the strong interaction between the idea of confidence and faith of one party in the performance of the other party's obligation and the general prohibition of '*venire contra factum proprium*'[612]. The development towards a transnational principle of liability related to this aspect of confidence is reinforced by the special role which confidence and faith play in the doctrine of international contract law[613].

b. *General Principles of Law as Reference Points for Valuation Processes Within the System of the New* Lex Mercatoria

Within the complex process of developing an autonomous system of transnational commercial law, general principles of law such as 'good faith' and '*pacta sunt servanda*'[614] perform an important 'classification and evaluation function'[615] with respect to the legal character and application of rules and standards contained in that system. This phenomenon is exemplified by the duty to re-negotiate.

609. *Cf. Paulsson*, Rev.d'Arb. 1990, at 55, 82.
610. *Cf. Hoffmann v. Red Owl Stores, Inc.*, 133 N.W. 2nd. 267 (Wis. 1965); *Kühne*, RabelsZ 36 (1972), at 261, 274.
611. *Cf. Harries*, Festschrift Zweigert, at 451, 463; *Kühne*, RabelsZ 36 (1972), at 261, 283; *Weise*, Lex Mercatoria, at 125.
612. *Cf. Wieacker*, Zur rechtstheoretischen Präzisierung des § 242 BGB, at 28; *Canaris*, Die Vertrauenshaftung im deutschen Privatrecht, at 287 *et seq.*; *Singer*, Das Verbot widersprüchlichen Verhaltens, at 35 *et seq.*
613. *Cf. supra* Chapter 2 II.G.3.d.
614. *Cf. Kahn*, in: Gaillard (ed.), Transnational Rules in International Commercial Arbitration, at 237, 241: '*Pacta sunt servanda constitue sans aucun doute la règle majeure du droit transnational avec son corollaire qu'est le principe de bonne foi*'.
615. *Cf. Dasser*, Lex Mercatoria, at 116; *cf. also Osman*, Lex Mercatoria, at 322 *et seq.*

The origin, contents and character of this duty are influenced by the principle of good faith and is also linked to other general principles such as '*clausula rebus sic stantibus*'. A new rule that is being discovered as an element of the NLM always has to be harmonized with the general principles that form the basic pillars of transnational commercial law[616]. Indeed, the constant interplay between legal rules and principles described above in the context of the UNIDROIT Principles[617] is also decisive for the evolution of the NLM in general[618] and for the structure of the lists in particular. As has been stated by an international arbitral tribunal:

> 'The application of international principles of law offers many advantages. They apply in a unique manner and they are independent of the particularities of any domestic legal system. They take into account the particular needs of international relations and allow a fruitful exchange between the systems which are often linked to conceptual distinctions in an exaggerated manner on the one hand and those who seek just and pragmatic solutions of individual cases on the other. It is thus an ideal opportunity to apply [in this arbitration] what is more and more called lex mercatoria'[619].

In the context of the NLM, general principles of law perform a function that is similar to that of domestic legal systems in that they provide the *substratum* for the development of new legal rules[620]. Because of their genetic function as the drivers of the NLM, the argument that general principles of law should not be included as sources of the NLM because general principles of *commercial* law do not exist must be rejected[621]. Every legal system, *whether commercial or not*, requires some basic standards and principles out of which new rules can be developed. It is their fundamental legal character and not their commercial nature which qualifies general principles of law as constituent elements of the NLM.

Frequently, the lists reproduce legal principles in their original Latin terminology. This 'Latin approach' is evidence that the dogmatic basis of these principles can be traced back to classical Roman law[622]. The reference to the Roman origins of many of the rules and principles contained in the list provides another important aspect of the research on which the list is based[623]. It is interesting to note in this context that the voluminous list of 1,000 principles, rules and aphorisms

---

616. *Cf. Schlesinger/Bonassies*, Rev.int.dr.comp. 1963, at 501, 517 *et seq.*; Dölle-*Wahl*, EKG, Art. 17, No. 32.
617. *See supra* I.A.7.b.
618. *Cf. Mayer*, Festschrift P. Lalive, at 543, 550 *et seq.*
619. ICC Award No. 8385, Clunet 1995, at 1061, 1066 (translation from French).
620. *Cf.* for the principle of good faith as a source of the 'estoppel doctrine' in common law *supra* I.A.7.b.
621. *See* for this argument *Goode/Kronke/McKendrick*, Transnational Commercial Law, No. 1.67.
622. *See* for the force of Latin legal maxims *Hyland*, Va. J.Int'l L 1993/94, 405, 408.
623. *Cf. Yntema*, in: Zweigert/Puttfarken (eds.), Rechtsvergleichung, at 162 *et seq.*; *Schipani*, University of Rome II, Department of Public Law Yearbook 1990–1991, at 583, 606 *et seq.*; *Zimmermann*, in: Hartkamp, *et al.* (eds.), Towards a European Civil Code, at 21, 27 *et seq.*

of 'Global Law' published by the *Garrigues* Chair of Global Law at the University of *Navarra* in Spain[624] contains only Latin principles and rules which are reprinted therein together with reference to international legal materials and the reprint of the original Latin text of the Roman Digest in which some of these principles and rules have their roots. This historic approach reflected in the Latin maxims finds support in the drafting process of the Dutch Civil Code. Even though this code is based on substantial comparative research[625], the drafters have emphasized the Roman origins of many of the rules and principles contained therein[626]. Also, references to the Roman origins of the rules and principles that are part of the NLM provide an ideal complement to the various sources of contemporary law such as the case law of international arbitral tribunals, international contract forms, general conditions of trade and the scientific discussion of the NLM doctrine. The historic references thereby add to the legitimacy of the NLM as an autonomous transnational legal system[627].

Apart from general principles of law and rules, the lists also contain generally recognized legal institutions such as the notion of prescription. To be workable in practice, these institutions need to be filled with concrete legal contents[628]. Thus, the idea of prescription can only be applied in international legal disputes if it relates to clearly defined periods of time. However, even without such concrete workable legal contents, the inclusion of such a legal institution in the list performs an important function within the system of the NLM in that it avoids from the outset any discussion on the existence of such an institution on the transnational plane. Also, the inclusion of the institution on the lists may ultimately lead to a consensus on the details of its contents.

4. The Open-Ended Character of the List

Even though the list performs an important function as a 'focal point'[629] for the Creeping Codification of the NLM, this should not be confused with a definite manifestation and petrifaction of transnational commercial law.

Gaillard maintains that the idea of drafting lists of principles and rules of the NLM is based on a misconception of the true nature of transnational commercial law. In his opinion, the contents of the NLM cannot be derived from a simple list,

624. *Domingo/Ortega/Rodriguez-Antolin/Zambrana*, Principios de Derecho Global, 1000 reglas, principios y aforismos jurídicos comentados, at 31 *et seq.*
625. *Cf. supra* Chapter 2 II.A.1.
626. *Cf. Feenstra*, Romeinsrechtelijke grondslagen van het Nederlands privaatrecht, No. 27.
627. *Cf.* for the 'Latin solution' of the Chamber for Complaints of the European Patent Office *Knütel*, ZEuP 1994, at 244, 245 *et seq.*; *see* for the Roman legal tradition of many rules and principles of the *lex mercatoria Knütel, id.*, at 274; *cf.* for the legitimacy of rules and principles of Roman law *Liebs*, Lateinische Rechtsregeln und Rechtssprichwörter, at 12; *cf. also Fouchard*, L'Arbitrage Commercial International, at 441 *et seq.*
628. *Cf. Ripert*, Rec.Cours 1933-II, at 569, 642; *Sandrock*, Am.Rev.Int'l Arb. 1992, at 30, 53.
629. *Cf. K. Schmidt*, Die Zukunft der Kodifikationsidee, at 60 for the judiciary of the state.

but instead result from the application of a certain comparative methodology[630]. The legal rules and principles that constitute the contents of the NLM may not be determined in advance, but only on an *ad hoc* basis, *i.e.* once a dispute has risen on the basis of the directives given by the parties or, in the absence of such agreement, by applying the functional comparative method[631]. *Gaillard* maintains that this approach does not require any further efforts by international arbitrators and counsel than the classical doctrines of private international law[632]. Likewise, *Goode* argues that the *ex ante* determination of the contents of the NLM is not in the interest of parties to international transactions and that this determination should be left to the arbitrator who has to decide a concrete case:

> 'No doubt it is possible after the event for an arbitrator, armed with all the relevant facts, to identify a rule of the lex mercatoria applicable to the case in hand. It is quite another to extrapolate from this ex post identifiability the ex ante ability to determine that the lex mercatoria would be suitable as a governing law for a dispute that has not yet arisen and the nature of which may be difficult, if not impossible, to foresee'[633].

This view must be rejected for two reasons. First, it underestimates the considerable problems that are related to the determination of the contents of the NLM[634]. These problems were exemplified in the Eurotunnel arbitration[635]. *Gaillard* maintains that it was the methodical task of the arbitrators in this case to ascertain the relevant jurisdictions from which the general principles, referred to in the complex choice of law clause of the construction contract, should be derived[636]. In actual practice, however, the arbitrators decided to have recourse to the UNIDROIT Principles as a pre-fabricated set of rules of authoritative persuasiveness[637]. Thus, the pragmatism of international arbitral practice lends itself much more to a collection of highly sophisticated rules and principles of transnational law than to the application of a transnational method of decision-making which requires 'access to a huge volume of comparative law studies'[638].

Secondly, the idea of codifying the NLM through either the drafting of lists or the functional comparative methodology does not constitute two antagonistic approaches to the same problem. It is true that the functional comparative method

630. *Gaillard*, in: van den Berg (ed.), Efficient Arbitration Proceedings: The Law Applicable in International Arbitration, at 570, 583 (reprinted in ICSID Rev.-FILJ 1995, at 208 *et seq.*; French version in Clunet 1995, at 5 *et seq.*); *Gaillard*, in: Berger (ed.), The Practice of Transnational Law, at 53, 56 *et seq.; Ortscheidt*, La réparation du dommage dans l'arbitrage commercial international, at 6.
631. *Gaillard, id.*; *cf. also Stein*, Lex mercatoria, at 175.
632. *Gaillard, supra* note 630, *id.*
633. *Goode*, ICLQ 2005, at 539, 552.
634. *Cf. supra* Chapter 2 II.B.1
635. *See supra* Chapter 2 I.B.
636. *Gaillard, supra* note 630, at 583.
637. *See supra* I.A.10.b.
638. *Gaillard, supra* note 630, at 585.

is a topical method that begins with the analysis of an individual legal problem[639]. The lists characteristically also allow a topical approach to the finding of the law. It has already been emphasized in this Study that it is one of the main tasks of scientific and practical research in the field of the NLM to avoid the creation of an inflexible, rigid or predetermined legal system that leaves little or no room for the further development of the NLM. This leads to a constant process of cross-fertilization between the decision-making of international arbitral tribunals and the list. The list derives a substantial input from the case load of international arbitration, while international arbitrators may use the list and the comparative references contained therein to develop or 'discover' new rules or principles of this transnational commercial legal system. This means that the lists are never 'completed' or 'closed'. Although in its initial form a list may not contain the solution to a certain legal issue of transnational law, a later version may include a principle or rule that has been acknowledged in international arbitral or contract drafting practice[640]. Here lies the decisive advantage of this non-formalized codification procedure as compared to the formalized approaches taken by the UNIDROIT Working Group and the *Lando* Commission. The work of these groups had to be 'finished' at some point in time. Even though the 2004 version of the Principles shows that there is a possibility for both the amendment and the updating of the UNIDROIT Principles[641], such process always requires the initiation of a new formalized procedure within the Working Group and within UNIDROIT. Updating the list through Creeping Codification, however, does not require a formalized procedure of that kind and can therefore be effected through a constant dialogue between arbitral practice, legal science and the academic institution that is responsible for the list. It is for this reason that the list contains a 'more or less complete collection of principles' which reflect 'the *lex mercatoria in its present form*'[642]. The progressing quality of comparative science necessarily leads to an increase in the sophistication of existing lists. As a consequence of this dialectical process between comparative science and (arbitral) practice[643], new principles will be added to the list and existing ones will be refined or even substituted by others[644]. In spite of the uncertainty that is necessarily connected with the drafting of the list as a process of constant evolution and change, the list still provides the

---

639. *Cf. supra* Chapter 2 II.A.1.a.
640. *Cf. Goldman*, Festschrift Lalive, at 241, 249 for the principles of defective contract formation, representation and form, which he initially did not consider to form part of the *lex mercatoria*.
641. *Bonell*, An International Restatement of Contract Law, at 24, 361 *et seq*.
642. *Mustill*, Arb.Int'l 1988, at 86, 110; *cf. also Stein*, Lex Mercatoria, at 161, speaking of a 'necessarily limited snap shot'.
643. *Cf.* for domestic law *K. Schmidt*, Die Zukunft der Kodifikationsidee, at 75 *et seq*.; classical dialectic methods can therefore be used in the context of topical legal processes; in this context, they serve to apply legal principles, on which a general agreement has been reached, in order to use the combination of these principles and the weighing of interests as a means to arrive at a resolution of legal problems, *see Horn*, NJW 1967, at 601, 607.
644. *Cf.* for this 'norm-creation-potential' as 'the real focal point of the discussion on the lex mercatoria', *Mertens*, Festschrift Odersky, at 857 *et seq*.

necessary prerequisite for the practical acceptance of the NLM: it creates 'a certain degree of predictability'[645] for the resolution of legal conflicts, thereby guaranteeing more legal certainty in transnational dispute resolution. This provides parties to international contracts with a certain basis for 'conflict avoidance' through planning and drafting techniques thereby depriving the NLM of the aura of a 'laissez-faire doctrine'.

At the same time, the goal of achieving legal certainty is not seen as an end in itself. Rather, the list technique leaves enough room for a teleological evolution of the NLM. The application of the NLM in practice therefore always oscillates between two extreme positions without ever reaching either: a decision in equity or a decision according to codified written law[646]. Both aspects influence the doctrine of a transnational autonomous law, but taken alone they would mean the failure of the NLM doctrine.

5. Creeping Codification Online: The TransLex Principles

The TransLex Principles, reprinted in Annex III to this Study and available at *www.trans-lex.org*, provide a unique online tool for the Creeping Codification of the NLM through the Internet. The TransLex Principles are based on the methodological approach and comparative research described in this Study. The functional comparative methodology[647] and the case law of international arbitral tribunals[648] form the two pillars on which the legitimacy of the TransLex Principles is based. They contain legal principles, standards and rules as constitutive elements of a transnational commercial legal system. This online approach to the Creeping Codification of the NLM serves three specific purposes:

- formulating of the rules and principles in black letter text so as to allow the user to apply the NLM in legal practice;
- reproducing the comparative law references for each principle or rule to help to save the time and money that practitioners and academics must invest in comparative research required to determine the contents of transnational law; and
- displaying the relevant materials *in full-text versions* immediately below the black letter text of each principle and rule to enable the user to make his own judgment about the 'comparative persuasiveness' of these sources.

---

645. *Langen*, Transnationales Recht, part I, Nos. 11 *et seq.; Samuel*, Jurisdictional Problems, at 248 mentions as one of the basic arguments against the *lex mercatoria* doctrine the lack of predictability of decision-making.
646. *Cf. Esser*, Grundsatz und Norm, at 343: 'Instead of the primitive "either-or" of domestic law and equity, a universal practice of general principles of law in the sense of Art. 38 No. 3 of the ICJ-Statute is required more and more' (translation by the author).
647. *Cf.* for details *supra* Chapter 2 II.A.1.
648. *Cf. supra* Chapter 2 II.D.2.

a. *History of the List*

The first version of the lists which form the basis of the TransLex Principles was published in 1992[649]. The list contained thirty-nine principles and rules of the NLM together with numerous comparative law references. The list was unstructured and not organized in any way. Its sole purpose was to prove the contents of the NLM at that specific point in time. The English version of the list, which was published in 1993, contained forty-four principles and rules[650].

It was *Norbert Horn*, one of the most important proponents of the NLM doctrine in Germany[651], who brought up the idea that the list could be more than just an unsystematic compilation of principles and rules of the NLM:

> 'One is puzzled by the list... because of its form: A concise listing of individual legal notions and legal principles. Almost each of them would deserve a scientific treatment of its own... The reader acknowledges with great interest the – according to my knowledge up to now most comprehensive – listing of such basic notions and legal principles. In my opinion, the list, in and of itself, constitutes an advancement of legal knowledge'[652].

The original German version of the first edition of this book, which was published in 1996, contained the third version of the list, now with sixty-nine principles and rules of the NLM[653]. Again, the list had no structure and was not organized in chapters or subdivisions. It was in that treatise that the idea of the 'Creeping Codification' of the NLM was developed and presented[654]. The English version of the German treatise, which was the first edition of this book, was published in 1999. It contained a new version of the list with seventy-eight principles and rules of the NLM.

b. *History of the Online Codification Platform 'TransLex' (www.trans-lex.org)*

There was an intrinsic problem with all lists published between 1992 and 1999. Their growth and character as a mere unorganized compilation of principles and

649. *Berger*, Internationale Wirtschaftsschiedsgerichtsbarkeit, at 374 *et seq.*
650. *Berger*, International Economic Arbitration, at 544 *et seq.*
651. *See De Ly*, International Business Law and Lex Mercatoria, at 234; *Marrella*, La Nuova Lex Mercatoria, at 690; *see also supra* Introduction, I.A.1, footnote 30.
652. Translation by the author of this book, the German original is published in *Berger*, in: CENTRAL (ed.), Jahresbericht 2007/2008, at 38. *See also Winiger*, ASA Bull. 1992, at 565: 'The compilation of substantive legal principles which are being used increasingly by international arbitrators in lieu of domestic laws, coupled with comprehensive references, is of particular value especially for the legal practitioner' (translation from the German original by the author).
653. *Berger*, Formalisierte oder 'schleichende' Kodifizierung des transnationalen Wirtschaftsrechts, at 217 *et seq.*
654. *See Berger, id.*

rules reduced their utility. That problem ran counter to the very purpose of the lists, namely the codification of the NLM in a way that makes them easily accessible for practitioners and academics around the globe.

aa. The Predecessor: The Transnational Law Database (Tldb)

In 1999, CENTRAL began to consider the use of modern communication technology for the implementation of the concept of the 'Creeping Codification' of the NLM. The idea of publishing a CD-ROM with the text of the list and the numerous full-text materials supporting each principle[655] was quickly abandoned. It was obvious that this technology would not be able to keep pace with the dynamic development of the NLM. Instead, the idea was born to set up a 'codification platform' on the Internet. To prepare for this project, a list was published by the Research Team in a CENTRAL publication on transnational law in late 1999 which was, for the first time, subdivided into fifteen chapters and which contained – also for the first time – the black letter text of each principle and rule contained in the list[656]. In May 2000, the CENTRAL Team, having conducted a global survey on the use of transnational commercial law in international practice, announced that it would 'publish a comprehensive Online Database on Transnational Commercial Law in early 2001'[657].

While the Internet has been regarded as a typical area of business life *for which* transnational legal structures have developed into a kind of '*lex informatica*' or '*lex electronica*'[658], the CENTRAL Research Team regarded the Web as the only technical environment *through which* the Creeping Codification of the NLM could be implemented. The CENTRAL Research Team quickly realized that the unique character of the World Wide Web avoids the defects inherent in traditional means of codification. The absence of a territorial localization of the Web conforms with the transnational character of the NLM, whose primary goal is to detach commercial law from the territorial constraints of domestic legal systems. The 'Open-Access' environment and global scope of the Web complies with the nature of the NLM as a 'public domain law'. Also, the Web permits easy and free access to the NLM on a global scale. Unlike printed texts, the technical options available on the Web, coupled with modern IT- and database technology, allow for easy everyday access, use, as well as the quick and continuous updating and dynamic evolution of the TransLex Principles. Through the Internet, CENTRAL can take account of the special character of the Creeping Codification concept

655. *See Berger*, CENTRAL-Datenbank zum transnationalen Wirtschaftsrecht, in: CENTRAL (ed.), Center for Transnational Law, 1997, at 18 *et seq.*

656. *See* Central List of Principles, Rules and Standards of the Lex Mercatoria, in: CENTRAL (ed.), Transnational Law in Commercial Legal Practice, at 146 *et seq.*

657. *Berger/Dubberstein/Lehmann/Petzold*, in: Berger (ed.), The Practice of Transnational Law, at 91, 113 with reference to previous reports on the progress of this project in CENTRAL's Annual Reports of 1998/1999 and 1999/2000; *see also Berger*, in: CENTRAL (ed.), Transnational Law in Commercial Legal Practice, 1999, at 121, 144.

658. *Ipsen*, Private Normenordnungen als Transnationales Recht?, at 104 *et seq.*; *Kahn*, in: Fouchard/Vogel (eds.), L'actualité de la pensée de Berthold Goldman, at 25, 26 *et seq.*

which is as flexible, spontaneous, and highly volatile as the NLM itself[659]. The use of the highly flexible technical environment of the Web assuages concerns that any attempt to 'catch' the NLM, which is floating in the transnational sphere, and to force it back into the straightjacket of a code-like list might ultimately result in compromising not only the autonomy, but also the inherent flexibility and highly dynamic character of the NLM[660].

A senior member of the CENTRAL Research Team, *Holger Dubberstein*, a lawyer and expert in IT and database programming, programmed the database as an Internet-based codification platform. The result of his excellent work, the 'Transnational Law Database' (Tldb, *www.tldb.de*)[661] was launched at an international conference on 'Transnational Law in the Age of Globalization' held at Münster University on October 26, 2001. At the conference, one of the speakers, *Gralf-Peter Calliess*, stated:

> '. . . in terms of providing free and easy access to systematic knowledge of Lex Mercatoria and thereby enabling self-reference, the CENTRAL Transnational Law Database launched today could be a milestone on the road to the New Law Merchant'[662].

After CENTRAL moved from Münster University to the University of Cologne in April 2002, the Tldb was renamed into 'Transnational Law Digest & Bibliography' in order to emphasize the 'Digest-like'[663] quality of the platform, while maintaining the acronym 'Tldb'. The platform was also transferred from a '.de'– to a '.net'-domain (*www.tldb.net*) to underline the transnational character of the codification platform.

bb. From the Tldb to the TransLex Principles

Over the next seven years, various problems in the handling of the Tldb manifested. The front-end of the Tldb became too complex, sacrificing the user-friendliness of the platform. At the same time, the back-end program which the members of the

659. *See Frischkorn*, Eur.J.L. Reform 2005, at 331, 343: 'By the time the list is prepared, the Lex Mercatoria may have changed.'
660. *See e.g. Fortier*, Arb.Int'l 2001, at 121, 126: 'I cannot help but wonder whether Berger's proposal does not end up impaled on the horns of the very "codification dilemma" that he himself invokes. One may legitimately ask whether *any* institutional framework is able to maintain the degree of openness and flexibility required to keep pace with the world of international commerce – particularly the world of e-commerce' (emphasis in the original); *Wasserstein Fassberg*, Chi.J.Int'l L. 2004, at 67, 82: 'This push towards formalised codification . . . requires lex mercatoria theorists to relax the qualifications for membership and compromise its autonomy in a way which ultimately belies the standard justification offered for its existence – the more formal and explicit the rules, the less organic, the less spontaneous, the less authentic they are'.
661. *See Berger*, Arb. Int'l 2002, at 83 *et seq.; Berger*, RIW 2002, at 256 *et seq.*; *Redfern/Hunter* on International Arbitration, No. 3-174.
662. *Calliess*, German L.J. 2001, *www.germanlawjournal.com/article.php?id=109.*
663. *See supra* note 551.

CENTRAL Team used to prepare and upload new documents became outdated and its use proved to be very time consuming. Also, the feedback from the users indicated that the message behind the acronym 'Tldb' was not readily understood by those academics and practitioners who were not familiar with CENTRAL and its research activities.

For all of these reasons, the decision was made at CENTRAL in early 2008 to set up a completely new online codification platform – TransLex – to which the list and the materials contained in the Tldb would then be transferred. The programming of TransLex was done by two members of the team with considerable experience in database programming, *Ulf Krause* and *Oliver Froitzheim*. The new TransLex-logo has four colours. These four colours represent the four areas of the TransLex platform at *www.trans-lex.org*:

- *TransLex Principles:* a list of almost 130 principles of transnational law, the 'New *Lex Mercatoria*'.
- *TransLex Bibliography:* a comprehensive bibliography on transnational law.
- *TransLex Materials:* a collection of texts of international conventions, model laws, restatements, domestic statutes, soft law instruments and many other materials.
- *TransLex Links:* a collection of selected links which are relevant for research in transnational law and international business law.

TransLex was launched at the final rounds of the *Willem C. Vis* Arbitration Moot Competition in Vienna in early April 2009. In fact, many student teams who have participated in that competition in the past have made extensive use of the Tldb, and the teams who participated in the final rounds of 2009 showed great interest in the new TransLex platform.

Like the UNIDROIT and *Lando* Principles[664], the TransLex Principles are of a multi-functional nature. They may be used:

(1) to determine the applicable rules in a dispute if the parties have chosen 'transnational commercial law', 'general principles of law', 'the *lex mercatoria*' or the like;
(2) to determine the applicable law, if, absent a choice of law by the parties, the arbitrators decide to apply this concept to the dispute before them;
(3) to allow for an autonomous interpretation of and for the filling of internal gaps in international conventions and other uniform law instruments;
(4) to allow for the 'internationally useful' construction of domestic law in international disputes;
(5) to ascertain the disputed meaning of key legal terms of transnational commerce, *e.g.* '*force majeure*', 'hardship', 'best efforts', 'time is of the essence', 'FOB', 'CIF' etc.;
(6) to supplement or correct a future European Civil Code in international commercial disputes;

664. *See supra* I.A.10 and I.B.2.c.

(7) to provide legal know-how about modern commercial law to developing and transition countries; and

(8) to provide information about transnational law to other sciences (politics, economics, sociology) which are exploring the clash between the territorial limitations of the law and the transnationalization of international commerce and trade in an era of globalization[665].

c. *Features of the TransLex Principles: The Online Codification Process*

Apart from its online character, the list contained in the TransLex Principles differs from the lists published in the four books mentioned above in various respects.

aa. Content and Structure of the List

A first major difference relates to the content and structure of the list. As of October 2009, the TransLex Principles contained 128 principles and rules of the NLM. The list begins with very general principles of good faith and the standard of reasonableness. It also contains very detailed and specific rules on such issues as agency, contract interpretation, the consequences of non-performance, *force majeure* and hardship, interest claims, unjust enrichment, expropriation, international commercial arbitration, and conflict of laws. The scope of the list thus goes far beyond international contract law. The principles and rules contained in the list, either on their own or in their combination, allow for the resolution of the vast majority of international business disputes. TransLex therefore does away with the longstanding criticism that the tremendous amount of academic attention devoted to it has only given rise to a very limited number of workable principles.

Unlike their predecessors which were published between 1992 and 1999, the TransLex Principles are not an unorganized compilation of principles and rules of the NLM. Instead, they are structured in fourteen chapters which are accessible through a drop-down menu. This is an example of the increasing systematization of the NLM described above[666]. Such systematization is by no means a new phenomenon. Even the ancient predecessors of the list, like the '*Rôles d'Oléron*'[667], were not an unsystematic compilation of rules and principles. Rather, they contained a coherent set of rules corresponding in broad terms to the chronology of a sea voyage[668].

By clicking on a principle of his choice, the user of the TransLex Principles gets instant access not only to its black letter text, but also to hundreds of comparative law references (doctrine, arbitral awards, court decisions, national legislation, international restatements, model laws, model terms), most of them

665. Purpose and Concept at *www.Trans-Lex.org/000010*.
666. *See supra* Chapter 2 II.G.1.b.
667. *See supra* C.1.
668. *Shephard, supra* note 560, at 217.

in full-text versions. It is one of the main tasks for the members of the CENTRAL Research Team to collect on a continuous basis new materials and upload them onto the platform. Reproduction of these sources has always been a key feature of the four lists published before the Tldb was launched and is also a key feature of TransLex. Apart from its online character and scope, which is not limited to contract law, it is that feature which distinguishes the TransLex Principles from the UNIDROIT and *Lando* Principles[669]. The experience with the American Restatement of the Law of Contracts[670] reveals the tremendous significance which these references have. It was for this reason that the *Lando* Commission decided to include notes with comparative law references (without, however, reproducing their full texts) in its Principles of European Contract Law and not to follow the example of the UNIDROIT Working Group[671]. The references guarantee the transparency which is necessary for a worldwide acceptance of the TransLex Principles and the rules and principles contained therein[672].

The documents which constitute the comparative law references are reproduced on the platform in PHP-format but can be downloaded as formatted and unlocked pdf-files. A sophisticated search engine developed specifically for the TransLex Principles by the CENTRAL technicians and equipped with a large variety of search filters allows the user to search for specific principles, rules or documents. When searching for a principle or rule, the search engine always produces the black letter text of the relevant principle as the first search result. While working with TransLex, users can suggest further references through the 'suggest a reference'-feature that was programmed into the platform for every principle or rule. This feature, together with the idea of a blog-like discussion forum on transnational law which will be implemented in the future, realizes the idea of a 'worldwide data-communication network' that was suggested in the German version of the first edition of this book[673]. TransLex also contains a 'genesis' function which is intended to create transparency of the 'codification' process by explaining the history of a given principle or rule throughout the codification process within TransLex. Embedded in the programming of the platform

669. *But see Brunner*, Force Majeure and Hardship under General Contract Principles, at 20 who argues that the drawback of the UNIDROIT Principles – the absence of comparative law materials – is considerably mitigated by the fact that the UNIDROIT Principles correspond to a large degree with the *Lando* Principles which contain such comparative law references. That, however, would require the burdensome process of constant comparisons between UNIDROIT and *Lando* Principles. The TransLex Principles combine the black letter text and comparative law references at a glance, *i.e.* within a single instrument.

670. *Cf. supra* Chapter 3 I.B.

671. *Cf. supra* I.B.2.b.

672. *Cf. Langen*, Transnationales Recht, Part I, No. 30: 'The judge may not be allowed to assume, without any further considerations, the equality of principles of different legal systems. This is indeed no longer reconcilable with legal certainty' (translation by the author); *cf. also Zimmermann*, JZ 1995, at 478, 480, who rightly characterizes the omission of any comparative references through the UNIDROIT Working Group as 'not very convincing'.

673. *Berger*, Formalisierte oder 'schleichende' Kodifizierung des transnationalen Wirtschaftsrechts, at 213 note 11.

but not yet activated is an 'annotation' feature which allows the CENTRAL Team to issue annotations and comments for individual principles or rules contained in the list.

bb. Formulation and Reformulation of the Principles and Rules Contained in the List

A second major difference relates to the way in which the principles and rules are formulated in the lists. This difference is due to the different purposes of the book- and the online-lists. The purpose of the book-lists was limited to furnishing proof of the existence of the 'constituent elements' of the NLM[674]. Therefore, those lists simply reflected the technical term of the relevant principle (*e.g.* '*bona fides*', '*pacta sunt servanda*', 'hardship', '*force majeure*') and provided comprehensive comparative references for each principle and rule contained in the lists. The book-lists did not contain the black letter text of the principles and rules contained therein. That approach was changed in the online-lists. The change was prompted by the UNIDROIT and *Lando* Principles which attempted for the first time to formulate the black letter text of the rules and principles of international contract law in a restatement-like fashion.

Contrary to the international restatements, however, the text of the TransLex Principles is not carved in stone but has always been, still is, and will always be subject to constant review, textual refinement and adaptation to new developments in international business practice by the CENTRAL Research Team. This is another indication of the special character of the Creeping Codification which relates not only to the continuous expansion of the lists, but also to the constant improvement of principles and rules already included in the lists. The changes are also reflective of the different underlying purpose of the online-lists. Rather than being mere archives of the nomenclature and abstract contents of the NLM, the online-lists are also intended to provide the international practitioner with a workable tool to apply the NLM in practice.

Three examples reflect the textual changes which many of the principles and rules contained in the online-lists have undergone over the past years. In the first version of the Tldb, the 'good faith principle' was formulated in the following words[675]:

> 'No. I.1 – Good faith and fair dealing in international trade
>
> The parties must act in accordance with the standard of good faith and fair dealing in international trade.'

In the current version of the TransLex Principles, the same principle is formulated in a broader fashion:

674. *Berger*, International Economic Arbitration, at 543.
675. *See* Central List of Principles, Rules and Standards of the Lex Mercatoria, *supra* note 656, at 148.

'No. I.1.1 – Good faith and fair dealing in international trade

(a) Parties to international business transactions must act in accordance with good faith and fair dealing in international trade. This standard applies to the negotiation, formation, performance, and interpretation of international contracts.

(b) The standards and requirements imposed on the parties by this Principle vary depending on the individual circumstances involved, such as the trade sector in which the parties are operating, their size and degree of professional sophistication, and the nature and duration of the contract.'

The textual and structural changes reflected in the two versions are not due to a change in the substantive meaning of the principle. Rather, they are intended to provide more guidance to international legal practice for the application of this very general and basic legal principle. At the same time, the new subsection (b) makes it clear that the application of the good faith principle is never a purely mechanical process, but always requires a determination of what is deemed to be a proper conduct of a party on an *ad hoc* basis, taking into account all circumstances of the concrete case[676]. This analysis must include the nature of the contact itself. Thus, the reference to the 'duration of the contract' in subsection (b) is meant to indicate that the time factor may play an important role as an 'amplifier' for the parties' duties imposed on them by the good faith principle. Thus, in long-term, 'relational'[677] contracts, the principle of good faith will almost always impose increased duties of good faith on both parties as compared to 'one off' exchange contracts.

A second example relates to the principle of nominalism. In the Tldb, that principle was phrased in the following words[678]:

'No. IX.3 – Nominal-Value Principle

Unless otherwise agreed by the parties, each party bears the risk of currency depreciation (nominal-value principle).'

In the TransLex Principles, the same principle is formulated as follows:

'No. V.2.3 – Nominalistic Principle

Unless otherwise agreed by the parties (*e.g.* in "value-stabilization clauses" or "index-linking clauses"), a claim for payment in a certain currency entitles the creditor only to the contractually specified amount of that currency (nominal value), irrespective of any fluctuations of the currency in which the debt is expressed between the date of concluding the contract out of which the claim arises and the date of payment.'

676. *See Nassar*, Sanctity of Contracts Revisited, at 161.
677. *See e.g. Macneil/Gudel*, Contracts: exchange transactions and relations, at 11 *et seq.*, 177 *et seq.*
678. *See* Central List of Principles, Rules and Standards of the Lex Mercatoria, *supra* note 656, at 159.

Again, the textual changes do not reflect a change in the substantive meaning of the principle. Rather, they were influenced by a recent study on *force majeure* and hardship in international contract law[679].

Finally, the '*force majeure*' principle, which has always been a key principle in the lists, was formulated in the original version of the Tldb in the following words[680]:

> 'No. 3 – Force majeure
>
> If non-performance of a party is due to an impediment which is beyond the reasonable control of that party and could not have reasonably been foreseen by that party at the time of conclusion of the contract, such as war, civil war, strike, acts of governments, accidents, fire, explosions, natural disasters etc., and neither the impediment nor its consequences could have been avoided or overcome by the non-performing party ("acts of God", "force majeure", "höhere Gewalt"), that party's non-performance is excused. If non-performance is temporary, performance of the contract is suspended during that time and that party is not liable for damages to the other party. If the period of non-performance becomes unreasonable and amounts to a fundamental non-performance, the other party may claim damages and terminate the contract.'

In the TransLex Principles, the same principle has undergone substantial textual and structural changes:

> 'No. VI.3 – Force majeure
>
> (a) If non-performance of a party is
>   i) due to an impediment which is beyond the reasonable control of that party and
>   ii) could not have reasonably been foreseen by that party at the time of conclusion of the contract, and
>   iii) neither the impediment nor its consequences could have been avoided or overcome by the non-performing party ("Acts of God", "Force Majeure", "höhere Gewalt"), and
>   iv) the non-performing party did not assume, explicitly or implicitly, the risk of the occurrence of the impediment that party's non-performance is excused.
>
> (b) If non-performance is temporary, performance of the contract is suspended during that time and that party is not liable for damages to the other party. If the period of non-performance becomes unreasonable and

---

679. The 'See principle history' section for this TransLex Principle indicates that 'the wording of the Principle was revised according to *Brunner*, Force Majeure and Hardship under General Contract Principles, Exemption for Non-Performance in International Arbitration 2009, at 451 *et seq.*'

680. *See* Central List of Principles, Rules and Standards of the Lex Mercatoria, *supra* note 656, at 156.

amounts to a fundamental non-performance, the other party may claim damages and terminate the contract.

(c) Unless otherwise agreed by the parties expressly or implicitly, Force Majeure events under subsection (a) above are impediments such as

i) war, whether declared or not, civil war or any other armed conflict, military or non-military interference by any third party state or states, acts of terrorism or serious threats of terrorist attacks, sabotage or piracy, strike or boycott, acts of governments or any other acts of authority whether lawful or unlawful, blockade, siege or sanctions, or

ii) accidents, fires, explosions, plagues, or

iii) natural disasters such as but not limited to storm, cyclone, hurricane, earthquake, landslide, flood, drought etc., or

iv) any event of a similar nature.

(d) Where the obligee has been prevented by a Force Majeure event as defined in (a) above from causing a limitation period to cease to run, the limitation period is suspended so as not to expire before one year after the relevant impediment has ceased to exist.'

As in the case of the good faith and nominalistic principle, most of the changes made do not reflect a change in the substantive meaning of the *force majeure* principle. Rather, the CENTRAL Research Team recognized that the text of the *force majeure* principle in the Tldb was not very user-friendly. To address that concern, the prerequisites and legal consequences of the *force majeure* principle were expressed in different subsections. The practical examples of *force majeure* events were likewise moved to a separate subsection and grouped into different subcategories of events. That subsection provides an example of changes that go beyond mere textual or structural improvements. Many of the examples contained in the current version of that subsection have been added as a consequence of the creeping codification process. For example, 'piracy' was added very early after the launch of the Tldb to take account of the increasing use of piracy, *e.g.* in the Gulf of Aden, offshore Lagos in Nigeria and in other places of the world[681]. The events 'acts of terrorism or serious threats of terrorist attacks', contained in subsection (c) (i), were added to the list as a reaction to a change in the *force majeure* drafting practice of many companies after 9/11. However, the wording of the introductory phrase of that subsection ('*such as*') and of subsection (iv) ('*any event of a similar nature*') make it clear that the list of *force majeure* events contained therein is non-exhaustive. Therefore, the changes made did not cause a change in the substantive content of the *force majeure* principles. Rather, they served to clarify its extended scope in international contract practice as a reaction to the changed realities of the global economic environment.

681. *See* for piracy activities the website of the Piracy Reporting Centre established in Kuala Lumpur, Malaysia, by the International Maritime Bureau (IMB), a specialized division of the International Chamber of Commerce (ICC), *www.icc-ccs.org/index.php?option=com_content&view=article&id=30&Itemid=12*.

d. *The Meaning of 'Codification' in the Context of the New* Lex Mercatoria

It becomes obvious from this description of the technical features of the Creeping Codification process why the term 'codification' used in the context of the Trans-Lex Principles must not be confused with the traditional notion of codification by domestic legislatures[682]. There is a natural temptation to fall into this trap because the code, once thought quintessential to private law in the state, is translated into realms outside the state[683]. Some even argue that the use of traditional 'codification' techniques might serve to alleviate concerns[684] raised by the proponents of the positivistic, monistic and state-centred theory of legal sources against the NLM doctrine[685].

That view must be rejected for three reasons. First, traditional codification techniques are being increasingly criticized today. They are useful as technical tools to ensure legal certainty and uniformity of legal rules within a given jurisdiction. However, codification is not considered as an efficient means of reshaping society or improving the law[686]. Reshaping and improving the law, however, are essential objectives for any codification of the NLM as law in action. It must also be noted that in today's multi-facetted society, which is developing at high speed, the idea of the 'code' has been disenchanted[687]. The recent developments in the EU which have lead to the creation of the DCFR[688], a code-like compilation of principles and rules of European private law, reveal that, in view of these intrinsic limits of traditional codification techniques, the term 'codification' may assume a new meaning in the near future[689]. Such a development can be observed in the area of public international law where the notions of 'codification'[690] and 'progressive development of the law' tend to merge, thereby giving a new and

682. *But see Herber*, IHR 2003, at 1 *et seq.* who seems to misunderstand that fundamental difference between the traditional notion of 'codification' and its meaning as 'privatized law-making' in the context of the NLM.
683. *See Michaels/Jansen*, Am.J.Comp.L. 2006, at 843, 887.
684. *See supra* Chapter 2.
685. *See Köndgen*, AcP 206 (2006), at 477, 501.
686. *Coing*, ZVglRWiss 81 (1982), 1, 15; *van den Berg*, De politiek van codificatie in Europa, at 8 (available at *www.recht.nl/doc/codificatie_in_europa.pdf*); *K. Schmidt*, Die Zukunft der Kodifikationsidee, at 64 *et seq.* (for a critical view on the German Commercial Code); *see* for an early critical view on codification techniques *Clarke*, The Science of Law and Lawmaking, at 41: '. . . neither for the layman nor for the lawyer, can it be said that the law can be successfully limited to one book of a few hundred pages [*i.e.* a Code]. The history of every Code that has ever been in operation – with its numerous volumes of commentaries, decisions of Courts as to its meaning, and revisions, repeals, and reenactments, gives the lie to the contention.'
687. *Caroni*, Gesetz und Gesetzbuch, at 125 *et seq.*
688. *See supra* Chapter 3 I.E. and Chapter 4 I.B.3.
689. *Ferrante*, in: Piergionvanni (ed.), From *Lex Mercatoria* to Commercial Law, at 121, 123. The DCFR has been characterized as a '*non-legislative codification* of European private law' and as a '*codification-like system* of *legal norms* with immediate application', *Jansen/Zimmermann*, NJW 2009, at 3401, 3406 (emphasis added).
690. *See supra* B.1.

progressive meaning to the traditional notion of 'codification' known from domestic law-making[691]. It is argued that even at the state level, such redefinition and modernization of the notion of 'codification' may involve the use of modern IT-technology:

> 'Codification – perhaps it comes back in a completely new way, detached from the traditional literary understanding of lawmaking and statutory texts; *perhaps as a database which is systematized and can be used in a systematic way through computer programs*[692].'

Secondly, the idea of traditional codes and codification techniques is closely linked to the nation state, while transnational law is intended to de-nationalize international business law. Thirdly, while codification is not per se inconsistent with the NLM[693], the traditional notions of 'legislature' and 'codification' have no place in the context of the NLM doctrine. The NLM is created 'bottom up' by the international business community. It is not imposed on the parties to international business transactions 'top down' by a formal law-making process[694]. Therefore, neither CENTRAL, UNIDROIT, nor any other academic or non-academic institution or organization can claim to be the 'legislator' of the NLM.

In fact, there is no single institution or formulating agency which possesses a 'law-making monopoly' for the NLM similar to that which state legislatures possess for domestic law and the reception of international law instruments. Rather, CENTRAL, through its TransLex Principles, acts as the 'formulator' or 'chronicler' of modern transnational commercial law. By formulating the principles and rules contained in the list and linking them to the comparative law materials, including arbitral case law and international Restatements such as the UNIDROIT and *Lando* Principles, in which they are reflected and which are reproduced on the platform, the TransLex Principles establish a presumption, *i.e.* prima facie evidence that the principles and rules reproduced in the list do in fact form part of the NLM[695]. It is for this reason that it has been suggested that the name of the NLM should rather be '*principia mercatoria*'[696]. It is precisely through this presumptive effect of the list that the Creeping Codification aims at making the application of transnational commercial law by international arbitrators easier.

---

691. *Lachs*, IJIL 1974, 1; *Singh*, IJIL 1978, 2; *Jain*, Codification and Progressive Development of International Law, at 4.
692. *Zeh*, in: Merten/Schreckenberger (eds.), Kodifikation gestern und heute, at 135, 144 (translation by the author, emphasis added).
693. *See Frischkorn*, Eur.J.L.Reform 2005, at 331, 349 *et seq.*
694. *See supra* Chapter 2 II.G.3.c.
695. *See Brunner*, Force Majeure and Hardship under General Contract Principles, at 20 *et seq.*
696. *See Highet*, 63 Tul. L. Rev. 1989, at 613, 616; *Marrella*, La Nuova Lex Mercatoria, at 636; *see also Lowenfeld*, in Lowenfeld, Collected Essays Over Three Decades, 2005, at 173, footnote 71, stating that '[t]here is some appeal to this point, though, . . . it is clearly too late to change the name of a concept so widely described if not always understood'.

That task that has been aptly described by an international arbitral tribunal as follows:

> 'It is always a more difficult and more demanding task for a tribunal to decide a case by the only reference to, and guidance by, general principles of law, lex mercatoria etc., instead of simply having regard and applying the solution as provided for in a particular national law, its case law and doctrine; this is so because an arbitrator, who can simply apply a national law, *may not have to scrutinize and to be concerned about the "validity" and "application-worthiness" of a particular provision*; he may and will simply apply the law (sometimes adding his own regrets: dura lex sed lex). However, an arbitrator who has to reflect on those rules and principles which truly deserve to be called "general principles", or forming part of the lex mercatoria (thus being carried by an international "communis opinio vel necessitas"), will have a much more difficult and responsible task to accomplish'[697].

e. *Updating and Developing the List*

The purpose of reproducing the comparative references in the TransLex Principles is not limited to providing the basis for the comparative persuasiveness of the principles and rules contained therein. They also serve as a comparative *substratum* for the further evolution of the list in general and for the development of specific rules from mere 'candidates'[698] to genuine components of the NLM. It lies in the very nature of the Creeping Codification process that the list is constantly updated and developed in order to provide an accurate 'snapshot' of the NLM. This specific character of the Creeping Codification was the major reason why the Web was chosen as a technical basis to implement this concept.

The process of adding a principle or rule[699] starts with a concrete legal problem that appears in an international business transaction which became public through a dispute before an international arbitration (with a resulting award that was published) or a domestic court decision. The corresponding legal principle or rule is then developed on the basis of the functional comparative methodology, *i.e.* using a topical, problem-oriented comparative approach[700]. This process accounts for the dual nature of the list, embracing both general principles of law as an abstract set of principles and the legal and/or commercial convictions of the international community of merchants. The process also considers the plurality of legal sources which account for the development of the NLM and which include public international law, uniform laws, the general principles of law, the rules

697. ICC Award No. 7375, reprinted in Mealey's Int'l Arb.Rep. Dec. 1996, A-1, A-5; *Marrella*, La Nuova Lex Mercatoria, at 417, footnote 53 (emphasis added).
698. *Strömholm*, Festschrift Zweigert, at 909, 910.
699. The flexibility of the 'creeping codification' may also lead to the striking of a principle or rule from the list. So far, this has happened very rarely.
700. *Cf. supra* Chapter 2 II.A.1.c.

developed by international 'formulating agencies', un-codified customs and usages, standard-form contracts, and published arbitral awards[701]. These sources constitute the 'raw material which has to be distilled into formally enacted or declared rules in order to become binding'[702], in order to become part of the NLM as an autonomous legal system.

As far as the discovery of general principles of law and legal rules is concerned, the UNIDROIT Principles and the *Lando* Principles of European Contract Law may serve as a starting point for the comparative analysis. The restatements are not a source of the NLM in the proper sense[703], but they provide an initial indication for the existence of certain legal principles and rules on the transnational plane[704]. Other lists of principles[705] may also be included in the research but must be meticulously verified, as some do not contain any comparative references[706], while others merely repeat the contents of other lists without verifying the comparative legitimacy of the individual rule, principle or standard. An example is the list set up by *Mustill*, himself an opponent of the NLM doctrine.

In order to ensure this legitimacy, the research must include classical legal systems from civil and common law countries and 'hybrid' legal systems such as the civil code of the Canadian province of Quebec, the laws of Scotland, South Africa or of the US state of Louisiana and the special laws of foreign trade contracts of the countries of the former Eastern Bloc and of the People's Republic of China[707]. Also, the comparative analysis includes Part I of the Civil Code of the Russian Federation promulgated on January 1, 1995[708]. The value of this law for comparative research is based on the fact that it is drafted upon the major codifications of civil law of continental Europe[709]. The drafting process of the new Russian

---

701. *See Lando*, ICLQ 1985, at 747, 748 *et seq.*
702. *Berman/Dasser*, in: Carbonneau (ed.), Lex Mercatoria and Arbitration, at 53, 58.
703. *But see Larroumet*, La Semaine Juridique 1997, at 147, 148 stating that the UNIDROIT Principles could be regarded as a potential source of the *lex mercatoria*; however, *see id.*, at 149 stating that the Principles may not contravene the law applicable to the contract which may be a domestic law, public international law or the *lex mercatoria*.
704. *See Goode*, ICLQ 1997, at 1, 26: 'More significant is their availability as a tool for courts and arbitrators seeking to identify current norms of contract established by mercantile usage or general principles of law, to ascertain what in modern legal thinking are conceived as best solutions to typical contract problems…'; *van Houtte*, Arb.Int'l 1995, at 382, note 4: 'The Principles will only be part of the lex mercatoria if they are recognized as such by the business community and by arbitrators'; *cf. also Perales Viscasillas*, Ariz.J.Int'l & Comp.L. 1996, at 383, 398; *Raeschke-Kessler*, in: Institute of International Business Law and Practice (ed.), UNIDROIT Principles of International Commercial Contracts: A New Lex Mercatoria?, at 167, 174 *et seq.*
705. *See supra* 1.
706. *See* for the significance of comparative references for the legitimacy of any attempt to 'codify' transnational commercial law *supra* Chapter 2 II.A.1.
707. *Cf.* for details *supra* I.A.3.b.aa.
708. *See generally Solotych*, Das Zivilgesetzbuch der Russischen Föderation, at 3 *et seq.*
709. *Cf. Glöckner*, WiRO 1994, at 367, 368; *Waehler*, Mitteilungen der Vereinigung für Deutsch-Russisches Wirtschaftsrecht Nos. 8/9 1994, at 24, 25 *et seq.*

law was dominated not so much by Anglo-American legal notions and ideas but by the legal systems of Germany, the Netherlands and Italy. As a consequence of this comparative drafting approach, the new Russian law takes account of recent developments and statutes in the field of private law in Europe[710]. Apart from its contents, the new Russian law is of particular significance for comparative research because it performs an important integrative function in the former Soviet Union. The law constitutes the beginning of a far-reaching and unified codification movement in the field of private law. Uzbekistan and Kazakhstan have adopted the Russian draft[711], and the Republic of Kirgistan has promulgated a new civil code that is based on a previous draft of the Russian law[712].

The results derived from this comparative research may then be verified on the basis of international conventions such as the CISG[713] and its predecessors, The Hague Sales Laws, and with reference to conventions of public international law, such as the Vienna Convention on the Law of Treaties of 1969. The CISG plays a pivotal role in this verification process for two reasons. First, the Convention is itself a first step towards the codification of the NLM in the field of international sales contracts[714]. Secondly, many of the principles and rules contained therein have been derived from the practice of international arbitral tribunals which in turn are a driving force behind the development of an autonomous and transnational commercial legal system[715].

The second aspect in the development of the list relates to the question of whether general principles or rules are in fact supported by the conviction of the general community of merchants[716]. Here, the verification process has to include the case law of international arbitral tribunals and those legal instruments which have been drafted by reputable international institutions, such as the ICC, and which constitute an amalgamation of commercial competence and experience. These 'code-like'[717] instruments include the 'Uniform Customs and Practices for Documentary Credits' issued by the ICC and in effect in a revised version since July 1, 2007 (UCP 600)[718], 'Uniform Rules for Demand Guarantees'[719],

710. *Glöckner, id.*; *Waehler, id.*
711. *Glöckner, supra* note 709, *id.*
712. *Waehler, see supra* note 709, at 29.
713. *Cf.* for the function of the UN Sales Convention as promoter of legal unification *Magnus*, ZEuP 1993, at 79, 80 *et seq.*; *see* for the work on the UNIDROIT Principles *Hartkamp*, in: Boele-Woelki, *et al.* (eds.), Comparability and Evaluation, at 85 *et seq.*
714. *Ferrari*, Riv.Tr.Dir.Pr.Civ. 1994, at 893, 903; *Perales Viscasillas*, Ariz.J.Int'l & Comp.L. 1996, at 383, 399; *see also Goode*, ICLQ 1997, at 1, 20 *et seq.*; *Raeschke-Kessler, supra* note 704, at 174 ('The CISG already provides a rather complete set of rules on a lex mercatoria'); *see also* ICC Award No. 5713, YCA 1990, at 70.
715. *Cf. Hascher*, note ICC Award No. 7197, Clunet 1993, at 1037, 1040.
716. *Cf. supra* Chapter 2 II.G.3.c.
717. *See Béguin*, McGill L.J. 1985, at 478, 485.
718. ICC Publ. No. 600; *cf. also ICC* (ed.), Commentary on UCP 600, ICC Publ. No. 680; *see* for the significance of the UCP as an element of the NLM *Kahn*, Annex I *infra*.
719. ICC Publ. No. 458, *cf. Berger*, DZWir 1993, at 1 *et seq.*; the Rules are considered part of the *lex mercatoria* in the ICC Award No. 8365, Clunet 1997, at 1078, 1080.

and the INCOTERMS[720]. Reference can also be made to the various projects of UNCITRAL, such as the Convention on Independent Guarantees[721] or the work on a Standard Communication Agreement Pertaining to Electronic Data Interchange (EDI and EDI-Lite) as reflected in the UNCITRAL Model Law on Electronic Commerce[722]. The various cross-border payment-schemes such as SWIFT, CHIPS[723] or CHAPS may provide important indications as to the existence of a commercial usage in the field of interbank payment[724]. Standard Contract Conditions such as the 'General Conditions For The Supply of Plant and Machinery For Export', drafted by the United Nations Economic Commission for Europe in March 1953[725] and the 'ORGALIME General Conditions for the Supply of Mechanical, Electrical and Related Electronic Products'[726] must also be included in the comparative research. Finally, the verification process has to focus on international standard form contracts and general conditions of trade such as the FIDIC Conditions[727]. The FIDIC-Red Book has greatly influenced the shaping of international construction law, as the new World Bank guidelines for procurement, which are incorporated into the World Bank's loan agreements with its borrowers, prescribe the use of 'Standard Bidding Documents', the principal document of which is almost entirely based on the FIDIC Red Book. This, of course, has given new authority to the influence of FIDIC on the shaping of international

720. ICC Publ. No. 560; the materials mentioned are partly reprinted at *von Caemmerer/Schlechtriem*, CISG, Annexes V–VII.
721. *Cf. Berger*, DZWir 1993, at 1 *et seq.*; *Horn*, The United Nations Convention on Independent Guarantees and the Lex Mercatoria, at 19.
722. UNCITRAL Model Law on Electronic Commerce 1996 with additional Art. 5*bis* as adopted in 1998, available at *www.uncitral.org/uncitral/en/uncitral_texts/electronic_commerce/1996Model.html; cf. Berger*, International Economic Arbitration, at 138 *et seq.*; *cf. also* the UNCID Rules, ICC Publ. No. 452; the rules developed by international institutions on EDI are regarded as part of a 'lex mercatoria numerica', *see Caprioli/Sorieul*, Clunet 1997, at 323, 330 (at 367 *et seq.* for the UNCITRAL Model Law).
723. *But see Libyan Arab Foreign Bank v. Bankers Trust Co.*, [1989] Q.B. 728 stating (per *Staughton* J.) that wire transfer through CHIPS or Fedwire is not a trade usage or custom; *see Goode*, ICLQ 1997, at 1, 8 *et seq.*
724. *Cf. Braeckmans*, TvPr. 1986, at 1, 10 *et seq.*
725. General Conditions For The Supply of Plant and Machinery For Export, prepared under the auspices of the United Nations Economic Commission for Europe, Geneva, March 1953, UN Publication Ref.: ME/188 bis/53.
726. ORGALIME General Conditions for the Supply of Mechanical, Electrical and Electronic Products, of August 2000, available at *www.orgalime.org/publications/conditions.htm*; ORGALIME is located in Brussels, Belgium, and groups the central trade federations of the mechanical, electrical, electronic and metalworking industries in twenty-two European countries and provides liaison between these organizations in the legal, technical and economic fields.
727. Fédération Internationale Des Ingénieurs-Conseils, Conditions of Contract for Works of Civil Engineering Construction, Part I: General Conditions with Forms of Tender and Agreement, Part II: Conditions of Particular Application with Guidelines for Preparation of Part II Clauses, 4th ed. 1987; *see* for the influence of FIDIC on the evolution of a genuine '*lex constructionis*' *Molineaux*, J.Int'l Arb. 1997, issue 1, at 59 *et seq.*

construction contract practice and also on the evolution of transnational commercial law in this area[728].

III. SUMMARY

The restatements of international contract law presented by UNIDROIT and the *Lando* Commission have paved the way for the codification of transnational commercial law. Today, informal and pragmatic rule-making prevails over formalized and overdogmatized doctrinal discussions. For the first time, a private group of academics and practitioners was able to show that the idea of a transnational commercial law is not an abstract subject developed in the academic ivory tower[729], but a practical working tool for the international practitioner. These projects have transformed the until now amorphous concepts of transnational commercial law into concrete and workable principles and rules for use by contracting parties, arbitral tribunals, and even national courts and legislatures[730]. Focusing on the question of *how to codify* the NLM instead of being trapped in *endless doctrinal discussions* on the existence of this legal system has led the NLM doctrine out of the status of stagnation in which it had been trapped in the past. The perspective has changed dramatically. The question is no longer '*lex mercatoria*: yes or no'? but rather '*lex mercatoria*: when and how'?[731].

The restatement projects have also done away with the well-known concern raised by international practitioners that the NLM is far too abstract to be used in practice. However, the drafting of the restatements is not the final word in the discussion on possible ways to codify transnational commercial law. In view of its particular legal nature, the NLM depends upon a new codification technique which provides sufficient openness and flexibility in order to take account of the rapid development of international trade and commerce. The Restatements of UNIDROIT and of the *Lando* Commission have nevertheless introduced a static element into the NLM doctrine. At first sight, this consequence seems to be inevitable since every codification necessarily implies the fixing of the law in statutory form. The restatements take account of this problem in so far as they contain provisions which allow the development of new solutions in accordance with their underlying general principles. Yet, these 'opening clauses' are only of limited use. They may help in individual cases but they also reveal the essential weakness of the restatement technique in that they contain an implied acknowledgment of the fact that transnational commercial (contract) law may not be put in statutory form. This need for openness and flexibility in a transnational commercial legal system is of another quality than in domestic legal systems, and the idea of a self-contained

728. *Molineaux, id.*
729. *Cf. supra* Chapter 2.
730. *Brower/Sharpe*, Va. J. Int'l L. 2004, at 199, 201.
731. *Bonell*, ZfRV 1996, at 152.

character of the major codifications of the last century has been abandoned[732]. The NLM as 'law in the making' requires a degree of codificatory flexibility and subtleness that goes far beyond that which the restatements may provide.

The idea of the 'Creeping Codification' of transnational law through an online codification platform avoids this essential weakness of the restatement technique. Contrary to the restatements, the updating and development of the TransLex Principles does not require a formalized procedure but is an ongoing process. The highly flexible, open-access environment of the World Wide Web, combined with the innovative technical features of modern database technology, allows for the quick and continuous updating and evolution of the list. Any adaptation of the list to the progressive development of transnational commercial law is instantly visible and accessible for the users around the globe. Due to the highly flexible and volatile character of the NLM, any attempt to codify this legal system can only produce a 'snapshot' of the reality of transnational commercial law, *i.e.* a reflection of the content of the NLM at a given moment in time. Since the TransLex Principles constitute an Internet-based codification platform, they can cope with that intrinsic problem of the NLM much better than any other, more traditional codification technique which must necessarily remain static and inflexible.

The TransLex Principles portray with a very high degree of precision the status of the NLM at any given point in time. At the same time, the highly dynamic character of the NLM is reflected in the technique of the Creeping Codification of transnational law which avoids the 'petrification' of the law which necessarily goes along with any traditional codification process.

732. *Cf. supra* Chapter 2 II.G.2.

Conclusion

Unification and creation of the law on the transnational plane are neither fashionable phenomena nor are they mere indications of the 'trends of the time'[1]. Instead, they reflect the commercial realities of modern international business practice. The increasing number of Codes of Conduct and other instruments of private governance[2] show that the privatization of rule- and law-making has become a reality in international business. The Academic DCFR[3] and the Resolution of the EU Parliament of December 12, 2007[4], which puts particular emphasis on the non-binding, soft law character of the DCFR, prove that even within the work towards a European Civil Code, the persuasive force of a compilation of non-statutory legal principles has been accepted as an efficient means to achieve the ambitious goal of the unification of European private law.

International business has always shown a tendency to favour practice-made rules of a transnational character. Thus, in the international construction industry, a suggestion has been made that a 'neutral *lex mercatoria*' should be applied in public sector procurement in order to create a true 'level playing field' for competition for public work and to test the prospects for a general informal harmonization of international construction law[5]. Arbitral case law also confirms that the transnational spirit of international arbitration provides fertile ground for the application of this concept in international commercial practice and that international arbitrators become increasingly aware of this phenomenon[6]. The development of a

1. *See Kötz*, RabelsZ 56 (1992), at 215 *et seq.*
2. *See supra* Chapter I III.B.
3. *See supra* Chapter 4 I.B.3.
4. EU Parliament Resolution of December 12, 2007 on European contract law, OJ No. C 323 E/364.
5. *Helps*, Int'l Constr.L.Rev. 1997, at 525, 537 with reference to the UNIDROIT and *Lando* Principles.
6. *Cf.* the statement of the sole arbitrator in ICC Award No. 8385, Clunet 1997, at 1061, 1066: *'L'application de principes internationaux offre beaucoup d'avantages. Ils s'appliquent*

'*lex petrolia*' for the international oil industry[7], a '*lex numerica*' or '*lex informatica*' for international data interchange[8], '*lex sportiva'* for international sports law[9] or a '*lex constructionis*'[10] for the international construction industry reveals that the transnationalization of commercial law has already transcended the traditional boundaries of general contract law[11].

Legal theory has to take account of this phenomenon in order to avoid any claims that it is out of touch with reality or antiquated. Therefore, modern conflict of laws doctrine faces the formidable task of redefining the relationship between autonomous international commercial law on one side and domestic law on the other[12]. Formulating this task also reflects the paradox of traditional conflict of laws doctrine. It was private international law, withdrawn from the competence of domestic legislatures by *Savigny* and handed over to legal science and the courts for further development[13]. Their economic inefficiency and the resulting legal uncertainty triggered the autonomous and decentralized evolution of the law through the international community of merchants[14].

In spite of the comprehensive and all-embracing approach towards the NLM as an autonomous 'third' legal system between domestic laws and public international law, every attempt to deal with transnational commercial law, as the basic and most controversial question of international commercial law, remains no more than an 'approach towards a new understanding'[15] of transnational commercial law. It is true that the discussion on the existence of an autonomous transnational commercial law raises a multitude of methodical, theoretical and

---

uniformément et sont indépendants des particularités de chaque droit national. Ils prennent en compte les besoins des relations internationales et permettent un échange fructueux entre les systèmes parfois exagérément liés à des distinctions conceptuelles et ceux qui cherchent une solution juste et pragmatique de cas particuliers. C'est donc une opportunité idéale pour appliquer [in this arbitration] *ce qui est de plus en plus nommé lex mercatoria*'; *cf. also* ICC Award No. 8365, Clunet 1997, at 1078, where the tribunal developed eight principles which, in its view, form part of the *lex mercatoria*; Paris Chamber of Arbitration Award No. 9246, YCA 1997, at 28, 31: '. . . the tribunal deems it . . . proper to refer to the body of rules of international commerce which have been developed by practice and affirmed by the national courts (lex mercatoria)'.

7. *See* Ad Hoc Award *The Government of the State of Kuwait v. The American Independent Oil Co. (AMINOIL)* of March 24, 1982, ILM 1982, at 976, 1036.
8. *See Caprioli/Sorieul*, Clunet 1997, at 323, 330 *et seq.*; *Mefford*, Ind.J.Gl.Legal Studies 1997, 221 *et seq.*
9. *Nafziger*, in: Blackshaw/Siekmann/Soek (eds.), The Court of Arbitration for Sport 1984–2004, at 409 *et seq.*; *Carbonneau*, Mich.J.Int'l L. 2004, at 1183, 1204 with reference to the case law of the Court of Sports Arbitration (CAS) in Lausanne, Switzerland; *Kaufmann-Kohler*, Arbitration at the Olympics: Issues of Fast-Track Dispute Resolution; *Röthel*, JZ 2007, at 756, 757; *van Hoecke*, R.I.E.J. 1995, at 62 *et seq.*; *Simon*, Droits 2001, at 97 *et seq.*; *Adolphsen*, Eine lex sportiva für den internationalen Sport?, in: Jahrbuch Junger Zivilrechtswissenschaftler 2002, at 281 *et seq.*
10. *Molineaux*, J.Int'l Arb. No. 1 1997, at 55, 64 *et seq.*
11. *See Ipsen*, Private Normenordnungen als Transnationales Recht?, at 65 *et seq.*
12. *von Hoffmann/Thorn*, IPR, § 2, No. 56 *in fine*.
13. *von Savigny*, System des heutigen Römischen Rechts, Vol. 8, at 28, note (g).
14. *Cf. supra* Chapter 1 I.A.
15. *Bärmann*, Festschrift Mann, at 547, 571.

practical issues which touch upon basic notions of legal theory and transnational decision-making. This Study has shown that the dogmatic arguments against the NLM 'are fading away'[16].

At the same time, the discussion on the viability of a transnational commercial legal system needs to be objectified. While any outright rejection of the theory fails to take into account commercial realities, any emphatic acclamation of the concept of commercial transnationalism lacks persuasiveness in that it fails to provide verifiable legal arguments. This resembles the initial scientific treatment of the phenomenon of reception of law in the early *ius commune*. At that time, there was a similar concern that the new legal situation would attract 'illusionists and visionaries'[17]. With respect to the NLM, this danger is increased by a sometimes lax and careless treatment of the concept of an autonomous world trade law. This is especially true with respect to the 'negative choice of law' of the parties[18]. Without a further inquiry into the motives and the will of the parties, the assumption of a 'negative choice' amounts to a fictitious agreement on the applicable law. This idea is often misused, even in international arbitral practice, to indicate the parties' will to have their contract transnationalized, thereby justifying the application of the NLM[19]. The NLM doctrine, the respect of which for the autonomy of the parties is one of its most prominent features, would be doomed to fail from the outset if its application would be based on such a violation of the will of the parties.

It has been emphasized in the Introduction to this Study that they need 'definitive' and 'provable' legal standards to negotiate their agreements or to resolve disputes, thereby reducing transaction costs[20]. Legal theory and legal practice alike, however, are confronted with the codification dilemma in the field of transnational commercial law. The NLM is a 'law in action' and depends upon a maximum degree of flexibility and openness. Its rules and principles cannot be fixed in 'statutory' form in the proper sense. The UNIDROIT Principles as well as the Principles of European Contract Law drafted by the *Lando* Commission reveal this dilemma. They provide a serious new indication for the consolidation of legal convictions pertaining to the existence of a transnational commercial legal system[21]. The great importance of these collections is that they exist. They can be taken to the court or the arbitral tribunal, can be referred to by page and article number, and people who are referred to their provisions can locate and review them without difficulty[22]. At the same time, however, they do not present the flexible

16. *Lando*, in: Festskrift till Stig Strömholm, at 567, 578.
17. *K. Schmidt*, in: Behrends (ed.), Privatrecht heute und Jherings evolutionäres Rechtsdenken, at 77, 104.
18. *See supra* Chapter 2 II.F.2.a.
19. *Cf. supra* Chapter 2 II.F.2.a.
20. *See Borchers*, in: Raisch/Shaffer (eds.), Introduction to Transnational Legal Transactions, at 139, 156 *et seq.*
21. *Cf. generally Lando*, in: Bonell/Bonelli (eds.), Contratti commerciali internazionali e Principi UNIDROIT, at 109, 114.
22. *Selden*, Ann.Surv.Int'l &Comp.L. 1995, at 111, 122; *cf. also Lalive*, in: Bonell/Bonelli (eds.), Contratti Commerciali Internazionali E Principi UNIDROIT, at 73, 89.

codification method that takes account of the peculiar character of the NLM which, being an open legal system, requires a codification technique that corresponds to the highly dynamic nature of the NLM.

The alternative presented in this Study is the idea of 'Creeping Codification' of the NLM through the TransLex Principles. This innovative approach is intended to provide international legal practice with an easily, freely and globally accessible Web-based platform to allow for the application of the NLM in everyday arbitration and drafting practice. If the '[t]he Internet is becoming the town square for the global village of tomorrow' (*Bill Gates* 2003[23]) then the World Wide Web must be regarded as the ideal forum for the codification of the NLM. It is the online character of the TransLex Principles which avoids the 'petrification' of the law that necessarily goes along with any traditional codification process. Unlike domestic law-making procedures, the Creeping Codification of the NLM is an ongoing, spontaneous and dynamic process which is never completed. This process requires a codification technique with a corresponding openness and dynamism. This dynamism can be guaranteed only through the use of the Internet. The open-access public domain created by the Internet, combined with modern database technology, provides the ideal *substratum* for the constant development and enrichment of the NLM through the process of Creeping Codification.

That process must not be confused with the traditional notion of codification by domestic legislatures. There is not and cannot be a single 'legislator' of the NLM which is created 'bottom up' by the community of merchants. Rather, by putting the principles and rules of the NLM in the form of black-letter rules with a synopsis of the relevant comparative law references, the TransLex Principles establish a presumption, *i.e.* prima facie evidence, that the principles and rules reproduced in the list do in fact form part of the NLM. With this approach, the TransLex Principles aim at alleviating the burden of arbitrators and contract lawyers who need to be concerned, in their daily work and in every single case, with the 'validity' and 'application-worthiness' of a particular principle or rule of the NLM.

Today, in an age of self-regulation and private governance, 'Cartesian pragmatism'[24] prevails over theoretic trench fighting about the nature and doctrinal underpinnings of the NLM doctrine. In economics, the 'Economics of Governance' theory concludes that private ordering is central to the performance of any economy, regardless of the particular conditions of lawfulness because in many instances, business actors can devise more satisfactory solutions to their problems and disputes than can professionals (lawmakers, courts) who are constrained to apply general rules on the basis of limited knowledge of the problem or the dispute[25].

---

23. Microsoft Encarta Reference Library 2003. 1993–2002 Microsoft Corporation (CD-Rom).
24. *See supra* Chapter 2 I.B, note 40.
25. *See Williamson*, The Economics of Governance, *www.aeaweb.org/annual_mtg_papers/2005/0107_1645_0101.pdf*, at 2 *et seq*; *see* for the conflict of the lack of democratic legitimacy and political accountability of decision-making and the increased effectiveness of rule-making within international institutions such as ISO and ICANN *Fukuyama,* America at the Crossroads, at 163 *et seq.*

As a consequence of these new legal and economic developments, the traditional theory of legal sources which is centred around the notion of sovereignty of the state[26] is being replaced by a legal pluralism which accepts that society's ability for self-organization and self-coordination is more than a mere factual pattern without independent legal significance.

In this age of private governance and legal pluralism, the NLM is not a myth or dream of the future. Today, transnational commercial law, the New *Lex Mercatoria*, is a fact of life[27].

26. *von Jhering*, Der Zweck im Recht, Vol. 1, at 249: 'Only those rules imposed by society deserve the name of law which have behind them the force of the law or . . . the force of the sovereign state, meaning that only those rules adopt the quality of legal norms that have been vested with this effect by the sovereign state or that the state is the only source of the law' (translation by the author).
27. *De Ly*, Diritto del Commercio Internazionale 2000, at 555, 570.

Bibliography

See for a comprehensive bibliography on transnational law the TransLex-Bibliography at www.trans-lex.org.

Abas, Piet, Rebus sic stantibus, Cologne, Berlin, Bonn, Munich 1993.

Abend, Martin, Die lex validitatis im internationalen Vertragsrecht, Heidelberg 1994.

Académie des privatistes européens (Academy of European Private Lawyers) (ed.), Code européen des contrats – Avant-Projet, 3rd ed., Milan 2002 *et seq.*

Acker, Wendelin/Bopp, Claudia, Führt eine zu enge Anwendung des AGB-Rechtes zu Nachteilen unserer Rechtsordnung im internationalen Rechtsverkehr?, Baurecht 2009, at 1040 *et seq.*

Addor, Felix, book review of: Berger, Internationale Wirtschaftsschiedsgerichtsbarkeit, 1992, in: 114 AJP 1993, at 357 *et seq.*

Aden, Menno, Die Anwendung materiellen Rechts durch den Schiedsrichter, 30 RIW 1984, at 934 *et seq.*

Adolphsen, Jens, Eine lex sportiva für den internationalen Sport?, in: Jahrbuch Junger Zivilrechtswissenschaftler 2002, at 281 *et seq.* (Stuttgart 2003).

Akademie für Staats- und Rechtswissenschaften der DDR, Institut für ausländisches Recht und Rechtsvergleichung (ed.), Internationale wissenschaftliche Konferenz: Grundzüge einer wissenschaftlichen Konzeption des allgemeinen Teils der rechtlichen Regelung internationaler Wirtschaftsverträge zwischen den Organisationen der Mitgliedsländer des RGW, Potsdam-Babelsberg 1986 [cited as: Akad.St.Rwiss.DDR (ed.) Grundzüge].

Alam-Eldin, Mohie Eldin I., Arbitral Awards of the Cairo Regional Centre for International Commercial Arbitration, The Hague 2000; Vol. II 1997–2000, The Hague 2003.

Alexy, Robert, Theorie der Grundrechte, Baden-Baden 1985; 5th ed., Frankfurt a.M. 2006.

Allen, Carleton Kemp, Law in the Making, 3rd ed., Oxford 1939.
Allison, Richard C./Coe, Jack J., Protecting Against the Expropriation Risk in Investing Abroad, New York 1988.
Allot, Antony N. (ed.), Restatement of African Law, London 1968.
American Arbitration Association (ed.), Resolving Commercial Financial Disputes, A Guide to Alternative Dispute Resolution, New York 1993.
American Law Institute (ed.), Restatement of the Law, Second: Contracts, Tentative Draft No. 1, Philadelphia 1964.
Ancel, Marc, Utilité et Méthodes du Droit Comparé, Neuchatel 1971.
Ancel, Pascal, Arbitrage et procedures collectives, Rev.d.Arb. 1983, at 255 *et seq.*
Angermüller, Niels O./Eichhorn, Michael/Ramke, Thomas, New Standards of Banking Supervision – A Look at the German Implementation Approach for the Second Pillar of Basel II, 20 J.I.B.L.R. 2005, at 45 *et seq.*
Arnaldez, Jean-Jacques, Comment to ICC Award No. 8365, 124 Clunet 1997, at 1080 *et seq.*
Arndt, Adolf, Gesetzesrecht und Richterrecht, in: Böckenförde/Lewald (eds.), Adolf Arndt, Gesammelte juristische Schriften, Munich 1976, at 59 *et seq.*
Asam, Herbert, UN-Kaufrechtsübereinkommen im deutsch-italienischen Rechtsverkehr, 35 RIW 1989, at 942 *et seq.*
Asante, Samuel, The Concept of Stability of Contractual Relations in the Transnational Investment Process, in: Hossain (ed.), Legal Aspects of the New International Economic Order, London, New York 1980, at 234 *et seq.*
Atienza, Manuel/Manero, Juan Ruiz, Über Prinzipien und Regeln, in: Festschrift Ernesto Garzón Valdés, Berlin 1992, at 109 *et seq.*
Atiyah, P.S./Smith, Stephen A., Atiyah's Introduction to the Law of Contract, 6th ed., Oxford 2005.
Aubin, Bernhard, Die rechtsvergleichende Interpretation autonom-internen Rechts in der deutschen Rechtsprechung, 34 RabelsZ 1970, at 458 *et seq.*

Baade, Hans W., Codes of Conduct for Multinational Enterprises: An Introductory Survey, in: Horn (ed.), Legal Problems of codes of Conduct for Multinational Enterprises, Deventer, Antwerp, Boston, London, Frankfurt a.M. 1980, at 407 *et seq.*
Bärmann, Johannes, Ist internationales Handelsrecht kodifizierbar?, in: Festschrift F.A. Mann, Munich 1977, at 547 *et seq.*
Baker, Stewart/Davis, Mark D., Arbitral Proceedings under the UNCITRAL Rules – The Experience of the Iran – United States Claims Tribunal, 23 G.Wash.J.Int'l L. & Ec. 1989, at 267 *et seq.*
von Bar, Christian, Internationales Privatrecht. Zweiter Band – Besonderer Teil, Munich 1991 [cited: IPR, Vol. II].
von Bar, Christian, Gemeineuropäisches Deliktsrecht, Vol. I: Die Kernbereiche des Deliktsrechts, seine Angleichung in Europa und seine Einbettung in die Gesamtrechtsordnungen, Munich 1996.
von Bar, Christian, Laudatio Ole Lando, in: Newsletter European Private Law, No. 2 1997, at 1 *et seq.*

von Bar, Christian, Die Struktur des Draft Common Frame of Reference, in: Schulze/von Bar/Schulte-Nölke (eds.), Der akademische Entwurf für einen Gemeinsamen Referenzrahmen, Tübingen 2008, at 35 *et seq.*

von Bar, Christian/Mankowski, Peter, Internationales Privatrecht. Band I – Allgemeine Lehren, 2nd ed., Munich 2003 [cited: IPR, Vol. I].

von Bar, Christian/Clive, Eric (eds.), Principles, Definitions and Model Rules of European Private Law: Draft Common Frame of Reference (DCFR) Full Edition, 6 Vols., Munich 2009.

von Bar, Christian/Clive, Eric/Schulte-Nölke, Hans (eds.), Principles, Definitions and Model Rules of European Private Law, Draft Common Frame of Reference (DCFR), Interim Outline Edition, Munich 2008.

von Bar, Christian/Clive, Eric/Schulte-Nölke, Hans (eds.), Principles, Definitions and Model Rules of European Private Law, Draft Common Frame of Reference (DCFR), Outline Edition, Munich 2009.

Baron, Gesa, Do the UNIDROIT Principles of International Commercial Contracts Form a New *Lex mercatoria*?, 15 Arb.Int'l 1999, at 115 *et seq.*

Bart, Jean, La *lex mercatoria* au moyen age: mythe ou réalité?, in: Leben/LoQuin/Salem (eds.), Souveraineté étatique et marchés internationaux à la fin du 20ème siècle – Mélanges en l'honneur de Philippe Kahn, Dijon 2000, at 9 *et seq.*

Bartels, Martin, Contractual Adaptation and Conflict Resolution, Antwerp, Boston, Frankfurt a.M., London 1985.

Basedow, Jürgen, Vertragsstatut und Arbitrage nach neuem IPR, Jahrbuch für die Praxis der Schiedsgerichtsbarkeit 1987, at 3 *et seq.*

Basedow, Jürgen, Lex Mercatoria und Internationales Schuldvertragsrecht – Eine rechtsökonomische Skizze – in: Festschrift für Norbert Horn, Berlin 2006, at 229 *et seq.*

Basten, Barbara, Zur Frage einer Konzernbildungskontrolle für Aktiengesellschaften als faktische Konzerntöchter, Diss. Cologne 1993.

Baur, Fritz, Neuere Probleme der privaten Schiedsgerichtsbarkeit, Berlin, New York 1980.

Baxter, Ian, International Conflict of Laws and International Business, 34 ICLQ 1985, at 538 *et seq.*

Baxter, Ian, International Business and Choice of Law, 36 ICLQ 1987, at 36 *et seq.*

Baxter, Ian, International Business Disputes, 39 ICLQ 1990, at 288 *et seq.*

Beater, Axel, Generalklauseln und Fallgruppen, (Reply to Ralph Weber, 192 AcP 1992, at 516 *et seq.*), 194 AcP 1994, at 82 *et seq.*

Beatson, Jack/Friedmann, Daniel, From 'Classical' to Modern Contract Law, in: Beatson/Friedmann (eds.), Good Faith and Fault in Contract Law, Oxford, New York 1997, at 3 *et seq.*

Beck, Alexander, Zu den Grundprinzipien der Bona Fides im Römischen Vertragsrecht, in: Festschrift Simonius, Basel 1955, at 9 *et seq.*

von Becker, Bernhard, Methodologische Probleme des qualifiziert-faktischen GmbH-Konzerns, Munich 1994.

Béguin, J., Le développement de la lex mercatoria menace-t-il l'ordre juridique international?, 33 McGill L.J. 1985, at 478 *et seq.*

Behrens, Peter, Voraussetzungen und Grenzen der Rechtsfortbildung durch Rechtsvereinheitlichung, 50 RabelsZ 1986, at 19 *et seq.*
Behrens, Peter, Die Europäisierung des Gesellschaftsrechts, 84 GmbHR 1993, at 129 *et seq.*
Bekker, Ernst Immanuel, Aus den Grenzmarken der geschichtlichen Rechtswissenschaft, 6 Zeitung der Savigny-Stiftung für Rechtsgeschichte 1885, at 68 *et seq.*
Bellstedt, Cristoph, Das Außenwirtschaftsvertrags-Gesetz der Volksrepublik China, 84 ZVglRWiss 1985, at 358 *et seq.*
Benditt, Theodore M., Law as Rule and Principle, New York 1978.
Benson, Bruce L., The Spontaneous Evolution of Commercial Law, 55 Southern Economic Journal 1989, at 644 *et seq.*
Béraudo, Jean-Paul, Les Principes d'Unidroit relatifs au droit du commerce international, La Semaine Juridique, 1995, I (3842), at 189 *et seq.*
van den Berg, Albert Jan, Wetsontwerp nieuwe arbitragewet, 6 TvA 1984 (Bijlage 21 Advocatenblad 1984), at 171 *et seq.*
van den Berg, Albert Jan/van Delden, R./Snijders, H.J., Arbitragerecht, Zwolle 1988.
Berg, Heyo, Diskussionsbericht zum Symposium 'Rechtsvereinheitlichung und Rechtsangleichung', Hamburg 15. und 16. Februar 1985, 50 RabelsZ 1986, at 233 *et seq.*
van den Berg, Peter A.J., De politiek van codificatie in Europa, available at www.recht.nl/doc/codificatie_in_europa.pdf.
Berger, Klaus Peter, The New Multilateral Investment Guarantee Agency: Globalizing The Investment Insurance Approach Towards Development, 15 Syr.J.Int'l L. & Com. 1988, at 13 *et seq.*
Berger, Klaus Peter, Die Eigenkapitalausstattung der Banken nach neuem EG-Recht, 44 BB 1989, at 1017 *et seq.*
Berger, Klaus Peter, Die Regelung der gerichtlichen Anfechtbarkeit internationaler Schiedssprüche in europäischen Schiedsgerichtsgesetzen, 35 RIW 1989, at 850 *et seq.*
Berger, Klaus Peter, Internationale Wirtschaftsschiedsgerichtsbarkeit, Berlin, New York 1992.
Berger, Klaus Peter, The International Arbitrators' Application of Precedents, 9 J.Int'l.Arb. 1992, No. 4, at 5 *et seq.*
Berger, Klaus Peter, Internationale Bankgarantien, DZWir 1993, at 1 *et seq.*
Berger, Klaus Peter, Zur Geltung einer Schiedsabrede kraft Handelsbrauchs, note on BGH (December 3, 1992 – III ZR 30/91), DZWir 1993, at 466 *et seq.*
Berger, Klaus Peter, Party Autonomy in International Economic Arbitration: A Reappraisal, 4 Am.Rev.Int'l Arb. 1993, at 1 *et seq.*
Berger, Klaus Peter, International Economic Arbitration, Deventer, Boston 1993.
Berger, Klaus Peter, Lex Mercatoria in der internationalen Wirtschaftsschiedsgerichtsbarkeit, Der Fall 'Companía Valenciana', 13 IPRax 1993, at 281 *et seq.*
Berger, Klaus Peter, Zur Wirksamkeit von Lösungsklauseln für den Konkursfall, 11 ZIP 1994, at 173 *et seq.*

Berger, Klaus Peter, Aufgaben und Grenzen der Parteiautonomie in der internationalen Wirtschaftsschiedsgerichtsbarkeit, 40 RIW 1994, at 12 *et seq.*

Berger, Klaus Peter, Die neuen UNIDROIT-Grundregeln für Internationale Handelsverträge, Indiz für ein transnationales Wirtschaftsrecht?, 94 ZVglRWiss 1995, at 217 *et seq.*

Berger, Klaus Peter, Der Aufrechnungsvertrag, Aufrechnung durch Vertrag – Vertrag über Aufrechnung, Tübingen 1996.

Berger, Klaus Peter, Formalisierte oder 'schleichende' Kodifizierung des transnationalen Wirtschaftsrechts, Berlin *et al.* 1996.

Berger, Klaus Peter, The Lex Mercatoria Doctrine and the UNIDROIT Principles of International Commercial Contracts, 28 Georgetown J.L. & P.Int'l Bus. 1997, at 943 *et seq.*

Berger, Klaus Peter, Die Einwirkung drittstaatlicher Eingriffsnormen auf internationale Verträge am Beispiel Islamischer Zinsverbote, in: Herrmann/Berger/Wackerbarth (eds.), Deutsches und Internationales Bank- und Wirtschaftsrecht im Wandel, Berlin, New York 1997, at 322 *et seq.*

Berger, Klaus Peter, The Lex Mercatoria Doctrine and the UNIDROIT Principles of International Commercial Contracts, 28 Law & Pol.Int'l Bus. 1997, at 943 *et seq.*

Berger, Klaus Peter, Der Zinsanspruch im internationalen Wirtschaftsrecht, 61 RabelsZ 1997, at 313 *et seq.*

Berger, Klaus Peter, Acts of State and Arbitration: Exchange Control Regulations, in: Böckstiegel (ed.), Acts of State and Arbitration, Cologne/Berlin/Bonn/Munich 1997, at 99 *et seq.*

Berger, Klaus Peter, Devisenrecht in der internationalen Wirtschaftsschiedsgerichtsbarkeit, 96 ZVglRWiss (1997), at 316 *et seq.*

Berger, Klaus Peter, CENTRAL-Datenbank zum transnationalen Wirtschaftsrecht, in: CENTRAL (ed.), Center for Transnational Law, Münster 1997, at 18 *et seq.*

Berger, Klaus Peter, Germany Adopts the UNCITRAL Model Law, 1 Int'l Arb.L. Rev. 1998, at 121 *et seq.*

Berger, Klaus Peter, International Arbitral Practice and the UNIDROIT Principles of International Commercial Contracts, 46 Am.J.Comp.L. 1998, at 129 *et seq.*

Berger, Klaus Peter, The Creeping Codification of the Lex Mercatoria, 1st ed., The Hague/London/Boston 1999.

Berger, Klaus Peter, CENTRAL-List of Principles, Rules and Standards of the Lex Mercatoria, in: CENTRAL (ed.), Transnational Law in Commercial Legal Practice, Münster 1999, at 121 *et seq.*

Berger, Klaus Peter, The New Law Merchant and the Global Market Place, in: Berger (ed.), The Practice of Transnational Law, The Hague, London, Boston 2001, at 1 *et seq.*

Berger, Klaus Peter, *Lex Mercatoria* Online: the CENTRAL Transnational Law Database at www.tldb.de, 18 Arb.Int'l 2002, at 83 *et seq.*

Berger, Klaus Peter, Lex Mercatoria Online, 48 RIW 2002, at 256 *et seq.*

Berger, Klaus Peter, Abschied von der Privatautonomie im unternehmerischen Geschäftsverkehr, 27 ZIP 2006, at 2149 *et seq.*

Berger, Klaus Peter, Transnational Law Digest & Bibliography: The Inside Story, in: CENTRAL (ed.), Jahresbericht 2007/2008, Cologne 2008, at 38 *et seq.*

Berger, Klaus Peter, Rechtliche Rahmenbedingungen der Globalisierung – vom Wettbewerb der Rechtsordnungen zu 'Private Governance', in: Bierbaum (ed.), So investiert die Welt, Wiesbaden 2008, at 33 *et seq.*

Berger, Klaus Peter, The Aftermath of the Financial Crisis: Why Arbitration Makes Sense for Banks and Financial Institutions, 3 LFMR 2009, at 54 *et seq.*

Berger, Klaus Peter, Private Dispute Resolution in International Business. Negotiation, Mediation, Arbitration, Vol. I: Case Study, Vol. II: Handbook, 2nd ed., The Hague 2009.

Berger, Klaus Peter/Dubberstein, Holger/Lehmann, Sascha/Petzold, Viktoria, The CENTRAL Enquiry on the Use of Transnational Law in International Contract Law and Arbitration, in: Berger (ed.), The Practice of Transnational Law, The Hague, London, Boston 2001, at 91 *et seq.*

Berger, Klaus Peter/Kleine, Lucas, AGB-Kontrolle im unternehmerischen Geschäftsverkehr, 62 BB 2007, at 2137 *et seq.*

Berger, Matthew, A Formulaic Approach to the Basel II Accord's First Pillar, 6 Hertfordshire Law Journal 2008, at 2 *et seq.*

Berman, Harold J./Kaufman, Colin, The Law of International Commercial Transactions (Lex Mercatoria), 19 Harv.Int'l L.J. 1978, at 221 *et seq.*

Berman, Harold J./Dasser, Felix, The 'New' Law Merchant and the 'Old': Sources, Content, and Legitimacy, in: Carbonneau (ed.), Lex Mercatoria and Arbitration, 2nd ed., The Hague 1998, at 53 *et seq.*

Bernardini, Piero, Is the Duty to Cooperate in Long-term Contracts a Substantive Transnational Rule in International Commercial Arbitration?, in: Gaillard (ed.), Transnational Rules in International Commercial Arbitration, Paris 1993 (ICC Publ. No. 480/4), at 137 *et seq.*

Bernardini, Piero, Adaption of Contracts in: Sanders (ed.), ICCA Congress Ser. No. 1, Deventer 1983, at 211 *et seq.*

Bernholz, Peter/Faber, Malte, Überlegungen zu einer normativen ökonomischen Theorie der Rechtsvereinheitlichung, 50 RabelsZ 1986, at 35 *et seq.*

Bernini, Giorgio, Les Techniques Permettant de Résoudre les Problèmes qui Surgissent lors de la Formation et de l'Exécution des Contrats à Long Terme, Rev.d.Arb. 1975, at 18 *et seq.*

Bernini, Giorgio, Adaptation of Contracts, in: Sanders (ed.), ICCA Congress Ser. No. 1, Deventer, Boston, London 1983, at 193 *et seq.*

Bernstein, Lisa, Opting out of the Legal System: Extralegal Contractual Relations in the Diamond Industry, 21 J.Legal Stud. 1992, at 115 *et seq.*

Bernstein, Lisa, Merchant Law in a Merchant Court: Rethinking the Code's Search for Immanent Business Norms, 144 U. Pa.L.Rev. (1996), at 1765 *et seq.*

Bianca, C. Massimo/Bonell, Michael Joachim, Commentary On The International Sales Law, Milan 1987 [cited as: Bianca/Bonell-*author*, Commentary on the International Sales Law].

Birk, Rolf, Die Umrechnungsbefugnis bei Fremdwährungsforderungen im Internationalen Privatrecht, 19 AWD 1973, at 425 *et seq.*

Black, Donald, The Behavior of Law, New York 1976.
Black, Henry Campell, Black's Law Dictionary, 8th ed., St. Paul 2004.
Blackman, M.S., Mercantile Law and Mercantile Practice, Cape Town 1985.
Blackstone, William, Commentaries on the Laws of England, Vol. I, 15th ed., London 1809.
Blagojevic, Borislav, Les Procèdes d'Unification ou d'Harmonisation les plus Appropriés dans les Relations entre Pays ayant des Régimes Economiques et Juridiques Différentes, UNIDROIT Annuaire 1967–1968, Vol. II, at 119 *et seq.*
Blase, Friedrich, Die Grundregeln des Europäischen Vertragsrechts als Recht grenzüberschreitender Verträge, Münster 2001.
Blaurock, Uwe, Wege zur Rechtseinheit im Zivilrecht Europas, in: Starck (ed.), Rechtsvereinheitlichung durch Gesetze, Göttingen 1992, at 90 *et seq.*
Blaurock, Uwe, Übernationales Recht des Internationalen Handels, 1 ZEuP 1993, at 247 *et seq.*
Blaurock, Uwe, Europäisches Privatrecht, 99 JZ 1994, at 270 *et seq.*
Blaurock, Uwe, The Law of Transnational Commerce, in: Ferrari (ed.), The Unification of International Commercial Law, 1998, at 9 *et seq.*
Blessing, Marc, Das neue internationale Schiedsgerichtsrecht der Schweiz – Ein Fortschritt oder ein Rückschritt? in: Böckstiegel (ed.), Die internationale Schiedsgerichtsbarkeit in der Schweiz (II), Cologne, Berlin, Bonn, Munich 1989, at 13 *et seq.* [cited as: *Blessing*, in: Böckstiegel (ed.), Schweiz (II)].
Blumenwitz, Dieter, Einführung in das anglo-amerikanische Recht, 7th ed., Munich 2003.
Böckstiegel, Karl-Heinz, Der Staat als Vertragspartner ausländischer Privatunternehmen, Frankfurt a.M. 1971 [cited as: *Böckstiegel*, Der Staat].
Böckstiegel, Karl-Heinz, Die Bestimmung des anwendbaren Rechts in der Praxis internationaler Schiedsgerichtsverfahren, in: Festschrift Beitzke, Munich 1979, at 443 *et seq.*
Böckstiegel, Karl-Heinz, Das UNCITRAL-Modellgesetz über die internationale Wirtschaftsschiedsgerichtsbarkeit, 30 RIW 1984, at 670 *et seq.*
Böckstiegel, Karl-Heinz, statement, in: Gaillard (ed.), Transnational Rules in International Commercial Arbitration, Paris 1993 (ICC Publ. No. 480/4), at 49.
Boele-Woelki, Katharina, Principles en IPR, Utrecht 1995.
Boele-Woelki, Katharina, Principle and Private International Law – The UNIDROIT Principles of International Commercial Contracts and the Principles of European Contract Law: How to Apply Them in International Contracts, 14 Unif.L.Rev. 1996, at 652 *et seq.*
Boele-Woelki, Katharina, Die Anwendung der UNIDROIT Principles auf internationale Handelsverträge, 17 IPRax 1997, at 161 *et seq.*
Boer, Ted M. de, The Relation between Uniform Substantive Law and Private International Law, in: Hartkamp/Hesselink/Hondius/du Perron/Vranken (eds.), Towards a European Civil Code, Nijmegen, Dordrecht, Boston, London 1994, at 51 *et seq.*
Boguslavsky, Mark M., L'Etat en tant que Partie a des Contrats de Concession ou d'Investissement Conclus avec des Sociétés Privées Etrangères,

in: UNIDROIT (ed.), New Directions in International Trade Law, 2 Vols., New York 1977, at 307 *et seq.*

Böhm, Franz, Privatrechtsgesellschaft und Marktwirtschaft, in: Mestmäcker (ed.), Freiheit und Ordnung in der Marktwirtschaft, Baden-Baden 1980, at 105 *et seq.*

Bonell, Michael Joachim, The Relevance of Courses of Dealing. Usages and Customs in the Interpretation of International Commercial Contracts, in: UNIDROIT (ed.), New Directions in International Trade Law, 2 Vols., New York 1977, at 109 *et seq.*

Bonell, Michael Joachim, The UNIDROIT Initiative for the Progressive Codification of International Trade Law, 27 ICLQ 1978, at 413 *et seq.*

Bonell, Michael Joachim, Das Autonome Recht des Welthandels – Rechtsdogmatische und Rechtspolitische Aspekte, 42 RabelsZ 1978, at 485 *et seq.*

Bonell, Michael Joachim, A 'Restatement' of Principles of International Commercial Contracts: An Academic Expertise or a Practical Need?, RDAI 1988, at 873 *et seq.*

Bonell, Michael Joachim, Uniform Law and Party Autonomy: What is Wrong with the Current Approach?, in: UNIDROIT (ed.), International Uniform Law in Practice, Rome 1988, at 433 *et seq.*

Bonell, Michael Joachim, Vertragsverhandlungen und culpa in contrahendo nach dem Wiener Kaufrechtsübereinkommen, 36 RIW 1990, at 693 *et seq.*

Bonell, Michael Joachim, Unification of Law by Non-Legislative Means: The UNIDROIT Draft Principles of International Commercial Contracts, 40 Am.J.Comp.L. 1992, at 617 *et seq.*

Bonell, Michael Joachim, Das UNIDROIT-Projekt für die Ausarbeitung von Regeln für internationale Handelsverträge, 56 RabelsZ 1992, at 274 *et seq.*

Bonell, Michael Joachim, The UNIDROIT Principles of International Commercial Contracts and the Principles of European Contract Law: Similar Rules for the Same Purposes?, 14 Uniform Law Review 1996, at 229 *et seq.*

Bonell, Michael Joachim, The UNIDROIT Principles of International Commercial Contracts and CISG – Alternative or Complementary Instruments?, 14 Uniform Law Review 1996, at 26 *et seq.*

Bonell, Michael Joachim, Die UNIDROIT Prinzipien der internationalen Handelsverträge: Eine neue Lex Mercatoria?, 37 ZRVgl. 1996, at 152 *et seq.*

Bonell, Michael Joachim, The UNIDROIT Principles in Practice: The Experience of the First Two Years, 15 Uniform Law Review 1997, at 34 *et seq.*

Bonell, Michael Joachim, The UNIDROIT Principles of International Commercial Contracts and the Principles of European Contract Law: A Comparison, in: Cranston (ed.), Making Commercial Law, Essays in Honour of Roy Goode, Oxford 1997, at 91 *et seq.* [cited as *Bonell*, in: Cranston (ed.), Essays in Honor of Roy Goode].

Bonell, Michael Joachim, The UNIDROIT Principles – A Modern Approach to Contract Law, in: Weyers (ed.), Europäisches Vertragsrecht, Baden-Baden 1997, at 9 *et seq.*

Bonell, Michael Joachim, A 'Global' Arbitration Decided on the Basis of the UNIDROIT Principles: *In re Andersen Consulting Business Unit Member Firms v. Arthur Andersen Business Unit Member Firms and Andersen Worldwide Société Coopérative*, 17 Arb.Int'l 2001, at 249 *et seq.*

Bonell, Michael Joachim, The UNIDROIT Principles and Transnational Law, in: Berger (ed.), The Practice of Transnational Law, The Hague, London, Boston 2001, at 23 *et seq.*

Bonell, Michael Joachim, The UNIDROIT Principles as a Means of Interpreting and Supplementing International Uniform Law, in: ICC Bull. 2002, Special Supplement, at 29 *et seq.*

Bonell, Michael Joachim, An International Restatement of Contract Law – The UNIDROIT Principles of International Commercial Contracts, 3rd ed., Irvington (New York) 2005.

Booysen, Hercules, Völkerrecht als Vertragsstatut internationaler privatrechtlicher Verträge, 59 RabelsZ 1995, at 245 *et seq.*

Borchers, Patrick J., The Triumph of Substantive over Rules of Choice in International Commercial Transactions: From the Lex Mercatoria to Modern Standards, in: Raisch/Shaffer (eds.), Introduction to Transnational Legal Transactions, New York, London, Rome 1995, at 139 *et seq.*

Borum, Oscar Alfred, Convention or Model Law, in: Festschrift für Ch. Fragistas, Thessaloniki 1966, at 1 *et seq.*

Bowden, Paul, L'interdiction de se contredire au détriment d'autrui (estoppel) as a Substantive Transnational Rule in International Commercial Arbitration, in: Gaillard (ed.), Transnational Rules in International Commercial Arbitration, Paris 1993 (ICC Publ. No. 480/4), at 125 *et seq.*

Boyd, Stewart, Interest for the Late Payment of Money, 1 Arb.Int'l 1985, at 153 *et seq.*

Braeckmans, H., Paralegale Normen En Lex Mercatoria, 23 TvPr 1986, at 1 *et seq.*

Brandner, Hans Erich/Ulmer, Peter, EG-Richtlinie über mißbräuchliche Klauseln in Verbraucherverträgen, 46 BB 1991, at 701 *et seq.*

Brazil, Patrick, UNIDROIT Principles of International Commercial Contracts in the Context of International Commercial Arbitration, 11 Mealey's Int'l Arb.Rep. 1996, April, at 31 *et seq.*

Bredin, Jean-Denis, Berthold Goldman, Toujours Vivant, in: Fouchard/Vogel (eds.), L'actualité de la pensée de Berthold Goldman, Paris 2004, at 15 *et seq.*

Bredow, Jens/Seiffert, Bodo, Incoterms 2000 – Kommentar und deutsch/englischer Text der ICC-Incoterms, Heidelberg 2000.

von Bredow, Wilfried, Abschied vom Westfälischen System? Die Zukunft der internationalen Staatenwelt, in: Lutz (ed.), Globalisierung und nationale Souveränität – Festschrift für Wilfried Röhrich, Baden-Baden 2000, at 159 *et seq.*

Broches, Aron, The Birth of UNCITRAL, in: Broches (ed.), Selected Essays, Dordrecht, Boston, London 1995, at 359 *et seq.*

Broom, Herbert, A Selection of Legal Maxims, 10th ed., London 1939.

Brower, Charles N./Sharpe, Jeremy K., The Creeping Codification of Transnational Commercial Law: An Arbitrator's Perspective, 45 Va. J. Int'l L. 2004, at 199 *et seq.*

Brunetti, Maurizio, The Lex Mercatoria in Practice: The Experience of the Iran-United States Claims Tribunal, 18 Arb.Int'l 2002, at 355 *et seq.*

Brunner, Christoph, Force Majeure and Hardship under General Contract Principles – Exemption for Non-Performance in International Arbitration, Alphen aan den Rijn 2009.

van Buchem-Spapens A.M.J./Nieuwenhuis, J.H, Inleiding privaatrecht, 2nd ed., Deventer 1988.

Bucher, Andreas, Transnationales Recht im IPR, in: Schwind (ed.), Aktuelle Fragen zum Europarecht aus der Sicht in- und ausländischer Gelehrter, Vienna 1986, at 11 *et seq.*

Bucher, Andreas, Die neue internationale Schiedsgerichtsbarkeit in der Schweiz, Basel, Frankfurt a.M., 1989.

Buchmann, Eva, Positive Comity im internationalen Kartellrecht, Munich 2004.

Bühler, Michael/Waitz von Eschen, Friedrich, Frankreich: Teilweise Aufhebung eines internationalen Schiedsspruchs mangels Begründung, 10 IPRax 1990, at 62 *et seq.*

Bühler, Theodor, Faktische Rechtsquellen, in: Festschrift für Hans Ulrich Walder, Zurich 1994, at 153 *et seq.*

Bühring-Uhle, Christian, The IBM-Fujitsu Arbitration: A Landmark in Innovative Dispute Resolution, 2 Am.Rev.Int'l Arb. 1991, at 113 *et seq.*

Bundesministerium der Justiz (ed.), Kommission zur Neuordnung des Schiedsverfahrensrechts, Bericht mit einem Diskussionsentwurf zur Neufassung des Zehnten Buchs der ZPO, Bonn 1994.

Bundesnotarkammer/Bundesrechtsanwaltskammer/Deutscher Anwaltverein/Deutscher Notarverein/Deutscher Richterbund, Law – Made in Germany. Global – effektiv – kostengünstig, available at www.lawmadeingermany.de.

Bungert, Hartwin, book review of: Berger, Internationale Wirtschaftsschiedsgerichtsbarkeit, 1992, in: 44 VersR 1993, at 36 *et seq.*

Bunni, Nael G., The FIDIC Forms of Contract, 3rd ed., Oxford 2005.

Buntenbroich, David, Menschenrechte und Unternehmen. Transnationale Rechtswirkungen 'freiwilliger' Verhaltenskodizes, Frankfurt a.M. 2007.

Burkart, Fabian, Interpretatives Zusammenwirken von CISG und UNIDROIT Principles, Baden-Baden 2000.

Buxbaum, Richard M., The Formation of Marketable Share Companies, in: Conrad/Vagts (eds.), Int'l Encycl.Comp.L., Vol. XIII/1, Tübingen 1974/2006, Chapter 3.

Buxbaum, Richard M./Hopt, Klaus J., Legal Harmonization and the Business Enterprise, Berlin/New York 1988.

Bydlinski, Franz, Handels- oder Unternehmensrecht als Sonderprivatrecht, Berlin *et al.* 1990.

Bydlinski, Franz, Juristische Methodenlehre und Rechtsbegriff, 2nd ed., Vienna, New York 1991.

von Caemmerer, Ernst/Schlechtriem, Peter, Kommentar zum Einheitlichen UN-Kaufrecht – das Übereinkommen der Vereinten Nationen über den internationalen Warenkauf; CISG-Kommentar, 2nd ed., Munich 1995 [cited as: von Caemmerer/Schlechtriem-*author*, CISG].

Cairo Regional Centre for International Commercial Arbitration (ed.), A Newsletter of CRCICA, No. 4, January 1997, Cairo 1997.

Calavros, Constantin, Das UNCITRAL-Modellgesetz über die internationale Handelsschiedsgerichtsbarkeit, Bielefeld 1988.

Calliess, Gralf-Peter, Lex Mercatoria: A Reflexive Law Guide To An Autonomous Legal System, 2 German L.J. No. 17 2001, available at: http://www.germanlawjournal.com/article.php?id=109.

Calliess, Gralf-Peter, The Making of Transnational Contract Law, 14 Ind.J.Gl.Legal Studies 2007, at 469 *et seq.*

Campbell, Dennis/Summerfield, Peter, Effective Dispute Resolution for the International Commercial Lawyer, Deventer, Boston 1989.

Canaris, Claus-Wilhelm, Die Vertrauenshaftung im deutschen Privatrecht, Munich 1971.

Canaris, Claus-Wilhelm, Systemdenken und Systembegriff in der Jurisprudenz, 2nd ed., Berlin 1983.

Canaris, Claus-Wilhelm, Die Feststellung von Lücken im Gesetz, 2nd ed., Berlin 1983.

Canaris, Claus-Wilhelm, Die Stellung der 'UNIDROIT Principles' und der 'Principles of European Contract Law' im System der Rechtsquellen, in: Basedow, Jürgen (ed.), Europäische Vertragsrechtsvereinheitlichung und deutsches Recht, Tübingen 2000, at 5 *et seq.*

Canaris, Claus-Wilhelm, Vorbemerkung, in: Académie des privatistes européens (Academy of European Private Lawyers) (ed.), Code européen des contrats – Avant-Projet, 3rd ed., Milan 2002, at XXVII *et seq.*

Caprioli, Eric A./Sorieul, Renaud, Le Commerce International Electronique: vers l'Emergence des Règles Juridiques Transnationales, 124 Clunet 1997, at 323 *et seq.*

Carbonneau, Thomas E., The Elaboration of Substantive Legal Norms and Arbitral Adjudication: The Case of the Iran-United States Claims Tribunal, in: Lillich (ed.), The Iran-United States Claims Tribunal 1981–1983, Charlottesville 1984, at 104 *et seq.*

Carbonneau, Thomas E., Rendering Arbitral Awards with Reasons: The Elaboration of a Common Law of International Transactions, 23 Col.J.-Transnat'l.L. 1985, at 579 *et seq.*

Carbonneau, Thomas E., 'A-Legality' and Arbitration: The German Supreme Court Joins the Fray, 4 Am.Rev.Int'l Arb. 1993, at 217 *et seq.*

Carbonneau, Thomas E., Diversity or Cacophony?: New Sources of Norms in International Law, 25 Mich.J.Int'l L. 2004, 1183 *et seq.*

Carbonnier, Jean, Réflexions marginales, in: Académie des privatistes européens (Academy of European Private Lawyers) (ed.), Code européen des contrats – Avant-Projet, 3rd ed., Milan 2002, at XIX *et seq.*

Caron, David B., The Nature of the Iran-United States Claims Tribunal and the Evolving Structure of International Dispute Resolution, 84 AJIL 1990, at 104 *et seq.*

Caroni, Pio, Gesetz und Gesetzbuch – Beiträge zu einer Kodifikationsgeschichte, Basel/Geneva/Munich 2003.

Carreau, Dominique/Juillard, Patrick, Droit international économique, 3rd ed., Paris 2007.

Carreau, Dominique/Flory, Thiébaut/Juillard, Patrick, Droit international économique, 1st ed., Paris 1978.

Carrington, Paul D./Haagen, Paul H., Contract and Jurisdiction, 8 The Supreme Court Review 1996, at 331 *et seq.*

CENTRAL (ed.), Transnational Law in Commercial Legal Practice, Münster 1999.

Cerina, Paolo, Interest as Damages in International Commercial Arbitration, 4 Am.Rev.Int'l Arb. 1993, at 255 *et seq.*

Charny, David, Nonlegal Sanctions in Commercial Relationships, 104 Harv.L. Rev. 1990, at 373 *et seq.*

Cheng, Bin, General Principles Of Law as Applied by International Courts and Tribunals, reprinted, Cambridge 2006.

Chieveley, Lord Goff of, The Future of The Common Law, 46 ICLQ 1997, at 745 *et seq.*

Chitty On Contracts, Vol. 1, 30th ed., London 2008.

Chloros, Aleck G., Principle, Reason and Policy in the Development of European Law, 17 Int'l Comp.L.Q. 1968, at 849 *et seq.*

Cian, Giorgio, Fünfzig Jahre italienischer Codice Civile, 1 ZEuP 1993, at 120 *et seq.*

Cistac, Gilles, Le Renouvellement du Role de l'Etat Contractant dans le Commerce International, Eléments pour une Théorie Générale, DPCI 1996, at 168 *et seq.*

Clagett, Bruce M., Present State of the International Law of Compensation for Expropriated Property and Repudiated State Contracts, in: The Southwestern Legal Foundation (ed.), Private Investors Abroad, Dallas 1989, at 12-1 *et seq.*

Clark, Charles E., The Restatement of the Law of Contracts, 43 Yale L.J. 1933/1934, at 643 *et seq.*

Clark, R. Floyd, The Science of Law and Lawmaking, New York 1898.

Coing, Helmut, Die juristische Auslegungsmethoden und die Lehren der allgemeinen Hermeneutik, Cologne, Opladen 1959 [cited as: *Coing*, Auslegungsmethoden].

Coing, Helmut, Die europäische Privatrechtsgeschichte der neueren Zeit als einheitliches Forschungsgebiet, 1 Ius Commune 1967, at 1 *et seq.*

Coing, Helmut, Materielles Recht und Verfahrensrecht in der internationalen Schiedsgerichtsbarkeit, in: Coing/Ellwood/Fouchard/Waehler/Vondracek/Koschucharoff/Lando/Migliazza (eds.), Materielles Recht und Verfahrensrecht in der internationalen Schiedsgerichtsbarkeit, Frankfurt a.M. 1972, at 9 *et seq.*

Coing, Helmut, Einführung, in: Coing/Schmitthoff/Hellner/Gleichmann (eds.), Methoden der Rechtsvereinheitlichung, Frankfurt a.M. 1974, at 7 *et seq.*

Coing, Helmut, book review of: Eugen Langen, Transnational Commercial Law, Leiden 1973, in: 80 JZ 1975, at 40 *et seq.*

Coing, Helmut, Aufgaben der Rechtsvergleichung in unserer Zeit, 35 NJW 1981, at 2601 *et seq.*

Coing, Helmut, Erfahrungen mit einer bürgerlich-rechtlichen Kodifikation in Deutschland, 81 ZVglRWiss (1982), at 1 *et seq.*

Coing, Helmut, La Détermination de la Loi Contractuelle en Droit International Privé Allemand, in: Klein/Vischer (eds.), Colloque de Bâle sur la Loi Régissant les Obligations Contractuelles, Basel, Frankfurt a.M., 1983, at 29 *et seq.*

Coing, Helmut, Probleme der internationalen Bankgarantie, 147 ZHR 1983, at 125 *et seq.*

Coing, Helmut, Zur Entwicklung des Schiedsvertrages im Ius Commune, in: Festschrift H. Hübner, Berlin, New York 1984, at 35 *et seq.*

Coing, Helmut, Grundzüge der Rechtsphilosophie, 5th ed., Berlin, New York 1993.

Commissione reale per la Riforma dei Codici – Commission Française d'Etudes de L'Union Legislative entre les Nations Alliées et Amies (ed.), Projet de Code des Obligations et des Contrats, Rom 1928.

Constantinesco, Léontin-Jean, Rechtsvergleichung, Vol. II, Die rechtsvergleichende Methode, Cologne, Berlin, Bonn, Munich 1972 [cited as: *Constantinesco*, Rechtsvergleichung].

Cooray, L.J.M., The Reception of Roman-Dutch law in Sri Lanka, 7 Comp. and Int'l L.J. of Southern Africa 1974, at 295 *et seq.*

Cooter, Robert, Structural Adjudication and the New Law Merchant: A Model of Decentralized Law, 14 Int'l Rev.L. & Econ. 1994, at 215 *et seq.*

Cooter, Robert D., Decentralized Law for a Complex Economy: The Structural Approach to Adjudicating the New Law Merchant, 144 U.Pa.L.Rev. 1996, at 1643 *et seq.*

Coquillette, Daniel R., Incipit Lex Mercatoria, Que, Quando, Ubi, Inter Quos Et De Quibus Sit. El Tratado De Lex Mercatoria En El Little Red Book De Bristol (Ca. 1280 AD), in: Petit (ed.), Del Ius Mercatorum Al Derecho Mercantil, Madrid 1997, at 143 *et seq.*

Corbett, E.C., FIDIC 4th – A Practical Legal Guide, London 1991.

Craig, W. Laurence/Park, William W./Paulsson, Jan, International Chamber of Commerce Arbitration, 3rd ed., Dobbs Ferry, NY, 2000.

Cremades, Bernardo, Multinational Companies and International Commercial Arbitration, in: Horn (ed.), Legal Problems of Codes of Conduct for Multinational Enterprises, Deventer, Antwerp, Boston, London, Frankfurt a.M. 1980, at 83 *et seq.*

Crook, John R., Applicable Law in International Commercial Arbitration: The Iran-US-Claims Tribunal Experience, 83 AJIL 1989, at 278 *et seq.*

Cross, Rupert/Harris, J.W., Precedents in English Law, 4th ed., Oxford 1991.

Dalhuisen, Jan H., Dalhuisen on International Commercial, Financial and Trade Law, Oxford/Portland 2000.

Dalhuisen, Jan H., Legal Orders and Their Manifestation: The Operation of the International Commercial and Financial Legal Order and Its Lex Mercatoria, 24 Berkeley J.Int'l L. 2006, at 129 *et seq.*

Dasser, Felix, Internationale Schiedsgerichte und Lex Mercatoria, Zurich 1989.

Dasser, Felix, Lex mercatoria: Werkzeug der Praktiker oder Spielzeug der Lehre?, Schweizerische Zeitschrift für internationales und europäisches Recht 1991, 299 *et seq.*

Dasser, Felix, Unfallverhütung bei Rechtskollisionen: Ergebnisorientierte Flexibilität im schweizerischen IPRG, in: Rechtskollisionen, Festschrift Anton Heini zum 65. Geburtstag, Zurich 1995, at 103 *et seq.*

Dasser, Felix, Lex Mercatoria – Critical Comments on a Tricky Topic, in: Appelbaum/Felstiner/Gessner (eds.), Rules and Networks – The Legal Culture of Global Business Transactions, Oxford *et al.* 2001, at 189 *et seq.*

Dasser, Felix, Mouse or Monster? Some Facts and Figures on the *Lex Mercatoria*, in: Zimmermann *et al.* (eds.), Globalisierung und Entstaatlichung des Rechts, Teilband II Nichtstaatliches Privatrecht: Geltung und Genese, Tübingen 2008, at 129 *et seq.*

Dauner-Lieb, Barbara, Auf dem Weg zu einem europäischen Schuldrecht?, 57 NJW 2004, at 1431 *et seq.*

Dauner-Lieb, Barbara, Viereinhalb Jahre Gesetz zur Modernisierung des Schuldrechts, 56 Anwaltsblatt 2006, at 430 *et seq.*

David, René, L'Unification internationale du droit privé, Brussels 1967.

David, René, L'Unification ou l'Harmonisation Législative sans Engagement International, UNIDROIT Annuaire 1967–1968, Vol. II, at 77 *et seq.*

David, René, The International Unification of Private Law, in: International Encyclopedia of Comparative Law, Vol. 2 (The Legal Systems of the World, Their Comparison and Unification), Chapter 5, Tübingen 1971.

David, René, Le Droit du Commerce International: Une Nouvelle Tache pour les Legislateurs Nationaux ou une Nouvelle 'Lex Mercatoria'?, in: UNIDROIT (ed.), New Directions in International Trade Law, 2 Vols., New York 1977, at 5 *et seq.*

David, René, Arbitration in International Trade, Deventer, Antwerp, Boston, London, Frankfurt a.M. 1985.

David, René, Le Droit Du Commerce International, Paris 1987.

David, René/Brierley, John E.C., Major Legal Systems in the World Today, London 1985.

de Groot, G.-R./Schneider, H., Das Werturteil in der Rechtsvergleichung, Die Suche nach dem besseren Recht, in: Boele-Woelki/Grosheide/Hondius/Steenhoff (eds.), Comparability and Evaluation, Dordrecht, Boston, London 1994, at 53 *et seq.*

Delaume, Georges, What is an International Contract? An American and a Gallic Dilemma, 28 ICLQ 1979, at 258 *et seq.*

Delaume, Georges, ICSID Arbitration: Practical Considerations, 1 J.Int'l Arb. 1984, at 101 *et seq.*

Delaume, Georges, Law and Practice of Transnational Contracts, New York, London, Rome 1988 [cited as: *Delaume*, Transnational Contracts].

Delaume, Georges, The Proper Law of State Contracts and the Lex Mercatoria: A Reappraisal, 3 ICSID Rev. FILJ 1988, at 79 *et seq.*

Delbrück, Jost, Globalization of Law, 1 Ind.J.Gl.Legal Studies 1993, at 9 *et seq.*

De Ly, Filip J.M., De Lex Mercatoria, Inleiding op de studie van het transnationaal handelsrecht, Antwerp 1989.

De Ly, Filip, International Business Law and Lex Mercatoria, Amsterdam/London/New York/Tokyo 1992.

De Ly, Filip J.M., Europese Gemeenschap en privaatrecht, Zwolle 1993.

De Ly, Filip J.M., Uniform Commercial Law and International Self-Regulation, Uniform Law Rev. 1997, at 519 *et seq.*

De Ly, Filip, *Lex Mercatoria* (New Law Merchant): Globalization and International Self-Regulation, 3 Diritto del Commercio Internazionale 2000, at 555 *et seq.*

Derains, Yves, Le Statut des Usages du Commerce International devant les Jurisdictions Arbitrales, Rev.d.Arb. 1973, at 122 *et seq.*

Derains, Yves, Possible Conflict of Law Rules and the Rules Applicable to the Dispute, in: Sanders (ed.), UNCITRAL'S Project for a Model Law on International Commercial Arbitration, Deventer, Antwerp, Boston, London, Frankfurt a.M. 1984, at 169 *et seq.*

Derains, Yves, L'Obligation de Minimiser le Dommage dans la Jurisprudence Arbitrale, RDAI 1987, at 375 *et seq.*

Derains, Yves, International Commercial Arbitration in Civil Law Countries, in: Sanders (ed.), ICCA Congress, Ser. No. 4, Deventer 1989, at 229 *et seq.*

Derains, Yves, Transnational Law in ICC Arbitration, in: Berger (ed.), The Practice of Transnational Law, The Hague, London, Boston 2001, at 43 *et seq.*

Dernburg, Heinrich, Geschichte und Theorie der Kompensation nach römischem und neuerem Rechte, 2nd ed., Heidelberg 1868 (reprint Aalen 1965).

Dernburg, Heinrich, System des Römischen Rechts, Pandekten Vol. I, Berlin 1911.

Devolvé, Jean-Louis, Arbitration in France: The French Law of National and International Arbitration 86 (1982).

Dezalay, Yves/Garth, Bryant G., Dealing in Virtue, International Commercial Arbitration and the Construction of a Transnational Legal Order, Chicago, London 1996.

Diamond, Aubrey L., Force Majeure and Frustration under International Sales Contracts, in: McKendrick (ed.), Force Majeure and Frustration of Contracts, London 1991, at 165 *et seq.*

Dickstein, Michael E., Revitalizing the International Law Governing Concession Agreements, 5/6 Int'l Tax. & Bus.Lawy. 1987/1988, at 54 *et seq.*

Diedrich, Frank, Autonome Auslegung von Internationalem Einheitsrecht, Baden-Baden 1994.

Dillard, Hardy, Some Aspects of Law and Diplomacy, 91 Rec.Cours 1957, at 449 *et seq.*

Dölle, Hans (ed.), Kommentar zum Einheitlichen Kaufrecht, Munich 1976 [cited as: Dölle-*author*, EKG].

Dolfen, Michael, Europäisches Privatrecht im Werden, in: Laum/Klein/Strauch (eds.), 175 Jahre Oberlandesgericht Köln, 1994, at 257 *et seq.*

Dolzer, Rudolf, International Agencies for the Formulation of Transnational Economic Law, in: Horn/Schmitthoff (eds.), The Transnational Law of International Commercial Transactions, Antwerp, Boston, London, Frankfurt a.M. 1982, at 61 *et seq.*

Dolzer, Rudolf, Indirect Expropriation of Alien Property, 1 ICSID Rev. I-FILJ 1986, at 41 *et seq.*

Domingo, Rafael/Ortega, Javier/Rodríguez-Antolín, Beatriz/Zambrana, Nicolás, Principios de derecho global – 1000 reglas, principios y aforismos jurídicos comentados, 2nd ed., Cizur Menor 2006.

Domke, Martin, Towards an 'International' Public Policy in Commercial Arbitration, in: Festschrift Bülow, Cologne, Berlin, Bonn, Munich 1981, at 49 *et seq.*

Dorner, Gerhard, BOT-Projekte in der nationalen und internationalen Praxis – Wechselwirkungen durch Vertragsvielfalt und Mehrparteienverbund, in: Nicklisch (ed.), Rechtsfragen privatfinanzierter Projekte, Heidelberg 1994, at 75 *et seq.*

Drobnig, Ulrich, Rechtsvergleichung und Rechtssoziologie, 18 RabelsZ 1953, at 294 *et seq.*

Drobnig, Ulrich, General Principles of European Contract Law, in: Volken/Šarčević (eds.), International Sale of Goods, Dubrovnik Lectures, New York, London, Rome 1986, at 305 *et seq.*

Drobnig, Ulrich, Internationale Schiedsgerichtsbarkeit und wirtschaftliche Eingriffsnormen, in: Festschrift Kegel, Stuttgart, Berlin, Cologne, Mainz 1987, at 95 *et seq.*

Drobnig, Ulrich, Ein Vertragsrecht für Europa, in: Festschrift Steindorff, Berlin, New York 1990, at 1141 *et seq.*

Drobnig, Ulrich, Substantive Validity, 40 Am.J.Comp.L. 1992, at 635 *et seq.*

Drobnig, Ulrich, The Use of the UNIDROIT Principles by National and Supra-National Courts, in: Institute of International Business Law and Practice (ed.), The UNIDROIT Principles of International Commercial Contracts – A New Lex Mercatoria?, Paris 1995 (ICC Publ. No. 490/1), at 223 *et seq.*

Drüke, Heiner, Die Haftung der Muttergesellschaft für die Schulden der Tochtergesellschaft, Cologne, Berlin, Bonn, Munich 1990.

Dünnweber, Inge, Vertrag zur Erstellung einer schlüsselfertigen Industrieanlage im internationalen Wirtschaftsverkehr, Berlin, New York 1984.

Duguit, Léon, Les Transformations du Droit Public, Paris 1913.

Duve, Christian/Keller, Moritz, Privatisierung der Justiz – bleibt die Rechtsfortbildung auf der Strecke? – Ein Beitrag zur Auflösung des Spannungsverhältnisses von Privatautonomie und Rechtsfortbildung in der Schiedsgerichtsbarkeit, 3 SchiedsVZ 2005, at 169 *et seq.*

Dworkin, Ronald, Taking Rights Seriously, Cambridge (Massachusetts) 1977.

Dworkin, Ronald, Law's Empire, Harvard 1986.

Ebenroth, Carsten Thomas/Karl, Joachim, Die Multilaterale Investitions-Garantie-Agentur, Heidelberg 1989.
Ebert, Kurt, Rechtsvergleichung, Bern 1978.
Ebke, Werner F., Internationales Devisenrecht, Heidelberg 1991.
Ebke, Werner F./Steinhauer, Bettina M., The Doctrine of Good Faith in German Contract Law, in: Beatson/Friedmann (eds.), Good Faith and Fault in Contract Law, Oxford, New York 1997, at 171 *et seq.*
Eckert, Hans-Werner, Die EG-Richtline über mißbräuchliche Klauseln in Verbraucherverträgen und ihre Auswirkungen auf das deutsche Recht, 47 WM 1993, at 1070 *et seq.*
Eckert, Hans-Werner, Der Referentenentwurf zur Umsetzung der EG-Richtlinie über mißbräuchliche Klauseln in Verbraucherverträgen, 7 ZIP 1994, at 1986.
Ehricke, Ulrich, Softwareverträge und internationale Schiedgerichtsbarkeit, 5 CR 1989, at 665 *et seq.*
Ehricke, Ulrich, Zur Einführung: Grundstrukturen und Probleme der lex mercatoria, 30 JuS 1990, at 967 *et seq.*
Ehrlich, Eugen, Das lebende Recht der Völker der Bukowina (1912), in: Ehrlich (ed.), Recht und Leben, Berlin 1967, at 43 *et seq.*
Ehrlich, Eugen, Grundlegung der Soziologie des Rechts (edited and revised by Manfred Rehbinder), 4th ed., Berlin 1989.
Eidenmüller, Horst, Recht als Produkt, 64 JZ 2009, at 641 *et seq.*
Eidenmüller, Horst/Faust, Florian/Grigoleit, Hans Christoph/Jansen, Nils/Wagner, Gerhard/Zimmermann, Reinhard, Der Gemeinsame Referenzrahmen für das Europäische Privatrecht – Wertungsfragen und Kodifikationsprobleme, 63 JZ 2008, at 529 *et seq.*
Eisemann, Frédéric, Zur Rechtswahl in der Schiedsgerichtsbarkeit bei Kaufverträgen, in: Festschrift Bülow, Cologne, Berlin, Bonn, Munich 1981, at 59 *et seq.*
Ekeberg, Birger, The Scandinavian Co-operation in the Field of Legislation, in: UNIDROIT (ed.), Unification of Law, Rome 1948, at 321 *et seq.*
Enderlein, Fritz, contribution, in: UNIDROIT (ed.), New Directions in International Trade Law, 2 Vols., New York 1977, at 447 *et seq.*
Enderlein, Fritz *et al.*, Handbuch der Außenhandelsverträge, Vol. 1, Der Außenhandelskaufvertrag, 3rd ed., Berlin, Heidelberg 1986 [cited as: *Enderlein*, Der Außenhandelskaufvertrag].
Engisch, Karl, Die Einheit der Rechtsordnung, Heidelberg 1935.
Engisch, Karl, Sinn und Tragweite juristischer Systematik, 10 Studium Generale 1957, at 173 *et seq.*
Erauw, J., Something Funny Happened to Foreign Law on its Way to the Forum, in: Sumampouw/Barnhoorn/Freedberg-Swartzburg/Tromm/Wade (eds.), Law and Reality, Dordrecht, Boston, London 1992, at 63 *et seq.*
Erler, Georg, Grundprobleme des internationalen Wirtschaftsrechts, Göttingen 1956.
Esser, Josef, Wandlungen von Billigkeit und Billigkeitsrechtsprechung im modernen Privatrecht, in: Summum ius – summa iniuria, Tübingen 1963, at 22 *et seq.*
Esser, Josef, Vorverständnis und Methodenwahl in der Rechtsfindung, Frankfurt a.M. 1970.

Esser, Josef, Grundsatz und Norm in der richterlichen Fortbildung des Privatrechts, 4th ed., Tübingen 1990 [cited as: *Esser*, Grundsatz und Norm].
Everling, Ulrich, Rechtsvereinheitlichung durch Richterrecht in der Europäischen Gemeinschaft, 50 RabelsZ 1986, at 193 *et seq.*

Fabricius, Fritz, Clive Schmitthoff – Leben, Beruf und Werk, in: Festschrift Schmitthoff, Frankfurt a.M. 1973, at 11 *et seq.*
Fabricius, Fritz, Internationales Handelsrecht und Weltfrieden, in: Festschrift Schmitthoff, Frankfurt a.M. 1973, at 101 *et seq.*
Farjat, Gérard, Réflexions sur les codes de conduite privés, in: Fouchard/Kahn/Lyon-Caen (eds.), Le droit des relations économiques internationales, Études offertes à Berthold Goldman, Paris 1982, at 47 *et seq.*
Farnsworth, Allan, UNCITRAL and the Progressive Development of International Trade, in: Festschrift Schmitthoff, Frankfurt a.M. 1973, at 145 *et seq.*
Farnsworth, Allan, Ingredients in the Redaction of the Restatement (Second) of Contracts, 81 Columbia Law Review 1981, at 5 *et seq.*
Farnsworth, Allan, Unification of Sales Law: Usage and Course of Dealing, in: Festschrift Sauveplanne, Deventer 1984, at 81 *et seq.*
Farnsworth, Allan, Duties of Good Faith and Fair Dealing under the UNIDROIT Principles, Relevant International Conventions and National Laws, Tul.J.Int.-Comp.L. 1995, at 56.
Farnsworth, Allan, Good Faith in Contract Performance, in: Beatson/Friedmann (eds.), Good Faith and Fault in Contract Law, Oxford, New York 1997, at 153 *et seq.*
Farnsworth, Allan, Contracts, 4th ed., New York 2004.
Feenstra, Robert, Romeinsrechtelijke grondslagen van het Nederlands privaatrecht – Inleidende Hoofdstukken, 6th ed., Leiden 1994.
Ferid, Murad, Internationales Privatrecht, 3rd ed., Frankfurt a.M. 1986.
Ferrante, Riccardo, Codification and *Lex Mercatoria*: The Maritime Law of the Second Book of the *Code de commerce* (1808), in: Piergiovanni (ed.), From *Lex Mercatoria* to Commercial Law, Berlin 2005, at 121 *et seq.*
Ferrari, Franco, L'ambito di applicazione della convenzione di Vienna sulla vendita internazionale, 48 Riv.Tr.Dir.Pr.Civ. 1994, at 893 *et seq.*
Ferrari, Franco, Le Champ d'Application des 'Principes pour les Contrats Commerciaux Internationaux' Élaborés par UNIDROIT, 47 Rev.int.dr.comp. 1995, at 985 *et seq.*
Ferrari, Franco, Interprétation Uniforme de la Convention de Vienne de 1980 sur la Vente Internationale, 48 Rev.dr.int.dr.comp. 1996, at 813 *et seq.*
Ferrari, Franco, Principi Generali Inseriti Nelle Convenzioni Internazionali Di Diritto Uniforme: L'Esempio Della Vendita, Del 'Factoring' E Del 'Leasing' Internazionali, 51 Riv.Tr.Dir.Pr.Civ. 1997, at 651 *et seq.*
Ferrari, Franco, Das Verhältnis zwischen den Unidroit-Grundsätzen und den allgemeinen Grundsätzen internationaler Einheitsprivatrechtskonventionen, 103 JZ 1998, at 9 *et seq.*
Fezer, Karl-Heinz, Die Pluralität des Rechts, 90 JZ 1985, at 762 *et seq.*

Ficker, Hans Claudius, L'Etat du Droit Comparé en Allemagne, 10 Rev.dr.int.dr. comp. 1958, at 701 *et seq.*

FIDIC (ed.), Conditions of Contract for Works of Civil Engineering Construction, Parts I & II, 4th ed. 1987, reprinted 1988 with editorial amendments, reprinted 1992 with further amendments.

Fikentscher, Wolfgang, Wirtschaftsrecht, Vol. I, Munich 1983.

Firsching, Karl, Übereinkommen über das auf vertragliche Schuldverhältnisse anzuwendende Recht (IPR-VertragsÜ) vom 11.6.1980, 1 IPRax 1981, at 37 *et seq.*

Fischer, Gerfried, Culpa in contrahendo im internationalen Privatrecht, 96 JZ 1991, at 168 *et seq.*

Fischer, Peter, Das Internationale Wirtschaftsrecht, 19 GYIL 1976, at 143 *et seq.*

Flessner, Axel, Interessenjurisprudenz im internationalen Privatrecht, Tübingen 1990.

Flume, Werner, Das Video-Urteil und das GmbH-Recht, 45 DB 1992, at 25 *et seq.*

Fontaine, Marcel, Les Clauses de Hardship – Aménagement Conventionnel de l'Imprévision dans les Contrats à Long Terme, DPCI 1976, at 7 *et seq.*

Fontaine, Marcel, Les Clauses de Force Majeure dans les Contrats Internationaux, DPCI 1979, at 469 *et seq.*

Fontaine, Marcel, Les Clauses Pénales dans les Contrats Internationaux, DPCI 1982, at 401 *et seq.*

Fontaine, Marcel, Content and Performance, 40 Am.J.Comp.L. 1992, at 645 *et seq.*

Fortier, L. Yves, The Occasional Unwarranted Assumption of Confidentiality, 15 Arb.Int'l 1999, at 131 *et seq.*

Fortier, L. Yves, The New, New *Lex Mercatoria*, or, Back To The Future, 17 Arb.Int'l 2001, at 121 *et seq.*

Fouchard, Philippe, L'Arbitrage Commercial International, Paris 1965.

Fouchard, Philippe/Kahn, Philippe/Lyon-Caen, Antoine (eds.), Le droit des relations économiques internationales, Études offertes à Berthold Goldman, Paris 1982.

Fragistas, Charalambos N., Arbitrage Etranger et Arbitrage International en Droit Privé, 49 Rev.crit.dr.int.priv. 1960, at 1 *et seq.*

Franzese, Lugio, Contratto Negozio E Lex Mercatoria Tra Autonomia Ed Eteronomia, 51 Riv.Tr.Dir.Pr.Civ. 1997, at 772 *et seq.*

Frey, Kaspar, Wie ändert sich das AGB-Gesetz, 14 ZIP 1993, at 572 *et seq.*

Friedl, Birgit, Haftung bei Abbruch von Vertragsverhandlungen im deutschen und anglo-australischen Recht, ZVglRWiss 97 (1998), at 161 *et seq.*

Friedmann, Wolfgang, The Changing Structure of International Law, London 1964.

Friedmann, Wolfgang, The Contractual Joint Venture, 7 Col. J. W. Bus. 1972, at 57 *et seq.*

Frischkorn, Michael, Definitions of the Lex Mercatoria and the Effects of Codifications on the Lex Mercatoria's Flexibility, 7 Eur. J. L. Reform (2005), at 331 *et seq.*

Fukuyama, Francis, America at the Crossroads: Democracy, Power, and the Neoconservative Legacy, New Haven 2006.

Fülbier, Andreas, Das Vertrags- und Wirtschaftsrecht des Gegenkaufs im internationalen Wirtschaftsverkehr, Berlin, New York 1992.

Furmston, Michael P., Breach of Contract, 40 Am.J.Comp.L. 1992, at 671 *et seq.*

Furmston, Michael P., The UNIDROIT Principles and International Commercial Arbitration, in: Institute of International Business Law and Practice (ed.), UNIDROIT Principles on International Commercial Contracts: A New Lex Mercatoria?, Paris 1995, at 199 *et seq.*

Gäbel, Johannes K., Neuere Probleme zur Aufrechnung im IPR, Munich 1983.

Gaillard, Emmanuel, L'interdiction de se contredire au détriment d'autrui comme principe général du droit du commerce international, Rev.d.Arb. 1985, at 241 *et seq.*

Gaillard, Emmanuel, The Use of Comparative Law in International Commercial Arbitration, in: Sanders (ed.), ICCA Congress Ser. No. 4, Deventer, Boston 1989, at 283 *et seq.*

Gaillard, Emmanuel (ed.), Transnational Rules in International Commercial Arbitration, Paris 1993 (ICC Publ. No. 480/4).

Gaillard, Emmanuel, Trente ans de Lex mercatoria, Pour une application selective de la méthode des principes généraux du droit, 122 Clunet 1995, at 5 *et seq.*

Gaillard, Emmanuel, Thirty Years of Lex Mercatoria: Towards the Discriminating Application of Transnational Rules, in: van den Berg (ed.), Planning Efficient Arbitration Proceedings/The Law Applicable in International Arbitration, ICC congress, Ser. No. 7, The Hague 1996, at 570 *et seq.* (reprinted in ICSID Rev.-FILJ 1995, at 208 *et seq.*).

Gaillard, Emmanuel, Transnational Law: A Legal System or a Method of Decision-Making?, in: Berger (ed.), The Practice of Transnational Law, The Hague, London, Boston 2001, at 53 *et seq.*

Gaillard, Emmanuel, Aspects philosophiques du droit de l'arbitrage internationale, 329 Recueil des Cours 2007, at 53 *et seq.*

Galgano, Francesco, The New Lex Mercatoria, 2 Ann.Surv.Int'l & Comp.L. 1995, at 99 *et seq.*

Gallo, Paolo, Unjust Enrichment: A Comparative Analysis, 40 Am.J.Comp.L. 1992, at 431 *et seq.*

Gamillscheg, Franz, Die Grundrechte im Arbeitsrecht, 164 AcP 1964, at 385 *et seq.*

Gandolfi, Giuseppe, Pour un Code Européen des Contrats, 91 RTD civ. 1992, at 707 *et seq.*

Gandolfi, Giuseppe, Introduction, in: Académie des privatistes européens (Academy of European Private Lawyers) (ed.), Code européen des contrats – Avant-Projet, 3rd ed., Milan 2002, at LV *et seq.*

Gannagé, Léna, Le contrat sans loi en droit international privé, in: Boele-Woelki/van Erp (eds.), General Reports of the XVIIth Congress of the International Academy of Comparative Law, Bruxelles/Utrecht 2007, at 275 *et seq.*

Gentinetta, Jörg, Konkordat der Schweizer Kantone zur Vereinheitlichung des Rechts der Schiedsgerichtsbarkeit, AWD 1970, at 113 *et seq.*

Gentinetta, Jörg, Die Lex Fori Internationaler Handelsschiedsgerichte, Bern 1973.

van Gerven, Walter, European Court of Justice Case Law as a Means of Unification of Private Law?, 20 Ford.Int'l L.J. 1997, at 680 *et seq.*

Giardina, Andrea, L'Application des Principes UNIDROIT aux Contrats Internationaux, in: Institute of International Business Law and Practice (ed.), UNIDROIT Principles of International Commercial Contracts: A New Lex Mercatoria?, Paris 1995, at 143 *et seq.*

Giovanoli, Mario, Télécommunications et Forme Ecrite dans les Contrats Internationaux, in: Mélanges Paul Piotet, Bern 1990, at 425 *et seq.*

Gleichmann, Karl, Methoden der Rechtsangleichung und Rechtsvereinheitlichung innerhalb der EWG, in: Coing/Schmitthoff/Hellner/Gleichmann (eds.), Methoden der Rechtsvereinheitlichung, Frankfurt a.M. 1974, at 35 *et seq.*

Glenn, Patrick H., The Capture, Reconstruction and Marginalization of 'Custom', Am.J.Comp.L. 1997, at 613 *et seq.*

Glöckner, Martin, Aus der Tätigkeit der IRZ-Stiftung, 3 WiRO 1994, at 367 *et seq.*

Glossner, Ottoarndt, The New York Convention on the Recognition and Enforcement of Foreign Arbitral Awards, in: Sanders (ed.), ICCA Congress Ser. No. 4, Deventer 1989, at 275 *et seq.*

Goldman, Berthold, La Compagnie de Suez, société internationale, Le Monde, October 4, 1956, at 3.

Goldman, Berthold, Frontières du Droit et Lex Mercatoria, 13 Archives de philosophie du droit 1964, at 177 *et seq.*

Goldman, Berthold, contribution, in: UNIDROIT (ed.), New Directions in International Trade Law, 2 Vols., New York 1977, at 498 *et seq.*

Goldman, Berthold, La Lex Mercatoria dans les Contrats et l'Arbitrage International: Réalités et Perspectives, 106 Clunet 1979, at 475 *et seq.*

Goldman, Berthold, The Applicable Law: General Principles of Law – The Lex Mercatoria, in: Lew (ed.), Contemporary Problems in International Arbitration, London 1986, at 113 *et seq.*

Goldman, Berthold, notes to: Cour d'Appel de Paris de 13.7.1989, Compañía Valenciana de Cementos Portland v. Société Primary Coal Ltd., Clunet 1990, at 433 *et seq.*

Goldman, Berthold, Nouvelles Réflexions sur la Lex Mercatoria, in: Festschrift Pierre Lalive, Basel, Frankfurt a.M. 1993, at 241 *et seq.*

Goldstajn, Aleksandar, The New Law Merchant, J.Bus.L. 1961, at 12 *et seq.*

Goldstajn, Aleksandar, The New Law Merchant Reconsidered, in: Festschrift Schmitthoff, Frankfurt a.M. 1973, at 171 *et seq.*

Goldstajn, Aleksandar, Usages of Trade and other Autonomous Rules of International Trade According to the UN (1980) Sales Convention, in: Volken/Šarčević (eds.), International Sale Of Goods, Dubrovnik Lectures, New York, London, Rome 1986, at 55 *et seq.*

Goldstajn, Aleksandar, Reflections on the Structure of the Modern Law of International Trade, in: Šarčević (ed.), International Contracts and Conflicts of Laws. A Collection of Essays, London *et al.* 1990, at 14 *et seq.*

Goode, Roy, Reflections on the Harmonisation of Commercial Law, 9 Unif.L.Rev. 1991, at 54 *et seq.*

Goode, Roy, Usage and its Reception in Transnational Commercial Law, 46 ICLQ 1997, at 1 *et seq.*

Goode, Roy, International Restatements of Contract and English Contract Law, 15 Unif.L.Rev. 1997, at 231 *et seq.*

Goode, Roy, Rule, Practice, and Pragmatism in Transnational Commercial Law, 54 ICLQ 2005, at 539 *et seq.*

Goode, Roy/Kronke, Herbert/McKendrick, Ewan, Transnational Commercial Law – Text, Cases, and Materials, New York 2007.

Goodrich, Herbert F., Restatement and Codification, in: Honnold (ed.), The Life of the Law, London 1964, at 170 *et seq.*

Gopalan, Sandeep, New Trends in the Making of International Commercial Law, 23 J.L. & Com. 2004, at 117 *et seq.*

Gordley, James, The Philosophical Origins of Modern Contract Doctrine, Oxford 1991.

Gordley, James, An American Perspective on the Unidroit Principles, Rome 1996.

Gotanda, Awarding Interest in International Arbitration, 90 AJIL 1996, at 40 *et seq.*

Gottschalk, Eckart, Neues zur Abgrenzung zwischen AGB und Individualabrede, 58 NJW 2005, at 2493 *et seq.*

Gottwald, Peter, Die sachliche Kontrolle internationaler Schiedssprüche durch staatliche Gerichte, in: Festschrift Nagel, Münster 1987, at 54 *et seq.*

Grabinski, Klaus, Die kollisionsrechtliche Behandlung des Durchgriffs, Frankfurt a.M. 1991.

Gramlich, Ludwig, Rechtsgestalt, Regelungstypen und Rechtsschutz bei grenzüberschreitenden Investitionen, Baden-Baden 1984.

Granzow, Joachim H., Das UNCITRAL-Modellgesetz über die internationale Handelsschiedsgerichtsbarkeit von 1985, Munich 1987.

Grasmann, Günther, Nachruf René David, 55 RabelsZ 1991, at 1 *et seq.*

Gray, Whitmore, E pluribus unum? A Bicentennial Report on Unification of Law in the United States, 50 RabelsZ 1986, at 111 *et seq.*

Grimm, Dieter, Historische Erfahrungen mit Rechtsvereinheitlichung – das frühe 19. Jahrhundert in Deutschland, 50 RabelsZ 1986, at 61 *et seq.*

Großfeld, Bernhard, Macht und Ohnmacht der Rechtsvergleichung, Tübingen 1984.

Großfeld, Bernhard, Grundfragen der Rechtsvergleichung, in: Festschrift Lukes, Cologne, Berlin, Bonn, Munich 1989, at 655 *et seq.*

Großfeld, Bernhard, Europäisches Gesellschaftsrecht, 46 WM 1992, at 2121 *et seq.*

Großfeld, Bernhard/Junker, Abbo, Das CoCom im internationalen Wirtschaftsrecht, Tübingen 1991.

Großmann-Doerth, Hans, Der Jurist und das autonome Recht des Welthandels, 58 JW 1929, at 3447 *et seq.*

Grundmann, Stefan, Das Europäische Bankaufsichtsrecht wächst zum System, Heidelberg 1990.

Grundmann, Stefan, Lex mercatoria und Rechtsquellenlehre, in: Jickeli/Kotzur/Noack/Weber (eds.), Jahrbuch Junger Zivilrechtswissenschaftler 1991, Stuttgart, Munich, Hannover, Berlin, Weimar 1992, at 43 *et seq.*

Gruson, Michael, The Remedies Opinion in International Transactions, Int.Bus.-Lawy. 1993, at 125 *et seq.*
Gutteridge, H.C., Comparative Law, Cambridge 1949.

Haanappel, P.P.C./Mackaay, Ejan, Nieuw Nederlands Burgerlijk Wetboek – Het Vermogensrecht, New Netherlands Civil Code – Patrimonial Law, Deventer, Boston 1997.
Häberle, Peter, Grundrechtsgeltung und Grundrechtsinterpretation im Verfassungsstaat – Zugleich zur Rechtsvergleichung als 'fünfter' Auslegungsmethode, 94 JZ 1989, at 913 *et seq.*
Hadding, Walther/Schneider, Uwe H. (eds.), Die Forderungsabtretung, insbesondere zur Kreditsicherung, in der Bundesrepublik Deutschland und in ausländischen Rechtsordnungen, Berlin 1986.
Hadding, Walther/Schneider, Uwe H. (eds.), Die Forderungsabtretung, insbesondere zur Kreditsicherung, in ausländischen Rechtsordnungen, Berlin 1999.
Hahn, Hugo J., Book Review of: Potacs, Michael, Devisenbewirtschaftung; Seuß, Melanie, Extraterritoriale Geltung von Devisenkontrollen; Unteregge, Udo, Ausländisches Devisenrecht und internationale Kreditverträge, 58 RabelsZ 1994, at 194 *et seq.*
Hall, Maximilian J. B., Basel II: Panacea or a missed opportunity?, 7 JBR 2006, at 106 *et seq.*
Hanisch, Hans, Das Genfer Abkommen über die Stellvertretung bei internationalen Wareneinkäufen von 1983, in: Festschrift Gieger, Bern 1989, at 251 *et seq.*
Hanotiau, Bernard, La Détermination et l'Evaluation du Dommage Réparable: Principes Généraux et Principes en Emergence, in: Gaillard (ed.) Transnational Rules in International Commercial Arbitration, Paris 1993 (ICC Publ. No. 480/4), at 209 *et seq.*
Harries, Heinrich, Die Rechtsscheinshaftung für fehlerhafte Rechtsgutachten bei internationalen Verträgen, in: Festschrift Zweigert, Tübingen 1981, at 451 *et seq.*
Harris D. J./Parry, Clive/Hopkins, Charity (eds.), An Index of British Treaties, Vol. 4: 1968–1988, London 1991.
Harrison, Reziya, Good Faith in Sales, London 1996.
Hart, Herbert L.A., The Concept of Law, Oxford 1961.
Hartard, Matthias, Die Europäische Wirtschaftliche Interessenvereinigung im deutschen, englischen und französischen Recht, Berlin, New York 1991.
Hartkamp, Arthur S., Voorwoord, in: Burgerlijk Wetboek 2009/2010, Ars Aequi Wetseditie, Nijmegen 2009, at V *et seq.*
Hartkamp, Arthur S., Judicial Discretion Under the New Civil Code of the Netherlands, 40 Am.J.Comp.L. 1992, at 551 *et seq.*
Hartkamp, Arthur S., The UNIDROIT Principles of International Commercial Contracts and the United Nations Convention on Contracts for the International Sale of Goods, in: Boele-Woelki/Grosheide/Hondius/Steenhoff (eds.), Comparability and Evaluation, Dordrecht, Boston, London 1994, at 85 *et seq.*

Hartkamp, Arthur S., The UNIDROIT Principles of International Commercial Contracts and the New Dutch Civil Code, in: CJHB/Brunner-Bundel, Deventer 1994, at 127 *et seq.*

Hartkamp, Arthur S., Principles of Contract Law, in: Hartkamp/Hesselink/Hondius/Joustra/du Perron/Veldman (eds.), Towards a European Civil Code, 3rd ed., Nijmegen 2004, at 125 *et seq.*

Hartmann, Max, Die philosophische Grundlage der Naturwissenschaften: Erkenntnistheorie und Methologie, Stuttgart 1959.

Hascher, Dominique, Note to ICC Award No. 7197, 120 Clunet 1993, at 1037 *et seq.*

Hattenhauer, Hans, Thibaut und Savigny – Ihre programmatischen Schriften, Munich 1973.

Hau, Wolfgang *see* Wolf/Lindacher/Pfeiffer.

Hauriou, Maurice, Die Theorie der Institution, in: Schriften zur Rechtstheorie 1965, No. 5.

Hauschka, Christoph, Die Tätigkeit der Europäischen Gemeinschaft im Gesellschaftsrecht zwischen Rechtsangleichung und Funktionen allgemeiner Gesetzgebung, 23 ZRP 1990, at 179 *et seq.*

Hay, Peter, Zum Wegfall der Geschäftsgrundlage im anglo-amerikanischen Recht, 164 AcP 1964, at 231 *et seq.*

van Hecke, Georges, Intergration Economique et Unification du Droit Privé, in: De Conflictu Legum, Bundel opstellen aangeboden aan R.D. Kollewijn, J. Offerhaus ter gelegenheid van hun zeventigste verjaardag, Brussels 1962, at 198 *et seq.*

van Hecke, Georges, Internationaal Privaatrecht, 2nd ed., 1989.

Hedemann, Justus Wilhelm, Reichsgericht und Wirtschaftsrecht, Ein Bild deutscher Praxis, Jena 1929.

Hedemann, Justus Wihelm, Die Flucht in die Generalklauseln, Eine Gefahr für Recht und Staat, Tübingen 1933.

Heinemann, Klaus, Pre-incorporation Transactions, Cologne, Berlin, Bonn, Munich 1990.

Heini, Anton, Die Rechtswahl im Vertragsrecht und das neue IPR-Gesetz, in: Festschrift Rudolf Moser, 1987, at 67 *et seq.*

Heini, Anton/Keller, Max/Siehr, Kurt/Vischer, Frank/Volken, Paul, IPRG-Kommentar, Zurich 1993 [cited as: Heini/Keller/Siehr/Vischer/Volken-*author*, IPRG-Kommentar].

Heini, Anton, Der materiellrechtliche ordre public im neuen schweizerischen Recht der internationalen Schiedsgerichtsbarkeit, in: Festschrift Habscheid, at 153 *et seq.*

Heinrichs, Helmut, Die EG-Richtlinie über mißbräuchliche Klauseln in Verbraucherverträgen, 47 NJW 1993, at 1817 *et seq.*

Helps, Dominic D.W., Harmonisation of Construction Law and Practice – Part I: The Current Position, Int'l Constr.L.Rev. 1997, at 525 *et seq.*

Herber, Rolf, 'Lex mercatoria' und 'Principles' – gefährliche Irrlichter im internationalen Kaufrecht, 3 IHR 2003, at 1 *et seq.*

Herber, Rolf/Czerwenka, Beate, Internationales Kaufrecht, Munich 1991.

Herdegen, Matthias, Internationales Wirtschaftsrecht, 8th ed., Munich 2009.
Herrmann, Gerold, The Contribution of UNCITRAL to the Development of International Trade Law, in: Horn/Schmitthoff (eds.), The Transnational Law of International Commercial Transactions, Antwerp, Boston, London, Frankfurt a.M. 1982, at 35 *et seq.*
Hesselink, Martijn W., The Principles of European Contract Law: Some Choices made by the Lando Commission, in: Hesselink/de Vries (eds.), Principles of European Contract Law, Deventer 2001, at 8 *et seq.*
Heuzé, Vincent, La Vente Internationale de Marchandises, Paris 1992.
Highet, Keith, The Enigma of the Lex Mercatoria, 63 Tul. L. Rev. (1988–1989), at 613 *et seq.*
Highet, Keith, The Enigma of the Lex Mercatoria, in: Carbonneau (ed.), Lex Mercatoria and Arbitration: A Discussion of the New Law Merchant, 2nd ed., New York 1998, at 133 *et seq.*
Hill, Richard, A Businessman's View of the UNIDROIT Principles, J.Int'l Arb. No. 2 1996, 163.
Hillgruber, Christian, Abschied von der Privatautonomie?, 28 ZRP 1995, at 6 *et seq.*
von Hippel, Fritz, Zur Gesetzmäßigkeit juristischer Systembildung, Berlin 1930.
Hirsch, Alain, Worldwide Legal Harmonization of Banking Law and Securities Regulation, in: Buxbaum/Hertig/Hirsch/Hopt (eds.), European Business Law, Berlin, New York 1991, at 347 *et seq.*
Hirte, Heribert, Wege zu einem europäischen Zivilrecht, Stuttgart/Munich 1996.
Hobe, Stephan, Global Challenge to Statehood: The Increasingly Important Role of Nongovernmental Organizations, 5 Ind. J. Global Legal Stud. 1997, at 191 *et seq.*
Hobeck, Paul, Anmerkung/Annotation to ICC-Award of January 29, 2001 (Arbitration No. 10279), 3 SchiedsVZ 2005, at 112.
van Hoecke, Mark, Des ordres juridiques en conflit: sport de droit, 35 R.I.E.J. 1995, at 62 *et seq.*
Hoeren, Thomas, Derogation im Zivilrecht, 61 The Legal History Rev. 1993, at 493 *et seq.*
van Hof, Jacomijn J., Commentary on the UNCITRAL Arbitration Rules, The Hague 1991.
von Hoffmann, Bernd, Internationale Handelsschiedsgerichtsbarkeit, Frankfurt a.M., Berlin 1970.
von Hoffmann, Bernd, Zur Auslegung von Formularbedingungen des internationalen Handelsverkehrs, 16 AWD 1970, at 247 *et seq.*
von Hoffmann, Bernd, 'Lex mercatoria' vor internationalen Schiedsgerichten, 4 IPRax 1984, at 106 *et seq.*
von Hoffmann, Bernd, Grundsätzliches zur Anwendung der 'lex mercatoria' durch internationale Schiedsgerichte, in: Festschrift Kegel, Stuttgart, Berlin, Cologne, Mainz 1987, at 215 *et seq.*
von Hoffmann, Bernd, Inländische Sachnormen mit zwingendem internationalem Anwendungsbereich, 9 IPRax 1989, at 261 *et seq.*

von Hoffmann, Bernd/Thorn, Karsten, Internationales Privatrecht, 8th ed., Munich 2007.

Holleaux, Georges, Rezension von Klein, Frederic Édouard, Considérations sur l'arbitrage en droit international privé, 45 Rev.crit.dr.int.priv. 1956, at 179 *et seq.*

Holmes, Oliver Wendell, The Path of the Law, in: Holmes (ed.), Collected Legal Papers, New York 1920, at 167 *et seq.*

Holtzmann, Howard M., Some Lessons of the Iran-United States Claims Tribunal, in: Pr.Inv.Abr. 1987, at 16-1 *et seq.*

Holtzmann, Howard M., Key Factors for the Success of Uniform International Commercial Legal Texts, in: Festschrift Pierre Lalive, Basel, Frankfurt a.M. 1993, at 257 *et seq.*

Hommelhoff, Peter, Zivilrecht unter dem Einfluß europäischer Rechtsangleichung, 192 AcP 1992, at 71 *et seq.*

Hondius, Ewoud H., European Contract Law: The Contribution of the Dutch, in: Weyers (ed.), Europäisches Vertragsrecht, Baden-Baden 1997, at 45 *et seq.*

Honnold, John (ed.), The Life of the Law: Readings on the Growth of Legal Institutions, New York 1964.

Honnold, John, Uniform Law for International Sales, Deventer, Antwerp, Boston, Frankfurt a.M. 1987 [cited as: *Honnold*, ULIS].

Hopt, Klaus, Handelsvertreterrecht, 4th ed., Munich 2009.

Horn, Norbert, Zur Bedeutung der Topiklehre Theodor Viehwegs für eine einheitliche Theorie des juristischen Denkens, 21 NJW 1967, at 601 *et seq.*

Horn, Norbert, Das Recht der internationalen Anleihen, Frankfurt a.M. 1972.

Horn, Norbert, A Uniform Approach to Eurobond Agreements, 9 L. & Pol.Int'l Bus. 1977, at 753 *et seq.*

Horn, Norbert, book review of: André Jacquemont, L'Emission des Emprunts Euro-Obligataires. Pouvoir Bancaire et Souverainetés Etatiques, 1976, in: 141 ZHR 1977, at 86 *et seq.*

Horn, Norbert, Codes of Conduct for MNEs and Transnational Lex Mercatoria: An International Process of Learning and Law Making, in: Horn (ed.), Legal Problems of Codes of Conduct for Multinational Enterprises, Deventer, Antwerp, Boston, London, Frankfurt a.M. 1980, at 45 *et seq.*

Horn, Norbert, Neuverhandlungspflicht, 181 AcP 1981, at 255 *et seq.*

Horn, Norbert, Vertragsdauer. Die Vertragsdauer als schuldrechtliches Regelungsproblem, in: BMJ (ed.), Gutachten und Vorschläge zur Überarbeitung des Schuldrechts, Vol.I, Cologne 1981, at 551 *et seq.*

Horn, Norbert, Normative Problems of A New International Economic Order, 16 JWTL 1982, at 338 *et seq.*

Horn, Norbert, Uniformity and Diversity in the Law of International Commercial, in: Horn/Schmitthoff (eds.), The Transnational Law of International Transactions, Antwerp, Boston, London, Frankfurt a.M. 1982, at 3 *et seq.*

Horn, Norbert, Die Anpassung langfristiger Verträge im internationalen Wirtschaftsverkehr. Vertragsklauseln und Schiedspraxis, in: Kötz/Marschall von Bieberstein (eds.), Die Anpassung langfristiger Verträge, Frankfurt a.M. 1984, at 9 *et seq.*

Horn, Norbert, Changes in Circumstances and the Revision of Contracts in Some European Laws and in International Law, in: Horn (ed.), Adaptation and Renegotiation of Contracts in International Trade and Finance, Antwerp, Boston, London, Frankfurt a.M. 1985, at 15 *et seq.*

Horn, Norbert, Procedures of Contract Adaptation and Renegotiation in International Commerce, in: Horn (ed.), Adaptation and Renegotiation of Contracts in International Trade and Finance, Antwerp, Boston, London, Frankfurt a.M. 1985, at 173 *et seq.*

Horn, Norbert, Das chinesische Außenwirtschaftsvertragsgesetz, 31 RIW 1985, at 688 *et seq.*

Horn, Norbert, Bankrecht auf dem Weg nach Europa, 1 ZBB 1989, at 107 *et seq.*

Horn, Norbert (ed.), Das Zivil- und Wirtschaftsrecht der DDR, Cologne 1990.

Horn, Norbert, Clive Schmitthoff, Nachruf, 45 NJW 1991, at 1399.

Horn, Norbert, Zinsforderung und Zinsverbot im Kanonischen, Islamischen und Deutschen Recht – Eine rechtsvergleichende Problemskizze, in: Festschrift Lange, Stuttgart 1991, at 769 *et seq.*

Horn, Norbert, Das Zivil- und Wirtschaftsrecht im neuen Bundesgebiet, 2nd ed., Cologne 1993.

Horn, Norbert, Entwicklungslinien des europäischen Bank- und Finanzdienstleistungsrechts, 6 ZBB 1994, at 130 *et seq.*

Horn, Norbert (ed.), Heymann, Handelsgesetzbuch (ohne Seerecht) : Kommentar, 2nd ed., Berlin, New York 1995–2005 [cited as: Heymann/*Horn*, HGB].

Horn, Norbert, Culpa in Contrahendo, 35 JuS 1995, at 377 *et seq.*

Horn, Norbert, Die UN-Konvention über unabhängige Garantien, Ein Beitrag zur lex mercatoria, 43 RIW 1997, at 717 *et seq.*

Horn, Norbert, The United Nations Convention on Indepedent Guarantees and Lex Mercatoria, Rome 1997.

Horn, Norbert, The Use of Transnational Law in the Contract Law of International Trade and Finance, in: Berger (ed.), The Practice of Transnational Law, The Hague, London, Boston 2001, at 67 *et seq.*

Horn, Norbert, Entgrenzung des Rechts durch wirtschaftliche Globalisierung, in: Brugger/Haverkate (eds.), Grenzen als Thema der Rechts- und Sozialphilosophie, ARSP Beiheft No. 84, Stuttgart 2002, at 179 *et seq.*

Horn, Norbert, Zwingendes Recht in der internationalen Schiedsgerichtsbarkeit, 6 SchiedsVZ 2008, at 209 *et seq.*

Horn, Norbert, Transnationales Handelsrecht: zur Normqualität der lex mercatoria, in: Bitter/Lutter/Priester/Schön, Ulmer (eds.), Festschrift für Karsten Schmidt, Cologne 2009, at 705 *et seq.*

Horn, Norbert, Enforcing Contractual Claims: From *Schmitthoff* to Investment Arbitration, in: Meessen (ed.), Economic Law as an Economic Good, Munich 2009, at 139 *et seq.*

Horn, Norbert/Schütze, Rolf A. (eds.), Wirtschaftsrecht und Außenwirtschaftsverkehr der Volksrepublik China, Berlin, New York 1987.

van Houtte, Hans, Arbitrage en toepasselijk recht, 19 TvPr 1982, at 703 *et seq.*

van Houtte, Hans, Changed Circumstances and Pacta Sunt Servanda, in: Gaillard (ed.), Transnational Rules in International Commercial Arbitration, Paris 1993 (ICC Publ. No. 480/4), at 105 *et seq.*

van Houtte, Hans, The UNIDROIT Principles of International Commercial Contracts, 11 Arb.Int'l 1995, at 373 *et seq.*

van Houtte, Hans, Les Principes UNIDROIT et l'Arbitrage Commercial International, in: Institute of International Business Law and Practice (ed.), The UNIDROIT Principles of International Commercial Contracts – A New Lex Mercatoria?, Paris 1995 (ICC Publ. No. 490/1), at 181 *et seq.*

van Houtte, Hans, The Law of International Trade, 2nd ed., London 2002.

Hudson, Manley O./Feller, A.H., The International Unification of Laws Concerning Bills of Exchange, 44 Harv.L.Rev. 1931, at 333 *et seq.*

Hübner, Ulrich, Die methodische Entwicklung des internationalen Wirtschaftsrechts, Konstanz 1980.

von Hülsen, Hans Viggo, Sinn und Methode der Rechtsvergleichung, insbesondere bei der Ermittlung übernationalen Zivilrechts, 72 JZ 1967, at 629 *et seq.*

Huet, Jérome, Synthesis, in: Institute of International Business Law and Practice (ed.), UNIDROIT Principles on International Commercial Contracts: A New Lex Mercatoria?, Paris 1995, at 273 *et seq.*

Hunter, Martin, Ethics of the International Arbitrator, 53 Arbitration 1987, at 219 *et seq.*

Hunter, Martin, Publication of Arbitration Awards and Lex Mercatoria, 54 Arbitration 1988, at 55 *et seq.*

Hunter, Martin, CENTRAL's Tenth Birthday, in: CENTRAL (ed.), Jahresbericht 2007/2008, Cologne 2008, at 32 *et seq.*

Hunter, Martin/Paulsson, Jan, A Code of Ethics for Arbitrators in International Commercial Arbitration?, 13 Int'l Bus.Lawy. 1985, at 153 *et seq.*

Hunter, Martin/Triebel, Volker, Awarding Interest in International Arbitration, 6 J.Int'l Arb. 1989, at 7 *et seq.*

Hußlein-Stich, Gabriele, Das UNCITRAL-Modellgesetz über die internationale Handelsschiedsgerichtsbarkeit, Cologne, Berlin, Bonn, Munich 1990.

Hyland, Richard, On Setting Forth the Law of Contract: A Foreword, 40 Am.J. Comp.L. 1992, at 541 *et seq.*

Hyland, Richard, Pacta Sunt Servanda: A Meditation, 34 Va. J. Int'l L. 1993/1994, at 406 *et seq.*

ICC (ed.), Formation of Contracts and Precontractual Liability, Paris 1993.

ICC (ed.), Commentary on UCP 600, Article-by-Article Analysis by the UCP 600 Drafting Group, Paris 2007 (ICC Publ. No. 680).

Iglesia Ferreirós, Aquilino, El Lobro Del Consulado Del Mar, in: Petit (ed.), Del Ius Mercatorum Al Derecho Mercantil, Madrid 1997, at 109 *et seq.*

ILA, Corporate Codes of Conduct, available at http://actrav.itcilo.org/actrav-english/telearn/global/ilo/code/main.htm.

Immenga, Ulrich, Thesen zur Privatrechtsangleichung, 4 EuZW 1993, at 169.

Ipsen, Nils Christian, Private Normenordnungen als Transnationales Recht?, Berlin 2009.

Jain, Tarun, Codification and Progressive Development of International Law, available at http://ssrn.com/abstract=1120849.

Jakobs, Horst Heinrich, Wissenschaft und Gesetzgebung im bürgerlichen Recht, Paderborn, Munich, Vienna, Zurich 1983.

Jakubowski, Jerzy, The Autonomy of the International Trade Law and its Influence on the Interpretation and Application of its Rules, in: Festschrift Schmitthoff, Frankfurt a.M. 1973, at 207 *et seq.*

James, Philip, Introduction to English Law, 10th ed., London 1979 [cited as: *James*, English Law].

Jander, Klaus H./du Mesnil de Rochement, Rudolf, Die Legal Opinion im Rechtsverkehr mit den USA, RIW 1976, at 332 *et seq.*

Jannott, Horst K., Überlegungen zu Bedeutung und Ausgestaltung von Schiedsgerichtsvereinbarungen in der Rückversicherung, in: Festschrift für Ernst C. Stiefel, Munich 1987, at 359 *et seq.*

Jansen, Nils/Michaels, Ralf, Private Law and the State – Comparative Perceptions and Historical Observations, 71 RabelsZ 2007, at 345 *et seq.*

Jansen, Nils/Zimmermann, Reinhard, Was ist und wozu der DCFR?, NJW 2009, at 3401 *et seq.*

Jarvin, Sigvard/Derains, Yves/Arnaldez, Jean-Jaques, Collection of ICC Arbitral Awards 1986–1990, Deventer, Boston 1994.

Jayme, Erik, The Rome Convention on the Law Applicable to Contractual Obligations, in: Šarčević (ed.), International Contracts and Conflicts of Laws, London *et al.* 1990, at 36 *et seq.*

Jayme, Erik, BOT-Projekte: Probleme der Rechtswahl, in: Nicklisch (ed.), Rechtsfragen privatfinanzierter Projekte, Heidelberg 1994, at 65 *et seq.*

Jellinek, Georg/Jellinek, Walter, Allgemeine Staatslehre, 3rd ed., Berlin 1929.

Jenks, Edward (ed.), A Digest of English Civil Law, London 1921.

Jennings, Robert Y., What is International Law and How Do We Tell It When We See It?, Schw.Jb.Int.R. 1981, at 59.

Jescheck, Heinrich, Entwicklungen, Methoden und Aufgaben der Strafrechtsvergleichung, Tübingen 1955.

Jessup, Philip C., Transnational Law, New Haven (CT) 1956.

von Jhering, Rudolf, Der Zweck im Recht, Volksausgabe, Vol. 2, 6th–8th ed., Leipzig 1923.

Joachim, Willi E., The 'Reasonable Man' in United States and German Commercial Law, 15 Comp.L.Yb.Int'l Bus. 1992, at 341 *et seq.*

Joerges, Christian, Das Rechtssystem der transnationalen Handelsschiedsgerichtsbarkeit, 138 ZHR 1974, at 549 *et seq.*

Joerges, Christian, Vorüberlegungen zu einer Theorie des Internationalen Wirtschaftsrechts, 43 RabelsZ 1979, at 6 *et seq.*

Jolidon, Pierre, La Sentence en Equité dans le Concordat Suisse sur l'Arbitrage, in: Reymond/E. Bucher (eds.), Recueil de Travaux Suisses sur L'Arbitrage International, Zurich 1984, at 259 *et seq.*

Jolivet, Emmanuel (ed.), UNIDROIT Principles: New Developments and Applications, Paris 2005 (ICC Publ. No. 662E).

Jomadar, Bushan K., The ISDA Master Agreement – The Rise and Fall of a Major Financial Instrument (August 24, 2007), available at SSRN: http://ssrn.com/abstract=1326520.

Jones, Peter, Reasonableness, Honesty and Good Faith, International Sales Quarterly, March 1995, at 8 *et seq.*

Joost, Detlev, Eine vergangene Zukunft der Rechtswissenschaft, 100 JZ 1995, at 11 *et seq.*

Juenger, Friedrich K., Zum Wandel des Internationalen Privatrechts, Juristische Studiengesellschaft Karlsruhe Schriftenreihe, No. 113, Karlsruhe 1974.

Juenger, Friedrich K., A Critique of Interest Analysis, 32 Am.J.Comp.L. 1984, at 1 *et seq.*

Juenger, Friedrich K., Lex mercatoria und Eingriffsnormen, in: Festschrift Rittner, Munich 1991, at 233 *et seq.*

Juenger, Friedrich K., American Conflicts Scholarship and the New Law Merchant, 28 Vand.J.Trans.L. (1995), at 487 *et seq.*

Juenger, Friedrich K., Contract Choice of Law in the Americas, 45 Am.J.Comp.L. 1997, at 195 *et seq.*

Juenger, Friedrich K., Afterword – The Lex Mercatoria and the Conflict of Laws, in: Carbonneau (ed.), Lex Mercatoria and Arbitration: A Discussion of the New Law Merchant, 2nd ed., New York 1998, at 265 *et seq.*

Juenger, Friedrich K., Some Random Remarks from Overseas, in: Berger (ed.), The Practice of Transnational Law, The Hague, London, Boston 2001, at 81 *et seq.*

Kadelbach, Stefan, Der Einfluß des EG-Rechts auf das nationale Allgemeine Verwaltungsrecht, in: von Danwitz *et al.* (eds.), Auf dem Weg zu einer Europäischen Staatlichkeit, Bonn 1993, at 131 *et seq.*

Kahn, Franz, Latente Gesetzeskollisionen, 30 Jher.Jahrb. 1891, at 107 *et seq.*

Kahn, Philippe, La Vente Commerciale Internationale, Paris 1961.

Kahn, Philippe, Lex mercatoria et euro-obligations, in: Fabricius (ed.), Law and International Trade – Festschrift für Clive M. Schmitthoff, Frankfurt a.M. 1973, at 215 *et seq.*

Kahn, Philippe, 'Lex mercatoria' et Pratique des Contrats Internationaux, in: Le Contrat Economique International, Bruxelles, Paris 1975, at 200 *et seq.*

Kahn, Philippe, Force majeure et contrats internationaux de longue durée, 102 Clunet 1975, at 467 *et seq.*

Kahn, Philippe, L'interprétation des contrats internationaux, 108 Clunet 1981, at 5 *et seq.*

Kahn, Philippe, Droit international économique, droit du développement, *lex mercatoria*: concept unique ou pluralisme des ordres juridiques?, in: Fouchard/

Kahn/Lyon-Caen (eds.), Le droit des relations économiques internationales, Études offertes à Berthold Goldman, Paris 1982, at 97 *et seq.*

Kahn, Philippe, Conclusion, in: Gaillard (ed.), Transnational Rules in International Commercial Arbitration, Paris 1993 (ICC Publ. No. 480/4), at 233 *et seq.*

Kahn, Philippe, Les Principes Unidroit comme Droit Applicable aux Contrats Internationaux, in: Bonell/Bonelli (eds.), Contratti commerciali internazionali e Principi Unidroit, Milan 1997, at 39 *et seq.*

Kahn, Philippe, La *lex mercatoria* et son destin, in: Fouchard/Vogel (eds.), L'actualité de la pensée de Berthold Goldman, Paris 2004, at 25 *et seq.*

Kahn, Rahmatullah, The Iran-United States Claims Tribunal, Controversies, Cases and Contribution, Dordrecht, Boston, London 1990 [cited as: *Kahn*, The Iran-US Claims Tribunal].

Kahn-Freund, Otto, Comparative Law as an Academic Subject, 82 L.Q.Rev. 1966, at 40 *et seq.*

Kahn-Freund, Otto, Comparative Law in Action, 20 Am.J.Comp.L. 1970, at 429 *et seq.*

Kalensky, Pavel, Quelques Considerations sur le Nouveau Code Tchécoslovaque du Commerce International, 22 Bulletin de Droit Tchécoslovaque 1964, at 299 *et seq.*

Kant, Immanuel, Metaphysik der Sitten, Königsberg 1797.

Kappus, Andreas, 'Conflict avoidance' durch 'lex mercatoria' und UN-Kaufrecht 1980, 36 RIW 1990, at 788 *et seq.*

Kappus, Andreas, Lex mercatoria und internationale Handelsschiedsgerichtsbarkeit – Einheitliches Sach- und Prozeßrecht für den Handelsstand, 1 WiB 1994, at 189 *et seq.*

Karl, Joachim, Das Multilateral Investitionsabkommen (MAI), RIW 1998, at 432 *et seq.*

Karrer, Pierre, Transnational Law of Interest in International Arbitration, in: Gaillard (ed.), Transnational Rules in International Commercial Arbitration, Paris 1993 (ICC Publ. No. 480/4), at 223 *et seq.*

Karrer, Pierre, Einstweiliger Rechtsschutz in Schiedssachen – Mut zum freien Ermessen, 14 IPRax 1994, at 56 *et seq.*

Kassis, Antoine, Théorie Générale des Usages du Commerce, Paris 1984.

Kaufmann, Arthur, Tendenzen im Rechtsdenken der Gegenwart, Tübingen 1976.

Kaufmann-Kohler, Gabriele, Arbitration at the Olympics: Issues of Fast-Track Dispute Resolution, The Hague *et al.* 2001.

Kaufmann-Kohler, Gabriele, The Arbitrator and the Law: Does He/She Know It? Apply It? How? And A Few More Questions, 21 Arb.Int'l 2005, at 631 *et seq.*

Kegel, Gerhard, Begriffs- und Interessenjurisprudenz im internationalen Privatrecht, in: Festschrift Lewald, Basel 1953, at 259 *et seq.*

Kegel, Gerhard, Internationales Privatrecht, 7th ed., München 1995.

Kegel, Gerhard, The Crisis of Conflict of Laws, 112 Rec.Cours 1964-II, at 91 *et seq.*

Kegel, Gerhard, Vaterhaus und Traumhaus: Herkömmliches internationales Privatrecht und Hauptthesen der amerikanischen Reformer, in: Festschrift für Günther Beitzke, Berlin/New York 1979, at 551 *et seq.*

Kegel, Gerhard/Schurig, Gerhard, Internationales Privatrecht, 9th ed., Munich 2004.

Kelsen, Hans, Reine Rechtslehre, 2nd ed., Vienna 1960.

Kessel, Christian/Jüttner, Andreas, Der Vorbehalt der Individualabrede im unternehmerischen Geschäftsverkehr, 63 BB 2008, at 1350 *et seq.*

Kessler, Joachim, Die Bindung des Schiedsgerichts an das materielle Recht, Cologne, Berlin 1964.

Kessler, Friedrich/Fine, Edith, Culpa in Contrahendo, Bargaining in Good Faith and Freedom of Contract: A Comparative Study, 77 Harv.L.Rev. 1963/1964, at 401 *et seq.*

Kindler, Peter, Neues deutsches Handelsvertreterrecht aufgrund der EG-Richtlinie, 36 RIW 1990, at 358 *et seq.*

Kischel, Uwe, State Contracts: völker-, schieds- und internationalprivatrechtliche Aspekte des anwendbaren Rechts, Stuttgart 1992.

Klausing, Friedrich, Wirtschaftsrecht, Marburg 1931.

Klein, Fréderic-Edouard, De L'Autorité de la Loi dans les Rapports Commerciaux Internationaux, in: Festschrift Mann, Munich 1977, at 617 *et seq.*

Klein, Peter, Die Möglichkeiten eines Weltprivatrechts, in: Festschrift für Ernst Zitelmann, Munich/Leipzig 1913, at 1 *et seq.*

Klinke, Ulrich, Bemerkungen zum Statut der Vollmacht unter Berücksichtigung niederländischen Rechts, 24 RIW/AWD 1978, at 642 *et seq.*

Knapp, Viktor, Die ungerechtfertigte Bereicherung in den Rechten der europäischen sozialistischen Länder, in: Festschrift Zweigert, Tübingen 1981, at 465 *et seq.*

Knütel, Rolf, Rechtseinheit in Europa und römisches Recht, 2 ZEuP 1994, at 244 *et seq.*

Köbler, Ralf, Die 'clausula rebus sic stantibus' als allgemeiner Rechtsgrundsatz, Tübingen 1991.

Köndgen, Johannes, Privatisierung des Rechts – *Private Governance* zwischen Deregulierung und Rekonstutionalisierung, 206 AcP 2006, at 477 *et seq.*

König, Detlef, Voraussehbarkeit des Schadens als Grenze vertraglicher Haftung (zu Art. 82, 86, 87 EKG), in: Leser/Marschall von Bieberstein (eds.), Haager Einheitliches Kaufgesetz, Karlsruhe 1973, at 76 *et seq.*

Kötz, Hein, Allgemeine Rechtsgrundsätze als Ersatzrecht, 34 RabelsZ 1970, at 663 *et seq.*

Kötz, Hein, Gemeineuropäisches Zivilrecht, in: Festschrift Zweigert, Tübingen 1981, at 481 *et seq.*

Kötz, Hein, Rechtsvereinheitlichung – Nutzen, Kosten, Methoden, Ziele, 50 RabelsZ 1986, at 1 *et seq.*

Kötz, Hein, Taking Civil Codes Less Seriously, 50 Modern Law Review 1987, at 1 *et seq.*

Kötz, Hein, Rechtsvergleichung und Rechtsdogmatik, 54 RabelsZ 1990, at 203 *et seq.*

Kötz, Hein, Alternativen zur legislatorischen Rechtsvereinheitlichung, 56 RabelsZ 1992, at 215 *et seq.*

Kötz, Hein, Europäisches Vertragsrecht, Part I, Tübingen 1996.
Kötz, Hein, European Contract Law, Vol. I: Formation, Validity, and Content of Contracts; Contract and Third Parties, Oxford 1997.
Kohler, J., De la méthode du Droit comparé, in: Congrès international de droit comparé, Tenu à Paris du 31 juillet au 4 août 1900, Procès-verbaux des séances et documents, Tome premier, Paris 1905, at 227 *et seq.*
Kokkini-Latridou, Dimitra, Een inleiding tot het rechtsvergelijkende onderzoek, Deventer 1988.
Koller, Ingo, Transportrecht, 6th ed., Munich 2007.
Kos-Rabcewicz-Zubkowski, Louis, Contribution, in: UNIDROIT (ed.), New Directions in International Trade Law, 2 Vols., New York 1977, at 459 *et seq.*
Kramer, Ernst A., Topik und Rechtsvergleichung, 33 RabelsZ 1969, at 1 *et seq.*
Kramer, Ernst A., Globalisierung der Wirtschaft – Internationalisierung des privaten Wirtschaftsrechts, 39 ÖBA 1991, at 621 *et seq.*
Kramer, Ernst A., Vielfalt und Einheit der Wertungen im Europäischen Privatrecht, in: Schluep *et al.* (eds.), Recht, Staat und Politik am Ende des zweiten Jahrtausends, Bern, Stuttgart, Vienna 1994.
Kramer, Ernst A., 'Fair Dealing in International Trade' et Vices du Consentement, in: Bonell/Bonelli (eds.), Contratti commerciali internazionali e Principi Unidroit, Milan 1997, at 161 *et seq.*
Krampe, Christoph, Qui tacet, consentire videtur – Über die Herkunft einer Rechtsregel, in: Festschrift Mikat, Berlin 1989, at 367 *et seq.*
Krebs, Peter, Die Begründungslast, 195 AcP 1995, at 171 *et seq.*
Kriele, Martin, Theorie der Rechtsgewinnung, Berlin 1976.
Kronke, Herbert, Transnational Commercial Law: General Doctrines, Thirty Years On, in: Baetge/von Hein/von Hinden (eds.), Die richtige Ordnung – Festschrift für Jan Kropholler, Tübingen 2008, at 39 *et seq.*
Kronstein, Heinrich, Arbitration is Power, 38 N.Y.U.L.Rev. 1963, at 661 *et seq.*
Kropholler, Jan, Die Anscheinshaftung im internationalen Recht der Stellvertretung, 19 NJW 1965, at 1641 *et seq.*
Kropholler, Jan, Internationales Einheitsrecht, Tübingen 1975.
Kropholler, Jan, Internationales Privatrecht, 6th ed., Tübingen 2006.
Kruse, Heinrich Wilhelm, Das Richterrecht als Rechtsquelle des innerstaatlichen Rechts, Tübingen 1971 (Recht und Staat issue 396).
Kühne, Günther, Der Vertrauensgedanke im Schuldvertragsrecht, vergleichende Betrachtungen zum deutschen und anglo-amerikanischen Recht, 36 RabelsZ 1972, at 261 *et seq.*
Kühne, Günther, Promissory Estoppel and Culpa In Contrahendo, 10 Tel Aviv University Studies in Law 1990, at 279 *et seq.*
Küpper, Wolfgang, Das Scheitern von Vertragsverhandlungen als Fallgruppe der culpa in contrahendo, Berlin 1988.
Kuijer, Martin, Een vergelijking van 'hardship' uit de UNIDROIT-regeling met de onvoorziene omstandigheden uit de artikel 6:258 van het BW, Ars Aequi 1996, at 16 *et seq.*

Labes, Hubertus, Schiedsgerichtsvereinbarungen in Rückversicherungsverträgen, Univ. Hamburg Diss. 1995.

Lagarde, Paul, Approche Critique de la Lex Mercatoria, in: Fouchard/Kahn/Lyon-Caen (eds.), Le Droit des Relations Économiques Internationales, Études offertes à Berthold Goldman, Paris 1982, at 125 *et seq.*

Lagarde, Paul, Le principe de proximité dans le droit international privé contemporain; cours général de droit international privé, 196 Recueil des Cours 1986-I, at 9 *et seq.*

Lagarde, Paul, notes to: Cour D'Appel de Paris, Companía Valenciana de Cementos Portland c. Primary Coal, Rev.d.Arb. 1990, at 666 *et seq.*

Lagarde, Paul, Le nouveau droit international privé des contrats après l'entrée en vigueur de la Convention de Rome du 19 juin 1980, 80 Rev. crit. dr. int. pr. 1991, at 288 *et seq.*

Lalive, Pierre, L'Etat en tant que Partie a des Contrats de Concession ou d'Investissement conclus avec des Sociétés Privégeres, in: UNIDROIT (ed.), New Directions in International Trade Law, 2 Vols., New York 1977, at 317 *et seq.*

Lalive, Pierre, The First World Bank Arbitration (Holiday Inns v. Morocco) – Some Legal Problems, 50 BYIL 1980, at 123 *et seq.*

Lalive, Pierre, Ordre Public Transnational (ou Réellement International) Et Arbitrage International, Rev.d.Arb. 1986, at 329 *et seq.*

Lalive, Pierre, L'Arbitrage International et les Principes Unidroit, in: Bonell/Bonelli (eds.), Contratti commerciali internazionali e Principi Unidroit, Milan 1997, at 71 *et seq.*

Lamaud, Emmanuel, Comparison between the CENTRAL List and the Vienna Convention for the International Sale of Goods – Specific Topics, Master Thesis, available at http://lawspace.law.uct.ac.za:8080/dspace/bitstream/2165/291/1/LamaudE_2006.pdf.

Lambert, Edouard, Sources du droit comparé ou supranational. Législation uniforme et jurisprudence comparative, in: Recueil d'études sur les sources du Droit: En l'honneur de Francois Gény, Vol. III, Vaduz 1934, at 478 *et seq.*

Lando, Ole, Unfair Contract Clauses and a Uniform Commercial Code, in: Cappelletti (ed.), New Perspectives for a Common Law of Europe, Florence 1978, at 267 *et seq.*

Lando, Ole, Conflict-of-Law Rules for Arbitrators, in: Festschrift Zweigert, Tübingen 1981, at 157 *et seq.*

Lando, Ole, European Contract Law, 31 Am.J.Comp.L. 1983, at 653 *et seq.*

Lando, Ole, The Lex Mercatoria in International Commercial Arbitration, 34 ICLQ 1985, at 34 *et seq.*

Lando, Ole, The Law Applicable to the Merits of the Dispute, in: Šarčević (ed.), Essays on International Commercial Arbitration, Boston, London 1989, at 129 *et seq.*

Lando, Ole, Principles of European Contract Law: An Alternative to or a Precusor of European Legislation?, 40 Am.J.Comp.L. 1992, at 573 *et seq.*

Lando, Ole, Principles of European Contract Law, 56 RabelsZ 1992, at 261 *et seq.*

Lando, Ole, Some Issues Relating to the Law Applicable to Contractual Obligations, 55 The King's College Law Journal 1996–1997, at 55 *et seq.*

Lando, Ole, Eight Principles of European Contract Law, in: Cranston (ed.), Making Commercial Law, Essays in Honour of Roy Goode, Oxford 1997, at 103 *et seq.* [cited as: *Lando*, in: Cranston (ed.), Essays in Honor of Roy Goode].

Lando, Ole, Lex Mercatoria 1985–1996, Festskrift till Stig Strömholm, 1997, at 567 *et seq.*

Lando, Ole, When Will a Person be Liable or Bound When Negotiating a Contract?, And og rett – Festskrift till Birger Stuevold Lassen, 1997, at 623 *et seq.*

Lando, Ole, The Harmonization of European Contract Law through a Restatement of Principles, Oxford 1997.

Lando, Ole, European Contract Law, in: Weyers (ed.), Europäisches Vertragsrecht, Baden-Baden 1997, at 81 *et seq.*

Lando, Ole, The Role of Party Autonomy and the Relevance of Usages, in: Bonell/Bonelli (eds.), Contratti commerciali internazionali e Principi Unidroit, Milan 1997, at 107 *et seq.*

Lando, Ole, Why Codify the European Law of Contract?, 5 Europ.Rev.Priv.L 1997, at 525 *et seq.*

Lando, Ole, CISG and its Followers: a Proposal to Adopt some International Principles of Contract Law, 53 Am.J.Comp.L. 2005, at 379 *et seq.*

Lando, Ole/Beale, Hugh, The Principles of European Contract Law, Dordrecht, Boston, London 1998.

Lando, Ole/Beale, Hugh (eds.), Principles of European Contract Law, Parts I and II, The Hague 2000.

Lando, Ole/Clive, Eric/Prüm, André/Zimmermann, Reinhard (eds.), Principles of European Contract Law, Part III, The Hague 2003.

Lange, Hermann, Schadensersatz und Privatstrafe in der mittelalterlichen Rechtstheorie, Münster, Cologne 1955.

Langen, Eugen, Studien zum Internationalen Wirtschaftsrecht, Munich 1963.

Langen, Eugen, Vom Internationalen Privatrecht zum Transnationalen Handelsrecht, 23 NJW 1969, at 358 *et seq.*

Langen, Eugen, Transnationales Recht, Heidelberg 1981.

Langefeld-Wirth, Klaus, Joint Ventures im internationalen Wirtschaftsverkehr, Heidelberg 1990.

Larenz, Karl, Richterliche Rechtsfortbildung als methodisches Problem, 19 NJW 1965, at 1 *et seq.*

Larenz, Karl, Über die Bindungswirkung von Präjudizien, in: Fasching (ed.), Festschrift für Hans Schima, Vienna 1969, at 247 *et seq.*

Larenz, Karl, Methodenlehre der Rechtswissenschaft, 6th ed., Berlin, Heidelberg, New York, Tokyo 1991 [cited as: *Larenz*, Methodenlehre].

Larroumet, Christian, La Valeur des Principes d'Unidroit Applicables aux Contrats du Commerce International (1), SemJud. 1997, at 147 *et seq.*

Lauterpacht, Hersch, Private Law Sources and Analogies of International Law, New York, Toronto 1927.

Laviec, Jean-Pierre, Protection et Promotion des Investissements, Paris 1985.

Lawson, Frederick H., The Field of Comparative Law, 2 Judicial Review 1949, at 16 *et seq.*

Leach, W. Barton, The Restatements as They Were in the Beginning, Are Now, and Perhaps Henceforth Shall Be, in: Honnold (ed.), The Life of the Law, 1964, at 162 *et seq.*

Lecheler, Helmut, Der Europäische Gerichtshof und die allgemeinen Rechtsgrundsätze, Berlin 1971.

Leclerc, Ginette, La Bonne Foi dans l'Exécution des Contrats, McGill L.J. 1992, at 1070 *et seq.*

Leenes, Ronald/Svensson, Jörgen, Large-Scale Computer Networks and The Future of Legal Knowledge-Based Systems, in: Hage/Bench-Capon/Cohen/van den Herik (eds.), Legal knowledge based systems, Lelystad, 1995, at 75 *et seq.*

Leflar, Robert A., Choice-Influencing Considerations in Conflicts Law, 41 N.Y.U.L.Rev. 1966, at 267 *et seq.*

Lenkaitis, Karlheinz/Löwisch, Stephan, Zur Inhaltskontrolle von AGB im unternehmerischen Geschäftsverkehr: Ein Plädoyer für eine dogmatische Korrektur, 30 ZIP 2009, at 441 *et seq.*

Lepaulle, Pierre, The Function of Comparative Law, 35 Harv.L.Rev. 1921/1922, at 838 *et seq.*

Lew, Julian D.M., Applicable Law in International Commercial Arbitration, New York 1978.

Lew, Julian D.M., The Case for the Publication of Arbitration Awards, in: Schultz/van den Berg (eds.), The Art of Arbitration: Essays on International Arbitration: Liber Amicorum Pieter Sanders, Deventer 1982, at 223 *et seq.*

Lew, Julian D.M., Interest on Money Awards in International Arbitration, in: Cranston (ed.), Making Commercial Law, Essays in Honour of Roy Goode, 1997, at 543 *et seq.* [cited as: *Lew*, in: Cranston (ed.), Essays in Honor of Roy Goode].

Lew, Julian D.M., Determination of Arbitrator's Jurisdiction and the Public Policy Limitations on that Jurisdiction, in: Lew (ed.), Contemporary Problems in International Arbitration, London 1986, at 84 *et seq.*

Lew, Julian D.M./Mistelis, Loukas A. (eds.), Arbitration Insights. Twenty Years of the Annual Lecture of the School of International Arbitration, Alphen aan den Rijn 2007.

Lewis, William Draper, How We Did It, in: Honnold (ed.), The Life of the Law, London 1964, at 150 *et seq.*

Lieb, Manfred, Grundfragen einer Schuldrechtsreform, 183 AcP 1983, at 327 *et seq.*

Liebs, Detlef, Lateinische Rechtsregeln und Rechtssprichwörter, 7th ed., Darmstadt 2007.

Lieckweg, Tanja, Das Recht der Weltgesellschaft, Systemtheoretische Perspektiven auf die Globalisierung des Rechts am Beispiel der lex mercatoria, Stuttgart 2003.

Llewellyn, Karl N., Präjudizienrecht und Rechtsprechung in Amerika, Leipzig 1933.

Loeber, Dietrich A., Rechtsvergleichung zwischen Ländern mit verschiedener Wirtschaftsordnung, 26 RabelsZ 1961, at 201 *et seq.*

Löffler, Reinhard, Vertragsstrafe und pauschalierter Schadensersatz im anglokanadischen Common Law und dem Recht der Provinz Quebec, Pfaffenweiler 1986.

Loewe, Roland, Commentaire donné au IVème Rencontre des Organisations s'occupant de l'Unification du Droit (Troisième Séance, April 23, 1968), in: UNIDROIT (ed.), Annuaire 1967–1968, Vol. II, Rome 1969, at 261 *et seq.*

Loquin, Eric, L'Amiable Composition en Droit Comparé et International, Paris 1980.

Loquin, Eric, Les Pouvoirs des Arbitres Internationaux à la Lumière de l'Evolution Récente du Droit de l'Arbitrage International, 110 Clunet 1983, at 293 *et seq.*

Loquin, Eric, Où en est la *lex mercatoria*, in: Leban/LoQuin/Salem (eds.), Souveraineté étatique et marchés internationaux à la fin du 20ème siècle – Mélanges en l'honneur de Philippe Kahn, Dijon 2000, at 23 *et seq.*

Lorenz, Stefan, Die culpa in contrahendo im französischen Recht, 2 ZEuP 1994, at 218 *et seq.*

Lorenz, Stefan, commentary on §§ 812 *et seq.* BGB *see* Staudinger.

Lorenz, Werner, Rechtsvergleichung als Methode zur Konkretisierung der allgemeinen Grundsätze des Rechts, 67 JZ 1962, at 269 *et seq.*

Lorenz, Werner, General Principles of Law: Their Elaboration in the Court of Justice of the European Communities, 12 Am.J.Comp.L. 1964, at 1 *et seq.*

Lorenz, Werner, Formularpraxis und Rechtsvereinheitlichung im internationalen Kaufrecht, Book Review of: Philippe Kahn, La Vente Commerciale Internationale, Bd. 4 der Bibliothèque de Droit Commercial, 126 ZHR 1964, at 146 *et seq.*

Lowenfeld, Andreas F., Lex Mercatoria: An Arbitrator's View, 6 Arb.Int'l. 1990, at 133 *et seq.*

Lowenfeld, Andreas F., Lex Mercatoria: An Arbitrator's View, in: Lowenfeld, Lowenfeld on International Arbitration – Collected Essays over Three Decades, Huntington (NY) 2005, at 149 *et seq.*

Luby, Stefan, Les Obligations dans les Relations Commerciales Internationales, in: Luby (ed.), Le Droit Civil Tchécoslovaque, Bratislava 1969, at 179 *et seq.*

Lüderitz, Alexander, Auslegung von Rechtsgeschäften, Karlsruhe 1966.

Lüderitz, Alexander, Anknüpfung im Parteiinteresse, in: Lüderitz/Schröder (eds.), Festschrift für Gerhard Kegel, Frankfurt a.M. 1977, at 31 *et seq.*

Lüderitz, Alexander, Internationales Privatrecht, 2nd ed., Frankfurt a.M. 1992.

Lüderitz, Alexander, Fortschritte im deutschen internationalen Privatrecht, in: Festschrift der Rechtswissenschaftlichen Fakultät zur 600-Jahr-Feier der Universität zu Köln, Cologne, Berlin, Bonn, Munich 1988, at 271 *et seq.*

Luhmann, Niklas, Funktionale Methode und juristische Entscheidung, 94 AöR 1969, at 1 *et seq.*

Luhmann, Niklas, Das Recht der Gesellschaft, Frankfurt am Main 1993.

Luithlen, Wolfgang, Einheitliches Kaufrecht und autonomes Handelsrecht, Fribourg (Switzerland) 1956.

Lutter, Marcus, Europäisches Gesellschaftsrecht, 2nd ed., Berlin *et al.*, 1984.

Lutter, Marcus, Die Auslegung angeglichenen Rechts, 97 JZ 1992, at 593 *et seq.*

Lutter, Marcus, Der Letter of Intent, 3rd ed., Cologne, Berlin, Bonn, Munich 1998.

Lynch, Katherine, The Forces of Economic Globalization, Challenges to the Regime of International Commercial Arbitration, The Hague, London, New York 2003.

Macaulay, Stewart, Chapter 9: Private Government, in: Lipson/Wheeler (eds.), Law and the Social Sciences, New York 1986, at 445 *et seq.*

Macneil, Ian R./Gudel, Paul J., Contracts: Exchange Transactions and Relations, 3rd ed., New York 2001.

Mänhardt, Franz/Posch, Willibald, Internationales Privatrecht, Privatrechtsvergleichung, Einheitsprivatrecht, 2nd ed., Vienna 1999.

Magnus, Ulrich, Aktuelle Fragen des UN-Kaufrechts, 1 ZEuP 1993, at 79 *et seq.*

Magnus, Ulrich, Die allgemeinen Grundsätze im UN-Kaufrecht, 59 RabelsZ 1995, at 469 *et seq.*

Malintoppi, M. Antonio, Les Relations entre l'Unification et l'Harmonisation du Droit et la Technique de l'Unification ou de l'Harmonisation par la Voie d'Accords Internationaux, UNIDROIT Annuaire 1967–1968, Vol. II, at 43 *et seq.*

Mallmann, Roman A., Bau- und Anlagenbauverträge nach den FIDIC-Standardbedingungen, Munich 2002.

Malynes, Gerard, Consuetudo, Vel Lex Mercatoria or The Ancient Law-Merchant, 1622, available at www.Trans-Lex.org/104970.

Mann, Frederick Alexander, Reflections on a Commercial Law of Nations, 33 BYIL 1957, at 20 *et seq.*

Mann, Frederick Alexander, Internationale Schiedsgerichte und nationale Rechtsordnung, 130 ZHR 1968, at 97 *et seq.*

Mann, Frederick Alexander, The Theoretical Approach towards the Law Governing Contracts between States and Private Persons, 11 Rev.belge dr.int. 1975, at 562 *et seq.*

Mann, Frederick Alexander, State Corporations in International Relations, in: Mann (ed.), Further Studies in International Law, Oxford 1990, at 199 *et seq.*

Mann, Frederick Alexander, The Aminoil Arbitration, in: Mann (ed.), Further Studies in International Law, Oxford 1990, at 252 *et seq.*

Mann, Frederick Alexander, Compound Interest as an Item of Damage in International Law, in: Mann (ed.), Further Studies in International Law, Oxford 1990, at 377 *et seq.*

Mann, Frederick Alexander, Introduction, in: Carbonneau (ed.), Lex Mercatoria and Arbitration: A Discussion of the New Law Merchant, 2nd ed., New York 1998, at XIX *et seq.*

Mantilla-Serrano, Fernando, International Arbitration and Insolvency Proceedings, Arb.Int'l. 1995, at 51 *et seq.*

Marceau, Gabrielle Z., Anti-Dumping and Anti-Trust Issues in Free Trade Areas, Oxford 1994.

Markert, Thomas, Rohstoffkonzessionen in der internationalen Schiedsgerichtsbarkeit, Baden-Baden 1989.

Marquardus, Johannes, Tractatus politico-iuridicus de iure mercatorum et commerciorum singulari, Frankfurt 1662.

Marrella, Fabrizio, La nuova lex mercatoria – Principi UNIDROIT ed usi dei contratti del commercio internazionale, Padova 2003.

Marrella, Fabrizio, Choice of Law in Third-Millennium Arbitrations: The Relevance of the UNIDROIT Principles of International Commercial Contracts, 36 Vand.J.Trans.L. 2003, at 1137 *et seq.*

Marrella, Fabrizio/Yoo, Christopher S., Is Open Source Software the New Lex Mercatoria?, 47 Va.J.Int'l L. 2007, at 807 *et seq.*

Martinek, Michael, Das internationale Kartellprivatrecht, Heidelberg 1987.

Martinek, Michael, Moderne Vertragstypen, Vol. II: Franchising, Know-how-Verträge, Management- und Consultingverträge, Munich 1992; Vol. III: Computerverträge, Kreditkartenverträge sowie sonstige moderne Vertragstypen, Munich 1993.

Martiny, Dieter, book review of: Klein/Vischer (eds.), Colloque de Bâle sur la Loi Régissant les Obligations Contractuelles, Frankfurt a.M., Basel 1983, in: 50 RabelsZ 1986, at 730 *et seq.*

Maskow, Dietrich, Beispiel für allgemeine vertragsrechtliche Regeln, in: Ak.St. Rwiss.DDR (ed.), Grundzüge, Potsdam-Babelsberg 1986, at 38 *et seq.*

Maskow, Dietrich, Hardship and Performance, 40 Am.J.Comp.L. 1992, at 657 *et seq.*

Maskow, Dierich/Stargardt, Monika, Thesen, in: Ak.St.Rwiss.DDR (ed.), Grundzüge, Potsdam-Babelsberg 1986, at 7 *et seq.*

Maskow, Dietrich/Wagner, Hellmut *et al.*, Kommentar zum Gesetz über internationale Wirtschaftsverträge, Heidelberg 1984.

Matteucci, Mario, La Coopération Internationale dans le Domaine du Droit Uniforme, UNIDROIT Annuaire 1965, at 53 *et seq.*

Matteucci, Mario, Contribution to the discussion, in: UNIDROIT Annuaire 1967–1968, Vol. II, at 267 *et seq.*

Matteucci, Mario, UNIDROIT – le premier cinquantenaire, Rev.dr.unif. 1976 I, at 14 *et seq.*

Matteucci, Mario, UNIDROIT, The First Fifty Years, in: UNIDROIT (ed.), New Directions in International Trade Law, 2 Vols., New York 1977, at XVII *et seq.*

Mayer, Pierre, Le Principe de Bonne Foi devant les Arbitres du Commerce International, in: Festschrift Pierre Lalive, Basel, Frankfurt a.M. 1993, at 543 *et seq.*

McAdams, Richard H., The Origin, Development, and Regulation of Norms, Mich.L.Rev. 1997, at 338 *et seq.*

McGregor, Harvey, Contract Code – Drawn up on Behalf of the English Law Commission, Milan 1993.

Medicus, Dieter, Abschied von der Privatautonomie im Schuldrecht?, Cologne 1994.

Meessen, Karl M., Internationale Verhaltenskodizes und Sittenwidrigkeitsklauseln, 35 NJW 1981, at 1131 *et seq.*

Meessen, Karl M., Zu den Grundlagen des internationalen Wirtschaftsrechts, 101 AöR 1985, at 398 *et seq.*

Mefford, Aron, Lex Informatica: Foundation of Law on the Internet, 5 Ind.J.Gl.Legal Studies (1977), at 221 *et seq.*

von Mehren, Robert B./Kourides, P. Nicholas, International Arbitrations between States and Foreign Private Parties: The Libyan Nationalization Cases, 75 Am.J.Int'l.L. 1981, at 476 *et seq.*

Meier, Sonja, Bereicherungsanspruch, Dreipersonenverhältnis und Wegfall der Bereicherung im englischen Recht, 1 ZEuP 1993, at 365 *et seq.*

Melis, Werner, Force Majeure and Hardship Clauses in International Commercial Contracts in View of the Practices of the ICC Court of Arbitration, 1 J.Int'l Arb. 1984, at 213 *et seq.*

Merkt, Hanno, Investitionsschutz durch Stabilisierungsklauseln: zur intertemporalen Rechtswahl in State Contracts, Heidelberg 1990.

Merry, Sally Engle, Legal Pluralism, 22 Law & Society Rev. 1988, at 869 *et seq.*

Mertens, Hans-Joachim, Das lex mercatoria-Problem, in: Festschrift für Walter Odersky, Berlin/New York 1996, at 857 *et seq.*

Mertens, Joachim, Nichtlegislatorische Rechtsvereinheitlichung durch transnationales Wirtschaftsrecht und Rechtsbegriff, 56 RabelsZ 1992, at 219 *et seq.*

Mertens, Joachim/Kirchner, Christian/Schanze, Erich, Wirtschaftsrecht, 2nd ed., Opladen 1982.

Merz, Hans, Die Quellen des schweizerischen Obligationenrechts von 1881, in: Festschrift Zweigert, Tübingen 1981, at 667 *et seq.*

Metzger, Axel, Extra legem, intra ius: Allgemeine Rechtsgrundsätze im Europäischen Privatrecht, Tübingen 2009.

Meyer, Olaf, Principles of Contract Law und nationales Vertragsrecht – Chancen und Wege für eine Internationalisierung der Rechtsanwendung, Baden-Baden 2007.

Meyer, Rudolf, Bona fides und lex mercatoria in der europäischen Rechtstradition, Göttingen 1994.

Meyer-Cording, Ulrich, Die Rechtsnormen, Tübingen 1971.

Michaels, Ralf/Jansen, Nils, Private Law Beyond the State? Europeanization, Globalization, Privatization, 54 Am. J. Comp. L. 2006, at 843 *et seq.*

Michalski, Lutz, Änderungen des AGB-Gesetzes durch die EG-Richtlinie über mißbräuchliche Klauseln in Verbraucherverträgen, 47 DB 1994, at 665 *et seq.*

Miller, Jeremy M., A Comparative Analysis of Codification, 12 W. St. U. L. Rev. (1984), at 93 *et seq.*

Ministerie van Justitie (Dutch Ministry of Justice) (ed.), Memorie van Toelichting (Ingedient bij de Tweede Kamer op 11 juli 1984, Kamerstuk 18 464),

Hernieuwde vaststelling van de regels omtrent arbitrage in het Wetboek van Burgerlijke Rechtsvordering, TvA August 1984, at 19 *et seq.*

Ministerie van Justitie (Dutch Ministry of Justice) (ed.), Memorie van Toelichting, 1st Memorial on the 1986 Dutch Arbitration Law, reprinted in TvA 1987, at 40 *et seq.*

Ministerie van Justitie (Dutch Ministry of Justice) (ed.), Memorie van Antwoord (Ingedient bij de Tweede Kamer op 16 februari 1986, Kamerstuk 18464 nr. 6), Hernieuwde vaststelling van de regelen omtrent de arbitrage in het Weboek van Burgerlijke Rechtsvordering, TvA March 1986, at 54 *et seq.*

Mitchell, Walter, Essays on the Early History of the Law Merchant, New York 1904.

Moehle von Hofmannswaldau, Dietrich, Schiedssprüche in der rechtswissenschaftlichen Diskussion, 13 TranspR 1990, at 15 *et seq.*

Molineaux, Charles, Moving Towards a Construction Lex Mercatoria, A Lex Constructionis, 14 J.Int'l Arb. 1997, No. 1, at 55 *et seq.*

Molineaux, Charles, book review of: Klaus Peter Berger, The Creeping Codification of the Lex Mercatoria, in: 17 J.Int'l Arb. 2000, No. 1, at 147 *et seq.*

Moller, Erik/Rolph, Elizabeth/Ebener, Patricia, Private Dispute Resolution in the Banking Industry, Santa Monica 1993.

Monaco, Riccardo, The Scientific Activity of UNIDROIT, in: UNIDROIT (ed.), New Directions in International Trade Law, 2 Vols., New York 1977, at XXVII *et seq.*

Montesquieu, Charles de Secondat, De l'Esprit des Lois, Geneva 1748.

Montrose, J. L., The Apparent Authority of an Agent of a Company, 50 L.Q.Rev. 1934, at 224 *et seq.*

Morrissey, Joseph F./Graves, Jack M., International Sales Law and Arbitration – Problems, Cases and Commentary, Alphen aan den Rijn 2008.

Morton, Alastair, The Greatest Tollgate in the World, 1 Int'l.Bus.Lawy. 1996, at 6 *et seq.*

Müller, Georg, Vorvertragliche und vertragliche Informationspflichten nach englischem und deutschem Recht, Heidelberg 1994 [cited as: *Müller*, Informationspflichten].

Müller, Peter, Die Vorbehalte in Übereinkommen zur Privatrechtsvereinheitlichung, Tübingen 1979.

Müller-Graff, Peter-Christian, Privatrecht und Europäisches Gemeinschaftsrecht, Baden-Baden, 2nd ed. 1991.

Müller-Graff, Peter-Christian, Europäisches Gemeinschaftsrecht und Privatrecht, 47 NJW 1993, at 13 *et seq.*

Müller-Graff, Peter-Christian, EC Directives as a Means of Private Law Unification, in: Hartkamp/Hesselink/Hondius/Joustra/Perron/Veldman (eds.), Towards a European Civil Code, 3rd ed., Nijmegen 2004, at 77 *et seq.*

Münchener Kommentar zum Bürgerlichen Gesetzbuch, edited by Rebmann/Säcker/Rixecker, Vol. 2: Schuldrecht Allgemeiner Teil, 5th ed., Munich 2007; Vol. 3: Schuldrecht Besonderer Teil I, 4th ed., Munich 2004; Vol. 10:

Einführungsgesetz zum Bürgerlichen Gesetzbuche, Internationales Privatrecht, 4th ed., Munich 2006 [cited as: MünchKomm-*author*].
Münzberg, Reinhard, Die Schranken der Parteivereinbarungen in der privaten internationalen Schiedsgerichtsbarkeit, Berlin 1970.
Mustill, Michael, The New Lex Mercatoria: The First Twenty-Five Years, 4 Arb.Int'l 1988, at 110 *et seq.*

Nadelmann, Kurt H., Uniform Legislation Versus International Conventions Revisited, UNIDROIT Annuaire 1967–1968, at 173 *et seq.*
Nafziger, James A.R., Lex Sportiva and CAS, in: Blackshaw/Siekmann/Soek (eds.), The Court of Arbitration for Sport 1984–2004, The Hague 2006, at 409 *et seq.*
Naslin, Jean, A Completely New Legal Experience, 1 Int'l.Bus.Lawy. 1996, at 8 *et seq.*
Nassall, Wendt, Die Auswirkungen der EU-Richtlinie über mißbräuchliche Klauseln in Verbraucherverträgen auf nationale Individualprozesse, 48 WM 1994, at 1645 *et seq.*
Nassar, Nagla, Sanctity of Contracts Revisited, Dordrecht, Boston, London 1995.
Nelle, Andreas, Internationales Institut für die Vereinheitlichung des Privatrechts (UNIDROIT), 30 JuS 1990, at 775 *et seq.*
Nelle, Andreas, Neuverhandlungspflichten, Munich 1994.
Neuhaus, Paul Heinrich, Die Grundbegriffe des Internationalen Privatrechts, 2nd ed., Tübingen 1976.
Neumayer, Karl H., Offene Fragen zur Anwendung des Abkommens der Vereinten Nationen über den internationalen Warenkauf, RIW 1994, at 99, 106.
Neumayer, Karl H./Ming, Catherine, Convention de Vienne sur les Contrats de Vente Internationale de Marchandises, Commentaire, Lausanne 1993.
Niederländer, Hubert, Nemo Turpitudinem Suam Allegans Auditur, Ein Rechtsvergleichender Versuch, in: Festschrift Gutzwiller, Basel 1959, at 621 *et seq.*
Nielsen, Jens, Ausgestaltung internationaler Bankgarantien unter dem Gesichtspunkt etwaigen Rechtsmißbrauchs, 147 ZHR 1983, at 145 *et seq.*
Nirk, Rudolf, Rechtsvergleichendes zur Haftung für culpa in contrahendo, 17 RabelsZ 1953, at 310 *et seq.*
Nöcker, Thomas, Das Recht der Schiedsgerichtsbarkeit in Kanada, Heidelberg 1988.
Nöcker, Thomas, Gesetzgebungstechnische Aspekte bei einer Übernahme des UNCITRAL-Modellgesetzes, 36 RIW 1990, at 28 *et seq.*
Noll, Peter, Gesetzgebungslehre, Reinbek 1973.
Nolting, Ekkehard, Hoheitliche Eingriffe als Force Majeure bei internationalen Wirtschaftsverträgen mit Staatsunternehmen?, 34 RIW 1988, at 511 *et seq.*
Norton, Patrick M., A Law of the Future or a Law of the Past? Modern Tribunals and the International Law of Expropriation, 85 AJIL 1991, at 474 *et seq.*
Note, General Principles of Law in International Commercial Arbitration, 101 Harv.L.Rev. 1988, at 1816 *et seq.*
Nottage, Luke, The Vicissitudes of Transnational Commercial Arbitration and the Lex Mercatoria: A View From the Periphery, 16 Arb.Int'l 2000, at 53 *et seq.*

de Nova, Rodolfo, Wann ist ein Vertrag 'international'?, in: Festschrift Ferid, Munich 1978, at 307 *et seq.*

Nussbaum, Arthur, Das Geld in Theorie und Praxis des Deutschen und Ausländischen Rechts, Tübingen 1925.

Nussbaum, Arthur, Grundzüge des Internationalen Privatrechts, Munich, Berlin 1952.

O'Connor, John F., Good Faith in English Law, Dartmouth 1990.

Oertmann, Paul, Bürgerliches Vermögensrecht, DJZ 1931, at 265.

Oetker, Hartmut, Die Verjährung, Baden-Baden 1994.

Oman, Charles, Changing International Investment Strategies in the North-South Context, CTC Rep. 1986, No. 22, at 47 *et seq.*

Oman, Charles, New Forms of Investment in Developing Countries, in: Moran (ed.), Investing in Development: New Roles for Private Capital?, New Brunswick (N.J.) 1986, at 131 *et seq.*

O'Neill, Philip/Salam, Nawaf, Is the Exceptio Non Adimpleti Contractus Part of the New Lex Mercatoria, in: Gaillard (ed.) Transnational Rules in International Commercial Arbitration, Paris 1993 (ICC Publ. No. 480/4), at 147 *et seq.*

Oppetit, Bruno, L'Adaptation des Contrats Internationaux aux Changements de Circonstances: La Clause de Hardship, Clunet 1974, at 794 *et seq.*

Ortscheidt, Jérôme, La réparation du dommage dans l'arbitrage commercial international, Paris 2001.

Osman, Filali, Les Principes Généraux de la Lex Mercatoria, Paris 1992, at 19 *et seq.*, [cited as: *Osman*, Lex Mercatoria].

Owsia, Parviz, Formation of Contract, A Comparative Study under English, French, Islamic and Iranian Law, London, Dordrecht, Boston 1994.

Palandt, Otto, Bürgerliches Gesetzbuch, 69th ed., Munich 2010 [cited as: Palandt-*author*, BGB].

Park, William W., Procedural Default Rules Revisited, in: Lew/Mistelis (eds.), Arbitration Insights. Twenty Years of the Annual Lecture of the School of International Arbitration, Alphen aan den Rijn 2007.

Parra-Aranguren, Gonzalo, The Centenary of the Hague Conference on Private International Law, in: Festschrift Pierre Lalive, Basel, Frankfurt a.M. 1993, at 97 *et seq.*

Patterson, Edwin W., The Restatement of the Law of Contracts, 33 Columbia Law Review 1933, at 397 *et seq.*

Paulsson, Jan, May a State Invoke its Internal Law to Repudiate Consent to International Commercial Arbitration?, 2 Arb.Int'l. 1986, at 90 *et seq.*

Paulsson, Jan, La Lex Mercatoria dans l'Arbitrage C.C.I., Rev.d.Arb. 1990, at 55.

Paulsson, Jan, Lex Mercatoria as Governing Law in Arbitration, 18 Int'l Bus.Lawy. 1990, at 4 *et seq.*

Paulsson, Jan, Arbitration without Privity, 10 ICSID Rev.-FILJ 1995, at 232 *et seq.*

Pawlowski, Hans-Martin, Methodenlehre für Juristen, 3rd ed., Heidelberg 1999.
Perales Viscasillas, Maria del Pilar, UNIDROIT Principles of International Commercial Contracts: Sphere of Application and General Provisions, Ariz.-J.Int'l & Comp.L. 1996, at 383 *et seq.*
Perelman, Chaim (ed.), Les notions à contenu variable en droit, Brussels 1984.
Perrot, Roger, Portrait d'un Ami, in: Fouchard/Vogel (eds.), L'actualité de la pensée de Berthold Goldman, Paris 2004, at 11 *et seq.*
Petersmann, Ernst-Ulrich, Constitutional Functions and Constitutional Problems of International Economic Law, Fribourg 1991.
Petit, Carlos, Mercatura y ius Mercatorum. Materiales para una Antropologia del Comerciante Premoderno, in: Petit, Carlos (ed.), Del Ius Mercatorum Al Derecho Mercantil, Madrid 1997, at 16 *et seq.*
Philipps, Günther, Erscheinungsformen und Methoden der Privatrechtsvereinheitlichung, Frankfurt a.M., Berlin 1965.
Picker, Randal C., Simple Games in a Complex World: A Generative Approach to the Adoption of Norms, U.Chi.L.Rev. 1997, at 1225 *et seq.*
Popescu, Tudor, Les Contrats économiques en Roumanie comme instruments d'exécution du plan, Annales de la Faculté de droit de Liège, Liège 1971.
Popescu, Tudor, Le Droit du Commerce International: Une Nouvelle Tache pour les Legislateurs Nationaux ou une Nouvelle 'Lex Mercatoria'?, in: UNIDROIT (ed.), New Directions in International Trade Law, 2 Vols., New York 1977, at 21 *et seq.*
Posner, Eric, The Regulation of Groups: The Influence of Legal and Nonlegal Sanctions on Collective Action, 63 U.Chi.L.Rev. 1996, at 133 *et seq.*
Pound, Roscoe, Do We Need a Philosophy of Law?, 5 Col.L.Rev. 1905, at 339 *et seq.*
Pound, Roscoe, Liberty of Contract, 19 Yale L.J. 1909/1910, at 454 *et seq.*
Pound, Roscoe, The Scope and Purpose of Sociological Jurisprudence, 25 Harv.L.-Rev. 1911/1912, at 591 *et seq.*
Pound, Roscoe, Law and Morals, Chapel Hill 1924 (reprint 1969).
Pound, Roscoe, Hierarchy of Sources and Forms in Different Systems of Law, 7 Tulane L.Rev. 1932/1933, at 475 *et seq.*
Pound, Roscoe, Introduction, 1 Am.J.Comp.L. 1952, at 1 *et seq.*
Prausnitz, Otto, Die Geschichte der Forderungsverrechnung, Marburg 1928.
Preis, Ulrich, Der persönliche Anwendungsbereich der Sonderprivatrechte, 158 ZHR 1994, at 567 *et seq.*
Prosser, William, Interstate Publication, 51 Mich.L.Rev. 1953, at 959 *et seq.*
Prütting, Hanns/Wegen, Gerhard/Weinreich, Gerd (eds.), BGB Kommentar, 4th ed., Cologne 2009 [cited as PWW-*author*].
Pryles, Michael, Application of the Lex Mercatoria in International Commercial Arbitration, 18 Mealey's Int'l.Arb.Rep. 2003, No. 2, February, at 1 *et seq.*
Puelinckx, A.H., Frustration, Hardship, Force Majeure, Imprévision, Wegfall der Geschäftsgrundlage, Unmöglichkeit, Changed Circumstances, 3 J.Int'l Arb., 1986, No. 2, at 47 *et seq.*

Quack, Friedrich, Wirtschaftsrecht, Munich 1973.

Raape, Leo/Sturm, Fritz, Internationales Privatrecht, 6th ed., Berlin, Frankfurt a.M. 1977.

Rabe, Dieter, Vorteilsausgleich im Zeitcharterrecht, TranspR 1989, at 356 *et seq.*

Rabe, Dieter, Schiedssprüche in der rechtswissenschaftlichen Diskussion, Eine Erwiderung auf Dietrich Moehle von Hoffmannswaldau, TranspR 1990, at 15 *et seq.*

Rabel, Ernst, Das Problem der Qualifikation, 5 RabelsZ 1931, at 241 *et seq.*

Rabel, Ernst, Zwei Rechtsinstitute für die internationalen privatrechtlichen Beziehungen, 60 JW 1932, at 2225 *et seq.*

Rabel, Ernst, Comparative Conflicts Law, 24 Indiana L.J. 1949, at 353, 355 *et seq.*

Rabel, Ernst, Deutsches und Amerikanisches Recht, 16 RabelsZ 1951, at 340 *et seq.*

Rabel, Ernst, The Conflict of Laws, A Comparative Study, Volume 2, 2nd ed., Ann Arbor 1960.

Rabel, Ernst, Aufgabe und Notwendigkeit der Rechtsvergleichung, in: Zweigert/Puttfarken (eds.), Rechtsvergleichung, Darmstadt 1978, at 85 *et seq.*

Rabel, Ernst, A Comparative Study of the Conflict of Laws (Schriften aus dem Nachlaß), 50 RabelsZ 1986, at 303 *et seq.*

Rabel, Ernst, International Tribunals for Private Matters (Schriften aus dem Nachlaß), 50 RabelsZ 1986, at 324 *et seq.*

Rabello, Alfredo Mordechai, La Théorie de la 'Culpa in Contrahendo' et la Loi Israélienne sur les Contrats 1973, 74 Rev.int.dr.comp. 1997, at 37 *et seq.*

Radbruch, Gustav, Über die Methode der Rechtsvergleichung, 2 Monatsschrift für Kriminalpsychologie und Strafrechtsreform 1905/1906, at 422 *et seq.*

Radbruch, Gustav, Der Geist des englischen Rechts, Heidelberg 1946.

Radbruch, Gustav, Einführung in die Rechtswissenschaft, improved reprint, Stuttgart 1958.

Radbruch, Gustav, Über die Methode der Rechtsvergleichung, in: Zweigert/Puttfarken (eds.), Rechtsvergleichung, Darmstadt 1978, at 72 *et seq.*

Raeschke-Kessler, Hilmar, Neuere Entwicklungen im Bereich der internationalen Schiedsgerichtsbarkeit, 42 NJW 1988, at 3041 *et seq.*

Raeschke-Kessler, Hilmar, Should an Arbitrator in an International Arbitration Procedure Apply the UNIDROIT Principles?, in: Institute of International Business Law and Practice (ed.), The UNIDROIT Principles of International Commercial Contracts – A New Lex Mercatoria?, Paris 1995 (ICC Publ. No. 490/1), at 167 *et seq.*

Raeschke-Kessler, Hilmar/Berger, Klaus Peter, Recht und Praxis des Schiedsverfahrens, 3rd ed., Cologne 1999.

Raiser, Ludwig, Das Recht der allgemeinen Geschäftsbedingungen, Hamburg 1935.

Raiser, Ludwig, Der Gegenstand des Wirtschaftsrechts, 143 ZHR 1979, at 338 *et seq.*

Ramberg, Jan, ICC Guide to Incoterms 2000 – Understanding and practical use, Paris 1999 (ICC Publ. No. 620).
Ramm, Thilo, Schiedsgerichtsbarkeit, Schlichtung und Rechtsprechungslehre, 22 ZRP 1989, at 136 *et seq.*
Redfern, Allan, International Commercial Arbitration: Winning the Battle, in: The Southwestern Legal Foundation (ed.), Private Investors Abroad, Dallas 1989, at 11–1 *et seq.*
Redfern, Alan/Hunter, Martin (eds.), Law and Practice of International Commercial Arbitration, 1st ed., London 1986.
Redfern and Hunter on International Arbitration (co-authored by Nigel Blackaby and Constantine Partasides with Alan Redfern and Martin Hunter), 5th ed., Oxford, New York 2009.
Rehfeldt, Bernhard, Die Wurzeln des Rechts, Berlin 1951.
Reich, Norbert, Europäisches Verbraucherschutzrecht, 2nd ed., Baden-Baden 1993.
Reimann, Mathias/Zimmermann, Reinhard (eds.), The Oxford Handbook of Comparative Law, Oxford 2008.
Reinhart, Gert, Rechtsvergleichung und Rechtsfortbildung auf dem Gebiet des Privatrechts, in: Festschrift der Juristischen Fakultät zur 600-Jahr-Feier der Ruprechts-Karls-Universität Heidelberg, Heidelberg 1986, at 599 *et seq.*
Reinhart, Gert, Fälligkeitszinsen und UN-Kaufrecht, IPRax 1991, at 376.
Reiterer, Irmgard, Die Aufrechnung, Graz 1976.
Reithmann, Christoph/Martiny, Dieter (eds.), Internationales Vertragsrecht, 6th ed., Cologne 2004.
Remien, Oliver, Illusion und Realität eines europäischen Privatrechts, 97 JZ 1992, at 277 *et seq.*
Remien, Oliver, Rechtseinheit ohne Einheitsgesetze? – Zum Symposium 'Alternativen zur legislatorischen Rechtsvereinheitlichung', 56 RabelsZ 1992, at 300 *et seq.*
Rheinstein, Max, book review of: Esser, Grundsatz und Norm in der richterlichen Fortbildung des Privatrechts, in: 24 U.Chi.L.Rev. 1957, at 597 *et seq.*
Rheinstein, Max, Comparative Law – Its Functions, Methods and Usages – in: Leser (ed.), Max Rheinstein, Gesammelte Schriften, Bd. I, Tübingen 1979, at 251 *et seq.*
Rheinstein, Max, Einführung in die Rechtsvergleichung, 2nd ed., Munich 1987.
Rieger, Thomas, Grundsätze der Unternehmensenteignung in der Rechtsprechung des Iran-United States Claims Tribunal, Diss. Cologne 1995.
Riese, Otto, Die Haager Konferenz über die internationale Vereinheitlichung des Kaufrechts vom 2. bis 25. April 1964 – Verlauf der Konferenz und Ergebnisse hinsichtlich der materiellen Vereinheitlichung, 29 RabelsZ 1965, at 1 *et seq.*
Riese, Otto, Über die Methoden der internationalen Vereinheitlichung des Privatrechts, 86 ZSR 1967, at 1 *et seq.*
Rigaux, François, Droit public et droit privé dans les relations internationales, Paris 1977.
Rigaux, François/Fallon, Marc, Droit international privé, 3rd ed., Brussels 2005.

Rinck, Gerd (ed.), Begriff und Prinzipien des Wirtschaftsrechts, Frankfurt a.M./Berlin 1971.

Ripert, Georges, Les Règles du Droit Civil Applicables aux Rapports Internationaux (Contribution à l'Etude des Principes Généraux du Droit Visés au Statut de la Cour Permanente de Justice Internationale), 44 Rec.Cours 1933, at 569 *et seq.*

Rittner, Fritz, Die sogenannte wirtschaftliche Betrachtungsweise in der Rechtsprechung des Bundesgerichtshofes, Karlsruhe 1975.

Rittner, Fritz, Die wirtschaftsrechtliche Ordnung der EG und das Privatrecht, 45 JZ 1990, at 838 *et seq.*

Rittner, Fritz/Dreher, Meinrad, Europäisches und deutsches Wirtschaftsrecht, 3rd ed., Heidelberg, München, Landsberg, Berlin 2008.

Rivkin, David R., Lex Mercatoria and Force Majeure, in: Gaillard (ed.) Transnational Rules in International Commercial Arbitration, Paris 1993 (ICC Publ. No. 480/4), at 161 *et seq.*

Robine, Eric, What Companies expect of International Commercial Arbitration, 9 J.Int'l Arb., No. 2 1992, at 31 *et seq.*

Roellecke, Gerd, Über richterliche Gewalt und höchstrichterliche Entscheidung, in: Roellecke (ed.), Zur Problematik der höchstrichterlichen Entscheidung, Darmstadt 1982, at 1 *et seq.*

Rohe, Mathias, Netzverträge, Tübingen 1998.

Rolland, Walter, Schuldrechtsreform – Allgemeiner Teil, 46 NJW 1992, at 2377 *et seq.*

Romano, Santi, L'ordinamento giuridico: studi sul concelto, le fonti e i caratteri del diritto, Pisa 1917.

Rosett, Arthur, Unification, Harmonization, Restatement, Codification, and Reform in International Commercial Law, 40 Am.J.Comp.L. 1992, at 683 *et seq.*

Rosett, Arthur, Improving the Uniform Commercial Code, Rome 1997.

Roth, Marianne/Happ, Richard, Interpretation of Uniform Law Instruments According to Principles of International Law, Unif.L.Rev. 1997, at 700 *et seq.*

Röthel, Anne, Lex mercatoria, lex sportiva, lex technica – Private Rechtsetzung jenseits des Nationalstaates?, 62 JZ 2007, at 755 *et seq.*

Rotondi, Mario, The Proposed Franco-Italien Code of Obligations, 2 Am.J. Comp.L. 1954, at 345 *et seq.*

Rowe, Michael C., The Contribution of the ICC to the Development of International Trade Law, in: Horn/Schmitthoff (eds.), The Transnational Law of International Commercial Transactions, Antwerp, Boston, London, Frankfurt a.M. 1982, at 51 *et seq.*

Rüber, Hans-Josef, Der Gerichtshof der Europäischen Gemeinschaften und die Konkretisierung allgemeiner Rechtsgrundsätze, Cologne 1970.

Rubin, Seymour J., Avoidance and Settlement of International Investment Disputes: Overview, in: Rubin/Nelson (eds.), International Investment Disputes: Avoidance and Settlement, Saint Paul, New York, Los Angeles, San Francisco, 1985, at 1 *et seq.*

Rubino-Sammartano, Mauro, Le 'Tronc Commun' des Lois Nationales en Présence (Réflexions sur le Droit Applicable par l'Arbitre International), Rev.d.Arb. 1987, at 133 *et seq.*

Rubino-Sammartano, Mauro, International Arbitration Law and Practice, 2nd ed., The Hague 2001.

Rudolf, Kenneth, Organizations Active in the Unification of Private Law, in: Raisch/Shaffer (eds.), Introduction to Transnational Legal Transactions, New York, London, Rome 1995, at 191 *et seq.*

Rühl, Helmut, Rechtsschöpfung durch die Wirtschaft, Mannheim, Berlin, Leipzig 1931.

Rüthers, Bernd, Die unbegrenzte Auslegung, Tübingen 1968 = 6th ed. 2005.

Salomon, Max, Grundlegung zur Rechtsphilosophie, Leipzig 1919.

Samuel, Adam, Jurisdictional Problems in International Commercial Arbitration. A Study of Belgian, Dutch, English, French, Swedish, USA and West German Law, Zurich 1989.

Sanders, A.J.G.M, The Characteristic Features of Southern African Law, 14 Comp. and Int'l L.J. of Southern Africa 1981, at 328 *et seq.*

Sanders, Pieter, Auf dem Weg zu einer europäischen Aktiengesellschaft, 6 AWD 1960, at 1 *et seq.*

Sanders, Pieter, Codes of Conduct and Sources of Law, in: Fouchard/Kahn/Lyon-Caen (eds.), Le droit des relations économiques internationales, Études offertes à Berthold Goldman, Paris 1982, at 281 *et seq.*

Sandrock, Otto, Über Sinn und Methode zivilistischer Rechtsvergleichung, Frankfurt a.M., Berlin 1966.

Sandrock, Otto (ed.), Handbuch der Internationalen Vertragsgestaltung, Vol. 1, Heidelberg 1980 [cited as: Sandrock-*author*].

Sandrock, Otto, Zügigkeit und Leichtigkeit versus Gründlichkeit, 91 JZ 1986, at 370 *et seq.*

Sandrock, Otto, Internationales Wirtschaftsrecht durch 'konsensuale Wirtschaftsregulierung'?, 152 ZHR 1988, at 66 *et seq.*

Sandrock, Otto, Verzugszinsen vor internationalen Schiedsgerichten: insbesondere Konflikte zwischen Schuld- und Währungsstatut, in: Glossner (ed.), 3 JPS 1989, at 64 *et seq.*

Sandrock, Otto, Die Fortbildung des materiellen Rechts durch die Internationale Schiedsgerichtsbarkeit, in: Böckstiegel (ed.), Rechtsfortbildung durch Internationale Schiedsgerichtsbarkeit, Cologne, Berlin, Bonn, Munich 1989, at 21 *et seq.*

Sandrock, Otto, book review of: Kahn, The Iran-US Claims Tribunal, in: 29 ArchVR 1991, at 104 *et seq.*

Sandrock, Otto, How Much Freedom Should an International Arbitrator Enjoy? – The Desire for Freedom from Law v. The Promotion of International Arbitration, 3 Am.Rev.Int'l Arb. 1992, at 30 *et seq.*

Sandrock, Otto/Ningelgen, Susanne/Schmidt, Michael Johannes, Schadensersatzansprüche wegen gescheiterter Vertragsverhandlungen nach mexikanischem Recht, 91 ZVglRWiss 1992, at 61 *et seq.*

Sandrock, Otto, Arbitration Agreements and Groups of Companies, in: Festschrift Pierre Lalive, Basel, Frankfurt a.M. 1993, at 625 *et seq.*

Sandrock, Otto, Internationale Kredite und die Internationale Schiedsgerichtsbarkeit, 48 WM 1994, at 405 *et seq.*, 445 *et seq.*

Santarelli, Umberto, La prohibición de la usura, de canon moral a regla jurídica. Modalidades y éxitos de un 'transplante', in: Petit, Carlos (ed.), Del ius mercatorum al derecho mercantil, Madrid 1997, at 237 *et seq.*

Saulle Durante, Maria Rita, L'Harmonisation des Principes Fondamentaux des Systèmes Nationaux comme Première Phase du Procède de L'Unification, UNIDROIT Annuaire 1967–1968, Vol. II, at 197 *et seq.*

von Savigny, Friedrich Carl, System des heutigen Römischen Rechts, Vol. 1, Berlin 1840; Vol. 8, Berlin 1849.

Schachter, Oscar, International Law in Theory and Practice: General Course in Public International Law, 178 Rec. Cours 1982-V, at 1 *et seq.*

Schack, Heimo, book review of: Jan Kropholler, Internationales Privatrecht, Tübingen 1990, in: 191 AcP 1991, at 373 *et seq.*

Schäfer, Martin, Entschädigungsstandard und Unternehmensbewertung bei Enteigungen im allgemeinen Völkerrecht, Heidelberg 1997.

Schanze, Erich, Investitionsverträge im internationalen Wirtschaftsrecht, Frankfurt a.M. 1986.

Schanze, Erich, Konzernspezifischer Gläubigerschutz: Vergleich der Regelungsansätze, in: Mestmäcker/Behrens (eds.), Das Gesellschaftsrecht der Konzerne im internationalen Vergleich, Baden-Baden 1991, at 473 *et seq.*

Schaub, Beate, Gewährleistung für Standardsoftware, Diss. Bielefeld 1993.

Schermaier, Martin Josef, Europäische Geistesgeschichte am Beispiel des Irrtumsrechts, ZEuP 1998, at 60 *et seq.*

Schiffer, Jan, Normen ausländischen 'öffentlichen' Rechts in internationalen Handelsschiedsverfahren, Cologne, Berlin, Bonn, Munich 1990.

Schilken, Eberhard, Wissenszurechnung im Zivilrecht, Bielefeld 1983.

Schimanski, Herbert, Bankvertragsrecht und Privatautonomie, 49 WM 1995, at 461 *et seq.*

Schindler, Thomas, Die Restatements und ihre Bedeutung für das amerikanische Privatrecht, ZEuP 1998, at 277 *et seq.*

Schipani, Sandro, The General Principles of Law and the Foreign Debt, in: 3 University of Rome II, Department of Public Law, Yearbook 1990–1991, at 583 *et seq.*

Schlechtriem, Peter, Einheitliches Kaufrecht – wissenschaftliches Modell oder praxisnahe Regelung, Heidelberg, Karlsruhe 1978.

Schlechtriem, Peter, Rechtsvereinheitlichung in Europa und Schuldrechtsreform in Deutschland, ZEuP 1993, at 230 *et seq.*

Schlechtriem, Peter, Good Faith in German Law and in International Uniform Laws, Rome 1997.

Schlechtriem, Peter, UNIDROIT Principles (Einheitliche Prinzipien für Verträge) und Werkvertragsrecht, in: Dem Baurecht ein Forum, Festschrift Götz von Craushaar, Düsseldorf 1997, at 157 *et seq.*

Schlegelberger, Franz (ed.), Rechtsvergleichendes Handwörterbuch für das Zivil- und Handelsrecht des In- und Auslandes, Vol. 6, Berlin 1938.

Schlesinger, Rudolf B., Research on the General Principles of Law Recognized by Civilized Nations, 51 AJIL 1957, at 734 *et seq.*

Schlesinger, Rudolf B., The Common Core of Legal Systems: An Emerging Subject of Comparative Study, in: XXth Century Comparative and Conflicts Law, Legal Essays in Honor of Hessel E. Yntema, Lyden 1961, at 65 *et seq.*

Schlesinger, Rudolf B. (ed.), Formation of Contracts: A Study of the Common Core of Legal Systems, Vols. I and II, New York, London 1968.

Schlesinger, Rudolf B./Bonassies, Pierre, Le fonds commun des systèmes juridiques, 15 Rev. int. dr. comp. 1963, at 501 *et seq.*

Schlesinger, Rudolf B./Gündisch, Hans Joachim, Allgemeine Rechtsgrundsätze als Sachnormen in Schiedsgerichtsverfahren, 28 RabelsZ 1964, at 4 *et seq.*

Schlosser, Peter, Das Internationale an der internationalen privaten Schiedsgerichtsbarkeit, 28 RIW 1982, at 857 *et seq.*

Schlosser, Peter, Das Recht der internationalen privaten Schiedsgerichtsbarkeit, Tübingen, 2nd ed., 1989.

Schlosser, Peter, Commentary on § 305 BGB *see* Staudinger.

Schlüter, Andreas, Management- und Consulting-Verträge, Berlin, New York 1987.

Schmidt, Harry *see* Ulmer/Brandner/Hensen.

Schmidt, Karsten, Die Zukunft der Kodifikationsidee, Heidelberg 1985.

Schmidt, Karsten, Jherings Geist in der heutigen Rechtsfortbildung, in: Behrends (ed.), Privatrecht heute und Jherings evolutionäres Rechtsdenken, Cologne 1993, at 77 *et seq.*

Schmidt, Karsten, Lex mercatoria: Allheilmittel? Rätsel? Chimäre?, in: Murakami/Marutschek/Riesenhuber (eds.), Globalisierung und Recht: Beiträge Japans und Deutschlands zu einer internationalen Rechtsordnung im 21. Jahrhundert, Berlin 2007, at 153 *et seq.*

Schmidt, Reiner, Wirtschaftsstandort Bundesrepublik aus verfassungs- bzw. verwaltungsrechtlicher Sicht – Öffentliches Wirtschaftsrecht als Wachstumshelfer im Binnenmarkt, WUR 1990, at 1 *et seq.*

Schmidtchen, Dieter, Territorialität des Rechts, Internationales Privatrecht und die privatautonome Regelung internationaler Sachverhalte, 59 RabelsZ 1995, at 56 *et seq.*

Schmidtchen, Dieter/Schmidt-Trenz, Hans-Jörg, New Institutional Economics of International Transactions. Constitutional Uncertainty and the Creation of Institutions as Exemplified by the Multinational Firm, in: 9 Jahrbuch für Neue Politische Ökonomie 1990, at 3 *et seq.*

Schmitthoff, Clive, The Science of Comparative Law, Cambridge L.J. 1939, at 94 *et seq.*

Schmitthoff, Clive, Modern Trends in English Commercial Law, Tidskrift, utgiven av Juridiska Foreningen i Finland, 1957, at 349 *et seq.*

Schmitthoff, Clive, International Business Law: A New Law Merchant, Current Law and Social Problems, 1961.

Schmitthoff, Clive, The New Sources of the Law of International Trade, 15 International Social Science Journal 1963, at 259 *et seq.*

Schmitthoff, Clive, Das neue Recht des Welthandels, 28 RabelsZ 1964, at 47 *et seq.*

Schmitthoff, Clive, The Law of International Trade, its Growth, Formulation and Operation, in: Schmitthoff, Clive (ed.), The Sources of the Law of International Trade, London 1964, at 3 *et seq.*

Schmitthoff, Clive, The Unification or Harmonization of Law by Means of Standard Contracts and General Conditions, UNIDROIT Annuaire 1967–1968, Vol. II, at 93 *et seq.*

Schmitthoff, Clive, Agency in International Trade, A Study in Comparative Law, 117 Rec.Cours 1970, at 115 *et seq.*

Schmitthoff, Clive, Methodik der Vereinheitlichungsbestrebungen des Handelsrechts durch die UNO, in: Coing/Schmitthoff/Hellner/Gleichmann (eds.), Methoden der Rechtsvereinheitlichung, Frankfurt a.M. 1974, at 19 *et seq.*

Schmitthoff, Clive, Die zukünftigen Aufgaben der Rechtsvergleichung, 83 JZ 1978, at 495 *et seq.*

Schmitthoff, Clive, Nature and Evolution of the Transnational Law of Commercial Transactions, in: Horn/Schmitthoff (eds.), The Transnational Law of International Commercial Transactions, Antwerp, Boston, London, Frankfurt a.M. 1982, at 19 *et seq.*

Schmitthoff, Clive, International Trade Usages, Institute of International Business Law And Practice Newsletter, Special Issue, Paris 1987 [cited as: *Schmitthoff*, Trade Usages].

Schmitthoff, Clive *et al.*, Schmitthoff's Export Trade: The Law and Practice of International Trade, 11th ed., London, 2007.

Schmitz, Rochus, Zinsrecht, Diss. Münster, Hamburg 1993.

Schmitz, Stephan, Allgemeine Rechtsgrundsätze in der Rechtsprechung des Iran-United States Claims Tribunal, Frankfurt a.M., Berlin, Bern 1992.

Schneider, Hans, Gesetzgebung, 3rd ed., Heidelberg 2002.

Schneider, Uwe H., Europäische und internationale Harmonisierung des Bankvertragsrechts, 45 NJW 1991, at 1985 *et seq.*

Schnitzer, Adolf F., Die Einordnung der internationalen Sachverhalte in das Rechtssystem, in: Festschrift Mann, Munich 1972, at 289 *et seq.*

Schoch, Friedrich, Die Europäisierung des Allgemeinen Verwaltungsrechts, 100 JZ 1995, at 109 *et seq.*

Schödermeier, Martin, Sonderprivatrecht für internationale Wirtschaftsverträge, Diss. Cologne 1989.

Schönle, Herbert, Intérêts moratoires, intérêts compensatoires et dommages-intérêts de retard en arbitrage international, in: Festschrift Pierre Lalive, Basel, Frankfurt a.M. 1993, at 649 *et seq.*

Scholten, G.J., Anticiperende interpretatie: een nieuwe interpretatiemethode?, 100 WPr. 1969, at 111 *et seq.*

Scholten, Johannes M.B., Het begrip Comitas in het internationaal privaatrecht van de Hollandse juristenschool der zeventiende eeuw, Amsterdam 1949.

Schröder, Gerhard, Die zivile Bürgergesellschaft. Anregungen zu einer Neubestimmung der Aufgaben von Staat und Gesellschaft, in: Die neue Gesellschaft/Frankfurter Hefte 4/2000, at 200 *et seq.*

Schröder, Jochen, Internationales Vertragsrecht, Das Kollisionsrecht der transnationalen Wirtschaftsverträge, 1st ed., Cologne 1984.

Schröder, Jochen/Wenner, Christian, Internationales Vertragsrecht, Das Kollisionsrecht der transnationalen Wirtschaftsverträge, 2nd ed., Cologne 1998.

Schüle, Adolf, Die Entscheidung des Internationalen Richters Ex Aequo Et Bono, in: Summum Ius – Summa Iniuria, Tübingen 1963, at 224 *et seq.*

Schütte, Ehrenfried, Schiedsklauseln und 'transnationales Recht', 33 VersR 1982, at 223 *et seq.*

Schütze, Rolf A., Zur Präzedenzwirkung von Schiedssprüchen in: Festschrift Glossner, Heidelberg 1994, at 333 *et seq.*

Schütze, Rolf A., Schiedsvereinbarung kraft Handelsbrauchs, note to BGH (December 3, 1992 – III ZR 30/91), in: WuB VII A. § 1027 ZPO 1.93.

Schütze, Rolf A./Tscherning, Dieter/Wais, Walter, Handbuch des Schiedsverfahrens, 2nd ed., Berlin, New York 1990.

Schulte-Nölke, Hans, Arbeiten an einem europäischen Vertragsrecht – Fakten und populäre Irrtümer, 62 NJW 2009, at 2161 *et seq.*

Schulte-Nölke, Hans, Editorial: Ein neuer Anlauf für ein Europäisches Vertragsrecht, 8 ZGS 2009, at 337.

Schulze, Reiner, Gemeineuropäisches Privatrecht und Rechtsgeschichte, in: Müller-Graff (ed.), Gemeinsames Privatrecht in der Europäischen Gemeinschaft, 2nd ed., Baden-Baden 1999, at 127 *et seq.*

Schulze, Reiner, Ein Jahrhundert BGB – Deutsche Rechtseinheit und Europäisches Privatrecht, 75 DRiZ 1997, at 369 *et seq.*

Schulze, Reiner, Auf dem Weg zu einem europäischen Zivilgesetzbuch?, 50 NJW 1997, at 2742 *et seq.*

Schulze, Reiner, Vergleichende Gesetzesauslegung und Rechtsangleichung, ZfRV 1997, at 183 *et seq.*

Schulze, Reiner/von Bar, Christian/Schulte-Nölke, Hans (eds.), Der akademische Entwurf für einen Gemeinsamen Referenzrahmen, Tübingen 2008.

Schumacher, Klaus, Fragen zum Anwendungsbereich des künftigen deutschen Schiedsverfahrensrechts, in: Festschrift Glossner, Heidelberg 1994, at 341 *et seq.*

Schumann, Hans, Keyword 'Abtretung', in: Schlegelberger (ed.), Rechtsvergleichendes Handwörterbuch für das Zivil- und Handelsrecht des In- und Auslandes, Vol. 2, Berlin 1929, at 34 *et seq.*

Schurig, Klaus, Kollisionsnorm und Sachrecht, Berlin 1981.

Schwab, Karl Heinz, book review of: Berger, Internationale Wirtschaftsschiedsgerichsbarkeit, 1992, in: 107 ZZP 1994, at 118 *et seq.*

Schwab, Karl Heinz/Walter, Gerhard, Schiedsgerichtsbarkeit, 7th ed., Munich 2005.

Schwander, Ivo, Lois d'application immédiate, Sonderanknüpfung, IPR-Sachnormen und andere Ausnahmen von der gewöhnlichen Anknüpfung im internationalen Privatrecht, Zurich 1975.

Schwarzenberger, Georg, The Principles and Standards of International Economic Law, 100 Rec. Cours 1966, No. 1, at 1 *et seq.*

Scialoja, Vittorio, Per un'alleanza legislativa fra gli Stati dell'Intesa, Nuova Antologia 1916, at 450 *et seq.*

Scott, Robert, A Relational Theory of Default Rules for Commercial Contracts, J.Legal Stud. 1990, at 597 *et seq.*

Sebastianutti, Paul, What is this thing called international financial law?, 3 LFMR 2009, at 64 *et seq.*

Sebastianutti, Paul, What is this thing called international financial law? Part 2, 3 LFMR 2009, at 155 *et seq.*

Sebastianutti, Paul, What Is This Thing Called International Financial Law? Part 3, 3 LFMR 2009, at 248 *et seq.*

Seckelmann, Robert, Zinsrecht, Baden-Baden 1992.

Seelmann, Kurt, Rechtsphilosophie, 4th ed., Munich 2007.

Seidl-Hohenveldern, Ignaz, General Principles of Law as Applied by the Conciliation Commissions Established under the Peace Treaty with Italy of 1947, 53 AJIL 1959, at 853 *et seq.*

Seidl-Hohenveldern, Ignaz, The Theory of Quasi-International and Partly International Agreements, 11 Rev. belge dr.int. 1975, at 567 *et seq.*

Seidl-Hohenveldern, Ignaz, Corporations in and under International Law, Cambridge 1987.

Seiffert, Wolfgang et al., Sozialistische Ökonomische Integration, East Berlin 1974.

von der Seipen, Christoph, Akzessorische Anknüpfung und engste Verbindung im Kollisionsrecht der komplexen Vertragsverhaltnisse, Cologne, Berlin, Bonn 1989.

Selden, Barton S., Lex Mercatoria in European and U.S. Trade Practice: Time to Take a Closer Look, 2 Ann.Surv.Int'l & Comp.L. 1995, at 111 *et seq.*

Shephard, James W., The *Rôles d'Oléron*: A *lex mercatoria* of the Sea?, in: Piergiovanni (ed.), From *Lex Mercatoria* to Commercial Law, Berlin 2005, at 207 *et seq.*

Shihata, Ibrahim, Legal Treatment of Foreign Investment: 'The World Bank Guidelines', Dordrecht, Boston, London 1993.

Shihata, Ibrahim, MIGA and Foreign Investment, Dordrecht, Boston, Lancaster 1988.

Siehr, Kurt, Sachrecht im IPR, Transnationales Recht und lex mercatoria, in: Holl/Klinke (eds.) Internationales Privatrecht, Internationales Wirtschaftsrecht, Cologne, Berlin, Bonn, Munich 1985, at 103 *et seq.*

Siehr, Kurt, Ökonomische Analyse des Internationalen Privatrechts, in: Festschrift Firsching, Munich 1985, at 269 *et seq.*

Siehr, Kurt, Internationale Rechtsvereinheitlichung von Innominatverträgen, in: Forstmoser/Tercier/Zäch (eds.), Innominatverträge, Zurich 1988, at 25 *et seq.*

Simon, Gérald, Existe-t-il un ordre juridique du sport?, 33 Droits 2001, at 97 *et seq.*
Singer, Reinhard, Das Verbot widersprüchlichen Verhaltens, Munich 1993.
Smid, Stefan, Einführung in die Philosophie des Rechts, Munich 1991.
Smid, Stefan, Deutscher Konkurs und internationales Schiedsverfahren, 3 DZWir 1993, at 485 *et seq.*
Smit, Hans, Substance and Procedure in International Arbitration: The Development of a New Legal Order, 65/2 Tul.L.Rev. 1991/1992, at 1318 *et seq.*
Smit, Hans/Galston, Nina M./Levitsky, Serge L. (eds.), International Contracts, New York 1981.
Solotych, Stefanie, Das Zivilgesetzbuch der Russischen Föderation – Erster Teil -, Textübersetzung mit Einführung, 2nd ed., Baden-Baden 1997.
Sonnenberger, Hans Jürgen, Treu und Glauben – ein supranationaler Grundsatz?, Festschrift Odersky, at 703 *et seq.*
Sornarajah, M., The UNCITRAL Model Law: A Third World Viewpoint, 6 J.Int'l Arb. 1989, at 7 *et seq.*
Sornarajah, M., International Commercial Arbitration, Singapore 1990.
Sossna, Ralf-Peter, Die Geschichte der Begrenzungen von Vertragsstrafen, Berlin 1993.
Sourioux, Jean-Luis, Codification et autres Formes de Systématisation du Droit à l'Epoque Actuelle – Le Droit Francais, in: Rev.Int.dr.comp. No. spécial vol. 10, 1988, at 145 *et seq.*
Spengler, Oswald, Der Untergang des Abendlandes, Düsseldorf 2007.
Spickhoff, Andreas, Internationales Handelsrecht vor Schiedsgerichten und staatlichen Gerichten, 56 RabelsZ 1992, at 116 *et seq.*
Spofford, Charles, Social Conflict and the Protection of Foreign Investment, in: The Southwestern Legal Foundation (ed.), Private Investors Abroad, Dallas 1964, at 653 *et seq.*
Staehlin, Estoppel und Vertrauensprinzip, in: Festschrift Simonius. Basel 1955, at 381 *et seq.*
Stammler, Rudolf, Wirtschaft und Recht nach der materialistischen Geschichtsauffassung: Eine sozialphilosophische Untersuchung, 5th ed., Berlin 1924 (reprint 1978).
Stargardt, Monika, Grundsätze der vertraglichen Regelung bei internationalen Wirtschaftsverträgen (IWV) in der DDR, 11 ZIP 1990, at 471 *et seq.*
Staudenmayer, Dirk, Die Richtlinien des Verbraucherprivatrechts – Bausteine für ein europäisches Privatrecht?, in: Schulte-Nölke/Schulze (eds.), Europäische Rechtsangleichung und nationale Privatrechte, Baden-Baden 1999, at 63 *et seq.*
Staudinger, Kommentar zum Bürgerlichen Gesetzbuch mit Einführungsgesetz und Nebengesetzen: §§ 305–310, UKlaG (Recht der Allgemeinen Geschäftsbedingungen), Berlin 2006 [cited as: Staudinger-*author*, BGB].
Stein, Peter, Preface, in: Académie des privatistes européens (Academy of European Private Lawyers) (ed.), Code européen des contrats – Avant-Projet, 3rd ed., Milan 2002, at XLVII *et seq.*

Stein, Ursula, Lex mercatoria: Realität und Theorie, Frankfurt a.M. 1995.

Steindorff, Ernst, Sachnormen im internationalen Privatrecht, Frankfurt a.M. 1958.

Steindorff, Ernst, Autonomy of Contracting Parties in Interstate Commerce – An Economic Evaluation, in: UNIDROIT (ed.), New Directions in International Trade Law, 2 Vols., New York 1977, at 87 *et seq.*

Steindorff, Ernst, Contribution, in: UNIDROIT (ed.), New Directions in International Trade Law, 2 Vols., New York 1977, at 517 *et seq.*

Stern, Klaus, Das Staatsrecht der Bundesrepublik Deutschland, Vol. I: Grundbegriffe und Grundlagen des Staatsrechts. Strukturprinzipien der Verfassung, 2nd ed., Munich 1984.

Steyn, Johan, Contract Law: Fulfilling the Reasonable Expectations of Honest Men, 113 L.Q.Rev. 1997, at 433 *et seq.*

Stoecker, Christoph, The Lex mercatoria: To what Extent does it Exist?, 7 J.Int'l Arb, No. 1 1990, at 101 *et seq.*

Stoll, Jutta, Rechtsnatur und Bestandsschutz von Vereinbarungen zwischen Staaten und ausländischen privaten Investoren, 27 RIW/AWD 1981, at 803 *et seq.*

Stone, Ferdinand F., The End to be Served by Comparative Law, 25 Tul.L.Rev. 1950/1951, at 325 *et seq.*

Storme, Matthias E., The Validity and the Content of Contracts, in: Hartkamp/Hesselink/Hondius/du Perron/Vranken (eds.), Towards a European Civil Code, Nijmegen, Dordrecht, Boston, London 1994, at 83 *et seq.*

Storme, Matthias E., Applications possibles et caractères généraux des principes de droit uniforme des contrats, 72 Rev.dr.int.dr.comp. 1995, at 309 *et seq.*

Story, Joseph, Commentaries on the Conflict of Laws, 8th ed. by Melville M. Bigelow, Boston 1883.

Stoufflet, Jean, Le crédit documentaire: étude juridique d'un instrument financier du commerce international, Paris 1957.

Straus, Michael, The Practice of the Iran-United States Claims Tribunal in Receiving Evidence from Parties and from Experts, 3 J.Int'l Arb. 1986, at 57 *et seq.*

Strömholm, Stig, Zum Begriff der 'Natur der Sache', Gedanken eines skandinavischen Juristen, RabelsZ 39 (1975), at 702 *et seq.*

Strömholm, Stig, Die tatsächlichen Grundlagen der Rechtsnormen, in: Festschrift Zweigert, Tübingen 1981, at 909 *et seq.*

Strohbach, Heinz, Spezielle Probleme, in: Ak.St.Rwiss.DDR (ed.), Grundzüge, Potsdam-Babelsberg, 1986, at 55 *et seq.*

Struycken, Antoon V.M, La Lex Mercatoria dans le Droit des Contrats Internationaux, in: L'Evolution Contemporaine du Droit des Contrats, Journées René Savatier, Paris 1986, at 209 *et seq.*

Sturm, Fritz, Bemühungen um ein einheitliches europäisches Vertragsrecht, 46 JZ 1991, at 555.

Symeonides, Symeon C., Choice of Law in the American Courts in 1995: A Year in Review, 44 Am.J.Comp.L. 1996, at 181 *et seq.*

Tallon, Denis, La Formation de Contrats: Recherche du Fonds Commun des Systèmes Juridiques. Réflexion sur un Projet de la Cornell Law School, 20 Rev.int.dr.comp. 1968, at 729 *et seq.*

Tallon, Denis, Damages, Exemption Clauses, and Penalties, 40 Am.J.Comp.L. 1992, at 675 *et seq.*

Tanega, Joseph, Securitisation Disclosures and Compliance under Basel II: Part I – A Risk-based Approach to Economic Substance Over Legal Form, 20 J.I.B.L.R. 2005, at 617 *et seq.*

Tanega, Joseph, Securitisation Disclosures and Compliance under Basel II: Part II – Applications of the Risk Symmetry Principle to Economic Substance Over Legal Form, 21 J.I.B.L.R. 2006, at 1 *et seq.*

Taupitz, Jochen, Privatrechtsvereinheitlichung durch die EG: Sachrechts- oder Kollisionsrechtsvereinheitlichung?, 98 JZ 1993, at 533 *et seq.*

Taupitz, Jochen, Europäische Privatrechtsvereinheitlichung heute und morgen, Tübingen 1993.

Teubner, Gunther, Das Recht als autopoietisches System, Frankfurt a.M. 1989.

Teubner, Gunther, Law as an Autopoetic System, Oxford 1993.

Teubner, Gunther, Globale Bukowina. Zur Emergenz eines transnationalen Rechtspluralismus, 15 Rechtshistorisches Journal 1996, at 255 *et seq.*

Teubner, Gunther (ed.), Global Law without a State, Dartmouth 1997.

Teubner, Gunther, Global Private Regimes: Neo-Spontaneous Law and Dual Constitution of Autonomous Sectors, in: Ladeur (ed.), Public Governance in the Age of Globalization, Ashgate 2004, at 71 *et seq.*

The Law Society of England and Wales (ed.), England and Wales: The Jurisdiction of Choice, available at www.lawsociety.org.uk/documents/downloads/jurisdiction_of_choice_brochure.pdf.

Thibaut, Anton Friedrich Justus, Über die Notwendigkeit eines allgemeinen bürgerlichen Rechts in Deutschland, Heidelberg 1814.

Thirlway, Hugh W.A, International Customary Law and Codification, Leiden 1972.

Thume, Karl-Heinz, Kommentar zur CMR, 2nd ed., Frankfurt a.M. 2007.

Tilmann, Winfried, Das AGB-Gesetz und die Einheit des Privatrechts, 142 ZHR 1978, at 52 *et seq.*

Tilmann, Winfried, Zur Entwicklung eines europäischen Zivilrechts, in: Festschrift Oppenhoff, Munich 1985, at 485 *et seq.*

Tilmann, Winfried, Wirtschaftsrecht, Berlin, Heidelberg, New York, Tokyo 1986.

Tilmann, Winfried, Zweiter Kodifikationsbeschluß des Europäischen Parlaments, 3 ZEuP 1995, at 534 *et seq.*

Toope, Stephen J., Mixed International Arbitration, Studies in Arbitration between States and Private Persons, Cambridge 1990 [cited as: *Toope*, Mixed Arbitration].

Treitel, Günter H., Remedies for Breach of Contract, in: von Mehren (ed.), International Encyclopedia of Comparative Law, Vol. VII, Tübingen 1976, at 121.

Triebel, Volker, Der Kampf ums anwendbare Recht, 58 Anwaltsblatt 2008, at 305 *et seq.*

Triebel, Volker/Petzold, Eckhart, Grenzen der lex mercatoria in der internationalen Schiedsgerichtsbarkeit, 34 RIW 1988, at 245 *et seq.*

Tschanz, Pierre-Yves, Le Nouveau Droit Suisse de l'Arbitrage International, 1 RDAI 1988, at 437 *et seq.*

Ulmer, Peter, Vom deutschen zum europäischen Privatrecht, 97 JZ 1992, at 1 *et seq.*

Ulmer, Peter/Brandner, Hans Erich, Hensen, Horst-Diether, AGB-Recht: Kommentar zu den §§ 305–310 BGB und zum UKlaG, 10th ed., Cologne 2006.

UNCITRAL (ed.), Legal Guide on Drawing up International Contracts for the Construction of Industrial Works, 1988.

UNIDROIT (ed.), Forty Years of Service in the Cause of the Unification of Law 1926–1966, Rome 1966.

UNIDROIT (ed.), Annuaire 1967–1968, Vol. II, Rome 1969.

UNIDROIT Secretariat, Progressive Codification of the Law of International Trade, in: United Nations Commission on International Trade Law, Yearbook I (1968–1970), at 285 *et seq.*

UNIDROIT (ed.), UNIDROIT Principles of International Commercial Contracts, Rome 1994; new edition 2004.

UNIDROIT (ed.), The Use of the UNIDROIT Principles in Practice, Results of the First Inquiry Undertaken by the Secretariat of Unidroit, Rome (undated).

Vagts, Detlef F., Company Law Harmonization in the European Community, in: Rubin/Hufbauer (eds.), Emerging Standards of International Trade and Investment, Totowa, N.Y., 1983, at 17 *et seq.*

Vasconcellos, Harald Michaelis de, Garantieklauseln und Risikoverteilung im internationalen Anlagenvertrag, Diss. Münster, Heidelberg 1987.

Verdross, Alfred, Die Sicherung von ausländischen Privatrechten aus Abkommen zur wirtschaftlichen Entwicklung mit Schiedsklauseln, 18 ZaöRV 1957/1958, at 635 *et seq.*

Verdross, Alfred, The Status of Foreign Private Interests Stemming from Economic Development Agreements with Arbitration Clauses, Pr.Inv.Abr. 1964, at 117 *et seq.*

Verdross, Alfred/Simma, Bruno, Universelles Völkerrecht, 4th ed., Berlin 1992.

Viehweg, Theodor, Topik und Jurisprudenz, 5th ed., Munich 1974.

Voigtel, Unter welchen Umständen ist die Existenz eines Contocurrent-Verhältnisses anzunehmen?, 3 Archiv für Theorie und Praxis des Allgemeinen deutschen Handelsrechts 1864, at 203 *et seq.*

Volken, Paul, Legal Opinions in International Transactions, in: Šarčević/Volken (eds.), International Contracts and Payments, London, Dordrecht, Boston 1991, at 125 *et seq.*

Voser, Nathalie, Best Practices: What Has Been Achieved and What Remains to Be Done?, in: Wirth (ed.), Best Practices in International Arbitration, ASA Special Series No. 26, Basel 2006, 1 *et seq.*

Voss, Jürgen, The Multilateral Investment Guarantee Agency. Status, Concept, Features, Implications, 21 JWTL 1987, at 5 *et seq.*

De Vries, Hans, Le caractère normatif des pratiques commerciales internationales, in: ICC (ed.), Hommage a Frédéric Eisemann, ICC Publ. Nr. 321, Paris 1978, at 115 *et seq.*

Waehler, Jan Peter, Zur Einführung eines neuen Zivilgesetzbuches in der Russischen Föderation, 8/9 Mitteilungen der Vereinigung für deutsch-russisches Wirtschaftsrecht e.V. 1994, at 24 *et seq.*

Wälde, Thomas, Negotiating for Dispute Settlement in Transnational Mineral Contracts: Current Practice, Trends and an Evaluation from the Host Country's Perspective, 7 Denver J.Int'l L & Pol. 1977/1978, at 33 *et seq.*

Wälde, Thomas W., book review of: Souveraineté étatique et marchés internationaux à la fin du 20ème siècle, A propos de 30 ans de recherche du CREDIMI, Mélanges en l'honneur de Philippe Kahn, 1 Transnational Dispute Management 2004, No. 1, available at www.transnational-dispute-management.com/samples/freearticles/tv1-1-bookreview_06.htm.

Walker, Gordon/Fox, Mark, Globalisation: An Analytical Framework, 3 Ind.J.Gl. Legal Studies 1996, at 375 *et seq.*

Wallace, Don, International Agencies for the Formulation of Transnational Economic Law: A Comment about Methods and Techniques, in: Horn/Schmitthoff (eds.), The Transnational Law of International Commercial Transactions, Antwerp, Boston, London, Frankfurt a.M. 1982, at 81 *et seq.*

Walter, Gerhard/Bosch, Wolfgang/Brönnimann, Jürgen, Internationale Schiedsgerichtsbarkeit in der Schweiz, Bern 1991.

Wank, Rolf, Grenzen richterlicher Rechtsfortbildung, Berlin 1978.

Wank, Rolf, Die juristische Begriffsbildung, Munich 1985.

Wasserstein Fassberg, Celia, The Empirical and Theoretical Underpinnings of the Law Merchant, 5 Chi.J.Int'l L. 2004, at 67 *et seq.*

Watt, Horatia Muir, Les Principes Généraux en Droit International Privé Français, 124 Clunet 1997, at 403 *et seq.*

Weber, Ralph, Einige Gedanken zur Konkretisierung von Generalklauseln durch Fallgruppen, 192 AcP 1992, at 516 *et seq.*

Weber, Rolf H., Gedanken zur Verzugsschadensregelung bei Geldschulden, in: Festschrift Keller, Zurich 1989, at 324 *et seq.*

Wehberg, Hans, Pacta Sunt Servanda, 53 AJIL 1959, at 775 *et seq.*

Weise, Paul-Frank, Lex Mercatoria, Materielles Recht vor der internationalen Handelsschiedsgerichtsbarkeit, Frankfurt a.M., Bern, New York, Paris 1990.

Weidhaas, Jutta/Swoboda, Michael, Schiedsgerichtsbarkeit und EDV-Verträge, 4 CR 1988, at 104 *et seq.*

Weitnauer, Hermann, Kausalitätsprobleme in rechtsvergleichender Sicht, in: Festschrift Wahl, Heidelberg 1973, at 109 *et seq.*

Weller, Heinz, Die Bedeutung der Präjudizien im Verständnis der deutschen Rechtswissenschaft, Berlin 1979.

Welzel, Hans, Die Frage nach der Rechtsgeltung, Munich 1966.

Wengler, Wilhelm, Les principes généraux du droit en tant que loi du contrat, 71 Revue Critique de Droit International Privé 1982, at 467 *et seq.*

Wenzel, Jens, Rechtsfragen internationaler Konsortialkreditverträge, Munich 2006.

Westberg, John A., The Applicable Law Issue in International Business Transactions with Governmental Parties – Rulings of the Iran-United States Claims Tribunal, 2 ISCID Rev.-FILR 1987, at 486 *et seq.*

Westberg, John A., Contract Excuse in International Business Transactions: Awards of the Iran-United States Claims Tribunal, 4 ISCID Rev. FILJ 1989, at 215 *et seq.*

Wetter, J.Gillis, Salient Clauses in International Investment Contracts, 20 Bus. Lawy. 1966, at 967 *et seq.*

Wetter, J.Gillis, Interest as an Element of Damages in the Arbitral Process, 5 IFLR, Dez. 1986, at 20 *et seq.*

Weyers, Hans-Leo (ed.), Europäisches Vertragsrecht, Baden-Baden 1997.

Wichard, Johannes Christian, Die Anwendung der UNIDROIT Prinzipien für internationale Handelsverträge durch Schiedsgerichte und staatliche Gerichte, 60 RabelsZ 1996, at 269 *et seq.*

Wieacker, Franz, Aufstieg, Blüte und Krise der Kodifikationsidee, in: Festschrift Böhmer, Bonn 1954, at 34 *et seq.*

Wieacker, Franz, Zur rechtstheoretischen Präzisierung des § 242 BGB, Tübingen 1956.

Wieacker, Franz, Historische Bedingungen und Paradigmen supranationaler Privatrechtsordnungen, in: Festschrift Zweigert, Tübingen 1981, at 575 *et seq.*

Wiedemann, Herbert, Rechtssicherheit – ein absoluter Wert?, in: Festschrift Larenz, Munich 1973, at 199 *et seq.*

Wiethölter, Rudolf, Materialization and Proceduralization in Modern Law, in: Teubner (ed.), Dilemmas of Law in the Welfare State, Berlin/New York 1986, at 221 *et seq.*

Wild, Peter E., Die Verrechnung im internationalen Privatrecht, St. Gallen 1992.

Will, Michael R., Verwirkung im Internationalen Privatrecht, 42 RabelsZ 1978, at 211 *et seq.*

Williamson, Oliver E., The Economics of Governance, 2005, available at www.aeaweb.org/annual_mtg_papers/2005/0107_1645_0101.pdf.

Williston, Samuel, Written and Unwritten Law, 17 ABAJ 1931, at 39 *et seq.*

Williston, Samuel, The Restatement of Contracts. 18 ABAJ 1932, at 775 *et seq.*

Winiger, Bénédict, book review of Berger, Internationale Wirtschaftsschiedsgerichtsbarkeit, 1992, in: ASA Bull. 1992, at 565.

Winship, Peter, The Convention on the Limitation Period in the International Sale of Goods: The United States Adopts UNCITRAL's Firstborn, 28 Int'l Lawy. 1994, at 1071 *et seq.*

Witz, Wolfgang, Der unbestimmte Kaufpreis, Neuwied, Frankfurt a.M. 1989.

Wolf, Manfred, Privates Bankvertragsrecht im EG-Binnenmarkt, 44 WM 1990, at 1941 *et seq.*

Wolf, Manfred, Auslegung und Inhaltskontrolle von AGB im internationalen kaufmännischen Verkehr, 153 ZHR 1989, at 300 *et seq.*

Wolf, Manfred/Lindacher, Walter F./Pfeiffer, Thomas, AGB-Recht – Kommentar, 5th ed., Munich 2009.

Wolff, Karl, Les principes généraux du droit applicables dans les rapports internationaux, 36 Rec.Cours. 1931-II, at 479 *et seq.*

Wood, Philip R., English and International Set-Off, London 1989.

Yarbrough, Beth V./Yarbrough, Robert M., International Contracting and Territorial Control: The Boundary Question, 150 JITE 1994, at 239 *et seq.*

Yntema, Hessel E., Die historischen Grundlagen des internationalen Privatrechts, in: Festschrift Rabel, Tübingen 1954, at 513 *et seq.*

Yntema, Hessel E., Roman Law as the Basis of Comparative Law, in: Zweigert/Puttfarken (eds.), Rechtsvergleichung, Darmstadt 1978, at 162 *et seq.*

Zajtay, Imre, Begriff, System und Präjudiz in den kontinentalen Rechten und im Common Law, 165 AcP 1965, at 97 *et seq.*

Zajtay, Imre, The Application of Foreign Law, in: Lipstein (ed.), Int'l Encycl. Comp.L., Vol. III (Private International Law), Chapter 14, Tübingen 1972.

Zajtay, Imre, Aims and Methods of Comparative Law, 7 Comp. and Int'l L.J. of Southern Africa 1974, at 321 *et seq.*

Zakariya, Hasan, Changed Circumstances and the Continued Validity of Mineral Development Contracts, in: Hossain (ed.), Legal Aspects of the New International Economic Order, London, New York 1980, at 263 *et seq.*

Zahi, Amor, L'Etat et l'arbitrage, Algiers 1984.

Zamora, Stephen, Is there Customary International Economic Law?, 32 GYIL 1989, at 9 *et seq.*

Zeh, Wolfgang, Kodifikation oder Kommunikation – Rechtssetzung in der Mediendemokratie, in: Merten/Schreckenberger (eds.), Kodifikation gestern und heute – Zum 200. Geburtstag des Allgemeinen Landrechts für die Preußischen Staaten, Berlin 1995, at 135 *et seq.*

Zekoll, Joachim, Common law und Civil Law im Privatrecht von Louisiana, 93 ZVglRWiss 1994, at 323 *et seq.*

Zepos, Pan J., The New Greek Civil Code of 1946, 28 J.Comp.Leg. (1946), at 56 *et seq.*

Zheng, Henry R., A Comparative Analysis of the Foreign Economic Contract Law of the People's Republic of China, 3 China Law Reporter 1985/1986, at 227 *et seq.*

Zimmermann, Reinhard, Das römisch-holländische Recht in Südafrika, Darmstadt 1983.

Zimmermann, Reinhard, The Law of Obligations – Roman Foundations of the Civilian Tradition, Munich 1990.

Zimmermann, Reinhard, Der europäische Charakter des englischen Rechts, 1 ZEuP 1993, at 4 *et seq.*

Zimmermann, Reinhard, Roman Law and the Harmonisation of Private Law in Europe, in: Hartkamp/Hesselink/Hondius/Joustra/du Perron/Veldman (eds.), Towards a European Civil Code, 3rd ed., Nijmegen 2004, at 21 *et seq.*

Zimmermann, Reinhard, Civil Code and Civil Law – The 'Europeanization' of Private Law within the European Community and the Re-Emergence of a European Legal Science, 1 Col.J.Europ.L. 1994/1995, at 63 *et seq.*

Zimmermann, Reinhard, Konturen eines Europäischen Vertragsrechts, 100 JZ 1995, at 477 *et seq.*

Zimmermann, Reinhard, Unjust Enrichment: The Modern Civilian Approach, Oxford Journal of Legal Studies 1995, at 403 *et seq.*

Zimmermann, Reinhard (ed.), Globalisierung und Entstaatlichung des Rechts, Teilband 2: Nichtstaatliches Privatrecht: Geltung und Genese, Tübingen 2008.

Zippelius, Reinhold, Juristische Methodenlehre, 10th ed., Munich 2006.

Zitelmann, Ernst, Die Möglichkeiten eines Weltrechts, in: 39 Allgemeine Österreichische Gerichts-Zeitung 1888, at 193 *et seq.*

Zitelmann, Ernst, Aufgaben und Bedeutung der Rechtsvergleichung, 5 DJZ 1900, at 329 *et seq.*

Zöllner, Wolfgang, Materielles Recht und Prozeßrecht, 190 AcP 1990, at 471 *et seq.*

Zumbansen, Peer, Piercing the Legal Veil: Commercial Arbitration and Transnational Law, EUI Working Paper LAW No. 2002/11, San Domenico 2002.

Zumbansen, Peer, Transnational Law, in: Smits (ed.), Encyclopedia of Comparative Law, Cheltenham *et al.* 2006, at 738 *et seq.*, also available at http://ssrn.com/abstract=1105576.

Zumbansen, Peer, The Law of Society: Governance Through Contract, 14 Ind.J.Gl.Legal Studies 2007, at 191 *et seq.*

Zumbansen, Peer, Law After the Welfare State: Formalism, Functionalism, and the Ironic Turn of Reflexive Law, 56 Am.J.Comp.L. 2008, at 769 *et seq.*

Zumbansen, Peer, Piercing the Legal Veil: Commercial Arbitration and Transnational Law, 8 Eur.L.J. 2002, at 400 *et seq.*

Zweigert, Konrad, Die dritte Schule im Internationalen Privatrecht, in: Ipsen (ed.), Festschrift für Leo Raape, Hamburg 1948, at 35 *et seq.*

Zweigert, Konrad, Rechtsvergleichung als universale Interpretationsmethode, 3 RabelsZ 1949/1950, at 5 *et seq.*

Zweigert, Konrad, Zur Armut des internationalen Privatrechts an sozialen Werten, 37 RabelsZ 1973, at 435 *et seq.*

Zweigert, Konrad, Die 'praesumptio similitudinis' als Grundsatzvermutung rechtsvergleichender Methode, in: Rotandi (ed.), Inchieste di diritto comparato, Rome 1973, at 735 *et seq.*

Zweigert, Konrad/von Hoffmann, Bernd, Zum internationalen Joint-Venture, in: Festschrift Martin Luther, Munich 1976, at 203 *et seq.*

Zweigert, Konrad/Kötz, Hein, Einführung in die Rechtsvergleichung auf dem Gebiete des Privatrechts, 3rd ed., Tübingen 1996.

Zweigert, Konrad/Puttfarken, Hans-Jürgen, Zur Vergleichbarkeit analoger Rechtsinstitute in verschiedenen Gesellschaftsordnungen, in: Zweigert/Puttfarken (eds.), Rechtsvergleichung, Darmstadt 1978, at 395 *et seq.*

Annexes

Annex I

Philippe Kahn

Vers la Quête de la Lex Mercatoria : L'apport de L'école de Dijon, 1957–1964

L'idée de l'existence de règles juridiques propres aux relations commerciales internationales créées en dehors ou à côté de celles émises par les Etats est apparue dans les années cinquante. Elle était exprimée de façon dispersée et floue. La naissance de ce mouvement et sa consolidation se sont faites à la suite d'observations portant sur les pratiques suivies par les opérateurs du commerce international. En France, l'idée a été fortement exprimée dans une série de travaux poursuivis à la Faculté de Droit de Dijon entre 1956 et 1964. C'est l'origine de l'école de Dijon de la *lex mercatoria.*

La première réflexion sur le problème est née d'un événement de portée internationale : la nationalisation du canal de Suez par les autorités égyptiennes et, par voie de conséquence, l'expropriation de la Compagnie Universelle du Canal de Suez, société exploitante du Canal.

Dans une opinion publiée dans le quotidien 'Le Monde' du 4 octobre 1956[1], *Berthold Goldman*, alors professeur à la Faculté de Droit de Dijon, essayait de démontrer qu'aucun des critères habituellement utilisés par les différents systèmes nationaux (lieu du siège social, incorporation, contrôle) ne conduisait à l'attribution à la compagnie de la nationalité égyptienne, ni même à celle d'une autre nationalité telle que française ou franco-anglaise. Elle était, selon lui, une société

1. *Voir www.Trans-Lex.org/000009*; pour une traduction anglaise *voir infra* Annex II.

internationale relevant directement de l'ordre juridique international. Son analyse reposait principalement sur l'objet et les résonances de son activité. Et il pouvait citer quelques précédents, par exemple la Banque de règlements internationaux ou la Croix-Rouge internationale, comme cas d'application de ce nouveau concept. *Berthold Goldman* reprendra cette idée dans un contexte plus large lors d'une étude parue dans le Journal du Droit international (Clunet) en 1963[2].

Dans la suite de cette première incursion dans un espace juridique transnational, *Berthold Goldman* dirigera, à Dijon, trois thèses : la première sur le crédit documentaire, la deuxième sur la vente commerciale internationale, la troisième sur l'arbitrage commercial international[3].

La thèse sur le crédit documentaire, soutenue par *Jean Stoufflet*, portait sur l'étude juridique d'un instrument financier du commerce international, notamment en réfléchissant sur le sens et le rôle joué par les règles et usances uniformes du crédit documentaire élaborées par la chambre de commerce international en 1933.

Les règles et usances uniformes du crédit documentaire sont, avec les Incoterms de la CCI (1936), un des premiers textes, à prétention universelle, élaborés en dehors des états. Et c'est l'aspect original de la thèse que d'avoir montré comment la régulation de cet instrument financier n'avait pas été créée *ex nihilo* dans un cabinet d'avocats ou un bureau d'administrateurs mais constituait une synthèse des usages et des pratiques des banques et aussi des pratiques des milieux commerciaux en général, transporteurs et assureurs y compris. Dans sa phase rédactionnelle, elle apparaît comme une norme unique, expression des solutions généralement reconnues et comme une formule contractuelle équilibrée. S'explique ainsi que ces règles et usances aient été adoptées par la plupart des institutions bancaires et par les banques nationales.

Ces règles et usances constituaient, après une connaissance et évaluation des pratiques, une véritable création par une institution privée représentative des intérêts commerciaux internationaux, toutes branches professionnelles confondues. On peut donc y voir, quelles que soient les controverses sur la nature de ces règles et sur leur autorité, une expression de ce que sera la *lex mercatoria.*

La thèse sur la vente internationale, soutenue par *Philippe Kahn*, marque, sans doute, une étape décisive dans la compréhension du phénomène qu'est la naissance d'un droit a-national dans l'espace constitué par les relations économiques internationales.

Ce n'était pas l'objet primitif de la thèse. Celle-ci devait porter sur les conventions de La Haye, du 15 juin 1955, sur les conflits de lois en matière de vente, et du 15 avril 1958, sur la loi applicable au transfert de propriété et sur la prorogation de for, et, à titre complémentaire, sur quelques particularités de droit matériel, tels

---

2. *Voir supra Klaus Peter Berger*, Introduction p. 1 *et seq.* pour un exposé plus complet de l'opinion de *Berthold Goldman* relative à Suez.
3. *Jean Stoufflet*, Le crédit documentaire : étude juridique d'un instrument financier du commerce international, Paris, Librairie technique 1957; *Philippe Kahn*, La vente commerciale internationale, Paris, Sirey 1961; *Philippe Fouchard*, L'arbitrage commercial international, Paris, Dalloz 1965.

le financement (voir thèse crédit documentaire) et les réglementations administratives relatives au commerce extérieur. Rien, a priori, ne conduisait à la *lex mercatoria*.

Les premières recherches documentaires de *Philippe Kahn*, orientées vers le droit français, ont montré que le droit civil ne connaissait pas de règles spécifiques de la vente internationale, que les grands arrêts de la cour de cassation portant, par exemple, sur l'autonomie de la volonté ou sur les clauses monétaires, avaient été rendus lors de litiges nés à propos de contrats de transport ou d'emprunt. De même la doctrine, en dehors des ventes maritimes, était peu développée[4]. Ce vide relatif a conduit l'auteur à chercher pourquoi le contrat le plus utilisé dans le commerce international, et contrat pivot de nombreuses activités (assurances, intermédiaires, transports), était si peu apparent dans le monde juridique. Certes, à l'époque, le système français était globalement orienté vers le positivisme juridique étatique avec sa pyramide : lois, jurisprudence, doctrine, cette dernière ayant pour mission de commenter et d'interpréter les premières. La théorie des conflits de lois suffisait à faire passer la vente interne (code civil) au régime de la vente internationale (désignation du droit étatique compétent). Sans doute quelques voix, sinon discordantes du moins marginales (*Edouard Lambert*[5] et ses élèves, *Georges Scelle*), avaient développé des visions plus larges des rapports internationaux privés et publics, mais restaient très minoritaires.

La réponse à l'interrogation : pourquoi ce vide officiel ? a été trouvée dans les travaux de la Commission économique pour l'Europe des Nations Unies. Son conseiller juridique, *Lazare Kopelmanas*, afin de faciliter les rapports commerciaux entre l'Europe de l'Ouest et l'Europe de l'Est, alors que les divergences politiques opposaient les deux blocs et paralysaient les échanges, a cherché un terrain d'entente sur un plan pratique.

Il a donc proposé d'élaborer en commun des conditions générales de vente, qui ne seraient pas des transpositions des ordres juridiques nationaux, mais qui reposeraient sur les pratiques et les contrats des opérateurs du commerce européen, exportateurs et importateurs localisés dans les pays de l'Europe de l'Ouest et de l'Europe de l'Est. Des groupes de travail étaient composés non pas de représentants des gouvernements mais d'opérateurs sous l'administration de la commission. Une riche documentation accompagnée de rapports techniques, portant sur les principaux problèmes rencontrés par les opérateurs, a permis de saisir l'existence d'une vie juridique se déroulant en dehors et à côté des états pour répondre à des besoins précis. C'est à partir de cette constatation que la commission et ses groupes de travail ont élaboré des conditions générales de vente produit par produit[6].

---

4. *M. Ishizaki*, Le droit corporatif des ventes de soies, les contrat-types américains et la codification lyonnaise dans leurs rapports avec les autres places, Paris, M. Giard, 1928.
5. *Cf. supra Klaus Peter Berger*, Chapitre 2 II.G.3.b.cc.(b).
6. Fourniture des matériels d'équipement à l'importation et à l'exportation, formules n°188 et n°574; contrats pour la vente de céréales CAF (maritime), 8 formules-FOB, 2 formules; conditions de vente uniformes pour les agrumes; exportation et importation de résineux n°410.

La compréhension de cette approche, à la fois méthodique et pratique, a conduit l'auteur de la thèse à compléter son information par la réunion et l'étude de nombreux contrats et contrats-type (contrat CAF de la London corntrade association, contrats portant sur des produits sidérurgiques, miniers, agricoles, forestiers, textiles, équipements etc . . .).

Il se dégage de cette recherche deux grandes conclusions :

1. On peut distinguer deux modèles de vente, la vente qui porte sur des biens non fongibles (biens d'équipement) et celle qui porte sur des biens fongibles (biens de production et biens de consommation).

2. Dans chacun de ces types de vente apparaissent un fond commun de règles et des règles plus spécifiques en fonction de la nature du produit, objet de la vente.

Ces règles sont élaborées et suivies sans lien direct ni hostilité envers les droits étatiques. Elles trouvent leur structuration et leur sanction à travers l'arbitrage commercial international qui, en quelque sorte, les légitime.

L'auteur de la thèse a cru pouvoir affirmer qu'il existait, au sens sociologique et non au sens juridique, une véritable société des vendeurs et des acheteurs du commerce international, sous-entendu au-delà de la thèse, une véritable société des opérateurs du commerce international.

L'idée allait être reprise par *Philippe Fouchard*, auteur de la thèse sur l'arbitrage commercial international avec une terminologie moins provocatrice, "communauté" se substituant à "société". L'avantage était d'utiliser une expression moins agressive face à la doctrine dominante du positivisme juridique hostile à toute atteinte aux droits étatiques. La méthode suivie par *Philippe Fouchard* est analogue à celle suivie par *Philippe Kahn* : réunir des documents issus de la pratique, principalement les clauses d'arbitrage incluses dans les contrats internationaux et les sentences arbitrales internationales elles-mêmes. Le deuxième point soulevait une difficulté particulière : la confidentialité de l'arbitrage, donc l'accès à des sentences significatives, hors les grandes sentences pétrolières que les media avaient rendues publiques. Toutefois, un adoucissement existait dans la mesure où, contrairement à la vente internationale dont la "juridiction de droit commun" était l'arbitrage, les sentences arbitrales pouvaient être soumises aux juridictions judiciaires par la procédure d'exequatur ou d'action en nullité, décisions judiciaires, elles, publiques.

Cependant, malgré cette difficulté, l'auteur a pu réunir un nombre significatif de sentences, soit sentences *ad hoc*, soit sentences rendues sous les hospices de nombreuses institutions d'arbitrage. Il a pu réunir également un nombre considérable de règlements d'arbitrage de ces institutions. Ce qui lui a permis d'avoir une vue d'ensemble de la situation de l'arbitrage commercial international telle qu'elle existait à l'époque.

Sa conclusion est que se dessine une internationalisation de l'arbitrage commercial aussi bien dans son organisation que dans son fonctionnement: non rattachement à un état (minimisation de la loi du siège de l'arbitrage), autonomie de la clause compromissoire, primauté des règles de procédure adoptées par la pratique internationale à travers les règlements d'arbitrage élaborés par les institutions d'arbitrage, liberté de choix du droit applicable (parties et arbitres) y compris l'application par l'arbitre d'un droit a-national etc...

Parmi les apports de la thèse à l'arbitrage international, on retiendra d'une part la démonstration que l'arbitrage était en train de devenir la juridiction de droit commun des litiges nés des opérations du commerce international, et d'autre part l'analyse de l'utilisation de leur pouvoir par les arbitres, qui les conduira à dégager des principes structurant les règles souvent floues issues des contrats et conditions générales employés par les opérateurs.

À ce stade, il ressort des trois thèses que se conjuguent activités opérationnelles et activités juridictionnelles pour que s'ouvre un espace de juridicité à proprement parler international, préjugeant un espace transnational (mondial?). Il faut retenir que les trois auteurs n'ont pas envisagé au début de leur travail une recherche sur la *lex mercatoria* supposée dans le débat. Ce sont les résultats de leur recherche qui les ont amenés à soutenir, chacun avec son mode d'expression, l'existence d'une juridicité professionnelle dans le domaine étudié du commerce international.

On retiendra également que la méthode suivie a été, dans les trois thèses, une méthode centrée sur l'analyse de documents issus de la pratique les conduisant à minimiser, sans les nier ou les oublier, les sources d'origine étatique ou interétatique. Il apparaît aussi de leurs observations que la notion d'ordre public, qu'il soit professionnel ou étatique, ne semble pas être une préoccupation des institutions, des contractants ou des arbitres.

La synthèse sera faite par *Berthold Goldman* dans son intervention, en 1964, au séminaire de philosophie du droit, consacré au droit subjectif, sous le titre : "Frontières du droit et *lex mercatoria*"[7]. Reprenant ses propres recherches sur la société internationale et les travaux de ses élèves, il constate « que les relations commerciales internationales, au sens large, paraissent échapper à l'emprise d'un droit étatique, voire d'un droit uniforme intégré dans la législation des états qui y ont adhéré, pour être aménagées et gouvernées selon des normes d'origine professionnelle, ou des règles coutumières et des principes que des sentences arbitrales révèlent à moins qu'elles ne les élaborent ». C'est ce phénomène qu'il proposera de dénommer *lex mercatoria* avec la fortune que l'on sait.

Si l'"école de Dijon" a bien fourni, dans cette période qui va de 1956 à 1964, les développements les plus élaborés, appuyés sur des justifications incontestables de l'existence d'une *lex mercatoria,* il faut rappeler que sa réflexion n'était pas isolée.

À la même époque, *Clive M. Schmitthoff* était arrivé à la même conclusion et à la même terminologie. Également, dans plusieurs pays, se rencontraient des personnalités ou des institutions qui s'interrogeaient sur ce nouveau droit professionnel. Les comptes rendus des discussions à propos de l'autonomie de la volonté, lors de la Conférence de La Haye de 1964 sur la vente internationale d'objets mobiliers corporels, sont significatifs; ou encore les travaux de la commission "Droit et vie

7. *Berthold Goldman*, "Frontière du droit et lex mercatoria" in Le Droit subjectif en question, p. 177, Paris, Sirey, 1964.

des affaires" de l'Université de Liège, qui jouera par la suite un rôle essentiel dans le développement et la compréhension de la *lex mercatoria*.

En tout cas, en 1964, est acquise la démonstration de l'existence d'un ensemble de normes d'origine professionnelle gouvernant les relations commerciales internationales. Le système reçoit sa dénomination "*lex mercatoria*", qui sera reprise tout au long d'une existence tumultueuse dont le destin n'est pas achevé[8].

8. *Philippe Kahn*, "La lex mercatoria et son destin" in L'actualité de la pensée de Berthold Goldman p. 25, Edition Panthéon Assas 2004.

Philippe Kahn

Towards the Quest for the Lex Mercatoria: The Contribution of the Dijon School, 1957–1964

– English Translation of the French Original –*

The idea of the existence of special legal rules governing international commercial relations which are created outside or adjacent to the realm of state law first emerged in the 1950s. It was expressed in a scattered and diffused way. The birth of this movement and its consolidation were the results of observations of the practices followed by the operators of international trade. In France, the idea was strongly advocated in a series of works undertaken at the Faculty of Law of Dijon between 1956 and 1964. This is the origin of the Dijon School of the *lex mercatoria.*

The first reflection on the problem was triggered by an event of international significance: the nationalization of the Suez Canal by Egyptian authorities and the subsequent expropriation of the company operating the canal, the Universal Company of the Suez Maritime Canal.

In an article published in the newspaper 'Le Monde' on 4 October 1956[1], *Berthold Goldman*, at that time Professor at the Law Faculty of Dijon, tried to demonstrate that none of the connecting factors usually used by the different national systems (seat of a company, place of incorporation, nationality of the persons controling the company) led to the attribution of an Egyptian nationality to the Company, nor even of another nationality including French or French-English. The Company was, according to him, an international company directly subject to the international legal order. His analysis was based primarily on the object and the impact of its activity. He was able to refer to some precedents, such as the Bank for International Settlements or the International Red Cross, as examples of applications of this new concept. *Berthold Goldman* took up this idea in a broader context in a study published in the Journal du Droit International (Clunet) in 1963[2].

After this first foray into a transnational legal space, *Berthold Goldman* supervised three theses at Dijon: the first about the documentary credit, the second about international commercial sales and the third about international commercial arbitration[3].

---

* Translated by *Thomas Claeßens* and *Klaus Peter Berger.*

1. *See* for an English translation of this article *infra* Annex II.
2. *Cf. supra Klaus Peter Berger*, Introduction p. 1 for a more complete account of *Berthold Goldman*'s article on the Suez Canal Company.
3. *Jean Stoufflet*, Le crédit documentaire: étude juridique d'un instrument financier du commerce international, Paris, Librairie technique 1957; *Philippe Kahn*, La vente commerciale internationale, Paris, Sirey 1961; *Philippe Fouchard*, L'arbitrage commercial international, Paris, Dalloz 1965.

The thesis about the documentary credit was submitted by *Jean Stoufflet* and was concerned with the legal analysis of an instrument to finance international trade. It reflected on the sense and the role of the Uniform Customs and Practice for Documentary Credit (UCP) issued by the International Chamber of Commerce (ICC) in 1933.

Together with the ICC Incoterms (1936) the UCP are one of the first legal texts with a claim to universal validity developed outside the states. And that is the original aspect of the thesis: it shows how the regulation of this financial instrument was not created *ex nihilo* in a lawyer's or an administration office, but that it constitutes a synthesis of the customs and practices of banks and the practices of commerce in general, including carriers and insurers. In their drafting phase, the UCP appeared as a unique set of rules, an expression of generally recognized solutions, and as a well-balanced contractual formula. That explains why these rules and customs have been adopted by most banking institutions and domestic banks.

Based on an appraisal and evaluation of commercial practices, the UCP constitute a genuine creation by a private institution representing the international business interests of all professional branches. Leaving aside the controversies as to the nature of these rules and their legal authority, one may regard them as an expression of what would be the *lex mercatoria.*

The thesis about international sales, submitted by *Philippe Kahn*, marks without a doubt a decisive stage in the process of understanding the phenomenon of the birth of an a-national law within the framework created by international economic relations.

This was not the original aim of the thesis. It was supposed to deal with the Hague Conventions, of 15 June 1955 on the Law Applicable to International Sales of Goods, and of 15 April 1958 on the Law Governing Transfer of Title [Convention on the Law Governing Transfer of Title in International Sales of Goods] and on the Jurisdiction of the Selected Forum [Convention on the Jurisdiction of the Selected Forum in the Case of International Sales of Goods], and, in addition, with some particularities of substantive law, such as the financing (see the thesis about the documentary credit) and the administrative regulations of foreign trade. Nothing was, at first, leading to the *lex mercatoria.*

Philippe Kahn's first documentary research was focussed on French law and showed that civil law did not know any specific rules of international sale. This researched also showed that the leading judgments of the Cour de Cassation on matters like the autonomy of will or on monetary clauses concerned disputes that arose out of contracts for carriage of goods or loans. In the same way legal doctrine, apart from maritime sales, was poorly developed[4]. This relative vacuum lead the author to search for the reasons why the most used contract in international business – and the pivotal contract for many business activities (insurances, intermediaries, transports) – was so poorly represented in the legal world. Surely

4. *M. Ishizaki*, Le droit corporatif des ventes de soies, les contrat-types américains et la codification lyonnaise dans leurs rapports avec les autres places, Paris, M. Giard, 1928.

enough, at this time, the French system was generally oriented towards the legal state positivism with its pyramid consisting of laws, jurisprudence, and doctrine, in which the last element had the purpose to comment on and interpret the first two. The theory of conflict of laws was sufficient to raise internal sales (governed by the Code Civil) on to the sphere of international sales (by indicating the applicable national law). No doubt some voices – if not openly disagreeing than at least at the edge of the spectrum (*Edouard Lambert*[5] and his pupils, *Georges Scelle*) – had developed broader visions of international private and public relations, but those views remained a small minority.

The answer to the question 'why this official vacuum?' was found in the works of the United Nations Economic Commission for Europe (UNECE). In order to facilitate the business relations between Western and Eastern Europe at a time when political differences separated the two blocs and paralyzed exchanges between them, the Commission's legal adviser, *Lazare Kopelmanas*, searched for a common ground on a practical plan.

He thus proposed to develop general conditions of sale, which would not be mere transpositions from the national legal orders, but which would be based on the practices and the contracts of European business operators, exporters, and importers located in the countries of Western and Eastern Europe. Working groups were set up and were composed not of government representatives, but of operators of international trade under the administration of the Commission. Rich documentation accompanied by technical reports on key issues faced by the operators made it possible to grasp the existence of a legal life outside or adjacent to the states in order to respond to specific needs [of international trade]. It was based on this observation that the Commission and its working groups, on a product by product basis, developed general conditions of sale[6].

The understanding of this approach, which is both methodical and practical, led the author of the thesis to complete his investigation by collecting and examining numerous contracts and model contracts (the CAF contract of the London Corntrade Association [today: Grain and Feed Trade Association, GAFTA], contracts for iron and steel products, agricultural, forestal and mining products, textiles, equipment etc . . .).

This research produced two main conclusions:

1. One can distinguish between two types of sale: the sale of non-fungible goods (capital goods) and the sale of fungible goods (production goods and consumption goods).
2. In each of these types of sales a common foundation of rules as well as more specific rules according to the nature of the product being sold appears.

5. *Cf. supra Klaus Peter Berger*, Chapter 2 II.G.3.b.cc.(b).
6. Supply and Erection of Plant and Machinery for Import and Export, Clauses No. 188 and No. 574; contracts for the sale of cereals CIF (by sea); 8 FOB-clauses, 2 clauses; uniform sale conditions for citrus fruits (General Conditions of Sale for Fresh Fruit and Vegetables including Citrus Fruit); Export and Import of Sawn Softwood, Clause No. 410.

These rules are developed and followed without direct connection to or with hostility towards state laws. They are structured and enforced through international commercial arbitration which, in a way, legitimizes them.

The author of the thesis thought he was able to prove the existence – in a sociological, not in a legal sense – of a real society of sellers and buyers of international commerce, implying that there is a veritable society of operators of international commerce beyond the thesis.

Philippe Fouchard, the author of the thesis about international commercial arbitration, would later take up this idea using a less provocative terminology, replacing 'society' with 'community'. The advantage of this step was to use a less aggressive expression *vis-à-vis* the prevailing doctrine of legal positivism, which was hostile towards any curtailment of state laws. The method followed by *Philippe Fouchard* was similar to that followed by *Philippe Kahn*: collecting documents from practice, mainly arbitration clauses included in international contracts and international arbitral awards themselves. The second point raised a particular difficulty: the confidentiality of arbitration, impeding access to significant awards apart from the big oil-related awards that the media had made public. However, there was a moderating effect insofar as, contrary to the international sale itself whose 'natural jurisdiction' was arbitration, arbitral awards could be subjected to the ordinary jurisdictions by way of an exequatur procedure or an action of nullity, judicial decisions which themselves are public.

Nevertheless, despite this difficulty, the author was able to gather a significant number of either *ad hoc* awards or awards rendered under the auspices of numerous arbitral institutions. He was equally able to collect a considerable number of arbitration rules from these institutions, which provided him with an overview of the *status quo* of international commercial arbitration as it existed at the time.

His conclusion was that an internationalization of commercial arbitration was beginning to emerge both with respect to its organization and to its functioning: non-attachment to a state (minimization of the law of the place of arbitration), autonomy of the arbitration clause, priority of procedural rules adopted by international practice thanks to arbitration rules developed by arbitral institutions, freedom of choice of law (parties and arbitrators) including the application of an a-national law by the arbitrator etc.

Among the contributions of the thesis about international arbitration, one will remember on the one hand the demonstration that arbitration was becoming the general dispute resolution mechanism for disputes arising out of international trade operations. Of equal importance was the analysis of the use of their power by the arbitrators which leads them to uncover structuring principles from the often vague contract provisions and terms and conditions used by the operators of international trade.

At this stage, the three theses combined reveal operational activities and jurisdictional activities which together open a space whose legal nature is international in the strictest of senses, suggesting the existence of a transnational (global?) legal sphere. It should be noted that at the beginning of their work, the three authors did not envisage a research project about the *lex mercatoria* at all. It was the result of their research that led them to assert, each of them with his own mode of expression, the existence of a professional juridicity in the studied field of international commerce.

It is noteworthy that the method followed in the three theses was focussed on the analysis of instruments issued by commercial practice, leading the authors to minimize, yet not to deny or forget, [the impact of] the state or interstate sources. It also appears from their observations that the notion of public policy, whether of practical or state origin, does not seem to be a concern for institutions, contracting parties or arbitrators.

The synthesis was made by *Berthold Goldman* in his contribution 'Frontiers of law and *lex mercatoria*'[7] at the Seminar on Philosophy of Law dedicated to the topic of subjective rights. Returning to his own research on the international company and the works of his pupils, he stated 'that international commercial relations, broadly defined, seem to escape from the grip of state law and even uniform law integrated into the legislation of contracting states. Instead, those relations seem to be managed and governed by norms of professional origin or customary rules, and by principles that arbitral awards discover if not develop.' It was this phenomenon that he would propose to call '*lex mercatoria*' with the success that we know.

If the 'Dijon School' has, in this period from 1956 to 1964, provided us with the most elaborate developments, supported by undeniable justifications for the existence of a *lex mercatoria*, it must be remembered that these reflections did not happen in isolation.

At the same time, *Clive M. Schmitthoff* was coming to the identical conclusion, using the same terminology. In several countries, personalities and institutions met and pondered about this new professional law. The minutes of the discussions about the autonomy of will, conducted at the 1964 Conference of the Hague on the International Sale of Goods, are significant; and so are the works of the commission '*Droit et vie des affaires*' of the University of Liège, which would subsequently play an essential role in the development and understanding of the *lex mercatoria*.

In any case, the demonstration of the existence of a set of norms of professional origin governing international trade relations was achieved in 1964. The system received its name '*lex mercatoria*' which would be used continuously throughout its tumultuous existence – an existence whose destiny is not yet complete[8].

---

7. *Berthold Goldman*, 'Frontière du droit et lex mercatoria' in Le Droit subjectif en question, p. 177, Paris, Sirey, 1964.
8. *Philippe Kahn*, 'La lex mercatoria et son destin', in L'actualité de la pensée de Berthold Goldman p. 25, Edition Panthéon Assas 2004.

Annex II

The Suez Company – an International Company*

By Berthold Goldman, Professor at the Law Faculty of Dijon

Since 26 July [1956] the Western powers have continuously denounced Egypt's violation of its international obligations. Yet even though they have denied the legality of the Canal Company's 'nationalization' by the Egyptian State – a measure based, at least in principle, on numerous precedents – they have discreetly left the infringements of the [private] rights of the Company unmentioned.

As Mr Roger Pinto has recently shown in this newspaper[1], the usurpation of the Company's power to manage the canal and Egypt's claim to take over this business from then on are contrary to the provisions and implications of the Constantinople Convention. One need not hesitate to add that its nationalization and the brutally enforced expropriation of all of its assets in Egypt and abroad – compensated with the promise of a future and unilaterally set indemnity – were as well illegal.

Although the Universal Company of the Suez Maritime Canal is tasked with the execution of a international public service, it can certainly be regarded as a legal entity of private law. Nevertheless it is subject neither solely to the Egyptian legal order nor, therefore, to the arbitrary decisions of the respective Egyptian state authority. There is no need to take sides in the very technical controversy about the 'nationality' of companies to be convinced of this fact. For, after all, the controversy as to how to determine the national legal order to which a company is subject concentrates on only three possible criteria: the Anglo-Saxon '*incorporation*' [theory], according to which a company has the nationality of the country whose law governed its birth and conferred upon it its structure; the '*real seat*' [theory], traditionally followed in France and in most other countries including Egypt; and finally the '*control*' [theory], which seeks to find real content hidden beneath the company's structural shape and according to which a company is subject to the law of the country whose citizens effectively control the company through their capital majority or by other means. This more recent notion emerged to replace or complete the real seat theory in its original countries when it became necessary to take measures of war towards companies which had a domestic real seat, but which were dependant on foreigners or enemies.

The Suez Company has not been '*incorporated*' in Egypt. Its articles of association, which Mr Lesseps deposited with the Paris notary Mr Mocquard on 2 December 1858, conform with French law. Further, Article 16 of the Convention of 22 February 1866 specifies that 'regarding the Company's constitution and the

* English translation of the article published in 'Le Monde' on 4 October 1956, p. 3; French original available at *www.Trans-Lex.org/img/monde.jpg*. The text was translated by *Thomas Claeßens* in collaboration with *Bernd Scholl.*

1. *See Le Monde* of 3 October 1956.

relationships between its associates, it is by virtue of a special convention governed by the laws which apply to corporations ["sociétés anonymes"] in France.' It is true that Article 3 of the articles of association provides that 'the Company has its seat in Alexandria and its *administrative domicile* in Paris'. Yet, a seat in Alexandria never existed and in Cairo the Company was only represented by a 'superior agent', as provided by the second firman of 5 January 1856. Its 'brain' operates in Paris, as do the organs legally vested with the power to express its will, namely the board of administration and the general assembly whose localisation defines the place of its real administrative seat. Lastly, regarding the control of the Company one has to keep in mind that, according to the articles of association, the board of administration is composed of 'thirty-two members representing the main nationalities interested in the enterprise', and that about half of the shares belong to French nationals and 44 % to the British Crown.

Therefore, despite careful assertions to the contrary in some constitutive texts which were commanded by the concerns of not hurting the Turkish government ['Sublime Porte'], the Canal Company is not, *in fact*, an Egyptian company. Did not the Sultan – as soon as in the 1860s, namely in the Convention of 18 March 1863 – even put the stress on its foreign nationality to impose on it the retrocession of 60,000 hectare land to the viceroy? And the mixed tribunals have, disregarding other opinions, always been careful to limit the link between the Company and the Egyptian sovereignty to particular matters and have several times decided that, because of its universal character, the Company avoided the application of rules essential to internal public policy (especially those monetary matters). The Egyptian Law on Corporations of 29 July 1947, finally, has never applied to the Company, and some of the matters covered by this law were added through a later freely negotiated convention between the Company and the royal government.

Moreover, it is not enough to say that in relation to Egypt, the Suez Company is a foreign company. It is true that one could consider it as French because of its 'place of incorporation', its real seat and, to some extent, because of the 'control' of the capital and the administration. Otherwise, from this last point of view, the Company can be viewed as having both the French and the British nationality, which is no less conceivable for a legal person than for an individual. And that alone would be enough to show the legal irregularity of the Egyptian nationalization. This nationalization would, without being in line with a general reform on the economic structures of the country, appear as a discriminatory measure against a single foreign company which is *based only on the reason that it is foreign.* Additionally, it would infringe the contractual rights acquired by this company, whereas the compensational indemnity itself was not contractually fixed.

But one must go even further: the Canal Company which is not Egyptian, is not French or British-French either. It is, through its capital structure and its management bodies as well as through the subject matter and the effects of its business activity, *an international company which is directly subject to the international legal order.* This is certainly a new concept – if not to say one in the process of being born – but its necessity has, to draw from an ancient reality, for many years been recognized. The fact that a company's birth and way of functioning are necessarily territorial does not pose an obstacle to that: one has rightfully cited the examples of the Bank for International Settlements or the International Red Cross – legal persons created in Switzerland and in accordance with Swiss law – which cannot, however, be considered as depending only on Swiss law. Towards them, as well as towards Suez, no one territorial state is entitled to exert exclusive powers. Their legal status, even if it materially conforms with the laws of one or several countries whose provisions it borrows, is of an essentially international origin and nature, resulting from conventions which are concluded between the territorial states and them, with other states or with international public organisms. Therefore, it cannot be within the competence of a territorial state to infringe company rights by a measure of nationalization, expropriation or by a withdrawal of concession.

These truths strike us as worthy of mentioning: if it was once odious to shield the big companies from the application of law, it would not be less odious today to deprive them from the law's protection.

Annex III

TransLex Principles

Please cite as: "*www.Trans-Lex.org/principles*".

Preface

This is a print out-version of the Center for Transnational Law's (CENTRAL) TransLex Principles. It contains the text of more than one hundred principles of transnational commercial law, the new lex mercatoria.

The CENTRAL Research Team has collected thousands of full-text references for each principle from legal doctrine, arbitral case law, domestic statutes and international uniform law. For online-access to these references and to more background information on the underlying concept of the "creeping codification of transnational law" please refer to the "Principles" Section of www.trans-lex.org.

For access to the largest bibliography on transnational law please refer to the TransLex Bibliography at www.trans-lex.org.

If you want more information on the Center for Transnational Law, please refer to www.central-koeln.de.

Please do not hesitate to contact us at info@trans-lex.org if you have any questions or suggestions.

Professor Dr. Klaus Peter Berger, LL.M.

Chapter Overview

Table of Contents

No. IV.3.3 – Competing terms; Battle of forms
No. IV.3.4 – Principle of ineffectiveness of unfair standard terms

Section 4: Form Requirements

No. IV.4.1 – Principle of informality

Section 5: Interpretation

No. IV.5.1 – Intentions of the parties
No. IV.5.2 – Context-oriented interpretation
No. IV.5.3 – Interpretation in favour of effectiveness of contract
No. IV.5.4 – Interpretation against the party that supplied the term
No. IV.5.5 – Falsa demonstratio rule
No. IV.5.6 – Rights and duties of the parties under "FOB", "FAS", "CIF", and "CF"

Section 6: Contractual Obligations

No. IV.6.1 – Express and implied obligations
No. IV.6.2 – Subsequent fixing of contract price
No. IV.6.3 – Fixing of price by third party
No. IV.6.4 – No contract to detriment of third party
No. IV.6.5 – Best efforts undertakings
No. IV.6.6 – Time is of the essence
No. IV.6.7 – Duty to renegotiate
No. IV.6.8 – (Re-) Negotiation Agreement/Clause
No. IV.6.9 – Duty to notify / to cooperate
No. IV.6.10 – Conditions
No. IV.6.11 – Plurality of debtors
No. IV.6.12 – Plurality of creditors
No. IV.6.13 – Duty of confidentiality

Section 7: Invalidity of Contract

No. IV.7.1 – Invalidity of contract that violates boni mores
No. IV.7.2 – Invalidity of contract due to bribery
No. IV.7.3 – Right to avoid the contract for mistake in fact or law

Section 8: Precontractual Liability

No. IV.8.1 – Principle of pre-contractual liability

Section 9: Limitation period

No. IV.9.1 – Limitation periods

Chapter V: Performance

Section 1: General Principles

No. V.1.1 – Place of performance
No. V.1.2 – Time of performance
No. V.1.3 – Early performance
No. V.1.4 – Principle of simultaneous performance
No. V.1.5 – Costs of performance

Section 2: Payment of Money Debts

No. V.2.1 – Payment in currency of place of payment
No. V.2.2 – Conversion of money debts
No. V.2.3 – Nominalistic principle

No. V.2.4 – Distribution of currency risk
No. V.2.5 – Payment of contract price through documentary credit

Chapter VI: Non-Performance

No. VI.1 – Termination of contract in case of fundamental non-performance
No. VI.2 – Deadline for notice of defects
No. VI.3 – Force majeure
No. VI.4 – Promise to pay in case of non-performance
No. VI.5 – Anticipatory breach

Chapter VII: Damages

No. VII.1 – Damages in case of non-performance
No. VII.2 – Principle of foreseeability of loss
No. VII.3.1 – Limits to claims for damages
No. VII.3.2 – Lost profits/Further damages
No. VII.4 – Duty to mitigate
No. VII.5 – Liability for damages for legal opinions
No. VII.6 – Duty to pay interest
No. VII.7 – Right to charge compound interest

Chapter VIII: Hardship

No. VIII.1 – Definition
No. VIII.2 – Legal consequences

Chapter IX: Unjust Enrichment/Restitution

No. IX.1 – Basic rule
No. IX.2 – Circumstances in which an enrichment is unjustified
No. IX.3 – Enrichment
No. IX.4 – Disadvantage
No. IX.5 – Disenrichment
No. IX.6 – No restitution in case of knowledge of illegality of performance
No. IX.7 – Relation to other remedies

Chapter X: Corporations

No. X.1 – Foreign corporate entities
No. X.2 – Piercing the corporate veil
No. X.3 – Liability in case of corporate de-facto successions
No. X.4 – Liability of corporate founders

Chapter XI: Expropriation

No. XI.1 – Compensation for expropriation

Chapter XII: Proof, Means of Evidence

No. XII.1 – Distribution of burden of proof
No. XII.2 – Proof of written contract
No. XII.3 – Circumstantial evidence
No. XII.4 – Prima facie evidence
No. XII.5 – Settlement Privilege
No. XII.6 – Attorney-Client Privilege

No. XII.7 – Most favoured nation treatment in case of unequal privilege protection

Chapter XIII: International Arbitration

Section 1: Arbitration Agreement

No. XIII.1.1 – Arbitration agreement
No. XIII.1.2 – Interpretation of Arbitration agreements
No. XIII.1.3 – Arbitration agreement and substantive claim before court
No. XIII.1.4 – Arbitration agreement and interim measures by court

Section 2: Arbitral Tribunal

No. XIII.2.1 – Number of arbitrators
No. XIII.2.2 – Arbitrator's duty to disclose
No. XIII.2.3 – Grounds for challenge of an arbitrator
No. XIII.2.4 – Kompetenz-Kompetenz; Separability of the arbitration clause
No. XIII.2.5 – Power of arbitral tribunal to order interim measures
No. XIII.2.6 – Decision making by panel of arbitrators

Section 3: Arbitral Procedure

No. XIII.3.1 – Arbitral due process
No. XIII.3.2 – Determination of rules of procedure
No. XIII.3.3 – Seat of arbitration
No. XIII.3.4 – Language of the arbitration
No. XIII.3.5 – Early legal guidance by the tribunal
No. XIII.3.6 – Hearings and written proceedings
No. XIII.3.7 – No suspension in case of bankruptcy of a party
No. XIII.3.8 – Default of a party

Section 4: Award; Termination of Proceedings

No. XIII.4.1 – Rules applicable to merits; decision ex aequo et bono
No. XIII.4.2 – Form and contents of award
No. XIII.4.3 – Settlement
No. XIII.4.4 – Termination of proceedings

Section 5: Confidentiality

No. XIII.5.1 – Confidentiality

Chapter XIV: Private International Law

No. XIV.1 – Law Applicable to an International Arbitration Agreement
No. XIV.2 – Closest connection-/Center of gravity-test
No. XIV.3 – Rule of validation/Lex validitatis

TransLex Principles

Chapter I: General Provisions

Section 1: Good Faith and Fair Dealing

No. I.1.1 – Good faith and fair dealing in international trade

(a) Parties to international business transactions must act in accordance with good faith and fair dealing in international trade. This standard applies to the negotiation, formation, performance and interpretation of international contracts.
(b) The standards and requirements imposed on the parties by this Principle vary depending on the individual circumstances involved, such as the trade sector in which the parties are operating, their size and degree of professional sophistication, and the nature and duration of the contract.

No. I.1.2 – Prohibition of inconsistent behaviour

(a) A party cannot set itself in contradiction to its previous conduct vis-à-vis another party if that latter party has acted in reasonable reliance on such conduct ("venire contra factum proprium"; "l'interdiction de se contredire au détriment d'autrui").
(b) Violation of this Principle may result in the loss, suspension, or modification of rights otherwise available to the party violating this Principle or to the creation of rights otherwise not available to the aggrieved party.

No. I.1.3 – Forfeiture of rights

A party that has not raised voluntarily a right to which it is entitled under the law for a certain period of time is precluded from asserting that right against another party that has justifiably relied on such conduct and will suffer injury if the former party is allowed to repudiate its conduct.

No. I.1.4 – Abuse of rights

A party may not exercise a right merely to damage the other party or to achieve a result which is disproportionate to the result intended by the legal principle out of which the right arises.

No. I.1.5 – No advantage in case of own unlawful acts

A party may not derive an advantage from its own unlawful acts ("nullus commodum capere potest de injuria sua propria", "ex injuria non oritur jus", "clean hands theory").

No. I.1.6 – No damage claim in case of consent

A party suffering damage or another prejudice may not raise claims arising out of this if it has consented to the act leading to the damage or prejudice ("volenti non fit iniuria").

Section 2: Reasonableness; Trade Usages; Professional Competence

No. I.2.1 – Standard of reasonableness

The parties always have to act according to what is reasonable in view of the particular nature of their transaction and the circumstances involved, in particular the economic interests and expectations of the parties.

No. I.2.2 – Trade usages

The parties are bound by any usages to which they have agreed and by any practice which they have established between themselves. Unless agreed otherwise, they are considered to have impliedly made applicable to their contract or its formation a usage of which the parties knew or ought to have known and which in international trade is widely known to, and regularly observed by, parties to contracts of the type involved in the particular trade concerned.

No. I.2.3 – Presumption of professional competence and equality of parties

(a) The professional competence and equality of the parties to an international commercial contract is presumed.
(b) Parties to such contracts may not argue that they were not aware of the significance of the contractual provisions and obligations to which they have agreed.

Section 3: Varia

No. I.3.1 – Limitation of transfer of rights

No one may transfer more rights than he actually has ("nemo plus iuris transferre potest quam ipse habet").

No. I.3.2 – Lex specialis-principle

Specialized laws prevail over general laws ("lex specialis derogat legi generali").

Chapter II: Agency

No. II.1 – Prerequisites and effects of agency

Where an agent acts on behalf of a principal within the scope of his authority which has been granted to him expressly or can be implied from the circumstances, his acts bind the principal and the third party unless it follows from the circumstances of the case that the agent undertakes to bind himself only.

No. II.2 – Agent acting on behalf of group of companies

A corporate entity acting on behalf of a group of corporate entities binds all entities that belong to the group.

No. II.3 – Agent acting without or outside his authority

The principal is not bound if an agent acts without or outside his authority (falsus procurator) unless he ratifies, expressly or impliedly through his conduct, the acts of the agent. In the latter case, the act produces the same effects as if it had initially been carried out with authority.

No. II.4 – Agency by estoppel / Apparent authority

Where the conduct of the principal causes the third party reasonably and in good faith to believe that the agent has authority to act on behalf of the principal and the agent is acting within the scope of that authority, the principal may not invoke against the third party the lack of authority of the agent ("agency by estoppel", "Anscheinsvollmacht").

No. II.5 – Attribution of knowledge to principal

Facts which the agent knows or ought to have known are attributable to the principal.

No. II.6 – Performance by agent

Unless a contrary intention appears from the language of the parties, or the nature of the transaction, a debtor may perform his part by an agent. Such a contrary intention is presumed, in the case of any duty involving personal confidence between the parties, or the exercise of the debtor's personal skill.

No. II.7 – General agent

An agent having authority to conduct a particular trade or business, or to act generally for his principal in a particular trade, business, or undertaking, has authority to do every lawful thing necessary or usually incidental thereto.

Chapter III: Set-Off; Assignment

No. III.1 – Set-off

If parties have mature and liquidated claims of an identical nature vis-à-vis each other, each party may declare the set-off of these claims. Set-off is not admissible if the contract contains an explicit or implicit (e.g. a "net cash against..." clause) prohibition of set-off. The parties may also agree on the set-off of these claims by contractual consent.

No. III.2 – Assignment of claim

(a) The creditor (assignor) may assign his claim by contract to the assignee. An assignment is not subject to any form requirements. The assignment is valid irrespective of whether the debtor has been notified of the assignment.
(b) A claim for the payment of a sum of money may be assigned in part. A claim for a non-monetary performance may be assigned in part only if the debtor consents to the assignment; or the claim is divisible and the assignment does not render performance significantly more burdensome for the debtor.
(c) An assignment is invalid if the assigned claim does not exist. A future claim may be the subject of an assignment but the transfer of the claim depends on its coming into existence and being identifiable as the claim to which the assignment relates.
(d) In a b2b-context, a contractual prohibition of, or restriction on, the assignment of a claim, agreed upon by the parties to the contract out of which the claim arises, does not affect the assignability of that claim.
(e) A claim is not assignable, if the parties intended that the promissee alone should be entitled thereto. Such an intention is presumed if the nature of the transaction involves personal confidence between the parties, or is otherwise such that personal consideration is of the essence of the contract.
(f) An accessory right securing payment of the assigned claim is transferred to the assignee without a new act of transfer notwithstanding any agreement between the assignor and the debtor or other party granting that right, limiting in any way the assignor's right to assign the receivable or the right securing payment of the assigned claim. If a non-accessory right is, under the law governing it, transferable only with a new act of transfer, the assignor is obliged to transfer such right and any proceeds thereof to the assignee.
(g) As soon as the assignment becomes effective the assignor ceases to be the creditor and the assignee becomes the creditor in relation to the claim assigned.
(h) The debtor may put forward against the assignee any defences which at the date the assignment becomes effective were available to him against the assignor.

Chapter IV: Contract

Section 1: General Principles

No. IV.1.1 – Freedom of contract

The parties are free to enter into contracts and to determine their contents (principle of party autonomy).

No. IV.1.2 – Sanctity of contracts

(a) A valid contract is binding upon the parties. It can only be modified or terminated by consent of the parties or if provided for by the law. The parties to a contract must, unless legally excused from performance, perform their respective duties under the contract ("pacta sunt servanda").
(b) A valid unilateral promise or undertaking on binding on the party giving it if that promise or undertaking is intended to be legally binding without acceptance.

Section 2: Conclusion of Contract; Standard Terms

No. IV.2.1 – Contractual consent

(a) A contract is concluded when one party has communicated to another an offer, and that other has accepted it, or when the parties have united in a concurrent expression of intention, designed to create a legal obligation.
(b) A valid contractual consent requires that the parties intend to be legally bound and that they have sufficiently identified the terms of the contract with respect to the parties and the subject matter.

No. IV.2.2 – Silence by offeree

(a) Silence by the offeree does not in and of itself amount to acceptance.
(b) Silence by the offeree amounts to acceptance if the offeree begins with the performance of his contractual obligations or is required to reject the offer due to a long-standing business relationship with the offeror or is subject to a practice which the parties have established between themselves or a trade usage requiring rejection of the offer ("qui tacet consentire videtur").

No. IV.2.3 – No repudiation of contractual consent by state party

A state or state controlled entity may not invoke its sovereignty or internal law to repudiate contractual consent.

No. IV.2.4 – Lapse of an offer

An offer lapses when

- **i)** the party to whom it is made fails to accept it within the time or in the manner prescribed by the offeror, or, if no time or manner is prescribed, within a time or in a manner reasonable under the circumstances,
- **ii)** the offeree communicates his refusal of the offer, or makes a counter-offer,
- **iii)** either party dies or, in case of a corporation, ceases to exist.

No. IV.2.5 – Holidays and non-business days

If a notice, letter or other communication cannot be delivered at the address of the addressee on the last day of a period set by law or contractual stipulation because that day falls on an official holiday or non-business day at the place of business of the addressee, the period is extended until the first business day which follows.

No. IV.2.6 – Modified acceptance

(a) A reply to an offer which purports to be an acceptance but contains additions, limitations or other modifications is a rejection of the offer and constitutes a counter-offer.
(b) However, a reply to an offer which purports to be an acceptance but contains additional or different terms which do not materially alter the terms of the offer constitutes an acceptance, unless the offeror without undue delay, objects to the discrepancy. If the offeror does not object, the terms of the contract are the terms of the offer with the modifications contained in the acceptance.
(c) Additional or different terms relating, among other things, to the price, payment, quality and quantity of the goods, place and time of delivery, extent of one party's liability to the other or the settlement of disputes are considered to alter the terms of the offer materially.

No. IV.2.7 – Writings in confirmation

If a writing which is sent within a reasonable time after the conclusion of the contract and which purports to be a confirmation of the contract contains additional or different terms, such terms become part of the contract, unless they materially alter the contract or the recipient objects to the discrepancy without undue delay.

Section 3: Contracting under Standard Terms

No. IV.3.1 – Scope of application; Definition

(a) Where one party or both parties use standard terms in concluding a contract, the general rules on formation apply, subject to the following principles.

(b) Standard terms are provisions which are prepared in advance for general and repeated use by one party and which are actually used without negotiation with the other party.

No. IV.3.2 – No surprising standard terms

No term contained in standard terms which is of such a character that the other party could not reasonably have expected it, is effective unless it has been expressly accepted by that party. In determining whether a term is of such a character regard shall be had to its content, language and presentation.

No. IV.3.3 – Competing terms; Battle of forms

(a) In case of conflict between a standard term and a term which is not a standard term the latter prevails.
(b) Where both parties use standard terms and reach agreement except on those terms, a contract is concluded on the basis of the agreed terms and of any standard terms which are common in substance unless one party clearly indicates in advance, or later and without undue delay informs the other party, that it does not intend to be bound by such a contract.

No. IV.3.4 – Principle of ineffectiveness of unfair standard terms

(a) A standard term that is unfair is not binding on the party who did not supply it.
(b) A standard term in a b2b-contract is unfair only if it is of such nature that its use grossly deviates from good commercial practice, contrary to good faith and fair dealing.
(c) If the contract can reasonably be maintained without the unfair term, the other terms remain binding on the parties.

Section 4: Form Requirements

No. IV.4.1 – Principle of informality

(a) Contractual declarations are valid even when they are not evidenced in writing unless mandatory rules of any applicable domestic law provide otherwise.
(b) Parties to international business contracts may not insist on undue formalism without any good reason.

Section 5: Interpretation

No. IV.5.1 – Intentions of the parties

The construction of a contract has to determine the common intention of the parties or, if no such intention can be determined, the meaning that reasonable parties of the same kind as the parties would give to it in the same circumstances, taking into account, in particular, the nature and purpose of the contract, the conduct of the parties and the meaning commonly given to contract terms and expressions in the trade concerned.

No. IV.5.2 – Context-oriented interpretation

Contractual stipulations shall be interpreted taking into account the whole contract in which they appear.

No. IV.5.3 – Interpretation in favour of effectiveness of contract

Where there is doubt about the meaning of a contract term, an interpretation should be preferred that makes the contract lawful or effective ("ut res magis valeat quam pereat"; "effet utile").

No. IV.5.4 – Interpretation against the party that supplied the term

Where, after the interpretation of a contract term that has been supplied by one party, doubts remain as to the meaning of that term, an interpretation against that party is to be preferred ("contra proferentem").

No. IV.5.5 – Falsa demonstratio rule

In case the parties have used the wrong term but mean the same thing, their common intention prevails ("falsa demonstratio non nocet").

No. IV.5.6 – Rights and duties of the parties under "FOB", "FAS", "CIF", and "CF"

If the parties have agreed on a sale "FOB", "FAS", "CIF" or "CF", the respective rights and duties of the parties under the contract are to be determined according to the latest version of the International Commercial Terms (INCOTERMS) issued by the International Chamber of Commerce (ICC) unless the parties have indicated that a different meaning is to be attributed to the term used.

Section 6: Contractual Obligations

No. IV.6.1 – Express and implied obligations

(a) The contractual obligations of the parties may be express or implied.
(b) Implied obligations stem from

- **i)** the nature and the purpose of the contract;
- **ii)** practices established between the parties and usages;

iii) good faith and fair dealing; or
iv) reasonableness.

No. IV.6.2 – Subsequent fixing of contract price

If the contract does not contain a provision fixing the price or a method for determining it, the parties are to be treated as having agreed to the price generally charged at the time of the conclusion of the contract for such performance in comparable circumstances in the trade concerned, or, if no such price is available, to a reasonable price.

No. IV.6.3 – Fixing of price by third party

If the contract provides that the price is to be fixed or determined by a third party, and this determination is manifestly unreasonable, a party may apply to a court or arbitral tribunal to have a reasonable price fixed, notwithstanding any agreements to the contrary.

No. IV.6.4 – No contract to detriment of third party

Contracts may not be concluded to the detriment of a third party ("res inter alios acta alteri non nocet").

No. IV.6.5 – Best efforts undertakings

If a party promises its "best efforts" in the performance of its contractual duties, that party owes to the promissee all efforts which can be expected from a reasonable party of the same kind in the same circumstances, taking into account the particular nature of the contract and the interests of the parties.

No. IV.6.6 – Time is of the essence

Unless otherwise agreed by the parties or contrary to the intrinsic nature of the contract, time limits and other contractual stipulations as to the timely performance of the parties' obligations have to be strictly complied with ("time is of the essence").

No. IV.6.7 – Duty to renegotiate

Each party has a good faith obligation to renegotiate the contract if there is a need to adapt the contract to changed circumstances and the continuation of performance can reasonably be expected from the parties.

No. IV.6.8 – (Re-) Negotiation Agreement/Clause

(a) Under an agreement or contract clause requiring the parties to (re-) negotiate in good faith (cf. No. I.1.1), both parties are legally obliged to cooperate in the (re-)

negotiation procedure in an efficient manner, i.e. in a manner aimed at successfully negotiating a solution. This requires above all earnest efforts, flexibility and a willingness to consider the needs and interests of the other party. Principle IV.8.1 c) applies accordingly.
(b) Such agreements/clauses impose an obligation on the parties to make best possible efforts (cf. No. IV.6.5) to reach an agreement within the framework of (a) above. They do not, however, require the parties to actually reach an agreement unless otherwise provided for in the agreement/clause*.

No. IV.6.9 – Duty to notify / to cooperate

(a) Each party is under a good faith obligation to notify in a timely fashion the other party of any problems that occur in the performance of the contract and of any other facts or circumstances on whose knowledge the other party is discernibly dependent, provided that such information can reasonably be expected from that party.
(b) Each party is under a good faith obligation to cooperate with the other party when such cooperation can reasonably be expected for the performance of that party's obligations.

No. IV.6.10 – Conditions

(a) A condition is a term in a contract, to the effect that on the occurrence, or non-occurrence of an uncertain event, act, or forbearance, a right shall arise, or cease to exist.
(b) A condition, on the occurrence of which a right is to arise, is called a "condition precedent" (or "suspensive"); a condition on the occurrence of which a right is to cease to exist, is called a "condition subsequent" (or "resolutive").

No. IV.6.11 – Plurality of debtors

Two or more parties who are liable for one and the same performance are (a) joint, or (b) partial debtors. Parties are liable as joint or partial debtors when they unite in making one and the same promise under the same contract or when they are liable for the same damage unless the contract or the law provides otherwise.

(a) Joint debtors

(aa) The creditor may claim performance from any one of the joint debtors until full performance has been reached.

(bb) If one joint debtor has performed, in kind or by way of set off, the liability to the creditor of the other joint debtor(s) is discharged to the extent of such

* For a list of obligations, which the parties to a (re-) negotiation clause are subject to, see *Berger*, Renegotiation and Adaptation of International Investment Contracts – The Role of Contract Drafters and Arbitrators, Vanderbilt Journal of Transnational Law 2003, at 1347, 1365 *et seq.*

performance or set-off. The same applies if one joint debtor concludes a settlement with the creditor.

(cc) As between themselves, joint debtors are liable in equal shares unless the contract or the law provides otherwise. If a joint debtor has performed more than his share, he may claim the excess from any of the other joint debtors to the extent of each debtor's unperformed share.

(dd) A joint debtor may invoke against the creditor any defence which another joint debtor can invoke, other than a defence personal to that other debtor. Invoking the defence has no effect with regard to the other joint debtors.

(b) Partial debtors

(aa) The creditor may claim from any partial debtor only that part of the performance for which he is liable and the partial debtor is bound to perform only to that extent.

(bb) Partial debtors are liable in equal shares unless the contract or the law provides otherwise.

No. IV.6.12 – Plurality of creditors

Two or more persons who may claim one and the same performance from the debtor are (a) joint, or (b) partial creditors.

(a) Joint Creditors

(aa) A joint creditor may claim full performance from the debtor and the debtor may render full performance to any of those joint creditors.

(bb) If one joint creditor has received performance, in kind or by way of set-off, the liability of the debtor to the other joint creditors is discharged to the extent of such performance or set-off. The same applies if one joint creditor concludes a settlement with the debtor.

(cc) As between themselves, joint creditors are entitled to performance in equal shares. If a joint creditor has received more than that creditor's share, that creditor must transfer the excess to the other creditors to the extent of their respective shares.

(dd) A release granted to the debtor by one of the joint creditors has no effect on the other joint creditors.

(ee) A debtor may invoke against a joint creditor any defence which he can invoke against another joint creditor, other than a defence personal to that other creditor. Invoking the defence has no effect with regard to the other joint creditors.

(b) Partial Creditors

(aa) A partial creditor may claim from the debtor only his share of the claim and the debtor owes to that partial creditor only that creditor's share of the claim.

(bb) Partial creditors are entitled to performance in equal shares unless the contract or the law provides otherwise.

No. IV.6.13 – Duty of confidentiality

Where information is given as confidential by one party in the course of negotiations, the other party is under a duty not to disclose that information or to use it improperly for its own purposes, whether or not a contract is subsequently concluded. Where appropriate, the remedy for breach of that duty may include compensation based on the benefit received by the other party.

Section 7: Invalidity of Contract

No. IV.7.1 – Invalidity of contract that violates boni mores

A contract that violates boni mores is void.

No. IV.7.2 – Invalidity of contract due to bribery

(a) Contracts based on or involving the payment or transfer of bribes ("corruption money", "secret commissions", "pots-de-vin", "kickbacks") are void.
(b) Any intentional offer, promise or transfer of any undue pecuniary or other advantage, whether directly or through intermediaries, to a foreign public official or private party, for the benefit of that official or private party or for a third party, in order that the official or private party acts or refrains from acting in relation to the performance of official or other duties, in order to obtain or retain business or other improper advantages in the conduct of international business constitutes bribery.

No. IV.7.3 – Right to avoid the contract for mistake in fact or law

(a) A party may avoid a contract retrospectively based on a mistake of fact or law existing at the moment the contract was concluded if:

i) the mistake was caused by information given by the other party, or
ii) the other party knew or ought to have known of the mistake and it was contrary to good faith and fair dealing to leave the mistaken party in error
iii) the other party made the same mistake

provided that the other party knew or ought to have known that a reasonable party in the same situation as the party in error would not have entered into the contract or would have concluded the contract on materially different terms.
(b) A party's right to avoid the contract for mistake is excluded if

i) the risk was assumed, or, under the particular circumstances, should be borne by it,
ii) it was grossly negligent in committing the mistake, or if

iii) the party, being aware of and reasonably capable of enforcing such a right, manifests an intention to confirm the transaction.

Section 8: Precontractual Liability

No. IV.8.1 – Principle of pre-contractual liability

(a) A party is free to negotiate a contract and is not liable for failure to reach agreement with the other side.
(b) A party who breaks off contract-negotiations in bad faith is liable for the losses caused to the other party ("culpa in contrahendo").
(c) It is bad faith, in particular, for a party to enter into or continue negotiations when intending not to reach an agreement with the other party while leaving the other party under the justified assumption that a contract would be concluded. The same applies if a party insists on contract terms so clearly unreasonable that they could not have been advanced with any expectation of acceptance, provided that there is some demonstrable advantage to be gained for that party by avoiding the contemplated transaction.

Section 9: Limitation period

No. IV.9.1 – Limitation periods

Contractual claims are subject to limitation periods.

Chapter V: Performance

Section 1: General Principles

No. V.1.1 – Place of performance

(a) If the place of performance is neither fixed by, nor determinable from, the contract, a party has to perform:

i) a monetary obligation, at the obligee's place of business;
ii) any other obligation, at its own place of business.

(b) If a party has more than one place of business, the place of business for the purpose of the preceding paragraph is that which has the closest relationship to the contract, having regard to the circumstances known to or contemplated by the parties at the time of conclusion of the contract.
(c) A party must bear any increase in the expenses incidental to performance which is caused by a change in its place of business subsequent to the conclusion of the contract.

No. V.1.2 – Time of performance

A party must perform its obligations:

i) if a time is fixed by or determinable from the contract, at that time;
ii) if a period of time is fixed by or determinable from the contract, at any time within that period unless circumstances indicate that the other party is to choose a time;
iii) in any other case, within a reasonable time after the conclusion of the contract.

No. V.1.3 – Early performance

(a) A party may decline a tender of performance made before it is due except where acceptance of the tender would not unreasonably prejudice its interests.
(b) A party's acceptance of early performance does not affect the time fixed for the performance of its own obligation.

No. V.1.4 – Principle of simultaneous performance

(a) The parties to a bilateral contract are required to render their respective performances simultaneously unless they have agreed or circumstances indicate otherwise.
(b) If simultaneous performance is required each party may withhold performance until tender of performance by the other party ("exceptio non adimpleti contractus").

No. V.1.5 – Costs of performance

Each party shall bear the costs of performance of its obligations, unless the parties have agreed otherwise.

Section 2: Payment of Money Debts

No. V.2.1 – Payment in currency of place of payment

Unless otherwise agreed by the parties, payment of a money debt may always be made in the currency of the place for payment.

No. V.2.2 – Conversion of money debts

Conversion of the currency of account into a different currency of payment has to be made according to the exchange rate prevailing at the time when payment is due. If the debtor is in arrear, the creditor may require payment either at the rate when payment is due or at the rate of the time of actual payment.

No. V.2.3 – Nominalistic principle

Unless otherwise agreed by the parties (e.g. in "value-stabilization clauses" or "index-linking clauses"), a claim for payment in a certain currency entitles the creditor only to the contractually specified amount of that currency (nominal value), irrespective of any fluctuations of the currency in which the debt is expressed between the date of concluding the contract out of which the claim arises and the date of payment.

No. V.2.4 – Distribution of currency risk

The distribution of the currency risk follows from Art. VIII (2)(b) IMF-Agreement.

No. V.2.5 – Payment of contract price through documentary credit

An agreement by the parties to payment through Documentary Credit (Letter of Credit, L/C) means any arrangement, however named or described, whereby a bank (the "Issuing Bank") acting at the request and on the instructions of a customer (the "Applicant") or on its own behalf,

- **i)** is to make a payment to or to the order of a third party (the "Beneficiary"), or is to accept and pay bills of exchange (Draft(s)) drawn by the Beneficiary, or
- **ii)** authorises another Bank to effect such payment, or to accept and pay such bills of exchange (Draft(s)), or
- **iii)** authorises another Bank to negotiate,

against stipulated document(s), provided they appear, on their face, to be in compliance with the terms and condition of the credit, to be determined according to international standard banking practices as reflected in the UCP issued by the International Chamber of Commerce.

Chapter VI: Non-Performance

No. VI.1 – Termination of contract in case of fundamental non-performance

(a) If a party's failure to perform its obligation amounts to a fundamental non-performance, the other party may terminate the contract.
(b) The right of a party to terminate the contract is exercised by notice to the other party.
(c) If performance has been offered late or otherwise does not conform to the contract the aggrieved party will lose its right to terminate the contract unless it gives notice to the other party within a reasonable time after it has or ought to have become aware of the offer or of the non-conforming performance.
(d) Termination of the contract releases both parties from their obligation to effect and to receive future performance.

(e) Upon termination of the contract either party may claim restitution of whatever it has supplied, provided that such party concurrently makes restitution of whatever it has received. If restitution in kind is not possible or appropriate allowance should be made in money whenever reasonable. However, if performance of the contract has extended over a period of time and the contract is divisible, such restitution can only be claimed for the period after termination has taken effect.
(f) Termination does not preclude a claim for damages for non-performance.
(g) Termination does not affect any provision in the contract for the settlement of disputes or any other term of the contract which is to operate even after termination.

No. VI.2 – Deadline for notice of defects

Notice of defects has to be given within two years of delivery of the goods.

No. VI.3 – Force majeure

(a) If non-performance of a party is

- **i)** due to an impediment which is beyond the reasonable control of that party and
- **ii)** could not have reasonably been foreseen by that party at the time of conclusion of the contract, and
- **iii)** neither the impediment nor its consequences could have been avoided or overcome by the non-performing party ("Acts of God"; "Force Majeure", "höhere Gewalt"), and
- **iv)** the non-performing party did not assume, explicitly or implicitly, the risk of the occurrence of the impediment

that party's non-performance is excused.
(b) If non-performance is temporary, performance of the contract is suspended during that time and that party is not liable for damages to the other party. If the period of non-performance becomes unreasonable and amounts to a fundamental non-performance, the other party may claim damages and terminate the contract.
(c) Unless otherwise agreed by the parties expressly or impliedly, Force Majeure events under subsection (a) above are impediments such as

- **i)** war, whether declared or not, civil war or any other armed conflict, military or non-military interference by any third party state or states, acts of terrorism or serious threats of terrorist attacks, sabotage or piracy, strike or boycott, acts of governments or any other acts of authority whether lawful or unlawful, blockade, siege or sanctions, or
- **ii)** accidents, fires, explosions, plagues, or
- **iii)** natural disasters such as but not limited to storm, cyclone, hurricane, earthquake, landslide, flood, drought etc., or
- **iv)** any event of a similar nature.

(d) Where the obligee has been prevented by a Force Majeure event as defined in (a) above from causing a limitation period to cease to run, the limitation period is suspended so as not to expire before one year after the relevant impediment has ceased to exist.

No. VI.4 – Promise to pay in case of non-performance

When the contract contains a clause providing that a party who fails to perform is to pay a specified sum to the aggrieved party for such non-performance ("penalty clause"; "clause pénale"; "Vertragsstrafeversprechen"), the aggrieved party is entitled to that sum irrespective of its actual loss. If the amount is grossly excessive in relation to the loss resulting from non-performance, and the other circumstances, the specified sum may be reduced by an arbitral tribunal or court to a reasonable amount notwithstanding any agreements of the parties to the contrary.

No. VI.5 – Anticipatory breach

When a party to a contract absolutely and unequivocally expresses an intention – expressly or tacitly – not to perform, or when it becomes otherwise clear, after the conclusion of the contract, that there will be a fundamental non-performance, the other party may terminate the contract. Principle VI.1 applies.

Chapter VII: Damages

No. VII.1 – Damages in case of non-performance

The aggrieved party is entitled to damages for loss caused by the other party's non-performance of its contractual obligations. It is entitled, subject to the provisions of Principle VII.2, to receive such a sum of money by way of damages as will, so far as possible, put him in the same position as if the contract had been performed.

No. VII.2 – Principle of foreseeability of loss

Claims for damages are limited to the loss which the non-performing party foresaw or could reasonably have foreseen at the time of the conclusion of the contract as being the likely result of its non-performance.

No. VII.3.1 – Limits to claims for damages

Damages may not exceed the actual loss and are available only for loss which is proved by the aggrieved party.

No. VII.3.2 – Lost profits/Further damages

(a) The party who suffers a loss from the failure of the other party to deliver is entitled to calculate his loss

i) based on the difference between the contract price and the price of a replacement transaction (e.g. substitute sale or substitute purchase) concluded within a reasonable time and in a reasonable manner or,
ii) based on the difference between the price in the unexecuted contract and the market price current at the date of default and at the place where the contract should have been performed, or, if there is no current price at that place, the current price at such other place that appears reasonable to take as a reference.

(b) The aggrieved party may only recover lost net profits. This requires that the benefits of avoiding performance – the operating or other costs avoided by the absence of performance – must be deducted from the value to be received through performance.
(c) A claim for compensation of further harm is not excluded by a claim raised under (a) above, provided that such harm was foreseeable under Principle VII.2 and is established with a reasonable degree of certainty.

No. VII.4 – Duty to mitigate

A party who relies on a breach of contract must take such measures as are reasonable in the circumstances to mitigate the loss, including loss of profit, resulting from the breach. If it fails to take such measures, the party in breach may claim a reduction in the damages in the amount which the loss should have been mitigated.

No. VII.5 – Liability for damages for legal opinions

A party is liable for damages if it solicits a legal opinion in the case according to the agreement of the parties and the other party, who has reasonably believed in the verity of the legal opinion, suffers damages because it has performed its obligation or has made other financial dispositions.

No. VII.6 – Duty to pay interest

(a) If the parties have not agreed otherwise, the debtor, who does not pay a sum of money when it falls due has to pay to the creditor interest on that sum from the time when payment was due.
(b) The rate of interest is to be determined on the basis of the average bank short-term lending rate to commercial borrowers prevailing for the currency of payment at the place of payment.

No. VII.7 – Right to charge compound interest

Compound interest may be charged on interest.

Chapter VIII: Hardship

No. VIII.1 – Definition

Any event of legal, economic, technical, political or financial nature

- **i)** which occurs after the conclusion of the contract,
- **ii)** which could not reasonably have been taken into account by the disadvantaged party at the time of the conclusion of the contract and
- **iii)** which fundamentally alters the equilibrium of the contractual obligations, thereby rendering the performance of the contract excessively onerous for that party provided that party has not, through express stipulation or by the nature of the contract, assumed the risk of that event

constitutes hardship ("Wegfall der Geschäftsgrundlage", "clausula rebus sic stantibus", "frustration of purpose").

No. VIII.2 – Legal consequences

(a) In case of hardship, the aggrieved party may claim renegotiation of the contract with a view to reach agreement on alternative contractual terms which reasonably allow for the consequences of the event.
(b) If the parties fail to reach agreement on these alternative terms within reasonable time, either party may apply to a court or arbitral tribunal in order to have the contract

- **i)** adapted to the changed circumstances (provided the applicable procedural law allows for such adaptation), or
- **ii)** terminated at a date and on terms to be determined by the court or arbitral tribunal.

Chapter IX: Unjust Enrichment/Restitution

No. IX.1 – Basic rule

(a) If a party is unjustifiably enriched (enriched party) without any legal ground,

- **i)** through performance by another, or
- **ii)** in any other manner,

at the expense of another party (disadvantaged party), the enriched party is bound to render restitution to the disadvantaged party.
(b) Restitution is the sum of money equal to the value of the enrichment to be determined according to the contractually agreed price or market price, including full compensation for the use (usufruct) of the subject matter of the enrichment.

No. IX.2 – Circumstances in which an enrichment is unjustified

An enrichment is unjustified in case of transfers of money, goods or services made

- **i)** on the basis of a contract or obligation or gratuitous disposition which is void or retrospectively avoided pursuant to Principle IV.7.3, or
- **ii)** without legal capacity to make them, or
- **iii)** under an express or implied reservation of a right of recovery, or
- **iv)** for a purpose which is not realized or does not materialize.

No. IX.3 – Enrichment

(a) A party is enriched by:

- **i)** an increase in assets or a decrease in liabilities;
- **ii)** receiving a service or having work done; or
- **iii)** use of another's assets.

(b) In determining whether and to what extent a party obtains an enrichment, no regard is to be had to any disadvantage which that party sustains in exchange for or after the enrichment.

No. IX.4 – Disadvantage

(a) A party is disadvantaged by:

- **i)** a decrease in assets or an increase in liabilities;
- **ii)** rendering a service or doing work; or
- **iii)** another's use of that party's assets.

(b) In determining whether and to what extent a party sustains a disadvantage, no regard is to be had to any enrichment which that party obtains in exchange for or after the disadvantage.

No. IX.5 – Disenrichment

The enriched party is not liable to reverse the enrichment to the extent that the enriched party has sustained a disadvantage by disposing of the enrichment or otherwise (disenrichment), unless the enriched party would have had the same disadvantage even if the enrichment had not been obtained.

No. IX.6 – No restitution in case of knowledge of illegality of performance

No one may claim restitution of what he has rendered to the other party while knowing the illegality of his performance ("nemo turpitudinem suam allegans auditur").

No. IX.7 – Relation to other remedies

This Principle does not affect any other right of recovery of the disadvantaged party arising under contractual or other rules.

Chapter X: Corporations

No. X.1 – Foreign corporate entities

The existence of foreign corporate entities is acknowledged.

No. X.2 – Piercing the corporate veil

(a) The separate legal personality of a corporation ("corporate veil") may be disregarded in appropriate cases in order to hold a shareholder liable for the corporation's debts.
(b) Appropriate cases are cases of:

- **i)** clear under-capitalization,
- **ii)** mingling of corporate and financial spheres, especially in case of total control of the parent company over the business and financial affairs of its subsidiary, or
- **iii)** fraud.

No. X.3 – Liability in case of corporate de-facto successions

In case of corporate de-facto succession liability continues.

No. X.4 – Liability of corporate founders

The founders are liable for debts incurred in the pre-incorporation phase.

Chapter XI: Expropriation

No. XI.1 – Compensation for expropriation

(a) A state may not nationalize or expropriate foreign private investment except for a purpose which is in the public interest, not discriminatory, carried out under due process of law and against appropriate compensation.
(b) Appropriate compensation must be based on the fair market value of the expropriated assets to be determined immediately before the time at which the taking occurred or the decision to take the asset became publicly known ("full compensation standard").
(c) Absent an agreement of the parties, if a going concern is expropriated, the amount of compensation is to be determined according to the "going

concern"-value, based on the discounted cash flow value of the enterprise ("discounted cash flow method", "DCF").
(d) Absent an agreement of the parties, if a non-profitable enterprise is expropriated, the amount of compensation is to be determined according to the liquidation value, i.e. the sum of the sale prices of the individual assets under condition of liquidation.
(e) Absent an agreement of the parties, if other assets are expropriated, the amount of compensation is to be determined according to their replacement value, i.e. the cash amount required to replace the individual assets of the enterprise in their actual state as of the date of the taking or the book value, i.e. the balance of the enterprise's assets and liabilities as recorded on its financial statements or the amount at which the taken tangible assets appear on the balance sheet of the enterprise.
(f) The standard of compensation may be adjusted to the individual circumstances of the case.
(g) Payment of compensation shall include interest and has to be made effectively, i.e. in freely convertible currency on the basis of the market rate of exchange existing for that currency on the valuation date or in any other currency accepted by the investor, and prompt, i.e. without undue delay or, in case of established foreign exchange stringencies, by payment in instalments within a period which will be as short as possible not exceeding five years from the time of the taking.

Chapter XII: Proof, Means of Evidence

No. XII.1 – Distribution of burden of proof

The burden of proof rests on the party who advances a proposition affirmatively ("actori incumbit probatio").

No. XII.2 – Proof of written contract

A written contract may be proven through any means of modern telecommunication (Telex, Telefax, btx, EDI etc.), if it provides a record of the information contained therein and can be reproduced in written form.

No. XII.3 – Circumstantial evidence

Principal facts may be proven by evidence of facts and/or circumstances from which the existence of those principal facts usually and reasonably follow according to the general experience of life.

No. XII.4 – Prima facie evidence

Prima facie evidence, which is based on a typical sequence of events that, according to the general experience of life, justifies the assumption of a certain cause or consequence, is admissible (res ipsa loquitur).

No. XII.5 – Settlement Privilege

(a) Privileged information is inadmissible as evidence in subsequent arbitration or court proceedings between the same parties, provided that the privilege objection

- **i)** is raised in the arbitration or court proceedings in good faith, and
- **ii)** does not relate to facts which one side would have been able to prove had there been no settlement negotiations between the parties.

(b) Privileged information relates to

- **i)** statements, views, admissions, proposals, suggestions, indications of readiness to accept a certain proposal for settlement, whether written or oral, submitted by a party during settlement negotiations, mediation/conciliation or any other ADR proceedings, or
- **ii)** statements made or views expressed by a third neutral involved in such proceedings, or
- **iii)** any document, witness statement or expert report submitted in or prepared by a party solely for these negotiations, mediation/conciliation or any other ADR process between the parties.

No. XII.6 – Attorney-Client Privilege

Any communication between a client and his attorney which is made in the course of or in anticipation of legal proceedings or which relates to the giving of legal advice, i.e. the seeking of advice as to legal rights and obligations as opposed to general business matters, and which originates in a confidence that it will not be disclosed, is privileged and may not be introduced as evidence in court or arbitration proceedings.

No. XII.7 – Most favoured nation treatment in case of unequal privilege protection

If the standard of privilege protection granted to one party under the applicable law is different from the standard granted to the other party under the applicable law, the arbitral tribunal – in the interest of procedural fairness and equal treatment of the parties – shall grant to both parties the privilege standard of the law of that party which accords the broadest privilege protection.

Chapter XIII: International Arbitration

Section 1: Arbitration Agreement

No. XIII.1.1 – Arbitration agreement

(a) An arbitration agreement is an agreement by the parties to submit to arbitration – whether administered (institutional arbitration) or not (ad hoc arbitration) – all or

certain disputes or disagreements which have arisen or which may arise between them in respect of a defined legal relationship, whether contractual or not.
(b) An arbitration agreement may be in the form of an arbitration clause in a contract or in the form of a separate agreement (submission agreement).
(c) The law applicable to the arbitration agreement is to be determined according to Principle XIV.1.

No. XIII.1.2 – Interpretation of Arbitration agreements

An international arbitration agreement must be construed with a view to preserve its validity and to uphold the will of the parties expressed therein to have their dispute decided by international arbitrators and not by domestic courts (in favorem validitatis).

No. XIII.1.3 – Arbitration agreement and substantive claim before court

(a) A court before which an action is brought in a matter which is the subject of an arbitration agreement shall, if a party so requests not later than when submitting his first statement on the substance of the dispute, refer the parties to arbitration unless it finds that the agreement is null and void, inoperative or incapable of being performed.
(b) Where an action referred to in paragraph (a) of this Principle has been brought, arbitral proceedings may nevertheless be commenced or continued, and an award may be made, while the issue is pending before the court.

No. XIII.1.4 – Arbitration agreement and interim measures by court

It is not incompatible with an arbitration agreement for a party to request, before or during arbitral proceedings, from a court an interim measure of protection and for a court to grant such measure.

Section 2: Arbitral Tribunal

No. XIII.2.1 – Number of arbitrators

(a) The number of arbitrators shall be one or three. The parties are free to determine the number of arbitrators.
(b) Failing such determination, the number of arbitrators shall be determined by the applicable arbitration law.

No. XIII.2.2 – Arbitrator's duty to disclose

(a) When a person is approached in connection with his possible appointment as an arbitrator, he shall disclose any circumstances likely to give rise, in the eyes of the parties, to justifiable doubts as to his impartiality or independence.

(b) An arbitrator, from the time of his appointment and throughout the arbitral proceedings, shall without delay disclose any such circumstances to the parties unless they have already been informed of them by him.
(c) An arbitrator who has made a disclosure considers himself or herself to be impartial and independent of the parties despite the disclosed facts and therefore capable of performing his or her duties as arbitrator. Therefore, disclosure does not, in and of itself, demonstrate grounds sufficient to disqualify the arbitrator.
(d) Non-disclosure by an arbitrator of certain facts or circumstances alone does not constitute a ground for challenge. Only the facts or circumstances that he did not disclose can do so.

No. XIII.2.3 – Grounds for challenge of an arbitrator

(a) An arbitrator may be challenged only if circumstances exist that, from the perspective of a reasonable third person having knowledge of the relevant facts, give rise to justifiable doubts as to his impartiality or independence, or if he does not possess qualifications agreed to by the parties.
(b) An arbitrator shall decline to accept an appointment or, if the arbitration has already been commenced, refuse to continue to act as an arbitrator if he or she has any doubts as to his or her ability to be impartial or independent.
(c) Justifiable doubts necessarily exist as to the arbitrator's impartiality or independence if there is an identity between a party and the arbitrator, if the arbitrator is a legal representative of a legal entity that is a party in the arbitration, or if the arbitrator has a significant financial or personal interest in the matter at stake.
(d) A party may challenge an arbitrator appointed by him, or in whose appointment he has participated, only for reasons of which he becomes aware after the appointment has been made.
(e) The parties are free to agree on a procedure for challenging an arbitrator, subject to mandatory court control of the challenge as provided for by the arbitration law in force at the seat of the arbitration.

No. XIII.2.4 – Kompetenz-Kompetenz; Separability of the arbitration clause

(a) The arbitral tribunal may rule on its own jurisdiction, including any objections with respect to the existence or validity of the arbitration agreement ("Kompetenz-Kompetenz").
(b) A plea that the arbitral tribunal does not have jurisdiction shall be raised not later than the submission of the statement of defence. A party is not precluded from raising such a plea by the fact that he has appointed, or participated in the appointment of, an arbitrator.
(c) The invalidity of the main contract does not automatically extend to the arbitration clause contained therein unless it is proven that the arbitration agreement itself is vitiated by fraud, or initial lack of consent (Principle of Separability).

No. XIII.2.5 – Power of arbitral tribunal to order interim measures

Unless otherwise agreed by the parties, the arbitral tribunal may, at the request of a party, order any party to take such interim measure of protection as the arbitral tribunal may consider necessary in respect of the subject matter of the dispute. The arbitral tribunal may require any party to provide appropriate security in connection with such measure.

No. XIII.2.6 – Decision making by panel of arbitrators

(a) In arbitral proceedings with more than one arbitrator, any decision of the arbitral tribunal shall be made, unless otherwise agreed by the parties, by a majority of all its members.
(b) Questions of procedure may be decided by a presiding arbitrator, if so authorized by the parties or all members of the arbitral tribunal.

Section 3: Arbitral Procedure

No. XIII.3.1 – Arbitral due process

(a) Throughout the proceedings, the parties shall be treated with equality.
(b) Each party shall be given a full opportunity to present his case at all stages of the proceedings ("audiatur et altera pars").
(c) The parties shall be given sufficient advance notice of any hearing and of any meeting of the arbitral tribunal for the purpose of taking evidence.
(d) All written pleadings, documents or other communications supplied to the arbitral tribunal by one party shall be communicated to the other party. Likewise, expert reports and other evidentiary documents on which the arbitral tribunal may rely in making its decision are to be communicated to both parties.
(e) The parties are entitled to be legally represented.

No. XIII.3.2 – Determination of rules of procedure

(a) Subject to the mandatory provisions of the arbitration law in force at the seat of the arbitration, the parties are free to agree on the procedure to be followed by the arbitral tribunal in conducting the proceedings, either by reference to a set of arbitration rules or by agreeing on specific rules for the conduct of the proceedings prior to or during the arbitration.
(b) Failing such agreement, the arbitral tribunal may conduct the arbitration in such manner as it considers appropriate, taking into account the parties' due process rights under Principle XIII.3.1. The power conferred upon the arbitral tribunal includes the power to determine the admissibility, relevance, materiality and weight of any evidence.

No. XIII.3.3 – Seat of arbitration

(a) The parties are free to agree on the seat of arbitration. Failing such agreement, the seat of arbitration shall be determined by the arbitral tribunal having regard to the circumstances of the case, including the convenience of the parties.
(b) Notwithstanding the provisions of paragraph a) of this Principle, the arbitral tribunal may, unless otherwise agreed by the parties, meet at any place it considers appropriate for consultation among its members, for hearing witnesses, experts or the parties, or for inspection of goods, other property or documents.
(c) The provisions of an arbitration law apply only if the seat of arbitration is in the territory of the state which has enacted that law, unless otherwise provided by that law (*lex loci arbitri*).

No. XIII.3.4 – Language of the arbitration

(a) The parties are free to agree on the language or languages to be used in the arbitral proceedings. Failing such agreement, the arbitral tribunal shall determine the language or languages to be used in the proceedings, taking into account the parties' due process rights under Principle XIII.3.1.
(b) This agreement or determination, unless otherwise specified therein, shall apply to any written statement by a party, any hearing and any award, decision or other communication by the arbitral tribunal.
(c) The arbitral tribunal may order that any documentary evidence shall be accompanied by a translation into the language or languages agreed upon by the parties or determined by the arbitral tribunal.

No. XIII.3.5 – Early legal guidance by the tribunal

(a) The arbitral tribunal shall identify to the parties, as soon as it considers it to be appropriate, the issues that it may regard as relevant and material to the outcome of the case, including issues where a preliminary determination may be appropriate.
(b) An arbitrator may assist the parties in reaching a settlement of the dispute at any appropriate stage of the proceedings. However, before doing so, the arbitrator shall receive an express agreement by the parties that acting in such a manner shall not disqualify the arbitrator from continuing to serve as arbitrator ("informed consent"). Such express agreement shall be considered to be an effective waiver of any potential conflict of interest that may arise from the arbitrator's participation in such process or from information that the arbitrator may learn in the process. If the assistance by the arbitrator does not lead to final settlement of the case, the parties remain bound by their waiver. Notwithstanding such agreement, the arbitrator shall resign if, as a consequence of his involvement in the settlement process, the arbitrator develops doubts as to his ability to remain impartial or independent in the future course of the arbitration proceedings.

No. XIII.3.6 – Hearings and written proceedings

Subject to any contrary agreement by the parties, the arbitral tribunal shall decide whether to hold oral hearings for the presentation of evidence or for oral argument, or whether the proceedings shall be conducted only on the basis of documents and other materials ("documents-only"). However, unless the parties have agreed that no hearings shall be held, the arbitral tribunal shall hold such hearings at an appropriate stage of the proceedings, if so requested by a party.

No. XIII.3.7 – No suspension in case of bankruptcy of a party

Arbitration proceedings are not suspended if one of the parties goes bankrupt.

No. XIII.3.8 – Default of a party

Unless otherwise agreed by the parties, if, without showing sufficient cause,

- **i)** the claimant fails to communicate his statement of claim, the arbitral tribunal shall terminate the proceedings;
- **ii)** the respondent fails to communicate his statement of defence, the arbitral tribunal shall continue the proceedings without treating such failure in itself as an admission of the claimant's allegations;
- **iii)** any party fails to appear at a hearing or to produce documentary evidence, the arbitral tribunal may continue the proceedings and make the award on the evidence before it.

Section 4: Award; Termination of Proceedings

No. XIII.4.1 – Rules applicable to merits; decision ex aequo et bono

(a) The arbitral tribunal shall decide the dispute in accordance with such rules of law as are chosen by the parties as applicable to the substance of the dispute. Any designation of the law or legal system of a given State shall be construed, unless otherwise expressed, as directly referring to the substantive law of that State and not to its conflict of laws rules.
(b) Failing any designation by the parties, the arbitral tribunal shall apply the law determined by the conflict of laws rules which it considers applicable.
(c) The arbitral tribunal shall decide ex aequo et bono or as amiable compositeur only if the parties have expressly authorized it to do so.
(d) In all cases, the arbitral tribunal shall decide in accordance with the terms of the contract and shall take into account the usages of the trade applicable to the transaction.

No. XIII.4.2 – Form and contents of award

(a) The award shall be made in writing and shall be signed by the arbitrator or arbitrators. In arbitral proceedings with more than one arbitrator, the signatures of the majority of all members of the arbitral tribunal shall suffice, provided that the reason for any omitted signature is stated.
(b) The award shall state the reasons upon which it is based, unless the parties have agreed that no reasons are to be given or the award is an award on agreed terms under Principle XIII.4.2.

No. XIII.4.3 – Settlement

(a) If, during arbitral proceedings, the parties settle the dispute, the arbitral tribunal shall terminate the proceedings and, if requested by the parties and not objected to by the arbitral tribunal, record the settlement in the form of an arbitral award on agreed terms.
(b) An award on agreed terms shall be made in accordance with the provisions of Principle XIII.4.1 and shall state that it is an award. Such an award has the same status and effect as any other award on the merits of the case.

No. XIII.4.4 – Termination of proceedings

(a) The arbitral proceedings are terminated by the final award or by an order of the arbitral tribunal in accordance with paragraph (b) of this Principle.
(b) The arbitral tribunal shall issue an order for the termination of the arbitral proceedings when:

- **i)** the claimant withdraws his claim, unless the respondent objects thereto and the arbitral tribunal recognizes a legitimate interest on his part in obtaining a final settlement of the dispute;
- **ii)** the parties agree on the termination of the proceedings;
- **iii)** the arbitral tribunal finds that the continuation of the proceedings has for any other reason become unnecessary or impossible.

(c) The mandate of the arbitral tribunal terminates with the termination of the arbitral proceedings, subject to provisions of the applicable arbitration law relating to the correction and interpretation or the setting aside of the award or the rendering of additional awards.

Section 5: Confidentiality

No. XIII.5.1 – Confidentiality

(a) The parties to arbitration proceedings, whether institutional or ad hoc, are under an obligation to keep confidential all awards and orders produced by the arbitral tribunal in the arbitration, together with all materials in the proceedings created for the purpose of the arbitration, as well as all materials submitted by another party in the framework of the arbitral proceedings not otherwise in the public domain, save and to the extent that disclosure may be required of a party

- **i)** by a legal duty vis-à-vis a third party, especially an official authority of a state ("public interest exception"),
- **ii)** to protect or pursue a legal right,
- **iii)** to enforce or challenge an award in bona fide legal proceedings before a state court or other judicial authority; or
- **iv)** is justified by an express or implied consent of the party who produced the document during the arbitration.

(b) This undertaking also applies to the arbitrators, the tribunal-appointed experts, the secretary of the arbitral tribunal and, in case of institutional arbitration, the arbitral institution.

Chapter XIV: Private International Law

No. XIV.1 – Law applicable to an international arbitration agreement

(a) The substantive validity of an international arbitration agreement is to be determined according to the law chosen by the parties of said agreement, or failing any indication thereof, according to the law in force at the place (seat) of the arbitration.
(b) The formal validity of an international arbitration agreement is to be determined according to the formal validity rules of the arbitration law of the country in whose territory the arbitration has its seat.

No. XIV.2 – Closest connection-/Centre of gravity-test

Absent a choice of law by the parties, the contract is governed by the law with which the contract has the closest connection ("centre of gravity test"; "engster Zusammenhang"; "liens les plus étroits").

No. XIV.3 – Rule of validation/Lex validitatis

If a contract has contacts to more than one jurisdiction and the parties have not agreed on the applicable law, it is in the presumed interest of the parties to apply the law, both as to form and to substance, that validates the contract ("favor negotii"; "lex validitatis"; "rule of validation").

Index

Index

www.ingramcontent.com/pod-product-compliance
Lightning Source LLC
LaVergne TN
LVHW020646300926
849161LV00004B/837

* 9 7 8 9 0 4 1 1 3 1 7 9 9 *